To David a. [...]

Best wishes for

a long and happy life.

With plenty of great fishing.

Sincerely

Richard Swan

11-19-86

 YO-CHP-593

Light Tackle Fishing Guides of North America

LIGHT TACKLE
FISHING
GUIDES
OF NORTH AMERICA

Richard Swan

Clear Water Press
Reno, Nevada

Copyright © 1986 by Richard Swan

All rights reserved. No part of this book may be reproduced, stored in a retrieval system, or transmitted, in any form, or by any means, electronic, mechanical, photocopying, recording, or otherwise, without the prior written permission of the publisher except in the case of brief quotations embodied in critical reviews and articles. All inquiries should be addressed to Clear Water Press, 218 California Ave., Suite 204, Reno, NV 89509

Cover Design by Brian Crane
Maps by Shelly Mayer
Cover Photo by Vance Fox
Typography by Type/Setting Network, Inc., Reno, NV
Printed and bound by Edwards Brothers, Ann Arbor, MI
Manufactured in the United States of America

ISBN 0-9617364-0-2 (hardcover)
ISBN 0-9617364-1-0 (paperback)

To Marilyn

Table of Contents

Maps

Acknowledgments

First, I want to thank my wife Marilyn for the long and tedious months of proofing the thousands of items in this directory. Only by doing such a project can one appreciate the importance and tedium of this task.

The following people all helped in important ways: Steve Campbell, Paul Bruun, Buck Wheeler, Larry Schoenborn, Bob Nauheim, Chris Child, Homer Circle, George Anderson, Bob Jacklin, Bill Humes, Brian O'Keefe, Tom Lippert, Jim Van Loan, Hal Janssen, and Sarah Swan. Without their advice and encouragement, this book would not be as it is. The staff who helped gather and process information also deserves special thanks. In particular, I appreciate the professional approach and hard work contributed by office manager Diane Cipperley-Fowler, copy editor and design consultant, David Morrison, computer indexer Theo McCormick, and typographer Linda Duarte.

This page would not be complete without mention of my parents, Ray and Rhea Swan, who taught me a deep appreciation of the outdoors through many family camping trips during my childhood. Finally, four close friends—Dean Ringsmuth, Ron Bushman, Arnie Sanders, and Duane Brian—and fishing guides Seldon Jones and Jack Allen kindled my interest in the sport of fishing to the point where I could sustain the energy to compile and write this book. For this I thank them—it has been a labor of love.

1. Introduction

Why this book was written

Great new opportunities await the light tackle fisherman all across North America. Many famous waters are being restored to their former greatness through better fish management and pollution control. Trophy regulations are increasing the number of big fish in many of the best lakes and streams. Economical jet transportation has improved access to virgin fishing areas in Alaska, Canada, and Mexico. The best way to try your luck on these new, or improved, waters is with a competent professional guide.

Nothing improves angling success like a good guide. He knows the water, the fish, and how to catch them. A guide can save you the days, or even weeks, you would spend learning each new lake or stream on your own. In addition, a guide's skillful use of his boats and aircraft will put you on fishing spots you can only dream of otherwise.

Although there are thousands of fishing guides in North America, it can be difficult to find a good one. Most guide operations are small, consisting of only one individual or a very few. Most have limited advertising budgets and must rely on word of mouth to reach their potential clients. Many of the best guides are booked months, or even years, in advance, and do not advertise at all.

How the guides were selected

The main purpose of this book is to provide anglers with a directory of light tackle fishing guides in North America. To achieve this, I wrote to each state and provincial government in the U.S. and Canada, asking for a list of licensed fishing guides. Thirteen states and eight provinces responded with names and addresses of 3785 licensed guides and out-fitters. An additional 1300 names were gleaned from magazine articles and ads, personal contacts, guide associations, and chambers of com-merce. A detailed questionnaire was sent to each of these 5085 guides; over 900 responses were received from thirty-five states, ten provinces, Mexico, Belize and the Bahamas.

From the returns, I selected those guides and outfitters who: filled out the questionnaire completely; returned it by the deadline date; and offered fishing by some method whereby an artificial fly or lure is cast to the fish and retrieved. Their responses were compiled, condensed, and edited to produce this book.

How complete is this directory? This question is difficult to answer, since many states and some provinces do not license fishing guides, and no complete national lists of light tackle guides exist. Undoubtedly, some unlicensed and unadvertised guides have not been included. On the other hand, since there is a large number of listings from outfitters, tackle shops, and lodges, which generally have one or more guides working for them, this directory represents many more guides then the 830 individual listings.

Why did only 17.7 percent of the guides return the questionnaire? In my opinion, a substantial proportion of the 3785 licensed guides and outfitters are not presently active. Of those who are, some may not have responded because they work for an outfitter who is listed; others may only guide for trolling or bait fishing; some, like famous doctors, have all the clients they can handle and do not want to be bothered with additional calls; still others most likely could not find time to fill out a three page questionnaire.

In spite of these many uncertainties, this is still the most comprehen-sive directory of light tackle guide services. In fact, it is to my knowledge the only directory available!

A second, but equally important, purpose of this book is to provide a fishing travel guide to the best-known and most fertile angling waters of North America. It is no coincidence that the most productive waters support not only the most and biggest fish, but also the most guides. The 830 listings in this book profile most of the outstanding fishing areas in North America. These listings, along with detailed notes, repre-sent a valuable summary of, and guide to, hundreds of blue ribbon waters across the continent.

To help you use the information in the directory, the fishing waters haved been mapped by state and province. These maps are designed to give you a convenient way to locate the waters discussed by the guides in their listings and notes. In addition, a cross-referenced index has been added, allowing you to easily look up information about guides and waters.

How to use this book as a guide directory

The directory is organized by region then alphabetically by state (or province), city, and, finally, by individual guide. You need only look for towns in the region you intend to fish to find prospective guides. The listing gives a brief profile which will help you quickly determine if a particular guide offers the type of fishing you want.

The following explanations will help you get the most out of this book.

Names: Each service is listed under an individual guide's name. If more than one guide works out of the same address, all may appear in the same listing.

Address and phone: Generally for the guide's base of operations. There are a few exceptions, particularly in Alaska where the mailing address may be in Anchorage while the actual lodge or camp may be in the back country.

Airport/Accommodations: The nearest airport with *scheduled* airlines, and the nearest accommodations.

Operation: The individual listed may operate as a guide, an outfitter, a lodge, or a tackle shop. Generally, an outfitter is defined as a guide who offers overnight trips, has one or more guides working for him, or supplies equipment. If he operates as a tackle shop or lodge, other guides may work through him or for him.

Water: Up to four, in order of frequency fished. Additional waters may be offered.

Fish: Up to four species, in order of frequency fished. Additional species may be available.

Type of Fishing: For the purposes of this book, light tackle fishing is defined as a method whereby a fly or lure is cast to the fish by spin-casting, bait-casting, or fly-casting. A fourth type of fishing, trolling, is listed only as a service to those guides who also offer it. If a guide lists *all* under **Type of fishing**, it means he offers all three methods of casting, not necessarily trolling.

Boats/Airplanes: Indicates equipment available.

Season: Refers to the times of the year when a guide is available for fishing.

Specialty: A brief statement by the guide indicating the type of guiding he does best.

Tackle Supplied: Indicates what tackle (rods and reels) the guide has available for the client's use. There may be a rental charge.

Rates: Are generally for two people per day. Always verify the rate when you make your reservations, and make sure you ask which items will be included. In some cases rates quoted will include lodging, meals, or fly-outs. This is particularly true in Alaska. On daily trips, ask if lunch is provided. If there is a distance to be traveled by car or boat, you should ask in advance who will be paying for it. All rates are subject to change. Keep in mind that rates may go up in 1987 due to huge increases in insurance costs which are currently affecting all U.S. businesses.

Guide's Notes: Guide's notes were provided by the guides and have been added after the regular listing. In most cases these notes provide valuable current information on important fisheries.

Author's Notes: Author's notes are provided in those cases where the author had personal experience with a guide or operation, or was able to procure information from a reliable source.

Accuracy of listings

The information in each listing was provided by the guide under whose name the operation is listed. The author cannot guarantee the accuracy of any information supplied by the guides. You should confirm all information in the listing with each individual guide, and obtain fishing regulations from local fish and game authorities. It is also possible that errors may have occcured in the preparation of this book. Any corrections or comments will be appreciated.

How to use this book as a guide to blue ribbon waters

The introduction to each state and province contains comments on waters and areas mentioned most by the guides in that state. These comments provide a brief outline of blue ribbon fishing in that region. You will find all these major waters mapped on the state maps, and most are described in detailed guide's notes. Use the index to locate these notes, which contain valuable information regarding species of fish, best methods to catch them, and peak fishing times. In some cases more than one guide has provided notes on a given water.

2. How to pick a light tackle fishing guide

How to recognize a good guide

Selecting a good guide is crucial to success on unfamiliar waters, but the job seldom gets the attention it requires. This task is not easy; it requires time, work, and, usually, some money. It is much more fun to dream about catching big fish than to research a guide's qualifications, but any extra effort spent on the selection process generally pays off on the water.

A good guide is honest, reliable, and hard-working. While he is in your employ, he puts your needs first and does his level best to provide the services you have requested.

Guiding also requires a combination of skills that is unique to this profession. A guide should be trained in water safety, lifesaving, and first aid. If he guides out of boats, he should be a competent captain. Good teaching skills are needed to explain and demonstrate new fishing techniques. Finally, a guide must know where the fish are and how to catch them.

Credentials

Before you hire a guide, an understanding of the terms *guide, outfitter*, and *licensed* will be helpful. A guide is a person who offers his guiding services for hire on a daytime-only basis. An outfitter is generally defined as an individual who offers overnight guided trips, supplies equipment, or who has one or more guides working for him. Furthermore, in some states, anyone holding a permit to guide on state or federal land where permits are required is also called an outfitter.

"Licensed guide" or "licensed outfitter" simply means that a guide or outfitter has been licensed by a governmental agency to engage in that activity. Only fourteen of the states I contacted required guides to be licensed. I found it surprising that Alaska, the state from which we received our fourth-largest response, did not license guides.

Among those states and provinces which issue licenses, actual requirements can vary considerably. In some states, a guide's license means only that an individual has paid a small fee and filled out an application. In other states, applicants may be required to take a written test, and/or be trained in first aid.

Guide Associations

In many states and provinces, there are guide associations which promote guided fishing and attempt to establish standards of behavior for their members. The Oregon Guides and Packers Association Code of Ethics is a good example of what these associations can stand for, and will give you an idea of what you should expect from a good guide operation.

OREGON GUIDES AND PACKERS CODE OF ETHICS

1. I will at all times conduct my operations and services in an ethical and businesslike manner.
2. Rates, accommodations and services will be clearly defined to prospective clients prior to booking and acceptance of deposits. I will not misrepresent rates, service accommodations nor otherwise mislead prospective clients through false or fictitious advertising.
3. I will maintain all my equipment to include livestock, camp gear, boats, vehicles and all other miscellaneous gear in good condition and working order.
4. I will employ only well-trained, courteous and sufficient personnel to adequately care for guests and render necessary services.
5. I will not allow any wanton waste of fish or game on a trip that is my responsibility. Also, I'll make every effort to keep all fish and game in a fresh and edible condition. Utmost care should be taken to preserve all trophies in a satisfactory condition.
6. An effort will be made on my part to honestly inform my clients on the general well-being and status of game and fish relative to the respective area, for their more knowledgeable understanding of the current situation relative to their specific booking and type of trip.
7. I will make a sincere effort to inform my clients with adequate information on the type of country, weather, travel involved, clothing requirements and hunting or fishing skill required if any, for them to fully enjoy their outdoor experience to the individual's satisfaction.
8. I will at all times provide for the safety of my clients and employed personnel, and when necessary will not hesitate to remind anyone of unsafe practices which have come to my attention.

9. I will fully cooperate with Federal, State and local fish and wildlife officials; I will advise my clients of all applicable conservation standards, fish and game laws, license requirements, statutes and regulations and will not condone their violation.
10. I will at all times cooperate fully with private landowners, public land management agencies and/or stockmen, other guides, and respect their rights and privileges.
11. I will always leave a clean camp, striving to maintain the environment in as good or better condition than when I arrived.

The Oregon Guides and Packers Association has a review board which investigates complaints about members pertinent to the Code of Ethics, and takes corrective action if warranted. If this self-policing policy works in practice, this type of organization could go a long way toward raising the level of guide service. The addresses of any guide associations in the areas you are interested in can usually be obtained from tackle shops or chambers of commerce.

Selecting a guide

There are huge differences between guides, both in the types of fishing they offer, and in the quality of their service. Because there is limited regulation of guides, and only a few groups like the Oregon Guides and Packers Association, there are few credentials which you can rely on to help you determine if a guide is competent. Guide selection is best accomplished through the following process.

Decide what type of fishing you want to do. Do not take this step lightly. If you want to dry fly fish spring creeks for large numbers of trout, or if you want to flip for trophy bass, be ready to tell this to a prospective guide. You're hiring a guide, not a mind reader.

Find out what your prospective guide's specialty is. This can be done by reading his brochure, by studying his listing if he is listed in this directory, or by asking about him at a tackle shop located near his home. At this point, if you still feel that this particular guide is a candidate, you should contact him directly for more information. You will want to ask specific questions like: What type of fishing is offered? What species will we be fishing for? What are our chances for success? Other important questions are: Do you carry liability insurance? Is the guide who will be guiding us trained in first aid? Has he been trained in lifesaving and water safety? Does he know CPR?

Once you are satisfied you have found a guide who meets your needs, you should check some references. As a general rule, one- or two-day trips call for two references, three- to five-day trips, three references; longer trips require four or more references. By references, I mean direct personal contact with a client who has recently been out with the guide.

Keep in mind that most people will tell you the guide was good if they caught a fair number of fish. Try not to let that distract you from finding out if the guide was knowledgeable, hard-working, and pleasant to be with.

Guide Equipment

Good equipment and the skill to operate it are basic to most guiding. Watercraft and aircraft are needed to fish in many areas, and are part and parcel of the guiding business. A guide's equipment inventory can give you a good idea of the nature and scope of his operation.

The watercraft most utilized for light tackle fishing are: bass boats, McKenzie river boats, inflatable rafts, jet sleds, canoes, bonefish skiffs, outboards, and floatplanes. You are probably familiar with most of these terms, with the possible exception of the following:

A *McKenzie river boat* is a dory designed and built to drift rivers. It is controlled by an oarsman who sits in the center seat and faces downstream, which allows him to negotiate obstacles and to properly position the fishermen—one in the front and one in the back—to cast to holding fish. It makes an extremely effective platform to cast from, and is by far the best way to learn to fly fish on the rivers of the west. With the help of a good guide, forty-fish days are a possibility for first-time fly fishermen who cast from one of these boats. The McKenzie's high bow keeps the fishermen dry; its maneuverability makes it an excellent craft for negotiating rapids.

A *jet sled* is similar to a johnboat, but has a sled-shaped bow and is powered by a special outboard with a water jet lower unit. A jet sled enables you to quickly cover long distances on rivers and still negotiate shallows and rapids. It is not as esthetically pleasing to fish from as a McKenzie, but it can get you into places which are inaccessible to other craft. It is used extensively on the west coast of the U.S., Canada, and Alaska.

A *bonefish skiff* or *flats skiff* is a special skiff built for fishing in salt water for bonefish, permit, tarpon, etc. It is designed to be easily and quietly poled while sight fishing for these exciting species on shallow saltwater flats. It is generally equipped with a powerful outboard, for moving from one fishing spot to another.

Aircraft most commonly used in guiding are the six-passenger Cessna 210 and the reliable eight-passenger de Havilland Beaver. Both are generally equipped with floats. Two other aircraft which are becoming popular because of their ability to get into small landing areas, are the Piper Super Cub equipped with fat tires, and the helicopter. Conventional floatplanes tend to head for the same good landing spots, so both of these are useful for avoiding the crowds.

Should you tip your guide?

If he does a good job, the answer is definitely yes. Guide fees are not high when compared to the cost per hour of other types of personally supervised recreation. When you tip, keep in mind that your guide probably has considerable equipment expense, and that most guides do not have the corporate safetynets, such as insurance and retirement plans, which many of us enjoy. A good tip helps him cover these costs and makes it possible for him to continue in business. In addition to tipping a guide, you can show your appreciation by letting others know what a good job he did. Also, please take the time to let us know about any guide who has done an outstanding job for you, so we can consider him for inclusion in our next edition.

The risks of guided fishing

Fishing by its nature involves specific dangers to participants, the most obvious of which is the possibility of drowning. Guided fishing does not eliminate these dangers. Not all guides carry liability insurance. If you are concerned about this issue you should discuss it directly with

Oregon boat builder Ray Heater on the Clackamas in one of his 16-ft. wooden dories.   *Ray Heater*

your guide. Clear Water Press and the author disclaim the competency of any listed guides or outfitters with regard to their ability to provide for the client's safety. Each reader should investigate, to his own satisfaction, the safety record, safety procedures, and financial integrity of any guide he employs, and must take sole responsibility for his own decisions.

3. Tips for the traveling fisherman

Good planning makes a great trip

The most important thing you can do to insure a successful fishing trip is to plan ahead. Across the country, fishing conditions can vary substantially from week to week. Spawning runs, insect hatches, and water levels all have dramatic impact on fishing conditions. You need to research the areas you are interested in fishing to decide which one will have the best conditions during your visit, and which species will be at their peak. You might even write or call some tackle shops and ask them questions or have them send guide books about the area. This research will not only increase your enjoyment on reaching your destination, but will intensify the planning period and make the whole trip more fun. You should make all reservations well ahead of time, especially for your guide. Remember, the best guides are often booked up months in advance.

Use travel agencies

To serve the considerable number of light tackle fishermen who are interested in fishing world class waters, a group of travel agencies has developed which specialize in fishing travel. These agents can be extremely helpful in planning your trip. They will analyze your needs and budget, and suggest what areas will be best for you. You pay nothing for these services; the agent receives a commission from the guides, lodges, and camps he represents.

There are two basic types of agents involved in fishing travel. Full service agencies offer a broad selection of trips to lodges and wilderness camps all over the continent, or the world; consequently, they can tailor a trip for you to a lodge which best suits your needs. Specialty operations, on the other hand, concentrate on certain kinds of fishing, like bass or fly, or a certain area, such as Alaska or Mexico. Specialty trips may be organizd by your local tackle shop or club, and are sometimes led by a well-known fisherman.

Conditions at lodges and outfitter operations change from year to year. Good agencies are constantly getting feedback on these changes from their clients, so I strongly urge you to use one of these agencies when planning and making reservations for your trip.

Here is a partial list of agencies specializing in fishing travel.

General Fishing Full Service Agencies

Fishing International, Santa Rosa, CA, (707) 542-4242, Bob Nauheim
Frontiers, Wexford, PA, (800) 245-1950, Chris Child
Sportsmans Safaris, Reno, NV, (702) 747-2747, Ted Kaphan
Angler Adventures, Lyme, CT, (203) 434-9624, Chip Bates

Specialty Fishing Full Service Agencies

Alaska Adventure, Anchorage, AK, (907) 274-3266, Jim Repine
Alaska Outdoors, Anchorage, AK, (907) 276-2670, Allen Swensen
Club Pacific, San Francisco, CA, (415) 752-0192, Mel Krieger
The Fly Shop, Redding, CA, (916) 222-3555, Mike Michalak
Kauffman's Fly Shop, Portland, OR, (503) 639-6400, Jerry Swanson
Marriott's Fly Fishing Store, Fullerton, CA, Bob Marriott, (714) 525-1827

Gear for your trip

A *pack rod* can be carried onto airplanes, and serves as a backup in case you lose your luggage or break a rod. I would not think of fishing Alaska's back country without a lightweight pack rod for grayling and Dolly Varden. These species are abundant all over Alaska, and hooked on a light rod can provide great enjoyment. If you expect to fish for salmon or rainbow and they do not co-operate, the grayling and Dollies will save the day. In other areas of the country, I keep a pack rod handy for small snook, sea trout, bass and bluegill. Several companies offer good pack rods. My favorites are the new graphites, because their fast action allows a wide range of lines to be used effectively on a single rod.

Neoprene waders have many advantages over conventional waders. They increase safety because they improve flotation and are slower to fill up with water if you take a fall. Neoprene's excellent insulation properties keep you warmer in cool or cold weather.

Polypropelene and pile garments wick moisture away from your skin and greatly increase comfort when worn under waders. If you should get wet, they will dry out very quickly, which is added protection against hypothermia. These materials are used in a variety of items including underwear, hats, sweat shirts, gloves, and jackets.

Neoprene gloves can keep you on the water in cold conditions by protecting the most exposed part of your body. They are definitely a must for Alaska and all cold weather fishing. A good pair will fit snugly and provide plenty of dexterity.

In all light tackle fishing situations, vision is critical. *Polaroid sunglasses* are an absolute must when you fish to visible fish like bonefish on saltwater flats, trout in gin-clear spring creeks, or steelhead holding behind the salmon redds in small shallow streams.

Your *survival kit* should include sun block, Kleenex tissue, bug dope, waterproof matches, space blanket, bug dope, rain coat, first aid kit, wader repair kit, extra pair of eyeglasses, sunglasses, and plenty of bug dope.

If you don't already have one, consider buying a small *thirty-five mm camera* that will fit in your vest pocket. I have a Minox, but I also like the Olympus. Carry several baggies with you and keep your camera sealed in a couple of them. It's not guaranteed to keep your camera dry if you fall in a river, but will protect it in most other circumstances.

Rubber bands are a cheap, effective way to protect your rod when you travel between fishing spots by car, boat, or light plane. Just break the rod down and attach the pieces at both ends with the rubber bands. The butt section will protect the tip from damage. This is standard practice when fishing out of floatplanes in Alaska, but I find it works well anywhere, when making short trips by boat or car.

Practice special skills before you go

Many trips will introduce you to new fishing situations and techniques. Find out what skills you will need, and start learning them before you depart. If you're going to try your hand at fly casting, go to a casting school, or at least get out and practice casting in your yard. Five hours of practice will work wonders, and heighten your anticipation.

Packing for air travel

When you pack for airline travel, carry a pack rod, a reel, a few flies or lures, and, if needed, a lightweight pair of waders with you on the plane, so you still will be able to fish if your luggage gets lost. In my experience, lost luggage almost always arrives within forty-eight hours; however, a rod of your own and a pair of waders that fit can make those two days a lot more tolerable.

Heading out for salmon.

Evan Swensen

4. Alaska: Still fabulous fishing!

In Alaska you can experience a fishing environment that has changed little since the turn of the century! Alaska's vast wilderness offers numberless streams still unviolated by bridges, dams, or access roads. Salmon runs are measured in millions, and practically all stocks are native. No wonder Alaska travel brochures carry the slogan, "Once you go to Alaska, you never come all the way back."

Alaska's huge fishing possibilities are best reviewed by dividing the state into four regions: northern, southwestern, south-central and southeastern. Each of these offers unique angling opportunities.

Northern Alaska, more than a quarter of a million square miles between Fairbanks and the Arctic Ocean, is a vast, roadless wilderness containing thousands of pristine lakes and streams. Fishing is for Arctic char, grayling, lake trout, salmon and sheefish. Gates of the Arctic and Kobuk Valley National Parks, and the Noatak National Preserve, adjoin each other in the northwest part of this region. Together, they contain over 16,000,000 acres of wilderness—an area roughly the size of West Virginia.

The Noatak, Kobuk, and Alatna rivers, which flow through this wilderness area, all offer excellent fishing. Other important rivers guided by the Alaskan outfitters listed here are the Niukluk and Unalakleet, both emptying into Norton sound, and the Chena and Chatanika rivers near Fairbanks. Although some prime spots in Alaska can actually get crowded, you will seldom have this problem in the north. Outfitters and lodges are based in the towns of Fairbanks, Bettles, Nome, Kotzebue and Unalakleet.

Southwestern Alaska, a fabulous network of lakes and streams, includes the famous Bristol Bay drainage, Lake Iliamna and the Wood

River/Tikchik Lakes area, as well as storied rivers like the Alagnak, Kvichak, and the Goodnews. Throughout the summer and fall, huge runs of salmon literally turn the rivers red. Big rainbows feast on the freshly-laid eggs, creating daily opportunities to catch trophy fish.

Visiting anglers will want to see the huge Kodiak Brown bears fishing for salmon in the Brooks River and visit the Valley of the Ten Thousand Smokes in Katmai National Park. Steelheaders may wish to try Kodiak Island's Karluk River, one of the finest steelhead and silver salmon fisheries in the world. In spite of an apparently inexhaustible number of fish in this region, the Alaskan Department of Fish and Game has wisely placed trophy regulations on much of this area. Fishing headquarters are Iliamna, Dillingham, and the town of Kodiak on Kodiak Island.

The south-central region of Alaska includes the world-renowned Kenai Peninsula. The Kenai is one of the few places in Alaska where the car-bound angler can reach a number of excellent lakes and rivers. The peninsula's most famous river is the Kenai, legendary for its record-sized king salmon. Accommodations are available in the towns of Soldotna and Kenai, and guide operations offer their services on a daily basis, allowing you to extend a business trip over a weekend and sample some great fishing.

The well-known Talkeetna River, about seventy miles north of Anchorage, is also accessible by car. Kings, silvers, rainbows, and grayling abound here. Daily guide services are available in the town of Talkeetna.

Southeastern Alaska consists of hundreds of miles of seacoast and a vast maze of islands from Yakutat Bay south to Ketchikan. Even though there are some light tackle angling opportunities in this region, such as steelheading on the Situk River near Yakutat, most guide operations concentrate on saltwater trolling. Consequently, we did not receive many responses from guides in this area. We have, however, listed a couple of lodges which are starting to offer saltwater fly fishing for salmon.

Fishing Alaska's back country is considerably more complex than a Sunday drive to your favorite bass lake. Even though the fishing is some of the finest in the world, most of it is only accessible by floatplane. Once on the water, a jet sled or other type of boat is generally needed to fish the good holes. Bear attacks, although rare, do occur, and should never be lightly dismissed.

So, choose your guide carefully! Dozens of lodges, camps, and float outfitters have recently started operations. In the next few years many of these will disappear, victims of poor management, undercapitalization, and bad (sometimes dishonest) business practices. Even well-established operations can offer unpleasant surprises, particularly if they have changed ownership or management. Choosing the wrong outfitter or lodge can be disastrous to your vacation, and even to your personal safety. It is wise to book your Alaska trip through a well-established agency specializing in fishing travel (see chapter 3). Make sure you get two or three additional references on the lodge or outfitter you choose.

Rates for guided fishing in Alaska may seem high; good lodges commonly charge $2500 to $3000 per person for a week's stay. Keep in mind that these rates usually include food, lodging, guide service, and floatplane fly-outs or riverboat transportation. To avoid an unpleasant end to your visit, be sure to ask in advance exactly what is included in the base price, and get it in writing before you mail your deposit.

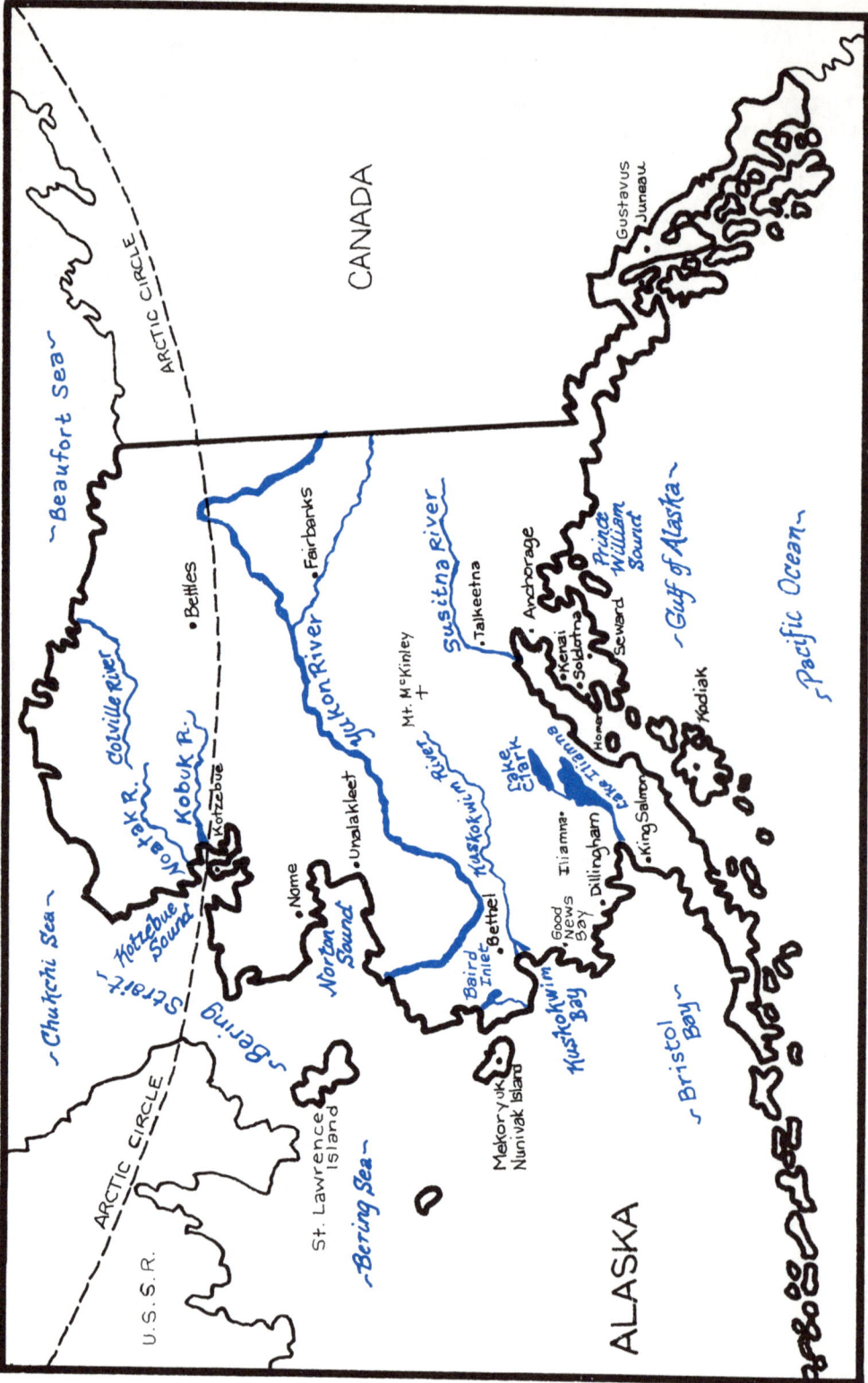

Alaska

ALAGNAK, ALASKA

ROCCANOVA, VIN-ALAGNAK LODGE (916) 487-6198
Address 4117 Hillcrest Way, Sacramento, CA 95821
Airport King Salmon 25m **Accommodations** On premises
Operation Outfitter, lodge **Type of Fishing** Fly, spin, troll
Fish 5 species of salmon, rainbow, grayling, char **Season** June-October
Water Alagnak River **Specialty** Fly & spin fishing **Aircraft** Floatplanes
Boats Johnboats **Tackle Supplied** Spin, troll
Experience 4 years **Rates** week: $2000/person

ANCHORAGE, ALASKA

ASH, CHUCK-BRIGHTWATER ALASKA (907) 243-1922
Address P.O. Box 110796, Anchorage, AK 99511
Airport Anchorage **Accommodations** Anchorage **Operation** Outfitter
Fish 5 species of salmon, rainbow, char, grayling **Season** May-Sept
Water Togiak, Goodnews, Koktuli Rivers, Naknek Drainage
Specialty Fly fishing float trips **Boats** Rafts **Type of Fishing** Fly, spin, troll
Experience 11 years **Rates** week: $1200/person

BRANHAM, CHRIS-BRANHAM ADVENTURES (907) 243-4901
Address Box 6184, Anchorage, AK 99502
Airport Anchorage **Accommodations** Anchorage
Operation Outfitter **Type of Fishing** Fly, spin
Fish King, coho salmon, rainbow, char, sheefish **Season** June-September
Water South west and south central Alaska waters **Tackle Supplied** Fly, spin
Specialty Fly-out lake and stream fishing **Aircraft** Floatplanes
Experience 40 years **Rates** week: $5000/2 people

EDWARDS, MIKE (503) 327-2350, (907) 522-1707
Address 263 Riverwood Dr., Jefferson, OR 97352
Airport Anchorage **Accommodations** Anchorage **Operation** Outfitter
Fish Rainbow, 5 species of salmon, char, sheefish **Season** June-Sept **Boats** Rafts
Water Kanektok, Kobuk Rivers, Lake Creek **Type of Fishing** Fly, spin
Specialty Fly fishing float trips **Aircraft** Floatplanes **Tackle Supplied** Fly, spin
Experience 4 years **Rates** week: $3000/2 people
Guides's Notes: Kobuk River, in Gates of the Arctic National Preserve, has it
all! Whitewater, wildlife, and sheefish. This unique Arctic sportfish attains its
greatest size - up to 60lbs. - in the Kobuk and average 10-20 lbs.

NORTHERN ALASKA

Beaufort Sea

Chukchi Sea

Colville River

Killik

Noatak River

Kobuk River

Walker Lake

N. Fork

Wild

John

Alatna

Bettles

ARCTIC CIRCLE

Yukon River

Forty Mile

Chatanika

Chena R.

Fairbanks

Tanana River

Koyukuk River

Yukon

Unalakleet R.

Unalakleet

Kotzebue

Kotzebue Sound

ARCTIC CIRCLE

Bering Strait

Fish

Niukluk

Nome

Norton Sound

U.S.S.R.

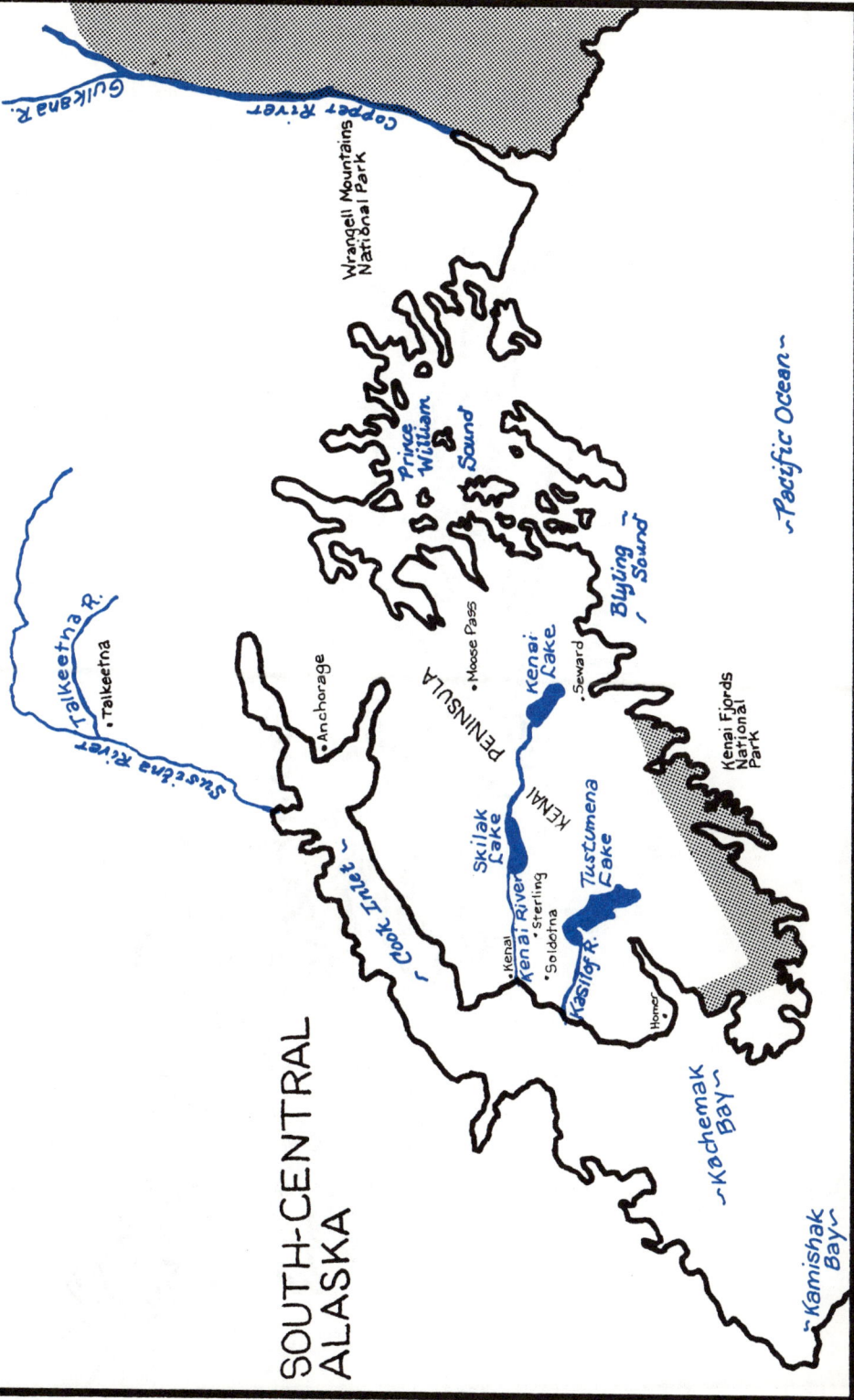

SOUTH-CENTRAL ALASKA

Gulkana R.

Copper River

Wrangell Mountains National Park

~Pacific Ocean~

Prince William Sound

Blying Sound

Talkeetna R.

Talkeetna

Susitna River

Anchorage

Moose Pass

Kenai Lake

Seward

Kenai Fjords National Park

~Cook Inlet~

PENINSULA

KENAI

Skilak Lake

Kenai River

Sterling

Soldotna

Kenai

Tustumena Lake

Kasilof R.

Homer

~Kachemak Bay~

~Kamishak Bay~

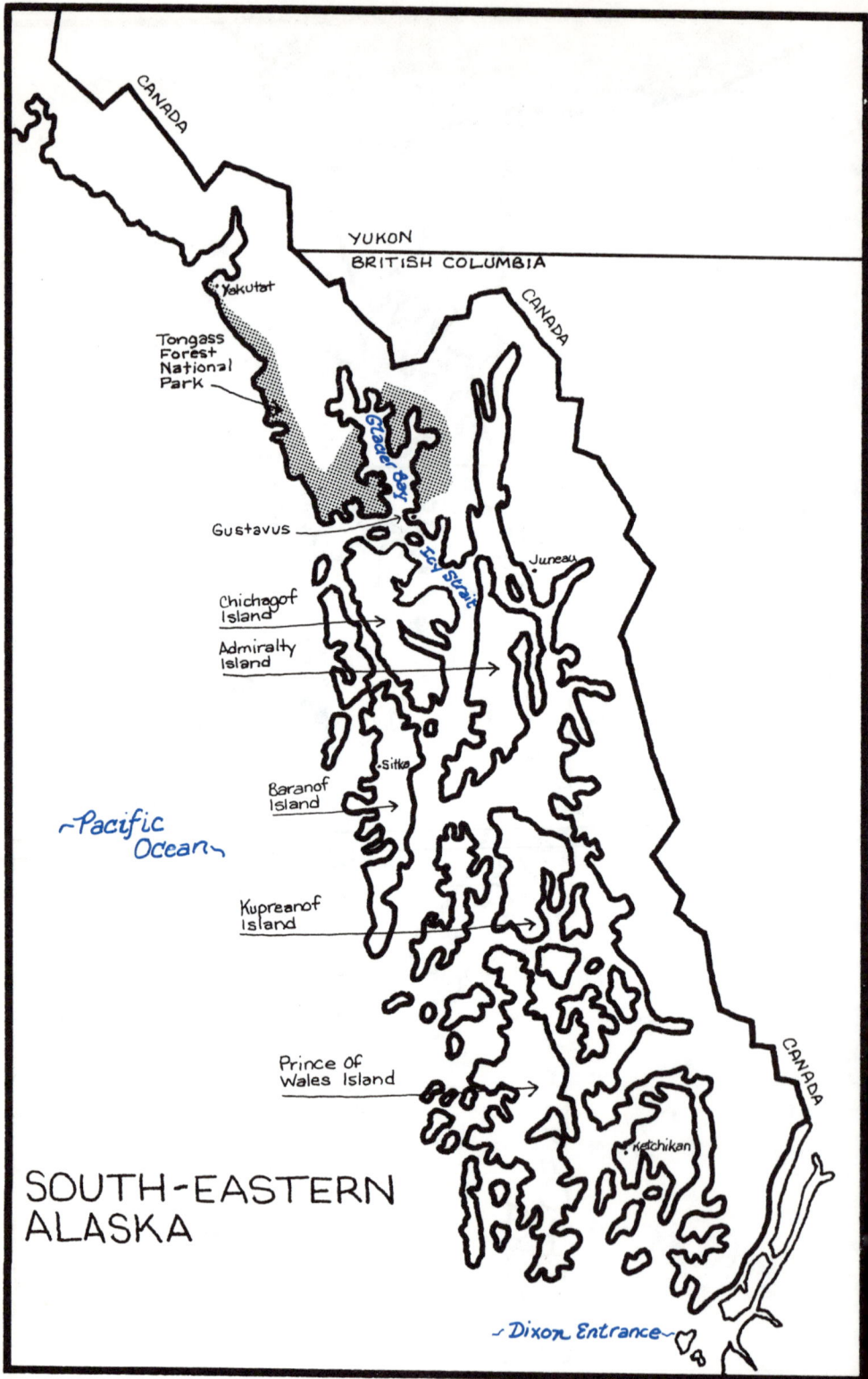

CANADA

YUKON
BRITISH COLUMBIA
CANADA

Yakutat

Tongass
Forest
National
Park

Glacier Bay

Gustavus

Icy Strait

Juneau

Chichagof
Island

Admiralty
Island

Baranof
Island

Sitka

Pacific
Ocean

Kupreanof
Island

Prince Of
Wales Island

Ketchikan

CANADA

SOUTH-EASTERN
ALASKA

Dixon Entrance

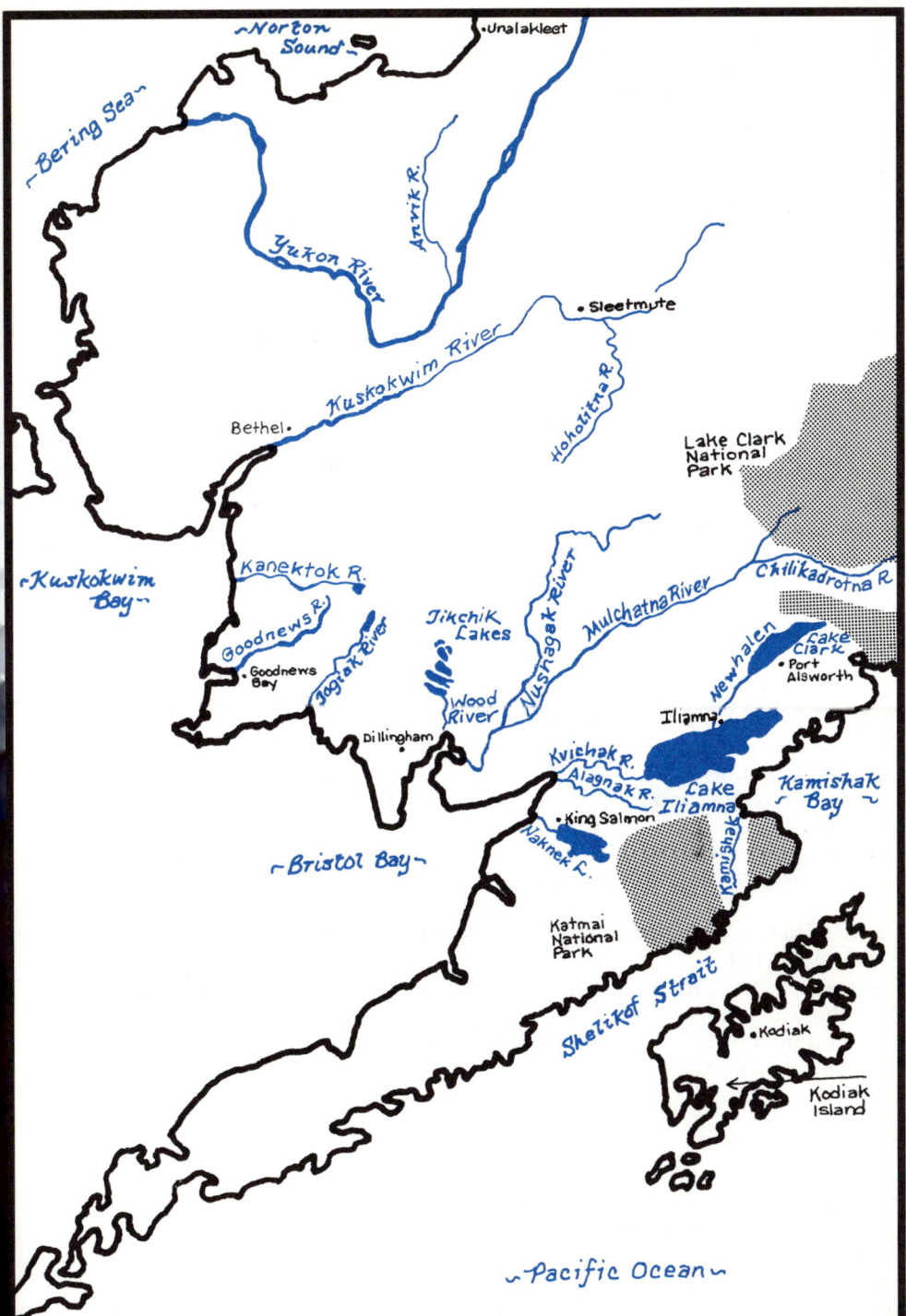

Norton Sound

~Bering Sea~

Unalakleet

Anvik R.

Yukon River

Sleetmute

Kuskokwim River

Hoholitna R.

Bethel

Lake Clark National Park

~Kuskokwim Bay~

Kanektok R.

Chilikadrotna R.

Goodnews R.

Jikchik Lakes

Nushagak River

Mulchatna River

Newhalen

Lake Clark

Goodnews Bay

Togiak River

Wood River

Iliamna

Port Alsworth

Dillingham

Kvichak R.

Alagnak R.

Lake Iliamna

Kamishak Bay

King Salmon

Naknek L.

Kamishak R.

~Bristol Bay~

Katmai National Park

Shelikof Strait

Kodiak

Kodiak Island

~Pacific Ocean~

SOUTH·WESTERN ALASKA

GAUDET, JOHN J.-JAKE'S ALASKA WILDERNESS OUTFITTERS (907) 248-0509

Address P.O. Box 104179, Anchorage, AK 99510
Airport Anchorage **Accommodations** Anchorage **Operation** Outfitter
Fish Salmon, trout, grayling, char **Season** June-Sept **Type of Fishing** Fly, spin
Water Bristol Bay area, Southwest Alaska **Specialty** Float fishing trips
Aircraft Floatplane **Boats** Rowboats, rafts **Tackle Supplied** Fly, spin
Experience 5 years **Rates** week: $4000/2 people

HAYES, RON-ALASKA RAINBOW LODGE (907) 248-2880

Address P.O. Box 101711, Anchorage, AK 99510
Airport King Salmon 30m **Accommodations** On premises
Operation Lodge, outfitter **Type of Fishing** Fly, spin **Water** Bristol Bay area
Fish 5 species of salmon, rainbow, char, grayling **Season** June-October
Specialty Fresh water fly and spin fishing **Aircraft** Floatplanes, landplane
Boats Rowboats, river sleds, canoe, McKenzie **Tackle Supplied** All
Experience 32 years **Rates** week: $3100/person
Guide's Notes: Our lodge is located on the **Kvichak River**, which boasts the largest Salmon run in the entire world. An average of eight million salmon pass by our front door every year.
Author's Notes: Our sources tell us that Ron Hayes runs a very high quality operation.

HYDE, RONALD B., SR-ALASKA RIVER SAFARIS (907) 333-2860

Address 4909 Rollins Drive, Anchorage, AK 99508
Airport Goodnews Bay 125m **Accommodations** On premises
Operation Guide, lodge **Type of Fishing** Fly **Boats** River sled, skiffs
Fish 5 species of salmon, grayling, trout **Season** June-October
Water Togiak River **Specialty** Fly fishing **Tackle Supplied** Fly, spin
Experience 22 years **Rates** week: $5500/2 people

MARINELLA, CONNIE & CHIP-WILD COUNTRY RIVER GUIDES (907) 349-9173

Address 12020 Timberlane Dr., Dept. G, Anchorage, AK 99502
Airport Anchorage 200m **Accommodations** Iliamna **Season** June-Oct
Operation Outfitter (Iliamna Area) **Specialty** Fly fishing float trips
Fish 5 species of salmon, char, rainbow, grayling **Type of Fishing** Fly
Water Lake Iliamna, Bristol Bay **Tackle Supplied** Fly, spin **Boats** Rafts
Experience 6 years **Rates** week: from $1550/person

MASON, MORT (907) 272-1206

Address 1235 R Street, Anchorage, AK 99501
Airport Anchorage **Accommodations** Anchorage
Operation Outfitter **Type of Fishing** All **Tackle Supplied** All
Fish 5 species of salmon, rainbow, char, grayling **Season** June-Oct
Water Iliamna and Cook Inlet Drainages **Boats** Bass boats, rafts
Specialty Fly-out fishing trips **Aircraft** Floatplanes, amphibian, landplanes

Young angler with King salmon from the Talkeetna River.   *Mark Noble/Alaska D.O.T.*

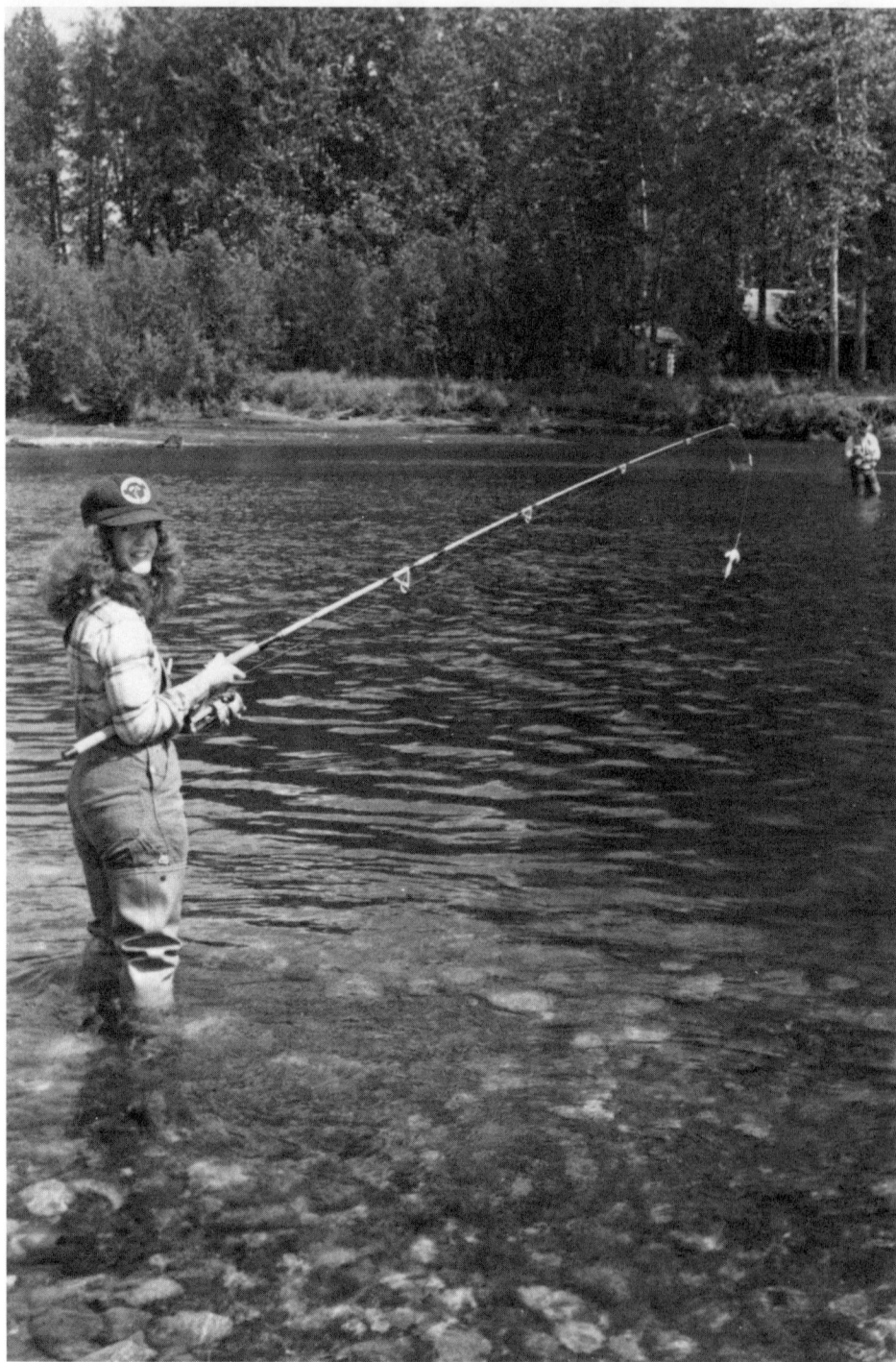

Spin-casting for silvers near Ketchikan.

Mark Noble/Alaska D.O.T.

Experience 29 years **Rates** varies
Guide's Notes: I also guide Lake Okeechobee, Florida for bass.

McGUIRE, TOM-TRAIL RIDGE AIR (907) 276-4485
Address P.O. Box 111377, Anchorage, AK 99511
Airport Anchorage **Accommodations** Anchorage **Operation** Outfitter
Fish King, silver salmon, rainbow, grayling **Season** Year-round
Water Susitna Drainage, Prince William Sound, Iliamna Streams
Specialty Fly fishing float trips **Aircraft** Floatplanes, landplane
Boats River sleds, rafts **Tackle Supplied** All **Type of Fishing** Fly, spin
Experience 7 years **Rates** varies

OWSICHEK, KEN-FISHING UNLIMITED, INC. (907) 243-5899, 781-2213
Address P.O. Box 190301, Anchorage, AK 99519-0301
Airport Anchorage 180m **Accommodations** Anchorage 180m
Operation Outfitter **Type of Fishing** Fly, spin **Tackle Supplied** Fly, spin
Fish 5 species of salmon, rainbow, char, grayling **Season** June-October
Water Bristol Bay, Iliamna, Tikchick, Katmai Areas, Kodiak Island
Specialty Fly-out float fishing trips **Aircraft** Floatplanes **Boats** River sleds, rafts
Experience 15 years **Rates** week: $6200/2 people

PETERSON, WILLIAM M. (907) 345-0762
Address 12101 Hillside Drive, Anchorage, AK 99516
Airport Anchorage **Accommodations** Anchorage **Tackle Supplied** Troll
Operation Outfitter, charter captain **Type of Fishing** Troll, spin, salt water fly
Fish King, silver salmon, halibut **Season** March-Oct **Boats** Rowboats, skiffs
Water Sitka area **Specialty** Trolling, salt water stream fishing
Experience 13 years **Rates** day: $450/2-6 people

SHARPE, ED & JUDY-WILDERNESS PLACE LODGE (707) 542-4242
Address C/O Fishing International, P.O. Box 2132, Santa Rosa, CA 95405
Airport Anchorage 65m **Accommodations** On premises **Aircraft** Floatplane
Operation Outfitter, lodge **Type of Fishing** All **Tackle Supplied** All
Fish Five species of salmon, rainbow, grayling, pike **Season** June-September
Specialty Wilderness lodge offering light tackle spin and fly fishing for trout
and salmon **Boats** River sleds, rafts **Water** Lake Creek, Yentna R., Fish Lakes
Experience 6 years **Rates** 5 days: $1075 week: $1395/person
Guides's Notes: Fishing Calendar Yentna River and Lake Creek

Fish	Available
King	June - mid July
Sockeye	July
Silver, Pink, Chum	Late July - Aug
Rainbow	Good all summer, peaks Sept thru early Oct
Grayling	All season

Our Lodge is located in the Alaskan wilderness on Lake Creek, 65 air miles
northwest of Anchorage. We offer excellent guided fishing on Lake Creek and
the nearby Yentna River.
Author's Notes: *Our contacts tell us this is a very nice lodge located in the
midst of excellent fishing. The price is relatively reasonable.*

BETTLES, ALASKA

KETSCHER, DAVID-WALKER LAKE WILDERNESS LODGE (907) 692-5252
Address P.O. Box 18, Bettles, AK 99726
Airport Bettles **Accommodations** Bettles
Operation Outfitter, lodge **Type of Fishing** Fly, spin, troll
Fish Sheefish, char, lake trout, grayling **Season** June-Sept.
Water Walker Lake, Noatak and Kobuk Rivers **Boats** Rafts, kayaks, canoe
Specialty Float trips for sheefish and arctic char **Tackle Supplied** Spin
Experience 12 years **Rates** varies
Guide's Notes: Two hundred and fifty miles from Fairbanks, over one hundred miles from the nearest road, and north of the Arctic Circle, Walker Lake Wilderness Lodge can be reached only by floatplane..... It is the only lodge inside the Gates of the Arctic National Park (a park larger than Massachusetts, Delaware, and Rhode Island combined). This isolation has protected our area from overcrowding and over-fishing.

Excursions by river boat or canoe across the great waters of **Walker Lake** take you to inlet streams and other secret fishing holes. In these waters we will be after lake trout averaging 6 to 12 pounds with trophy fish coming well above the 30 pound mark, Arctic char in the 5 pound class with many between 10 and 15 pounds, and lots of fast Arctic grayling action.

It is from the fish-filled **Kobuk River** that the world's record sheefish are caught. Sometimes called the tarpon of the north, the mighty sheefish are Alaska's most exotic big game fish......Sheefish may take to the air in powerful acrobatic leaps. They average 15 to 20 pounds and many trophy fish reach the 40 to 50 pound range.

North Fork River   The trip in July originates at the Eskimo village of Anaktuvuk Pass, while the August trip begins amidst the fall splendor of Summit Lake. Wildlife abounds and can be observed with little effort. The river is not difficult; however, sharp turns and obstacles will keep you alert. Nearby lakes are full of pike and the creeks provide excellent grayling fishing.

On **The Alatna River**, we begin at the mouth of Arrigetch Valley and canoe down the Alatna River with numerous side trips for fishing and photography. The Alatna is a safe, gentle river meandering through scenic mountains and bluffs, with veils of creeks cascading down rocky falls.

Born in the melting snows of the Brooks Range and running 400 miles west to Kotzebue Sound, the magnificent **Noatak River** lies completely above the Arctic Circle. For three weeks we'll float it's entire 400-mile length, passing through an amazing ecological variety--jagged Arctic mountains, treeless tundra plains, steep canyons and finally into the spruce forest. We'll meet Natives of the village of Noatak near Kotzebue Sound, the only human settlement along the entire river. And of course, there will be plenty of time for hiking and fishing for grayling, northern pike, Arctic char, salmon and lake trout.

We will float down the **Kobuk River** via raft and kayak. Short stretches of whitewater make for unparalleled excitement. Further downriver, we'll stop to fish for migratory salmon and sheefish and float by Eskimo fish camps. The beaches are a rockhound's paradise, with jasper and jade especially common.

Also evident is an amazing abundance of birdlife, including ravens, Arctic terns, kingfishers, eagles and other predatory birds. At the finish, we'll briefly visit the native village of Kobuk before heading to Kotzebue.

Wild River Intimate, serene and relatively unused--originates at Wild Lake, a lovely body of water which is full of lake trout, northern pike and grayling for the angler. Canoe this cheerful river as it invites the traveler to become part of the panorama of rugged mountain peaks and stretches of lush green tundra.

The **Nigu** and the **Killik** are two of the North Slope's most scenic rivers....Wildlife abounds and many of the mountain Eskimos (Nunamiut) from Anaktuvuk Pass trap wolves, foxes, lynx and wolverine here in the winter. Arctic sand dunes line the riverbanks as do a myriad variety of wildflowers. Below Sunday Rapids, many of the rock outcroppings adjacent to the river are rich in various fossils. Upon our arrival at Umiat, we'll fly back to the land of the trees, south of the brooks.

The **Nigu** is born of the melting snows north of the Noatak River. There, north of the Arctic Divide, you are the only visitor. Caribou, grizzlies and wolves are frequently encountered. Fishing is good for lake trout, Arctic char and grayling.

Walker Lake Area Fish Schedule

Fish	Available	Peak
Sheefish	July 7 - Sept 15	July 21 - Sept 7
Arctic Char	June - Sept 15	June 1 - July 31, Sept 1-14
Lake Trout	June - Sept 15	June 1 - July 31, Sept 1-14
Northern Pike	June - Sept 15	June - Sept 15
Arctic Grayling	June - Sept 15	June - Sept 15
Chum Salmon	June 21 - Sept 7	July 8 - Aug 21

DENALI PARK, ALASKA

CASTLE, LYNN-SILVERTIP LODGE ON THE UNALAKLEET (907) 683-2261
Address Box 517, Denali Park, AK 99755
Airport Unalakleet 7m **Accommodations** Unalakleet 7m
Operation Outfitter, lodge **Type of Fishing** Fly, spin **Tackle Supplied** All
Fish King, silver salmon, grayling, sheefish **Season** June-Sept
Water Unalakleet, Kanektok and Anvik Rivers **Boats** River sleds, rafts
Specialty Fly/spin fishing **Aircraft** Floatplane, landplanes
Experience 21 years **Rates** day: $400
Guide's Notes: Four hundred miles northwest of Anchorage by plane, across the magnificent Alaska Range, lies a remote Eskimo village called Unalakleet. From there, it is only 10 miles more by boat to SILVERTIP'S finest fishing lodge.

The season starts in mid-June and extends to October 1. You can hook trophy size Arctic char, grayling, Dolly Varden and four species of salmon. Because the lodge is within 10 miles of the Bering Sea, our fresh-run salmon are the strongest and hardest fighting fish you will ever encounter!

King salmon, which run from the last two weeks in June through mid-July, can weigh more than 60 pounds. They are a thrill to take on both spinning and fly rods. As Winston Moore writes of SILVERTIP'S Unalakleet in THE PAN ANGLER: "It's the best I've been able to find for big fish."

Over one million pink (humpback) salmon enter the **Unalakleet River** in early July and remain until early August. They aggressively take lures and flies, in fact, have a reputation for striking "anything that hits the water." You can catch these fish one after another "until your arms fall off."

By very late June and lasting until early August a truly vastly underrated and realtively unknown fighting fish has made its way to our doorstep. The chum (or calico) salmon is an extremely strong fighter for its size (averaging 7-10 lbs.) and, in fact, is a tremendous jumper. Many professional anglers who have fished with us feel the chum salmon are easily the match of the legendary silvers.

The Unalakleet River features one of the most intense silver (coho) salmon runs in Alaska. These famous hard-hitting, jumping fish enter the river the first part of August and stay through mid-September. Their weight ranges from 8 to 20 pounds. They are equally responsive to lures and flies. Many anglers feel that the silvers are the most exciting of all the Pacific salmon. A fighting silver on a fly rod is what it is all about!

Unalakleet's large Arctic grayling, which are 2 pounds average and 3 pounds trophy, are always in the water in abundance. These small "sailfish of the north" love flies and ultralight gear.

Schools of Arctic char move in and out of the ocean along with the different runs of salmon. The average size is 4 to 6 pounds, with 10 pounds considered a trophy. During the last week of July and the first week of August these Arctic char swarm by the tens of thousands into Unalakleet's pink salmon spawning beds. At this time the char fishing is literally "a fish a cast" on both flies and lures.

DILLINGHAM, ALASKA

BERGMANN, BUS-B & B FISHING ADVENTURES
(209) 358-4576, (305) 743-7021
Address 6598 Fruitland Ave., Atwater, CA 95301
Airport Dillingham **Accommodations** Dillingham
Operation Outfitter **Type of Fishing** Fly, spin **Season** June-Sept
Fish 5 species of salmon, rainbow, Dolly Varden, grayling
Water Bristol Bay Drainage **Specialty** Wilderness float trips **Boats** Rafts
Experience 12 years **Rates** week: $2250/person
Guide's Notes: Catch and release, maximum of 4 people on wilderness float trips.
Author's Notes: *Bus is known for high quality Alaskan float trips and also guides in the Florida Keys where he is highly respected as a light tackle salt water guide.*

BROADY, JIM-ALEKNAGIK MISSION LODGE (206) 763-7708
Address 200 West 34th, Suite 908, Anchorage, AK 99503
Airport Dillingham 20m **Accommodations** On premises

Operation Outfitter, lodge **Type of Fishing** Fly, spin **Tackle Supplied** Fly, spin
Fish Rainbow, salmon, Arctic char, northern pike **Season** June-October
Water Bristol Bay, Iliamna water shed **Boats** River sleds, rafts, Johnboats
Specialty Daily fly-out (floatplane) fishing **Aircraft** Floatplanes, landplane
Experience 15 years **Rates** week: $6000/2 people
Author's Notes: Our contacts indicate this is a very good operation.

DUNCAN, DAVE AND SONS (509) 962-1060
Address High Valley Ranch, Rt. 1, Box 740, Ellensburg, WA 98926
Airport Dillingham **Accommodations** Dillingham **Operation** Outfitter
Fish Rainbow, char, 5 species of salmon **Season** June-September
Water Chosen River, Kodiak Island, Yakutat area **Type of Fishing** All
Specialty Remote float fishing trips **Aircraft** floatplanes
Boats River sleds, rafts **Tackle Supplied** Fly, spin
Experience 6 years **Rates** week: $2200/person
Author's Notes: Dave Duncan has a reputation for high quality tent camps and float trips.

EGDORF, DAVE-WESTERN ALASKA SPORT FISHING
(907) 842-5480, (406) 222-0451
Address P.O. Box 10142, Dillingham, AK 99576
Airport Dillingham **Accommodations** Dillingham
Operation Outfitter **Type of Fishing** Fly, spin **Tackle Supplied** Fly, spin
Fish Rainbow, king, coho salmon, char **Season** June-Oct
Water Bristol Bay watershed area **Boats** Rowboats, river sleds, rafts
Specialty Fly fishing for rainbow trout **Aircraft** Floatplanes
Experience 6 years **Rates** week: $2400/person
Author's Notes: Dave Egdorf has gained a reputation as a quality outfitter and guide.

MARTIN, BILL-ROYAL COACHMAN LODGE (907) 346-2595
Address P.O. Box 1887, Anchorage, AK 99510
Airport Dillingham 65m **Accommodations** Dillingham 65m
Operation Outfitter, lodge **Type of Fishing** All
Fish 5 species of salmon, rainbow, grayling, char **Season** June-Oct
Water West Bristol Bay area, Kanektok River **Tackle Supplied** All
Specialty Fly fishing **Aircraft** Floatplanes **Boats** River sleds, rafts
Experience 14 years **Rates** week: $3250/person

McMILLAN, RON-BRISTOL BAY LODGE (907) 248-1714
Address 3318 West 30th Street, Anchorage, AK 99517
Airport Dillingham 45m **Accommodations** On premises
Operation Outfitter, lodge (Dillingham area) **Type of Fishing** Fly, spin
Fish Rainbow, chinook, coho salmon, grayling **Season** June-September
Water Wood-Tikchiks, Nushagek, Togiak Rivers **Tackle Supplied** Fly, spin
Specialty Fly-out fishing trips **Aircraft** Floatplanes **Boats** River sleds, rafts
Experience 8 years **Rates** week: $6500/2 people

Author's Notes: *Bristol Bay Lodge is well known and our contacts tell us its good reputation is well deserved.*

STOCKHOLM, KEN R.-WOOD RIVER LODGE (907) 479-0308
Address 4437 Stanford Drive, Fairbanks, AK
Airport Dillingham 50m **Accommodations** On premises
Operation Outfitter, lodge (Dillingham Area) **Type of Fishing** All
Fish Rainbow, grayling, char, all salmon species **Season** June-Sept
Water Wood, Nushagak, and Togiak Rivers, Tikchik Lake **Tackle Supplied** All
Specialty Fly/spin stream fishing **Aircraft** Floatplanes **Boats** River sleds, rafts
Experience 13 years **Rates** day: $450 week: $2995/person
Guide's Notes: Wood River Lodge is located in the heart of Alaska's best fishing area.

Guests are flown out each day (weather permitting) in our float-equipped aircraft to the best spots for the type of fishing you prefer. Excellent fishing for reds, char, grayling, and rainbow is available 50 feet from the Lodge's front door!

The **Wood River-Tikchik Lakes** area of Southwest Alaska is one of the most beautiful locations in the state. The Lodge overlooks the **Agulowak River** which connects two of the largest lakes in the system. The lakes and rivers are crystal clear and unpolluted. Guests are likely to see a variety of wildlife that exists nowhere as in Alaska.

FAIRBANKS, ALASKA

NELSON, MIKE-ALASKA WILDERNESS EXPEDITIONS, INC. (907) 479-5496
Address P.O. Box 73297, Fairbanks, AK 99707
Airport Fairbanks **Accommodations** Fairbanks **Operation** Outfitter
Fish King, silver salmon, rainbow, grayling **Season** May-Sept
Water Gulkana, Deshka, Chena and Chatanika Rivers **Type of Fishing** Fly, spin
Specialty Fly/spin float trips **Aircraft** Floatplanes, landplanes **Boats** Rafts
Experience 5 years **Rates** day: $150 week:$1200-1500/2 people
Guide's Notes: For a day or the weekend the **Chatanika and Chena Rivers** offer easy relaxation and fun fishing for grayling.

Experience Alaska's Historic Gold Country first hand, as we travel one of its most exciting waterways, **the Forty-Mile River**. We'll fly in to the headwaters to begin our adventure, then explore old mining cabins and artifacts as we raft our way downstream through the 'chute' and around the 'kink'. Be sure to bring a rod and reel as the grayling fishing has been excellent; and, of course, we'll take time out for you to try your hand at gold panning.

The **Gulkana River** offers good to excellent fishing for king salmon, red salmon, rainbow trout and grayling. We will begin at Paxson Lake and immediately upon entering the river get a taste of its white-water, before relaxing in the more placid stretches where we can savor the scenic wilderness and wildlife which includes moose, bear, wolf, fox, beaver and eagle. The peace and tranquility of the float are again interrupted by frothing white-water as we prepare to make camp at Canyon Falls. A short trek to **Canyon Lake** for excellent grayling fishing may be included, time permitting.

Surrounded by lush green foliage, the gently flowing **Deshka River** provides an excellent opportunity for anglers of all ages to experience Alaskan fishing at its finest for king salmon, silver salmon, pink salmon, rainbow trout, and grayling.

FORT RICHARDSON, ALASKA

RUDD, JOHN H.-FISH HAWK CHARTERS (907) 694-5875
Address P.O. Box 592, Fort Richardson, AK 99505
Airport Kenai 4m **Accommodations** Soldotna 1m
Operation Outfitter **Type of Fishing** Spin, baitcast
Fish King, silver salmon, rainbow **Season** May-Sept.
Water Kenai River **Specialty** River fishing
Boats River sleds and river boats **Tackle Supplied** Spin, baitcast
Experience 6 years **Rates** 1/2 day: $190

GUSTAVUS, ALASKA

ROSENBRUCH, JIMMIE-GLACIER GUIDES, INC. (907) 697-2252
Address P.O. Box 66, Gustavus, AK 99826
Winter Address P.O. Box 460, Santa Clara, UT 84765
Airport Gustavus **Accommodations** Gustavus
Operation Outfitter **Type of Fishing** Spin, troll
Fish Salmon, halibut, char, trout **Season** June-Aug.
Water Glacier Bay, Icy Straits **Specialty** Charter vessel fishing
Boats 14 ft. skiffs with outboards**Tackle Supplied** troll
Experience 25 years **Rates** day: $500/2 people

HOMER, ALASKA

IVERSON, KEITH-SADIE COVE WILDERNESS LODGE (907) 235-8256
Address P.O. Box 2265, Homer, AK 99603
Airport Homer **Accommodations** On premises
Operation Outfitter, lodge **Type of Fishing** All
Fish Halibut, 5 species of salmon, Dolly Varden **Season** May-Sept.
Water Kachemak Bay area **Specialty** Salt water fishing **Aircraft** Floatplanes
Boats Sm. cabin cruiser, rowboats, skiff **Tackle Supplied** All
Experience 12 years **Rates** day: $200/person-guide-lodge-meals

McBRIDE, MICHAEL-KACHEMAK BAY WILDERNESS LODGE (907) 235-8910
Address China Poot Bay via, Homer, AK 99603

Airport Homer **Accommodations** On premises **Operation** Outfitter, lodge
Fish Silver, pink, king salmon, halibut, rainbow **Season** April-December
Water Kachemak & Kamishak Bays & watersheds **Tackle Supplied** Spin
Specialty Wilderness lodge fishing **Aircraft** Floatplanes
Boats Rafts, Boston Whalers **Type of Fishing** All
Experience 20 years **Rates** day: $300 5 days: $1500
Guide's Notes: Our Brown Bear Camp is located about 100 air miles, or about
a one hour bush flight, from the lodge. You will fly directly over smoking
Augustine Island, an active volcano. Ervin Bauer, an editor for "Outdoor Life"
magazine, veteran Alaskan traveler, and respected big game photographer, wrote
in the January 1979 issue. "I have never disembarked at a place like Chenik
Lagoon Camp. Not even on journeys to Antarctica, the northwest shores of
Hudson Bay, or even the Himalaya Mountains have I felt so suddenly surrounded
by wilderness." Our camp adjoins the **McNeil River Brown Bear Sanctuary**,
home of the greatest concentration of the world's largest carnivores.

Salmon, trout and flounder may be caught from the beaches. King salmon
and halibut are also abundant; we'll arrange charter trips for these two.
*Author's Notes: The McBride's Lodge has won lots of national awards. Clearly
a top notch operation.*

ILIAMNA, ALASKA

CARRELL, DEAN-TUWALA QUAH LODGE (707) 542-4242
Address C/O Fishing International, 4000 Montgomery Dr, Santa Rosa, CA 95405
Airport Iliamna 30m **Accommodations** On premises **Operation** Outfitter, lodge
Fish King, silver, sockeye salmon, Dolly Varden, lake trout **Type of Fishing** All
Season June-Sept. **Water** Lake Iliamna Area **Boats** Jet sled
Aircraft Floatplanes **Specialty** Fly and spin fishing for salmon and trout
Experience 2 years **Rates** week: $2195/person
Guide's Notes: First, there's the home river, a classic coastal stream that carves
its way through a forested wilderness from its origin at Tuwala Quah Lake to
where it meets the sea 15 miles downstream. This is a pure salmon river of
exceptional character offering mile after mile of beautiful runs, riffles and pools
accessible from the lodge by comfortable jet boats.

Fly fishers will enjoy the easy wading conditions and mid-range casts that
will cover battalions of chrome-plated salmon still carrying sea lice. Early in
the season the sockeye and kings begin nosing their way upstream, boiling as
they move into classic holding pools. No heavily weighted, trick fly lines here--
just a sink-tip with a bright streamer will take salmon after salmon. Spin casters
will literally raise havoc with these aggressive, eager takers with wobblers,
spinners and spoons.

Next come the silvers, acrobatic and fresh from the sea they'll provide the
kind of action that every angler should experience at least once in his life. If
the salmon wear you down (and they will!) try for Dolly Varden sea run char
and lake trout.

de Havilland Beaver, a favorite vehicle of Alaska guides. *Richard Swan*

Curry Harbor into a nice rainbow on Lake Iliamna tributary. *Richard Swan*

The fly-out program at Tuwala Quah focuses on the outstanding rainbow fishing this area of Alaska offers. Something totally unique to this area is a small, shallow lake where anglers cast to surface feeding 3 to 9 pound rainbows from float tubes or john boats.

Author's Notes: This is one of the top lodges in the state.

CONVENTE, KLAUS D.-RED QUILL LODGE (908) 571-1215
Address Box 49, Iliamna, AK 99606
Winter Address P.O. Box 2308, Kailua-Kona, HI 96745
Airport Iliamna **Accommodations** On premises
Operation Outfitter, lodge, tackle shop **Type of Fishing** Fly, spin
Fish Rainbow, Dolly Varden, grayling, 5 species of salmon **Season** June-Oct.
Water Bristol Bay, Lake Iliamna **Specialty** Fly fishing **Aircraft** Floatplanes
Boats Rafts, canoes, river and lake boats **Tackle Supplied** Fly, spin
Experience 8 years **Rates** day: $500 week: $6200 2 people

COMFORT, BYRON-ILIAMNA LAKE RESORT (907) 571-1387
Address Box 208, Iliamna, AK 99606
Airport Iliamna **Accommodations** On premises
Operation Outfitter, lodge, tackle shop **Type of Fishing** Fly, spin
Fish Rainbow, sockeye, king, silver salmon, char **Season** June-Oct.
Water New Halen, Nushagak, Kamishak, Aleknagik Rivers
Specialty Fly and spin fishing **Aircraft** Floatplanes, landplanes
Boats Outboard aluminum boats **Tackle Supplied** All
Experience 18 years **Rates** day: $150 week: $900-3000/person
Guide's Notes: Iliamna Area Fishing Calendar. In **June**, fishing is excellent for rainbow, Arctic char and grayling. These fish are primarily feeding on the sockeye fry from the previous season and will hit both dry and wet flies as well as spinners. The large king salmon make their showing in the rivers in early June. Dolly Varden, lake trout, bull trout, and northern pike are available as well as chum and pink salmon that show up the last of June.

During **July**, rainbow, char and grayling are still going strong in the streams. They still hit dry flies but are beginning to have a preference for wet flies, especially the rainbow. The king salmon run peaks about the 20th of July but they are still here in great numbers. Between the 1st and 4th of July, the sockeye or red salmon make their appearance as millions invade our streams from the Bristol Bay area. Many of the other species of fish in the streams that have a run of sockeye begin to retreat to the big lake. If you have never seen this run of sockeye salmon in the Iliamna area, there is no way that we could adequately describe it, as the streams are bank to bank fish. These are great fighting fish and equally great on the table. Both the chum and pink salmon are in the streams and give some really fantastic fishing. So here in July we have four of the five species of Pacific Salmon available. Also the Dolly Varden, bull trout, lake trout and northern pike are readily available. The weather is usually great in July.

Like July, **August** is a month of variety. The sockeye are well along in their spawning stages and are literally turning the streams red with their brilliant bright red body colors. Rainbow, char and grayling fishing is still good in many of the streams away from the lake, but on the streams full of sockeye its not until late in the month that they begin to venture in. There is still some king salmon fishing available until about mid August. Most of these giants are in full color as they are well into their spawning stage but there is still a lot of fight left in these mighty creatures. Another fisherman of the brown four legged kind can be seen on many of the salmon streams. This true Alaskan Fisherman usually has little concern for we two legged fishermen as his hearty appetite is being satisfied by the abundant easy to obtain sockeye salmon. Be sure to have a camera and preferably a telephoto lens available. You should be able to get photos that you will talk about for years to come. Early August marks the return of the silver salmon. These fish will average 10-12 lbs. in size and are excellent fighters. It is not unusual to catch 30-40 of these beautiful fighters in a day's fishing. The pink and chum salmon are still around as well as the dollies, bull trout, lake trout, and northern pike. Weather is usually fantastic.

September marks the return of the famous Iliamna wild rainbow trout into the streams from the big lake. The bottoms of the streams are usually orange from the roe left from the spawning sockeye and the rainbow, char and grayling are gorging themselves with this plentiful delicacy. Egg pattern flies and Okie Drifter lures will catch these monsters without fail. Silver salmon fishing is absolutely fantastic. Lake trout, dollies, bull trout and northern pike are still plentiful, but the month is most famous for its big rainbow trout. The last two weeks of September usually go to getting a little cooler and rain a little more frequent.

In our opinion, some of the very best fishing is in October. This is especially true of the big trophy rainbow trout. We have found that the very best time to catch them is just before freeze up which can occur almost any time now. During this first week of October, we are fishing for rainbow, char, grayling, silver salmon, Dolly Varden, lake trout, bull trout and northern pike. Weather conditions can be cold and harsh at this time and it is definately not one for other than the hearty fisherman that would really like to get one of the monster rainbows the area is famous for.

Author's Notes: Iliamna Lake Resort is a new operation which opened its doors in 1985. The facilities and food are excellent, however, I did not have a chance to evaluate their guide services.

GERKEN, TED-ILIASKA LODGE (907) 571-1221
Address Box 228, Iliamna, AK 99606
Airport Iliamna **Accommodations** On premises **Operation** Outfitter, lodge
Fish Rainbow, char, grayling, 5 species of salmon **Season** June-Oct.
Specialty Fly fishing **Aircraft** Floatplanes, landplanes **Type of Fishing** Fly
Boats River sleds **Tackle Supplied** Fly **Water** Iliamna area
Experience 9 years **Rates** week: $3100/person
Author's Notes: I have visited Ted's lodge. The accommodations and food are excellent. The lodge sets on a point over-looking Lake Iliamna. I can personally recommend this operation as excellent for the serious fly fisherman.

GOLL, CHRIS-RAINBOW RIVER LODGE (907) 243-7894
Address 4127 Raspberry Rd., Anchorage, AK 99502
Airport Iliamna 30m **Accommodations** On premises
Operation Lodge, outfitter **Type of Fishing** Fly, spin, troll
Fish Rainbow, king, coho, char, pike **Season** May-October
Water Copper R., Pike L., all waters in Bristol Bay region
Specialty Fly fishing **Aircraft** Floatplanes, landplane
Boats River sled, rafts, 22' cruiser **Tackle Supplied** Fly, spin, troll
Experience 18 years **Rates** week: $2650/person
*Author's Notes: I have never been to Chris Goll's lodge but after a visit in June,
1985, former President Jimmy Carter wrote the following to Chris Goll:*
   *...[It was] "one of the most enjoyable weeks of our lives. Everything about
   our stay at Rainbow River Lodge was memorable, but the hospitality we
   received from you and the staff served to tie together all the week's adventures.....As you know, I have fished in a lot of places in the world from
   Canada to New Zealand, but I've never seen anything to equal the Rainbows
   of the Copper River. They're a real challenge with wet or dry fly, nymph or
   streamer, but their size, number and fighting ability in the crystal clear water
   make the Copper worthy to be called a trophy stream. I'm grateful that you
   and the other outfitters in the area are determined to preserve the unique
   quality of the fishing. I am sure that I will never land the equal of the 30-inch
   Rainbow that finally took my yellow stonefly nymph nor the many large
   trout we caught on dry flies during the great caddis hatches."*

JOHNSON, BRUCE-KOKSETNA LODGE (206) 778-9811
Address P.O. Box 164, Iliamna, AK 99606
Airport Iliamna **Accommodations** On premises
Operation Guide, lodge **Type of Fishing** Fly, spin, troll
Fish Rainbow, king, silver, red salmon, char **Season** June-Oct.
Water Lake Iliamna, Nushagak River, Tikchik Lake, Kodiak Island
Specialty Fly/spin fishing **Aircraft** Floatplanes, landplanes
Boats River sleds **Tackle Supplied** Fly, spin
Experience 20 years **Rates** week: $2800/person

LOESCHE, RAY-RAINBOW KING LODGE (907) 571-1277
Address P.O. Box 106, Iliamna, AK 99606
Winter Address P.O. Box 3446, Spokane, WA 99220
Airport Iliamna **Accommodations** On premises **Operation** Outfitter, lodge
Fish King, silver, sockeye, rainbow **Season** May-Oct **Tackle Supplied** Fly, spin
Water 75 streams in the Iliamna area **Type of Fishing** Fly, spin
Specialty Stream fishing **Aircraft** Floatplanes, landplane **Boats** River sleds, rafts
Experience 20 years **Rates** week: $3700/person
*Author's Notes: The facilities, food, and equipment of this lodge are deluxe.
Gourmet meals are served each evening on white table clothes. Ray Loesche is
known for running a tight ship. New equipment for 1986 includes 2 de Havilland
Otter floatplanes which can spot a jet boat on a river which has just received
a fresh run of salmon. The next morning, Ray's guests will be fishing that stream.*

JUNEAU, ALASKA

ANDERSON, DALE-ADMIRALTY INN (907) 789-3263
Address 9040 Glacier Hwy, Juneau, AK 99801
Airport Juneau 20m **Accommodations** On premises
Operation Outfitter, lodge **Type of Fishing** Saltwater trolling
Fish Salmon, halibut, trout **Season** May-Sept **Specialty** Saltwater fishing
Water Icy Strait, Chatham Strait, Lynn Canal, Stephens Passage
Boats Rowboat, canoes, inboards **Tackle Supplied** Fly, spin, troll
Experience 5 years **Rates** week: $1750/person
Author's Notes: This lodge is known as a high quality operation. They have, to date, offered mainly trolling for salmon. However, they are now developing a salt water fly fishery for salmon.

KATMAI, ALASKA

SARP, TONY-KATMAI LODGE (206) 337-0326
Address 2825 90th SE, Everett, WA 98204
Airport King Salmon 15m **Accommodations** On premises
Operation Outfitter, lodge **Type of Fishing** All
Fish 5 species of salmon, grayling, trout, pike **Season** June-Oct.
Water Alagnak River **Specialty** Fly fishing **Aircraft** Floatplanes
Boats River sleds, rafts **Tackle Supplied** Spin, baitcast
Rates week: $1800-2400/person
Guide's Notes: Katmai Lodge is located on the **Branch River (Alagnak)** which originates in Nonvianuk Lake in Katmai National Monument. This area sits a few miles South of Lake Iliamna in the heart of the Bristol Bay watershed. The Alagnak River is not only within the designated trophy region, it is listed as an official wild scenic river. The clear waters of the Alagnak will keep even the most active angler busy with salmon, trout, char and grayling action.

The Lodge is located about eight miles from tidewater. When you stand on the banks of the Alagnak, you will know you are in the wilds of Alaska.

Catches comprise, depending on the season, Arctic char, northern pike, grayling, huge rainbow trout, Dolly Varden and all five species of salmon. The Alagnak features one of the largest sockeye runs in Bristol Bay, numbering in the millions and king salmon that run in the 70 pound class. We have hooked them larger, but have never been able to beach them because most of our fishing has been on flies and fly rods. If you have never caught a sockeye on a fly, you don't know what you have missed. Their fight is, by most standards, better than steelhead. The average fisherman can catch 25 to 40 sockeye a day.

We have landed and relased 12-20 pound trophy rainbows and northern pike that weigh in the high 20's, large for anywhere in Alaska. Even more exciting is the water--crystal clear, with its origin from Nonvianuk Lake. It does not run silt-laden as most Alaskan glacial rivers. The Branch is Alaska's only designated trophy fish area as well as a wild and scenic river.

Our silver salmon average 8-12 pounds, with trophy fish up to 20 pounds. August and September is the time to come up for silvers. They are the most aerobatic of the Pacific Salmon. A favorite of the fly fisherman, who can average up to 40 fish a day.

Our chum salmon average 9-12 pounds, with trophy fish well over 20 pounds. The chum salmon is probably one of the most overlooked sport salmon available. These fish are extremely powerful as they come in fresh from the sea. One may literally catch a fish on every other cast. Casts are made directly to the fish, as they are very visible as they travel up the river. They are migrating in very shallow water, making it an exciting fishery.

Author's Notes: Our friends tell us this is a top quality operation catering to serious fishermen. The river on which Katmai Lodge is located, the Branch River, is also called the Alagnak.

KENAI, ALASKA

GAINES, HARRY (907) 283-4618, 262-5097
Address Box 624, Kenai, AK 99611
Airport Kenai **Accommodations** On premises **Operation** Guide,lodge
Fish 4 species of salmon, rainbow, Dolly Varden grayling **Season** April-Oct.
Water Kenai River **Specialty** River fishing-trolling for salmon
Boats River sleds **Tackle Supplied** Spin, baitcast **Type of Fishing** Spin
Experience 15 years **Rates** day: $500 1/2 day: $250
Author's Notes: Harry has a very good reputation not only as a guide but also for his efforts to preserve the fishing on the Kenai.

WALKER, ROBERT AND DORIS-COPPER FLYFISHING LODGE (907) 262-7814
Address Route 1 Box 260, Kenai, AK 99611
Airport Kenai **Accommodations** On premises **Operation** Outfitter, lodge
Fish Rainbow **Season** June-Oct **Type of Fishing** Fly **Tackle Supplied** Fly
Water Copper River (designated as trophy fly fishing only)
Specialty Fly fishing the Copper River **Boats** River sleds
Experience 30 years **Rates** day: $275/person week: $1900/person

YEAGER, JOHN A.-JAY'S RIVER GUIDE (907) 283-3874
Address P.O. Box 2694, Kenai, AK 99611
Airport Kenai **Accommodations** Kenai **Operation** Guide, Outfitter
Fish King, red, silver salmon **Season** May-Sept **Type of Fishing** Spin
Water Kenai & Kasilof Rivers **Specialty** Drift fish & back troll for salmon
Boats River sleds, McKenzies, rafts **Tackle Supplied** Spin, troll
Experience 5 years **Rates** 1/2 day: $260

KETCHIKAN, ALASKA

MARQUART, MICHELLE-WATER FALL RESORT (800) 544-5125
Address P.O. Box 6440-FG, Ketchikan, AK 99901

Airport Ketchikan **Accommodations** On premises
Operation Outfitter, lodge **Type of Fishing** All
Fish Salmon, halibut, bottom fish **Season** June-Sept
Water Ulloa Channel, Bucareli Bay, Meares Passage
Specialty Salt water troll and mooching **Aircraft** Floatplanes
Boats Cabin cruisers, skiffs **Tackle Supplied** All
Experience 5 years **Rates** week: $2955/person
*Author's Notes: Homer Circle, fishing editor of SPORTS AFIELD, made this
comment to me about Water Fall Resort:*
    *"You don't need to be an expert fisherman to catch trophy size king and
silver salmon here. Excellent facilities with food to match!"*

McQUARRIE, LARRY-COAST WISE QUALITY CHARTERS
(206) 268-0950, 268-0515
Address P.O. Box 601, Westport, WA 98595
Airport Ketchikan **Accommodations** On premises
Operation Outfitter, lodge **Type of Fishing** Fly, spin, troll
Fish 5 species of salmon, steelhead, halibut, rockfish **Season** May-Sept.
Water Southeast Alaska salt water and tidal streams
Specialty Salt water salmon and halibut charter fishing
Boats Charter boats, rafts **Tackle Supplied** Troll
Experience 12 years **Rates** day: $600 week: $3500 2 people
**Guide's Notes: Description of fishing salt water and fresh water of Southeast
Alaska.**
    In saltwater, our daily bread and butter are "Feeder" (immature) King salmon
from 10 to 30 pounds, and halibut ranging from 20 to over 200 pounds, both
of which are found in abundance in our area at any time of year. This is spiced
by runs of different species of salmon timed throughout the season. "Spawner"
(mature) king salmon to 60+ pounds peak in May and are available through
June. Pink (Humpback) salmon to 6 pounds arrive in hordes during July and
are available throughout the remainder of the season. Coho (Silver) salmon to
20+ pounds begin to show in early August and build to a peak in September.
Chum salmon and sockeye salmon provide an incidental saltwater catch in
June and July/August respectively.
    In saltwater we use plug-cut or whole herring almost exclusively and present
the baits by mooching and trolling. The exception to this occurs in late August
and September when we will use flies for coho when conditions are right.
    Freshwater fishing begins in May and early June for the beautiful steelhead
in the many tidal streams of our area. Pink (Humpback) salmon swarm into
our streams in July, offering wide-open fly and spin fishing throughout the rest
of the season. Sockeye salmon also provide considerable excitement in many
of our streams during July and August.
    These fish are not fussy; small, bright fly patterns with a bit of tinsel or nearly
any small red spinner such as a Mepps No. 2 will take limits (6 fish) easily.
Yarn flies with pencil leads and typical steelhead casting equipment work well.

KING SALMON, ALASKA

CUSAK, MIKE-KING SALMON LODGE (707) 542-4242
Address C/O Fishing International, 4000 Montgomery Dr, Santa Rosa, CA 95405
Airport King Salmon 50m **Accommodations** On premises
Fish 5 species of salmon, rainbow **Season** June-Sept **Operation** Outfitter, lodge
Water Bristol Bay watershed **Aircraft** Floatplane **Type of Fishing** All
Specialty Light tackle spinning and fly fishing **Boats** River sleds
Experience 4 years **Rates** week: $3200/person
Guide's Notes: Trout fishermen will have their choice of miles of undisturbed trout streams whose crystaline pools and rocky riffles run thick with magnificent wild Alaskan rainbow trout--some of which will top fifteen pounds! Boasting a four-month long season, these rivers produce on all kinds of tackle--from delicate dry flies in June and July to brightly polished spinners and spoons, wet flies, and egg patterns in September.

Great runs of Pacific salmon abound in the Bristol Bay region, and Mike's guests are treated to the full spectrum of all of these--from the searing runs of red hot silver salmon, to the explosive power and endless stubborn strength of fresh Chinook. Arctic char, both resident and sea-run may be found in these rivers, as well as the light tackle artistry of Arctic grayling, lake trout and northern pike.

Author's Notes: *This is one of the top lodges in Alaska. Every aspect is rated excellent and the food, we are told, is outstanding.*

MATTHEWS, DICK, ALASKA'S ENCHANTED LAKE LODGE (206) 643-2172
Address 3722 West Lake Sammawish S.E., Bellevue, WA 98008
Airport King Salmon 70m **Accommodations** On premises
Operation Lodge, Guide **Type of Fishing** Fly, spin, troll
Fish Rainbow, 5 salmon species, grayling, char **Season** June-Oct.
Water Bristol Bay streams & rivers, Iliamna Region, Cook Inlet Coast, Katmai Park **Specialty** The Rolls Royce of Alaskan fly-out fishing **Aircraft** Floatplanes
Boats Jet boats, rafts, sport boat **Rates** week: $3300/person
Author's Notes: *This operation is recognized as one of the leading fishing lodges in the state.*

KODIAK ISLAND, ALASKA

SIKES, ROBIN & MARTHA-KARLUK LODGE (707) 542-4242
Address C/O Fishing International, 4000 Montgomery Dr, Santa Rosa, CA 95405
Airport Kodiak 75m **Accommodations** On premises **Operation** Outfitter, lodge
Fish King, silver, steelhead **Season** May-Oct **Type of Fishing** All
Water Karluk River **Boats** Jet sled **Specialty** Light tackle spinning and fly fishing
Experience 6 years **Rates** week: $1695/person
Guide's Notes: "**The Karluk River** boasts one of the heaviest salmon runs in the world, plus a good run of steelhead in the late fall. King salmon enter the river system in late May and average 25 to 30 pounds. Silver salmon (coho)

averaging 12 pounds begin their migration in late August with continued heavy runs into October. Though some steelhead are taken in early September, the best steelheading takes place in late September and early October.

In front of the lodge, anglers fish the dropping tides by wading to exploding pods of salmon fresh from the sea. In the lagoon, one casts lightly dressed flies or spinners to milling schools of anxious fish. In the easily waded river, fishermen work over pockets holding salmon and steelhead." (Fishing International)
Author's Notes: The Karluk River on Kodiak Island is world famous. The Karluk Lodge has been highly recommended by contacts whose judgement we respect.

KOTZEBUE, ALASKA

JACOBSON, JAKE AND PAT (907) 442-3120, 486-3954
Address P.O. Box 124, Kotzebue, AK 99752
Winter Address P.O. Box 1313, Kodiak, AK 99615
Airport Kotzebue **Accommodations** Kotzebue **Operation** Outfitter, guide
Fish Sheefish, char, grayling, 5 species of salmon **Season** July-Oct
Water Selawik, Kobuk, Noatak Rivers **Type of Fishing** All
Specialty Fly-in bank fishing **Aircraft** Floatplanes, landplanes
Experience 18 years **Rates** day: $300 week: $2000

MEKORYUK, ALASKA

SHAVINGS, SR., EDWARD-NUNIVAK ISLAND GUIDE SERVICE
(907) 227-8213
Address P.O. Box 31, Mekoryuk, AK 99630
Airport Bethel 100m **Accommodations** Mekoryuk **Operation** Outfitter
Fish Char, Dolly Varden, pink, silver salmon **Season** June-Sept.
Water Nunivak Island **Specialty** Fly fishing float trips
Boats Skiffs **Tackle Supplied** Fly, baitcast **Type of Fishing** All
Experience 17 years **Rates** 10 days: $2000

MOOSE PASS, ALASKA

HACKETT, STEVE-ALASKA TREKS 'N VOYAGES (907) 288-3610, 224-3960
Address P. O. Box 600, Moose Pass, AK 99631
Airport Seward 1m **Accommodations** Seward 1m
Operation Outfitter **Type of Fishing** Fly, spin, troll
Fish Salmon, trout, sheefish, grayling **Season** June-Sept.
Water Kobuk, John, Mulchatna, Chilikadrotna Rivers
Specialty Sea kayaking and river paddle raft trips
Boats Rafts, kayaks **Aircraft** Floatplanes, landplanes
Experience 6 years **Rates** day: $150

NOME, ALASKA

ELMORE, JOHN-CAMP BENDELEBEN (907) 443-2880

Address P.O. Box 1045, Nome, AK 99762
Airport Nome 73m **Accommodations** On premises
Operation Outfitter, lodge, tackle shop **Type of Fishing** All
Fish Grayling, char, coho, chum salmon **Season** June-Sept.
Water Niukluk and Fish Rivers **Specialty** Fly and river fishing
Boats River sleds, canoes **Tackle Supplied** Spin
Experience 19 years **Rates** day: $300/person
Guide's Notes: You start fishing right in front of camp. We use jet powered river boats and fish from the boat and by wading or walking the banks of the **Niuklik River**.

Grayling are plentiful and range from 14 to 22 inches with more 20 inch trophy grayling coming from our area than any other area of the state. They are a joy to fly fish. Nymphs, Wooly Worms, Muddlers, Polar Shrimp and dry fly patterns are their favorites. They also like small spinners such as #0 - #1 - #2 silver, red and white or black Mepps. Ultra light tackle brings out the best in the Arctic grayling, which are plentiful all summer long.

Arctic char range in size from 2 to 10 pounds with most of them averaging between 2 to 5 pounds. They are frantic fighters. The best lures are bright colored wet flies, red and white spoons or hammered brass with red, pink or orange. There are char in the river all summer, however, the non spawners follow the salmon fry migration to the sea in late June and follow the adult salmon back up river about mid August. The fall spawning char remain in the river all summer and develop the vivid colors so desirable in the char. The best char fishing is from ice out to late June and mid August thru freeze up in October.

King salmon run from the last week of June to the middle of July with a few stragglers through August. They are not as numerous as the other species, but are available. They run 15 pounds to 45 pounds and take bright colored spoons with orange, pink or red coloration. A real thrill to catch and a real challenge on a fly rod.

Chum salmon run up to 15 pounds. They start running about July 1st, thinning out by late August. They are plentiful and great sport. They enjoy the same lures as the other salmon.

Pink salmon run up to 6 or 7 pounds. Their run coincides with the chum salmon run. They run in vast numbers and love the same lures you use for other salmon and trout. Again match the tackle to the size of the fish. You will have great fun catching pinks on 6 to 8 pound line or a 6 weight fly outfit. You will wear yourself out catching them.

Pike are not as numerous as the other species but are available for those who want to fish them. They like Dardevle type lures as well as surface plugs. They are caught in the sloughs that are connected to the river system.

Author's Notes: *John Elmore has some excellent references. This is not a luxurious lodge but a basic operation for the serious fisherman.*

PORT ALSWORTH, ALASKA

JOHNSON, WILLIAM A.-LAKESIDE LODGE (907) 781-2202, 262-5245
Address Port Alsworth, AK 99653
Airport Anchorage 180m **Accommodations** On premises
Operation Outfitter, lodge **Type of Fishing** Fly, spin, troll **Aircraft** Floatplanes
Fish Rainbow, grayling, char, 3 species of salmon **Season** June-Oct
Specialty Fly fish and float scenic streams and rivers or troll lakes
Water Clark, Iliamna, Twin, Nicabuna Lakes **Boats** Row boats, rafts
Experience 7 years **Rates** day: $195-325/person

LANG, MARK-ALASKA'S WILDERNESS LODGE (800) 874-2880
Address 1 Lang Road, Port Alsworth, AK 99653-0001
Airport Anchorage 180m **Accommodations** On premises
Operation Guide, lodge **Type of Fishing** All **Tackle Supplied** All
Fish 5 species of salmon, grayling, rainbow, char **Season** June-Oct.
Water Bristol Bay Drainage **Boats** Row boats, red shanks
Specialty Light Tackle fishing **Aircraft** Floatplanes
Experience 6 years **Rates** week : $2595 (includes 6 fly-outs)
Author's Notes: I have not stayed at this lodge. However, a friend and I got stuck overnight on the shores of Lake Iliamna (the floatplane that was supposed to pick us up was grounded due to weather). Three of the owners of this lodge were camped out by the mouth of the river. They graciously invited us into their camp to have dinner and sleep in their cook tent. If the lodge treats guests as well as the owners treated us, it is an outstanding operation.

Tent camp on Lake Iliamna.   *Richard Swan*

VAN VALIN, GLEN-VAN VALIN'S ISLAND LODGE (907) 781-2230
Address Lake Clark, Port Alsworth, AK 99653
Airport Iliamna 50m **Accommodations** On premises
Operation Outfitter, lodge **Type of Fishing** All
Fish Rainbow, grayling, 5 species of salmon **Season** June-Sept.
Water Bristol Bay drainage **Boats** Rafts, cruisers **Tackle Supplied** All
Specialty Fly fishing float trips **Aircraft** Floatplanes
Experience 15 years **Rates** week: $5100/2 people
Author's Notes: I have never visited Mr. Van Valin's lodge on Lake Clark, but Homer Circle, Fishing Editor of SPORTS AFIELD, told me "They have excellent facilities, two of the finest private guides in Alaska, trophy sized salmon and rainbows, and with fly-out trips each day, you can't miss."

SLEETMUTE, ALASKA

HURLBER, VERNON-HOLITNA LODGE (800) 544-2244
Address General Delivery, Sleetmute, AK 99668
Airport Sleetmute 20m **Accommodations** On premises
Operation Guide, lodge **Type of Fishing** Fly, spin
Fish King salmon, sheefish, char, pike **Season** May-Sept
Water Holitna River, Tikchik, Iliamna Lakes, Bristol Bay area
Specialty Fly fishing **Aircraft** Floatplane, landplane
Boats River sleds, canoes, rafts **Tackle Supplied** Fly, spin
Experience 12 years **Rates** day: $800 week: $5000/2 people

SOLDOTNA, ALASKA

BAKER, TOM-FUNNY RIVER FISH CAMP (907) 262-9207
Address Star Route 2 Box 1270, Soldotna, AK 99669
Airport Soldotna 12m **Accommodations** On premises
Operation Guide, lodge **Type of Fishing** Spin, baitcast
Fish King, coho, sockeye, rainbow, Dolly Varden **Season** May-Oct.
Water Kenai, Kasilof Rivers **Specialty** Back troll and drifting for king salmon
Boats River sleds, power boats **Tackle Supplied** Spin, baitcast
Experience 5 years **Rates** day: $350 1/2 day: $200/2 people
Guide's Notes: King slamon fishing on the **Kenai River** generally begins in mid-May and runs through the 31st of July. "First run" fishing for kings is usually best during the last week of May and the first two weeks of June. "Second run" kings is generally best the last two weeks of July. Sockeye (red) salmon usually show up by the 4th of July with angling for them good until the end of July. By then, the coho (silver) are showing up. They are available through October. Humpback salmon, locally known as "Humpies" or in the lower 48, known as pink salmon, run the Kenai on even years. 1986 is a "Humpy Year." These small salmon (to 8 lbs) are great fun on ultra-light tackle.

BERG, RODNEY (907) 262-6064, 262-7550
Address 266 Redwood Court, Soldotna, AK 99669
Airport Soldotna **Accommodations** Soldotna **Operation** Charter Captain
Fish King, silver salmon, rainbow, halibut **Season** May-Oct
Water Kenai River, Cook Inlet, Kasilof River **Type of Fishing** Baitcast, troll
Specialty Light tackle fishing for king, silver salmon
Boats River sled, McKenzie **Tackle Supplied** Baitcast, troll, spin
Experience 4 years **Rates** day: $85-200

BYRNS, GLEN-FRONTIER RIVERS (907) 262-5931
Address P.O. Box 3460, Soldotna, AK 99669
Airport Soldotna **Accommodations** On premises**Operation** Outfitter, lodge
Fish King, coho salmon, rainbow, grayling **Season** April-Oct
Water Kenai River, Cook Inlet, Prince William Sound **Type of Fishing** All
Specialty Fly and drift fishing **Aircraft** Floatplane, landplane
Boats River sleds, canoes, McKenzies, rafts **Tackle Supplied** All
Experience 18 years **Rates** day: $500 week: $3,200 (includes room and board)
Guide's Notes: Fishing Calendar for Kenai River

Fish	Available	Peak
King Salmon	May 20 - July 31	June 15 - July 31
Sockeye Salmon	June 10 - July 31	July
Coho Salmon	Aug 1 - Oct 30	Aug 15 - Sept 15
Rainbow Trout	June 15 - Oct 30	Aug - Oct
Dolly Varden	May - Oct	July - Sept
Halibut	April - Sept	June - Aug

Drifting the Kenai in a McKenzie.

R. Valentine Atkinson

CORAY, DAVID A.-SILVER SALMON CREEK LODGE (907) 262-4839
Address Box 3234, Soldotna, AK 99669
Airport Soldotna 80m **Accommodations** On premises
Operation Outfitter, guide, lodge **Type of Fishing** Fly, spin, troll
Fish Silver, king salmon, halibut, Dolly Varden **Season** May-Sept.
Water Cook Inlet, Silver Salmon Creek, Shelter Creek
Specialty Stream bank fly and spin fishing **Boats** Canoes, rafts, cabin cruiser
Tackle Supplied Fly, spin **Experience** 4 years

DeVITO, SPENCER (907) 283-7437
Address Box 317, Soldotna, AK 99669
Airport Kenai 5m **Accommodations** Kenai 5m
Operation Outfitter, Charter Captain **Type of Fishing** Fly, spin, troll
Fish King, silver salmon, rainbow, Dolly Varden **Season** May-Sept.
Water Kenai, Kuskatan Rivers, Cook Inlet, Kenai Peninsula **Tackle Supplied** All
Specialty Float and drift fishing **Aircraft** Landplanes **Boats** Lunds aluminum
Experience 26 years **Rates** day: $100-200:varies

HINER, TIM (907) 262-9729
Address P.O. Box 2122, Soldotna, AK 99669
Airport Soldotna **Accommodations** Soldotna
Operation Guide, Charter Captain **Type of Fishing** Spin, troll, baitcast
Fish King, silver, pink, red salmon **Season** May-Sept
Water Kenai River **Specialty** Guided half day river trips
Boats River sleds, canoes **Tackle Supplied** Spin, baitcast
Experience 9 years **Rates** day: $400 1/2 day: $200

JOHNSON, JIM, PAT AND DON (907) 262-5357
Address Box 3773, 44526 Sterling Hwy, Soldotna, AK 99669
Airport Soldotna **Accommodations** Soldotna **Operation** Guide, Charter Captain
Fish King, silver salmon **Season** May-Sept **Type of Fishing** Baitcast
Water Kenai River **Specialty** River drift fishing and backtrolling
Boats River boats **Tackle Supplied** Baitcast, spin
Experience 7 years **Rates** 1/2 day: $220

KISHBAUGH, CHICK-ALASKA OUTDOOR SERVICES (907) 262-4589
Address Box 1066, Soldotna, AK 99669
Airport Soldotna **Accommodations** Soldotna **Operation** Outfitter
Fish Salmon, rainbow, char, grayling **Season** May-Nov **Type of Fishing** All
Water Kenai River and Peninsula, Iliamna/Bristol Bay, Lake Clark
Specialty Individually tailored fishing trips **Aircraft** Floatplane
Boats River sleds, canoes, McKenzies, rafts **Tackle Supplied** Spin
Experience 6 years

STERLING, ALASKA

SUITER, LARRY-FREEBIRD FISH CAMP (907) 262-5685
Address P.O. Box 454, Sterling, AK 99672
Airport Soldotna 12m **Accommodations** On premises
Operation Outfitter, lodge **Type of Fishing** Spin, baitcast
Fish King, silver salmon, rainbow, Dolly Varden **Season** May-Oct
Water Kenai River **Specialty** Drifting for King, silver salmon
Boats River sleds, McKenzies**Tackle Supplied** Spin, baitcast
Experience 5 years **Rates** day: $150 1/2 day: $125

TALKEETNA, ALASKA

MAHAY, STEPHEN (907) 733-2223, 733-2307
Address Box 133, Talkeetna, AK 99676
Airport Anchoage 120m **Accommodations** Talkeetna
Operation Guide, Outfitter **Type of Fishing** All **Tackle Supplied** All
Fish King, silver salmon, rainbow, grayling **Season** May-Oct
Water Talkeetna, Susitna, Chulitna Rivers, Chunilna Creek
Specialty Drop-off fishing tours and trips **Boats** Rafts, jetboats
Experience 8 years **Rates** day: $80-200 week: $2000 1/2 day: $80

Guide Dennis Reagen's son Israel (left) with fishing buddy Carlo Beronio and 6½-lb. steelhead from the Klamath.   *Dennis Reagen*

5. The West Coast States: Super mixed bag!

California, Hawaii, Oregon, Washington

The west coast states offer a fabulous array of light tackle fishing. A substantial number of guides reported back from these states, indicating that plenty of help is available to put the visiting fisherman over lots of hard-fighting fish.

Some of the largest bass in North America swim within 15 miles of San Diego, southern California's fastest-growing city. Florida strain largemouth were planted here in the sixties and have since grown to record-breaking size. There are more excellent bass lakes to the north, some within an hour's drive of downtown Los Angeles. Along the coast you will encounter many saltwater species such as bonito, yellowtail, and kelp bass.

You could spend a lifetime fishing central and northern California. Trout abound in the mountain streams, particularly in Hat Creek and on the Fall River, which are world class spring creeks in the Mt. Lassen area. Steelhead and salmon are available in outstanding coastal streams such as the Klamath, the Eel, and the Smith, as well as the Sacramento River system. At lower elevations, bass are abundant in most lakes; largemouth and striped bass can be found in the Sacramento Delta. Clear Lake, about one hundred miles north of San Francisco, is one of the largest natural lakes in California and has superb bass and crappie fishing.

The California Department of Fish and Game in cooperation with Cal Trout, a local organization similar to Trout Unlimited, has imposed wild trout angling regulations on a number of California waters. These measures have produced some excellent results, and bode well for the future.

Oregon may be the best-kept secret in American sport fishing. Superb angling is available on the Deschutes, one of the top trout and steelhead waters in the U.S. Oregon's best-known coastal streams—the Rogue, the Umpqua, and the Siletz—offer tremendous steelhead and salmon fishing. Runs occur all year, so you can plan a trip any time.

The McKenzie River, which empties into the Willamette about a hundred miles south of Portland, is another blue ribbon stream with excellent trout and steelhead possibilities. Further south is Klamath Lake and its little-known tributaries, the Williamson and Wood rivers. These streams, which are like big spring creeks, are tremendously productive and each year give up a number of big browns and rainbows in the ten pound class. If you like to fish for bass, try the outstanding smallmouth bass fishing that is available on the Umpqua River near Roseburg, or on the eastern side of the state in the famous Hells Canyon of the Snake.

Washington has long been known for great fishing. Its most famous steelhead river is the Skykomish, favorite of the Washington guides in this book. Second in popularity was the Sauk/Skagit system, well known for summer and winter run steelhead. There are dozens of other excellent steelhead and salmon streams in northwest Washington, especially on the Olympic Peninsula, where the Sol Duc, the Hoh, and the Bogachiel course down out of the cool rain forests of the Olympic Mountains.

To the south, more steelhead and salmon fishing can be found on the Cowlitz, Kalama, and Lewis rivers, which empty into the mighty Columbia near Longview. Like the Oregon streams, these rivers have fresh runs practically all year.

If you are a trout fisherman, head east to the Naches or Yakima rivers. Here, excellent hatches occur all through summer and into late fall. Bass fishermen and those interested in pike or walleye should plan to visit Potholes Reservoir, Banks Lake, and Franklin Roosevelt Lake, which are also located in the central part of the state.

Traveling fishermen will be happy to note that some of the best fishing in Washington is close to Seattle/Tacoma international airport. The Skykomish, for example, is only a forty-five minute drive from downtown Seattle. Lake Sammamish, known for good smallmouth fishing, is within the city limits of nearby Bellevue.

California

ANDERSON, CALIFORNIA

ADKINS, VICTOR-RIVERVIEW INN AND MARINA (916) 365-0772
Address Route 1 Box 1978, Anderson, CA 96007
Airport Redding 8m **Accommodations** On premises
Operation Guide, Inn **Type of Fishing** All **Season** Year-round
Water Sacramento River, Shasta Lake **Specialty** Back trolling and floating
Boats River sled **Tackle Supplied** All **Fish** Salmon, steelhead, trout, bass
Experience 45 years **Rates** day: $200
Guide's Notes: Sacramento River--We have four runs of salmon with the average fish weighing 28 pounds and running from 12 pounds to 60 pounds. Our fishing is year-round, with the largest run August through November. Big fish are caught December through March. Steelhead fishing is best August through November but fish are in the river all year. Trout are availble year-round. Striped bass fishing is best April through May.

MOORE, OKIE DICK (916) 365-2331
Address Route 1 Box 2231, Anderson, CA 96007
Airport Redding 3m **Accommodations** Anderson 5m
Operation Guide **Type of Fishing** Baitcast, troll
Fish Salmon, steelhead, trout, bass **Season** Year-round
Water Sacramento River, Shasta, Whiskeytown, Trinity Lakes
Specialty Back trolling **Boats** River sled, bass boats
Experience 21 years **Rates** day: $200

ARCATA, CALIFORNIA

SIMPSON, LARRY-TIME FLIES, INC. (707) 822-8331
Address 815 J Street, Arcata, CA 95521
Airport Arcata 6m **Accommodations** Arcata 6m **Operation** Guide, tackle shop
Fish Steelhead, salmon **Season** Aug-Mar **Type of Fishing** Fly, baitcast
Water Klamath, Eel, Smith Rivers **Specialty** Fly fishing & floating for steelhead
Boats River sleds, McKenzies **Tackle Supplied** Fly, baitcast
Experience 10 years **Rates** day: $175
Guide's Notes: The Klamath River is California's second largest river system. Originating in Oregon, the river drains the rugged coast range before winding through forests of giant redwoods and finally entering the Pacific. The lower forty miles of the river is particularly remote, much of the river being only accessible by boat.

CALIFORNIA

Crescent
City

Klamath

Eureka

Trinity

Mad R.

Eel River

S. Fk. Eel R.

Shasta
Lake

Redding

Russian River

Sacramento R.

Susanville

Oroville
Lake

Chico

Feather R.

Yuba R.

American R.

Sacramento

Lake
Tahoe

San Francisco

Oakland

Delta of the
Sacramento
River

San Jose

Stockton

Crowley
Lake

Yosemite
National
Park

5

Bishop

Owen's R.

Kings
Canyon
National
Park

Sequoia
National
Park

Owen's
Lake
(dry)

Lake
Nacimiento

San Luis
Obispo

Isabella
Lake

Weldon

Pyramid
Lake

Kern R.

Cachuma L.

Lake
Piru

Castaic
Lake

Santa Barbara

Lake
Casitas

Burbank

San Gabriel
River

San Gabriel
Reservoir

Van Nuys

Fullerton

Los Angeles

Yorba Linda
Santa Ana

Pacific Ocean

Colorado R.

Lake
Havasu

Lake Hodges

San Vicente Lake

El Capitan Lake

San Diego

Lower Otay Lake

NORTHERN CALIFORNIA

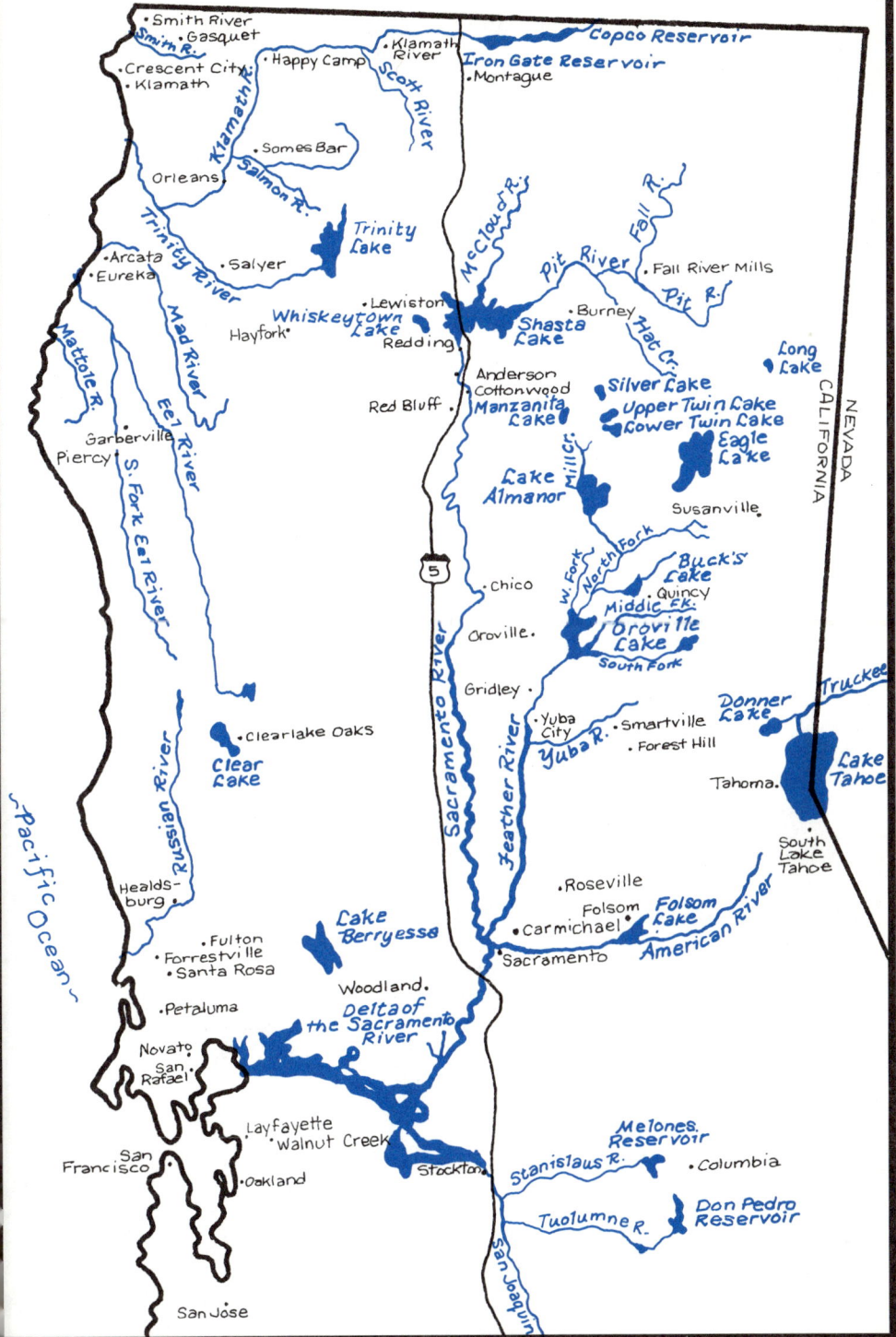

The Klamath boasts a reputation of being one of the finest steelhead streams in the world, having a huge run of fish entering the river in the late summer and fall months. This is the ideal time for the fly fisher. The weather is mild, the river is low and the fish are eager! There are two main runs of steelhead in the Klamath during this time of year. The larger fish are four to ten pounds (and sometimes bigger). While these fish do not average particularly large for steelhead, they are very abundant and tremendously strong fighters. The other run of fish is made up of "half-pounders." These are two year old steelhead of about 12″ to 18″ in length and from 3/4 pound to 3 pounds in weight. These fish are particularly abundant in August and September in the lower river. They are amazing battlers on light tackle, usually prone to lots of jumps and strong runs. The "half-pounders" are quick to take a fly, hooking twenty or thirty in a morning or evening is not uncommon when the run is on.

The Klamath also hosts large runs of shad, coastal cutthroat trout, king and silver salmon. Any of these fine gamefish are a possibility when wetting a line in the Klamath.

Fly Tackle--We recommend an 8 1/2 ′ or 9′ fly rod that balances with a size 6 or 7 fly line. Such a fly rod is ideal for Klamath steelhead fly fishing. Experienced fly fishers may want to try lighter rods, especially for the 12″ to 18″ "half-pounders" that can be abundant. Fly lines in weight forward tapers are best. Both floating and 10′ fast sinking tip lines are useful. A fast sinking shooting taper is handy at times, particularly late in the season. The fly reel should be of the single action type with a strong, smooth drag and adequate capacity to hold 100 yards of 20 pound test braided dacron backing in addition to your fly line.

Leaders--Leaders should be 7 1/2′ to 9′ in length and tapered to about 6 pound test (2x or 1x).

Flies--A few of the proven favorites are: Brindle Bug, Silver Hilton, Burlap, Skunk, Wooly Worm, in sizes 6 through 10.

BISHOP, CALIFORNIA

THORESON, GERALD (619) 873-7703
Address P.O. Box 1483, Bishop, CA 93514
Airport Bishop **Accommodations** Bishop **Operation** Guide
Fish Brown, rainbow **Season** Apr-Oct **Type of Fishing** Spin, baitcast, troll
Water Crowley, Silver, Upper and Lower Twin Lakes **Specialty** Lake trolling
Boats 17 foot Glasspar **Tackle Supplied** Spin, baitcast, troll
Experience 2 years **Rates** day: $150/2 people

BURBANK, CALIFORNIA

IOVINO, DON (818) 848-6180
Address 3220 Wyoming Street, Burbank, CA 91505
Airport Burbank 20m **Accommodations** Burbank

Operation Outfitter **Fish** Largemouth & striped bass **Season** Year-round
Water Lakes Casitas, Cachuma, Piru, Castaic lake **Type of Fishing** Spin, baitcast
Specialty Plastic worm fishing-doodle method **Boats** Bass boats
Experience 8 years **Rates** day: $240/2 people (within a 50 mile radius)
*Author's Notes: Don has developed a method of bass fishing with plastic worms
which he calls doodling. This is a deep jigging technique and is very effective.
Don guides the local bass lakes around Los Angeles. He has won several bass
championships and is well known in bass circles. If he is booked up he can
set you up with another guide. In fact, he can book you with bass guides
throughout the southwest from California to Texas.*

BURNEY, CALIFORNIA

QUIGLEY, BOB-HAT CREEK & FALL RIVER FLY SHOP (916) 335-4700
Address Route 2 Box 294, Burney, CA 96013
Airport Redding 20m **Accommodations** Burney **Operation** Guide, tackle shop
Fish Rainbow, brown **Season** April-Nov **Type of Fishing** Fly, spin
Water Hat Creek, Fall, McCloud Rivers, Manzanita Lake **Tackle Supplied** Fly
Specialty Fly fishing float and wade trips **Boats** Rowboats, river sled
Experience 10 years **Rates** day: $165 1/2 day: $110
*Author's Notes: Bob Quigley guides on **The Fall River**, which is one of the
finest spring creeks in the west. The Fall has huge rainbows up to 10 pounds
and prolific hatches including a hatch in mid-June of the giant mayfly, Hexagenia
Limbata. However, true to spring creek form, the water is gin clear and the
fishing can be very difficult. Small flies and long leaders are the rule. Bob
Quigley has been fishing and guiding the Fall for over 10 years. He is also a
nationally known fly-tier and has developed several original patterns to fish
the Fall and other spring creeks. He is a highly capable guide.*

CARMICHAEL, CALIFORNIA

WATSON, BARRY (916) 944-0498
Address 3244 California Avenue, Carmichael, CA 95608
Airport Sacramento 15m **Accommodations** Carmichael
Operation Guide **Type of Fishing** Fly, spin, baitcast
Fish Steelhead, salmon, shad, bass **Season** Year-round
Water American, Sacramento, Eel, Klamath Rivers **Tackle Supplied** All
Specialty Drift boat fishing trips **Boats** McKenzies, 15' aluminum
Experience 3 years **Rates** day: $165 1/2 day: $90
Guide's Notes: Sacramento Area Fish Calendar

Fish	Available	Peak	Method
Steelhead	Sept - Mar	Dec - Jan	Lures, bait (roe), flies
Salmon	Sept - Oct		Lures, roe
American Shad	May - June	June	Flies
Striped Bass	Mar - May	April	Bait, lures

CHICO, CALIFORNIA

JENSEN, MILT-MERGANSER OUTFITTERS (916) 343-2616
Address 843 Colusa Street, Chico, CA 95928
Airport Chico **Accommodations** Chico **Operation** Guide, outfitter
Water Yellow Creek, McCoy Res., Long, Butt Lakes **Type of Fishing** Fly
Specialty Fly fishing float/wade trips **Fish** Rainbow, brown, brook, bass
Boats Rowboats, float tubes **Tackle Supplied** Fly **Season** Mar-Oct
Experience 2 years **Rates** day: $300 1/2 day: $160
Guide's Notes: Yellow Creek--Spring creek fishing for brown trout almost exclusively. Very fussy and fine fishing with fine tippets and tiny dry flys.

Butt Estuary--Really the crown jewel in my program. Very large rainbow and brown trout on small nymphs with fine leaders. This fishery has to be experienced to be believed. August and early September are best.

McCoy and Long Lakes--Classic weedy, shallow, cool waters and agressive rainbow trout and brookies provide fine sport when conditions permit. Weather dictates availability.

Author's Notes: Hal Janssen tells me Milt is very knowledgeable and an excellent guide.

CLEARLAKE OAKS, CALIFORNIA

CLOW, KEITH (707) 998-1921
Address P.O. Box 1401, Clearlake Oaks, CA 95423
Airport Sacramento 110m **Accommodations** Clearlake Oaks
Operation Guide **Type of Fishing** Spin, baitcast **Fish** Black, sm bass
Water Clear, Berryessa, Powell, Mead Lakes **Specialty** Instructional fishing trips
Boats Bass boats, 18' ranger **Tackle Supplied** Spin, baitcast **Season** Year-round
Experience 15 years **Rates** day: $225-275
Guide's Notes: Clear Lake is probably the best bass fishery in northen California. The record weight in a 2 day draw tournament, 40 pounds + came from Clear Lake. The lake is the largest natural lake in California, and 7 to 9 pound fish are not uncommon. The lake record is 13 pounds.

COTTONWOOD, CALIFORNIA

SITTON, JERRY-JERRY'S GUIDE SERVICE (916) 365-1282
Address P.O. Box 1271, Cottonwood, CA 96022
Airport Redding 12m **Accommodations** Cottonwood
Operation Outfitter, guide **Type of Fishing** All **Tackle Supplied** All
Fish Salmon, steelhead, bass **Season** Year-round **Water** Sacramento River
Specialty Trolling and drifting **Boats** 19' commander river boat
Experience 7 years **Rates** day: $170

CRESCENT CITY, CALIFORNIA

DAMM, DAROL L.-THE DAMM DRIFTER (707) 464-7192
Address 2303 Parkway Drive, Crescent City, CA 95531
Airport Arcata 70m **Accommodations** Crescent City
Operation Guide, outfitter, tackle shop **Type of Fishing** Spin, baitcast
Fish Steelhead, salmon **Season** August-February
Water Smith, Chetco, Klamath, Mad Rivers **Specialty** Float trips
Boats Rowboat, jet boat, McKenzies **Tackle Supplied** Spin, baitcast
Experience 5 years **Rates** day: $150
Guide's Notes: I fish on the **Klamath River** with jet boats starting in August
and going through October for salmon and steelhead. In November, we start
fishing for the big winter fish (salmon) on the **Smith, Chetco (OR), and Elk
Rivers**. By mid-December, we start using drift boats and gear everything towards
trophy steelhead on the **Smith, Mad, Chetco (OR), and Sixes Rivers (OR)**. We
do a lot of "hot shot" fishing and also do some bait drifting. Whatever it takes
to put fish in the box.

EUREKA, CALIFORNIA

BREWER, JIM (707) 443-0936
Address 111 Brauning Road, Eureka, CA 95501
Airport Arcata 10m **Accommodations** Eureka
Operation Guide, outfitter **Fish** Steelhead, salmon **Season** Oct-May
Water Eel, Mad, Smith, Mattole Rivers **Specialty** Float trips and bank guiding
Boats McKenzies **Tackle Supplied** Spin, baitcast **Type of Fishing** Spin, baitcast
Experience 5 years **Rates** day: $150 1/2 day: $75

CHANDLER, RAY-CAL-ORE RIVER GUIDES (707) 442-6125
Address 2440 Bainbridge Street, Eureka, CA 95501
Airport Arcata 10m **Accommodations** On premises **Operation** Outfitter, lodge
Fish Salmon, steelhead, shad, sturgeon **Season** Aug-March
Water Klamath, Smith, Eel Rivers **Specialty** Fly and drift fishing
Boats River sled, McKenzie **Tackle Supplied** All **Type of Fishing** Fly, spin
Experience 4 years **Rates** day: $150 1/2 day: $100/2 people

FALL RIVER MILLS, CALIFORNIA

NORMAN, ROBERT (916) 336-6787
Address P.O. Box 652, Fall River Mills, CA 96028
Airport Redding 70m **Accommodations** Fall River Mills
Operation Guide **Fish** Rainbow, brown **Season** April-November
Water Fall, McCloud Rivers, Hat Creek **Specialty** Fly fishing float/wade trips
Boats Jet boats **Tackle Supplied** Fly **Type of Fishing** Fly

Experience 6 years **Rates** day: $145 1/2 day: $105
Guide's Notes: I guide fly fishing only for Fall River, Hat Creek, and the McCloud River. The peak times for **Fall River** are from the opener (3rd Saturday in April) to the end of July. There is an excellent spinner fall on the upper Fall during this period, also there are pale Morning Duns hatching between 10am and 2pm every day weather permitting and caddis hatches in the evenings. Starting about May 15th the Fall River gets a good green drake hatch between 10am and 2pm, this goes on for about 3 weeks. Throughout this period there's excellent nymphing.

The lower Fall River has an excellent Hexagenia hatch that starts about June 15th and lasts about 5 to 6 weeks. This hatch offers exciting dry fly fishing right at dark and allows an angler to take fish 5 to 8 pounds on a dry fly.

Fall River fall fishing is excellent from September 15 to November 15. There are fabulous hatches of mayflies and Caddis, also very good Green Drake hatches (better than the spring hatch). Fall River requires long fine leaders (14' to 18' leaders) and 5x and 6x tippets. The average fish on Fall River is 15".

Hat Creek provides excellent evening hatches in May and June which slow down in July and August. The evening hatches in May and June are mayflies and caddis (very heavy), fabulous dry fly fishing, long leaders and fine tippets (14' to 20' leaders) are a must. Hat Creek has a good hatch of salmon fly and golden stones the first two weeks of May, followed by an excellent Green Drake emergence mid-May to June 1st. Nymphing is excellent May - June and again in mid September to the close of the season. There are great caddis hatches all fall.

McCloud River provides excellent nymphing and streamer fishing all season. Golden stones come off heavy in June. McCloud River has good Caddis hatches all season. The brown trout migrate into the McCloud from Shasta Lake in the fall. The fish are big, 5 to 10 pounds. The water is generally low at this time offering a good chance to stick big fish.

FOLSOM, CALIFORNIA

SIEMENS, JIM (916) 985-4333
Address 116 Winchester Court, Folsom, CA 95630
Airport Sacramento **Accommodations** Sacramento
Operation Guide **Type of Fishing** Spin, baitcast **Fish** Salmon, trout, striper
Water American, Sacramento Rivers, Donner, Shasta Lakes **Season** Year-round
Specialty Lake trolling **Boats** Bass boats **Tackle Supplied** All
Experience 6 years **Rates** day: $130 1/2 day: $70

FOREST HILL, CALIFORNIA

SLAGLE, KEN (916) 367-2351
Address Box 635, Forest Hill, CA 95631
Airport Sacramento 10m **Accommodations** Sacramento 10m
Fish Bass, salmon, steelhead, trout **Season** Spring & Fall

Operation Guide **Boats** River sleds, bass boats **Tackle Supplied** All
Water Sacramento, Feather, Yuba Rivers, Donner Lake
Specialty River and lake fishing **Type of Fishing** Spin, baitcast
Experience 5 years **Rates** day: $150

FORESTVILLE, CALIFORNIA

MOSSHOLDER, RICHARD-RICH'S GUIDE SERVICE (707) 887-2659, 482-8545
Address 8001 Trenton Road, Forestville, CA 95436
Airport Eureka 50m **Accommodations** Klamath 2m **Operation** Guide, outfitter
Fish Salmon, steelhead **Season** July-Mar **Type of Fishing** All
Water Klamath, Smith, Russian Rivers **Specialty** Up river sled and drift fishing
Boats Rowboat, river sleds, McKenzies **Tackle Supplied** All
Experience 4 years **Rates** day: $150 week: $750 1/2 day: $90

FULLERTON, CALIFORNIA

SANTORI, GREG-MARRIOTT'S FLY FISHING STORE (714) 525-1827
Address 2634 W. Orangethorpe, Dept. O, Fullerton, CA 92633
Airport Los Angeles 23m **Accommodations** Fullerton
Operation Guide, tackle shop **Type of Fishing** Fly
Fish Rainbow, bonita **Season** Year-round **Specialty** Fly fishing
Water San Gabriel River, Deep Creek, King Harbor **Tackle Supplied** Fly
Experience 2 years **Rates** day: $125-250
Guide's Notes: The West Fork of San Gabriel is a small river in the San Gabriel
Mountains which is managed as a catch and release, fly fishing only stream.
· **Deep Creek** is located in the San Bernadino Mountains and is also managed
as a fly fishing-only stream. It has an excellent population of rainbows. Fish
can be taken all year long but the best fishing is from September to May.
Standard fly patterns that work well on both streams include Adams, Humpy,
Royal Wulffs, and all Caddis patterns.
   King Harbor bonita fishing begins as early as December and runs into March.
We cast streamer patterns from small outboard boats to the fish which average
3 to 5 pounds. On good days 50 fish per boat is common and strikes are right
on the surface.
*Author's Notes: Marriott's Fly Fishing Store, formerly Hackle and Tackle, is
one of the top fly shops in California.*

GARBERVILLE, CALIFORNIA

MULLINS, GREGORY-BEAR CREEK GUIDE SERVICE (707) 986-7734
Address P.O. Box 364, Garberville, CA 95440
Airport Arcata 70m **Accommodations** Garberville
Operation Outfitter **Type of Fishing** Spin, baitcast **Season** Year-round

Fish Steelhead, salmon, trout **Specialty** Float/drift boat trips
Water South, North, Main Fork of the Eel, Mattole Rivers
Boats River sled, McKenzie **Tackle Supplied** Spin, baitcast
Experience 4 years **Rates** day: $150 week: $450 1/2 day: $75

GASQUET, CALIFORNIA

EUDEMILLER, JOE-VILLAGE TACKLE SHOP (707) 457-3475, 457-3160
Address 10340 Highway 199, Gasquet, CA 95543
Airport Crescent City 18m **Accommodations** Gasquet
Operation Outfitter, tackle shop **Type of Fishing** Spin, baitcast
Fish Steelhead, salmon **Season** Year-round **Specialty** Drift boating for salmon
Water Smith, Klamath, Chetco (OR), Rogue (OR) Rivers
Boats River sleds, McKenzies **Tackle Supplied** All
Experience 11 years **Rates** day: $150 1/2 day: $85

GRIDLEY, CALIFORNIA

PYLE, RICHARD E. (916) 846-6420
Address P.O. Box 831, Gridley, CA 95948
Airport Sacramento 40m **Accommodations** Colusa
Operation Guide **Type of Fishing** Spin, baitcast, troll **Tackle Supplied** All
Fish Bass, sturgeon, salmon, steelhead **Season** Sept-June **Boats** Bass boats
Water Sacramento, Feather Rivers **Specialty** River and lake trolling
Experience 6 years **Rates** day: $150

HAPPY CAMP, CALIFORNIA

GRENVIK, TIM-THOMPSON CREEK GUIDE SERVICE (916) 493-2430
Address P.O. Box 875, Happy Camp, CA 96039
Airport Medford, OR 110m **Accommodations** Happy Camp
Operation Guide, Outfitter **Type of Fishing** All **Boats** McKenzies
Fish Steelhead, rainbow, brook **Season** Year-round
Water Klamath River, Clear, Elk Creeks, Marble Mountain area
Specialty Fly fishing and drift fishing plugs for steelhead
Experience 5 years **Rates** day: $70/person 1/2 day: $35/person
Guide's Notes: Klamath River and Tributaries
   Steelhead--We drift fish the Klamath from September to January. During September and October there is an excellent run of "half pounders" which are 12 - 18" fish. Bigger steelies arrive November to January. Lures work good any time. Fly fishing is best during October and November. The tributaries hold steelhead all summer. They are most easily caught with spinners, however, the determined fly fisherman can catch them on flies.
   Trout--We drift the river for resident trout from April through June. The tributaries open the end of May and provide action all summer. Wilderness

lakes open in June. Fishing the outlets from these lakes can be fun and rewarding. Rainbow and eastern brook are the major species of trout. Salmon flies (early May), stoneflies and mayflies are the major hatches.

HEAD, TOM E.-WILDERNESS PACKERS GUIDE SERVICE
(916) 493-2364, 493-2793
Address Indian Creek Road, Box 764, Happy Camp, CA 96039
Airport Medford, OR 110m **Accommodations** Happy Camp
Operation Outfitter **Type of Fishing** All **Tackle Supplied** Fly, spin
Fish Lake, mountain, rainbow, brook trout **Season** March-November
Water Happy Camp mountain area lakes and streams
Specialty Fly or spin lake and stream fishing **Boats** Rafts
Experience 1 year **Rates** day: $100 1/2 day: $65

HENDERSON, BILL (916) 493-2422
Address P.O. Box 90, Happy Camp, CA 96039
Airport Medford, OR 110m **Accommodations** Happy Camp
Operation Guide **Specialty** Fly and drift fishing
Fish Steelhead, salmon **Season** Aug-Mar **Type of Fishing** All
Water Klamath, Smith, Chetco (OR), Trinity Rivers
Boats River sled, McKenzies **Tackle Supplied** Fly, spin
Experience 5 years **Rates** day: $160 1/2 day: $80
Guide's Notes: We catch salmon and steelhead. Lures used are Wee Warts and Hot Shots. Flies are, to name a few, Silver Hilton, Brindle Bug, Moss Back, Green Butted Skunk, Wooly Worm, and Brown Hackle Peacock. Peak time is September, October, and November.
Author's Notes: Larry Schoenborn, owner of Larry's Sport Center in Oregon City, Oregon, and producer of the excellent television show, "Fishing the West," tells me Bill is a top notch guide.

HAYFORK, CALIFORNIA

OSWALD, JOHN & GAIL TANAKA (916) 623-4456
Address Box 115, Hayfork, CA 96041
Airport Redding 60m **Accommodations** Hayfork **Operation** Outfitter
Fish Steelhead, samon, shad, trout **Season** Year-round **Type of Fishing** All
Water Trinity, Eel, Sacramento, Smith Rivers **Tackle Supplied** Spin, baitcast
Specialty Driftboating for steelhead and salmon **Boats** McKenzies, raft
Experience 5 years **Rates** day: $165 1/2 day: $125
Guide's Notes: Trinity River--July-September: The salmon fishing can be exciting. The run peaks in mid-September. At this point, steelheading turns on and fishing varies from fair to excellent as the runs come into the river.

Eel River System--From the first rain until late March when this system is fishable, it is my choice. Large salmon are taken from October until January. In December the steelhead show up and are in the river until late March. Large steelhead are taken throughout the winter. Fish to 21-3/4 pounds have come to our net. At this time we may also fish the Mad and Van Duzen Rivers.

HEALDSBURG, CALIFORNIA

SHEEHY, WES (707) 433-5933

Address 319 Fuchsia Way, Healdsburg, CA 95448
Airport Santa Rosa 17m **Accommodations** Local
Operation Guide **Type of Fishing** All **Season** Nov-July
Fish Smallmouth, largemouth, spotted bass, rainbow
Water Lake Berryessa, Lake Sonoma, Clear Lake
Specialty Casting for bass and fly rodding for bass
Boats Bass boats **Tackle Supplied** All
Experience 2 years **Rates** day: $125
Guide's Notes: Good fishing is available from November to May with the season lasting November to July.

   Lake Berryessa--November is the peak month for trophy smallmouth bass which are surface feeding on thread fin shad at Lake Berryessa. Three to six pound fish are common and can be caught with surface lures and streamers at this time. We encourage children down to 3 1/2 years of age to join us (trolling).
Author's Notes: Bob Nauheim of Fishing International says "Wes is the best bass guide in Northern California and one of the best anywhere."

KLAMATH, CALIFORNIA

MORRIS, JOHN "CHUB" (707) 482-5591

Address 1661 W. Klamath Beach., Box 589, Klamath, CA 95548
Airport Crescent City 25m **Accommodations** Klamath
Operation Guide **Type of Fishing** All **Water** Klamath River
Fish Steelhead, salmon **Season** March-Oct **Boats** Jet boats
Specialty Inboard jet river drifting and trolling **Tackle Supplied** All
Experience 16 years **Rates** day: $150 week: $900 1/2 day: $100

KLAMATH RIVER, CALIFORNIA

RUCKER, NEIL & JOANN-BEAVER CREEK LODGE (916) 465-2646, 465-2246

Address P.O. Box 121, 16606 Hwy 96, Klamath River, CA 96050
Airport Medford, OR 50m **Accommodations** On premises
Operation Outfitter, lodge **Type of Fishing** Fly, spin
Fish Steelhead, native trout, salmon **Season** Year-round
Water Klamath, Sacramento, Trinity Rivers
Specialty Fly fishing float or back packing trips and drift boat fishing
Boats Canoes, rafts, dory, McKenzies **Tackle Supplied** Fly, spin
Experience 10 years **Rates** day: $140 week: $980

LAYFAYETTE, CALIFORNIA

WOOLLEY, PETE-FLY FISHING OUTFITTERS (415) 284-3474
Address 3533 Mt. Diablo Blvd., Layfayette, CA 94549
Airport Oakland 18m **Accommodations** Layfayette
Operation Outfitter, tackle shop **Type of Fishing** Fly
Fish Trout, steelhead, salmon, shad **Season** Year-round
Water Fall, Klamath, Eel, Trinity, Russian Rivers, Hat Creek
Specialty Fly fishing **Boats** McKenzie, john boats **Tackle Supplied** Fly
Experience 6 guides- varies **Rates** day: $120-180
Author's Notes: Pete Woolley runs an excellent fly fishing shop in Layfayette, California (San Francisco Bay Area). He does not personally guide, but he does book guides in the Northern California area.

LEWISTON, CALIFORNIA

BURTON, HERB-TRINITY ALPS ANGLING EXPERIENCE (916) 623-6757
Address P.O. Box 176, Lewiston, CA 96052
Airport Redding 40m **Accommodations** Lewiston
Operation Guide, outfitter **Type of Fishing** All
Fish Salmon, steelhead, rainbow, brown **Season** Year-round
Water Trinity River, Trinity, Lewiston high mountain lakes
Specialty Float fishing trips for salmon and steelhead
Boats McKenzies, rafts, prams **Tackle Supplied** All
Experience 9 years **Rates** day: $150 week: $945 1/2 day: $120
Guide's Notes: Trinity River:
  Spring Run Chinook--Few rivers along the entire west coast support spring-summer salmon runs. Beginning in late May and lasting through August, the Trinity River is blessed with a hardy spring-summer chinook salmon run. Arriving as fresh and bright as the spring and summer seasons, the 6-8 pound "Kings" aggressively respond to light-weight drift fishing techniques and have a hard core reputation for pushing the highest quality tackle to its limits. This is a pleasant time of year for fellow salmon anglers to get out and enjoy the flourishing spring-summer beauty along the Trinity River, not to mention dig in your heels on a fresh-run salmon.
  Fall Run Chinook and Coho--With the first substantial rain in early September, large numbers of fall chinook salmon begin arriving in the upper Trinity River and provide high quality drift-spin fishing. Highly regarded for their strength and determined fighting ability, the Trinity River fall "Kings" generally run 8-15 pounds and are quite capable of wearing out the arm of even the most avid angler. Arriving shortly behind the fall chinook is a brief run of coho salmon that provides interesting sport.
  Steelhead--Below the town of Lewiston, the Trinity River changes character from smooth, gliding waters into long, tapering riffles intermittent with deep emerald pools, transforming itself into one of the west coast's leading steelhead

rivers. From early September through mid-March, the Trinity supports fine runs of both native and hatchery strain steelhead. These fish arrive in the upper river in excellent condition and respond well to a variety of fishing styles. Early fall steelhead in the 3-6 pound range can be expected, with traditional late winter native fish pressing 6-9 lbs. Excellent fly fishing opportunities exist throughout the season with the months October through January being the optimum times to stretch a line (both floating and sinking line techniques fish well). Light-weight spin-drifting fishing techniques are effective any time during steelhead season. One should be reminded the Trinity's water flows are monitored from Trinity to Lewiston Lakes; therefore, the river remains fishable throughout much of the winter.

Brown Trout--Without a doubt, the Trinity River is the west coast's sleeper for exceptionally large and wary brown trout. Flowing rich and placid in its upper waters around the small town of Lewiston, the Trinity River begins its long, 140-mile journey west, gaining volume and velocity and becoming a major network of tributaries and rivers before intercepting the Klamath River. The upper river supports an excellent population of Brown Trout that provides challenging year-round fishing. Streamer fishing often yields browns in the 16 - 20 " range, while fish 4 - 6 pounds are not uncommon. Quality streamer fishing begins in early spring (mid-May) and lasts well into November. Dependable mayfly hatches occur throughout the late fall and winter seasons (Dec-Jan-Feb) and provide exciting dry fly opportunities for trophy browns -- an excellent winter trout option!

Sacramento River--Often referred to as one of the finest and most diverse fisheries in the west; the mighty upper Sacramento River drains much of the Shasta-Trinity National Forest before flowing southerly through the Sacramento Valley. Sacramento "Redsides" are brightly colored, hard-fighting native rainbows averaging 1-4 pounds. Fly fishermen can depend on intense early spring (Mar-Apr-May) caddis hatches that activate quality angling, while spin fishing is effective throughout the year. During the fall-winter seasons, Sacramento steelhead, averaging 4-6 pounds, are also available and offer exciting angling opportunities.

Lewiston Lake--One of the major lake systems that feeds the Trinity River. A highly regarded tailwater fishery that produces excellent aquatic hatches of all kinds the entire year. Our emphasis is the Fall-Winter, and Spring Midge-Mayfly hatches. Trophy Rainbow and Brown Trout can be found cruising the shallow tapering flats and feeding on various aquatics. These spirited fighters can challenge the best nymph and dry fly purists.

Trinity Lake Smallmouth Bass--Surrounded by the majestic Trinity Alps and inspiring evergreen landscape lies beautiful Trinity Lake-- the headwaters of the famed Trinity River, and one of the west's finest smallmouth bass fisheries. Each spring (Mar-Apr-May), large numbers of smallmouth bass and some very respectable largemouth as well, begin using the lake's shallows to spawn and provides exciting angling for a variety of bass fishing techniques. Casting a variety of bizarre style plugs and crank baits along the lake's many rocky, tapering shoals is one of the more effective ways to hook into Trinity Lake smallmouths, although at times, fly fishing with hi-speed sinking lines and eel-like patterns can be equally, if not more, effective. Casting a fly while surrounded by spring's snow capped Trinity Alps into the glassy waters of Trinity Lake and feeling the solid grab of a feisty smallmouth is truly one of the most exciting ways to catch bass. Trinity Lake smallmouth are hard-fighting quarry and average 1-3 pounds with many in the trophy class. Trinity Lake currently holds the California state record for smallmouth--a whopping 9lb-1oz!!!!

Blessed with a diversified watershed, anglers are able to fish our local waters 12 months out of the year. In fact, some of our finest and most consistent steelhead and trout fishing occurs during the winter and early spring seasons, prior to the general trout opener.

Northern California Area Fishing Calendar

Season	Fish	Water	Method
Jan - Feb	Steelhead	Trinity River	Spin-Fly
		Sacramento River	Spin
	Trout	Lewiston Lake	Excellent Fly
		Sacramento River	Excellent Spin
		Keswick Lake	Spin-Fly
Mar - Apr	Steelhead	Trinity River	Spin-Fly
		Sacramento River	Fly
	Trout	Lewiston Lake	Excellent Fly
		Trinity Lake Trib	Fly-Spin
		Sacramento River	Excellent Fly
		Keswick Lake	Spin-Fly
	Bass	Trinity Lake	Spin
		Shasta Lake	Spin
May - June	Trout	High mountain Lakes	Excellent Fly
		Trinity River	Fly-Browns
		Sacramento River	Spin-Fly
		Lewiston Lake	Fly
	Bass	Trinity Lake	Spin-Fly
		Shasta Lake	Spin-Fly
	Shad	Yuba River	Spin-Fly
July - Aug	Salmon	Trinity River	Spin
	Trout	Trinity River	Fly-Browns
		Sacramento River	Spin-Fly
		Trinity Lake Trib.	Spin-Fly
		High Mtn. Lakes	Spin-Fly
		Keswick Lake	Spin-Fly
Sept - Oct	Salmon-Steelhead	Trinity River	Spin-Fly
		Sacramento River	Spin-Fly

Season	Fish	Water	Method
Sept - Oct	Trout	Lewiston Lake	Excellent Fly
		High Mtn Lakes	Spin-Fly
		Trinity Lake Trib.	Spin-Fly
		Keswick Lake	Spin-Fly
		Sacramento River	Spin-Fly
Nov - Dec	Steelhead	Trinity River	Spin-Fly
		Sacramento River	Spin-Fly
	Trout	Lewiston Lake	Excellent Fly
		Keswick Lake	Spin-Fly
		Sacramento River	Spin

LOS ANGELES, CALIFORNIA

MARLEY, PATRICK (213) 557-2288, 559-5592
Address 1900 Avenue of the Stars, Los Angeles, CA 90067
Airport Los Angeles **Accommodations** Los Angeles
Operation Guide, outfitter **Type of Fishing** Spin, baitcast
Fish Black bass **Season** Year-round **Tackle Supplied** Spin, baitcast
Water Castaic, Casitas, Isabella, Cachuma Lakes **Boats** Bass boats
Specialty Black bass fishing with artificial lures
Experience 10 years **Rates** day: $250 week: $1200
Guide's Notes: Excellent fishing year-round. We go to the lake with action guaranteed, you catch fish or no cost for guide trip. We fish over 40 lakes.

MONTAGUE, CALIFORNIA

BONTRAGER, ROBERT (916) 459-5155, 459-3414
Address P.O. Box 92, Montague, CA 96064
Airport Medford, OR 50m **Accommodations** Yreka 14m **Operation** Guide
Fish Salmon, steelhead, trout **Season** Year-round **Type of Fishing** All
Water Klamath, Smith Rivers (CA), Chetco, Rogue, Elk Rivers (OR)
Specialty Float trips and bank fishing **Boats** McKenzies **Tackle Supplied** All
Experience 10 years **Rates** day: $150

MUIR BEACH, CALIFORNIA

GALLAND, DICK-CLEARWATER TROUT TOURS (415) 381-1173
Address Box 274, Star Route, Muir Beach, CA 94965
Airport San Francisco 35m **Accommodations** On premises
Operation Outfitter, lodge **Type of Fishing** Fly

Fish Rainbow, brown, steelhead, shad, cutthroat **Season** May-November
Water Hat Creek, McCloud, Pit, Feather, Truckee Rivers **Boats** Float tubes
Specialty Guided weekend & week-long trips with focus on improving fly fishing techniques
Rates 2 days: $195/person
Guide's Notes: The McCloud River A classic pool and drop river in a magnificent wooded canyon. Fed by Mt. Shasta's glaciers, the McCloud regularly produces 16 to 24 inch browns and rainbows, typically on nymphs and streamers.

Hat Creek Managed since 1968 for wild trout only, it's spring-fed, richly alkaline waters support a diverse insect population and thousands of trout per mile. These trout can be maddeningly selective. If you are an accomplished caster, with good line control and a fondness for delicate tippets and fussy trout, join Mike for this special spring creek weekend.

Martis & Milton Lakes Two trophy trout lakes within an hour of Truckee.

Davis Lake is famous for growing big trout. In the fall, the browns move into the shallows and creek channels to begin spawning. The rainbows follow them in as they begin feeding up for winter. We probe these flats and channels, often casting to visible fish tailing in the weed beds for nymphs. We fish from shore and from float tubes, which are provided.

Feather River Using trout weight outfits and sinking lines, we catch bright steelhead fresh from the sea. Most are four to six pounds, but larger ones are not uncommon. This weekend is strictly catch and release.

Snorkeling a Trout Stream Have you ever wondered how your dry fly looks to a trout? How a nymph swims underwater? Where trout hold in a riffle? On this outing we get down on the trout's level with mask and snorkel to explore the riffles, runs and pools of Deer Creek. This stream rises on the slopes of Mt. Lassen and runs with clear steady flows all summer. With a fisheries biologist as our guide, we will look for nymphs, sneak up on feeding rainbows, and explore the whole watery world of the trout. We may see big salmon holding in the deep pools. The daytime temperatures are very warm and water temperatures between 65 and 70 degrees make our explorations quite pleasant.

Author's Notes: This is a new high quality operation. I personally know Joe Heuseveldt who guides the trips on the Truckee River and Davis Lake. Joe is an outstanding fisherman and guide. He is the most knowledgeable fly fisherman I know in the Tahoe/Truckee area.

NOVATO, CALIFORNIA

DUNLOP, NICHOLAS (415) 892-6710
Address 2060 Vineyard Road, Novato, CA 94947
Airport Fulton 20m **Accommodations** Novato
Operation Guide, outfitter **Type of Fishing** All **Tackle Supplied** All
Fish Steelhead, salmon **Season** Sept-Apr **Boats** McKenzies, rafts
Water Eel, Klamath, Russian, Smith Rivers **Specialty** Drift fishing float trips
Experience 4 years **Rates** day: $160 1/2 day: $100/2 people

ORLEANS, CALIFORNIA

FOSS, AL "THE DRIFTER" & LIL (916) 627-3224, (714) 528-0030
Address P.O. Box 442, Orleans, CA 95556
Airport Eureka 90m **Accommodations** Orleans
Operation Guide, outfitter **Type of Fishing** All **Tackle Supplied** All
Fish Steelhead, salmon, shad, sturgeon **Season** Sept-May
Water Klamath, Smith, Eel, Mad Rivers **Boats** McKenzies, 17' fiberglass
Specialty White water drift fishing and fly fishing trips
Experience 54 years **Rates** day: $100-210/1-3 persons

GLAZE, EDWARD-SANDY BAR RANCH RESORT (916) 627-3379
Address P.O. Box 295, Orleans, CA 95556
Airport Eureka 90m **Accommodations** On premises
Operation Guide, tackle shop, cabins **Type of Fishing** All
Fish Steelhead, salmon, shad, sturgeon, trout **Season** Year-round
Water Klamath River **Specialty** River drift and fly fishing trips
Boats McKenzie, river sled **Tackle Supplied** All
Experience 6 years **Rates** day: $150 1/2 day: $90

HEMUS, BOB & JOHN TORRES-KLAMATH RIVER OUTDOOR EXPERIENCES
(916) 469-3391, 469-3351
Address P.O. Box 369, Orleans, CA 95556
Airport Eureka 85m **Accommodations** Orleans **Operation** Outfitter
Fish Steelhead, salmon, sturgeon, shad **Season** Sept.-May
Water Klamath, Salmon, Smith, Chetco (OR), Trinity, Eel Rivers
Specialty Drift boat float trips, guided bank fishing trips
Boats McKenzies, rafts **Tackle Supplied** All **Type of Fishing** Baitcast
Experience 5 years **Rates** day: $120-150 1/2 day: $70-80

OROVILLE, CALIFORNIA

TIBBETTS, JOHN T. (916) 589-1017
Address 181 Skyline Blvd., Oroville, CA 95965
Airport Sacramento 60m **Accommodations** Oroville
Operation Guide **Type of Fishing** Spin, baitcast
Fish Salmon, steelhead, stripers **Season** May-October
Water Feather, Sacramento Rivers **Specialty** Jet boat fishing
Boats River sleds **Tackle Supplied** Spin, baitcast, troll
Experience 9 years **Rates** $60/person (min. $150)

PARADISE, CALIFORNIA

NELSON, JOHN W. (916) 877-3773, 696-2673, 365-8418
Address 6271 Graham Road, Paradise, CA 95969

Airport Redding 15m **Accommodations** Anderson 5m
Operation Guide **Type of Fishing** All **Boats** River sleds
Fish Salmon, trout, steelhead **Season** Year-round **Tackle Supplied** All
Water Sacramento, Feather Rivers **Specialty** River boat fishing trips
Experience 5 years **Rates** day: $170 week: $700

PETALUMA, CALIFORNIA

BRADEN, MARVIN "HAL" (707) 762-6809
Address 827 B Street, Petaluma, CA 94952
Airport San Francisco 52m **Accommodations** Petaluma
Operation Guide **Type of Fishing** All **Tackle Supplied** All
Fish Salmon, steelhead, shad, trout **Season** Sept-May **Boats** McKenzies
Water Klamath, Smith, Eel, Russian Rivers **Specialty** Drift boat fishing
Experience 5 years **Rates** day: $160

PIERCY, CALIFORNIA

CAMERON, DON-EEL RIVER BOATWORKS (707) 247-3339
Address P.O. Box 118, Piercy, CA 95467
Airport Eureka 90m **Accommodations** Garberville 12m
Operation Guide, boat shop **Type of Fishing** Fly, baitcast, troll
Fish Salmon, steelhead, cod, bottom fish **Season** Summer & Winter
Water Eel River, Shelter Cove, Pacific Ocean **Specialty** Drift and fly fishing
Boats McKenzies, dory, river sled **Tackle Supplied** All
Experience 15 years **Rates** day: $150 1/2 day: $100

QUINCY, CALIFORNIA

BARTH, BILL-SIERRA SAFARIS (916) 283-3172
Address P. O. Box 1595, Quincy, CA 95971
Airport Reno, NV 76m **Accommodations** Quincy **Operation** Guide, outfitter
Fish Trout, small and largemouth bass **Season** Year-round **Type of Fishing** All
Water Buck's Lake, Lakes Alamanor and Oroville, Feather River
Specialty Fly fishing and lake trolling **Boats** Pontoon boats **Tackle Supplied** All
Experience 10 years **Rates** day: $100-150 1/2 day: $60-90
Guide's Notes: Handicapped and kids welcome!

RED BLUFF, CALIFORNIA

GRAVIER, BARRY (916) 527-7024
Address P.O. Box 0, Red Bluff, CA 96080
Airport Redding 20m **Accommodations** Red Bluff **Operation** Guide

Fish Salmon, steelhead, bass, shad, trout **Season** Year-round
Water Sacramento River, Shasta Lake, Mill, Deer Creek
Specialty Trolling for salmon, drifting for trout and steelhead
Boats River sleds **Tackle Supplied** Spin, troll **Type of Fishing** All
Experience 10 years **Rates** day: $170 week: $1190 1/2 day: $170

HUNERBERG, DENNIS W. (916) 527-7370
Address 19055 Ridge Road, Red Bluff, CA 96080
Airport Redding 20m **Accommodations** Red Bluff
Operation Guide **Type of Fishing** Spin, baitcast
Fish King salmon, sturgeon, striper **Season** Year-round
Water Sacramento River **Specialty** Lure and bait fishing
Boats River sleds **Tackle Supplied** Spin, baitcast
Experience 6 years **Rates** day: $170 1/2 day: $130

REDDING, CALIFORNIA

DAVIS, ELVIN (916) 241-6806
Address 2315 Heryford Lane, Redding, CA 96001
Airport Redding **Accommodations** Redding **Operation** Guide
Fish Bass, brown, rainbow **Season** Year-round **Type of Fishing** All
Water Shasta, Trinity, Oroville Lakes, Cow Creek **Boats** Bass boats
Specialty Lake fishing and stream fly fishing **Tackle Supplied** All
Experience 19 years **Rates** day: $175 week: $500

DUNN, HARDY A. (916) 241-5744
Address 2085 Quartz Way, Redding, CA 96001
Airport Redding **Accommodations** Redding
Operation Guide **Type of Fishing** Spin, baitcast **Boats** River sleds
Fish Salmon, steelhead, trout **Season** Year-round **Tackle Supplied** Spin, baitcast
Water Sacramento River **Specialty** Salmon backtrolling and steelhead drifting
Experience 16 years **Rates** day: $170

JACKSON, BRAD-THE FLY SHOP (916) 222-3555
Address 4140 Churn Creek Road, Dept. U, Redding, CA 96002
Airport Redding **Accommodations** Redding
Operation Guide, tackle shop **Type of Fishing** Fly **Boats** John boats
Fish Rainbow, brown **Season** April-Nov **Tackle Supplied** Fly
Water Fall, McCloud, Sacramento Rivers, Hat Creek **Specialty** Fly fishing
Experience 35 years **Rates** day: $160
Guide's Notes: Fall River is California's most productive wild trout fishery.
Open to the public for only the last decade, its limited access and gin-clear
water provide delicate and demanding fly fishing. Its meandering flow through
miles of meadow, dominated by Mount Shasta, and its trophy trout make Fall
River the premium Golden State trout fishing experience.

Light tackle, long leaders, and precise fly patterns are absolutely necessary. The peak dry fly activity is from early May through late June, above average dry fly and nymph fishing continue throughout the season. Accomodations are available streamside and nearby, and there are other fishing opportunities in the vicinity.

The McCloud River derives its flow from the snow-covered slopes of Mount Shasta. Above McCloud Reservoir it is a meandering meadow stream, small and brush lined. Downstream it flows into a deep canyon of alternating large pools and stretches of pocket-water. It is managed as a wild trout stream, primarily rainbows and occasional brown trout.

The Nature Conservancy Preserve on the McCloud is a three mile section of river with a limit of ten fishermen per day, and strict catch-and-release regulations. The scenery, solitude and fishing combine to make this an exceptional opportunity. Peak fishing is late May through August. Nymphing and streamers provide plenty of action through the remainder of the season.

Hat Creek is the showcase of California's wild trout project. A beautiful limestone stream with occasional pocket water stretches, it's textbook progression of insect hatches and diverse water types make it our choice for instructional trips.

This nutrient rich water results in fast-growing fish occasionally reaching trophy size. To further encourage this, the California Department of Fish and Game allows only fish larger than 18" to be harvested and no bait or barbed hooks. From the salmonfly hatch in May to the prolific mayfly hatches of early July rising fish are abundant.

Klamath River--The deep canyons and swift, rugged water of the Klamath River provide fly fishermen with the most consistent steelhead fishing in the Pacific Northwest. Beginning in August and continuing through November, the famous "1/2 pounders" of the Klamath take flies aggressively and floating lines are often the rule. Fish to six pounds are not uncommon, though many more in the acrobatic fourteen to fifteen inch class are taken. McKenzie river-type boats provide access to remote water and scenery which make this fall angling experience unforgettable.

Author's Notes: Brad Jackson is one of the owners of The Fly Shop, one of the best fly fishing shops in the West. They publish a mail order catalog whch offers a huge selection of quality fly fishing gear. Their local guide service covers much of the Northern California area. They also offer specialty fly fishing trips to the famous waters of Alaska, British Columbia, Belize, Christmas Island and even Bhutan, a small kingdom in the Himalayas. These trips are all accompanied by someone from the Fly Shop staff. Personal experience allows me to recommended this operation highly.

VILLA, BILL-SHASTA FISHING SERVICE (916) 244-1284
Address 980 Market Street, Redding, CA 96001
Airport Redding **Accommodations** Redding
Operation Guide, tackle shop **Boats** River sleds, rafts
Fish Steelhead, trout, shad, king salmon **Season** Year-round

Water Sacramento, Klamath, Trinity, Eel Rivers **Type of Fishing** Fly, spin
Specialty Fly and ultra light spin fishing **Tackle Supplied** Fly, spin
Experience 25 years **Rates** day: $90/person $150/2people
Guide's Notes: Northern California Area Fishing Calendar

Fish	Available	Method
Steelhead	Sept - Feb	Fly or Spin
Trout	May - Aug	Fly
Salmon	Oct - Nov	Fly
Shad	May - Aug	Fly or Spin
Largemouth Bass	Mar - Aug	Fly or Spin
Smallmouth Bass	Apr - June	Fly or Spin
Striped Bass	Apr - June	Fly or Spin
Crappie	Apr - Aug	Fly
Bluegill	Apr - Sept	Fly

Author's Notes: Bill is recognized as a knowledgeable and very capable guide.

ROSEVILLE, CALIFORNIA

GIRDVAIN, R.R. "WHITEY" (916) 791-4389
Address 10090 Willey Court, Roseville, CA 95678
Airport Sacramento 23m **Accommodations** Sacramento 23m
Operation Charter Captain **Type of Fishing** Spin, baitcast, troll
Fish Mackinaw, rainbow, brown trout, salmon, bass
Water Shasta, Donner, Oroville Lakes, Sacramento River
Specialty Lake and river trolling **Boats** Outboard ski barge and houseboat
Tackle Supplied Spin, baitcast **Season** Year-round
Experience 7 years **Rates** day: $130 1/2 day: $80

SACRAMENTO, CALIFORNIA

HICKEY, BILL-CHARLIEBILL FISHING AND GUIDE SERVICE (916) 682-4258
Address 7641 Bar Du Lane, Sacramento, CA 95829
Airport Sacramento 10m **Accommodations** Sacramento 10m
Operation Guide, outfitter **Type of Fishing** All
Fish Salmon, trout, steelhead, bass, shad **Season** Year-round
Water American, Sacramento, Feather, Yuba Rivers **Specialty** Float trips
Boats River sleds, McKenzies **Tackle Supplied** All
Experience 9 years **Rates** day: $75/person 1/2 day: $50/person
*Author's Notes: Bill Hickey has a very good reputation for guiding Sacramento's
local rivers. Salmon, steelhead, and shad fishing can be excellent right in the
city limits. What a great way to add some pleasure to a business trip to the
capital city of California.*

SALYER, CALIFORNIA

BROWN, ORVILLE "BROWNIE"-BROWNIE'S GUIDE SERVICE (916) 629-2156
Address Hwy 229, East Salyer P.O. Box 527, Salyer, CA 95563
Airport Arcata 5m **Accommodations** On premises
Operation Guide, campground **Type of Fishing** Drift, fly, baitcast
Fish Steelhead, salmon **Season** Year-round **Boats** McKenzies
Water Trinity River **Specialty** Drift boat fishing **Tackle Supplied** Baitcast
Experience 5 years **Rates** day: $85

SAN DIEGO, CALIFORNIA

HECHT, ROSS R.-POINT LOMA SPORTFISHING ASSOCIATION (619) 223-1627
Address 1403 Scott Street, San Diego, CA 92106
Airport San Diego **Accommodations** San Diego **Operation** Charter Captain
Boats Power boats 45'-90' **Type of Fishing** Spin, baitcast, troll
Fish Tuna, wahoo, yellowtail, marlin **Season** Year-round
Water Pacific Ocean **Specialty** Deep sea fishing **Tackle Supplied** Baitcast, troll
Rates day: $150

MORRIS, PAUL-FISHERMAN'S LANDING (619) 222-0391
Address 2838 Garrison Street, San Diego, CA 92106
Airport San Diego **Accommodations** San Diego
Operation Charter Captain, booking office **Type of Fishing** Baitcast, sea trolling
Fish Albacore, yellowtail, tuna, wahoo **Season** Year-round **Water** Baja California
Boats Charter boats **Tackle Supplied** troll, baitcast
Rates Varies

MURPHY, JIM (619) 271-8781
Address 8008 Flanders Drive, San Diego, CA 92126
Airport San Diego **Accommodations** San Diego
Operation Guide **Type of Fishing** Spin, baitcast
Fish Largemouth, spotted, sand bass, halibut **Season** Year-round
Water Lower Otay, Hodges, San Vicente Lakes, San Diego Bay
Specialty Topwater largemouth and instructional fishing
Boats Bass boats **Tackle Supplied** Spin, baitcast
Experience 3 years **Rates** day: $200 1/2 day: $125 week: $1400
Guide's Notes: The species we fish for are largemouth bass (all Florida Strain), catfish, bluegills, and trout. Our season runs all year because of our fantastic weather with peak times being February to October. The best lures to use are topwater, plastic worms, spinner baits, and crank baits. The largest bass taken this year was 20 lbs, 4 oz from lake Hodges.

WATSON, PETE-BASS GUIDES OF SAN DIEGO (619) 578-0041, 292-9920
Address 6374 Caminito Telmo, Dept. B, San Diego, CA 92111
Airport San Diego **Accommodations** San Diego
Operation Guide **Type of Fishing** All **Tackle Supplied** All
Fish Bass **Season** Year-round **Water** San Diego area lakes and bay
Specialty Largemouth bass fishing with artificial lures **Boats** Bass boats
Experience 3 years **Rates** day: $200
Guide's Notes: San Diego Area Bass Lakes--Lower Otay, Sutherland, El Capitan, San Vicente, and Hodges.

Largemouth bass--Year round fishing is generally good, the best fishing is in the spring, March through May, especially for lunker spawning fish. In fall, during September and October you can expect great topwater action. We fish mainly with baitcasting and spinning rods. Fly rods work well, also, especially when topwater action is good. Primary baits include plastic worms, spinners, topwater lures, and crank baits.

Bluegill and Crappie--Most lakes have an excellent population of Bluegill and crappie. Summertime and spring fishing for these can be exciting with other artificial or live bait-ultralight spinning and fly rods are best.

San Diego Bay Bass--We also guide in San Diego Bay for spotted bay bass and sand bass. Best fishing is generally in winter months. Lead head jigs with plastic grubs work well when fishing over grass beds.

SAN JOSE, CALIFORNIA

HOLMES, DARRELL (408) 266-8731
Address 1405 Sieta Court, San Jose, CA 95118
Airport San Jose **Accommodations** San Jose **Operation** Guide
Fish Large and smallmouth bass **Type of Fishing** Spin, baitcast
Water Nacimiento Res., Berryessa, Clear Lake, the Delta **Season** Year-round
Specialty Lake bass casting **Boats** Bass boats **Tackle Supplied** Spin, baitcast
Experience 3 years **Rates** day: $200

RAMEZANE, DOUG (408) 268-0650
Address 6224 Cloverhill Drive, San Jose, CA 95120
Airport Redding 115m **Accommodations** Yreka 15m
Operation Guide **Type of Fishing** All **Season** Sept-June
Water Klamath River, Copco, Iron Gate Reservoirs **Fish** Rainbow
Specialty River fishing **Boats** Row boats **Tackle Supplied** Spin
Experience 2 years **Rates** 1/2 day: $55

SAN RAFAEL, CALIFORNIA

ALMQUIST, FRANK-NORTHFORK STEELHEAD GUIDE SERVICE (415) 456-9389
Address 41 Meadows Ave., San Rafael, CA 94901

Airport San Francisco 30m **Accommodations** San Rafael
Operation Outfitter **Type of Fishing** All **Fish** Steelhead, salmon
Water Coastal rivers and streams, Russian, Eel Rivers **Season** Nov-March
Specialty Drift boat fishing **Boats** McKenzie **Tackle Supplied** All
Experience 3 years **Rates** day: $150 week: $750

SIATOS, SI-OUTDOOR FAMILY (415) 472-5341
Address P.O. Box 4339, San Rafael, CA 94913-4339
Airport San Francisco 25m **Accommodations** San Rafael
Operation Guide, outfitter **Type of Fishing** All
Fish Trout, bass **Season** Year-round **Water** Northern California area
Specialty Trolling, fly and bait fishing **Boats** Rafts
Experience 5 years **Rates** day: $100 week: $700 1/2 day: $75

SANTA BARBARA, CALIFORNIA

BERNTH, HOWARD "HOWDY" (805) 688-5195
Address Star Route-Cachuma Village, Santa Barbara, CA 93105
Airport Santa Barbara 25m **Accommodations** Santa Ynez 6m
Operation Guide **Type of Fishing** Spin, baitcast, troll
Fish Large and smallmouth bass, trout **Season** Year-round
Water Cachuma Lake, (Santa Barbara County) **Specialty** Bass fishing
Boats Bass boats **Tackle Supplied** Spin, baitcast, troll
Experience 21 years **Rates** day: $140 1/2 day: $70

SANTA ROSA, CALIFORNIA

ELLIS, JACK (707) 526-9077
Address 926-B West Avenue, Santa Rosa, CA 95407
Airport Eureka 60m **Accommodations** Santa Rosa
Operation Guide **Type of Fishing** All **Tackle Supplied** All
Fish Steelhead, salmon, trout, shad **Season** Year-round **Boats** McKenzies
Water Eel, Klamath, Smith, Trinity Rivers **Specialty** Steelhead fishing
Experience 6 years **Rates** day: $180
Guide's Notes: Northern California Fishing Calendar

Fish	Available	Fish	Size
Steelhead & Salmon	Aug - Mar	Winter Steelhead	8 - 20 lbs
Trout	Apr - Sept.	Winter Salmon	10 - 50 lbs
Shad	July	Fall Steelhead	1 - 8 lbs
		Fall Salmon	2 - 20 lbs

I offer spring and summer drift trips on the Sacramento, Yuba and Feather Rivers. Trout run 1-6 pounds and shad 1-5 pounds.
Author's Notes: *Jack is an outdoor writer and a staff photographer for WESTERN OUTDOORS magazine. His articles and photographs have been published in several well-known magazines such as FLY FISHERMAN, FIELD AND STREAM, and CALIFORNIA ANGLER.*

Jack Ellis, California guide, photographer, and writer, with King salmon. *Jack Ellis*

GALLOWAY, SCOTT K.-SOLITUDE GUIDING & PACKING SERVICE
(707) 545-7049
Address 1808 Peterson Lane, Santa Rosa, CA 95401
Airport Sonoma 5m **Accommodations** Santa Rosa
Operation Outfitter **Type of Fishing** All **Specialty** All water fishing
Fish Trout, steelhead, bass, salmon, sturgeon **Season** Year-round
Water Marble Mtn. Wilderness, Klamath, Scott, Salmon Rivers
Boats Rowboat, canoe, bass boats, rafts **Tackle Supplied** All
Experience 3 years **Rates** day: $100 week: $475 1/2 day: $50

PIZZA, JOHN P. (707) 539-9534, 923-2174
Address P.O. Box 9156, Santa Rosa, CA 95405
Airport Eureka 60m **Accommodations** Santa Rosa **Operation** Guide
Fish Steelhead, salmon, trout, shad **Season** Year-round **Type of Fishing** All
Water Eel, Smith, Russian Rivers, No. California coastal streams
Specialty Drift boat trips **Boats** McKenzies, rafts **Tackle Supplied** All
Experience 3 years **Rates** day: $160

SMARTVILLE, CALIFORNIA

WAGGONER, ED (916) 639-2393
Address 8839 Hwy 20, Smartsville, CA 95977
Airport Sacramento 45m **Accommodations** Marysville 15m
Operation Guide **Type of Fishing** All **Specialty** Jet boat river trips
Fish Steelhead, salmon, striped bass, trout **Season** Sept-May
Water Yuba, Feather, Sacramento Rivers
Boats River sled, canoes **Tackle Supplied** Spin, baitcast
Experience 9 years **Rates** day: $160

SMITH RIVER, CALIFORNIA

EARLY, GARY B. (707) 487-0525
Address 200 Salmon Harbor Road #3, Smith River, CA 95567
Airport Crescent City 10m**Accommodations** Crescent City 10m
Operation Guide **Fish** Salmon, steelhead **Season** Year-round
Water Eel, Klamath, Smith, Chetco (OR), Rogue (OR) Rivers
Specialty Drift and jet boats trips **Type of Fishing** All
Boats Rowboats, river sleds, McKenzies **Tackle Supplied** All
Experience 6 years **Rates** day: $200

GIST, WADE (707) 487-6015
Address Route 2 Box 1282 A, Smith River, CA 95567
Airport Crescent City 10m **Accommodations** Crescent City 10m
Operation Guide **Fish** Salmon, steelhead, trout **Season** July-Mar

Water Smith, Chetco (OR), Klamath, Eel Rivers **Type of Fishing** Fly, baitcast
Specialty Bait & lures on fly trips **Boats** McKenzies **Tackle Supplied** Baitcast
Experience 4 years **Rates** day: $150

LINDSTROM, GARY (707) 487-0935
Address Hwy 101 North, Smith River, CA 95567
Airport Crescent City 10m **Accommodations** Crescent City 10m
Operation Guide **Fish** Salmon, steelhead **Season** June-March
Water Smith, Chetco (OR), Rogue (OR) Rivers **Specialty** Float trips
Boats McKenzies **Tackle Supplied** All **Type of Fishing** All
Experience 15 years **Rates** day: $200

REAGAN, DENNIS-WILDERNESS OUTFITTER (707) 487-6445
Address P.O. Box 788, Smith River, CA 95567
Airport Medford, OR 50m **Accommodations** Smith River
Fish Salmon, steelhead, trout, shad **Season** Year-round **Type of Fishing** All
Water Smith, Chetco (OR), Klamath, Trinity Rivers **Operation** Guide, outfitter
Specialty Drift boat river fishing **Boats** McKenzies, rafts **Tackle Supplied** All
Experience 10 years **Rates** day: $150

SOMES BAR, CALIFORNIA

THROGMORTON, BRAD-SOMES BAR LODGE (916) 469-3399
Address General Delivery, Somes Bar, CA 95568
Airport Arcata 80m **Accommodations** On premises
Operation Outfitter, lodge **Type of Fishing** All **Boats** McKenzies
Fish Steelhead **Season** Sept-March **Tackle Supplied** Baitcast
Water Klamath, Salmon River **Specialty** Fly fishing and lures
Experience 11 years **Rates** day: $150

WATSON, MICHAEL-TI BAR GUIDE SERVICE (916) 469-3349
Address General Delivery, Somes Bar, CA 95568
Airport Arcata 80m **Accommodations** Somes Bar
Operation Guide, outfitter **Type of Fishing** Spin, baitcast
Fish Steelhead, salmon **Season** Sept-March **Tackle Supplied** All
Water Klamath, Salmon, Eel, Smith Rivers **Boats** McKenzies, rafts
Experience 10 years **Rates** day: $160

SOUTH LAKE TAHOE, CALIFORNIA

MULLER, RICK (916) 544-4358
Address Box 8773, S. Lake Tahoe, CA 95731
Airport S. Lake Tahoe **Accommodations** S. Lake Tahoe **Season** Year-round
Operation Guide, charter captain **Type of Fishing** Spin, baitcast, troll
Fish Mackinaw, rainbow, brown, kokanee **Boats** 19' Bayliner

Water Lake Tahoe **Specialty** Trolling and drifting for mackinaw
Experience 1 years **Rates** day: $180 1/2 day: $90
Guide's Notes: Most of our fishing is deep trolling for mackinaw, however, lately we have been finding some good action casting to rainbows in deep open water. This type of fishing requires locating small windrows of debris (pollen from the trees, small twigs, dust, and insects) which have combined on the water to form sort of a natural chum line. Fish feed on the small insects which are trapped in these slicks. This type of fishing can be very exciting for rainbows from 2 - 4 pounds, however it does require calm conditions.
Author's Notes: Similar fishing is described by Larry Presnall who fishes Lake Michigan out of Wisconsin.

RICKARDS, DENNY-ROCKY POINT RESORT (916) 577-7815
Address Box 10153, Dept. E, South Lake Tahoe, CA 95731
Airport S. Lake Tahoe **Accommodations** S. Lake Tahoe **Operation** Guide, lodge
Fish Brown, rainbow, cutthroat, brook **Season** Apr-Oct **Type of Fishing** All
Water East Walker, East & West Carson (NV), Truckee Rivers, Klamath Lake (OR)
Specialty Fly fishing-lakes or streams **Boats** Bass boats **Tackle Supplied** All
Experience 7 years **Rates** day: $125 1/2 day: $75
Guide's Notes: Our best fishing for brown, rainbow, cutthroat and brook is May, June, September and October. I recommend nymphs, streamers and dries for fish 1 to 6 pounds. The best lures are Rapalas.
Author's Notes: Denny was highly recommended as a very competent guide by my friend Jack Martin of the Outdoorsman in South Lake Tahoe.

SMITH, WILL (916) 541-0253
Address Box 9778, South Lake Tahoe, CA 95731
Airport South Lake Tahoe **Accommodations** South Lake Tahoe
Operation Charter Captain **Type of Fishing** Spin, trolling
Fish Lake and rainbow trout, salmon **Season** May-September
Water Lake Tahoe **Specialty** Lake trolling and drifting
Boats 20' open **Tackle Supplied** Spin, troll, baitcast
Experience 20 years **Rates** 1/2 day: $80/2 people

SUSANVILLE, CALIFORNIA

EVANS, RON (916) 257-9265
Address 265 North Sacramento St., Susanville, CA 96130
Airport Reno, NV 85m **Accommodations** Susanville
Operation Guide, outfitter **Type of Fishing** Spin, baitcast, troll
Fish Rainbow **Season** May-January **Water** Eagle Lake **Boats** 16' Runabout
Specialty Lake fly fishing and lure fishing **Tackle Supplied** All
Experience 2 years **Rates** day: $120 week: $700
Guide's Notes: Eagle Lake rainbow--June, August and September to end of December for the best fishing. Summer temperature about 85 degrees--fall and winter 40 degrees to zero.

TAHOMA, CALIFORNIA

JOHNSON, RANDY (916) 525-6575
Address P.O. Box 26, Dept. D, Tahoma, CA 95733
Airport Reno, NV 50m **Accommodations** On premises
Operation Guide, lodge **Type of Fishing** Fly **Tackle Supplied** Fly
Fish Brown, rainbow, brook **Season** May-Sept
Water Truckee R., Desolation Wilderness, Miller Lake Region, Truckee area
res. **Specialty** Fly fishing rivers & still water **Boats** Rowboats, float tubes
Experience 3 years **Rates** day: $120 2-3 hours: $45

VAN NUYS, CALIFORNIA

LAWSON, CAPTAIN ROY (818) 782-4161
Address 6050 Venture Canyon Ave., Van Nuys, CA 91401
Airport Burbank 5m **Accommodations** Van Nuys
Operation Guide, Charter Captain **Type of Fishing** All
Fish Freshwater bass and stripers, halibut, yellowtail, calico bass
Season Year-round **Water** Pacific Ocean, Casitas, Castaic, Pyramid Lakes
Specialty Trophy largemouth bass and stripers on light tackle and fly gear
Boats 24' & 45' Sportfishers, bass boat **Tackle Supplied** All
Experience 10 years **Rates** varies
Guide's Notes: Southern California Fishing Calendar

Water	Season	Fish	Size
Fresh Water	Winter/Spring	Largemouth Trophy Bass	to 14 lbs
		Striped Bass	to 25 lbs
Salt Water	Spring	Halibut	to 28 lbs
Salt Water	Summer/Fall	Bass, Yellowtail	to 25 lbs
		Tuna	to 150 lbs
		Marlin	125 - 250 lbs
		Albacore	to 35 lbs

I also guide light tackle and fly rod charters in saltwater for bass, bonita, tuna, and yellowtail. We have guided our clients to 12 IGFA world records.

WALNUT CREEK, CALIFORNIA

RESHATOFF, JACK (415) 934-1186
Address 19 Hanson Lane, Walnut Creek, CA 94596
Airport Oakland 15m **Accommodations** Walnut Creek
Operation Guide **Type of Fishing** Spin, baitcast **Fish** Bass, striper, trout, carp
Water Delta, Indian Valley, New Melones Reservoirs, Clear Lake
Specialty Plug casting **Boats** Bass boats **Tackle Supplied** All **Season** Year-round
Experience 3 years **Rates** day: $150
Guide's Notes: Good fishing for largemouth and striped bass all year.

WELDON, CALIFORNIA

QUINN, BOB AND TIESE-KENNEDY MEADOWS PACK TRAINS
(619) 378-2232
Address Box 1300, Weldon, CA 93283
Airport Los Angeles 200m **Accommodations** Ridgecrest 45m
Operation Outfitter **Type of Fishing** Fly **Specialty** Fly fishing pack trips
Fish Native golden, rainbow and german brown trout **Season** May-Nov.
Water North and South Forks of the Kern River **Tackle Supplied** Fly
Experience 3 years **Rates** day: $100/person

YORBA LINDA, CALIFORNIA

CONTINI, BRUCE-SO. CALIFORNIA GUIDE SERVICE (714) 996-1544
Address 17302 Chestnut, Yorba Linda, CA 92686
Airport Santa Anna 25m **Accommodations** Yorba Linda
Operation Guide, outfitter **Type of Fishing** Spin, baitcast, troll
Fish Bass, stripers **Season** March-October **Tackle Supplied** Spin, baitcast
Water Lakes Hodges, Havasu, Casitas, Pyramid **Boats** Bass boats
Specialty Freshwater largemouth bass fishing
Experience 3 years **Rates** day: $85
Guide's Notes: Southern California fresh water lakes are known for their great largemouth bass fishing. I also guide trips to Lake Havasu (AZ) and Lake Pyramid. These two lakes have a good reputation for large stripers.

YUBA CITY, CALIFORNIA

OWEN, RUSSELL (916) 674-0292
Address 2769 Roosevelt Road, Yuba City, CA 95991
Airport Sacramento 50m **Accommodations** Yuba City
Operation Guide **Type of Fishing** All **Boats** River sleds, McKenzies
Fish Trout, bass, steelhead, salmon, shad **Season** Year-round
Water Feather, Sacramento, Yuba, Eel, Klamath, Smith Rivers
Specialty Jet boats and drift boat fishing **Tackle Supplied** All
Experience 10 years **Rates** day: $180 week: $1000
Author's Notes: I fished with Russ last fall and found him to be a capable guide.

HAWAII

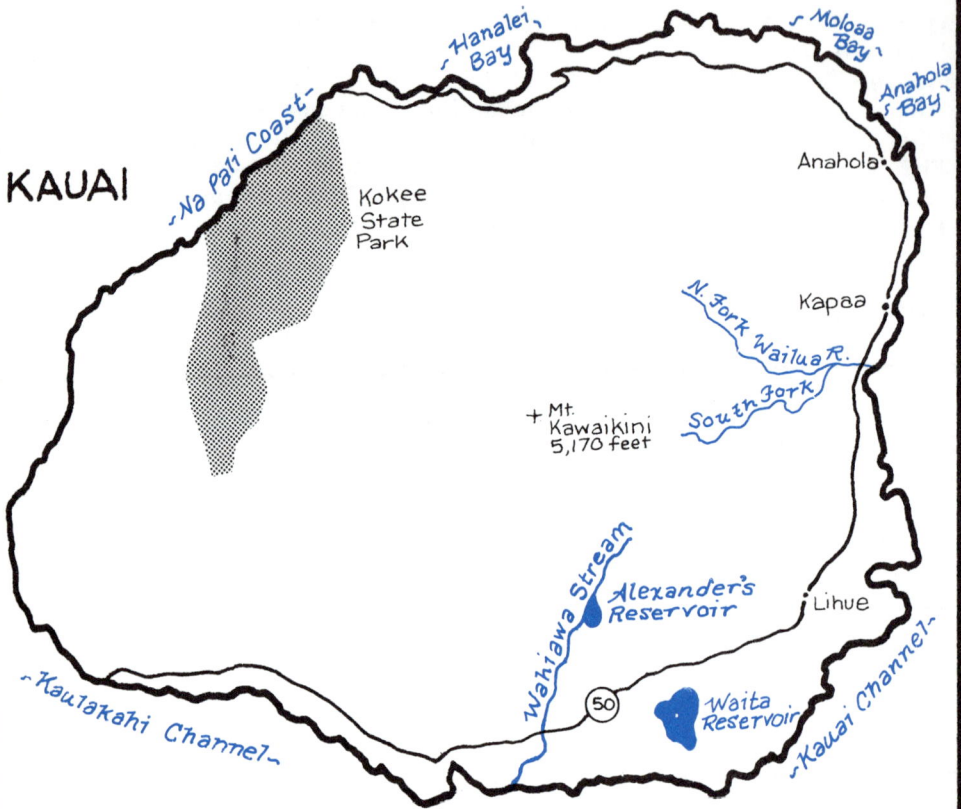

KAUAI

- ~Hanalei Bay~
- ~Moloaa Bay~
- ~Anahola Bay~
- ~Na Pali Coast~
- Kokee State Park
- Anahola
- Kapaa
- N. Fork Wailua R.
- South Fork
- + Mt. Kawaikini 5,170 feet
- Wahiawa Stream
- Alexander's Reservoir
- Lihue
- ~Kaulakahi Channel~
- 50
- Waita Reservoir
- ~Kauai Channel~

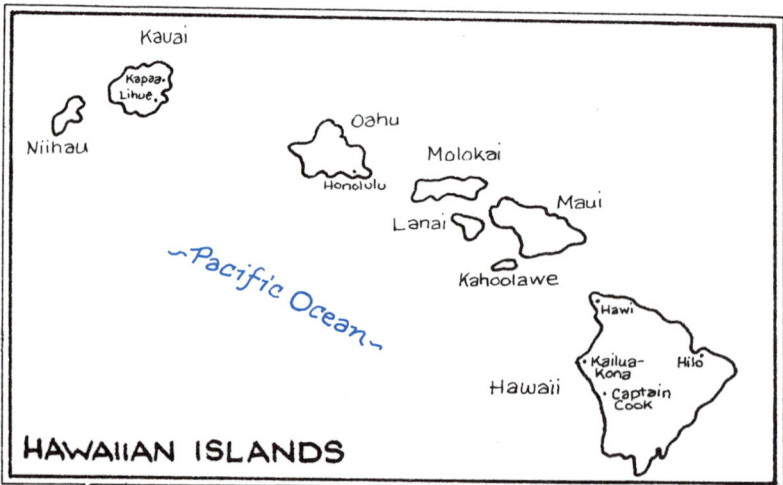

- Kauai
- Kapaa•
  Lihue•
- Niihau
- Oahu
- Honolulu
- Molokai
- Lanai
- Maui
- Kahoolawe
- ~Pacific Ocean~
- Hawi
- Kailua-Kona•
- Hilo
- •Captain Cook
- Hawaii

HAWAIIAN ISLANDS

Hawaii

KAUAI, HAWAII

PETERSON, ROYCE E.-BASS GUIDES OF KAUAI (808) 822-1405

Address 5657 Ohelo Road, Kapaa, Kauai, Hawaii 96746
Airport Lihue 8m **Accommodations** Kauai
Operation Guide **Type of Fishing** All
Fish Black Bass, tucanary (peacock bass), sm bass **Season** Year-round
Water Alexander Dam, Waita Reservoir, Manuhohonohu Reservoir
Specialty Fishing from boats with baitcasting, spinning, or fly casting gear
Boats Flat-bottom aluminum boats **Tackle Supplied** Spin, baitcast
Experience 3 years **Rates** 1/2 day: $125/2 people $85/person
Guide's Notes: Bass fishing on the island of Kauai is generally a surprise to most people. The bass have been stocked for about 20 years here and include largemouth, smallmouth, and tucanary (peacock bass). Tucanary bass are imported from South America and flourish only in the Hawaiian Islands as far as North America is concerned.

Fishing is good year-round because of the steady weather and mild climate found in the islands. We use all the standard lures that catch bass in the areas that most visitors come from. The surprise is the amount of hard-fighting bass that we catch. Pressure is very low on the reservoirs that we fish because most natives fish the ocean and are not aware of the fresh water fishing.

Author's Notes: *We fished with Royce in July of '85 while on a family vacation. The peacock bass were on the spawning beds and were very aggressive. I highly recommend spending a day fishing with Royce when you visit Kauai. The fishing is excellent and the scenery is spectacular.*

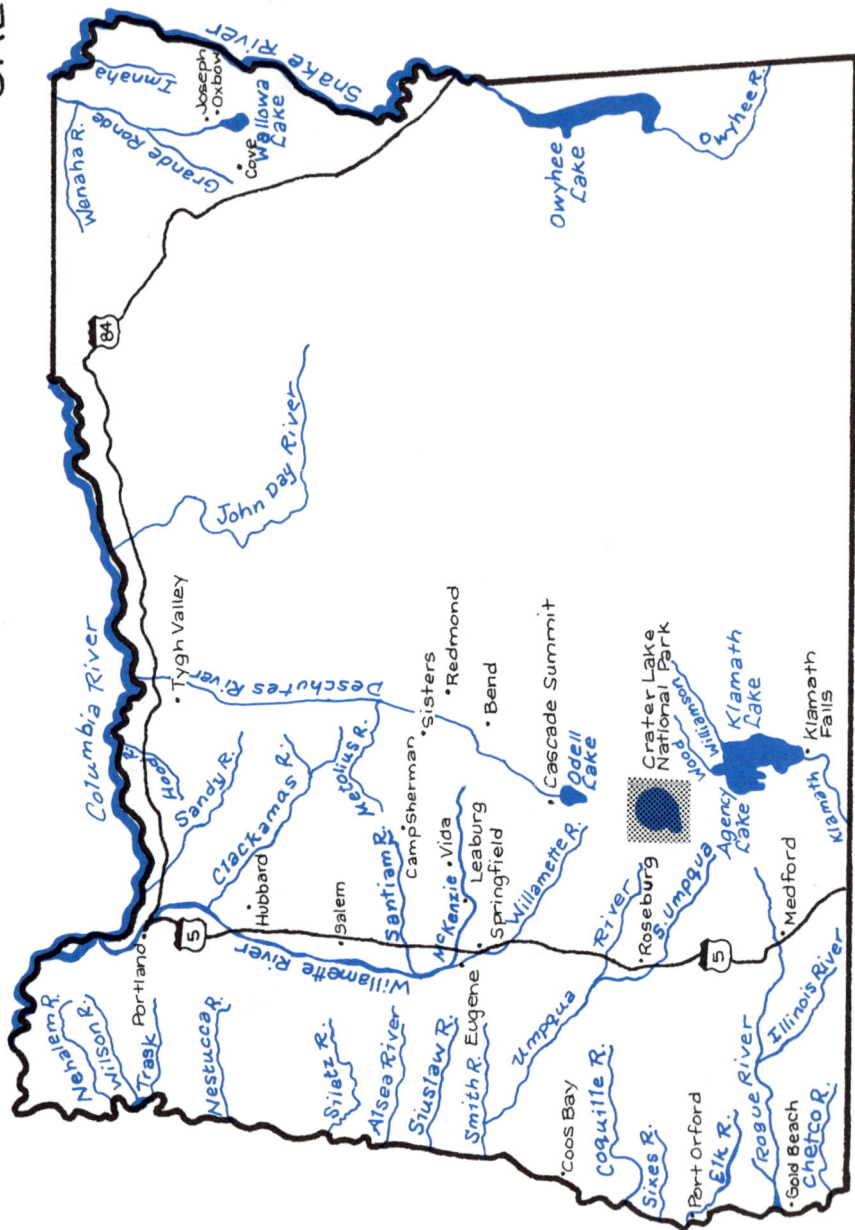

Oregon

CAMP SHERMAN, OREGON

PETERSON, PAUL & GARY KISH-CAMP SHERMAN STORE & FLY SHOP (503) 595-6262
Address P.O. Box 125, Camp Sherman, OR 97730
Airport Redman 40m **Accommodations** Camp Sherman
Operation Outfitter, tackle shop **Type of Fishing** All
Fish Rainbow, western brook char **Season** Year-round
Water Metolius, Deschutes, McKenzie Rivers **Tackle Supplied** All
Specialty Fly fishing for trophy western brook char **Boats** McKenzies
Experience 6 years, 1 year **Rates** day: $150 1/2 day: $100
Guide's Notes: We fly fish for large, wild, redside rainbows in private, secluded water on the Metolius. During early and late hours world class western brook char (a cousin of the Eastern Brookie), ranging from five to eighteen pounds, can be taken on large dry flies.

In May and June green drake and big golden stonefly patterns are effective as their hatches bring to the surface the river's largest trout.

After the mid-summer midge and caddis activity is completed, August into September is the time to fish hopper patterns along the rivers many banks.

Fishing ends in October with the emergence of the giant October caddis. After that, it's time to saddle up the horses and go chase deer and elk but that's a whole 'nother story........

Author's Notes: Paul Peterson's operation was recommended to us by Brian O'Keefe, a former guide now working with the Simms Co. These trophy char described above run to 20 lbs and average 8 to 10 lbs. Western brook char, also called bull trout, are found only in a few western rivers including the Flathead Drainage in Montana, in addition to the Metolius. Recently fish biologists have, according to Paul, reclassified them as a separate species of char. Paul says in the Fall of 1985 he and Gary Kish recorded 21 consecutive days of guiding on which their clients landed brook char over five lbs.

CHILOQUIN, OREGON

NELSON, JOHN-WILLIAMSON RIVER GUIDE SERVICE (503) 783-2466
Address Star Rte, Box 9, Chiloquin, OR 97624
Airport Chiloquin **Accommodations** Chiloquin **Operation** Outfitter
Fish Rainbow, brown **Season** Late April-Oct **Type of Fishing** All
Water Williamson, Wood Rivers, Agency, Klamath Lakes, Spring Creek
Specialty Fly fishing **Boats** Canoe, McKenzie **Tackle Supplied** All
Experience 7 years **Rates** day: $150

Guide's Notes: Williamson River and Agency Lake The peak times are June through September. The most effective flies are leeches, wooly buggers and caddis patterns. The best lures are Roostertails and Panther Martins, and Mepps. Fish average 2 to 5 pounds with rainbows over 8 pounds not unusual.

The **Wood River** is a tributary of Agency Lake and has similar fishing to the Williamson. As the waters of Klamath Lake warm up in late May and early June, large numbers of rainbow trout move upstream into the Williamson and Wood Rivers. These fish add to the resident population of trout in these streams to form a concentration of big trout. Add to this trophy management regulations by the Department of Fish and Game (a two fish a day limit), and you have the formula for fantastic fishing.

Author's Notes: Local sources tell me John is a capable guide. This area has not received much national attention because there were no accommodations. Recently Bud Speezee has opened up the Waterwheel Campground, for information call him at (503) 783-2738.

CORVALLIS, OREGON

McELDOWNEY, CRAIG (503) 757-1383
Address 6450 Oak Creek Drive, Corvallis, OR 97330
Airport Eugene 40m **Accommodations** Corvallis
Operation Guide **Type of Fishing** All **Tackle Supplied** All
Fish Steelhead, salmon, trout, sturgeon **Season** Year-round
Water Alsea, Siletz, Santiam, Deschutes, Willamette Rivers, Yaquina Bay
Specialty Fly fishing, drift fishing **Boats** River sleds, McKenzies
Experience 2 years **Rates** day: $120 1/2 day: $60
Guide's Notes: Fishing Calendar

Fish	Available	Method
Winter Steelhead	Dec - Feb	Drift Fishing, plugging
Summer Steelhead	July - Sept	Fly fishing, drift, plugging
Spring Chinook Salmon	Apr - May	Drift, plugging, backbouncing
Sea-run Cutthroat	Aug - Sept	Fly fishing, trolling
Fall Chinook & Coho Salmon	Oct - Nov	Plugging, casting, trolling
Deschutes Rainbow	June	Fly fishing(salmon fly hatch)
Willamette Trout	May - Oct	Fly fishing, trolling
Yaquina Sturgeon	Mar - Apr	Still fishing

Note: The above list attempts to indicate prime times. Some fisheries such as steelhead and sturgeon are active on a year round basis.

Author's Notes: Larry Schoenborn, producer of the television show "Fishing the West" tells me Craig is a very good guide.

COVE, OREGON

LANE, GARY & KAREN WELLS (503) 568-4663, 252-6413
Address Route 1, Cove, OR 97824

Airport Boise, ID 150m **Accommodations** Cove **Operation** Outfitter
Fish Trout, salmon **Season** Year-round **Boats** McKenzies, rafts, dory
Water Grande Ronde, Owyhee Rivers **Tackle Supplied** All
Specialty Fly fishing float trips **Type of Fishing** All
Experience 12 years **Rates** day: $130 week: $795
Guide's Notes: We also offer wilderness float trips in Alaska.

EUGENE, OREGON

ADKINS, RON (503) 484-4180
Address 555 Stonegate, Eugene, OR 97401
Airport Eugene **Accommodations** Eugene **Operation** Guide
Fish Steelhead, chinook **Season** Year-round **Type of Fishing** All
Water North Umpqua, McKenzie, Siletz and Siuslaw Rivers
Boats Jet sled, McKenzies **Tackle Supplied** All
Experience 10 years **Rates** day: $125

BAKER, RAY (503) 343-7514
Address P.O. Box 5586, Eugene, OR 97405
Airport Eugene **Accommodations** Eugene
Operation Outfitter **Type of Fishing** All
Fish Trout, steelhead, salmon **Season** Year-round
Water Deschutes, Umpqua and McKenzie Rivers
Specialty Fly fishing float and power boat trips
Boats River sled, McKenzie, rafts **Tackle Supplied** All
Experience 30 years **Rates** day: $175
Author's Notes: A reliable reference tells me Ray runs a very good operation.

DOPPELT, ROBERT-OREGON RIVER EXPERIENCES (503) 342-3293
Address 1935 Hayes, Eugene, OR 97405
Airport Eugene **Accommodations** Eugene
Operation Guide, Outfitter **Type of Fishing** Fly
Fish Steelhead, brown trout **Season** May-October **Tackle Supplied** Fly
Water Rogue, Deschutes, Umpqua Rivers, Salmon River (Idaho)
Specialty Fly fishing float trips **Boats** McKenzies, rafts
Experience 9 years **Rates** day: $160 week: $800

GUARD, R.H.-THE CADDIS FLY (503) 342-7005
Address 191-A East 5th Ave., Dept. A, Eugene, OR 97401
Airport Eugene **Accommodations** Eugene **Boats** Drift boats
Operation Outfitter, tackle shop **Type of Fishing** All
Fish Steelhead, trout **Season** Year-round **Tackle Supplied** All
Water McKenzie, Umpqua, Deschutes, Santiam Rivers
Rates day: $135 week: $450-650 1/2 day:$50-75
Guide's Notes: The famous **McKenzie River**, Herbert Hoover's old fishing hole
offers world class rainbow fishing. The peak time of the year is May and June.

The most effective flies are green caddis patterns in size #10 Little Yellow Stonefly sizes #18-14, and yellow Elk Hair Caddis #16-12. The **Willamette River** has a great March Brown hatch in March and May. Spruce fly streamers, sizes #10-8 are good for big native cutthroat.

Both rivers have runs of summer steelhead. Muddlers and Silver Hiltons size #6 are best. They also eat big green caddis flies.

Author's Notes: I have fished with Bob Guard in Alaska. He is an excellent fisherman and a very good guide.

HAAS, GALAND (503) 342-1222, 266-2974
Address P.O. Box 10754, Eugene, OR 97440
Airport Eugene **Accommodations** Eugene
Operation Outfitter **Specialty** Fly fishing **Type of Fishing** All
Fish Rainbow, steelhead, salmon, bass **Season** Year-round
Water Rogue, Deschutes, McKenzie Rivers, Salmon (ID)
Boats River sled, McKenzies **Tackle Supplied** All
Experience 15 years **Rates** day: $150 1/2 day: $100 week: $660
Guide's Notes: McKenzie River: Rainbow trout, summer steelhead, spring chinook salmon. Peak times for trout are May to mid-July - caddis hatches. Chinook salmon run May-June. Summer steelhead are available June-October.

Deschutes River: Native rainbow trout, summer steelhead. The peak times are May-July for native rainbows with the stonefly hatch in late May through mid-June. Caddis hatch June through August. Summer steelhead run late July through August.

Rogue River: Summer steelhead, fall chinook salmon, sturgeon. Peak time for all species is September through October.

Umpqua River: Summer and winter steelhead. Summer steelhead prime time is June through August. Winter steelhead prime time is November through March.

High Cascade Lakes-Davis Lake, Crane Prairie, Hosmer: Rainbow trout, brown trout, Atlantic salmon. Prime times are May through August. The hatches are damsel and caddis. We also use streamers, leeches, and fresh water shrimp flies.

Oregon Coastal Rivers: Chetco, Elk, Sixes, Coquille, Smith, Siuslaw, Alsea, Siletz, Nestucca, Trask, Wilson, Kilchis, and Nehalem: Fall chinook salmon, winter and summer steelhead. Prime time for chinook salmon is October through November. Winter steelhead run November through March. Summer steelhead are available May through June.

Salmon River, ID: Summer steelhead-trophy size. Prime time is October through November. Fly fishing and lures.

Author's Notes: Our contacts in Oregon tell us Galand is a top notch guide.

HOUGHTON, BOB (503) 344-9024
Address 2840 Ferry Street, Eugene, OR 97405
Airport Eugene **Accommodations** Eugene **Operation** Outfitter
Fish Trout, steelhead, salmon, shad **Season** Year-round

Water McKenzie, Rogue, Deschutes, Umpqua Rivers
Specialty Fly fishing float trips **Tackle Supplied** All
Boats McKenzies, river sled, rafts **Type of Fishing** Fly, baitcast
Experience 12 years **Rates** day: $140

THOMAS, WADE (503) 686-1106
Address 210 Palomino. Eugene, OR 97401
Airport Eugene **Accommodations** Eugene **Operation** Outfitter
Boats McKenzie **Tackle Supplied** All **Type of Fishing** Fly
Fish Rainbow, steelhead **Season** April-October
Water McKenzie River **Specialty** Fly fishing
Experience 14 years **Rates** day: $120

FORT KLAMATH, OREGON

**SPARACINO, RANDY & CYNTHIA-TAKE IT EASY FLY FISHING RESORT
(503) 381-2328**
Address P.O. Box 408, Fort Klamath, OR 97626
Airport Klamath Falls 30m **Accommodations** On premises
Operation Outfitter, lodge, tackle shop **Type of Fishing** Fly
Fish Rainbow, brook, brown, steelhead **Season** Mid-April-October 15
Water Williamson, Rogue Rivers, two spring creeks **Boats** McKenzies, jet sleds
Specialty Fly fishing spring creeks and drift fishing **Tackle Supplied** Fly
Experience 15 years **Rates** day: $150/2 people
Guide's Notes: We have good to excellent fishing on the **Williamson** from late
May through September. The peak is mid-July to mid-August. Excellent spring
creek fishing runs from April to November.
*Author's Notes: Take It Easy Ranch has been written up in FLY FISHING, FLY
FISHERMAN, and FISHING THE WEST. In 1983 they were given an award for
being the best fly fishing resort in the state of Oregon by OREGON MAGAZINE.
Cynthia's cooking has been written up in several magazines. Personal friends
that have visited Take It Easy Ranch tell us it is an excellent operation.*

GOLD BEACH, OREGON

SMITH, RON (503) 247-6676, 247-7691
Address P.O. Box 862, Gold Beach, OR 97444
Airport Coos Bay 60m **Accommodations** Gold Beach
Operation Guide **Type of Fishing** Fly **Boats** River sled, McKenzie
Fish Steelhead, chinook salmon **Season** Year-round
Water Rogue, Chetco, Elk, Sixes Rivers **Tackle Supplied** All
Specialty Power boat and drift boat river trips
Experience 4 years **Rates** day: $150 1/2 day: $100

Guide's Notes: Fishing Calendar

Fish	Water	Available	Lures
Spring Chinook	Rogue River	Apr - June	Bait, Spinners
Summer Steelhead	Rogue River	July - Oct	Flies, bait, lures
Fall Chinook	Rogue, Elk Chetco Rivers	Aug - Dec	Bait, lures
Winter Steelhead	Rogue, Elk Chetco Rivers	Dec - Mar	Bait, lures

JOSEPH, OREGON

STEEN, JAMES (503) 432-5315
Address P.O. Box 216, Joseph, OR 97846
Airport Lewiston, ID 80m **Accomodations** Joseph
Operation Outfitter **Type of Fishing** All **Specialty** Float trips
Fish Trout, steelhead, bass, sturgeon **Season** February-September
Water Hells Canyon, Snake and Grand Ronde Rivers, Wallowa Lake
Boats McKenzies, rafts, rowboats **Tackle Supplied** All
Experience 12 years **Rates** day: $200 week: $1000

WICK, KEN-OUTBACK RANCH OUTFITTERS (503) 432-1721, 432-6202
Address P.O. Box 384, Joseph, OR 97846
Airport Lewiston, ID 80m **Accomodations** Joseph **Operation** Outfitter
Fish Trout, bass, steelhead, sturgeon **Type of Fishing** All
Water Snake, Wenaha, Wallowa, Imnaha, Grande Ronde Rivers
Specialty High lake horseback fishing trips **Season** April-December
Boats Rafts **Experience** 16 years **Rates** day: $90

The Williamson River above Klamath Lake.   *R. Valentine Atkinson*

LEABURG, OREGON

HELFRICH, JEFF R. (503) 896-3219, 896-3370
Address 89825 Greenwood Drive, Leaburg, OR 97489
Airport Eugene 30m **Accomodations** Leaburg
Operation Outfitter **Type of Fishing** Fly, baitcast
Fish Trout, steelhead, salmon **Season** Year-round **Tackle Supplied** All
Water Middle Fork of the Salmon, Rogue, McKenzie, Siuslaw Rivers
Specialty Fly fishing camp trips **Boats** McKenzies, rafts
Experience 6 years **Rates** day: $140

MEDFORD, OREGON

SMITH, BILLY FLOYD-EAGLE SUN, INC. (503) 772-9910
Address P.O. Box 873, Medford, OR 97501
Airport Medford **Accomodations** Medford **Operation** Outfitter
Fish Steelhead, salmon, trout, bass **Season** Year-round
Water Rogue, Klamath, Chetco, Smith Rivers **Type of Fishing** All
Specialty Fly fishing float trips **Tackle Supplied** All
Boats Rowboats, river sled, McKenzie
Experience 9 years **Rates** day: $140

MOUNT HOOD, OREGON

PARKER, CLINT & JIM DOYLE-JIM DOYLE GUIDE SERVICE
(503) 352-7547
Address 5430 Hwy 35, Mt. Hood, OR 97041
Airport Portland 60m **Accommodations** Mt. Hood
Operation Outfitter, tackle shop **Type of Fishing** All
Fish Steelhead, salmon, trout, sturgeon **Season** Year-round
Water Deschutes, Hood, Sandy Rivers **Boats** McKenzies, raft
Specialty Light tackle fishing and fly fishing **Tackle Supplied** All
Experience 8 years **Rates** day: $140

OXBOW, OREGON

ARMACOST, GARY-HELLS CANYON ADVENTURES
(503) 785-3352, 1-800-422-3568
Address P.O. Box 159, Oxbow, OR 97840
Airport Boise, ID 160m **Accomodations** Halfway 17m
Operation Outfitter **Type of Fishing** Baitcast **Water** Snake River
Fish Steelhead, trout, bass, catfish **Season** Year-round
Boats River sled, rafts **Specialty** Overnight jet boat charters
Experience 3 years **Rates** day: $160 (overnight)

PORT ORFORD, OREGON

HANNAH, DENNY-HANNAH FISH CAMPS (503) 332-0443, 759-3535
Address 94893 Elk River Road, Dept. L, Port Orford, OR 97465
Airport Eugene 50m **Accommodations** On Premises
Fish Salmon, steelhead, sm bass, sturgeon, stripers **Season** Year-round
Water Rogue, Illinois, Elk, Sixes, Coquille, Umpqua Rivers
Specialty Fly fishing float trips for smallmouth bass and drifting eggs
for salmon with light tackle **Operation** Outfitter, camp **Type of Fishing** All
Boats River sleds, McKenzies **Tackle Supplied** Spin, baitcast
Experience 19 years **Rates** day: $250 week: $900/person
Guide's Notes: Fishing Calendar for Oregon Costal Rivers

Water	Fish	Available
Rogue	Salmon	Sept - Oct
	Steelhead	Jan - Mar
Umpqua	Smallmouth bass	June - Sept
	Striped bass, Sturgeon	Apr - Sept
Illinois	Steelhead	Jan - Mar
Elk	Steelhead	Jan - Mar
	Salmon	Nov - Dec
Sixes, Coquille	Steelhead	Jan - Mar

Author's Notes: *Denny comes highly recommended by Paul Bruun, a well
known outdoor writer and top guide out of Jackson Hole, Wyoming. With four
separate fishing camps, Denny covers much of the best fishing in Oregon. In
addition to steelhead and salmon, of particular interest is the smallmouth and
striped bass fishing which he offers on the* **Umpqua**. *Denny tells me they caught
over 3000 smallmouths from the section between Roseburg and Reedsport last
year. The peak time for this fishing is July and August.*

PORTLAND, OREGON

CLARK, EUGENE (503) 656-2795
Address 4110 West Cornwall Street, West Linn, OR 97068
Airport Portland 20m **Accommodations** West Linn **Operation** Outfitter
Fish Steelhead, trout, salmon, sturgeon **Season** Year-round
Water Clackamas, Deschutes, Columbia, Willamette Rivers
Specialty Trolling, fly, and anchored fishing **Type of Fishing** All
Boats Rowboats, McKenzie, rafts **Tackle Supplied** All
Experience 16 years **Rates** day: $150 1/2day: $75

HAZEL, JOHN & RANDY STETZER, GORDON NASH-KAUFMANN'S STREAMBORN (503) 639-6400
Address 12963 SW Pacific Hwy, Tigard, OR 97223
Airport Portland 10m **Accommodations** Tigard **Season** May-Nov.
Operation Tackle shop **Type of Fishing** Fly **Fish** Steelhead, trout
Water Deschutes River **Specialty** Fly fishing specialists

Experience 6 full time guides who work through the shop

Guide's Notes: The **Deschutes** has long been known locally for its superb rainbow and steelhead fishing, but it has only been recently that national attention has been focused on its unique and outstanding fishery.

The Deschutes is a large stream, but you will soon become familiar with its long slow runs, deep pools, spring creek-like weed beds, rushing riffles, boulder pockets and exciting white water. The Deschutes has it all.

The Deschutes flows through one of the finest semi-wilderness canyons in the West, slicing its way for 100 miles through high desert until it meets the mighty Columbia. This section of river is crossed by highways only in the center, leaving about 40 miles of wild river on both ends accessible only by drift boat or boot power. The lower 40 miles is mostly steelhead water, while the upper 40 is prime trout water. Beginning in September the upper 40 miles will also support steelhead.

Rainbow trout are deep and heavy, averaging a pound. Two and three pound fish are common. Locals refer to them as "redsides" for they will remind you of a Picasso coloring book.

When is the best time to fish the Deschutes? It depends whether you want trout, steelhead, or a chance at both, and, whether you prefer fishing large or small flies, subsurface or dry.

Giant salmonflies, or stoneflies, become active in mid May, begin hatching in late May, and continue on the surface thru late June. This famous hatch attracts anglers from all over the country. Many 20" fish are hooked with big dries and heavily weighted nymphs. Caddis and cranefly hatches can also produce wild surface action.

June is the most popular time on the river but we feel July offers the most consistent dry fly fishing. Ovi-positing caddis sometimes return to the water in clouds. Hoppers begin to entice big fish toward shoreline areas and numerous mayflies are present.

August offers a potpourri of excitement for both the nymph and dry fly artist. Hoppers are at their peak, stonefly, mayfly, and caddis hatches abound and some big trout begin gorging themselves on midges.

Hoppers are still plentiful in early September, but as the larger size terrestrials and aquatic insects taper off, fish begin to concentrate on the micro caddis and midges. The exception to this is the October Caddis hatch. These rusty orange insects attain a length of 1-1 1/2 inches. About dusk these oversize beauties bring up some hefty trout and steelhead.

Steelhead steal the limelight during August. Most anglers desert the upper river and devote their efforts to early arriving steelhead. This first wave of fish are wild battlers and usually very receptive to the fly.

The steelhead run continues to build right through October. The river traffic cools down with the temperature but the fishing thermometer keeps rising.

If you are strictly interested in steelhead we suggest and August-October trip on the lower river. If you wish to combine trout and steelhead we would suggest an upper river float during September or October.

The would-be steelheader must have faith and patience, for you don't always catch a lot of them, but they're all big. Deschutes fish will average 5 to 10 pounds. Three fish days are not uncommon but neither are zero fish days. When conditions are right steelhead can be enticed to the dry fly. Many anglers "in the know" believe the Deschutes to be the finest blue-ribbon stream in the lower 48. We know it is. Where else can you consistently catch fish the length of your arm with flies?

Those anglers wishing to enjoy a private catch and release fishing spree on the Deschutes river with all the comforts of home should consider booking our house for a few days. We provide food, lodging, guide, raft and local transportation. The tying bench is well stocked. Our house is centrally located in Maupin, providing ideal access to both trout and steelhead areas. We can fish about 35 miles of river from a gravel road and reach numerous other areas with a short walk or float, returning each night to the warmth and comfort of a bed, shower, and barbecue. Rates are $125 per person per day food, lodging and guide service included with a three person minimum.

Author's Notes: Kaufmann's is the largest specialty fly shop in the U.S. They are nationally known as an outstanding operation and put out a great mail order catalog. They offer local guide service through six guides who work out of their Portland and Seattle stores. They also offer a full service travel agency which organizes fully planned fly fishing trips to world famous fishing waters.

MEUSLING, JOHN (J.R.) (503) 981-8306
Address Box 128/9713 Broadacres Rd NE, Hubbard, OR 97032-0128
Airport Portland 24m **Accomodations** Woodburn 3m
Operation Outfitter **Type of Fishing** All **Season** Year-round
Fish Steelhead, trout, sturgeon, salmon
Water Deschutes, Nestucca, Wilson and Nehalem Rivers
Specialty Fly fishing trout and steelhead trips
Boats River sleds, McKenzie **Tackle Supplied** All
Experience 10 years **Rates** day: $125-250

MILLER, BILL-NORTHWEST GUIDES AND OUTFITTERS (503) 649-6008
Address 18325 SW Division, Aloha, OR 97007
Airport Portland 25m **Accomodations** Aloha **Operation** Outfitter
Fish Steelhead, salmon, trout, bass **Season** Year-round
Water Deschutes, Wilson, Nestucca and Nehalem Rivers
Specialty Drift and fly float trips **Type of Fishing** All
Boats River sled, McKenzies, rafts **Tackle Supplied** All
Experience 10 years **Rates** day: $55-$85/person
Guide's Notes: Fishing Calendar

Fish	Water	Available	Peak
Steelhead	Oregon Coast	Nov - Apr	Dec - Feb
Salmon	Oregon Coast	Oct - Dec	Nov
Salmon	Oregon Coast	Mar - May	April
Trout	Upper Deschutes	May - Oct	
Steelhead	Lower Deschutes	July - Oct	

PETERSEN, JOHN "PETE" (503) 245-1358, 666-6803
Address 5160 SW Beaverton-Hillsdale Hwy, Portland, OR 97221
Airport Portland **Accomodations** Portland **Operation** Outfitter
Fish Trout, steelhead, bass, salmon **Season** Feb.-Sept.
Water Deschutes, Rogue, Nestucca, Nehalem Rivers
Specialty 1-5 day fly fishing drift trips **Tackle Supplied** Fly, baitcast
Boats River sled, bass boats, McKenzies, rafts **Type of Fishing** Fly
Experience 13 years **Rates** day: $230 week: $595/person

STEWART, DOUGLAS-STEWART CUSTOM TACKLE (503) 254-2359
Address 17310 NE Halsey, Portland, OR 97230
Airport Portland **Accommodations** Portland **Tackle Supplied** All
Operation Outfitter, tackle shop **Type of Fishing** All
Fish Steelhead, trout, salmon **Season** Year-round
Water Deschutes, Sandy, Trask, Kilchis Rivers
Specialty Fly fishing float trips **Boats** McKenzie, rafts
Experience 10 years
Guide's Notes: Fishing Calendar

Water	Fish	Available	Peak	Flies/Lures
Deschutes	Steelhead	July-Oct	Aug-Sept	Max Canyon, Purple Peril, Skunk, Steelees, Wee Warts
Deschutes	Trout	May-Oct	Sept-May	Stone Nymph, Soft Hackles, Tied Down Caddis, Leadwing Coachman, Roostertails
Sandy and Clackamas	Salmon	Dec-Mar	July-Oct	Eggs, Corkies, Yarn, Polar Shrimp, Skycomish Sunrise, Teeny Nymphs, Max Canyon
Coast Rivers	Steelhead	Nov-Feb		Pink & Polar Shrimp, Glo Bugs, Teeny Nymphs, Eggs, Corkies, Yarn

Author's Notes: Doug has written articles for FLY FISHERMAN and owns an Orvis Shop in Portland.

TOMAN, BOB & JERRY, STEVE KOLER & JACK SMITH
LARRY'S SPORTS CENTER (503) 656-0321
Address #60 Oregon City Shopping Center, Oregon City, OR 97045
Airport Portland 10m **Accommodations** Oregon City
Operation Guide, tackle shop **Type of Fishing** All
Fish Salmon, steelhead **Season** Year-round **Tackle Supplied** All
Water Clackamas, Sandy, Wilson, Trask, Nestucca, Deschutes
Specialty Drift fishing, back trolling for salmon, light tackle spinning and fly fishing on the Deschutes **Boats** River sleds, McKenzies
Experience 4-10 years **Rates** day: $80-110/person

Author's Notes: *Larry's Sport Center is one of the largest tackle stores in the U.S. Larry Schoenborn, the owner, is also the producer of the well known television program "Fishing the West." Larry tells me "All of these guys are excellent."*

SISTERS, OREGON

GABER, JOE & PEGGY-CASCADE ADVENTURES (503) 549-1047
Address P.O. Box 873, Sisters, OR 97759
Airport Redmond 20m **Accomodations** Sisters
Operation Outfitter, tackle shop **Type of Fishing** All
Fish Steelhead, trout, salmon, sturgeon
Water McKenzie, Deschutes, Rogue, Owyhee Rivers
Specialty Fly fishing in high lakes **Season** April-Dec.
Boats River sled, McKenzies, rafts **Tackle Supplied** All
Experience 6 years **Rates** day: $175-250 week: $800-900

SPRINGFIELD, OREGON

BENTSEN, DAN (503) 726-6613
Address 1421 Fairview, Springfield, OR 97477
Airport Eugene 5m **Accomodations** Eugene **Operation** Guide
Fish Steelhead, trout, salmon, bass **Season** Year-round
Water Deschutes, Rogue, McKenzie, Umpqua Rivers
Specialty Plugging for steelhead **Type of Fishing** Fly, spin
Boats Rowboat, McKenzie, rafts **Tackle Supplied** All
Experience 8 years **Rates** day: $175 1/2 day: $125 week: $1000

HELFRICH, DEAN (503) 747-8401
Address 2722 Harvest Lane, Springfield, OR 97477
Airport Eugene 5m **Accomodations** Eugene 5m **Operation** Outfitter
Fish Trout, steelhead, salmon **Season** Year-round
Water Rogue, McKenzie, Deschutes Rivers, Middle Fork Salmon(ID)
Specialty Fly fishing float trips with dory boats **Type of Fishing** Fly, spin
Boats River sled, McKenzies, rafts **Tackle Supplied** All
Experience 30 years **Rates** day: $175

HELFRICH, KEN (503) 741-1905
Address 378 South 69th Place, Springfield, OR 97478
Airport Eugene 5m **Accomodations** Eugene 5m
Operation Outfitter **Type of Fishing** Fly **Tackle Supplied** All
Fish Rainbow, cutthroat, steelhead, salmon **Season** Year-round
Water McKenzie and Rogue Rivers, Salmon (ID)
Specialty Fly fishing river float trips **Boats** McKenzies, rafts
Experience 17 years **Rates** day: $150 1/2 day: $100 week: $1000

SPENCER, BOB (503) 747-8153
Address 656 North 71st Street, Springfield, OR 97478
Airport Eugene 5m **Accomodations** Eugene 5m
Operation Outfitter **Type of Fishing** All
Fish Trout, steelhead, salmon **Season** Year-round
Water McKenzie, Deschutes, Willamette, Coastal Rivers
Specialty Scenic whitewater fly fishing and raft trips
Boats McKenzie, rafts **Tackle Supplied** All
Experience 7 years **Rates** day: $130 1/2day: $75 week: $650

TYGH VALLEY, OREGON

ZAPFFE, SKIP (503) 544-2615
Address Route 1 Box 312, Tygh Valley, OR 97063
Airport Portland 95m **Accommodations** Maupin 20m
Operation Outfitter **Type of Fishing** All **Specialty** Fly fishing
Fish Steelhead, trout, salmon **Season** Year-round
Water Deschutes, Salmon and Snake (ID), Cowlitz (WA) Rivers
Boats McKenzies, river sleds, rafts **Tackle Supplied** All
Experience 25 years **Rates** varies- $80-140/person

VIDA, OREGON

CUNNINGHAM, JAMES (503) 896-3750
Address 45304 Goodpasture Road, Vida, OR 97488
Airport Eugene 40m **Accommodations** Vida **Boats** McKenzie
Operation Guide **Type of Fishing** Fly **Season** Year-round
Fish Rainbow, steelhead, salmon **Specialty** Fly fishing driftboat trips
Water McKenzie, Rogue Rivers, Umpqua, coastal streams
Experience 10 years **Rates** day: $125 week: varies
Guide's Notes: The McKenzie River really has 3 different phases to the fishing
season which begins April 28th and closes October 31st:
   Late Spring Fishing-- From April 28th to early June. The best fishing for this
time of the season generally takes place below Leaburg Dam to Eugene. The
fishing can be outstanding. The records for both the biggest fish caught, as well
as the most fish caught come from this lower stretch of the river. Oftentimes,
some of the mayfly hatches and nymphing occur during these early weeks.
   Early and Mid-Summer Fishing-- Mid-June through August. The best fishing
during this period generally takes place on the upper stretches of the McKenzie
between Blue River and Leaburg Lake. This is also the prime time for fishing
the river during good weather, although showers (known in Oregon as "liquid
sunshine") can still occur. Fishing is a little slower because the fish tend to be
less active during the warmer months; the best time of the day is mid-morning
or evening hours. This is the best period of the year for those of you who enjoy
the sunshine, leisurely lunches with freshly fried fish and good conversation.

Late Summer and Early Fall--September through closing day, October 31st. The best fishing during the late season generally takes place on the upper stretches of the McKenzie between McKenzie Bridge and Leaburg Lake. If you have never experienced Indian Summer on the river, I encourage you to do so. Trout fishing picks up once again and there are still a number of steelhead left in the river. The tourists are gone, the weather is pleasant, and the fall colors are magnificent. Try it!

HELFRICH, DAVE (503) 896-3786
Address 47555 McKenzie Hwy, Vida, OR 97488
Airport Eugene 36m **Accomodations** Vida
Operation Outfitter **Type of Fishing** Fly **Specialty** Fly fishing float trips
Fish Trout, steelhead, cutthroat **Season** April-November
Water McKenzie, Rogue Rivers, Middle Fork of the Salmon (ID)
BoatsMcKenzies, kayaks, pontoons **Tackle Supplied** Fly
Experience 36 years**Rates** week: $725/person, varies
Guide's Notes: The Rogue River--Beginning high in the Cascade Mountains near Crater Lake, the Rogue River carves its way through Oregon's coastal mountains on its way to the Pacific Ocean.

Eighty-four miles of this remarkable river are named in the 1968 "Wild and Scenic Rivers Act," which protects certain rivers in the United States which possess outstanding scenic, recreational, geologic, fish and wildlife, historic and cultural values.

Fishing is for the fighting fall-run steelhead, on flies and light tackle. At noon your catch will be broiled for you over hardwood coals for a leisurely lunch, the fillets supplemented with stores we carry in the boats.

In September the weather is likely to be warm and mild. The fish will range from a half pound to three pounds. From mid-October through November early winter steelhead up to eight and ten pounds are coming in. The weather is likely to be cool, and we may get rain.

The McKenzie River--The McKenzie River begins at Clear Lake, not far from the summit of the Cascade Mountains. Its crystal waters flow for about 80 miles, until it joins the Willamette River near Eugene.

The upper portions of the river plummet over roaring waterfalls. The large middle section of the river, where we offer both fishing and scenic trips, flows through forests of Douglas fir and Western red cedar, abounding in excellent fishing and a variety of whitewater.

The McKenzie has been world-famous for its rainbow trout for more than a half century. Although it is now walled by the McKenzie Highway, it remains crystal-clear and unspoiled. The McKenzie season is late April to October.

SCOTT, NEIL-HEAVEN'S GATE COTTAGES (503) 822-3214
Address 50055 McKenzie Highway, Vida, OR 97488
Airport Eugene 36m**Accommodations** On premises
Operation Outfitter, cottages **Type of Fishing** All
Fish Trout, steelhead **Season** Year-round **Specialty** Fly fishing
Water McKenzie, Rogue, Deschutes Rivers
Boats McKenzies, rafts, kayaks **Tackle Supplied** All
Experience 5 years **Rates** day: $75 1/2day: $60/2 people

Washington

ARLINGTON, WASHINGTON

BUTORAC, JOE-TROPHY TRIPS (206) 435-8624
Address P.O. Box 98, Arlington, WA 98223
Airport Seattle 47m **Accommodations** Arlington **Operation** Guide
Fish Steelhead, cutthroat, salmon **Season** Year-round **Boats** Rafts
Water Sauk, Skagit, Wenatchee, Skykomish Rivers **Tackle Supplied** Fly
Specialty Fly fishing only for steelhead **Type of Fishing** Fly
Experience 2 years **Rates** day: $195
Guide's Notes: Steelhead Fishing Calendar

Water	Available
Skykomish	Feb - Mar
Sauk	Mar - Apr
Skagit	Mar - Apr
Wenatchee	Aug - Oct

Author's Notes: Our contacts tell us Joe is an outstanding guide.

BELLEVUE, WASHINGTON

COOK, GEORGE-KAUFMANN'S STREAMBORN (206) 643-2246, 747-4993
Address 15015 Main St., Bellevue, WA 98007
Airport Seattle 15m **Accommodations** Bellevue
Operation Guide **Type of Fishing** Fly **Tackle Supplied** Fly
Fish Rainbow, brown, Lahontan cutthroat **Season** March-Sept
Water Columbia basin region of central Washington **Boats** Float tubes
Specialty Fly-fishing central Washington lakes for trophy cutthroat and rainbow
Experience 4 years **Rates** day: $185
Guide's Notes: We have a total of four guides working out of Kaufmann's
Bellevue store so if I'm not available we can cover you with another guide.

   Central Washington Lakes Fishing begins in March and runs through October
prime time is April and May. Rainbows, browns, and cutthroats run 18 to 27
inches. We fish with streamers and specialize in night fishing for large browns,
rainbows, and cutthroats. We have excellent nymph fishing with both floating
and sinking lines in April and May.
Author's Notes: George guides groups to Christmas Island, Alaska, and New
Zealand. He has also worked as a full time guide for 4 years in the Bristol Bay
region of Alaska. He has an excellent reputation.

WASHINGTON

Strait of Georgia

VANCOUVER ISLAND

CANADA

Strait of Juan De Fuca

San Juan Islands

Anacortes

Nooksack R.

Sedro Woolley

Skagit River

Stillaguamish

Sauk

Skykomish R.

Silvana

Arlington

Ross Lake

Skagit R.

Lake Wenatchee

Snoqualmie R.

Lynnwood

Kirkland

Seattle

Bellevue

Issaquah

Lake Sammamish

Kent

Puget Sound

Bremerton

Port Angeles

Sol Duc

Forks

Bogachiel R.

Hoh River

Queets R.

Pacific Ocean

Tacoma

Columbia R.

Wenatchee

Spokane

Spokane River

Columbia R.

Franklin Roosevelt Lake

Banks Lake

Moses Lake

Potholes Reservoir

Soda Lake

90

Snake River

Yakima River

Yakima R.

Naches R.

Yakima

+ Mt. Rainier

Cowlitz R.

Klickitat River

Columbia River

Joutle River

Silver Lake

Longview

Kalama

+ Mt. Saint Helens

Kalama R.

N. Fk. Lewis R.

Woodland

Ridgefield

Vancouver

Columbia River

5

5

BREMERTON, WASHINGTON

ALEXANDER, JACK-KITSAP SPORT SHOP (206) 373-9589, 373-3355
Address 630 N. Callow Ave, Bremerton, WA 98312
Airport Seattle 30m **Accommodations** Bremerton
Operation Tackle shop, guide **Type of Fishing** All **Boats** McKenzies
Fish Steelhead, spring chinook, Dolly Varden, rainbow **Season** June-March
Water Hoh, Soleduck, Bogachiel, Queets Rivers **Tackle Supplied** All
Specialty Back trolling and light tackle fishing for steelhead and salmon
Experience 17 years **Rates** day: $170

FORKS, WASHINGTON

JACOBSEN, HERB-HERB JACOBSEN GUIDE SERVICE
(206) 374-2162, (218) 847-2925 (MN)
Address P.O. Box 87, Forks, WA 98331,
or 334 Elizabeth St., Detroit Lakes, MN 56501
Airport Port Angeles 50m **Accommodations** Forks **Operation** Guide
Fish Salmon, steelhead, trout **Season** Year-round **Type of Fishing** All
Water Rivers of Olympic Peninsula, Rogue River (OR), Bristol Bay (AK)
Specialty Whitewater float trips for salmon, trout and steelhead using flies and
other tackle **Boats** River sleds, McKenzies **Tackle Supplied** All
Experience 17 years **Rates** day: $180/Forks week: $2000/Alaska
Guide's Notes: I also guide in Oregon and Alaska.

Steve Probasco holds up an eastern Washington rainbow.   *Ken Bamford*

JOHNSON, NORRIE (206) 374-3204
Address P.O. Box 314, Forks, WA 98331
Airport Port Angeles 55m **Accommodations** Forks
Operation Guide **Type of Fishing** River float fishing **Boats** McKenzie
Fish Steelhead, king, silver, jack **Season** Sept-Feb **Tackle Supplied** Baitcast
Water Bogachiel, Hoh, Sol Duc, Calawah Rivers **Specialty** Drift fishing bait
Experience 8 years **Rates** day: $170

OLSEN, CHRIS (206)374-6146, (503)474-2775
Address (May-Nov)1245 Shanks Creek Rd, Sunny Valley, OR 97497 (Dec-Apr)
P.O. Box 945, Forks, WA 98331
Airport Seattle **Accommodations** Forks **Operation** Outfitter
Fish Steelhead, salmon, trout **Season** Year-round **Type of Fishing** Fly, baitcast
Water Hoh, Rogue (OR), Middle Fork Salmon (ID) Rivers **Boats** McKenzie, raft
Specialty Drift fishing for winter steelhead **Tackle Supplied** Fly, baitcast, troll
Experience 20 years **Rates** varies

ISSAQUAH, WASHINGTON

KISER, TED (206) 226-6066
Address P.O. Box 581, Issaquah, WA 98027
Airport Seattle **Accommodations** Issaquah
Operation Outfitter **Type of Fishing** Fly, baitcast
Fish Steelhead, salmon, trout, sm bass **Season** Mar-Aug
Water Cowlitz, Deschutes (OR), John Day (OR), Snoqualmie Rivers
Specialty Spring salmon bait fishing, whitewater float trips
Boats Riversleds, McKenzies, rafts **Tackle Supplied** Baitcast
Experience 15 years **Rates** day: $175 week: $1750

KALAMA, WASHINGTON

JOHNSON, RICK-STEELHEAD OUTFITTERS (206) 673-4813
Address 5500 Kalama River Rd, Kalama, WA 98625
Airport Portland, OR 40m **Accommodations** Kalama
Operation Outfitter, tackle shop **Type of Fishing** All
Fish Steelhead, chinook, cutthroat, rainbow **Season** Year-round
Water Kalama, Cowlitz, Klickitat, Lewis Rivers
Specialty Steelhead fly fishing from drift boats
Boats Riversleds, McKenzies, rafts **Tackle Supplied** All
Experience 21 years **Rates** day: $180
Guide's Notes: Winter (December - February) Drift fishing for winter run
steelhead. Excellent chance to put a trophy on the wall.
   Spring (March - May) Drift fishing for spring chinook and steelhead. These
fish are the wildest fighting fish in the northwest.

Summer (June - August) Fly fishing or drift fishing for summer run steelhead. Shirt sleeve "steelheading" at its best.

Fall (September - November) Fly fishing for sea run cutthroat and fall steelhead. Some of our best fly fishing.

KENT, WASHINGTON

BOYER, JEFF (206) 631-6740
Address 23262 132nd Place Southeast, Kent, WA 98042
Airport Seattle 10m **Accommodations** Kent **Operation** Guide
Fish Bass, walleye, 3 species of salmon **Season** Feb.-Nov.
Water Silver Lake, Banks Lake, Moses Pot Holes, Lake Sammamish
Specialty Bass fishing **Type of Fishing** Spin, baitcast, troll
Boats Bass boats **Tackle Supplied** Spin, baitcast, troll
Experience 4 years **Rates** day: $110-200
Guide's Notes: Silver Lake, (Cowlitz Co.): March - November. Western Washington's best bet for trophy largemouth bass. Best trophy months are March - May, October - November. Fantastic surface action May - September.

Lake Sammamish: May - July--Possibly the best smallmouth lake in the state. This fishery is still in the growing stages, with plenty of action from 1 to 3-1/2 pounders. Surface bite is great in June-July. Largemouth are an added bonus.

Potholes Reservoir: May - October--Fantastic action for both largemouth and smallmouth throughout season. Walleye, perch, and crappie also abundant. Truly a warm water species paradise.

Banks Lake: May - August--Super largemouth lake, especially if you like topwater action. Smallmouth and walleye also coming on strong now. Clear water, beautiful scenery, and hot action.

Moses Lake: May - October--Another excellent largemouth, smallmouth fishery. Especially good in late season. This combined with Potholes makes a great two day trip.

Columbia River, Umatilla and Celilo Pools: July - September--Walleye heaven! Best area in the state to boat a trophy. Walleye run 4 pounds up to state records. Washington and Oregon records have each been shattered several times here the past three years. Current record holders are both from this area; a 17-9 for Oregon, an 18-1/2 for Washington. Smallmouth also available for a nice change of pace.

Lake Washington: July - October--Opening day of sockeye kicks off this lake's guide season. Sockeye normally start mid-July into August. King salmon open mid-August, with silvers following in September. Sockeye run 5-10 pounds, adult silvers 6-13, and kings approach 20 pounds. Jumbo perch and bass also available as an attractive diversion. A rare opportunity to enjoy quality salmon fishing in calm waters.

Author's Notes: Larry Schoenborn, who produces the television show "Fishing the West", tells us that Jeff is the best bass guide in Washington.

LYNNWOOD, WASHINGTON

GAYESKI, NICK-WESTERN FLYFISHER, INC. (206) 775-4496
Address 19512 37th Ave West, Lynnwood, WA 98036
Airport Seattle 20m **Accommodations** Lynnwood
Operation Outfitter, tackle shop **Type of Fishing** Fly **Specialty** Fly fishing
Fish Steelhead, rainbow, cutthroat **Season** Year-round **Boats** Rafts
Water Sauk/Skagit, Wenatchee, Skykomish, N. Fork of Stillaguamish Rivers
Experience 3 years **Rates** day: $180

RIDGEFIELD, WASHINGTON

GRUELLE, SR., MEL-MELS 4 RIVER GUIDE SERVICE (206) 887-4891
Address P.O. Box 143, Ridgefield, WA 98642
Airport Portland 20m **Accommodations** Ridgefield
Operation Guide **Type of Fishing** All **Boats** River sleds, McKenzies
Fish Steelhead, salmon, sturgeon, shad **Season** Year-round
Water North Fork Lewis, East Fork Kalama, Washougal Rivers
Specialty River guiding, drift and jet boat **Tackle Supplied** Spin, baitcast
Rates day: $130

SEATTLE, WASHINGTON

FARRAR, JOHN-KAUFMANN'S STREAMBORN (206) 367-2243, 643-5717
Address 1413 NE 162nd St., Seattle, WA 98155
Airport Seattle **Accommodations** Seattle
Operation Outfitter **Type of Fishing** Fly **Tackle Supplied** Fly
Fish Steelhead, rainbow, sea run cutthroat **Season** Year-round
Water Skykomish, Sauk/Skagit, Wenatchee, Grand Ronde Rivers
Specialty Fly fishing float trips **Boats** Rafts, river sleds, McKenzies
Experience 6 years **Rates** day: $180 week: $650 1/2 day: $100
Guide's Notes: Fishing Calendar

Water	Fish	Available	Flies
Skykomish, Sauk/Skagit	Winter Steelhead	March-April	Wet
Skykomish, Wenatchee, Grand Ronde, Yakima, Columbia, Snake	Summer Steelhead	June-Nov	Wet & Dry
Yakima	Rainbow & Cutthroat	Aug-Oct	Wet & Dry
Skykomish, Stillaguamish	Sea run cutthroat	Aug-Oct	Wet & Dry

Author's Notes: Two close friends who live in Washington tell me John is one of the top guides in the state and that he ranks with the best in the nation. If you are visiting from abroad you might be interested to know John speaks Hungarian, German, French, and Spanish. John, of course, is often booked up and out on the river, however, you can always contact him through Kaufmann's Streamborn in Bellevue Washington, (206) 643-5717.

SEDRO WOOLLEY, WASHINGTON

HUNGER, F.C.-ED'S SPORT SHOP (206) 826-3646, 336-3232
Address 3094 Lyman Hamilton Hwy, Sedro Woolley, WA 98284
Airport Bellingham 40m **Accommodations** Sedro Woolley
Operation Guide **Type of Fishing** All **Tackle Supplied** All
Fish Steelhead, salmon, trout **Season** Year-round
Water Sauk/Skagit, Nooksack, Cowlitz Rivers **Boats** River sleds, McKenzies
Specialty Steelhead, king salmon, coho drifting and back bounce
Experience 2 years **Rates** day: $120-150
Guide's Notes: Steelhead season is from December 1st through March 31st with
a special catch and release season in April. Fishing at this time is excellent.
King salmon season is from July through September with the peak in August
and September. Trout and coho trips are available on request between steelhead
and king salmon seasons.

SILVANA, WASHINGTON

WAGNER, BILL (206) 652-6850
Address 1406 226th St NW, Box 132, Silvana, WA 98287
Airport Seattle 45m **Accommodations** Silvana
Operation Outfitter **Type of Fishing** Fly, baitcast
Fish Steelhead, chinook, coho, chum **Season** Year-round
Water Skykomish, Sauk, Sol Duc, Bogachiel, Hoh Rivers **Boats** McKenzies
Specialty Drift fishing, fly fishing float trips **Tackle Supplied** Fly, baitcast
Experience 4 years **Rates** day: $150 week: $900
*Author's Notes: Bill was recommended to us by Larry Schoenborn of the well
known television show "Fishing the West."*

VANCOUVER, WASHINGTON

GIPPLE, BRUCE (206) 573-8342
Address 2295 NE 97th St., Vancouver, WA 98665
Airport Portland, OR 20m **Accommodations** Vancouver **Operation** Outfitter
Fish Salmon, steelhead, trout, sturgeon **Season** Year-round **Tackle Supplied** All
Water Rivers in Western Washington **Type of Fishing** Baitcast
Specialty Fishing with novices in mind **Boats** River sled, McKenzie
Experience 8 years **Rates** day: $150

WOODLAND, WASHINGTON

WALLACE, STU-LARRY'S SPORTS CENTER (206) 225-9530
Address 1511 N. Georig, Woodland, WA 98674
Airport Portland 40m **Accommodations** Woodland **Season** Year-round
Fish Steelhead, king, silver, cutthroat **Operation** Guide, tackle shop

Water North Fork Lewis, East Fork Lewis, Kalama, Cowlitz Rivers
Specialty Drift fishing, back trolling **Type of Fishing** Spin, baitcast
Boats River sleds, McKenzies **Tackle Supplied** Spin, baitcast
Rates day: $150-175
Guide's Notes: East Fork Lewis is primarily a steelhead fishery becoming world renown for big steelhead. Fish are available year round. The peak winter run is from January through February. The peak summer run is from June through August.

   North Fork Lewis Chinook salmon are available mid-March through June. Summer run steelhead are available June - August. The winter run for steelhead is January through February.
Author's Notes: Stu is the manager at Larry's Sports Center. They have two guides that work out of the shop.

YAKIMA, WASHINGTON

FAIRBANKS, GARY-GARY'S FLY SHOP (509) 457-3474
Address 1505 1/2 Fruitvale Blvd, Yakima, WA 98902
Airport Yakima **Accommodations** Yakima
Operation Guide, tackle shop **Type of Fishing** Fly **Tackle Supplied** Fly
Fish Rainbow, steelhead, brown, cutthroat **Season** April-Oct.
Water Yakima, Naches, Wenatchee River, Lenice Lake
Specialty Fly fishing **Boats** McKenzies, rafts, float tubes
Experience 3 years **Rates** day: $125
Guide's Notes: Fishing Calendar

Water	Fish	Peak
Yakima	Trout	Sept - Oct
Wenatchee	Steelhead	Sept - Oct
Naches	Trout	May - Aug

Author's Notes: Gary has a very good reputation both as a guide and a fly shop owner.

6. The Mountain States: Float Trips!

Colorado, Idaho, Montana, Nevada, Utah, Wyoming

In the Rocky Mountain states, you will find some of the finest trout fishing in all the world. The Missouri, Snake, Colorado, and Platte rivers all rise near the Continental Divide, which traverses these states. These four rivers and their tributaries represent more than half of the blue ribbon trout streams in the United States; their drainages include almost all of Idaho, Montana, Wyoming, and Colorado.

One of the most popular ways for the visiting angler to fish these streams is a guided float trip. As the boat drifts along amid changing panoramas, it is hard to keep your mind on fishing. Nonetheless, thirty-fish days are common and seventy-fish days are possible, even for beginners.

An alternative to the float trip is a guided pack trip to fish the high mountain lakes and streams in a true wilderness setting. On these trips you will see spectacular scenery and plenty of game. The outfitter takes care of the food, the horses, and sets up camp—all you do is concentrate on having fun.

West Yellowstone, Montana, occupies the geographical center of a 200-mile circle, sometimes called the Golden Circle or Golden Triangle, encompassing Yellowstone and Grand Teton National Parks, the Henry's Fork area of eastern Idaho, and the famous trout streams of southwestern Montana. The Golden Circle contains the heaviest concentration of outstanding trout waters in the United States. Montana's share of this great fishing includes the blue ribbon waters of the Yellowstone, Gallatin, Big Hole, Jefferson, Ruby, Beaverhead, Missouri, and world-famous Madison rivers.

Flowing out of Yellowstone Park, the Madison courses north towards a confluence with the Gallatin and Jefferson which forms the mighty Missouri. Over forty guides listed in this directory claimed the Madison as one of their most-fished rivers. This response suggests that the Madison could be the most-guided river in North America. Studies show that it also has one of the highest catch rates of any river in Montana; this, along with its beauty and accessibility, accounts for the Madison's popularity.

If you are concerned about crowds, the Beaverhead, Jefferson, Big Hole and Missouri rivers all boast bigger fish and more elbow room than the Madison. The Livingston area claims some of the finest spring creek fishing in the country (see especially, Livingston Spring Creeks, under George Anderson, Livingston, Montana). The Bighorn River near Fort Smith is another viable choice. Since it was opened to the public in 1981, this section of the Bighorn has shared the limelight with the Madison as one of the country's best trout streams.

Missoula, about 200 miles northwest of Yellowstone, is the center of another important Montana fishing area. Rock Creek, the Clark Fork, the Flathead, the Blackfoot, and the Bitterroot rivers all offer excellent fishing; Rock Creek is considered one of the best trout streams in the country.

A large number of Montana guides mention the Smith River, which empties into the Missouri west of Great Falls. Said to be a great float river, the Smith is best floated in June before the water drops.

Idaho is another premier trout fishing state. Among its best streams is the Henry's Fork of the Snake. The Henry's Fork begins at the outlet of Henry's Lake in eastern Idaho and flows about ninety miles to its confluence with the Snake near Idaho Falls. The most famous part, known as the Railroad Ranch, is located in the Last Chance area north of Ashton. This classic dry-fly section was recently given to the people of Idaho by the Harriman family to be maintained as a state park. For many confirmed fly fishermen, this part of the Henry's Fork is Mecca. Hundreds of large rainbow trout can be seen rising to the prolific hatches that come off the Henry's Fork from May to September.

In addition to the Henry's Fork, the angler visiting southeastern Idaho should try the fishing on Henry's Lake, the Snake River in the Swan Valley region, and the Teton River section near Driggs. Visitor accommodations can be found in Last Chance, Island Park, or in West Yellowstone, Montana, about thirty miles to the north.

The Salmon, flowing through the central part of Idaho, was the river most frequently mentioned by the Idaho guides listed in this book. Both the main Salmon and its famous Middle Fork are considered two of the most exciting and beautiful float rivers in the world. Trout fishing can be very good on the Salmon system; the main river has a good steelhead run in late September and October.

The Clearwater River, which empties into the Snake near Lewiston, is second favorite of the Idaho guides. It has very good trout fishing in its headwaters, which include the well-known Kelly Creek, and supports a good run of steelhead in its lower reaches. Other excellent Idaho trout streams are Silver Creek, the Big Wood, and the Little Wood, all in the Sun Valley area. Silver Creek is owned by the Nature Conservancy and is managed by the state as quality wild trout water.

Wyoming has a number of blue ribbon trout streams. Starting from the northwest corner of the state, they include the waters of Yellowstone and Grand Teton National Parks, and the Snake, Yellowstone, Shoshone, Gros Ventre and Buffalo Rivers. All of these provide great fly fishing in the months of July, August, and September. Headquarters for fishing them is Jackson Hole.

Two more famous trout streams, the Green and the New Fork, are located about eighty miles south of Jackson Hole. Both are good float rivers and offer big browns and rainbows. Pinedale serves as headquarters for fishing these two blue ribbon streams.

The North Platte in southeastern Wyoming is another outstanding stream. The Wyoming Department of Game and Fish claims it is one of the most productive rivers in the state; they estimate it supports 3100 fish per mile. This means it is one of the best-kept secrets in the U.S. The North Platte is managed as a wild trout stream and no bait fishing is allowed from the Colorado state line to the town of Saratoga, which is a good place to fish it from.

Colorado is the birthplace of four major river systems: the Colorado, the Platte, the Arkansas, and the Rio Grande. Each of these great rivers has some very good to excellent trout fishing in its headwaters. Guide returns from this state were sparse, but indicate that some of the best stream fishing in the state is located on the tributaries of the Colorado.

The Frying Pan, Roaring Fork, Crystal, and Gunnison rivers were mentioned most by the guides listed here. These are all blue ribbon streams with strict regulations. Both the Frying Pan and Roaring Fork can be fished all year except during spring run off, a bonus for those who do not mind cold weather.

The famous Black Canyon of the Gunnison National Monument is located fifteen miles northeast of Montrose. No roads go into the canyon, so this wilderness fishing can be reached only by hiking or float trip. Fishing is for large browns and rainbows from two to eight pounds.

Nevada, known as a desert state, can surprise you with some excellent fishing. Lake Mead and Lake Mohave on the Nevada/Arizona border offer some exciting largemouth and striped bass fishing. The striped bass feed on the surface from July until October, providing action for anglers using topwater plugs and lures. There are other opportunities for guided fishing in the northeastern part of the state on Wilson and Wild Horse Reservoirs, and in the Ruby Lakes National Wildlife Preserve near Elko. Fishing is for brookies and rainbows at higher elevations, and bass at lower elevations.

A summary of Nevada's best waters would not be complete without mention of Pyramid Lake, near Reno. This lake supports a large population of cutthroat trout which run three to sixteen pounds. Fish are caught from shore from September to April with fly rods and spinning gear. Presently, the Paiute Indians who regulate the fishing do not allow guides to operate on the lake because of liability reasons; however, this may change. Updates can be obtained from tackle shops in Reno.

Only one Utah guide responded to our questionnaire. He is based out of Blanding, in the southeast corner of the state, and guides on Lake Powell. This lake offers largemouth bass, walleye, and striped bass. I have not fished Powell, but friends tell me it is spectacular.

Colorado

ALAMOSA, COLORADO

QUINTANA, EUGENIO-WILDERNESS OUTFITTER (303) 589-2187
Address 5659 Road 9.6 South, Alamosa, CO 81101
Airport Alamosa **Accommodations** Alamosa
Operation Outfitter **Type of Fishing** Fly **Season** June-Nov
Fish German browns, rainbow, brook and native trout
Water Green Lake, South Fork Conejos River, No Name, Glacier Lakes
Specialty Fly fishing in lakes or streams with fly fishing instructor
Experience 9 years **Rates** day: $65/person
Guide's Notes: We pack into the **South San Juan Wilderness** by horse back for lake and stream fly fishing. This is a very scenic area along the Continental Divide.

ANTONITO, COLORADO

EWING, CHARLES-CONEJOS CANYON OUTFITTERS (303) 376-5832
Address RFD, Antonito, CO 81120
Airport Alamosa 55m **Accommodations** Antonito **Operation** Outfitter
Fish Cutthroat, brook, rainbow, brown trout **Season** June-Sept **Boats** Rafts
Water Green, Trail, Blue, Ruybalid Lakes **Type of Fishing** Fly, spin
Specialty High country lake and small stream fly and spinner fishing
Experience 8 years **Rates** day: $90 week: $980 1/2 day: $50
Guide's Notes: High Country stream fishing is good from July 4th until it snows. High lakes are usually very good the last two weeks in June; sporadically good until mid August; then usually very good for flies and lures thru September and October. Some lakes produce 2-4 pound brookies, some a mix of brook and rainbow, and some cutthroat.

ASPEN, COLORADO

ODIER, GEORGE-FOTHERGILL'S LTD (303) 925-3288
Address 534 E. Cooper Avenue, Aspen, CO 81611
Airport Aspen **Accommodations** Aspen **Operation** Outfitter
Season Year-round **Water** Roaring Fork, Frying Pan Rivers **Fish** Rainbow, brown
Specialty Bank fishing **Tackle Supplied** Fly **Type of Fishing** Fly
Experience 24 years **Rates** day: $135 1/2 day: $90
Guide's Notes: The **Roaring Fork and Frying Pan Rivers** are nationally known rivers, and have been placed under strict regulations (gold waters). The Roaring

COLORADO

Fork is primarily a "nymphing river," while the Frying Pan is good for both dries and wets. The Roaring Fork runs through Aspen, and goes on to the Colorado for 41 miles. The Frying Pan is approximately 10 miles long and runs into the Roaring Fork 16 miles downstream from Aspen. Hatches on both rivers are primarily caddis, with fair hatches of a variety of Mays, that include a terrific Green Drake hatch. Rainbows dominate, but browns are now close behind; average sizes are 10 to 14 inches on both rivers with fish in the 16 to 20 inch range quite common. These two rivers are well known to great numbers of fly fishermen.

Author's Notes: Fothergill's is a nationally known fly shop which is now owned by George Odier. George has recently authored a book entitled SWIMMING FLIES, which offers many new and interesting insights on sub-surface fly fishing. If you visit Aspen, a stop at Fothergill's Shop is recommended.

BAYFIELD, COLORADO

SUNDBLOM, DALE-MEADOWLARK RANCH (303) 884-2966
Address 19786 C.R. 501, Bayfield, CO 81122
Airport La Plata 35m **Accommodations** On premises **Operation** Outfitter, lodge
Fish Cutthroat, brook, rainbow, northern pike **Season** June-Sept.
Water Flint, Emerald, Ute, Vallecito Lakes **Type of Fishing** Fly, spin
Specialty Fly fishing pack trips to remote wilderness lakes **Boats** Rafts
Experience 4 years **Rates** day: $70
Guide's Notes: Wimenuche Wilderness Lakes have excellent fly fishing and spincasting for trout during July-September. **Vallecito Lake** has good fishing for 6-20 pound pike in early August and has a kokanee salmon run in early October.

BRECKENRIDGE, COLORADO

DAWSON, BILLY-BRECKENRIDGE GENERAL STORE
(303) 453-2611, 453-1025
Address 1125 Main, Box 1938, Breckenridge, CO 80424
Airport Denver 85m **Accommodations** Breckenridge
Operation Outfitter, charter captain, tackle shop **Type of Fishing** All
Fish Brown, cutthroat, rainbow, brook **Season** Apr-Oct **Tackle Supplied** All
Water Middle Fork South Platt, Blue R., Lake Dillon, Ten Mile
Specialty Fly fishing trophy fish, lake fishing **Boats** Bass boat
Experience 2 years **Rates** day: $175/2 people 1/2 day: $100/2 people

BUENA VISTA, COLORADO

ROBERTS, GLEN-HORN FORK GUIDES (303) 395-8363
Address 29178 County Road 361, Buena Vista, CO 81211
Airport Denver 115m **Accommodations** Buena Vista

Operation Outfitter **Type of Fishing** Fly, spin **Water** High country lakes **Fish** Cutthroat, brook, brown, rainbow **Season** June-Aug. **Specialty** Wilderness area fly fishing **Tackle Supplied** Fly, spin **Experience** 14 years **Rates** day: $170/2 people week: $1100/2 people **Guide's Notes:** Fishing is primarily for cutthroat trout in remote, above tree-line lakes within the **Collegiate Peaks Wilderness**. Best flies are the Double Ugly (a local pattern), Rio Grande King, and Orange Asher. The best lure is the Black Panther Martin.

CARBONDALE, COLORADO

NIELSEN, CHUCK & JUDY-SOPRIS VALLEY GUIDES & OUTFITTING (303) 963-2628
Address 16613 Colorado Hwy 82, Carbondale, CO 81623 **Airport** Aspen 23m **Accommodations** Basalt 6m **Operation** Outfitter **Fish** Brown, rainbow, brook, native cutthroat **Season** Year-round **Water** Frying Pan, Roaring Fork, Colorado, Crystal, White River drainages **Specialty** Stream fly fishing, artificial and bait lures, mountain streams by horse packing or by using jeeps **Type of Fishing** All **Experience** 9 years **Rates** day: $100 **Guide's Notes: Carbondale/Aspen Area** Spring fishing can occur year round in our famous Roaring Fork River, also in Blue Ribbon areas of the Frying Pan, Colorado, and Crystal Rivers. It is especially active during January and February to April before the spring melt muddies these waters. You can fly into Aspen, enjoy skiing, but also take a little time off to fish the rivers. The rivers begin to muddy around May to June or early July. Whitefish are most active and German browns of good size are commonly caught. After spring run-off, and snow melt, we take pack trips for fishing and photography into wilderness areas: Sopris, Frying Pan; and White River, up to Marvine Lake. Fishing is done by fly or spin casting methods. There are many high lakes up in these areas to pack into on horses or by jeep.

CRESTED BUTTE, COLORADO

CESARIO, ROGER G. (303) 929-5201
Address Box 1116, Crested Butte, CO 81224 **Airport** Aspen 55m **Accommodations** Paonia 30m **Operation** Outfitter **Fish** Rainbow, brown, cutthroat, brook trout **Season** March-Nov. **Water** West Muddy Creek, Gunnison, East Rivers, private lakes **Specialty** Fly fishing walk trips **Type of Fishing** Fly **Experience** 3 years **Rates** day: $75 week: $375 1/2 day: $50 **Guide's Notes: Gunnison River** Our specialty is walk trips into the famous Black Canyon of the Gunnison and fishing for large (2-10 pounds) brown and rainbow trout. Patterns used are Petronarcys California (stonefly) wet or dry in sizes 2-4-6-8, Elk Hair Caddis, Hares Ear Nymph, and Wooly Bugger. Fishing is good July-October with the peak season August-September.

Spadafora Ranch owns river bottom on approximately 3 miles of West Muddy Creek for private fly fishing. We recommend using small tan stoneflies, hair-wing dry flies such as Stonefly or Elk Hair Caddis, Wooly Bugger or in late summer grasshopper patterns. We fish for rainbow and cutthroat trout up to 3 pounds.

DURANGO, COLORADO

NEELY, JOHN R.-OVER THE HILL OUTFITTERS (303) 247-9289
Address 3624 Co. Rd. 203, Durango, CO 81301
Airport LaPlata 20m **Accommodations** Durango **Operation** Outfitter
Fish Rainbow, brook, cutthroat **Season** June-Nov **Type of Fishing** Fly
Water Hermosa, Florida Rivers, Weminuche Wilderness Area Lakes
Specialty Fly fishing **Tackle** Fly
Experience 26 years **Rates** day: $150 week: $1750

GLENWOOD SPRINGS, COLORADO

SCHULTZ, KURT E. (303) 945-7120
Address 0010 Ponderosa Dr., Glenwood Springs, CO 81601
Airport Glenwood Springs **Accommodations** Glenwood Springs
Operation Outfitter **Type of Fishing** All **Specialty** Fly fishing
Fish Rainbow, cutthroat, brook, brown trout **Season** May-Sept.
Water Frying Pan River including all tributaries
Boats Rowboats, McKenzies, rafts **Tackle Supplied** Fly,spin
Experience 15 years **Rates** day: $150-200 week: $750 - 1200 1/2 day: $75

GRAND JUNCTION, COLORADO

LAMICQ, JOHN (303) 243-1082
Address 635 191/2 Rd., Grand Junction, CO 81503
Airport Grand Junction **Accommodations** Grand Junction
Operation Outfitter **Type of Fishing** All **Specialty** Lake trolling
Fish Stripers, brown, native, mackinaw **Season** Dec-Aug
Water Lake Powell (UT), Flaming Gorge (UT), Pyramid, Roan Creek
Boats Rowboats, bass boat **Tackle Supplied** Spin, baitcast, troll
Experience 30 years **Rates** day: $250 week: $1000

GUNNISON, COLORADO

MAPES, DAVE-QUAKING ASPEN GUIDES AND OUTFITTERS (303) 641-0529
Address P.O. Box 485, Gunnison, CO 81230
Airport Gunnison **Accommodations** Gunnison
Operation Outfitter **Type of Fishing** Fly, spin

Fish Cutthroat, rainbow, brook, brown trout **Season** June-Sept
Water Gunnison Gorge, Gunnison R., high mountain lakes and streams
Specialty Fly fishing float trips **Boats** Rafts **Tackle Supplied** Fly, spin
Experience 10 years **Rates** day: $100 week: $600

NELSON, JOHN C.-THE GUNNISON COUNTRY GUIDE SERVICE (303) 641-2830
Address 49221 E. Hwy 50, Gunnison, CO 81230
Airport Gunnison **Accommodations** Gunnison **Operation** Outfitter
Fish Cutthroat, brook, rainbow, brown trout **Season** June-Nov.
Water Crystal, Henry, Costo Lakes, Crystal Creek **Type of Fishing** All
Specialty Horse pack trips to alpine lakes and secluded streams **Boats** Rafts
Experience 9 years **Rates** day: $120 week: $1000 1/2 day: $70

LAMAR, COLORADO

HARBOUR, DOUG-COLORADO CARAVANS, LTD (303) 336-7268
Address 808 S. 9th, Lamar, CO 81052
Airport Lamar **Accommodations** Lamar **Operation** Outfitter
Fish Walleye, white bass, crappie **Season** May-Aug **Type of Fishing** Troll
Water Nee Noshe and John Martin Reservoirs **Specialty** Trolling and casting
Boats Bass boat **Tackle Supplied** Troll, baitcast
Experience 7 years **Rates** day: $200
Guide's Notes: Nee Noshe and John Martin Reservoirs The best walleye action
is during mid-May through the end of June. White bass is best from June to
August.

LEWIS, COLORADO

HONAKER, PAT-HONAKER OUTFITTERS (303) 565-9695
Address 20745 County Rd. 19, Lewis, CO 81327
Airport Cortez 50m **Accommodations** Lewis **Operation** Outfitter
Fish Rainbow, brown, cutthroat, native **Season** Year-round
Water West Dolores, Stoner Creek, Fish Creek, Navajo Lake
Specialty Fly fishing and bait fishing **Type of Fishing** All
Experience 6 years **Rates** day: $80 week: $350 1/2 day: $50

MEEKER, COLORADO

COOK, RICK-R CIRCLE C OUTFITTERS (303) 878-4612
Address 23586 County Rd. 8, Meeker, CO 81641
Airport Grand Junction 120m **Accommodations** Meeker **Operation** Outfitter
Fish Rainbow, brook, cutthroat, brown **Season** Year-round
Water Baily Lake, Trappers Lake, Lake Avery, Wall Lake
Specialty High mountain lake fishing **Type of Fishing** Fly, baitcast, troll
Boats Rowboat, canoes, rafts **Tackle Supplied** Fly, spin, baitcast
Experience 15 years **Rates** day: $150 week: $800 1/2 day: $100

FRITZLAN, CALVIN S.-FRITZLAN'S GUEST RANCH (303) 878-4845
Address 1891 County Rd 12, Meeker, CO 81641
Airport Grand Junction 130m **Accommodations** On premises
Operation Outfitter, lodge **Type of Fishing** All
Fish Rainbow, brook, cutthroat, whitefish **Season** May-Nov
Water Marvine, Rainbow, Mary Lock, Sable Lakes **Boats** Rafts
Specialty Fly fishing on lakes and streams with dry and wet flies
Experience 30 years **Rates** day: $65 week: $410
Guide's Notes: Marvine Lakes is an 8 mile ride from the Marvine campground.
We provide tent camping at its best from June 15 to September 15. This enables
you to get in on the late night early morning fishing. 1 1/2 pound cutthroats
and up to 3 pound rainbows were taken this year. Best fishing is June, July,
and September. The Lake turns over in August and slows the fishing some.
Excellent fishing, fantastic scenery and only a two hour ride to the Flat Tops.

JETT, KEN-RIPPLE CREEK LODGE (303) 878-4725, 989-4950
Address 39020 County Road 8, Meeker, CO 81641
Airport Steamboat Springs 75m **Accommodations** On premises
Operation Outfitter, lodge **Type of Fishing** All
Fish Trout **Season** June-Nov. **Water** White River
Experience 23 years **Rates** day: $100

MONTROSE, COLORADO

MAGTUTU, GABE-DOUBLE HAUL FLOAT TRIPS, INC. (303) 249-3323
Address 719 S. 6th Street, Montrose, CO 81401-5726
Airport Montrose **Accommodations** Montrose **Operation** Guide
Fish Rainbow, brown **Season** March-Oct **Type of Fishing** Fly, spin
Water Gunnison Gorge, Rio Grande **Specialty** Wilderness float fishing
Rates day: $200 3 day wilderness float: $625/person
Guide's Notes: Gunnison River Our season is governed by the run-off in the
Gunnison Basin. Fishing is usually excellent from June to September. The
Gunnison offers a variety of types of water. We fish large stonefly patterns
down deep during the day and have some super dry fly action with caddis
patterns during the evening. Hoppers are also effective. We specialize in dutch
oven cooking for streamside meals. We offer a wilderness experience.
Author's Notes: I have received excellent reports on Gabe's guide service.

PENROSE, COLORADO

HALL, KINNEY-BACK COUNTRY GUIDES & OUTFITTERS (303) 275-6274
Address Upper Bearer Creek Road, Penrose, CO 81240
Airport Colorado Springs 50m **Accommodations** Penrose **Operation** Outfitter
Fish Brown, rainbow, brook, cutthroat **Season** Year-round
Water Bearer Creek, North Crestone, Sand and Mesa Lakes
Specialty Horse back trips into remote areas **Type of Fishing** All

Experience 15 years **Rates** day: $80-120
Guide's Notes: We pack our guests into remote high mountain lakes that are still frozen over until the first of July or later. We recommend visiting during August, September or possibly late July. These lakes contain trout of various species. We also fish streams with wild trout that get very little pressure. These streams are open year round, but we recommend May through September because of the comfort of camping out.

SOUTH FORK, COLORADO

EHARDT, LARRY-WILDERNESS ADVENTURES, INC. (303) 873-5216
Address Box 265, South Fork, CO 81154
Airport Alamosa 55m **Accommodations** South Fork
Fish Trout **Season** June-Nov **Type of Fishing** All **Operation** Outfitter
Water Remote high country lakes and streams **Tackle Supplied** All
Experience 17 years **Rates** day: $40/person 1/2 day: $30/person

STEAMBOAT SPRINGS, COLORADO

MEEK, FRANK-STRAIGHTLINE OUTDOOR SPORTS (303) 879-7568
out of state: 1-800-354-5463
Address P.O. Box 3510, 744 Lincoln Ave., Steamboat Springs, CO 80477
Airport Steamboat Springs **Accommodations** Steamboat Springs
Operation Outfitter, tackle shop **Type of Fishing** Fly, spin
Fish Rainbow, brown, cutthroat, brook trout **Season** Year-round
Water Elk, Yampa Rivers, high mountain ponds, lakes and streams
Specialty High mountain fly fishing, rivers, streams and lakes
Boats Johnboat, float tube **Tackle Supplied** All
Experience 10 years **Rates** day: $100/person 1/2 day: $60/person

Idaho

ASHTON, IDAHO

LAWSON, MIKE-HENRY'S FORK ANGLERS, INC. (208) 558-7525, 624-3595

Address Star Route, Last Chance, Ashton, ID 83420
Airport Idaho Falls 75m **Accommodations** Island Park 1m
Operation Outfitter, tackle shop **Type of Fishing** Fly
Fish Rainbow, brown, brook, cutthroat **Season** March-Oct.
Water Henry's Fork of the Snake, Madison R., Yellowstone R., Firehole R.
Specialty Fly fishing instruction and float trips
Boats Bass boat, McKenzies, rafts, johnboats **Tackle Supplied** Fly, spin
Experience 12 years **Rates** day: $185 1/2 day: $110
Guide's Notes: The Henry's Fork of the Snake

Stoneflies--The salmonfly hatch begins on the Henry's Fork during the last week of May. It progresses upstream moving several miles each day. It usually reaches Box Canyon the first week of June. The best stretches of the rivers are the fast water areas. Box Canyon, Coffee Pot Rapids, the stretch between Riverside Campground and Lower Mesa Falls, and the stretches above and below Ashton are all good areas for the salmonfly hatch on the Henry's Fork.

Falls River contains healthy populations of salmonflies. The hatch usually starts on Falls River about the second week of June.

A smaller stonefly, the Golden Stone hatches just following the larger salmonflies on the same stretches of river. The Golden Stones are imitated on size 8 or 10 hooks while the salmonflies are size 4 or 6.

Caddis Many different species of caddis hatch on the Henry's Fork as well as other western rivers. Generally caddis populations are heavier in the faster stretches of the rivers. Most of the caddis hatches occur the first part of the season.

June and early July offers the best caddis hatches on the Henry's Fork. Last Chance and the upper section of the Harriman State Park have excellent evening caddis hatches. The stretch of river between Ashton and St. Anthony also have very productive caddis hatches. The entire stretch of Falls River also has some excellent caddis hatches.

Mayflies No other river in the west has as many different mayfly hatches as the Henry's Fork. The following mayflies are the major hatches that occur throughout the season on this magnificent river.

Pale Morning Dun(Ephemerella infrequens): Hatches occur June 10 through June 30. Duns emerge about 10am. Spinners fall at dusk and in the morning hours. Size 16 or 18. The Harriman State Park and the Last Chance area as well as the stretch between Ashton and St. Anthony are the best areas on the Henry's Fork to fish this hatch.

IDAHO

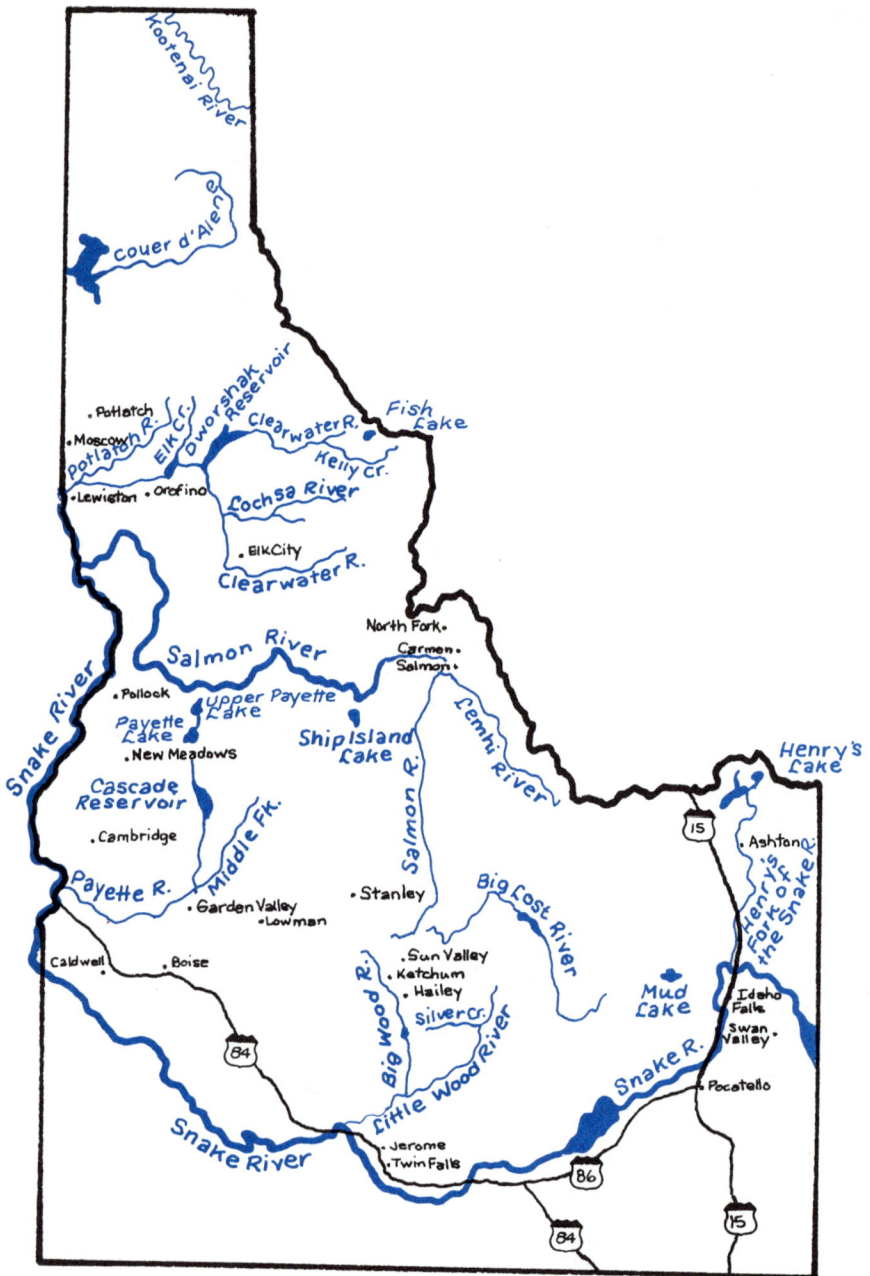

Kootenai River

Couer d'Alene

Potlatch
Moscow
Potlatch R.
Elk Cr.
Dworshak Reservoir
Clearwater R.
Fish Lake
Lewiston
Orofino
Kelly Cr.
Lochsa River
ElkCity
Clearwater R.

North Fork
Carmen
Salmon

Salmon River

Snake River
Pollock
upper Payette Lake
Payette Lake
New Meadows
Ship Island Lake
Lemhi River

Henry's Lake

Cascade Reservoir
Salmon R.

Cambridge
Middle Fk.

15
Ashton

Payette R.
Garden Valley
Lowman
Stanley
Big Lost River

Henry's Fork of the Snake

Caldwell
Boise
Sun Valley
Ketchum
Hailey
Big Wood R.
Silver Cr.

Mud Lake
Idaho Falls
Swan Valley

84
Little Wood River
Snake R.
Pocatello

Snake River
Jerome
Twin Falls

86
15
84

HENRY'S FORK
OF THE SNAKE RIVER
(Harriman State Park Area)
Map Courtesy of
HENRY'S FORK ANGLERS INC.

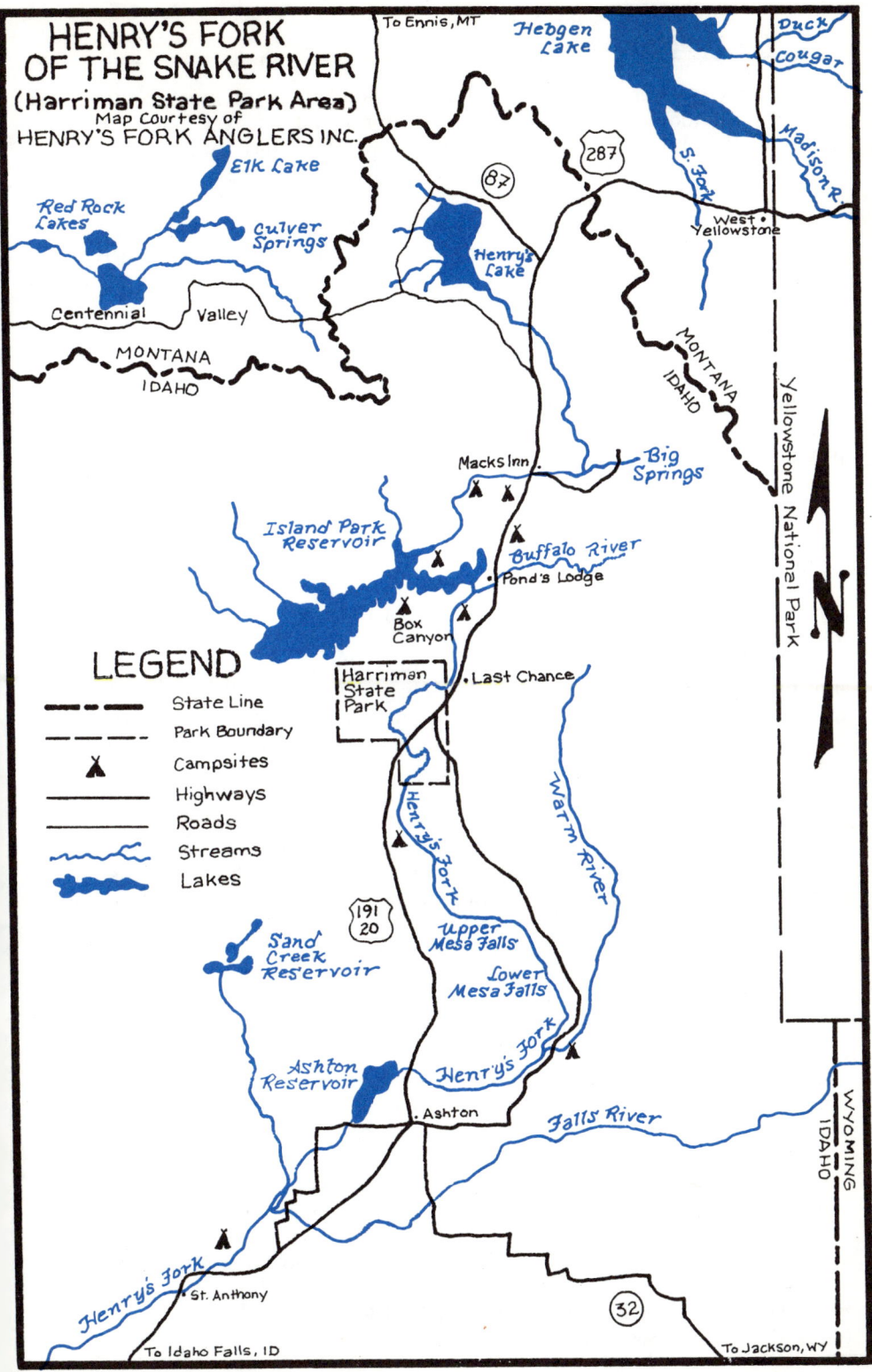

To Ennis, MT

Hebgen Lake

Duck

Cougar

287

Elk Lake

Red Rock Lakes

Culver Springs

87

Henry's Lake

S. Fork

Madison R.

West Yellowstone

Centennial   Valley

MONTANA
IDAHO

MONTANA
IDAHO

Yellowstone National Park

Macks Inn

Big Springs

Island Park Reservoir

Buffalo River

Pond's Lodge

Box Canyon

LEGEND

— · — · —	State Line
– – – –	Park Boundary
⛺	Campsites
———	Highways
———	Roads
∼∼∼	Streams
〰	Lakes

Harriman State Park

Last Chance

Warm River

Henry's Fork

Sand Creek Reservoir

191
20

Upper Mesa Falls

Lower Mesa Falls

Ashton Reservoir

Henry's Fork

Ashton

Falls River

WYOMING
IDAHO

Henry's Fork

St. Anthony

32

To Idaho Falls, ID

To Jackson, WY

N

Western Green Drake (Ephemerella grandis): This is the most exciting of all the mayfly hatches. Best fishing occurs from June 23 to July 1. The Last Chance area and the upper section of the Harriman State Park contain the highest populations of Green Drakes. Dun emerge about 11 am. Cool, cloudy days are best. Spinners are not usually important. Size 10 or 12.

Brown Drake (Ephemera simulans): The greatest populations of these large mayflies are in the slow, silty sections of the Harriman State Park. Peak hatching activity occurs June 25 through July 5. Duns emerge at dusk. Spinners also fall at dusk. Size 8 or 10.

Small Western Drake (Ephemerella flavilinea): Duns emerge late afternoon July 1 through July 25. Best hatches occur on cloudy days. Spinners fall mornings.

Pale Morning Dun (Ephemerella inermis): This mayfly hatches on the better western rivers during mid summer. Best hatches on the Henry's Fork occur July 15 through September 1. Duns emerge at mid morning. Spinners fall mornings and evenings. Size 18 or 20.

Tiny Blue Quill (Baetis parvus): Duns emerge early afternoon. Spinners fall at dusk. This hatch is best in the upper section of Harriman State Park. Size 20 or 22.

Tiny Blue Winged Olive (Pseudocloeon edmundsi): Hatches occur July 15 through October 15. Blanket hatches carpet the water in Harriman State Park and the stretch below Ashton during the latter part of September.

White Wing Black (Tricorythodes minutus): These tiny mayflies hatch early mornings on the quiet sections of the Henry's Fork as well as several lakes in the area. Spinners fall about 8 am. Best hatches occur during August. Hebgen Lake offers exciting dry fly fishing to cruising trout, locally called "gulpers." Size 20 or 22.

Speckled Spinner (Callibaetis nigritus): Spinners fall about 10am on the quiet sections of the Henry's Fork. Most lakes also have great hatches. Duns hatch sporadically during the morning hours. July and August are the peak months.

Mahogany Dun (Paraleptophlebia bicornuta): This hatch produces some excellent fishing during the month of September on the Henry's Fork. Duns emerge about 10am. Spinners fall in the evening. Size 16 or 18.

Iron Blue Quill (Baetis tricaudatus): If you ever visit the west during the off season you may encounter some fine fishing during this hatch. It occurs on most western streams during March and April and again in the fall during October and November. Duns emerge during late morning. Spinners are not important. Size 18 is best.

Author's Notes: *Mike Lawson owns and operates the outstanding Henry's Fork Anglers fly shop and guide service in Last Chance, Idaho, only a few hundred yards from the world famous Henry's Fork of the Snake River. The Henry's Fork is a superb but extremely demanding stream. It has left more than a few "fishing experts" talking to themselves as hundreds of trout refuse their offerings while gorging themselves on the real thing. Mike employs very knowledgeable sales clerks and guides who can help take some of the mystery out of fishing this great river and make fishing it a very special and satisfying experience.*

SIMMONS, DON-THREE RIVERS FISHING RANCH
(412) 935-1577, 1-800-245-1950

Address C/O Frontiers, P.O. Box 161, Wexford, PA 15090
Airport Idaho Falls 75m **Accommodations** On premises
Operation Outfitter, lodge **Type of Fishing** Fly
Fish Rainbow, brown, cutthroat **Season** June-Oct **Boats** McKenzies
Water Henry's Fork, Fall River, Teton River **Specialty** Fly fishing
Experience 20 years **Rates** week: $1200/person
Author's Notes: This is a very special lodge. The rooms, the food, the facilities and the grounds are very nice. The fishing compares with the best in the world and the guide services can help you make the best of it.

CAMBRIDGE, IDAHO

HUGHES, JERRY-HUGHES RIVER EXPEDITIONS (208) 257-3477
Address P.O. Box 217, Cambridge, ID 83610
Airport Boise 100m **Accommodations** Cambridge
Operation Outfitter **Type of Fishing** Fly, spin
Fish Cutthroat, rainbow, steelhead, bass **Season** June-Sept.
Water Middle Fork of the Salmon, Snake R./Hells Canyon, Salmon River Canyon
Specialty Combination backcountry, white water fishing trips
Boats McKenzies, rafts **Tackle Supplied** Spin, fly
Experience 20 years **Rates** varies
Guide's Notes: Middle Fork of the Salmon River Late June through mid-September. My favorite times are August and September. Catch and release regulations for Westslope cutthroat and rainbow trout. Blue ribbon fishery. Drift boats or rafts. Dry flies.

Snake River through Hells Canyon Late June through September. Early summer fishing is best for smallmouth bass. As we move into mid-summer and fall, rainbow trout fishing becomes the best. After early September we begin to have steelhead migrating into the Canyon. Snake River is a very large river to fish with flies, but it can offer excellent fly fishing on low water conditions. Spin casting or level line gear works well on all conditions. I recommend bringing both spring/level line gear and fly fishing gear. Rafts only.

Salmon River Canyon Mid-September through October. Salmon River steelhead run 5-18 pounds. Average fish run 5-8 pounds. Catch and release for native fish, and we can take hatchery fish which make up approximately 70-85% of the run. We fish with flies, lures, and plugs. We often fish all three styles on a given day.

Author's Notes: Jerry is certainly one of the best whitewater outfitters in Idaho. He offers float trips on the big rivers like the Salmon and Snake. He has been selected four times to guide National Geographic Society exhibitions on Idaho's famous rivers.

CALDWELL, IDAHO

MEHOLCHICK, STAN-JUNIPER MOUNTAIN OUTFITERS (208) 454-1172
Address Route 3 Box 50, Caldwell, ID 83605
Airport Boise 23m **Accommodations** Caldwell

Operation Outfitter **Type of Fishing** Fly, spin
Fish Trout **Season** May-November **Tackle Supplied** Fly, spin
Water South Fork Salmon, Middle Fork Payette, Gold Fork Rivers
Specialty Stream and river fishing for trout **Boats** Rowboats, canoes
Experience 8 years **Rates** day: $200

CARMEN, IDAHO

McFARLAND, MITCH-BIGHORN OUTFITTERS (208) 756-3407
Address Box 66, Carmen, ID 83462
Airport Idaho Falls 160m **Accommodations** Salmon 12m
Operation Outfitter **Type of Fishing** Fly, spin
Fish Rainbow, dolly varden, cutthroat, golden **Season** July-Aug.
Water Ship Island L., Clear Creek, Goat L., Reflection L.
Specialty High mountain lake fishing trips
Experience 10 years **Rates** day: $75 week: $500 1/2 day: $50

ELK CITY, IDAHO

YORK, TRAVIS-WALLY YORK AND SON, INC. (208) 842-2367
Address P.O. Box 319, Elk City, ID 83525
Airport Lewiston 140m **Accommodations** Elk City
Operation Outfitter **Specialty** Fly and Spin fishing from the banks
Fish Trout, cutthroat, brown, rainbow **Season** July-Aug **Type of Fishing** All
Water Unit 17 Selway Bitteroot Wilderness lakes and streams, Unit 20 Salmon
River Wilderness Area, River of No Return **Tackle Supplied** All
Experience 30 years **Rates** day: $130 week: $900 1/2 day: $60

GARDEN VALLEY, IDAHO

ROTTHOFF, DAN-GARDEN VALLEY OUTFITTERS, INC. (208) 462-3751
Address Garden Valley, ID 83622
Airport Boise 48m **Accommodations** On premises **Operation** Outfitter, lodge
Fish Cutthroat, rainbow **Season** Year-round **Type of Fishing** All
Water Bernard, Sheepherder Lakes, Bull Creek, Payette River **Boats** Rafts
Specialty Pack trips to back country lakes and streams **Tackle Supplied** All
Experience 17 years **Rates** day: varies week: $250/person

JEROME, IDAHO

PAUL, ANN-SALMON RIVER LODGE (208) 324-3553
Address P.O. Box 348, Jerome, ID 83338
Airport Salmon 100m **Accommodations** On premises **Operation** Lodge, outfitter

Fish Steelhead, trout **Season** March-Nov **Type of Fishing** All
Specialty Steelhead fishing using jet boats to transport
Boats Jet boats **Tackle Supplied** Spin, baitcast **Water** Main Salmon R.
Experience 18 years **Rates** day: $85 1/2 day; $60

KETCHUM, IDAHO

CRABTREE, PHIL-MIDDLE FORK RAPID TRANSIT (208) 726-5666
Address P.O. Box 2368, Ketchum, ID 83340
Airport Boise 140m **Accommodations** Stanley 1m
Operation Outfitter **Specialty** Fly fishing **Boats** Rafts
Fish Cutthroat, rainbow **Season** March-November
Water Middle Fork Salmon River **Type of Fishing** Fly, spin
Experience 5 years **Rates** varies

LEWISTON, IDAHO

ARFORD, ERROL-KELLY KREEK FLY FISHING OUTFITTERS (208) 743-4910
Address 616 7th Street, Lewiston, ID 83501
Airport Lewiston 120m **Accommodations** Lewiston 120m
Operation Outfitter **Type of Fishing** Fly **Water** Kelly Creek, Clearwater River
Fish Cutthroat, steelhead **Season** Aug-Nov **Specialty** Fly fishing
Experience 6 years **Rates** day: $100 week: $400 1/2 day: $40

BARKER, JOHN A.K.-BARKER RIVER TRIPS (208) 743-7459
Address 2124 Grelle, Lewiston, ID 83501
Airport Lewiston **Accommodations** Lewiston
Operation Outfitter **Type of Fishing** Fly, spin
Fish Steelhead **Season** Oct-Dec **Boats** McKenzies, rafts
Water Salmon, Clearwater, Snake **Specialty** Float fishing for steelhead
Experience 16 years **Rates** day: $100
Guide's Notes: Float and drift boat fishing for steelhead. Day trips on the
Clearwater River near Orofino, Idaho. Extended float trip fishing 3-7 days on
the lower **Salmon River**.

BEAMER, WALLY-BEAMER'S LANDING (208) 743-4800
Address P.O. Box 1223, Lewiston, ID 83501
Airport Lewiston 31m **Accommodations** On premises **Boats** Rafts, outboard
Season June-Jan **Type of Fishing** Spin, baitcast **Operation** Outfitter, lodge
Fish Steelhead, rainbow, sm bass, sturgeon **Tackle Supplied** Baitcast
Water Snake River Hells Canyon, Salmon, Clearwater and Grande Ronde Rivers
Specialty Power boat on rapid rivers, trolling and drift fishing
Experience 12 years **Rates** day: $75/2 people
*Author's Notes: Wally runs an excellent operation. He recently appeared on
the television program "Fishing the West," produced by Larry Schoenborn.*

LOWMAN, IDAHO

SHAW, ELLEN-SOUTH FORK LODGE (208) 259-3321
Address Highway 21 MP 72, Lowman, ID 83637
Airport Boise 72m **Accommodations** On Premises
Operation Lodge, outfitter **Type of Fishing** Fly, baitcast
Fish Trout **Season** May-Sept **Water** South Fork of Payette River
Specialty Float and fly fishing **Boats** Rafts **Tackle Supplied** All
Experience 2 years **Rates** day: $50 week: $300 1/2 day: $30

MOSCOW, IDAHO

VAUGHN, HARRY W. (208) 882-5367
Address 1376 Walenta Drive, Moscow, ID 83843
Airport Spokane, WA 70m **Accommodations** Moscow
Operation Outfitter **Type of Fishing** All **Tackle Supplied** All
Fish Cutthroat, steelhead, kokanee, chinook **Season** Year-round
Water Clearwater, Lochsa Rivers, Dworshak Dam Reservoir, Cour d'Alene Lake
Specialty Fly fishing, trolling lakes **Boats** Rowboats, outboards
Experience 19 years **Rates** day: $150 week: $650 1/2 day: $90

NEW MEADOWS, IDAHO

THRASH, JAMES-SALMON MEADOWS LODGE (208) 347-2357
Address HC 75 Box 3410, New Meadows, ID 83654
Airport Boise 120m **Accommodations** On premises
Operation Lodge, outfitter **Type of Fishing** Fly, spin **Tackle Supplied** Fly
Fish Cutthroat, rainbow, brook **Season** June-Nov **Specialty** Fly fishing
Water Enos Jungle, Lake Rock, and various high mountain lakes
Experience 4 years **Rates** day: $125 week: $995
Guide's Notes: High Mountains Lakes July 1-September. Cutthroat and rainbow
trout to 5 pounds, beautiful scenery and uncrowded fishing.

NORTH FORK, IDAHO

CUMMINGS, NANCY AND CLIFF-CUMMINGS LAKE LODGE
(208) 865-2422
Address Cummings Lake, Box 810, North Fork, ID 83466
Airport Missoula, MT 120m **Accommodations** On premises
Operation Lodge, outfitter **Type of Fishing** All **Water** Cummings Lake
Fish Trout **Season** June-Aug **Specialty** Lake fishing **Boats** Rowboats, rafts
Experience 35 years **Rates** varies

OROFINO, IDAHO

CRANE, LEO AND VIRGINIA-CLEARWATER OUTFITTERS (208) 476-5971
Address 4088 Canyon Creek Road, Orofino, ID 83544

Airport Lewiston 150m **Accommodations** Pierce 50m
Operation Outfitter **Type of Fishing** Fly, spin
Fish Cutthroat, rainbow, Dolly Varden **Season** July-Sept
Water Little Fork of Clearwater River, Larkins, Mud Lakes, Dworshak Res.
Specialty Fly fishing pack trips **Boats** Rafts, pontoon boat
Experience 21 years **Rates** day: $100 2nd day: $80/person
Guide's Notes: The **Little North Fork of the Clearwater River** is an angler's paradise and offers some of the best fly fishing in the world.

Rainbow and cutthroat trout and Dolly Varden char average about 10', however, fish up to 14 and 16 inches or more are not at all uncommon.

"Crowded" is a word that just doesn't apply out here; you'll be with your own small group and during your entire trip it's very doubtful whether we'll run across anybody else at all.

Dworshak Lake is famous for smallmouth bass and also boasts of kokanee salmon, rainbow and cutthroat trout and Dolly Varden char.

STOCKTON, MIKE-ELK RIVER OUTFITTERS (208) 476-7074
Address Box 265, Orofino, ID 83544
Airport Spokane, WA 150m **Accommodations** Elk River 1m
Operation Outfitter **Type of Fishing** Spin, baitcast, troll
Fish Trout, kokanee, sm bass **Season** Year-round
Water Dworshak Reservoir, Elk river, Elk Creek
Specialty Lake fishing, camping trips **Boats** Rowboats
Experience 7 years **Rates** day: $80 week: $280 1/2 day: $25

POLLOCK, IDAHO

WOODS, NOLAN "RED"-RED WOODS OUTFITTERS (208) 628-3673
Address HC 2, Box 580, Pollock, ID 83547
Airport Boise 121m **Accommodations** Riggins 11m
Operation Outfitter **Type of Fishing** All **Tackle Supplied** Spin, baitcast, troll
Fish Steelhead, bass, trout, sturgeon **Season** Sept-Mar **Boats** River sled
Water River of No Return, Snake, Salmon Rivers **Specialty** Jet boat fishing
Experience 5 years **Rates** day: $110 week: $700 1/2 day: $70

POTLATCH, IDAHO

NYGAARD, JACK O.-LOCHSA RIVER OUTFITTERS (208) 875-0620
Address Route 2, Box 30, Potlatch, ID 83855
Airport Missoula, MT 126 **Accommodations** Orofino
Operation Outfitter **Type of Fishing** All **Boats** McKenzies, rafts
Fish Steelhead, brook, cutthroat **Season** Year-round
Water Clearwater R, Sponge, Long, Fish Lakes **Specialty** Float trips
Experience 27 years **Rates** day: $200
Guide's Notes: Clear Water River Steelhead fly fishing during September and October; lure fishing November thru April.

SALMON, IDAHO

McAFEE, DICK-CASTLE CREEK OUTFITTERS
Address P.O. Box 2008, Salmon, ID 83467
Airport Boise 120m **Accommodations** Challis 57m
Operation Outfitter **Type of Fishing** Fly, spin
Fish Cutthroat, rainbow, brook, Dolly Varden **Season** July-Aug.
Water Martingdale Lakes, West Fork Lakes, Castle Lake, Blue Lake
Specialty Fully guided horse pack trips into high lake areas
Experience 10 years **Rates** day: $130

MYERS, JERRY-SILVER CLOUD EXPEDITIONS (208) 756-6215
Address P.O. Box 1006, Salmon, ID 83467
Airport Boise 230m **Accommodations** Salmon
Operation Outfitter **Type of Fishing** Fly, spin
Fish Steelhead, cutthroat, Dolly Varden **Season** Mar-Apr / Sept-Nov
Water Wilderness section of Salmon River **Boats** Rafts
Specialty Fly and spin casting float trips **Aircraft** Landplanes
Experience 9 years **Rates** week: $750/person
Guide's Notes: Salmon River The steelhead runs on the Salmon River have made a dramatic comeback and this fall's season is forecasted to be the best in 20 years! These anadromous rainbow (they migrate 800 miles to the Pacific and return to the Salmon to spawn) range in size from 6 to 24 pounds. By combining a wild and scenic 60 miles of spectacular river canyon with these fighting fish, we provide a unique and serene fishing vacation.

We spend 5 nights and slightly over 5 days leisurely floating through the largest wilderness in the U. S. outside of Alaska. Most of our fishing is done from shore or wading into the shallow reaches of the deeper holes. Casting from the drifting rafts is also productive. Fly rods or casting gear work equally well depending on your preference. Steelhead will rise to a dry fly early in the season. Spoons produce fish throughout the season and generally work best for those less accustomed to fly casting.

Both wild, and hatchery introduced steelhead, are caught in the Salmon. Distinguished only by a shorter dorsal fin, the hatchery fish make the same arduous migration and fight just as tenaciously as their wild counterparts. All native steelhead are released unharmed and we limit hatchery fish to 2 per person. The wild steelhead runs are gaining strength, bolstered by increased hatchery releases and improved migration conditions.

Bring an 8 or 9 weight fly rod equipped with both a floating and a sinking or sink tip line. Casting rods and reels should be heavy enough to handle big fish. Fly casting leaders should have a tippet strength of 8 to 10 pounds. Casting or spinning reels should be loaded with 8 to 12 pound test monofilament.

LATHAM, TONY-RAINBOW RIVER CO. (208) 756-4701
Address Rt. 1, Box 48 A, Salmon, ID 83467
Airport Missoula, MT 150m **Accommodations** Salmon
Operation Outfitter **Type of Fishing** All **Tackle Supplied** Spin
Fish Steelhead **Season** Oct-March **Water** Salmon River (Idaho)

Specialty Steelhead McKenzie river boat fishing **Boats** McKenzies
Experience 4 years **Rates** day: $120 week: varies 1/2 day: $100
Guide's Notes: The **Salmon River** steelhead run has been rebuilt to levels of the 1930's. These hardy summer run fish arrive in good numbers in early October and winter over in the area through March. Most fish are in the 25" class but 30" is common. We consider 3 to 5 fish per day good fishing. Ten per day is unusual but possible.

TONSMEIRE, JOE & FRAN-WILDERNESS RIVER OUTFITTERS (208) 756-3959
Address P.O. Box 871, Salmon, ID 83467
Airport Idaho Falls 150m **Accommodations** Salmon **Operation** Outfitter
Fish Trout, steelhead **Season** March-Nov **Type of Fishing** Fly, spin
Water South and Middle Fork of Flathead, Salmon Rivers
Specialty Float trips that offer both fly and lake fishing
Boats Rowboats, rafts **Tackle Supplied** Fly, spin
Experience 15 years **Rates** day: $100 week: $800/person

WAITE, JOHN-JOHN WAITE TACKLE (208) 756-4192, 894-2279
Address Box 1944, Salmon, ID 83467
Airport Missoula, MT 140m **Accommodations** Salmon
Operation Outfitter, tackle shop **Type of Fishing** Fly, spin, baitcast
Fish Steelhead, rainbow, brook, cutthroat **Season** Year-round **Boats** McKenzies
Water Salmon, Lemhi, Pahsimori Rivers, high mountain lakes
Specialty Dry line and dry fly steelheading **Tackle Supplied** Fly, spin, baitcast
Experience 6 years **Rates** day: $225 1/2 day: $175
Guide's Notes: Summer steelhead are best September through November with trout June through August. Steelhead drift fishing is good November through April while chinook salmon run June and July.

STANLEY, IDAHO

BAUGH, RANDALL-VALLEY RANCH OUTFITTERS (208) 774-2255
Address Box 107, Stanley, ID 83278
Airport Hailey 58m **Accommodations** Stanley
Operation Outfitter **Type of Fishing** Fly, baitcast **Fish** Cutthroat, rainbow
Water Salmon River, various lakes in the Sawtooth and White Cloud Mountains
Specialty Lake fishing in high mountain lakes **Season** March-Nov
Experience 12 years **Rates** day: $80 week: $1150 1/2 day: $40

BITTON, JEFF-MYSTIC SADDLE RANCH (208) 774-3591
Address Mystic Saddle Ranch, Stanley, ID 83340
Airport Boise 125m **Accommodations** On premises
Operation Outfitter, ranch **Type of Fishing** Fly, spin
Fish Cutthroat, rainbow, brook, golden **Season** June-Aug
Water Salmon River, Sawtooth Wilderness Area
Specialty Dry fly fishing **Tackle Supplied** Fly, spin
Experience 15 years **Rates** day: $90 week: $950

SUN VALLEY, IDAHO

MASON, BILL-SNUG FLY FISHING (208) 622-9305 726-4671
Address Box 127, Sun Valley, ID 83353
Airport Hailey 11m **Accommodations** Sun Valley
Operation Outfitter, tackle shop **Type of Fishing** Fly **Tackle Supplied** Fly
Fish Rainbow, brown, brook, cutthroat **Season** June-February
Water Silver Creek, Big Wood, Big Lost, Little Wood Rivers
Specialty Fly fishing wade trips **Boats** Rowboats, float tubes
Experience 16 years **Rates** day: $180 1/2 day: $145
Guide's Notes: The Big Wood River runs through the Wood River Valley, and
we refer to it as our bread and butter stream. Not only is it easy to fish for all
anglers, it is accessible and the fish quantity is extremely high. The size of
trout can be surprising. Hatches are strong, continuing into the late fall.

A sister stream to the Big Wood, approximately 40 miles away from Sun
Valley, is the **Little Wood River**. This is our Brown Trout fishery with fish up
to eight pounds being caught and released by anglers.

Flowing into the Little Wood river, 30 miles from Sun Valley, is the legendary
Silver Creek, which needs no introduction. Generally regarded as one of the
best trout streams in the United States, this stream, over the past ten years, has
had the most remarkable comeback of any stream that I know of today. There
was a time period when the stream was abused and not managed well. However,
under the catch and release regulations, not only is the fish size staggering, but
the population residing in this stream is enormous.

This phenomenal stretch of gently flowing water is acknowledged by experts
the world over to be on a par with (and a sister to) the famous chalk streams
of England that inspired and nurtured the development of the dry fly. Silver
Creek's rich, sparkling waters challenge the ability of the technician to make
perfectly correct fly patterns, attached to the lightest of leaders, presented in
delicate delivery, to the immense population of well-fed, discriminating trout.
Because of this, Silver Creek provides the ultimate angling experience, wherein
the degree of difficulty relates in direct proportion with the degree of satisfaction.

Silver Creek, being a spring creek, is fishable when the season opens at the
end of May. It is not subject to any runoff, high water, or discoloration.

The Big Wood and Copper Basin are streams that transfer the mountain snows
down into the lower valleys. Consequently, depending on the weather, these
streams become fishable from July 1st on.

The Little Wood can be subject to runoff, but, in most cases, is fishable from
the beginning to the end of the season.

Fishing and Hatching Schedule

May 26 - June 20 Silver Creek is the main fishable water. Hatches are good
and consistent. There is midday activity with (E. infrequens), Pale Morning
Duns. Imitate hatches with gray/yellow No Hackle, Lt. Olive floating Nymph,
Lt. Cahill regular or parachute #16-18. You may also see Blue Winged Olives
#18-20, and in selected areas (Ephemera simulans), Brown Drake #10.

June 20 - July 20 All river systems should be fishable as runoff subsides.
Silver Creek continues with above hatches with addition of (Calibeatis coloradensis), Speckled Spinner #16. The most exciting fishing is on Big Wood

and Copper Basin. Hatches identical. (Acroneuria californica), Golden Stonefly #8 and (Isoperla patricia), Small Yellow Stonefly #12 are very strong. There are also great hatches of (E. doddsi), Green Western Quill #12 late afternoon. Midday should see (Epeorus longimanus), Gray Duns #14, imitated by Adams, Blue Duns, Small Western quill, as well as (Epeorus deceptive), Cream Duns #16.

July 21 - September 1 Silver Creek literally explodes with Tricos, White Winged Black Spinner #22 and (Beatis parvus), Olive Brown Spinner #22. Midday activity has good (Calibeatis), Speckled Spinner #16 hatches. The Big Wood has good daily hatches of (E. doddsi), Green Western Quill #12, (Rithrogenia Hageni), Gray Duns #16 and (Epeorus deceptiva), Cream Duns #16 will be seen most.

September 1 - October 30 This is the most pleasant time of year. Silver Creek continues with great hatches-Trico, Beatis, etc. as mentioned above. Latter part of month produces fishable hatches of (Paraleptophlebia debilis), Slate Mahogany Duns #16, and Beatis Tricaudatus, Blue Winged Olive in dun stage. Big Wood continues with midday hatches of (E. doddsi), Green Western Quill #12, (E. tabilis), Slate Brown Duns #16, and (E. coloradensis), Slate Olive Duns #14. Little Wood River begins to pick up with its brown trout, using streamers and hopper imitations. Midday hatch of Beatis good.

Note: Some conventional patterns that work well on Big Wood, Little Wood and Copper Basin are: Adams, Quill Gordon, Royal Wulff, Lt. Cahill, and various hopper imitations.

Middle Fork of the Salmon The Middle Fork of the Salmon River is one of the most famous float rivers in North America. As the last major, pure river system left, the Middle Fork flows nearly one hundred miles through scenic, roadless wilderness, mixing the excitement of white water with the peace of crystal clear riffles and pools. The Middle Fork drops twenty-six hundred vertical feet, punctuated by well-known rapids like Velvet, Powerhouse, Tappan, Pistol Creek, Haystack and Rubber.

In addition to white water floating, the Middle Fork itself may be the most pristine cutthroat fishery left in the United States today. Because of special regulations, the river contains an abundancy of fish. Consequently, it is an easy place to catch fish for all levels of fly fishermen.

One of the most popular ways to take this trip is to encourage a group of friends to join you for the six days.

Author's Notes: Sun Valley is known best as a world class ski resort. Those that fish the area know the fishing is also world class. Bill Mason is knowledgeable about local conditions and runs a quality operation.

MILLS, DAVID AND SHEILA-ROCKY MOUNTAIN RIVER TOURS
(208) 726-9300
Address P.O. Box 790, Sun Valley, ID 83353
Airport Boise 150m **Accommodations** Stanley 43m
Operation Outfitter **Type of Fishing** Fly **Boats** Rafts
Fish Cutthroat **Season** July-Sept **Water** Middle Fork of Salmon
Specialty Fly fishing float and whitewater trips
Experience 9 years **Rates** 6 days: $1790/2 people

ROSS, JIM-WILD RIVERS IDAHO (208) 726-8097
Address P.O. Box 2599, Sun Valley, ID 83353
Airport Hailey 12m **Accommodations** Ketchum 1m
Operation Outfitter **Type of Fishing** Fly, spin
Fish Steelhead, salmon, trout **Season** March-Nov.
Water Salmon River, Middle Fork to Riggins **Boats** Rafts
Specialty Steelhead float trips **Tackle Supplied** Fly, spin
Experience 15 years **Rates** week: $1500/2 people

VAN BRAMER, TODD-SUN VALLEY OUTFITTERS (208) 622-3400
Address P.O. Box 3400, Sun Valley, ID 83353
Airport Hailey 12m **Accommodations** Sun Valley **Operation** Guide, retail shop
Fish Rainbow, brown, brook **Type of Fishing** Fly, spin **Season** June-Oct
Water Silver Creek, Big Wood R., Copper Basin, Warm Springs
Specialty Fly fishing wade trips **Boats** Float tubes **Tackle Supplied** All
Experience 4 years **Rates** day: $165 1/2 day: $125

SWAN VALLEY, IDAHO

WARNER, SPENCE-SOUTH FORK LODGE TACKLE SHOP (208) 483-2112
Address Box 22, Swan Valley, ID 83449
Airport Idaho Falls 37m **Accommodations** Irwin 7m
Operation Outfitter, tackle shop, lodge **Type of Fishing** All
Fish Brown, cutthroat **Season** April-Oct **Water** South Fork of Snake River
Specialty Fly fishing, spin fishing, bait fishing float trips
Boats River sled, McKenzies, raft **Tackle Supplied** All
Experience 20 years **Rates** day: $85/person 1/2 day: $25/hour
Guide's Notes: The **South Fork of the Snake River** runs from Yellowstone Park
through Jackson Hole and into the Swan Valley, Idaho region. The new state
record brown trout was caught here last year (32 lbs). Its water holds record
browns but there are many more cutthroats. The fly fishing usually begins the
first week in July with the coming of the stoneflies and lasts to mid-October.
Spin fishing is good throughout the year with big browns hitting Rapalas in
November. Good flies are: Elk hair caddis, stonefly patterns, Adams, Cahills,
Wooly Worms, hoppers, and Muddler patterns. Spin fishing lures are: Rapalas,
Black and Brown Roostertails, Panther Martins, Mepps, and assorted spoons.

Montana

ALBERTON, MONTANA

FREEMAN, JEFFRY-HOLE WALL LODGE (406) 728-5203 (Ext. 1284)
Address P.O. Box 134, Alberton, MT 59820
Airport Missoula 55m **Accommodations** On premises
Operation Outfitter, lodge **Type of Fishing** All **Boats** Rafts
Fish Cutthroat, rainbow, bull trout, brook **Season** Year-round
Water Fish Creek drainage **Specialty** Fly and lake fishing
Experience 10 years **Rates** day: $130 week: $910 1/2 day: $70

ANACONDA, MONTANA

CRUM, KEITH (MIKE) (406) 563-8229, 563-7608
Address 909 East Park Street, Anaconda, MT 59711
Airport Butte 25m **Accommodations** Anaconda
Operation Outfitter **Type of Fishing** Fly, spin **Boats** McKenzies, rafts
Fish Rainbow, brown, cutthroat, grayling **Season** May-September
Water Big Hole, Beaverhead River, Clark's Fork, Rock Creek
Specialty Fly fishing float trips **Tackle Supplied** Fly, spin
Experience 7 years **Rates** day: $130 1/2 day: $40 week: $1100

BELGRADE, MONTANA

WARWOOD, DAVE (406) 388-4463, 646-9292
Address 15100 Rocky Mountain Road, Belgrade, MT 59714
Airport Bozeman 3m **Accommodations** Belgrade **Operation** Outfitter
Fish Rainbow, cutthroat, brown, grayling **Season** Year-round
Water Yellowstone River, Hebgen, Yellowstone Lakes, Madison River
Specialty Horseback pack trips for fly fishing and lake trolling
Boats 16' Outboards **Tackle Supplied** All **Type of Fishing** All
Experience 13 years **Rates** day: $75 week: $700 1/2 day: $45

BIGFORK, MONTANA

BUCHANAN, FRED W. (406) 837-6933
Address 385 Crane Mountain Road, Bigfork, MT 59911
Airport Kalispell 23m **Accommodations** Bigfork
Operation Outfitter **Type of Fishing** Fly, spin, trolling

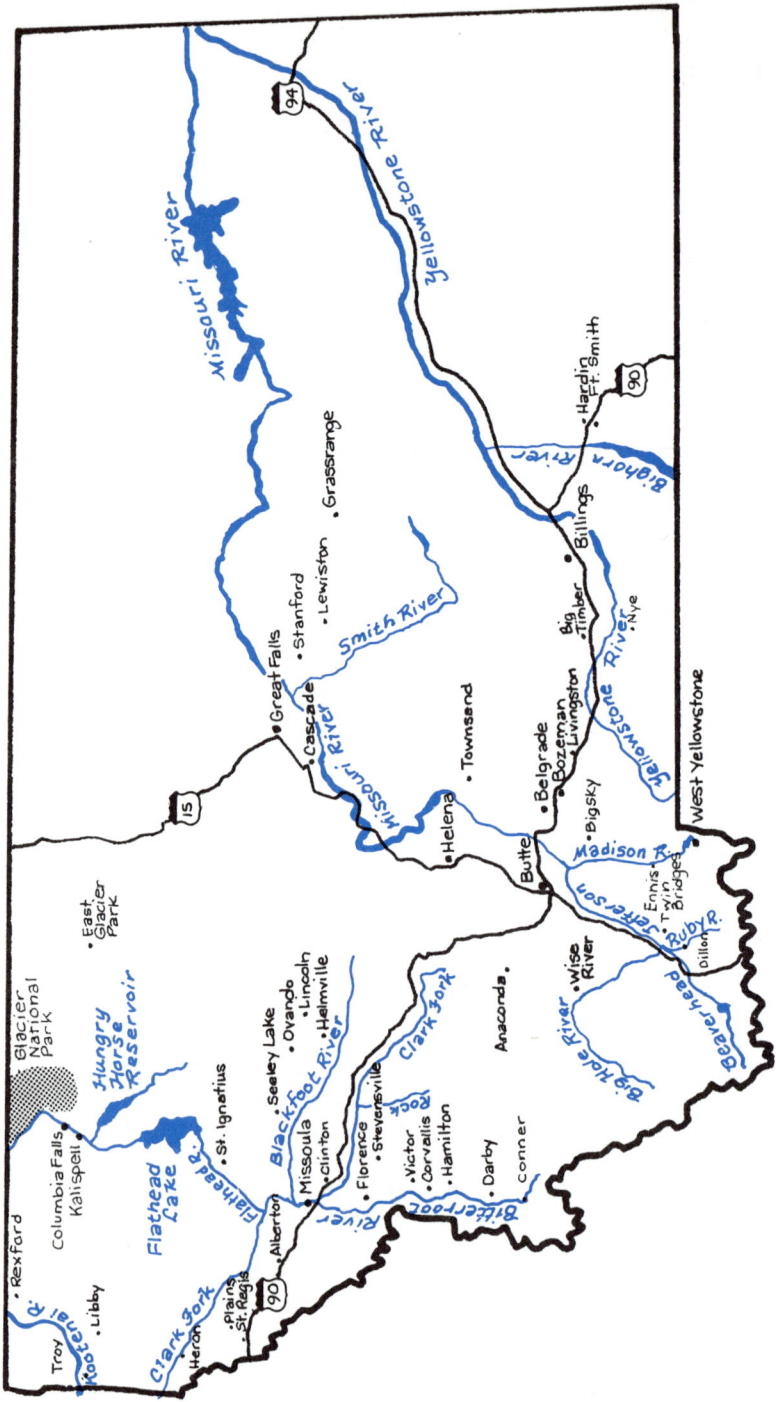

MONTANA

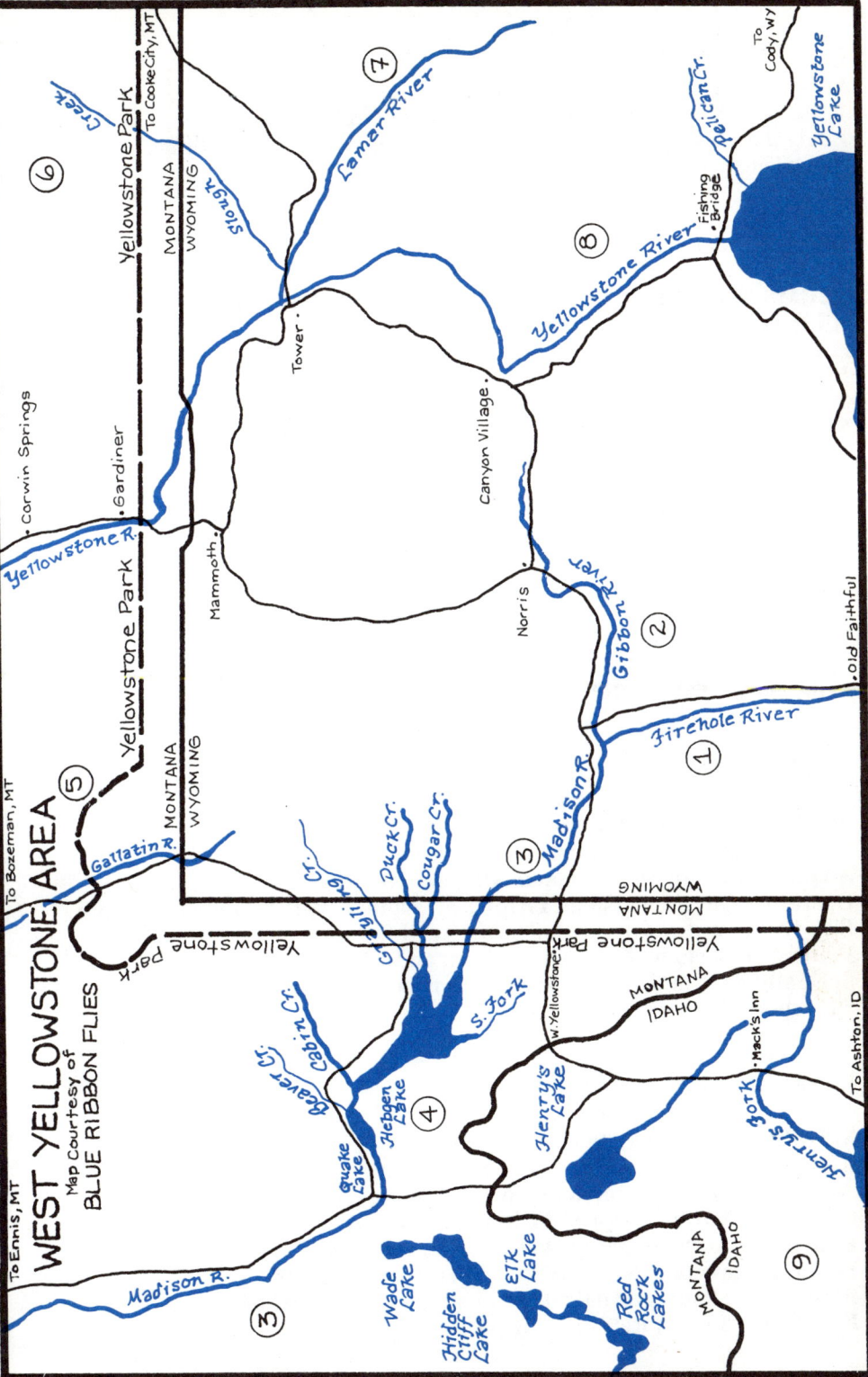

WEST YELLOWSTONE AREA
Map Courtesy of
BLUE RIBBON FLIES

Fish Trout, bass **Season** May-November
Water Flat Head Lake, Swan River **Specialty** Lake trolling
Boats Bass boats, Cabin Cruisers **Tackle Supplied** Spin, trolling
Experience 20 years **Rates** day: $140 1/2day: $75

BIG SKY, MONTANA

REHMS, JIM AND JOYCE-HANGING-J-RANCH (916) 888-8224
Address Box 237, Big Sky, MT 59716
Airport Bozeman 40m **Accommodations** Big Sky **Operation** Guide, outfitter
Fish Trout **Season** Year-round **Type of Fishing** All **Boats** River sleds
Water Gallatin, Jefferson, Madison, Missouri Rivers
Specialty Fly and lure fishing using jet boats **Tackle Supplied** All
Experience 36 years **Rates** day: $150

SCHAPP, ROBERT L.-LONE MOUNTAIN RANCH (406) 995-4644
Address Box 145, Big Sky, MT 59716
Airport Bozeman 40m **Accommodations** Big Sky
Operation Outfitter **Type of Fishing** Fly, spin
Fish Brown, rainbow, cutthroat, brook **Season** May-October
Water Gallatin, Madison, Firehole, Yellowstone Rivers
Specialty Fly fishing **Boats** McKenzies **Tackle Supplied** Fly
Experience 14 years **Rates** day: $140

BIG TIMBER, MONTANA

BOVEE, BOB-HIDDEN LAKE OUTFITTERS (406) 932-6582
Address Box 1233, Big Timber, MT 59011
Airport Bozeman 80m **Accommodations** Ennis 20m
Operation Outfitter **Type of Fishing** Fly, spin **Tackle Supplied** Fly, spin
Fish Rainbow, brown, brook **Season** April-October
Water Yellowstone, Madison, Bighorn and Boulder Rivers
Specialty Pack and float trips **Boats** Rowboats, McKenzies, rafts
Experience 10 years **Rates** day: $75

BOZEMAN, MONTANA

BIRRER, MARK (406) 586-5072, 586-7045
Address 145 North Spruce Drive, Bozeman, MT 59715
Airport Bozeman **Accommodations** Bozeman
Operation Outfitter **Type of Fishing** Fly **Boats** Rowboats, McKenzies, tubes
Fish Trout, Arctic grayling **Season** February-November
Water Yellowstone, Madison Rivers, Hyalite, Harrison Lakes
Specialty Fly fishing drift float and float tubing trips **Tackle Supplied** Fly, spin
Experience 3 years **Rates** day: $165 1/2 day: $90

Author's Notes: I have known Mark four years. Although I have not fished with him, I can say he is a knowledgeable and conscientious guide.

GADOURY, ALLAN W.-6X OUTFITTERS (406) 586-3806
Address 9631 Cougar Drive, Bozeman, MT 59715
Airport Bozeman **Accommodations** Bozeman **Operation** Outfitter
Fish Rainbow, brown, cutthroat, brook **Season** Year-round **Type of Fishing** Fly
Water Armstrong, Nelson's, Depuy's Spring Creeks, Yellowstone River
Specialty Fly fishing spring creeks **Boats** McKenzies **Tackle Supplied** Fly
Experience 13 years **Rates** day: $160 + rod fee/person

KAVANAGH, DENNIS-MONTANA FLYCAST (406) 587-5923
Address 309 West Harrison, Bozeman, MT 59715
Airport Bozeman **Accommodations** Bozeman
Operation Outfitter **Type of Fishing** Fly, spin **Boats** McKenzies
Fish Brown, rainbow, cutthroat, grayling **Season** May-October
Water Madison, Gallatin, Yellowstone Rivers, Spring Creeks
Specialty Fly fishing float trips **Tackle Supplied** Fly, spin
Experience 5 years **Rates** day: $175 week: $830/person

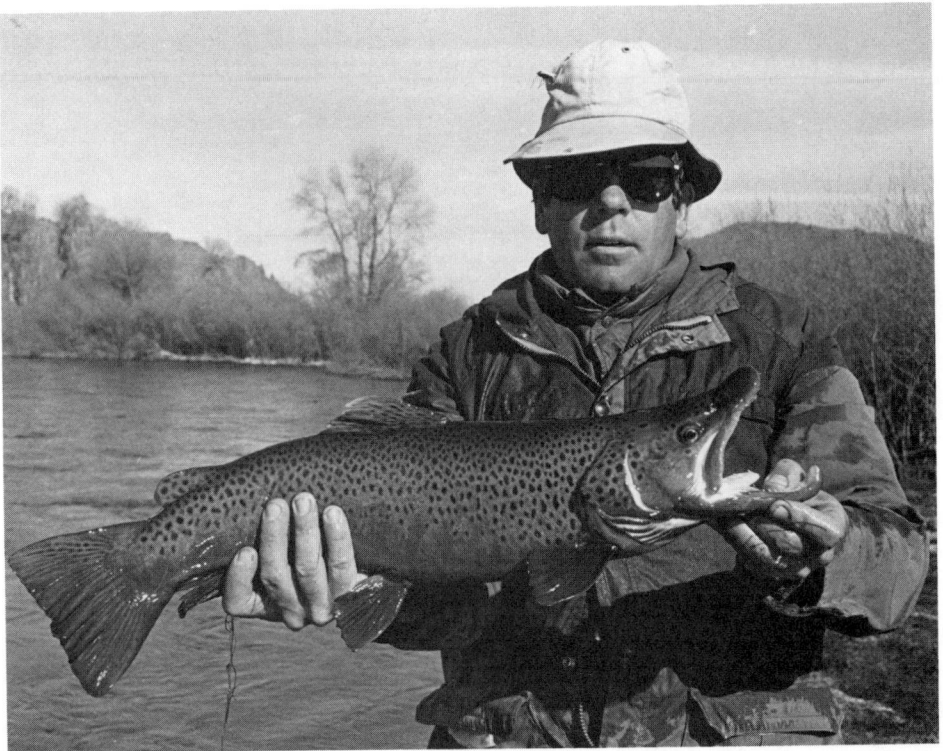

Fall brown from the Bighorn.   *Rip Woodin*

KUMLIEN, DAVID L.-MONTANA TROUTFITTERS (406) 587-4707
Address 2720 West Main Street, Bozeman, MT 59715
Airport Bozeman **Accommodations** Bozeman
Operation Outfitter **Type of Fishing** Fly **Season** April-October
Fish Rainbow, cutthroat, brown **Specialty** Fly fishing float trips
Water Madison, Yellowstone, Gallatin, Big Hole Rivers
Boats McKenzies, rafts, float tubes **Tackle Supplied** Fly, spin
Experience 10 years **Rates** day: $185
*Author's Notes: David Kumlien has an excellent Orvis fly shop in Bozeman.
My contacts in Montana tell me his guide services are also good.*

LILLY, GREG-THE RIVERS EDGE (406) 586-5373
Address 2012 North 7th Avenue, Dept. T, Bozeman, MT 59715
Airport Bozeman **Accommodations** Bozeman **Operation** Outfitter, tackle shop
Fish Trout **Season** Year-round **Type of Fishing** Fly
Water Yellowstone, Madison, Big Hole, Jefferson Rivers, Gallatin Rivers
Specialty Float fishing, wade fishing **Boats** McKenzies **Tackle Supplied** Fly
Experience 15 years **Rates** day: $175
*Author's Notes: Greg Lilly's operation is one of the best in Montana. His fly
shop, which he manages along with Dave Corcoran, is one of the finest in the
country. They also produce a mail order catalog. He carries on in the tradition
of his dad, Bud Lilly, who is now retired from the fly fishing business, but
Greg tells me he has not retired from the sport. Both Greg and Dave are personally
available to guide on local streams.*

BUTTE, MONTANA

ATCHESON, JR., JACK (406) 782-3498, 782-3470
Address 3210 Ottawa, Butte, MT 59701
Airport Butte **Accommodations** Butte
Operation Outfitter, Guide **Type of Fishing** All **Tackle Supplied** All
Fish Brown, rainbow, cutthroat, grayling, brook **Season** Year-round
Water Bighorn, Madison, Beaverhead, Jefferson, Smith Rivers
Specialty Fly and spin river fishing **Boats** McKenzies, rafts
Experience 25 years **Rates** day: $300

CAMERON, MONTANA

MERIGOLD, ROSS A. (406) 682-4804
Address Box 563 Slide Inn, Cameron, MT 59720
Airport Bozeman 100m **Accommodations** On premises
Operation Guide, Outfitter **Type of Fishing** Fly
Fish Rainbow, brown **Season** May-September
Water Madison River **Specialty** Walk and wade day trips
Experience 7 years **Rates** day: $175 1/2 day: $100
*Author's Notes: Ross offers wade trips on my favorite section of the Madison.
He has an excellent reputation.*

Greg Lilly and Dave Corcoran on the Madison. *Greg Lilly*

CASCADE, MONTANA

CARDINAL, PETE-MISSOURI RIVER ANGLER (406) 468-2743
Address Box 95, Cascade, MT 59421
Airport Great Falls 45m **Accommodations** Cascade
Operation Outfitter, tackle shop **Type of Fishing** Fly
Fish Rainbow, brown **Season** Year-round **Specialty** Fly fishing float trips
Water Missouri River **Boats** McKenzies **Tackle Supplied** Fly
Experience 3 years **Rates** day: $133-175
Guide's Notes: The Missouri River is one of Montana's richest resources. It is formed by the confluence of the Gallatin, Jefferson and Madison Rivers near Three Forks, Montana. Once wild and primitive, the mighty Mo has been tamed by a series of three dams. The often muddy and warm upper Missouri River exits below the final dam (Holter) as blue-ribbon water, rejuvenated, purified and cool; a trout river reborn.

Steady flow releases over the past decade have allowed aquatic insect and fish populations to develop that are unmatched by any other river in the state and perhaps the nation. Only the Beaverhead and Bighorn Rivers have comparable fish populations. Ask any knowledgeable biologist or fisherman, however, and the Missouri below Holter Dam emerges as the finer fishery. Reasons cited include a healthier trout population uneffected by nitrogen narcosis, a more diverse aquatic environment with abundant baitfish populations, and greater accessibility to the fisherman with an easier fishing environment.

Despite its immense size, the Missouri flows over fine gravels and lush weed beds resembling a giant spring creek. From July thru September, the massive, consistant hatches provide dry fly angling opportunities unmatched by any other water.

The Missouri River is primarily a rainbow trout fishery. These hard battling leapers average 15 to 19 inches.

Missouri River Hatch Schedule

Time	Activity	Pattern	Sizes
April - May 15	Stonefly	Golden Stone	12 - 14
	Mayfly	Hares Ear	12 - 16
	Baitfish	Any Sculpin	2 - 16
	Midge	Pupae and Adults	18 - 24
May - July	Caddis	Tan & Olive Pupae & Elk Hair	12 - 16
	Mayfly	Olive Emergers & Comparaduns	16 - 20
	Craneflies	Olive Wooly Worm & Buggers	6
	Terrestrials	Flying Ants and Beetles	12 - 18
July 15 - Sept	Caddis	Olive & Brown Elk Hair	16 - 20
	Mayfly	Black & White and Olive Spinners	18 - 26
	Terrestrials	Flying Ant, Beetles and Hoppers	12 - 18
Oct - Nov	Mayfly	Olive Duns & Comparduns	18 - 22
	Midges	Pupae & Adult	18 - 24
	Baitfish	Any Sculpin	2-6
Terrestrials	Hoppers	12 - 14	

Author's Notes: I fished the Missouri a couple of years ago and was very impressed. This is an awesome, blue ribbon trout stream, and it gets very little pressure. Pete Cardinal is located in Cascade, MT, adjacent to some of the best water.

CLINTON, MONTANA

EKSTROM, DAN (406) 825-6295
Address Box 885, Clinton, MT 59825
Airport Missoula 30m **Accommodations** Missoula 30m
Operation Outfitter **Type of Fishing** Fly, spin **Season** June-August
Fish Brown, rainbow **Water** Rock Creek, Upper Clark Fork
Specialty Fly fishing and pack-in lake fishing
Experience 15 years **Rates** day: $75 week: $525

COLUMBIA FALLS, MONTANA

CHEEK, ROLAND (406) 892-5560
Address P.O. Box 1880, Columbia Falls, MT 59912
Airport Missoula 10m **Accommodations** Columbia Falls
Operation Outfitter **Type of Fishing** Fly, spin, baitcasting
Fish Cutthroat, Dolly Varden **Season** July-September **Boats** Rafts
Water South Fork of Flathead **Specialty** Float/fish combo pack-in
Experience 15 years**Rates** week: $3200

ROLFING, STEVE-GREAT NORTHERN LLAMA CO. (406) 755-9044
Address 1795 Middle Road, Columbia Falls, MT 59912
Airport Missoula 10m **Accommodations** Columbia Falls
Operation Outfitter **Type of Fishing** Spin, fly **Fish** Rainbow, cutthroat
Season June-August **Water** Bond, Trinkus and other Alpine Lakes
Specialty Lake shore spinning and fly fishing **Tackle Supplied** Spin
Experience 4 years **Rates** day: $180

CONDON, MONTANA

SCHAEFFER, RICHARD-HOLLAND LAKE LODGE (406) 754-2282
Address Box 2083, Condon, MT 59826
Airport Missoula 80m **Accommodations** On premises
Operation Outfitter, lodge **Type of Fishing** Fly, spin
Fish Trout **Season** June-Nov **Water** Bob Marshall Wilderness lakes
Specialty Mountain stream and lake fly fishing **Boats** Rafts
Experience 5 years **Rates** day: $200 week: $1400

CONNER, MONTANA

ZIKAN, SR., BOB (46) 821-4541
Address P.O. Box 555, Conner, MT 59827

Airport Missoula 80m **Accommodations** Conner **Operation** Outfitter
Fish Rainbow, brown, cutthroat, Arctic grayling **Season** April-November
Water Big Hole, Bitterroot, Beaverhead Rivers **Type of Fishing** Fly, spin
Specialty River float trips **Boats** Rafts **Tackle Supplied** Fly, spin
Experience 10 years **Rates** day: $150 week: $840

CORVALLIS, MONTANA

WRIGHT, TOM AND PETERS, GARY (406) 961-4453
Address 1341 Summerdale Road, Corvallis, MT 59828
Airport Missoula 45m **Accommodations** Missoula 45m
Operation Outfitter **Type of Fishing** Spin, baitcasting
Fish Trout **Season** July-August **Specialty** Lake fly fishing
Water High Montana lakes in Idaho and Montana **Boats** Rafts
Experience 8 years **Rates** day: $160/2 people (4 day minimum)

CORWIN SPRINGS, MONTANA

DUFFY, CHARLES G. (406) 848-7287
Address Box 863, Corwin Springs, MT 59021
Airport Bozeman 85m **Accommodations** Gardiner 8m
Operation Outfitter **Type of Fishing** All **Tackle Supplied** Spin, baitcast
Fish Cutthroat, Rainbow, Brown, Brook **Season** June-September
Water Yellowstone River and Hell Roaring Creek drainages, Yellowstone
National Park **Specialty** Fly and spin fishing from shore
Experience 14 years **Rates** day: $100 week: $700

DARBY, MONTANA

ALLAMAN, KEN (406) 821-3763
Address West Fork, Darby, MT 59829
Airport Missoula 80m **Accommodations** Darby **Operation** Outfitter, guide
Fish Brook, cutthroat, rainbow **Season** June-September
Water West Fork of Bitterroot River, Mountain lakes and streams
Specialty Small mountain wilderness streams **Type of Fishing** Fly, spin
Experience 15 years **Rates** day: $200

LEWIS, JERRY A. (406) 821-3872
Address Box 213, Darby, MT 59829
Airport Missoula 85m **Accommodations** Darby
Operation Outfitter, guide **Type of Fishing** Fly, spin, baitcasting
Fish Rainbow, brown, grayling, cutthroat **Season** Year-round
Water Bitterroot, Big Hole Rivers **Tackle Supplied** Fly, spin
Specialty Fly, float and bait fishing **Boats** Rafts
Experience 9 years **Rates** day: $125

MUIR, DAN (406) 821-4560
Address Box 414, Darby, MT 59829
Airport Missoula 85m**Accommodations** Darby
Operation Outfitter**Type of Fishing** All
Fish Rainbow, cutthroat, brook, brown **Season** March-August
Water Bitterroot River, Como, Painted Rocks Lake
Specialty Fly fishing &bait fishing **Tackle Supplied** All
Experience 10 years **Rates** day: $75 6 days: $450 1/2 day: $40

DILLON, MONTANA

JOHNSON, BILL (406) 683-4975
Address 1500 Clark Lane, Dillon, MT 59725
Airport Butte 65m **Accommodations** Dillon
Operation Outfitter **Type of Fishing** Fly, spin **Season** Year-round
Water Beaverhead, Big Hole Rivers, High mountain lakes
Specialty Float fishing and pack trips **Fish** Trout, grayling
Boats Rowboats, canoes, rafts **Tackle Supplied** Fly, spin
Experience 20 years **Rates** day: $100 week: $750 1/2 day: $60

KIPP, RUSS-MONTANA HIGH COUNTRY TOURS (406) 683-4920
Address 315 South Argenta, Dillon, MT 59725
Airport Bozeman 110m **Accommodations** Dillon **Season** May-Dec
Operation Outfitter **Type of Fishing** Fly, spin **Tackle Supplied** Fly
Water Beaverhead, Big Hole, Smith Rivers **Boats** Rafts
Specialty Float trips for fly fishermen **Fish** Trout, grayling
Experience 10 years **Rates** day: $150 week: $1000 1/2 day: $90

McNEILL, BOB AND CHRIS (406) 683-5494
Address 3405 10 Mile Road, Dillon, MT 59725
Airport Butte 65m **Accommodations** Dillon
Operation Guide, outfitter **Type of Fishing** Fly, spin **Boats** Rowboats
Fish Rainbow, brown, native trout, grayling **Season** June-September
Water Beaverhead, Big Hole, Jefferson Rivers **Specialty** Fly fishing
Experience 13 years **Rates** day: $150 week: $700

MOSOLF, TIM (406) 683-5400
Address 2900 Highway 41 North, Dillon, MT 59725
Airport Butte 65m **Accommodations** Dillon
Operation Guide, outfitter **Type of Fishing** Fly, spin **Tackle Supplied** Fly
Fish Brown, rainbow, cutthroat, brook **Season** May-November
Water Beaverhead, Big Hole, Jefferson, Madison Rivers
Specialty Fly fishing float trips **Boats** McKenzies, rafts, johns, tubes
Experience 7 years **Rates** day: $185 1/2 day: $100

PIERCE, TOM AND JUDY (406) 681-3178
Address 16100 Highway 324, Dillon, MT 59725

Airport Butte 100m **Accommodations** Dillon 35m
Operation Outfitter **Type of Fishing** Fly, spin, baitcast
Fish Brown, rainbow, cutthroat, brook **Season** June-October
Water Horse Prairie Creek, Beaverhead, Big Hole, Jefferson Rivers
Specialty Fly fishing **Boats** Rafts **Tackle Supplied** All
Experience 12 years **Rates** day: $100

REITSE, DENNIS (406) 683-6232
Address 614 Barnett Avenue, Dillon, MT 59725
Airport Butte 65m **Accommodations** Dillon
Operation Outfitter **Type of Fishing** Fly **Tackle Supplied** Fly
Fish Brown, rainbow, brook, grayling **Season** May-November
Water Beaverhead, Big Hole, Madison, Smith Rivers
Specialty Fly fishing float trips **Boats** McKenzies, rafts, johns
Experience 8 years **Rates** day: $170 1/2 day: $100
Author's Notes: Dennis knows the Beaverhead extremely well and has a very good reputation.

THROCKMORTON, TERRY (406) 683-4005
Address 325 South Dakota, Dillon, MT 59725
Airport Butte 65m **Accommodations** Dillon
Operation Outfitter **Type of Fishing** Fly, spin, baitcasting
Fish Brown, rainbow, brook, grayling **Season** May-October
Water Beaverhead, Big Hole, Madison Rivers **Boats** Rafts, johns
Specialty Fly fishing float trips **Tackle Supplied** Fly
Experience 2 years **Rates** day: $160 week: $1000

TOLLET, TIM-FRONTIER ANGLERS (406) 683-5276
Address 427 South Atlantic, Dillon, MT 59725
Airport Butte 65m **Accommodations** Dillon
Operation Outfitter, tackle shop **Type of Fishing** Fly
Fish Brown, rainbow, brook, grayling **Season** May-November
Water Beaverhead, Big Hole, Jefferson Rivers, Poindexter Slough
Specialty Fly fishing float and wade fishing trips
Boats McKenzies, rafts, johns **Tackle Supplied** Fly
Experience 9 years **Rates** day: $185 1/2 day: $100
Author's Notes: Tim Tollet runs his outfitter operation out of his tackle shop in Dillon. His guides are on the Beaverhead or other local rivers every day. This is a top-notch operation.

TROTH, AL AND ERIC (406) 683-2752
Address Box 1307, Dillon, MT 59725
Airport Butte 65m **Accommodations** Dillon
Operation Outfitter **Type of Fishing** Fly
Fish Brown, rainbow, brook, grayling **Season** June-November
Water Beaverhead, Big Hole, Jefferson, Bighorn Rivers
Specialty River fly fishing, floats and tube fishing trips
Boats Rowboats, McKenzies, rafts **Tackle Supplied** Fly

Experience 23 years **Rates** day: $175 week: $1225 1/2 day: $130
Author's Notes: Al Troth is a nationally known fly fisherman and fly tier. He
has a reputation as a demanding guide.

EAST GLACIER, MONTANA

BECK, WILLIAM A.-BEAR CREEK RANCH (406) 226-4489
Address P.O. Box 151, East Glacier, MT 59434
Airport Glacier Int'l 65m **Accommodations** On premises
Operation Outfitter, lodge **Type of Fishing** Fly, spin
Fish Trout, cutthroat, Dolly Varden, rainbow **Season** May-September
Water Flathead River, Bear Creek, high country lakes **Tackle Supplied** Fly, spin
Specialty Fly fishing rivers, streams, and lakes by horseback
Experience 6 years **Rates** day: $100 week: $1200 1/2 day: $60

EAST MISSOULA, MONTANA

DOTY, PATRICK-ROCKY MOUNTAIN WHITEWATER (406) 728-2984
Address 612 Minnesota, East Missoula, MT 59802
Airport Missoula 6m **Accommodations** Missoula **Operation** Outfitter
Fish All species of trout **Season** March-Oct **Type of Fishing** All
Water Clark Fork, Blackfoot, Bitterroot, Smith, Big Hole Rivers
Specialty Fly fishing, spin fishing, white water float trips **Boats** Rafts
Experience 4 years **Rates** day: $150 week: $600

EMIGRANT, MONTANA

WILTSHIRE, ROBERT (406) 333-4779
Address P.O. Box 216, Emigrant, MT 59027
Airport Bozeman 50m **Accommodations** Chico Hot Springs 3m
Operation Outfitter **Type of Fishing** Fly, spin, baitcasting
Fish Trout **Season** March-Nov **Water** Yellowstone, Smith Rivers
Specialty Fly fishing float trips **Boats** Rafts **Tackle Supplied** Fly, spin
Experience 9 years **Rates** day: $170 week: $1400 1/2 day: $90

ENNIS, MONTANA

BROWN, RANDY (406) 682-7481
Address 301 E. Ennis St., Ennis, MT 59729
Airport Bozeman 50m **Accommodations** Ennis
Operation Outfitter **Type of Fishing** All **Fish** Rainbow, brown
Water Madison, Big Hole, Beaverhead Rivers **Season** Year-round
Specialty Fly fishing **Boats** McKenzie, flats skiff **Tackle Supplied** All
Experience 6 years **Rates** day: $200

Author's Notes: I have several good friends who fish with Randy. They all say he is a very good guide. During the winter months Randy guides bonefish and tarpon in the Florida Keys.

D'AMBRUOSO, ROBERT-HEADWATERS TACKLE SHOP (406) 682-7269
Address Route 1, Box 207, Ennis, MT 59729
Airport Bozeman 55m **Accommodations** Ennis
Operation Outfitter, tackle shop, lodge **Type of Fishing** Fly
Fish Trout **Season** Mar-Nov **Tackle Supplied** Fly
Water Madison, Big Hole, Bighorn, Jefferson Rivers
Specialty Fly fishing float trips and instruction **Boats** McKenzies
Experience 11 years **Rates** day: $170 week: $1100 1/2 day: $100
Author's Notes: Bob owns and runs an excellent tackle shop in Ennis.

RATHIE, RANDY-SEPTEMBER RANCH (406) 682-7598
Address P.O. Box 82, Ennis, MT 59729
Airport Bozeman 55m **Accommodations** On premises
Operation Outfitter, lodge **Type of Fishing** Fly, spin
Fish Brown, rainbow, grayling **Season** March-November
Water Madison, Big Hole, Beaverhead, Jefferson Rivers **Boats** McKenzies, rafts
Specialty Fly fishing float trips **Tackle Supplied** Fly, spin
Experience 18 years **Rates** day: $140 1/2 day: $90
Author's Notes: Contacts who have fished with Randy tell me he knows the rivers and works hard to put his clients into fish.

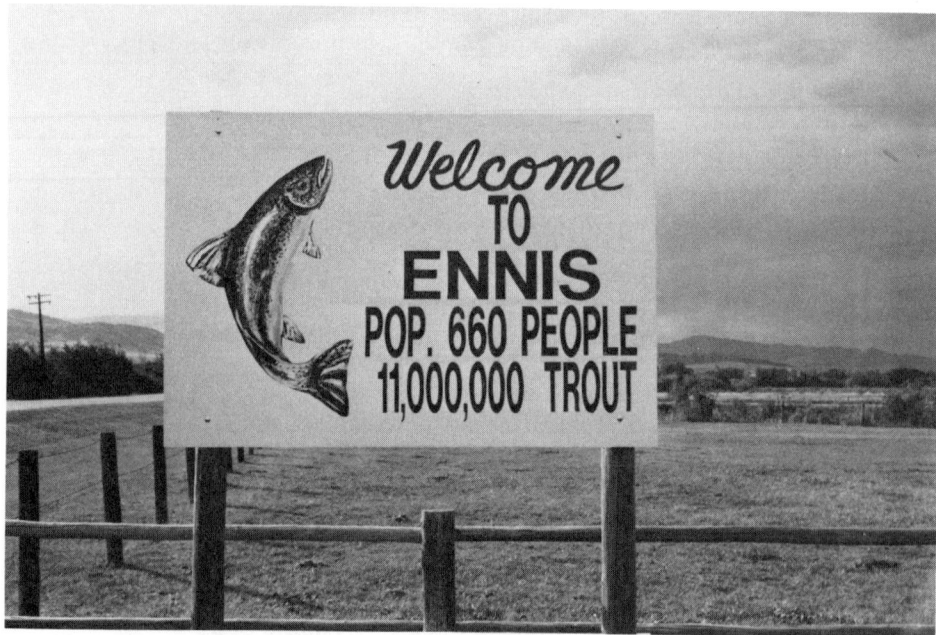

Ennis, Montana, headquarters for fishing the Madison.   *Richard Swan*

WALKER, BOB-T LAZY B RANCH (406) 682-7288
Address Route 1 Box 75, Ennis, MT 59729
Airport Bozeman 55m **Accommodations** On premises
Operation Outfitter, lodge **Type of Fishing** Fly
Fish Rainbow, brown, cutthroat, brook **Season** May-Nov
Water Madison, Jefferson, Big Hole, Bighorn Rivers
Specialty Fly fishing float trips **Boats** McKenzies **Tackle Supplied** Fly, spin
Experience 10 years **Rates** day: $75-140

FLORENCE, MONTANA

SCOTT, BRUCE A. (406) 273-6419
Address P.O. Box 352, Florence, MT 59833
Airport Missoula 30m **Accommodations** Missoula 30m
Operation Outfitter **Type of Fishing** Fly, spin, baitcasting
Fish Rainbow, cutthroat, brook **Season** June-Sept **Boats** Rafts
Water High mountain lakes and streams, Selway Wilderness Area
Specialty Wilderness pack-in lake fishing **Tackle Supplied** Fly, spin
Experience 10 years **Rates** day: $75 week: $525/person

FORT SMITH, MONTANA

Author's Notes: Fort Smith is a very small town 70 miles southeast of Billings which has become the center for anglers fishing the famous Bighorn River. The town offers tackle shops, a couple of restaraunts, and limited accommodations. The following detailed notes on the Bighorn River were provided by George Anderson of Livingston who is the owner of the Yellowstone Angler, which offers guided fishing on the Bighorn.

FISHING THE BIGHORN

The Bighorn may be the finest river in the continental U.S. today for trophy sized brown and rainbow trout. A decision by the U.S. Supreme Court opened the river, which runs through the Crow Indian Reservation, to fishing in 1981. Fishermen must, however, stay within the high water mark (below the vegetation line) and since the Bighorn is a large river the best means of access is by boat. We use boats mainly for transportation and stop so that you can fish the best runs. The wading is relatively easy with the bottom consisting mostly of small rocks and gravel.

Access is gained at four public access areas on the river above Hardin, Montana. The first access is at the Afterbay Dam at Ft. Smith, and another public access is approximately 3 miles downstream from there. Both the Afterbay access and the 3 mile access provide good fishing for wading fishermen that are willing to do a little walking. A third access called the "Bighorn Access" is located off the highway 12 miles from Ft. Smith (back towards Hardin). There is a sign on the highway that marks this access, and camping is allowed there.

The fourth access point is 24 miles downstream from the Bighorn Access at Two Leggins Bridge. This is also a Fish & Game access site, and is about 9 miles out of Hardin..

The Bighorn is a large river that is difficult to cross except at a few spots, and then only in low water. There is a variety of water to fish, from smooth flats and smaller side channels to long heavy runs perfect for streamer fishing. There are lots of drop offs, channels and riffle corners at the heads of runs and pools that provide ideal water to fish with nymphs and dry flies.

Although a lot has been written about the great fishing on the Bighorn, the fishing is not always easy. Experienced fishermen will nearly always catch some good fish, but beginners and less experienced fishermen often have a tough time. Reading the water is of extreme importance as fish lie in very different places depending on changes in water flow levels. Finding fish when the water is high is especially difficult, but once you learn where to look for fish the fishing can be fantastic even with the water high. When the fishing is hot, it is possible for a good fisherman to catch and release a dozen or more fish over 18 inches, and with a few of these being fish in the 3-5 pound class. Later in the summer when the insect hatches come with intensity, the dry fly fishing is superb. Complex water currents and flat water make the dry fly fishing as challenging as the Henry's Fork, but there are many huge browns and rainbows sipping in everything that comes down their driftline and a good cast and presentation will put you into many 20" plus fish.

WHEN TO COME

The Bighorn River is controlled by the 550' high Yellowtail Dam, and the upper 10 miles of the river always stays clear and fishable, unaffected by spring runoff. Because of the colder water temperatures from water running out of the bottom of the reservoir, the best fishing comes later in the year than most of our other streams here in Montana. Prime time seems to be mid-July through the middle of October.

The dry fly fishing starts early on the Bighorn. Terrific hatches of midges start in late March. The Baetis hatches get going in mid-April and continue through June. May is an excellent month to fish the river. In early mid-July, golden stoneflies show up and produce some exciting action. In late July and early August the fantastic caddis hatches start and provide the finest dry fly fishing of the season, running through late September.

The nymph fishing is good all year but especially good from June through September.

Fall is a great time to look for those big browns if you like to fish streamers, and although the browns don't actually spawn in the Bighorn until late November and sometimes early December, the streamer fishing can be hot at any time from mid-September on through the end of December. Insect hatches, mostly Baetis, continue on throughout the fall, and I have seen flies on the water and fish rising as late as the end of December! These afternoon hatches late in the fall can provide some very pleasant dry fly fishing. If you are planning a trip late in the fall, say after mid-October, remember that the weather can be mighty cold at times, so be prepared!

HATCHES AND FLY PATTERNS

The insect hatches start in late March when midges and then baetis mayflies (Dark Blue Duns in size 18) get the fish looking to the surface for some of their food. The good consistent hatches don't come until mid-July through August when heavy infrequens (Pale Morning Dun #16) hatches and a variety of caddis start to appear on the river. There are a number of mayflies present in late summer and fall and a great quantity of these are species of baetis that one can match with Blue Wing Olive patterns in sizes 16-22. The Pale Morning Duns (infrequens and inermis) are best tied on sizes 14-18. Heavy caddis hatches occur from mid-August through mid-September. One of the best hatches is a small Black Caddis (#16-18) that fills the air and drives the fish into a frenzy. Many other species of caddis are present, from large speckled sedges to smaller brown and gray varieties. Henryville, Hemingway, and Elk Hair Caddis patterns in sizes 14-18 will fill the bill. Some smaller stoneflies hatch in July, August and September, but there are no larger stoneflies present here like the "Salmonflies" on the Yellowstone or Madison.

Hoppers and attractor patterns like the Royal Wulff etc. do not work as well here as they do on the Yellowstone or other streams. The Bighorn is slower, flatter water more like the Henry's Fork. The fish are quite selective and you must match closely the flies on the water and present them well in order to catch the larger fish. Hopper fishing is good only occasionally.

Nymph fishing is probably the most productive method of fishing the Bighorn and the primary food you want to imitate are the scuds (shrimp). We have found that colors like bright red and orange are especially deadly, but bring some olive, tan and pinkish scuds as well. Sizes should be 8-12. Other nymphs work very well and here are some of my favorites: George's Rubber Leg Brown Stone #6-8, Peeking Caddis #10-12, Casual Dress #6-8, Hare's Ear #12-16, Pheasant Tail #12-16, Caddis Pupa-olive or brown #12-14, Red Fox Squirrel #10-14, and Girdle Bugs-black or brown in sizes #4-8.

Streamers are dynamite on big trout, especially late in the fall. Olive or Black Wooly Buggers can be good anytime and the Black Girdle Bugger #2-4 is one of my favorites.

Matuka patterns like the Dk. Spruce and Lt. Spruce, olive and brown are good in sizes #2-6. There are no sculpins in the Bighorn and most of the baitfish are either dace or sucker minnows. For this reason we tend to use patterns like Zonkers (silver or olive in #2-4), Black Nose Dace #2-6, and other mylar bodied streamers. Marabou Muddlers, white or black and also the Bighorn Special streamers are also good in sizes 2-6. Another streamer pattern that is a killer is the Rabbit Fur Sculpin pattern in olive or brown, sizes 1/0 to 6, depending on your equipment and line size. (George Anderson-Yellowstone Angler)

CRAIG, MIKE-BIGHORN ANGLER (406) 666-2233

Address Park Dale Court, Fort Smith, MT 59035
Airport Billings 92m **Accommodations** On premises
Operation Outfitter, lodge, tackle shop **Type of Fishing** Fly, spin
Fish Brown, rainbow **Season** March-Nov **Water** Bighorn River
Specialty Fly fishing float trips **Boats** McKenzies **Tackle Supplied** Fly

Experience 4 years **Rates** day: $185
Author's Notes: Mike Craig's operation is located right next to the Bighorn in Fort Smith. He has a very good reputation

DOWNEY, BRAD (406) 666-2233
Address Box 551, Fort Smith, MT 59035
Airport Billings 92m **Accommodations** Fort Smith
Operation Guide **Fish** Trout **Season** April-Nov
Water Bighorn, Madison, Yellowstone, Big Hole Rivers
Specialty Fly fishing float trips **Type of Fishing** Fly
Boats McKenzie, rafts w/motors **Tackle Supplied** Fly
Experience 5 years **Rates** day: $200

ROHRBACHER, BILL-BIG HORN RIVER OUTFITTERS (406) 666-2351
Address P.O. Box 483YRS, Fort Smith. MT 59035
Airport Billings 92m **Accommodations** On premises
Operation Outfitter, lodge, tackle shop **Type of Fishing** Fly , spin
Fish Brown, rainbow, brook, cutthroat **Season** March-December
Water Bighorn, Madison, Missouri, Yellowstone Rivers **Boats** McKenzies
Specialty Fly fishing and upland water fowl hunting **Tackle Supplied** Fly, spin
Experience 4 years **Rates** day: $175 1/2 day: $100

SCHULLER, DAVID A. (406) 666-2311
Address Box 565 Yrs, Fort Smith, MT 59035
Airport Billings 90m **Accommodations** Fort Smith
Operation Guide **Type of Fishing** Fly **Water** Bighorn River
Fish Brown and rainbow trout **Season** April-December
Specialty Fly fishing float trips **Boats** McKenzie **Tackle Supplied** Fly, spin
Experience 4 years **Rates** day: $175

GARDINER, MONTANA

HOPPE, WILLIAM H. (406) 848-7651
Address Box 75 Jardine Route, Gardiner, MT 59030
Airport Bozeman 90m **Accommodations** Gardiner **Operation** Outfitter
Fish Cutthroat, rainbow, brown, eastern brook **Season** Year-round
Water Yellowstone River, Hellroaring, Slough Creeks, mountain lakes
Specialty Fly fishing and spin fishing from the shore
Tackle Supplied Fly, spin **Type of Fishing** Fly, spin
Experience 12 years **Rates** day: $200 week: $1200 1/2 day: $100

JOHNSON, WARREN-HELLS A'ROARING OUTFITTERS (406) 848-7578
Address Box 399, Gardiner, MT 59030
Airport Bozeman 90m **Accommodations** On premises
Operation Outfitter, lodge **Type of Fishing** Fly, baitcast
Fish Cutthroat, brook, rainbow, brown **Season** March-September
Water Yellowstone, Hellroaring, Lamar Rivers **Tackle Supplied** Fly, spin
Specialty Fly fishing trips-pack in on horseback
Experience 10 years **Rates** day: $200 week: $1200 1/2 day: $100

PARKS, RICHARD C.-PARK'S FLY SHOP (406) 848-7314
Address P.O. Box 196, Gardiner, MT 59030
Airport Bozeman 90 m **Accommodations** Gardiner
Operation Outfitter, tackle shop **Type of Fishing** Fly, spin
Fish Brown, cutthroat, rainbow **Season** April-November
Water Yellowstone, Gibbon Rivers, Slough Creek
Specialty Fly fishing float and wading trips
Boats McKenzies **Tackle Supplied** All
Experience 24 years**Rates** day: $150 1./2 day: $95
Guide's Notes:

Fishing Calendar for Yellowstone River and Tributaries

River	Fish	Peak
Yellowstone River		
above Canyon	Cutthroat	July - Aug
Canyon to Gardiner	Cutthroat, rainbow, brown	July - Oct
below Gardiner	Cutthroat, rainbow, brown	Mar - Apr, July - Nov
Pelican Creek	Cutthroat	July - Aug
Lamar River	Cutthroat, rainbow	July - Sept
Slough Creek	Cutthroat, rainbow	July - Aug
Soda Butte Creek	Cutthroat, rainbow	July - Aug
Gardiner River	Cutthroat, rainbow, brown, brook	July - Oct
Mill Creek	Cutthroat, rainbow, brook	July - Oct
Shields River	Rainbow, brown	July - Oct
Boulder River	Cutthroat, rainbow, brown	July - Oct

Yellowstone Area Lakes

Lakes	Fish	Peak
Yellowstone Lake	Cutthroat	June - July & Sept
Trout Lake	Cutthroat, rainbow	June - July & Sept
Dailey Lake	Rainbow	April - June & Sept - Oct
Blacktail Lakes	Brook	June & Sept - Oct
Shoshone Lake	Brown, brook, grayling	June & Sept - Oct
Lewis Lake	Brown, brook, grayling	June & Sept - Oct
Heart Lake	Cutthroat, brown, mackinaw	June - July & Sept - Oct
Grebe Lake	Rainbow, grayling	June - Oct
Henry's Lake	Cutthroat, rainbow, brook	June - Sept
Wade Lake	Rainbow, brown	April - Oct
Cliff Lake	Rainbow	June - Oct
Hebgen Lake	Rainbow, brown	April - Oct
Meadow Lake	Rainbow, brown	April - Oct

GRASS RANGE, MONTANA

OLSEN, ROY G. (406) 428-2195
Address Box 836, Grass Range, MT 59032
Airport Billings 100m **Accommodations** Lewiston 50m **Operation** Outfitter
Fish Trout, paddle fish **Season** Year-round **Type of Fishing** Fly, spin, troll
Water Missouri R., private & public reservoirs & ponds **Tackle Supplied** All

Specialty Pond fishing for trout & paddle fish **Boats** Canoes, bass boats
Experience 3 years **Rates** day: $75 week: $375 1/2 day: $45

GREAT FALLS, MONTANA

MADSEN, CRAIG (406) 761-1677
Address 820 Central Avenue, Great Falls, MT 59401
Airport Great Falls **Accommodations** Great Falls
Operation Guide, outfitter **Type of Fishing** Fly, spin
Fish Trout, brown, rainbow, cutthroat **Season** April-October
Water Smith, Missouri, Blackfoot, Yellowstone Rivers
Specialty Fly fishing float trips **Aircraft** Helicopters
Boats River sleds, canoes, McKenzies, rafts **Tackle Supplied** Fly
Experience 7 years **Rates** day: $195 week: $950 1/2 day: $175

PASQUALE, RICK-R + L FLY FISHING OUTFITTERS (406) 453-3301
Address 825 8th Ave South, Great Falls, MT 59405
Airport Great Falls 3 **Accommodations** Great Falls
Operation Outfitter, tackle shop **Type of Fishing** Fly **Boats** Canoe, rafts
Fish Trout **Season** May-November **Water** Missouri, Smith Rivers
Specialty Fly fishing only, day trips on Missouri, overnights on Smith
Experience 5 years **Rates** day: $200, two-day overnight: $450

HAMILTON, MONTANA

RAINBOLT, WYNN M. (406) 363-4159
Address SW 770 Gold Creek Loop, Hamilton, MT 59840
Airport Missoula 50m **Accommodations** Hamilton 10m
Operation Outfitter **Fish** Trout **Season** April-Oct
Water Bitterroot, Big Hole, Yellowstone Rivers, Bob Marshall Wilderness
Specialty Fly fishing- float or walking trips **Type of Fishing** Fly
Boats McKenzies, rafts, outboard **Tackle Supplied** Fly
Experience 11 years **Rates** day: $175 1/2 day: $125

RENNAKER, DWAIN (406) 363-1829
Address SE 1835 Old Darby Road, Hamilton, MT 59840
Airport Missoula 50m **Accommodations** Hamilton 10m
Operation Outfitter **Type of Fishing** Fly, spin, baitcasting
Fish Rainbow, cutthroat, brown, brook **Season** July-December
Water Elk, El Capitan, Grizzly, Bell Lakes **Boats** Rafts
Specialty Mountain lake fishing, canyon creeks
Experience 25 years **Rates** week: $700/person

HARDIN, MONTANA

KELLY, G. ALAN-EAGLE OUTFITTERS (406) 665-3799
Address P.O. Box 492, Hardin, MT 59034

Airport Billings 50m **Accommodations** On premises
Operation Outfitter, lodge **Type of Fishing** Fly, spin
Fish Rainbow, brown **Season** Year-round **Water** Bighorn River
Specialty River float trips **Boats** McKenzies, river sleds
Experience 4 years **Rates** day: $350

HELENA, MONTANA

BAY, MIKE (406) 442-9671
Address 31 Division Street, Helena, MT 59601
Airport Helena **Accommodations** Helena
Operation Outfitter **Type of Fishing** Fly, spin
Fish Brown, rainbow, cutthroat, brook **Season** May-Nov
Water Smith, Missouri, Yellowstone, Blackfoot Rivers
Specialty Fly fishing trips **Boats** McKenzies, rafts **Tackle Supplied** Fly
Experience 12 years **Rates** day: $180 week: $1050

O'LOONEY, DOUGLAS-MONTANA FLY GOODS CO. (406) 442-2630
Address 330 North Jackson, Helena, MT 59601
Airport Helena **Accommodations** Helena
Operation Outfitter, tackle shop **Type of Fishing** Fly **Tackle Supplied** Fly
Fish Rainbow, cutthroat, brown, grayling **Season** Year-round
Water Missouri River, Clark's Fork and headwaters **Boats** McKenzies, rafts
Specialty Fly fishing float and wading trips-catch and release
Experience 7 years **Rates** day: $125-175

TEDESCO, FRED-WESTERN RIVERS FLY SHOP (406) 443-7431
Address 120 East 6th Avenue, Helena, MT 59601
Airport Helena **Accommodations** Helena
Operation Outfitter, tackle shop **Type of Fishing** Fly, spin
Fish Rainbow, brown, cutthroat, brook **Season** February-December
Water Smith, Missouri, Madison, Yellowstone Rivers **Boats** McKenzies, rafts
Specialty Fly fishing floats trips **Tackle Supplied** Fly, spin
Experience 14 years **Rates** day: $125-175

HELMVILLE, MONTANA

ANDERSON, JAMES L. (406) 793-5675
Address Rural Route, Helmville, MT 59843
Airport Missoula 65m **Accommodations** Missoula 65m
Operation Outfitter **Type of Fishing** Fly
Fish Cutthroat, Dolly Varden **Season** June-November
Water Flathead River, Young's, Danaher Creeks
Experience 20 years **Rates** day $160 week: $1120

HERON, MONTANA

WILLIS, RUS (406) 847-5523
Address Star Route 1 Box 16, Heron, MT 59844

Airport Missoula 150m **Accommodations** Noxon 20m
Operation Outfitter **Type of Fishing** Fly, spin
Fish Cutthroat, rainbow, brown, brook **Season** June-August
Water Bull River, Clark Fork, Kootenai **Boats** Canoes
Specialty Fly fishing float trips **Tackle Supplied** Fly, spin
Experience 8 years **Rates** day:$150 1/2 day: $75

HUNGRY HORSE, MONTANA

LEE, EUGENE P.-WILDERNESS RANCH AND LODGE (406) 837-6749
Address Box 391, Hungry Horse, MT 59919
Airport Kalispell 85m **Accommodations** On premises
Operation Guide, outfitter, lodge **Type of Fishing** Fly, spin
Fish Cutthroat, Dolly Varden **Season** July-August
Water S. Fork of Flathead River and Lake **Aircraft** Landplane
Specialty Dry fly fishing floating or wading **Boats** Rafts
Experience 30 years **Rates** day: $125

KALISPELL, MONTANA

CURTISS, RON-CURTISS OUTFITTERS (406) 257-6215
Address 326 Bench Drive, Kalispell, MT 59901
Airport Kalispell **Accommodations** On premises
Operation Outfitter **Fish** Cutthroat, Dolly Varden **Season** July-Aug
Water South Fork of the Flathead, Bob Marshall Wilderness area
Specialty Fly fishing float trips **Boats** Rafts **Type of Fishing** Fly, spin
Experience 17 years **Rates** $950/person/6 days
Guide's Notes: Upper South Fork of the Flathead River. This river rises and
flows within the Bob Marshall Wilderness Area. There are no access roads and
therefore the only way to reach this river is to pack over and into the mountains
the river runs through. These unique circumstances make the South Fork
America's most inaccessable and unchanged river.

The South Fork is alive with native cutthroat trout, and also has Dolly Varden
trout and whitefish. Any good trout tackle will take them, but it is surely a fly
fisherman's dream! The upper river flows past wide gravel bars and through
boulder-strewn chutes. Continuing down, the river valley narrows and the river
forms white water riffles and cascades down into deep emerald green pools.
The South Fork's water is clear and cold, and you will see a multitude of fish
and colored rocks on the bottom of pools that stand over twenty feet deep.

Fishing on the South Fork is primarily for cutthroat trout in the ten to eighteen
inch class, with a few fish running larger. There is also fishing for whitefish
and Dolly Varden trout that can go up to ten pounds. The cutthroat trout readily
take dry flies; some favorite patterns are Royal, Wulff, Goofus Bug, Irresistible,
Brown Wulff, Gray Wulff, Joe's Hopper, Humpies and similar flies in sizes 8
and 10. An excellent fly that can be fished either wet or dry is the Muddler
Minnow in size 4 or 6. Light weight fly rods are normally used and tippets of
about 8' and four pound test work well.

Spin fisherman will find that light action rods work well with about four pound line. Favorite lures are all Mepps type spinners in 0 or 1, and small spoons.

Our fishing is excellent. It is seldom that anyone fails to catch twenty trout a day and three times that many is not unusual. The South Fork is not a white water river, although it has a few exciting chutes. Most of it flows along at an ideal pace for fishing, relaxing and enjoying the water and surrounding scenery. During the entire trip expect to see all kinds of wildlife including elk, moose, deer, mountain goat, and eagles, as well as many smaller birds and animals.

LEWISTOWN, MONTANA

SNYDER, ELDON AND BARB-DN & 3 OUTFITTERS (406) 538-8591
Address R.R. 1, Box 1602, Lewistown, MT 59457
Airport Lewistown **Accommodations** Lewistown
Operation Outfitter **Type of Fishing** All **Specialty** Fly fishing
Fish Rainbow, cutthroat, native trout, paddlefish **Season** June-Sept
Water Judith, Missouri Rivers, Spring Creek, East Fork Dam
Experience 21 years **Rates** day: $80/person

LIMA, MONTANA

RUSH, KEITH-LAKEVIEW GUEST RANCH (406) 276-3300
Address Monida Star Route, Lima, MT 59739
Airport West Yellowstone 45m **Accommodations** On premises
Operation Outfitter, tackle shop, lodge **Type of Fishing** Fly, spin
Fish Rainbow, brown, brook, cutthroat **Season** Year-round
Water Beaverhead, Big Hole, Madison, Gallatin Rivers
Specialty High mountain lake pack-in fishing trips
Boats Rowboats, canoes, rafts **Experience** 36 years **Rates** varies

LINCOLN, MONTANA

HOEFFNER, KENNY-K LAZY THREE RANCH (406) 362-4258
Address Box 267, Lincoln, MT 59639
Airport Helena 60m **Accommodations** On premises
Operation Guide, outfitter, lodge, camp **Type of Fishing** Fly
Fish Rainbow, cutthroat, brook **Season** July-Sept **Boats** Rafts
Water Blackfoot, Flathead, Sun Rivers **Tackle Supplied** Fly, spin
Specialty Pack-trips fishing of mountain streams and lakes
Experience 19 years **Rates** day: $80/person

LIVINGSTON, MONTANA

ANDERSON, GEORGE-YELLOWSTONE ANGLER (406) 222-7130
Address Route 89 South, P.O. Box 660, Dept. C, Livingston, MT 59047

Airport Bozeman 35m **Accommodations** Livingston
Operation Outfitter, tackle shop **Type of Fishing** Fly **Boats** McKenzies
Fish Brown, rainbow, cutthroat **Season** March-November
Water Yellowstone, Bighorn, Madison Rivers, Spring Creek
Specialty Fly fishing float and wading trips **Tackle Supplied** Fly
Experience 15 years **Rates** day: $175
Guide's Notes: The Livingston Spring Creeks The "springs creeks" in the Livingston Area are spring-fed, limestone type meadow streams that flow into the Yellowstone River eight miles south of Livingston. These streams are relatively short in overall length and are formed entirely by natural springs. They are not affected by any normal spring runoff as are our "freestone" streams.

Habitat and food conditions are outstanding, and these streams are able to support fantastic numbers of wild trout. Access is limited by the landowners, who charge a fee and limit the number of rods per day so that the streams are not overcrowded.

The fishing can be so good that one doesn't have to cover a lot of water to find good fish. When the heavy insect hatches occur, it is not uncommon to see dozens of rising trout within casting distance. People have been known to fish one pool or riffle for hours at a time, and be constantly into good fish! Only catch-and-release fly fishing is permitted. These streams offer some of the finest small stream trout fishing to be found anywhere in the world today.

Be sure to make your reservations as early as possible since the prime time on these streams gets booked very early, as much as 6-12 months in advance. You can make these reservations by calling direct.

Armstrong Spring Creek (the O'Hair Ranch) - Call Mrs. Allyn O'Hair (406) 222-2979. 10 rods allowed per day. Rod fee $30

DePuy's Spring Creek - Call Mrs. Warren DePuy (406) 222-0221. 10 rods allowed per day. Rod fee $30 per day.

Nelson's Spring Creek - Call Mrs. Edwin Nelson (406) 222-2159. 5-6 rods allowed per day. Rod fee $30 per day.

People always ask me which is the best stream, and it seems like I'm hedging when I say I think they are all great fishing. These streams offer different types of fishing and water, but all are excellent. They get basically the same hatches of insects throughout the season.

Armstrong Spring Creek is perhaps the easiest to fish because of its wide, shallow riffles and pools. Most of the fish caught are rainbows with many in the 14-18 inch class. A few good sized browns are present but not often caught. There are about 1-1/2 miles of fishable water on Armstrong creek, and the scenery, with the Absaroka mountains as a backdrop, is spectacular. All the spring creeks share this magnificent scenery.

Armstrong Spring Creek on both the O'Hair and DePuy property is now open year round and only a partial rate of $15 is charged in the "off season" from November 1st to May 1st. During February, March and April we have many mild days when the temperature is up in the 40's and 50's and the fishing then can be excellent. The stream temperature never drops below 55 degrees so the fish are active and feed steadily throughout the winter and spring. There are few fishermen around before the 1st of June so chances are you'll have the stream to yourself during these late winter and spring months.

De Puy's Spring Creek is actually the lower portion of Armstrong creek before it runs into the Yellowstone River. There is more water available than on the O'Hair ranch, some of which includes ponds and sloughs that harbor some BIG trout. There is a good amount of stream, much of which is easy fishing although some is deep and narrow and more difficult to fish. In certain stretches you will find some more browns, many over 2 pounds. In general most of the fish caught are rainbows, similar to the fish found upstream on O'Hair's. There are also many cutthroats in the lower reaches of DePuy's and the creek does get a spawning run of cutthroats from the Yellowstone in late June and July. There are approximately 3 miles of fishable water on DePuy's. You will see lots of waterfowl here including ducks, geese, and swans. Beaver and muskrat are common.

Nelson's Spring Creek is a real classic, and favored by many of the best fly fishermen. There is perhaps 3/4 of a mile of water available to fish, but an awful lot of good big trout are packed into this stretch. The fishing is more difficult with flatter pools that demand the utmost in delicate presentation, fine tippets, and small flies. Lots of rainbows in the 16 to 18 inch class with some larger. There are always a few big fish around, and they are tough to catch. Browns and cutthroats are present in fair numbers and there is some influx of spawning cutthroats from the Yellowstone in July. Browns and rainbows from the Yellowstone rarely run into the spring creeks to spawn but do spawn effectively in the main river and side channels.

Hatches March and April provide some heavy hatches of small dark blue dun #18-20 that is a Baetis. The same fly hatches again in October and November. Few hatches occur in late May when the season opens but the fish are easy to catch on nymphs. In mid June we start to see good hatches of the larger olive dun mayflies, size 16-18. These are the Ephemerella Infrequens, Inermis etc. We also see a variety of smaller blue wing olives, sizes 18-24, which are mostly Baetis. During July and August we get strong hatches of a cream colored Baetis that provides some of the best dry fly fishing all year. A Light Cahill is a good match in size 18-20. Midge hatches occur nearly all the time and many good fish feed on midges even though there are larger mayflies on the water. Prime time for dry fly fishing is mid June through mid August. Hatches continue on into the fall, but are of less intensity and are more sporadic than during this prime time period.

Nymph fishermen should concentrate on gray, olive, and brownish mayfly nymphs in sizes 16-22. Midge larva and pupa imitations are deadly. There are great numbers of scuds and sowbugs in the spring creeks, and their imitations are very effective especially at times when there are very few insect hatches. Although the Yellowstone has great hatches of stoneflies and caddis early in the season, you will see very few of these insects on the spring creeks. Caddis are present at times early in the season, but are not usually present in numbers great enough to interest the fish. Terrestrials like ants catch a lot of trout, but hoppers are not very effective with a few exceptions along grassy banks when the wind is blowing a gale.

Author's Notes: *In a relatively short time, George Anderson has built a reputation as one of the top outfitters and fly shops in the U.S. He has written articles for* FLY FISHERMAN *and other fly fishing publications, and gives talks and seminars to fly fishing clubs across the country.*

George recently moved his fly shop to a brand new facility just outside Livingston on the main road to Yellowstone Park. Take time to stop by when you are in the area.

BAILEY, JOHN-DAN BAILEY'S (406) 222-1673
Address 209 West Park Street, Livingston, MT 59047
Airport Bozeman 35m **Accommodations** Livingston **Operation** Outfitter
Fish Brown, rainbow, cutthroat **Season** Year-round **Type of Fishing** Fly
Water Yellowstone, Missouri, Madison, Gallatin Rivers **Boats** McKenzies
Specialty Fly fishing float trips and stream fishing **Tackle Supplied** Fly
Experience 10 years **Rates** day: $165
Author's Notes: The famous Dan Bailey's in Livingston is now owned and operated by Dan's son, John, who carries on in the Dan Bailey's tradition of excellence. Their mail order catalog has one of the best selections of flies available.

BUDESKI, GENE AND LINDA (406) 222-7536
Address Box 45, Livingston, MT 59047
Airport Bozeman 45m **Accommodations** Livingston 10m
Operation Outfitter **Type of Fishing** Fly, spin, baitcasting
Fish Trout **Season** June-November **Boats** McKenzies
Water Yellowstone, Shields, Madison, Smith Rivers
Specialty Fly float trips and pack-in mountain lake fishing
Experience 10 years **Rates** day: $150 week: $800 1/2 day: $100

FRANCIS, JIM (406) 222-3637
Address Route 38 Box 2213, Livingston, MT 59047
Airport Bozeman 25m **Accommodations** Livingston 10m
Operation Outfitter **Type of Fishing** Fly **Fish** Trout **Season** May-Nov
Water Yellowstone, Missouri, Madison Rivers, Armstrong Creek
Specialty Fly fishing float trips **Boats** McKenzies **Tackle Supplied** Fly
Experience 15 years **Rates** day: $165 1/2 day: $100

GAMBLE, DAVID B. (406) 333-4944, 222-2734
Address Route 38 Box 2249, Livingston, MT 59047
Airport Bozeman 25m **Accommodations** Livingston 10m
Operation Outfitter **Type of Fishing** Fly, spin **Tackle Supplied** Fly, spin
Fish Rainbow, brown, brook, cutthroat **Season** May-November
Water Yellowstone, Madison Rivers, private lakes
Specialty Fly fishing float trips and lake fishing **Boats** McKenzies
Experience 5 years **Rates** day: $145 week: $100

LAHREN, LARRY-CAYUSE OUTFITTERS (406) 222-3168
Address Box 1218, Livingston, MT 59047
Airport Bozeman 35m **Accommodations** Bozeman 35m
Operation Guide, outfitter **Type of Fishing** All **Boats** Rowboats
Fish Cutthroat, brown, rainbow **Season** May-November
Water Yellowstone, Little Mission, West Boulder Rivers

Specialty River fly fishing float trips **Tackle Supplied** All
Experience 10 years **Rates** day: $150 week: $500 1/2 day: $75
Guide's Notes: We also offer pack trips to archaeological sites in the Yellowstone Valley.

RICE, PAUL (406) 222-1522
Address Route 85 Box 4194, Livingston, MT 59047
Airport Bozeman 35m **Accommodations** Livingston
Operation Guide **Fish** Trout **Season** March-Nov
Water Yellowstone, Madison, Shields, Bighorn Rivers
Specialty Fly and spin fishing float trips **Type of Fishing** Fly, spin
Boats McKenzies, canoes **Tackle Supplied** Fly, spin
Experience 3 years **Rates** varies

TRAVIS, THOMAS (406) 222-0783
Address P.O. Box 1320, 914 East Clark, Livingston, MT 59047
Airport Bozeman 35m **Accommodations** Livingston
Operation Outfitter **Type of Fishing** Fly, spin
Fish Brown, rainbow, cutthroat, brook **Season** March-November
Water Yellowstone, Madison, Bighorn, Missouri Rivers
Specialty Fly or spin fishing float trips **Tackle Supplied** Fly, spin
Boats Canoes, bass boats, McKenzies, rafts, tubes
Experience 15 years **Rates** day: $170 week: $1190

WILLIAMS, DON A. (406) 222-1386
Address Box 2, Billman and Miller Lane, Livingston, MT 59047
Airport Bozeman 35m **Accommodations** Livingston
Operation Guide, outfitter **Type of Fishing** Fly **Tackle Supplied** Fly
Fish Rainbow, brown, cutthroat, brook **Season** Year-round
Water Yellowstone, Madison, Missouri Rivers, Spring Creeks
Specialty Fly fishing float or shore fishing trips **Boats** McKenzies
Experience 28 years **Rates** day: $160

McLEOD, MONTANA

JARRETT, BILL-HOWLEY MOUNTAIN GUEST RANCH (406) 932-5791
Address Box 4, McLeod, MT 59052
Airport Billings 125m **Accommodations** On premises
Operation Outfitter, guest ranch **Type of Fishing** All
Fish Cutthroat, rainbow, german brown **Season** June-September
Water Boulder, Yellowstone Rivers, Absuroka Lakes
Specialty Fly fishing **Boats** Rafts **Tackle Supplied** Fly, spin
Experience 22 years **Rates** week: $950

REID, CHUCK-BURNT LEATHER RANCH (406) 932-6155
Address West Boulder Rd, McLeod, MT 59052
Airport Bozeman 56m **Accommodations** On premises

Operation Guide, outfitter, ranch **Type of Fishing** Fly
Fish Brown, rainbow, cutthroat **Season** May-October
Water West Boulder River, Alpine, Hays, Culver Lakes
Specialty Fly fishing wading the West Boulder RIver
Experience 14 years **Rates** week: $1500

MISSOULA, MONTANA

ANDERSON, RICHARD C.-STREAMSIDE ANGLERS (406) 728-1085
Address 501 South Orange Street, Missoula, MT 59801
Airport Missoula **Accommodations** Missoula
Operation Outfitter, tackle shop **Type of Fishing** Fly
Fish Trout (all species) **Season** May-Oct **Tackle Supplied** Fly
Water Rock Creek, Smith, Bitterroot, Blackfoot Rivers
Specialty Fly fishing float trips and overnights **Boats** Rafts
Experience 12 years **Rates** day: $150

MANN, CARL-THE MONTANA FISHERMAN (406) 721-6839
Address 3100 Brooks, Missoula, MT 59801
Airport Missoula **Accommodations** Missoula
Operation Outfitter, tackle shop **Type of Fishing** All
Fish Rainbow, brown, lake trout **Season** April-October
Water Clark Fork, Bitterroot, Blackfoot Rivers, Flathead Lake
Specialty River fly float fishing and lake trout trolling
Boats Rafts, 16' Micro Crafts **Tackle Supplied** All
Experience 6 years **Rates** day: $150-250
Author's Notes: Carl has a well known taxidermy business in addition to his guide service. He has a very good reputation in both fields.

NICHOLS, JERRY R.-WESTERN WATERS (406) 728-5885
Address 333 Knowles Road, Missoula, MT 59801
Airport Missoula **Accommodations** Missoula
Operation Guide, outfitter **Type of Fishing** Fly, spin **Tackle Supplied** All
Fish Rainbow, cutthroat, brown, paddle fish**Season** March-Nov.
Water Clark Fork, Madison, Smith, Big Hole, Beaverhead Rivers
Specialty Day or extended fly or spin fishing trips **Boats** McKenzies, rafts
Experience 10 years **Rates** day: $90 week: $500

NYE, MONTANA

MOART, STEVE & MIKE, DEWEY CHARVAT-MONTANA SCHOOL OF FLY FISHING (406) 328-6282
Address Montana School of Fishing, Box 467, Nye, MT 59061
Airport Logan 90m **Accommodations** On premises
Operation Outfitter, tackle shop, ranch **Type of Fishing** Fly
Fish Brown, rainbow, cutthroat, brook **Season** May-October
Water Yellowstone, Bighorn, Stillwater Rivers

Specialty Fly fishing schools, guided float and pack trips
Boats Canoes, McKenzies, rafts **Tackle Supplied** Fly
Experience 7 years **Rates** varies

OVANDO, MONTANA

HOOKER, JACK (406) 793-5666
Address White Tail Ranch, Ovando, MT 59854
Airport Missoula 70m **Accommodations** Lincoln 30m **Operation** Outfitter
Fish Cutthroat **Season** July-Aug **Specialty** Wilderness pack trips
Water Flathead, White, Danaher Rivers, Young's Creek **Type of Fishing** Fly
Experience 30 years **Rates** day: $100

PLAINS, MONTANA

KUESTER, ORVALL-ROCKY POINT OUTFITTERS (406) 826-3221
Address 837 Swamp Creek Road, Plains, MT 59859
Airport Missoula 85m **Accommodations** On premises
Operation Guide, outfitter, lodge **Type of Fishing** All **Boats** Rowboats, rafts
Fish Rainbow, cutthroat, hybrid and lake trout **Season** June-February
Water Clark Fork, Thompson Rivers, Flathead Lake **Specialty** Lake trolling
Experience 18 years **Rates** day: $120 week $700 1/2 day: $60

REXFORD, MONTANA

HAND, B.C."BARNEY"-KOOTENAI EXPEDITIONS (406) 296-2031
Address Box 117 Rondo Road, Rexford, MT 59930
Airport Kalispell 62m **Accommodations** On premises
Operation Outfitter, lodge **Type of Fishing** Fly, spin, troll **Boats** Rafts
Fish Rainbow, cutthroat, Dolly Varden **Season** June-Aug **Tackle Supplied** All
Water Kootenai, Flathead Rivers **Specialty** Fly or spin float fishing trips
Experience 14 years **Rates** day: $150 week: $900

SEELEY LAKE, MONTANA

BURNS, VIRGIL & BARB-BOB MARSHALL WILDERNESS RANCH (406) 745-4466
Address Seeley Lake, MT 59868
Airport Missoula 80m **Accommodations** On premises
Operation Outfitter, lodge **Type of Fishing** Fly, spin
Fish Cutthroat, rainbow, Dolly Varden **Season** June-Oct.
Water Bob Marshall Wilderness area lakes, rivers and streams
Specialty Fly fishing pack trips **Tackle Supplied** Fly
Experience 25 years **Rates** day: $200

Author's Notes: *The following is a quote from Jim Zumbo, Editor-at-large of*
OUTDOOR LIFE MAGAZINE:
> *"I've had the good fortune of knowing many outfitters, but Virgil and Barb*
> *rank at the very top. They know the outdoors, and they know how to please*
> *their clients."*

RICH, JACK AND C.B.-DOUBLE ARROW OUTFITTERS (406) 677-2317
Address Box 495, Seeley Lake, MT 59868
Airport Missoula 50m **Accommodations** On premises
Operation Outfitter, lodge**Type of Fishing** Fly, spin
Fish Cutthroat, Dolly Varden, rainbow, brown **Season** May-Sept.
Water South Fork of the Flathead, Blackfoot, Clearwater Rivers
Specialty Fly fishing pack trips and river rafting **Boats** Rafts
Experience 10 years, 40 years **Rates** day: $70-100

SHERIDAN, MONTANA

HUTCHISON, JACK D.-HUTCHISON'S ANGLING SUPPLIES (406) 842-5868
Address 310 South Main Street, Sheridan, MT 59749
Airport Butte 50m **Accommodations** Sheridan
Operation Outfitter, tackle shop **Type of Fishing** Fly, spin
Fish Brown, rainbow, brook, grayling **Season** May-November
Water Big Hole, Madison, Jefferson, Ruby, Beaverhead Rivers
Specialty Fly fishing float trips **Boats** McKenzies **Tackle Supplied** Fly, spin
Experience 20 years **Rates** day: $175 1/2 day: $130

NAISBITT, JOHN & STEVE SHIMEK-TOBACCO ROOT RANCH (406) 842-5655
Address Rt 1, Box 24, Sheridan, MT 59749
Airport Butte 50m **Accommodations** On premises
Operation Ranch, outfitter **Type of Fishing** Fly **Tackle Supplied** Fly
Fish Brown, rainbow, brook, cutthroat **Season** June-Oct.
Water Big Hole, Ruby, Madison, Beaverhead Rivers
Specialty Fly fishing and fly fishing floats **Boats** Rowboat
Experience 4 years **Rates** day: $200

ST. IGNATIUS, MONTANA

RUGG, RAY (406) 745-4160
Address Route 1 Box 50-G, St. Ignatius, MT 59865
Airport Missoula 45m **Accommodations** St. Ignatius
Operation Outfitter **Type of Fishing** All **Season** July-Aug
Fish Rainbow, cutthroat, brook, golden **Specialty** Mountain lake pack trips
Water Lakes of Selway-Bitterroot area and Great Burn Unit area
Experience 15 years **Rates** week: $1000/2 people

ST. REGIS, MONTANA

SIMONS, JACK (406) 649-2329
Address Star Route Box 450, St. Regis, MT 59866
Airport Missoula 72m **Accommodations** St. Regis
Operation Outfitter, guide **Type of Fishing** All
Fish Rainbow, brook, cutthroat **Season** Year-round
Water Clark's Fork River, Moore, Heart, Hub Lakes
Specialty Float trips on the Clark's Fork River
Boats Rowboats, river sleds **Tackle Supplied** All
Experience 32 years **Rates** 4 hours: $25/person

STANFORD, MONTANA

PRIDE, MERRITT (406) 566-2486, 646-9677
Address Box 15, Stanford, MT 59479
Airport West Yellowstone 12m **Accommodations** West Yellowstone 12m
Operation Outfitter **Type of Fishing** Fly, spin **Tackle Supplied** Fly, spin
Fish Cutthroat, golden trout **Season** July-Sept **Specialty** Fly fishing
Water Yellowstone Park, Lee Metcalf Wilderness area
Experience 8 years **Rates** week: $850/person

STEVENSVILLE, MONTANA

LAMBERSON, BOB (406) 777-5969
Address P.O. Box 25, Stevensville, MT 59870
Airport Missoula 35m **Accommodations** Hamilton 20m
Operation Outfitter **Type of Fishing** Fly, spin, baitcasting
Fish Brook, cutthroat, rainbow **Season** March-August
Water Bitterroot area mountain lakes and streams
Specialty Lake fly and spin fishing
Experience 13 years **Rates** day: $136 (minimum 5 days)

THOMPSON FALLS, MONTANA

HOLDEN, ANTHONY (406) 827-4752 (Ask for Tom Albertson)
Address P.O. Box 754, Thompson Falls, MT 59873
Airport Missoula 100m **Accommodations** Rimrock 12m
Operation Outfitter **Fish** Trout, bass, pike, salmon
Water Clark's Fork, Thompson Rivers, Lake Kocawusa
Specialty Pack in to high lakes for trout **Season** Year-round
Boats Rowboats, canoes, bass boats, rafts **Type of Fishing** All
Experience 7 years **Rates** day: $200 week: $1400 1/2 day: $100

THREE FORKS, MONTANA

ANDERSON, ALLAN L. (406) 285-3488
Address RR 1 Boz 192, Three Forks, MT 59752
Airport Bozeman 30m **Accommodations** Three Forks
Operation Outfitter **Fish** Brown, rainbow **Season** June-Sept
Water Missouri, Jefferson, Madison, Yellowstone Rivers
Specialty Spin & fly fishing float trips **Type of Fishing** Fly, spin
Boats McKenzies, canoes **Tackle Supplied** Fly, spin
Experience 7 years **Rates** day: $150 week:$700 1/2day: $100

TOWNSEND, MONTANA

ANDERSON, AUDIE (406) 266-3095
Address Box 622, Townsend, MT 59644
Airport Helena 35m **Accommodations** Townsend
Operation Outfitter **Type of Fishing** Fly, spin, baitcast
Fish Cutthroat, brook **Season** September-December
Water Edith, Hidden, Groce Lakes, Birch Creek
Specialty Guided back country pack trips
Experience 4 years **Rates** day: $125 week $700

TROY, MONTANA

DARE, CLIFFORD E. (406) 295-4487
Address RR #2, Troy, MT 59935
Airport Kalispell 100m **Accommodations** Troy
Operation Outfitter **Type of Fishing** Fly, spin
Fish Rainbow, cutthroat, brook, char, whitefish **Season** April-Oct.
Water Kootenai, Bull, Yaak Rivers, Lake Creek **Boats** McKenzies
Specialty Fly fishing float trips **Tackle Supplied** Fly, spin, baitcast
Experience 2 years **Rates** day: $150 1/2 day: $100

JENSON, HOLGER-FIX RANCH (406) 295-5159
Address Route 1, (Yaak), Troy, MT 59935
Airport Kalispell 100m **Accommodations** On premises
Operation Outfitter, ranch **Type of Fishing** All
Fish Cutthroat, rainbow, brook, kokanee salmon **Season** May-Sept
Water Yaak, Kootenai Rivers, Koocanusa, Burke Lakes
Specialty Fly and spin fishing rivers and alpine lakes
Boats Rowboats, river sleds, canoe **Tackle Supplied** All
Experience 7 years **Rates** day: $400

THOMPSON, ALEX (406) 295-4228
Address Route 2, Troy, MT 59935
Airport Kalispell 100m **Accommodations** Troy

Operation Outfitter **Type of Fishing** Fly, baitcast, troll
Fish Cutthroat, trout **Season** Year-round **Boats** Rowboats
Water Various area lakes, rivers and streams
Specialty Fly fishing and lake trolling **Tackle Supplied** Baitcast
Experience 10 years **Rates** day: $110 week: $750 1/2 day: $55

TWIN BRIDGES, MONTANA

WALDIE, SCOTT-FOUR RIVERS FISHING CO. (406) 684-5651
Address 205 South Main Street, Twin Bridges, MT 59754
Airport Butte 40m **Accommodations** Twin Bridges
Operation Guide, ranch **Type of Fishing** Fly
Fish Brown, rainbow **Season** May-Oct **Tackle Supplied** Fly
Water Big Hole, Beaverhead, Madison, Jefferson Rivers
Specialty Fly fishing float trips **Boats** McKenzies, rafts
Experience 14 years **Rates** day: $200
Guide's Notes: Nestled in the Ruby Valley at the foot of the Tobacco Root Mountain, Twin Bridges is host to four outstanding trout streams. The Ruby River joins the Beaverhead just south of town, while the waters of the Big Hole and Beaverhead merge north of Twin Bridges to form the Jefferson. Although close to one another geographically, each river offers a unique fly fishing experience.

The **Big Hole** is a blue-ribbon trout stream affording some of the best dry fly fishing available. The season kicks off in mid-June with the fabled salmon fly hatch. Mayfly, caddis and hoppers continue to produce excellent surface action into October.

The meandering **Beaverhead River** also has its moments in the dry fly world with high numbers of caddis and the unique crane fly hatch. Streamers and wet flies, however, take the most fish from beneath the Beaverhead's deep willow banks.

The **Ruby** offers prime brown trout habitat in its lower reaches and large populations of rainbow trout above the Ruby Reservoir. The upper river is excellent for both dry fly purists and the beginning fly fisherman.

The **Jefferson** is little changed from the time Lewis and Clark first journeyed its cottonwood-lined banks and gazed at the surrounding peaks. Beyond the spectacular scenery, float fishing on the Jefferson offers the angler a chance to catch some of the biggest brown trout in the area. Streamers and rubber-leg nymphs will probably be the patterns of choice.

If I may be permitted to paraphrase Dickens, rivers have their best of times and they have their worst of times. The following is a brief summary of those rivers that surround Four Rivers Fishing Company.

Big Hole River--The Big Hole kicks off the fishing season in our part of Southwestern Montana in mid-June with the Salmon fly hatch. While the quality of the fishing at this time can be spectacular, its excellence is dependent on unpredictable weather and water conditions. I hate to see anglers plan their vacations around a variable. If you wish to take the risk, the best dates in recent years are the fifteenth through the twenty-second. After the third week of June, the fishing slows for a few days. Then the river comes alive again and plays host to the finest dry fly fishing to be found anywhere and stays that way until the last week of July. The patterns of choice will be Golden Stones, Caddis, Royal Wulffs, and Royal Humpies.

August has its moments as the "hoppers" are out by the millions but this is certainly the river's slowest month. The guides then switch allegiance to the Madison and the Beaverhead.

The Madison--The Madison's season starts during the first ten days of July with the salmon fly hatch, a much more predictable hatch than the one on the Big Hole. It fishes well through July, but is probably at its dry fly best throughout August. Again, like the Big Hole and all other freestone streams, Caddis, Stone fly nymphs and attractor patterns will be the best bets.

The Beaverhead--Although there can be some fine fishing in late June and July, the river doesn't really come into its own until August when it is possible to take the really large fish with dry flies. But even amid all the intense Caddis activity, most of the fish are taken out from beneath the willows with rubber-legged patterns and large streamers.

The Jefferson--The "Jeff" unfortunately is the victim of return irrigation water from the lower Beaverhead and Ruby. To say the river is spotty would paint a rather optimistic picture. However, over the last six years, my best days of fishing have been on the Jefferson but that comes from having the privilege of living near by. Hopefully, during your stay, the river will clear and you will witness some fishing that will long be remembered.

The Ruby--The upper Ruby is not usually fishable until mid to late July depending on the run-off. It is an excellent stream for the beginner as the fish are numerous and eager. The lower Ruby is unpredictable because the outflows of Ruby Reservoir can muddy it overnight and it is a stream that is a long time clearing. But it can be an excellent fishery using small streamers and Caddis. Four Rivers works as an agent with several of the Ranchers who own prime stretches of the river. The rod fee is twenty dollars and worth every nickel. These are catch and release waters and limited to four fishermen a day.

As you have noticed, I have not discussed fall fishing on any of these rivers and this is because they all fall under the heading of "excellent." Though each of our local streams have weeks throughout the summer months where they are at their peak, they all fish consistently well in autumn. The Beaverhead is the only exception as the months of September and October are its best times.

Author's Notes: Located at the confluence of 4 of the finest fishing rivers in the nation, Scott Waldie operates an excellent tackle shop and outfitter service.

VICTOR, MONTANA

ODELL, DAVE-ANGLERS AFLOAT (406) 642-3103
Address 2620 Smith Ck Ln, Victor, MT 59875
Airport Missoula 30m **Accommodations** Hamilton 12m
Operation Outfitter **Type of Fishing** Fly **Tackle Supplied** Fly
Fish Rainbow, brown, cutthroat, brook **Season** March-Nov
Water Bitterroot, Blackfoot, Clark Fork Rivers, Rock Creek
Specialty Fly fishing float trips with dry flies **Boats** Rafts
Experience 7 years **Rates** day: $160 1/2 day: $140

Guide's Notes: The Rivers We Fish--Bitterroot--Flowing down from the snow-capped peaks of the Selway-Bitterroot and Anaconda-Pintlar wilderness areas, this crystal clear stream has everything. Within its 80 miles of wooded floodplain are a maze of creeks, springs, braided channels and backwater sloughs that offer the angler an endless variety of fishing opportunities. The Bitterroot's east and west forks are also outstanding fisheries. Dependable insect hatches and gin-clear water result in superb flyfishing for fish up to four pounds, with a possible chance at even larger browns. The Bitterroot is one of the few rivers where trout can be caught on dry flies during all four seasons. Trout will often rise to artificials even when there is no hatch. This is our home river, and our intimate knowledge of its fish and wetlands assures you of access to some of Montana's best flyfishing of the Bitterroot throughout the year.

Rock Creek--Swift, narrow and rocky, this blue ribbon stream cuts an impressive canyon through heavily forested mountains on its fifty mile journey to the Clark Fork. Rock Creek is the crown jewel of special management trout waters in western Montana. A twelve mile section for catch and release, and other creel restrictions, have resulted in a trout population explosion. We know of no other stream in Montana that can equal the flyfishing thrills and non-stop excitement of our Rock Creek floats.

Blackfoot--Wild and free flowing, the scenic Blackfoot is a photographer's delight. This majestic river flows through open ranchland and box canyons with sheer cliffs and colorful walls. Rock-filled rapids, emerald pools and swift runs give the Blackfoot a character all of its own. Some fine summer fishing exists on the main river and many of the clear side streams. Sightings of bald eagles, bear and deer add to the excitement of your trip through this wild country.

Clark Fork--The Clark Fork of the Columbia, Montana's largest river, is a real sleeper. Along its length, almost every conceivable type of fishing water exists. Below Missoula, the lower river resembles the mighty Yellowstone in size, but has little fishing pressure. Lunker rainbows over four pounds live in the massive slickwater pools of the lower river. Thrill seekers should explore the Alberton Gorge, which provides a unique combination of whitewater rapids, fantastic geologic scenery and good fishing. Streamer fishermen in search of wily browns will find the meandering willowlined banks above Missoula to their liking.

When to Come

Spring: The first good fishing of the year occurs before the spring runoff in March and April. This is usually the best time of year to land a trophy-size brown. Although the weather can be temperamental at times, the fishing is great! Dry fly fisherman will delight in the progression of stonefly, mayfly and caddis hatches that occur. If you are one of those anxious anglers who can't wait for the summer season, this is the time for you.

Summer: Our peak season begins in June with the arrival of the famous salmonfly hatch on Rock Creek and other streams. Every angler should have the chance to witness this miraculous hatch of America's largest aquatic insects.

July produces some of the year's best fishing. Streams are dropping and clearing and and insect hatches are prolific. Heavy concentrations of golden stoneflies, green drakes and caddisflies often carpet the water simultaneously, and large trout feed on the surface with reckless abandon. Fishing on the Bitterroot and Rock Creek is red hot.

By August, all western Montana Rivers are clear and wadable. The water temperature is good for swimming and the weather is sunny and dry. Hoppers and other terrestrial imitations work well on most rivers, particularly the Blackfoot and upper Bitterroot. The spruce moth hatch on Rock Creek provides some unbelievable dry fly action.

Fall: Fall is a time for solitude, dazzling gold colors and superb fishing. The first cold fronts in early September set off a series of mayfly hatches that continue into November. Pods of hungry rainbows and large spawning browns fatten themselves for winter on scores of these tiny insects. Serious anglers will appreciate the challenge and rewards of stalking for dimpling trout with a delicate dry-fly. Fall fishing can also be combined with hunting for a total sporting experience. Some of the largest rainbows of the season are landed during this time on the Bitterroot and lower Clark Fork Rivers.

WEST YELLOWSTONE, MONTANA

Author's Notes: Trout fishing in Southwest Montana is considered to be some of the finest in the world. The area is sometimes referred to as the Golden Triangle because of the large number of blue ribbon streams and excellent lakes located there. The area is served during the summer months by scheduled airlines into West Yellowstone located at the western entrance to Yellowstone National Park and by year-round connections available into Bozeman, Montana, located 70 miles north of Yellowstone Park. Other important towns in the general area which offer lodging, guide service, and tackle shops are Ennis, Twin Bridges, Dillon, Livingston, Gardiner MT, and Jackson Hole, WY.

HULL, DAN & BRAD RICHEY-MADISON RIVER OUTFITTERS (406) 646-9644
Address P.O. Box 1106, 112 Canyon, Dept. M, West Yellowstone, MT 59758
Airport West Yellowstone **Accommodations** West Yellowstone
Operation Outfitter, tackle shop **Type of Fishing** Fly
Fish Rainbow, brown, cutthroat **Season** May-Oct **Tackle Supplied** Fly
Water Madison, Bighorn, Yellowstone Park, Big Hole, Gallatin, Yellowstone
Specialty Fly fishing float and wade trips **Boats** McKenzies
Experience 12 years **Rates** day: $160-wade/$180-float
Author's Notes: Brad Richey and Dan Hull's shop is one of the finest in the state. A stop here is recommended when you're in the area. Their guide services, I am told, are on a par with the rest of their operation.

JACKLIN, BOB-JACKLIN'S FLY SHOP (406) 646-7336
Address 105 Yellowstone Avenue, West Yellowstone, MT 59758
Airport West Yellowstone **Accommodations** West Yellowstone
Operation Outfitter, tackle shop **Type of Fishing** Fly
Fish Brown, rainbow, cutthroat, brook **Season** Year-round
Water Madison, Big Hole, Missouri Rivers, Henry's Fork (ID)
Specialty Fly fishing float trips and wade trips
Boats Rowboats, McKenzies, rafts **Tackle Supplied** Fly
Experience 14 years **Rates** day: $185

Guide's Notes: The Madison River--July has been noted as the "month the Madison goes wild." Usually over the fourth of July weekend the nationally renowned Salmon Fly Hatch will start on the lower Madison near Ennis, Montana. Each day the Salmon fly hatch will move progressively upstream. Over a two-week period, which is the approximate duration of this hatch, the trout will feed on either the nymph or the adult stage of this large aquatic insect.

The most practical way to fish the river during the hatch is to float. Our guides float the river every day. In most cases the boat is used for transportation. This allows the angler to cover the choicest waters thoroughly. Fishing from a drift boat is also rewarding. The guide maneuvers the boat into position, allowing the anglers to place their flies in those hard-to-reach areas.

When the Salmon Fly hatch has passed on the Madison, the fishing is certainly not over. Caddis, mayflies and small stone flies continue to hatch throughout the month and into August. Our guides continue to float the river throughout the season. Action is usually steady on this Montana Blue Ribbon stream. Wild brown and rainbow trout, the Rocky Mountain Whitefish and an occasional grayling share this fast-moving powerful river.

Yellowstone Park--A short drive into Yellowstone Park brings you to the Upper Madison, the Firehole and the Gibbon rivers, plus a multitude of small lakes and streams which await the ambitious angler.

Towards the **end of May**, each year, the general fishing season opens in Yellowstone National Park. The Firehole River is one of the best streams to fish when the Park opens. The Firehole's temperature is not constant and may vary from one section of the river to the next. The hatches are usually of short duration, but frequent. Small dry flies or nymphs, down to size 20, normally work best.

Yellowstone Lake opens each year about **June 15th**. Fishing along the shoreline of the Lake with a large nymph or wet fly will produce Yellowstone Black Spotted Cutthroat Trout, native to the Yellowstone drainage only.

Mid July offers an abundance of fishable water. The high water of early spring has spent itself to an even flow. Alpine lakes are open and in prime shape for the back country fly fisherman.

July 15th is the normal opening for the Yellowstone River in the Park between Yellowstone Lake and the Upper Falls. This section of the river is a unique fishery. The wild, native black spotted cutthroat trout average in size between 15 and 19 inches. Set aside as a no-kill area, this portion of the river has a gravel bottom with a smooth, even flow of water. Insect hatches are quite predictable and the cutthroat trout are not usually selective.

The long, hot summer days of **August** bring low water conditions and a change in tactics for the fisherman. The Upper Madison, Firehole and many of the small streams in the area are low and clear. Using grasshopper patterns, ants, crickets, and other terrestrial imitations will produce. Through the month of August and well into September, using hoppers is challenging and rewarding. At mid-day, trophy size trout will take up feeding stations near the banks of many rivers and streams, inhaling grasshoppers as they fall into the water.

The Yellowstone River in the Park is still in its prime, with actively feeding fish and good insect activity. The Buffalo Ford area along the upper river is one of the most productive areas to catch some of these brightly colored native trout.

The Gallatin River starts in the high elevations and flows north very close to highway 191, for about 50 miles. Due to the river's late run-off and cold temperatures, the Gallatin is most productive from August into late fall. Fishing at mid-day, during bright sun, is most effective for this river.

In the high country, due to the cooler conditions at this time of year, much of the insect activity is focused during the middle of the day. Small may flies and caddis hatch on the Firehole, Madison, Henry's Fork, and many of the smaller streams. In most cases these hatches will be short, lasting only an hour or two. The flies are generally of a smaller size at this time of year.

About the **middle of September**, the brown trout will start their annual spawning run. Fishermen from all over the country long for an opportunity to fish for these migrating spawners. The average size spawner is from 2 to3 pounds, with a 4 or 5 pounder not uncommon. The best method is to fish with a sinking line, using streamers in sizes 2 or 4.

Most of the fishing from the **beginning of October into November** is on the upper Madison near town. Brown trout on their spawning run will work upstream, looking for the choicest spawning areas. The portion of the Madison that runs through Yellowstone National Park is one of the hot spots during October. From the junction of the Gibbon and Firehole rivers, to the Park line, there is about 20 miles of prime river. Most of this section of the river is paralleled by road. The Firehole and Gibbon rivers are also good fall fisheries and have their run of spawning brown trout. The South Fork of the Madison, near town, is another choice section of river to fish in the fall.

Author's Notes: Bob Jacklin is a nationally known outfitter and tackle shop owner. His operation is respected as one of the best of its kind in Montana.

MARINO, BOB-NORTH FORK OUTFITTERS (208) 558-7388, (604) 797-0596
Address 84 Rosemont Ave., Elmwood Park, NJ 07407
Airport Bozeman 90m **Accommodations** West Yellowstone 30m
Operation Outfitter, tackle shop **Fish** All species of trout **Season** June-Sept
Water Madison, Galatin, Firehole, Yellowstone Rivers
Specialty Fly fishing (walk and float trips) **Type of Fishing** Fly
Boats Rowboats, canoe, McKenzies, raft **Tackle Supplied** Fly
Experience 4 years **Rates** day: $180 week: $1100 1/2 day: $100

MATTHEWS, CRAIG-BLUE RIBBON FLIES (406) 646-9365
Address 309 Canyon St., Box 1037, West Yellowstone, MT 59758
Airport West Yellowstone **Accommodations** West Yellowsotne
Operation Outfitter, tackle shop **Type of Fishing** Fly
Fish Trout, grayling **Season** Year-round **Tackle Supplied** Fly
Water Madison, Yellowstone, Gallatin Rivers, Yellowstone Park waters
Specialty Fly fishing, float/wade combination **Boats** McKenzies
Experience 6 years **Rates** day: $180 1/2 day: $105
Guide's Notes: Float trips take place in McKenzie river boats with one or two anglers. A typical float would be a 10-12 mile float on the Madison River. Floats are designed to get the anglers to stretches of rivers inaccessible to wading fishermen.

Walk-wade trips enable the fisherman to move from river to river. You might expect to fish different sections of a river or different streams during a day.

You may start fishing on a spring creek or pond, then move to a larger stream and end up fishing the evening Caddis hatch on the Madison or Gallatin, for example. Some fishermen like to begin the day fishing from float tubes for "Gulpers", then move to the Madison, Gallatin, Gibbon or Yellowstone in the afternoon for Caddis or Hopper fishing.

Fall trips mean big water, big flies and big fish. Most of our fall trips (September, October and November) begin early in the morning working Streamers, Nymphs, or Large Soft Hackles through the mist covered runs and riffles. By 9 a.m. or 10 a.m. we are headed down to the Madison or Yellowstone with the drift boat for a day's float. Crisp, cold mornings and warm, sunny afternoons can be expected, although raw, cloudy, damp days fish the best and one must be prepared to face even snow squalls in the fall season.

Blue Ribbon offers guided fishing trips every month of the year. Some spectacular fishing can be experienced in February, March, April and May, and you'll be alone! Dry fly fishing is productive during all months but November, December, and the first two weeks of January.

Rivers and streams of the Yellowstone Area (See map on page 137)

Firehole River (1) The Firehold River in Yellowstone Park is unique among trout streams due to the geothermal features that influence its water temperature and quality. Its character is typified by smooth weed-filled flats interspersed with riffles over a lava rock bottom. Summer temperatures in some sections can climb high enough to cause trout to migrate long distances to seek cooler tributaries, such as Nez Perce and Sentinal Creeks. Hatches are best in the spring and fall when water temperatures are cooler, although rising trout can be found at any time of the year. Owing to the thermal influences, major hatches occur 2-3 weeks earlier than the same hatches on other area waters.

Gibbon River (2) The Gibbon River combines with the Firehole to form the Madison River. Its upper and lower reaches are smooth, meadow meandering stretches. The middle section is faster pool and riffle water. This section can be fished with any good high floating dry fly or nymphed successfully at most times. The meadow sections can be more difficult fishing, as the fish are much warier. Frequent Caddis hatches can be found here, and matching the hatch is then in order.

Madison River (3) The Upper Madison in Yellowstone Park consists mostly of smooth-flowing flats. Caddis flies, Pale Morning Duns, and some stoneflies can be found emerging during the summer months. Late summer also finds the fish ready and willing to accept a well presented grasshopper pattern. In the smooth flats, presentation is the most important key to success. A run of spawning brown trout also draws many anglers to this section of the river in the fall.

The Madison below Quake Lake is an essentially continuous riffle until it reaches the town of Ennis. This section is well known for the "Salmon Fly" hatch it receives each year, although it is oftentimes unpredictable. It also has very prevalent Caddis fly hatches, as well as good emergences of Pale Morning Duns, Western Black Quills (Rhithrogena Sp.), and Western Quill Gordons (Epeorus Albertae). These species can be found hatching during June and July. The Salmon Fly hatch progresses upstream along the entire river, sometime between mid-June and early July. Nymph fishing with large weighted nymphs is excellent prior to and during the hatch. Because the nymphs migrate to the shore to hatch, both nymphs and dry imitations should be fished close to the margins of the river.

Hebgen Lake (4) This reservoir is an impoundment of the Madison River. In the spring it offers food fishing from the shoreline, casting streamers out and retrieving them rapidly. Summer brings hatches of speckled spinners (Callibaetis Sp.) and White Winged Blacks (Tricorythodes Sp.). The Spinner Falls are tremendous, and the fish make such a disitnctive "gulp" that the fishing has acquired the name "Gulper Fishing." These Spinner Falls are best fished from float tubes in the Madison arm of the lake.

Gallatin River (5) The Gallatin is a freestone river that receives far less angling pressure than the other well-known rivers. It experiences a much more predictable "Salmon Fly" hatch than the Madison, and offers excellent fishing during the emergence. The fish, as typical of most fast freestone streams are not terribly selective. Caddis fly and Mayfly hatches occur, for instance, the Small Western Green Drake (Ephemerella Coloradensis), and most high floating dry flies will take fish.

Slough Creek (6) This river offers excellent fishing for large cutthroats and rainbows (hybrids are also common). The lower water (below the campground) has the largest trout, but the walk into the upper meadows offers a true wilderness setting. Hatches are common and not difficult to match, with the fish not particularly selective except for the slow water areas. The lower water has hatches of Caddis, Midges, Western Quill Gordons, and Western Ginger Quills to name a few insects. Standard dry flies will usually produce well during these July and August hatches, with 18"-20" fish not uncommon. Slough is a late clearing stream, so seeking current information is advisable.

Lamar River (7) The Lamar is similar water to lower Slough Creek; pools and riffles. Rainbows and Cutthroats are present and not overly difficult to catch. The Lamar is another late clearing stream, so it is at its best in July, August and September. Local thunderstorms often turn the river brown, rendering it unfishable.

Yellowstone River (8) The Yellowstone in the park is an extremely important cutthroat fishery; in fact, above the falls no other trout are present. The fish are generally easily caught, but at times they can become quite selective. Hatches are common. Opening day is July 15.

Henry's Fork of the Snake (9) The Henry's Fork has its genesis at the outlet of Henry's Lake. It is a particularly famed trout stream below island park reservoir where it first enters the Box Canyon and again at the popular Railroad Ranch section. Box Canyon is a fast, turbulent section of water best known for its mid-June Salmon Fly hatch. Below the canyon the river slows and widens, becoming a literal "insect factory". Large rainbows free rise to profuse Caddis and Mayfly hatches here and present the angler with the ultimate hatch-matching challenge.

Author's Notes: *Craig Matthews, owner of Blue Ribbon Flies, has built a reputation as having one of the finest selections of flys and fly tying materials in Montana. I have not had the opportunity to fish with his guides, but I am certain they are very competent.*

TERWILLIGER, FRED-BUD LILLY'S TROUT SHOP (406) 646-7801
Address 39 Madison Avenue, West Yellowstone, MT, 59758
Airport West Yellowstone **Accommodations** West Yellowstone
Operation Outfitter, tackle shop **Type of Fishing** Fly, spin
Fish Brown, rainbow, cutthroat **Season** May-Oct **Boats** McKenzies
Water Madison, Firehole, Yellowstone Rivers, Henry's Fork (ID)
Specialty Fly fishing float trips **Tackle Supplied** Fly, spin
Experience 10 years **Rates** day: $175

WISE RIVER, MONTANA

DECKER, DAVID W.-THE COMPLETE FLY FISHER (406) 832-3175
Address Box 105, Wise River, MT 59762
Airport Butte 40m **Accommodations** Wise River
Operation Outfitter, tackle shop, lodge **Type of Fishing** Fly
Fish Trout **Season** June-Oct **Specialty** Fly fishing float trips
Water Big Hole, Beaverhead, Jefferson, Wise, Madison Rivers
Boats Rafts with bass boat seats **Tackle Supplied** Fly
Experience 9 years **Rates** day: $220 week (5 days 6 nights): $1200/person
*Author's Notes: David Decker operates a first class lodge comparable to the
best anywhere including Alaska. Food, lodging and guide service are all rated
excellent. Catch and release is encouraged.*

FELLIN, CRAIG-BIG HOLE RIVER OUTFITTERS (406) 832-3252
Address Box 167, Wise River, MT 59762
Airport Butte 45m **Accommodations** On premises **Operation** Outfitter, lodge
Fish Brown, rainbow, brook, grayling **Season** March-October
Water Big Hole, Beaverhead, Madison Rivers **Type of Fishing** Fly
Specialty Fly fishing float trips **Boats** Rafts **Tackle Supplied** Fly
Experience 7 years **Rates** day: $210
*Author's Notes: Our contacts in Montana tell us Craig runs an excellent oper-
ation.*

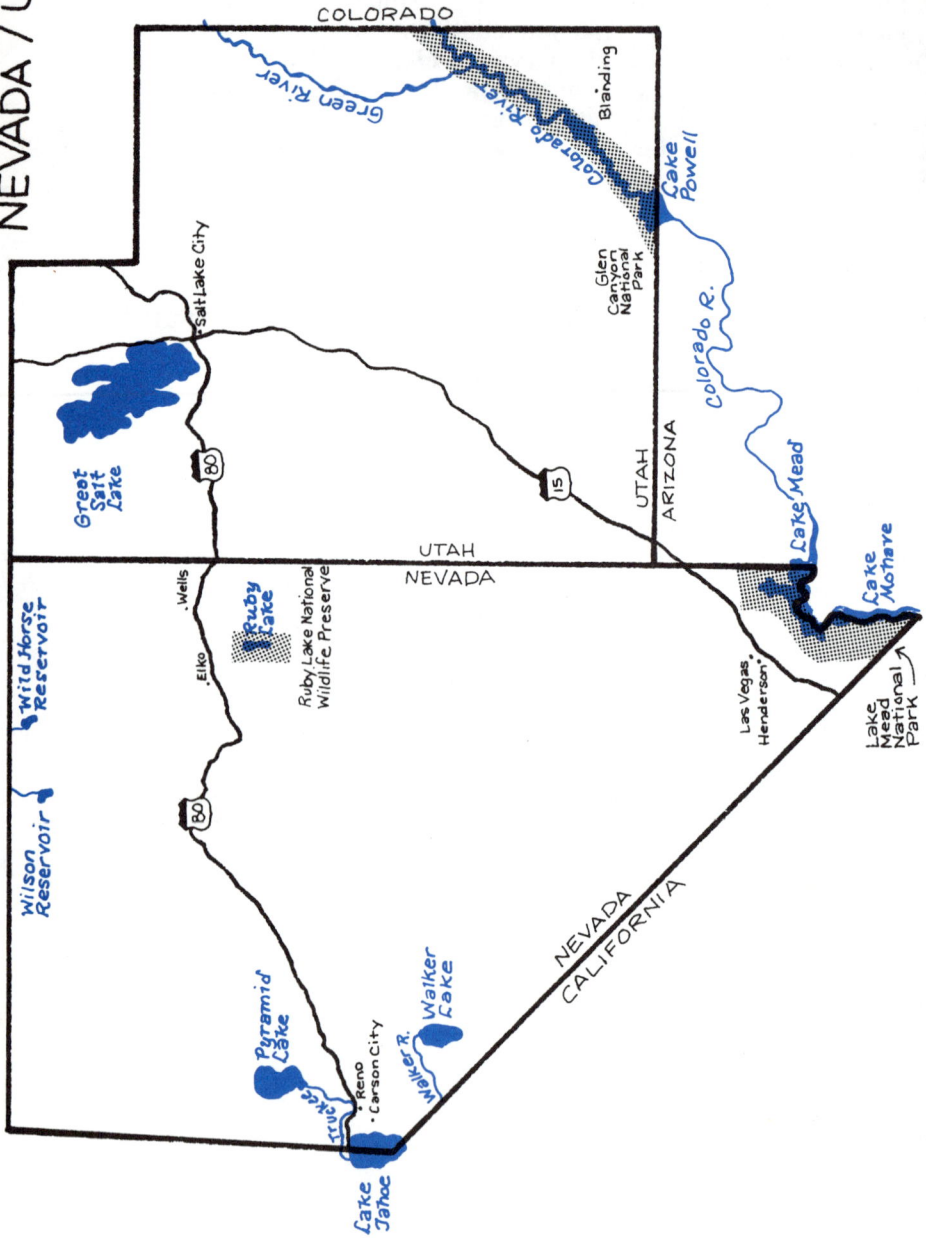

Nevada

ELKO, NEVADA

GIBSON, BILL-ELKO GUIDE SERVICE (702) 738-7539
Address 227 North Belloak Court, Elko, NV 89801
Airport Elko **Accommodations** Elko **Operation** Outfitter
Fish Bass, rainbow, brook **Season** March-Oct **Type of Fishing** Fly, spin
Water Ruby Marsh, Ruby Mtn High Lakes, Wilson,Wild Horse Reservoirs
Specialty Lm bass on Ruby Marsh **Boats** Rowboat, canoes **Tackle Supplied** All
Experience 10 years **Rates** day: $250
Guide's Notes: Elko Area Fishing Calendar

Fish	Available
Rainbow Trout	Year-round
Brook Trout (high country)	June - Sept
Largemouth Bass	June - Oct

HENDERSON, NEVADA

CIERI, AL (702) 565-1595
Address P.O. Box 215, Henderson, NV 89015
Airport Las Vegas 10m **Accommodations** Las Vegas 10m
Operation Guide, charter captain **Type of Fishing** All
Water Lake Mead, Lake Mohave, Colorado River, Lake Powell
Specialty Lake fishing **Fish** Largemouth bass, striped bass
Season Year-round **Boats** Bass boat **Tackle Supplied** All
Experience 30 years **Rates** day: $200
Guide's Notes: Lake Mead provides year round action on stripers and largemouth bass. Peak season is from April through October. Topwater action is solid from July through October.

GOFF, JAMES-FISH, INC. (702) 565-8396
Address 18 Brown Street, Henderson, NV 89015
Airport Las Vegas 10m **Accommodations** Las Vegas 10m **Operation** Guide
Fish Lm bass, striped bass **Season** April-Nov **Specialty** Topwater stripers
Water Lake Mead, Lake Mohave **Type of Fishing** Spin, baitcast, troll
Boats Bass boats **Tackle Supplied** All
Experience 5 years **Rates** day: $150

JONES, KAREN A.-SUNSET MARINE AND TACKLE (702) 565-0696, 451-4968
Address 2236 Marlboro Dr., Henderson, NV 89015
Airport Las Vegas 15m **Accommodations** Henderson
Fish Largemouth bass, striped bass, rainbow trout **Season** Year-round

Water Lake Mead, Lake Mohave **Type of Fishing** Spin, baitcast, troll
Specialty Lake fishing with lures or bait **Operation** Guide, tackle shop
Boats Bass boat **Tackle Supplied** Spin, baitcast, troll
Experience 5 years **Rates** day: $150 1/2 day: $100
Guide's Notes: Fishing Calendar for Lake Mead and Lake Mohave
Largemouth Bass:

Winter - Fish deep off outside points - jig and pig - purple or brown patterns
Spring - Spawn occurs as early as February on some parts of lake
    through early May. Cast worms, lizards, crawdads, etc., in
    light colors to spawning beds.
Summer - Early morning use top water lures in shad or crawdad patterns.
    Afternoon fish crankbaits and worms deep off points and reefs.
Fall - Worms, topwater plugs, crankbaits, etc. Excellent time of year.

Stripers:

Winter - Trolling or fishing very deep with anchovies is the best method.
Spring - The spawn occurs from mid May through mid June. Crank baits or
    anchovies in water 25 to 60 feet deep are most effective
Summer and Fall- Fish are running the shad to the surface creating all
    topwater action through late November

LAS VEGAS, NEVADA

TANNER, ZOLAN E.-TANNERS GUIDE SERVICE (702) 452-7890
Address 2221 Rigney Lane, Las Vegas, NV 89115
Airport Las Vegas **Accommodations** Las Vegas **Operation** Guide
Fish Striped bass, largemouth bass, trout **Season** March-Oct.
Water Lake Mead, Lake Mohave, Colorado River
Specialty Plug fishing, trolling, bait **Type of Fishing** Spin, baitcast, troll
Boats Outboards **Tackle Supplied** Spin, baitcast, troll
Experience 8 years **Rates** day: $175

RENO, NEVADA

BROOKS, BART
Address 316 California, #702, Reno, NV 89509
Airport Reno **Accommodations** Reno **Operation** Guide
Fish Trout **Season** June-November
Water Mountain streams and lakes **Type of Fishing** All
Specialty Fly fishing local waters for trout **Boats** Raft
Experience 2 years **Rates** day: $175

STANLEY, DAVE-RENO FLY SHOP (702) 851-0151, 853-4991
Address 6473 S. Virginia St., Reno, NV 89511
Airport Reno 3m **Accommodations** Reno **Season** Year-round
Operation Guide, tackle shop **Type of Fishing** Fly
Fish Brown, rainbow, cutthroat **Boats** Rowboats, McKenzies

Water Truckee River, Martis, Milton, Davis Lake **Tackle Supplied** Fly
Specialty Fly fishing walk wade trips and fly fishing lake trips
Experience 5 years **Rates** day: $150 1/2 day: $90
Author's Notes: Dave knows the trout waters in the Reno area as well as anyone and has an excellent reputation. He is the owner of the Reno Fly Shop which is one of the finest fly shops in the state of Nevada.

RUBY VALLEY, NEVADA

KRENKA, HENRY-HIDDEN LAKE OUTFITTERS (702) 779-2268, 779-2278
Address Ruby Valley, Ruby Valley, NV 89833
Airport Elko 45m **Accommodations** Elko 45m **Operation** Outfitter
Fish Native trout, cutthroat **Season** June-Oct. **Type of Fishing** All
Water Robison, Hidden, Cold Lakes **Specialty** Fly fishing, spinners & bait fishing
Experience 4 years **Rates** day: $150
Guide's Notes: Fishing in the **Ruby Alpine Lakes** and some stream fishing for native and cutthroat trout. Fishing months are June through October. Best fishing is late June and late September.

WELLS, NEVADA

BROUGH, WILDE-HUMBOLDT OUTFITTERS (702) 752-3714
Address Clover Valley, Wells, NV 89835
Airport Elko 70m **Accommodations** Wells **Operation** Outfitter
Fish Rainbow, brook **Season** June-Oct. **Type of Fishing** All
Water Steele Lake, Leach & Weeks Creeks, Hole-in-the-Mountain Beaver dams
Specialty High Mountain fishing
Experience 10 years **Rates** day: $150 week: $600

Utah

BLANDING, UTAH

RATH, RUSTY (801) 684-2261
Address Halls Crossing, Blanding, UT 84511
Airport Salt Lake City 380m **Accommodations** Blanding
Operation Guide **Type of Fishing** Spin, baitcast
Fish Lm Bass, walleye, striped bass, pike **Season** Year-round
Water Lake Powell (UT) central and northern area
Specialty Baitcasting with plastic worms and crank baits in a bass boat
Boats Bass boat, power boats
Experience 4 years **Rates** day: $165

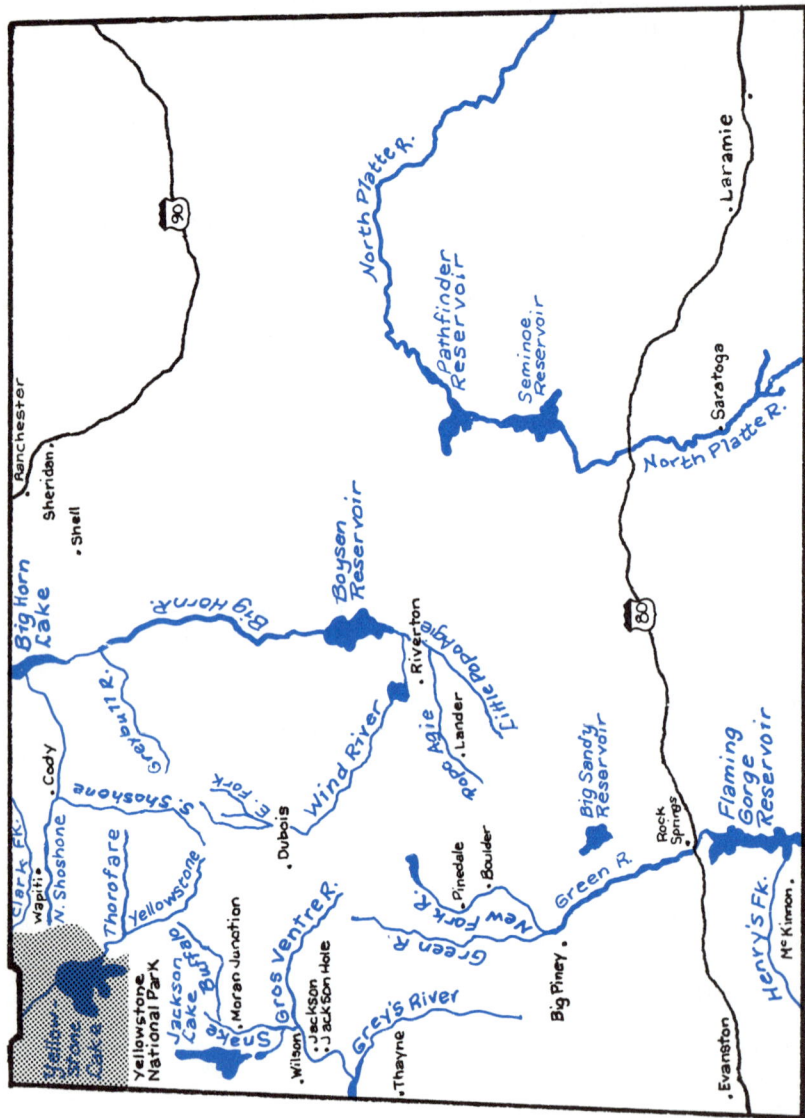

Wyoming

BOULDER, WYOMING

SNOW, HANK (307) 537-5278
Address P.O. Box 146, Boulder, WY 82923
Airport Jackson 80m **Accommodations** Pinedale 12m
Fish Cutthroat, rainbow, brook, golden **Season** June-September
Water Pine, Pole, Boulder Creeks, East Fork R. **Operation** Outfitter
Specialty Fly fishing pack trips **Type of Fishing** Fly, spin
Experience 26 years **Rates** day: $300/2 people
Guide's Notes: We have 20 horses for pack trips.

CODY, WYOMING

FELTS, RICK-GRIZZLY RANCH (307) 587-3966
Address North Fork Route, Cody, WY 82414
Airport Cody 26m **Accommodations** On premises **Operation** Outfitter, ranch
Fish Rainbow, cutthroat **Season** July-Sept **Type of Fishing** Fly, spin
Water Shoshone, Yellowstone Rivers **Specialty** Fly fishing
Experience 17 years **Rates** day: $100

GOOD, DONALD-SHEEP MESA OUTFITTERS (307) 587-4305, 587-4014
Address 2143 Peake Avenue, Cody, WY 82414
Airport Cody **Accommodations** Cody **Operation** Outfitter
Type of Fishing All **Fish** Cutthroat, rainbow, brook
Water Yellowstone, Lamar, Shoshone, Clarks Fork Rivers
Specialty Fly fishing streams and rivers **Season** July-Aug
Experience 29 years **Rates** day: $180 week: $1260

GRIFFITH, CRAIG A.-GREYBULL RIVER OUTFITTERS (307) 789-7126
Address P.O. Box 1431, Evanston, WY 82930
Airport Cody 3m **Accommodations** Cody 3m **Operation** Outfitter
Fish Cutthroat, rainbow, brown **Season** July-Oct **Type of Fishing** All
Water Greybull River Drainage **Tackle Supplied** Fly
Specialty Pack trips and fishing from a wilderness base camp
Experience 28 years **Rates** day: $100/person week: $700/person
Guide's Notes: Horses and mules are available for pack trips.

JOHNSON, DEAN-JOHNSON OUTFITTERS (307) 587-4072
Address Box 1535, Cody, WY 82414
Airport Cody **Accommodations** Cody

Operation Outfitter **Type of Fishing** All **Specialty** Fly and spin fishing
Fish Cutthroat, rainbow, brook, brown **Season** July-August
Water Thorofare, Yellowstone, Shoshone Rivers, Beartooth Areas
Experience 19 years **Rates** day: $200

LINEBERGER, RON-C OVER T RANCH (307) 587-6016
Address 2319 Southfork Road, Cody, WY 82414
Airport Cody 30m **Accommodations** Cody 30m
Operation Outfitter, ranch **Type of Fishing** Fly, spin
Fish Cutthroat, rainbow,brown, brook **Season** July-Sept
Water Shoshone, Greybull, Yellowstone Rivers
Specialty Fly fishing pack trips **Tackle Supplied** Fly, spin
Experience 8 years **Rates** day: $200 1/2 day: $100
Guide's Notes: Southfork River has its high country peak in mid-July and the
ranch area in mid-August. **Greybull River** peaks around August 15 and the
Yellowstone River peaks July 15 - August 1.

THORNE, DR. OAKLEIGH-VALLEY RANCH (307) 587-4661
Address Valley Ranch Road, Cody, WY 82414
Airport Cody 40m **Accommodations** On premises
Operation Outfitter, ranch **Type of Fishing** Fly, spin **Tackle Supplied** Fly, spin
Fish Cutthroat, brown, rainbow, brook trout **Season** Year-round
Water South Fork, Shoshone River, Yellowstone National Park
Specialty Overnight horse back fly fishing trips to lakes in National Forest
Experience 10 years **Rates** day: $200 week: $1400

TILDEN, JOE AND ALLISON-CASTLE ROCK RANCH (307) 587-2076
Address 412 RD 6NS, Cody, WY 82414
Airport Cody **Accommodations** On premises
Operation Outfitter, ranch **Type of Fishing** Fly
Fish Rainbow, cutthroat, brown **Season** July-Sept **Tackle Supplied** Fly
Water Shoshone, Clarks Fork, Buffalo Ford **Specialty** Float/wade fly fishing
Experience 15 years **Rates** day: $200 week: $1300
Guides's Notes: The peak on these rivers is August 1 - September 10. Good fly
patterns are Wooly Worms, Adams, and Hoppers, sizes 20-12.

DUBOIS, WYOMING

FOX, BAYARD-BITTERROOT RANCH (307) 455-2778
Address Bitterroot Ranch, Dubois, WY 82513
Airport Riverton 80m **Accommodations** On premises
Operation Outfitter, ranch **Type of Fishing** Fly, trolling
Fish Cutthroat, rainbow, brown, grayling **Season** June-November
Water Wind, Wiggins Fork, East Fork Rivers, Wind River Lakes
Specialty Fly fishing rivers **Boats** Canoes **Tackle Supplied** Fly
Experience 15 years **Rates** week: $1200
Guide's Notes: Wind River, East Fork, Wiggins Fork There is fishing here for
cutthroat, rainbow and brown trout as well as grayling. The best stream fishing
is in August and September. Dry fly patterns including yellow Humpy, Royal

Wulff, Renegade, etc., are often effective. It is often more effective to fish a weighted nymph upstream like a Charles Brooks stone or a Montana Nymph, relying on the motion of a floating line to signal a strike.

KINNEMAN, DAN (307) 455-2208
Address Box 1079, Dubois, WY 82513
Airport Riverton 80m **Accommodations** Dubois
Operation Guide, outfitter **Type of Fishing** Fly, spin
Fish Brown, rainbow, brook, cutthroat **Season** April-September
Water Wind River Range **Specialty** Fly fishing rivers and lakes
Experience 16 years **Rates** day: $250

RANDLE, DON-SODA FORK OUTFITTERS (307)455-2351
Address Box 911, Dubois, WY 82513
Airport Riverton 80m **Accommodations** Dubois **Operation** Outfitter, lodge
Fish Cutthroat, rainbow, golden, brook **Season** June-November
Water Buffalo, Yellowstone, Shoshone, Wind Rivers **Type of Fishing** All
Specialty Fly and spin cast fishing on streams and lakes **Tackle Supplied** All
Experience 6 years **Rates** day: $30 week: $100/person 1/2 day: $18
Guide's Notes: The drainages we fish include the **Wind River, Shoshone River, Yellowstone River and Buffalo Fork.** The fish species include cutthroat, brook, rainbow, German brown, mackinaw and California golden trout. We use both spin-cast and fly fishing techniques with both types of artificial lures constantly changing from day-to-day throughout the May to October fishing period.

RICE, GARY-ZK OUTFITTERS (307) 455-2210
Address P.O. Box 284, 20 King Fisher Rd, Dubois, WY 82513
Airport Riverton 80m **Accommodations** Dubois **Operation** Outfitter
Fish Cutthroat, golden, brook, rainbow **Season** June-September
Water Wind River Range, Fitzpatrick Wilderness area
Specialty Fly and spin fishing pack trips **Type of Fishing** Fly, spin
Experience 15 years **Rates** day: $200 week: $1250

STETTER, LARRY-DOUBLE BAR J RANCH (307) 455-2725
Address Box 695, US 26/287 Dubois, WY 82513
Airport Riverton 80m **Accommodations** On premises
Operation Outfitter, ranch **Type of Fishing** Fly, spin
Fish Brook, cutthroat, rainbow, brown **Season** June-Nov
Water Teton, Wind, Green River drainages, Yellowstone area
Specialty Fishing remote mountain lakes and streams
Boats Rafts **Tackle Supplied** Fly, spin
Experience 27 years **Rates** day: $200 week: $1200
Guide's Notes: We have horses for access to remote lakes and streams. Excellent fishing with a variety of species caught each day. There are many golden trout lakes available on pack trips.

WHITE, MARLAN "BUD"-STAR MOUNTAIN OUTFITTING (307) 455-2816
Address Box 274, Dubois, WY 82513
Airport Riverton 80m **Accommodations** Dubois

Operation Outfitter **Type of Fishing** All **Tackle Supplied** All
Fish Trout **Season** Year-round **Boats** Canoes, rafts, party boat
Water Lakes and streams throughout Northwestern Wyoming
Specialty Fishing back pack and horse pack trips
Experience 25 years **Rates** day: $100 week: $700 1/2 day: $100

JACKSON, WYOMING

ALLEN, JOE-STONE DRUG INC. (307) 733-8025 733-6222
Address P.O. Box 2950, 300 Flat Creek Dr., Jackson, WY 83001
Airport Jackson Hole 10m **Accommodations** Jackson
Operation Outfitter, tackle shop **Type of Fishing** Fly, spin
Fish Cutthroat, lake trout, brown, rainbow **Season** March-November
Water Snake River, Jackson Lake **Boats** Rafts **Tackle Supplied** Fly, spin
Experience 33 years **Rates** day: $200/2 people
Guide's Notes: We offer five four-day trips into Heart Lake each year by horse
back for trophy lake trout. We troll for these fish, which run from 15 to 45
pounds, with light trolling tackle.
*Author's Notes: Local contacts tell me Joe probably knows the Snake River
better than any guide in the area.*

ASHBURN, RICHARD H.L. (307) 733-3649
Address Box 1437, Jackson, WY 83001
Airport Jackson Hole 10m **Accommodations** Jackson
Operation Outfitter **Type of Fishing** Fly, spin
Fish Cutthroat **Season** May-November
Water Yellowstone, Snake Rivers **Specialty** Fly fishing
Experience 7 years **Rates** day: $200
Guide's Notes: Horses are available for pack trips

BRUUN, PAUL-ROD & REEL FLY FISHING FLOAT TRIPS (307) 733-5173
Address Box 1385, Dept. F, Jackson, WY 83001
Airport Jackson Hole 10m **Accommodations** Jackson
Operation Guide, tackle shop **Type of Fishing** Fly, spin **Tackle Supplied** Fly
Fish Cutthroat, rainbow, brown trout **Season** July-October
Water Snake, Green, New Fork Rivers, Yellowstone Park area
Specialty Fly fishing float trips **Boats** McKenzies, rafts, johnboats
Experience 12 years **Rates** day: $200
*Author's Notes: Paul is a nationally known guide and outdoor writer. Friends
tell me he is one of the best guides in the Wyoming/Montana region.*

HAECKER, RICHARD-R.R. HAECKER OUTFITTER, INC. (307) 733-6195
Address Box 818, Jackson, WY 83001
Airport Jackson Hole 10m **Accommodations** Jackson
Operation Outfitter **Type of Fishing** Fly, spin
Fish Cutthroat trout **Season** June-October
Water Yellowstone, Thorofare Rivers and drainages
Specialty Fly fishing **Tackle Supplied** Fly, spin

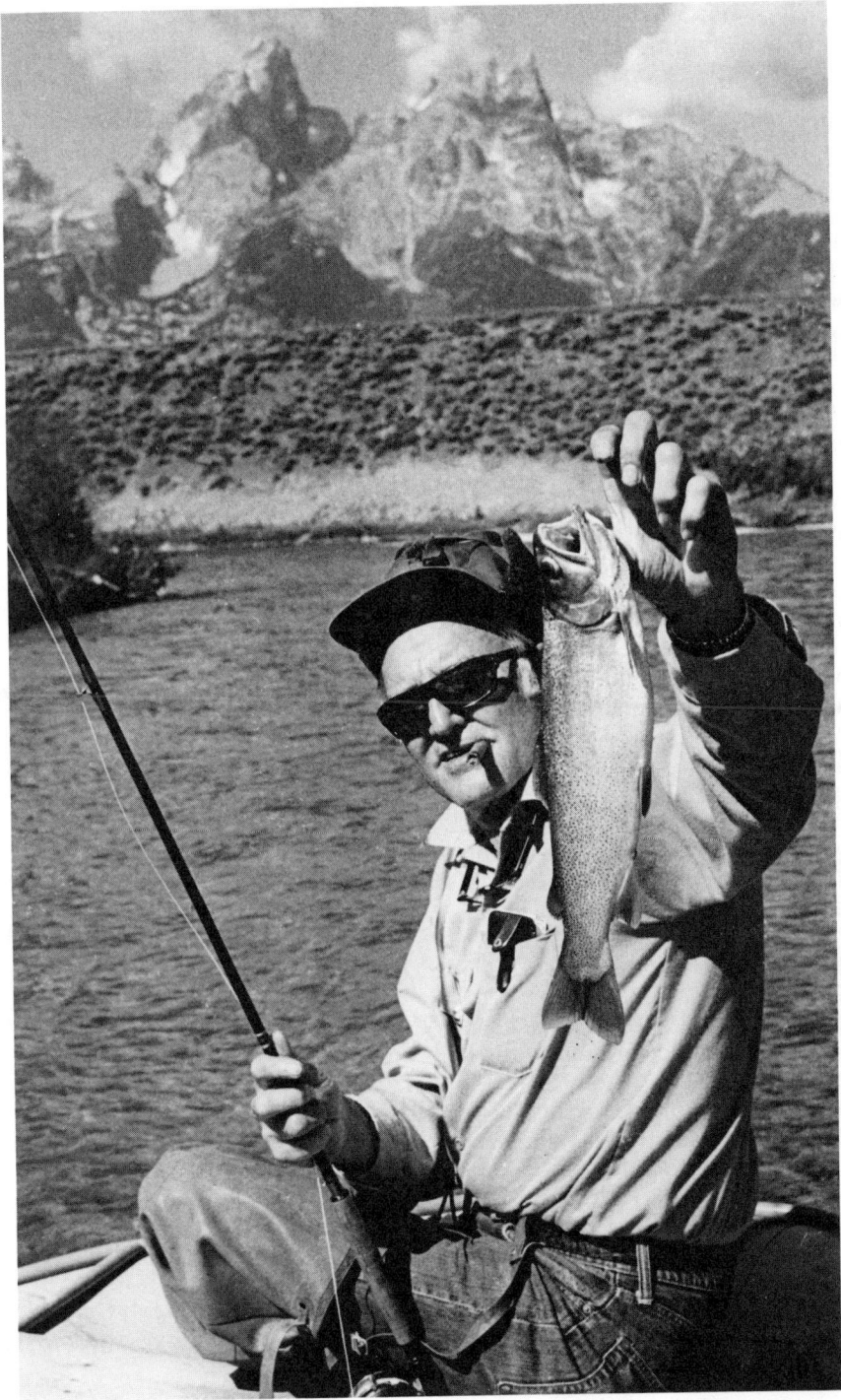

A nice Snake River rainbow.   *Paul Bruun*

Experience 8 years **Rates** varies
Author's Notes: Richard is known locally as a very capable guide.

JAMES, BRUCE-JACK DENNIS SPORTS (307) 733-3270
Address Box 1939, Jackson, WY 83001
Airport Jackson Hole 6m **Accommodations** Jackson
Operation Guide, tackle shop **Type of Fishing** Fly
Fish Cutthroat, rainbow, brown **Season** June-August
Water Snake, Green Rivers **Specialty** Fly fishing float trips
Boats Rafts, johnboats **Tackle Supplied** Fly, spin
Experience 8 years **Rates** day: $175
Author's Notes: Bruce is the head guide for Jack Dennis' tackle shop. Jack Dennis, the owner, gained national recognition with fly fisherman when he authored the well known book, WESTERN TROUT FLY TYING MANUAL. Both the store and the guide services have excellent reputations.

JONES, JAMES R.-HIGH COUNTRY FLIES (307) 733-7210
Address Box 3432, 75 E. Broadway, Jackson, WY 83001
Airport Jackson **Accommodations** Jackson
Operation Outfitter **Type of Fishing** Fly, spin **Specialty** Fly fishing
Fish Cutthroat, rainbow, brown **Season** May-Nov **Boats** McKenzies
Water Grand Teton N. Park, Green R., New Fork, Yellowstone Park
Experience 2-10 years **Rates** day: $175/1 or 2 people
Guide's Notes: Fishing Calendar

Water	Fish	Available	Flies/Lures
Snake River	Cutthroat	Jul 15 - Oct 31	Humpy, Royal Wulffs,
		Peak Aug 1-Sept 30	Trudes, grasshoppers
Green River	Brown, Rainbow	June 20 - Sept 30	Gray Drakes, caddis
New Fork	Brown, Rainbow	June 1- Aug 30	Streamers, nymphs

Author's Notes: Jim runs an excellent shop and has very capable guides working for him.

MONTGOMERY, TOM-JACK DENNIS OUTDOOR SHOP
(307) 733-6584, 733-3270
Address Box 1962, Dept. S, Jackson, WY 83001
Airport Jackson **Accommodations** Jackson
Operation Guide, outfitter, tackle shop **Type of Fishing** Fly **Season** Mar-Nov
Fish Cutthroat, brown, rainbow **Specialty** Fly fishing float trips
Water Snake, Green Rivers (WY), Beaverhead, Big Hole, Madison Rivers (MT)
Boats Canoe, McKenzie, raft, johnboat **Tackle Supplied** Fly
Experience 10 years **Rates** day: $200 week: $1400
Guides's Notes: Fishing Calendar

Water	Best Fishing	Flies
Snake	Late Aug - Sept	Mostly dries
Green, Big Hole, Beaverhead	Mid June - July	Dries and wets

Author's Notes: Very reliable sources tell us Tom is one of the best guides in the area. He also is a first class photographer.

WILSON, MICHAEL V.-FIGHTING TROUT FLY FISHING EXPEDITONS (307) 733-3491

Address Box 306, Jackson, WY 83001
Airport Jackson **Accommodations** Jackson **Operation** Outfitter
Fish Cutthroat, browns, brook, rainbow **Season** Year-round
Water Snake, Yellowstone, Firehole, Lewis, Gros Ventre Rivers
Specialty Fly fishing trips for trout and salmon **Type of Fishing** All
Boats Canoes, McKenzies, rafts **Tackle Supplied** All
Experience 28 years **Rates** day: $210 week: $1000

WIND, ALAN-MOUNTAIN SERVICE CO. (307) 733-8369

Address P.O. Box 2636, Jackson, WY 83001
Airport Jackson **Accommodations** Jackson
Operation Outfitter, tackle shop **Type of Fishing** All
Fish Cutthroat, brown, rainbow, lake trout **Season** Jan.-Nov.
Water Snake, Green, Yellowstone National Park, New Fork Rivers
Specialty Fly fishing float and walk-in trips
Boats Rowboats, McKenzies, rafts **Tackle Supplied** All
Experience 5 years **Rates** day: $200 1/2 day: $150

JACKSON HOLE, WYOMING

RONEY, WILLIAM R.-CRESENT H RANCH (307) 733-3999, 733-5714

Address 1055 Gregory Lane, Box 1611, Jackson Hole, WY 83001
Airport Jackson 15m **Accommodations** On premises
Operation Guide, lodge **Type of Fishing** Fly, spin
Fish Cutthroat, brown, rainbow, brook **Season** April-October
Water Green River, Snake River (ID) **Tackle Supplied** Fly, spin
Specialty Fly fishing float trips for large trout **Boats** McKenzies
Experience 12 years **Rates** day: $160-185 1/2 day: $110-120

LANDER, WYOMING

ALLEN, JIM AND PHIL-ALLEN BROTHERS WILDERNESS OUTFITTING (307) 332-2995

Address P.O. Box 243, Lander, WY 82520
Airport Riverton 25m **Accommodations** Lander 35m
Operation Outfitter, lodge **Type of Fishing** Fly, spin
Fish Golden, cutthroat, brook, rainbow **Season** June-September
Water Wind, South Fork, Little Wind, Popo Agie Rivers
Specialty Pack trips to high mountain lakes and streams
Experience 16 years **Rates** day: $200 week: $1400

FOCHT, RAY-D.T. OUTFITTING (307) 332-3123, 332-5434

Address 336 Focht Road, Lander, WY 82520

Airport Riverton 30m **Accommodations** On premises
Operation Outfitter, bunkhouse **Type of Fishing** Fly, spin **Season** July-Sept
Water Popo Agie River, lakes along Continental Divide, Dunoir **Fish** Trout
Specialty Horse pack trips into high country **Tackle Supplied** Fly, spin
Experience 45 years **Rates** day: $120 week: $840

MC NIVEN, KEVIN-YZ OUTFITTERS (307) 332-9149
Address Rt. 61, Box 480, Lander, WY 82520
Airport Riverton 25m **Accommodations** Lander 7m
Operation Outfitter **Type of Fishing** Fly, spin, bait
Fish Cutthroat, rainbow, golden, brook **Season** June-August
Water Popo Agie River, Wind River drainages **Tackle Supplied** Fly, spin
Specialty High country fishing pack trips on horse back
Experience 15 years **Rates** day: $100 week: $500

MC KINNON, WYOMING

GUTZ, HENRY J. (307) 874-6145, (801) 784-3483
Address Box 25, Mc Kinnon, WY 82938
Airport Rock Springs 65m **Accommodations** Manila, UT 7m
Operation Guide **Type of Fishing** Troll **Boats** Deep V hull
Fish Lake trout **Season** March-Nov **Tackle Supplied** Troll, jigging
Water Flaming Gorge Reservoir **Specialty** Trolling
Experience 4 years **Rates** day: $200

MORAN, WYOMING

KORN, WALTER M. & PAT-BOX K RANCH (307) 543-2407
Address Box 110, Moran, WY 83013
Airport Jackson 11m **Accommodations** On premises
Operation Lodge, outfitter **Type of Fishing** Fly, spin
Fish Cutthroat, lake trout, brook, rainbow **Season** June-September
Water Yellowstone, Buffalo, Snake Rivers, Bridger, Crater Lakes
Specialty Spin casting and fly fishing
Experience 37 years **Rates** week: $690
Author's Notes: Friends in the area tell us Walt is an excellent guide.

PINEDALE, WYOMING

BRIGHT, MR. KIMBERLY-BOULDER LAKE LODGE (307) 367-2961
Address Box 1100, Pinedale, WY 82941
Airport Jackson 100m **Accommodations** On premises
Operation Lodge, Outfitter **Type of Fishing** All **Boats** Canoes
Fish Cutthroat, brook, brown, rainbow **Season** May-October
Water Bridger Wilderness Area Lakes **Specialty** Wilderness fly fishing
Experience 4 years **Rates** day: $72

BURKE, WARREN-BIG SANDY RANCH
Address Big Sandy Ranch, Pinedale, WY 82941
Airport Jackson 100m **Accommodations** On premises **Season** June-Sept
Operation Outfitter, ranch **Type of Fishing** Fly **Fish** Brook, brown trout
Water Big Sandy Reservoir **Specialty** River fishing at the ranch
Experience 25 years **Rates** day: $48/person includes meals and room

MILLER, DICK-THE FISHING GUIDE (307) 367-4760
Address 610 S. Fremont, Pinedale, WY 82941
Airport Jackson 80m **Accommodations** Pinedale **Operation** Outfitter
Fish Brown, rainbow, lake trout **Season** May-Oct **Type of Fishing** All
Water Green, New Fork Rivers, area lakes **Tackle Supplied** All
Specialty Dry fly fishing float trips **Boats** Rowboats
Experience 25 years **Rates** day: $180

SINGEWALD, TIM R.-DC Bar Ranch (307) 367-2268
Address P.O. Box 561, Pinedale, WY 82941
Airport Jackson 77m **Accommodations** On premises
Operation Ranch, outfitter **Type of Fishing** All
Fish Cutthroat, brown, golden, grayling **Season** June-Sept
Water Green River, Bridger Wilderness Area lakes and streams
Specialty Pack trips into wilderness area
Boats Canoe, McKenzies, rafts, johnboats **Tackle Supplied** Fly, spin
Experience 3 years **Rates** day: $190 week $990

SKINNER, BOB, COURTNEY, MONTE, & OLE-SKINNER BROS., INC.
(307) 367-4675, 367-2270
Address Box 859, Pinedale, WY 82941
Airport Jackson 80m **Accommodations** Pinedale 2m **Operation** Outfitter
Fish All species of trout **Season** July-Sept **Type of Fishing** Fly, spin
Water Bridger Wilderness Area **Specialty** Fishing and scenic pack trips
Experience 30 years **Rates** day: $150

WEBB, BILL-GREEN RIVER OUTFITTERS (307) 367-2416
Address P.O. Box 727, Pinedale, WY 82941
Airport Jackson 77m **Accommodations** Pinedale **Operation** Outfitter
Fish Brown, rainbow, brook, cutthroat **Season** March-November
Water Green, New Fork Rivers, Gros Ventre Mountains **Type of Fishing** All
Specialty Fly fishing float trips **Boats** Rowboats, rafts, johnboats
Experience 6 years **Rates** day: $200
Guide's Notes: The species of trout in the **Green** and **New Fork Rivers** include brown, rainbow, brookie, with occasional mackinaw and arctic grayling. Hatches begin on the New Fork and Green in June and run through September.

Lunch of T-bone steaks, Green River bean salad, pop, refreshments, and fruit are offered on float trips.

RANCHESTER, WYOMING

VANCE, NATE-TETON WILDERNESS OUTFITTING (307) 655-2451
Address P.O. Box 442, Ranchester, WY 82839
Airport Cody 40m **Accommodations** Cody 40m **Operation** Outfitter
Fish Native cutthroat trout **Season** July **Tackle Supplied** All **Type of Fishing** All
Water Yellowstone, Thorofare Rivers, Bridger Lake, Open Creek
Specialty Pack into wilderness areas to fly fish rivers, streams and lakes
Experience 10 years **Rates** day: $180 includes food and lodging
Guide's Notes: Teton Wilderness I fish the Teton Wilderness during the month of July when the native cutthroat trout are making their spawning run from Yellowstone Lake. The entire month affords spectacular trout fishing in an unpeopled area in the remote wilderness. We pack in and ride in on horseback.

Fishermen have the option of fishing the water body we camp close to for their particular trip or to take dayrides to neighboring waters. Fishermen fish the rivers from the banks or with waders and the lakes with float tubes.

RIVERTON, WYOMING

BLACK, JIGGS-JIGGS PACK AND GUIDE SERVICE (307) 856-3047
Address Riverview Rt, Box 2066, Riverton, WY 82501
Airport Jackson 65m **Accommodations** Jackson 14m
Operation Outfitter **Type of Fishing** Fly, spin **Specialty** Fly fishing
Fish Cutthroat, brook, rainbow, golden **Season** June-Nov
Water Yellowstone, Buffalo, Shoshone Rivers, Angles Lakes
Experience 20 years **Rates** day: $150 week: $1050 1/2 day: $100

ROCK SPRINGS, WYOMING

WILMETTI, BOB-SWEETWATER GAP RANCH (307) 362-2798
Address Box 26, Rock Springs, WY 82901
Airport Rock Springs 100m **Accommodations** On Premises
Operation Lodge, outfitter **Type of Fishing** All
Fish Rainbow, brook, golden, lake trout **Season** June-October
Water High mountain lakes in Wind River Mountains
Specialty High mountain lake and stream fishing (fly and bait)
Experience 23 years **Rates** day: $110 week: $350

SARATOGA, WYOMING

HUGHES, RICK (307) 326-8540
Address P.O. Box 1372, 412 South First, Saratago, WY 82331
Airport Laramie 90m **Accommodations** Saratoga
Operation Outfitter, tackle shop **Type of Fishing** All
Fish Brown, rainbow, brook, walleye **Season** March-Nov

Water North Platte River, Saratoga Lake, Seminoe Reservoir
Specialty Float trips **Boats** Bass boats, rafts **Tackle Supplied** All
Experience 10 years **Rates** day: $155 week: $950 1/2 day: $85
Guide's Notes: North Platte River, Saratoga Lake--We fish for brown, rainbow, brook and cutthroat trout, walleye, and northern pike. We use Panther Martin and Rooster tail lures, and we fish them from April-October along with minnows and worms. August starts the fly fishing which ends in November. We float fish most of the time, but we offer float tube, wader, trolling and stream fishing. July is our most productive month.

SMITH, BOB AND TOM WIERSEMA-GREAT ROCKY MOUNTAIN OUTFIT-TER (307) 326-8750

Address 216 E. Walnut, Box 1636, Saratoga, WY 82331
Airport Laramie 85m **Accommodations** Saratoga
Operation Outfitter, tackle shop **Type of Fishing** Fly, spin
Fish Brown, rainbow, cutthroat, brook **Season** June-Oct
Water North Platte, Green, Encampment, New Fork Rivers
Specialty Fly and spin fishing float trips
Boats Rowboats, rafts **Tackle Supplied** Fly, spin
Experience 12 years **Rates** day: $160-225 week: $800 1/2 day: $100
Guide's Notes: North Platte River--The Wyoming Game & Fish lists the North Platte as the premier trout stream of Wyoming. From the Colorado state-line north to Saratoga, the North Platte is restricted to artificials only, with a slot limit and has no stocked fish. Fish populations are estimated at up to 3100 catchable trout per mile. The North Platte River is situated in Southeastern Wyoming bordered by the magnificent Snowy Range and the Sierra Madres. The river has great diversity of scenery and habitat, from high mountain streams with forest and cliffs, to semi-arid desert with towering sandstone bluffs.

April-May--Early season dry fly and streamer action, for spawning rainbows. A great way to start the season.

June 15-August 1--Great spin fishing for rainbows, cutthroat and browns.

July 15-Late September--Prime dry fly and hopper season on the North Platte, Encampment and other nearby streams.

Late Sept-October--Spawning browns caught on streamers and dry flies. Great time to combine fishing with bird or antelope hunting.

SHELL, WYOMING

STEPHENS, PRESS (307) 765-4377

Address Beaver Creek Road, Shell, WY 82441
Airport Jackson 85m **Accommodations** Dubois **Operation** Outfitter
Fish Cutthroat, brook, golden, rainbow **Season** July-September
Water Wind, Yellowstone, Snake, Shoshone Rivers **Type of Fishing** Fly
Specialty Stream and lake fly fishing pack trips
Experience 15 year **Rates** day: $100
Guide's Notes: I pack into remote wilderness areas of your public land, and am fully permitted by the U.S. Forest Service and National Park Service. I

stress the solitude of the backcountry and the good fishing that accompanies a well-run and memorable camping experience.
Author's Notes: Press was awarded Guide of the Year by the Jackson Hole Outfitters and Guide Association in 1979.

SHERIDAN, WYOMING

JORDAN, W. SCOTT (307) 672-0338 672-8332
Address 1045 1/2 N. Sheridan, Sheridan, WY 82801
Airport Billings, MT 85m**Accommodations** Fort Smith
Operation Outfitter **Type of Fishing** Fly **Tackle Supplied** Fly
Fish Brown, Rainbow **Season** Year-round **Boats** McKenzies, 16' drift boats
Water Bighorn River (MT) **Specialty** Fly fishing float trips
Experience 4 years **Rates** day: $175 1/2 day: $110

THAYNE, WYOMING

LLOYD, DAVID H.-TETON COUNTRY OUTFITTERS (307) 883-2627
Address P.O. Box 478, Thayne, WY 83127
Airport Jackson 11m **Accommodations** Jackson 11m
Operation Outfitter **Type of Fishing** All
Fish Cutthroat, brook, brown **Season** March-August
Water Gros Ventre River Drainage and tributaries
Specialty Fly and spin fishing streams and lakes
Boats Rafts **Experience** 20 years **Rates** day: $75

WAPITI, WYOMING

BLEVINS, DOUG-RAND CREEK OUTFITTERS (307) 587-5077
Address Box 128, Wapiti, WY 82450
Airport Cody 25m **Accommodations** Wapiti
Operation Outfitter, lodge **Type of Fishing** All
Fish Trout **Season** Year-round **Specialty** Stream fishing
Water North and South Forks of the Shoshone River, Yellowstone Park
Experience 14 years **Rates** day: $110/person

WILSON, WYOMING

BRESSLER, JOE-BRESSLER EXPEDITIONS (307) 733-8497
Address Box 766, Wilson, WY 83014
Airport Jackson 15m **Accommodations** Jackson 8m **Operation** Outfitter
Fish Cutthroat, brown, rainbow **Season** January-Sept **Type of Fishing** Fly
Water Snake, Green, New Fork, Salt Rivers **Specialty** Fly fishing only
Boats McKenzies, Boston Whalers **Tackle Supplied** Fly

Experience 4 years **Rates** day: $185
Guide's Notes: Like rivers anywhere, there are many factors to peak time such as snow run off, rains, etc. But I'd have to say peak time is July and August and even the first two weeks of September. We have tremendous mayfly and caddis hatches which run through the middle of September. It's mostly dry fly fishing, but there are always days when nymph fishing is far more productive.

BRESSLER, VERN (307) 733-5407
Address Box 394, Wilson, WY 83014
Airport Jackson 15m **Accommodations** Jackson 15 **Operation** Outfitter
Fish Cutthroat, rainbow, brown **Season** June-Nov **Type of Fishing** Fly
Water Green, New Fork, Salt, Snake Rivers, Teton River (ID)
Specialty Fly fishing **Boats** Dory, rafts, johnboats, runabout **Tackle Supplied** Fly
Experience 25 years **Rates** day: $200/2 people
Guide's Notes: The best fishing we have available, July 1 through October 31, is the **Teton River** and the **South Fork of the Snake**. I have permits for over 50 miles of each river. The South Fork is known for its big brown and cutthroat trout. The Teton has rainbow and cutthroat. **The Green and New Fork** are brown, rainbow, and cutthroat water. **The Salt** has cutthroat, brown, and rainbow. These rivers come in during July and we fish them to the end of October.

DeROSA, A.J.-FAT BOY FISHING (307) 733-3061
Address Box 121, Wilson, WY 83014
Airport Jackson 10m **Accommodations** Jackson 10m
Operation Outfitter **Type of Fishing** Fly
Fish Brown, rainbow, cutthroat trout **Season** March-Nov.
Water Snake, Green, Bighorn (MT), Yellowstone Rivers
Specialty Float fishing using wooden boats
Boats Drift boats **Experience** 7 years
Guide's Notes: Snake River in Jackson Hole is excellent for dry fly fishing for cutthroat in August and September.

The **Bighorn in Montana** is excellent dry fly fishing for browns and rainbow from April to May and streamer fishing for browns during October and November.

MOODY, JAY-FLY FISHING GUIDE SERVICE (307) 733-3782
Address P.O. Box 644, Wilson, WY 83014
Airport Jackson 10m **Accommodations** Jackson 5m
Operation Guide, outfitter **Type of Fishing** Fly, spin
Fish Cutthroat, rainbow, brown, brook **Season** May-October
Water Snake, Green, Yellowstone Rivers, Henry's Fork
Specialty Fly fishing-all aspects **Boats** Canoes, rafts **Tackle Supplied** Fly, spin
Experience 7 years **Rates** day: $150 1/2 day: $90
Guide's Notes: Spring Creek fishing is best in July and August. The **Snake River** has great dry fly fishing from mid-July to October. It is a fabulous float fishing river. The **Green River** is a great float fishing river for rainbows and browns from July until mid-August. **Yellowstone Park** is an easy day's drive. The **Firehole River** is good in June and July and the Yellowstone River is best

July 15 - September. The **Madison River** is good all season. Fabulous backpack fishing available to those interested in hiking a bit. Float tube fishing abounds in my area.

RICE, PAUL (307) 733-6917
Address Star Rt. 362 B, Wilson, WY 83014
Airport Jackson 15m **Accommodations** Jackson 7m
Operation Outfitter **Type of Fishing** Fly
Fish Cutthroat, browns, rainbows, brooks **Season** June-October
Water Snake, Green, New Fork Rivers **Specialty** Fly fishing float trips
Boats Rowboat, McKenzie, raft **Tackle Supplied** Fly, spin
Experience 9 years **Rates** day: $175 1/2 day: $125
Guide's Notes: Green and New Fork Rivers fish very well late June through July and into early August. Salmon fly hatches and caddis hatches are excellent. The **Snake River** generally fishes best August through September with great hopper fishing from mid-August on. The best wet fly patterns for the area are Kiwi Muddler and Yuk Bug. The best dry fly patterns are Royal Wulff, Pale Morning Dun, Joe's Hopper and Yellow Humpy. The Snake River is ideal for the novice fly fisherman. The Green and New Fork provide large brown trout for the experienced fly caster.
Author's Notes: Local contacts tell us Paul is one of the best guides in the area.

7. The Southwest: Stripers on top, and more!

Arizona, New Mexico, Texas

The amount of quality fishing in the southwest will probably surprise you. These arid states boast three blue ribbon trout waters, one of which is world class. Several of this region's excellent striped and largemouth bass lakes are rated among the nation's best.

The Colorado, Arizona's most famous river, enters the state near Page flowing clear and cool from the huge impoundment known as Lake Powell. It traverses the northwest corner of the state, passing through the Grand Canyon, then turns south below Hoover Dam and its impoundment, Lake Mead. Two other man-made lakes, Havasu and Mohave, mark the Colorado's 350-mile passage to the Mexican border.

The Colorado produces great fishing along its entire course through Arizona. In the north, it offers outstanding trout fishing from Lee's Ferry to Glen Canyon Dam. Trout fishing can also be good within the Grand Canyon, particularly on or near tributaries. Lakes Mead, Mohave, and Havasu are all excellent largemouth and striped bass fisheries, with some good opportunities for trout in the cooler water below the dams.

Several Arizona guides work the chain of reservoirs along the Salt River. These lakes, including Apache, Canyon, and Theodore Roosevelt lakes, in addition to Lake Pleasant on the Agua Fria and San Carlos Lake on the Gila, host good striper fishing and some excellent black bass fishing. All are located quite close to the cities of Phoenix and Tucson, a boon to the business traveler. Fishing in Arizona runs all year, with many peak times in the cooler months.

New Mexico's most famous water is the San Juan River, located in the northwest corner of the state near Farmington. The San Juan has been gaining national fame for several years as more people discover the huge brown, rainbow, and cutthroat trout that live there. This is unquestionably a world class trout stream. The San Juan flows at a constant temperature out of Navajo Reservoir, so fishing is good all year. Friends tell me some of the very biggest fish are caught in December.

More great trout fishing is available near Questa, where the Rio Grande flows through the famous gorge known as the Rio Grande Box. This portion of the Rio Grande holds huge rainbows and browns, but there are no access roads—it is trophy fishing in a wilderness setting. Additional trout fishing is to be had in nearby mountain streams.

The muddy Chama River flows into the Rio Grande about sixty miles below the Box, bringing an end to trout fishing. Near the town of Truth or Consequences, another 200 miles south, the river is dammed to create Elephant Butte Reservoir. This is an excellent bass water, but we did not hear from any guides who operate on it. Another dam below Elephant Butte forms Caballo Reservoir, which is also good bass water. The Rio Grande then continues on its southerly course toward El Paso, Texas.

The Lone Star State is known for its bass fishing, particularly in the big impoundments like Sam Rayburn and Toledo Bend on its eastern border. However, we had a difficult time finding guides who work these well-known waters. Most of the Texas guides who responded to our questionnaire were light tackle saltwater guides who fish the south Texas coast from Galveston to Port Isabel. They fish the inshore areas of the Gulf of Mexico primarily for redfish, seatrout, kingfish, and flounder. This area has received little national attention, but offers some outstanding light tackle possibilities.

Arizona

BULLHEAD CITY, ARIZONA

MORELAND, CHESTER-SMITTY'S BAIT AND TACKLE (602) 754-3407
Address 408 Main St., Bullhead City, AZ 86430
Airport Bullhead **Accommodations** Bullhead **Operation** Guide, tackle shop
Fish Striped bass, trout, lm bass, catfish **Season** Year-round
Water Colorado River, Lake Mohave, Top Pack Marsh, Lake Mead
Specialty Bass and trout fishing **Type of Fishing** Spin, baitcast, troll
Boats Bass boat **Tackle Supplied** Spin, baitcast, troll
Experience 2 years **Rates** 1/2 day: $75
Guide's Notes: Fishing Calendar

Water	Fish	Available
Colorado River	Trout	Nov - Feb
Lake Mohave	Largemouth bass	Mar - June
Lake Mohave	Stripers	Apr - Sept
Lake Mead	Largemouth bass	Mar - June
Lake Mead	Stripers	Apr - Sept

CLAYPOOL, ARIZONA

DOVER, DAVE W. (602) 425-3825
Address Box 457, Claypool, AZ 85532
Airport Cutter 16m **Accommodations** Claypool
Operation Guide **Type of Fishing** Spin, baitcast **Tackle Supplied** Spin, baitcast
Fish Lm bass, sm bass, crappie, catfish **Season** Year-round
Water San Carlos, Roosevelt, Apache, Canyon Lakes **Boats** Bass boat
Specialty Bass fishing with sinner baits, worms, jigs, crank baitcast
Experience 2 years **Rates** day: $125 1/2 day: $70
Guide's Notes: January through April we have excellent fishing for largemouth bass and is the best time for large fish. Bass fishing is good in this area all year. June through August provides very good nighttime bass fishing.

LAKE HAVASU CITY, ARIZONA

AMADEI, GEORGE (602) 453-6912
Address 3451 Candlewood Drive, Lake Havasu City, AZ 86403
Airport Lake Havasu City **Accommodations** Lake Havasu City
Operation Guide **Type of Fishing** All **Fish** Striped bass
Water Lake Havasu, Colorado River, south of Parker Dam to Mexico

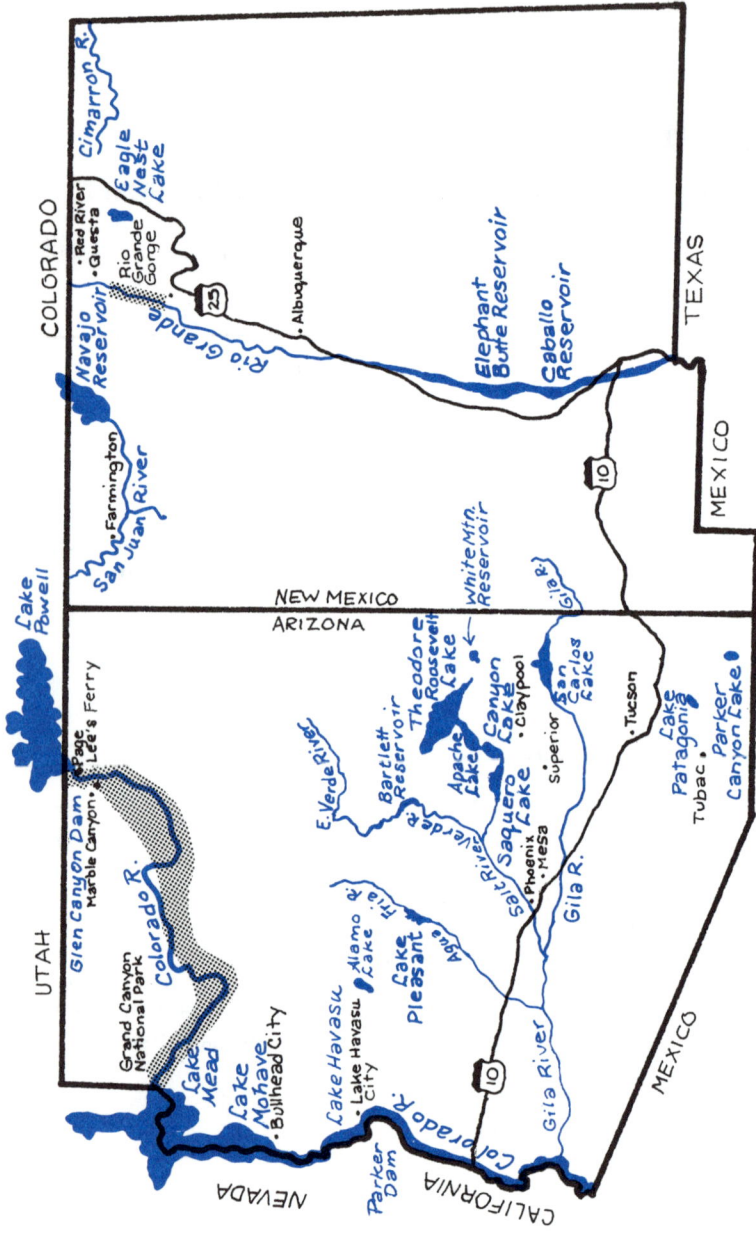

ARIZONA / NEW MEXICO

Specialty Top water fishing and crank baits **Season** March-Nov
Boats Bass boat, outboard **Tackle Supplied** All
Experience 6 years **Rates** day: $210 1/2 day: $110
Guide's Notes: 95% of my time is spent in Havasu National Wildlife Refuge. I recommend using top water plugs and 7-1/2 foot poles with baitcasting reels.

McCORMICK, PAT J. (602) 453-2277
Address 2169 Chaparal Drive, Lake Havasu City, AZ 86403
Airport Lake Havasu City **Accommodations** Lake Havasu City
Operation Outfitter **Type of Fishing** Spin, baitcast, troll **Boats** Bass boats
Fish Striped bass, lm bass, trout, catfish **Season** Year-round
Water Lake Havasu, Colorado River, Alamo Lake **Tackle Supplied** Spin, baitcast
Specialty Drift fishing in river, either casting with lures or bottom bouncing bait
Experience 5 years **Rates** day: $225 1/2 day: $150
Guide's Notes:

Fishing Calendar for Lake Havasu and The Colorado River

Fish	Available	Lure/Method
Striped Bass	Nov - Jan	Spoons and bait fished deep
Striped Bass	Feb - Apr	Casting Cordell Spots, Zara Spooks Red Fins; Fish moving to river
Largemouth Bass	Feb - Apr	Jig Pig; pre-spawn period
Striped Bass	May - June	Casting or bait fishing; fish up river
Largemouth Bass	May - June	Spinner Baits, worms, topwater plugs
Striped Bass	July - Oct	Good topwater
Largemouth Bass	July - Oct	Good topwater

MIDLER, MARSHALL (602) 453-6634
Address 2971 Yuma Drive, Lake Havasu City, AZ 86403
Airport Lake Havasu City **Accommodations** Lake Havasu City
Operation Charter Captain **Tackle Supplied** Spin, baitcast **Water** Lake Havasu
Fish Striped bass, catfish **Season** Year-round **Type of Fishing** Spin, baitcast, troll
Specialty Plug casting, bottom fishing, or trolling for striped bass **Boats** Pontoon
Experience 1 year **Rates** 1/2 day: $25 for men, $12.50 for kids and women
Guide's Notes: Lake Havasu Striped bass, catfish--peak times are April to October but we catch fish all year round.

MARBLE CANYON, ARIZONA

SULLIVAN, RUSSELL (602) 355-2250
Address Badger Creek, Marble Canyon, AZ 86036
Airport Marble Canyon **Accommodations** Marble Canyon
Operation Guide, charter captain **Type of Fishing** Fly, spin **Season** Sept.-May
Water Colorado R. from Lee's Ferry to Glen Canyon Dam **Fish** Rainbow, brook
Specialty Lure and fly fishing **Boats** Outboard **Tackle Supplied** Spin
Experience 17 years **Rates** day: $150 1/2 day: $120
Guide's Notes: Colorado River (Lee's Ferry to Glen Canyon Dam) Trout fishing only, 1 day charters. Trout range from 1 to 15 pounds with 3 - 5 pound trout

common. Park Service Campground is 1 mile from Lee's Ferry where all my fishing trips begin.

MESA, ARIZONA

PRICE, GEORGE (602) 835-9799
Address 2244 E. Jacaranda, Mesa, AZ 85203
Airport Phoenix 20m **Accommodations** Mesa **Operation** Guide
Type of Fishing All **Fish** Black bass **Season** Year-round
Water Roosevelt, Pleasant, Canyon, San Carlos Lakes
Specialty Lake fishing for bass **Boats** Bass boat **Tackle Supplied** All
Experience 4 years **Rates** day: $165 1/2 day: $100
Guide's Notes: Roosevelt, Pleasant, Canyon, and San Carlos Lakes I lake fish for black bass, crappie and catfish. The bass are excellent spring, summer and fall. With winter being a little slow, you'll need to fish deep. The summer fishing is excellent but extremely hot weather.

PAGE, ARIZONA

CLARK, CHARLIE (602) 645-5127
Address Box 2702, Page, AZ 86040
Airport Page **Accommodations** Page **Operation** Guide
Fish Trout, bass, walleye **Water** Colorado River, Lake Powell
Specialty One day drift trips on Colorado River **Season** Year-round
Boats Outboard **Tackle Supplied** Spin, baitcast **Type of Fishing** All
Experience 8 years **Rates** day: $85/person
Guide's Notes: Colorado River (below Lake Powell) Fly fishing with nymphs only (scud patterns sinking orange wooly). The only fish caught on the river are rainbows, cutthroats and a few brook trout. The river went to lures only January 1, 1986.

JOHNSON, BILL (602)645-2433, 645-9236
Address P.O. Box 1432, Page, AZ 86040
Airport Page **Accommodations** Page **Boats** Bass boats, outboard
Operation Guide **Type of Fishing** All **Tackle Supplied** Spin, baitcast
Fish Lm bass, striper, walleye, crappie **Season** Year-round
Water Lake Powell **Specialty** Artificial bait casting
Experience 2 years **Rates** day: $165 1/2 day: $100
Guide's Notes: Lake Powell Springtime, March 1 through June 15. This peak time covers pre-spawn, spawn, and post-spawn. Great fishing going for largemouths, walleye, crappie.

Fall, September 1 through November 15. The second peak time provides great topwater action for largemouth bass and stripers working shad on the surface.

PHOENIX, ARIZONA

DIAZ, RICHARD-PRO BASS GUIDE SERVICE (602) 877-2018
Address 8947 W. Whitton, Phoenix, AZ 85037
Airport Phoenix **Accommodations** Phoenix **Operation** Outfitter
Fish Lm bass, crappie, white bass, striped bass **Season** Year-round
Water Lake Pleasant, Alamo, Roosevelt, Bartlett Lakes **Boats** Bass boats
Specialty Artificial bait, live bait, spin cast, flipping, trolling
Tackle Supplied Spin, baitcast, troll **Type of Fishing** Spin, baitcast, troll
Experience 4 years **Rates** day: $60-75 1/2 day: $35-50

KIMBALL, GARY H. (602) 956-4802
Address 3810 N. 43rd Place, Phoenix, AZ 85018
Airport Phoenix **Accommodations** Phoenix **Operation** Outfitter
Fish Lm bass, sm bass, crappie **Season** Year-round
Water San Carlos Indian Resv., Apache, Roosevelt, Pleasant Lakes
Specialty Bass boat, float tube, fish fries **Type of Fishing** Spin, baitcast
Boats Bass boats, float tube **Tackle Supplied** Spin, baitcast
Experience 3 years **Rates** day; $185/person 1/2 day: $125/person

SCHMIDT, TED A.-ARIZONA ADVENTURES (206) 263-2626, 863-4427
Address 13044 N. 8th Ave., Phoenix, AZ 85029
Airport Phoenix **Accommodations** Phoenix
Operation Outfitter **Type of Fishing** Baitcast, troll
Fish Lm bass, sm bass, trout, striped bass, walleye **Season** Year-round
Water San Carlos L., Lake Powell, Lee's Ferry, White Mountain Lakes
Specialty Bass fishing from bass boats in central Arizona and Lake Powell
Boats Rowboats, bass boats **Tackle Supplied** Spin, baitcast, troll
Experience 5 years **Rates** day: $100 week: $600 1/2 day: $65

SCOTTSDALE, ARIZONA

CISSEL, NEAL (602) 945-6122
Address 8715 E. Amelia Ave., Scottsdale, AZ 85251
Airport Sky Harbor 15m **Accommodations** Scottsdale
Operation Guide **Type of Fishing** Spin, troll
Fish Lm bass, sm bass, walleye, crappie **Season** Sept-July
Water Lake Pleasant, Alamo, Bartlett, Canyon, Apache, Roosevelt Lakes
Specialty Lake fishing **Boats** Bass boat **Tackle Supplied** Spin, troll, baitcast
Experience 5 years **Rates** day: $200 1/2 day: $175

SUPERIOR, ARIZONA

MILLER, TED-SUNLAND MARINE (602) 689-2713
Address 150 Smith Dr., Superior, AZ 85273

A fly rod striper from the Colorado.   *Paul Bruun*

Airport Phoenix 50m **Accommodations** Globe 17m
Operation Guide **Type of Fishing** Spin, baitcast **Boats** Bass boats
Fish Largemouth, smallmouth, striped bass **Season** Year-round
Water Roosevelt, San Carlos Lake, Colorado River, Lakes Powell, Mead, Mohave
Specialty Light tackle casting to structure **Tackle Supplied** Spin, baitcast
Experience 5 years **Rates** day: $200 plus gas
Guide's Notes: We fish all year. During the period from late January to mid-April
the fish are in shallow water. We take them flipping with spinner baits. During
summer and fall, we fish deep structure using Garland jigs and Westy Worms.
The average fish is 2 pounds and big fish (about one a week) are 5 pounds.
Author's Notes: Our contacts tell us Ted is an excellent fisherman and guide.

TUBAC, ARIZONA

MILLER, FRANK (602) 398-2283
Address P.O. Box 1235, Tubac, AZ 85646
Airport Tucson 45m **Accommodations** Rio Rico 14m **Operation** Outfitter
Fish Lm bass, sm bass **Season** Year-round **Type of Fishing** Spin, baitcast
Water Patagonia, Arivaca, Roosevelt, Parker Canyon Lakes **Boats** Bass boats
Specialty Lake bass fishing **Tackle Supplied** Spin, baitcast
Experience 5 years **Rates** day: $175 week: $500 1/2 day: $75

TUCSON, ARIZONA

GASSAWAY, H. LEE (206) 888-0443
Address 4166 Ninidito Pl., Tucson, AZ 85705
Airport Tucson **Accommodations** Tucson **Operation** Outfitter
Type of Fishing Baitcast **Specialty** Black bass lake fishing
Fish Bass, crappie, catfish **Season** Year-round **Tackle Supplied** Spin, baitcast
Water San Carlos, Roosevelt, Alamo, Patagonia Lakes **Boats** Rowboat, bass boat
Experience 3 years **Rates** day: $150 week: $500 1/2 day: $100/person
Guide's Notes: San Carlos Lake is very good and getting better. Currently 10
fish limits are often going over 40 pounds. There have been over 100 fish going
from 7 - 9 + pounds caught this year. The next 3 years will be better as the
lake is just "coming back" after a draw down.

HOMEN, MANNY (602) 299-9353
Address 5798 E. Paseo Cimarron, Tucson, AZ 85715
Airport Tucson **Accommodations** Tucson **Operation** Guide
Type of Fishing Baitcast, troll **Specialty** Lake bass with worms and jigs
Fish Lm bass, sm bass, striped bass **Season** Year-round
Water Roosevelt, San Carlos, Apache Lakes, Lakes Mohave and Mead
Boats Bass boat, outboard **Tackle Supplied** Baitcast, troll
Experience 4 years **Rates** day: $150 week: $500 1/2 day: $100

New Mexico

FARMINGTON, NEW MEXICO

LANE, HARRY (505) 327-9550

Address 209 N. Monterey, Farmington, NM 87401
Airport Farmington **Accommodations** Farmington
Operation Tackle shop, guide **Type of Fishing** Fly
Fish Rainbow, brown, cutthroat **Season** Year-round **Water** San Juan River
Boats Wading only **Specialty** Fly fishing for trout on the San Juan
Experience 1 year **Rates** day: $175/2 people
Guide's Notes: San Juan Fishing Calendar Rainbow, brown and cutthroat are available year round. Peak nymph fishing is early November through December. Peak dry fly fishing is July and September. Hatches include midges (#22-28), baetis mayflies (#18), and infrequen mayflies (#16). Other entomology includes leeches and aquatic worms. Patterns are Brown Leeches (#4-6), Wooly Worms (#4-8), Glo-Bugs (#10-12), Hare's Ears (#14-16), Grey Olive Midges (#22-28), infrequen or Light Hendrickson (#16).

RIZUTO, CHUCK-RIZUTO'S HACKLE SHOP & GUIDE SERVICE
(505) 326-0664, 632-2708
Address 200 Sunset Place, Farmington, NM 87401
Airport Farmington **Accommodations** Farmington
Operation Outfitter, tackle shop **Type of Fishing** Fly, spin
Fish Rainbow, cutthroat, brown, lm & sm bass **Season** Year-round
Water San Juan River, Navajo Reservoir **Specialty** Fly fishing and float trips
Boats McKenzies, bass boats **Tackle Supplied** Fly, spin
Experience 11 years **Rates** day: $200
Guide's Notes: San Juan River We feel the San Juan River is the best year around river anywhere. We have 4 miles of fly fishing only. You can keep one fish over 20 inches. The average fish size seems to be 18 inches. We have rainbow, cutthroat and brown trout in the river with 5 to 8 lbs being very common. Most of the fishing is nymph fishing, however, July through October there is some dry fly fishing with grasshoppers and mayfly-midges. Peak times are May through November but I would say September, October and November are the best. River temperature is 42 degrees year round and that's very cold. At Navajo Lake we have some of the finest small and largemouth bass fly fishing anywhere.
Author's Notes: Chuck helped film and appeared on the ESPN television program "The Fishing Hole" which covered the fishing on the San Juan. He is very knowledgeable on this blue ribbon stream.

QUESTA, NEW MEXICO

GLINES, CECIL-EL RIO GUIDE SERVICE (505) 586-0652
Address P.O. Box 23, Questa, NM 87556
Airport Albuquerque 140m **Accommodations** Questa
Operation Outfitter, tackle shop **Type of Fishing** All
Fish Brown, rainbow, cutthroat, brook, pike **Season** Year-round
Water Rio Grande Box, mountain lakes and streams, Eagle Nest Lake
Boats Rowboats, canoe, outboard **Tackle Supplied** All
Specialty Rio Grande Box, wild and scenic river mountain lakes & streams
Experience 3 years **Rates** day: $100 week: $550 1/2 day: $60
Guide's Notes: The Rio Grande is the very best in early spring (April - May) and late fall (September - October). This is before the run-off begins and after it ends. This also holds true for most mountain streams in the area. During run-off season, mountain lakes are the best fishing i.e., Cabresto Lake, Latir Lakes, Goose Lake, Middle Fork Lake, and Eagle Nest Lake in my immediate area.

RED RIVER, NEW MEXICO

BEACHAM, VAN-LOS RIOS ANGLERS (505) 754-2735, 754-6630
Address Main St., Box 10, Red River, NM 87558
Airport Santa Fe 80m **Accommodations** Red River
Operation Outfitter, tackle shop **Type of Fishing** Fly, spin, troll
Fish Brown, rainbow, cutthroat, northern pike **Season** Year-round
Water Rio Grande Gorge, San Juan, Cimarron Rivers, high lakes & streams
Specialty 2 to 5 day float fishing with flies and some light spin fishing
Boats Bass boat, McKenzie, rafts **Tackle Supplied** All
Experience 6 years **Rates** day: $135 week: $1400 1/2 day: $75
Guide's Notes: San Juan River - Quality waters - Tailwater river offering excellent fly fishing for trophy rainbows, cutthroats, and browns. Good all year. Best time late fall and early spring.

Rio Grande Gorge - Wilderness Canyon is very remote and scenic. We offer 2 to 5 day floats for fly and spincast. September 1 - Thanksgiving is the best time for big browns, some big rainbows, and cutthroats. From Thanksgiving - March 31st we offer one day trips only.

Cimarron River - Rio Costilla Excellent small high country streams offering fine dry fly fishing Memorial Day through September 30th. There are beautiful browns in the Cimarron and cutthroats in the Rio Costilla.

TEXAS/OKLAHOMA

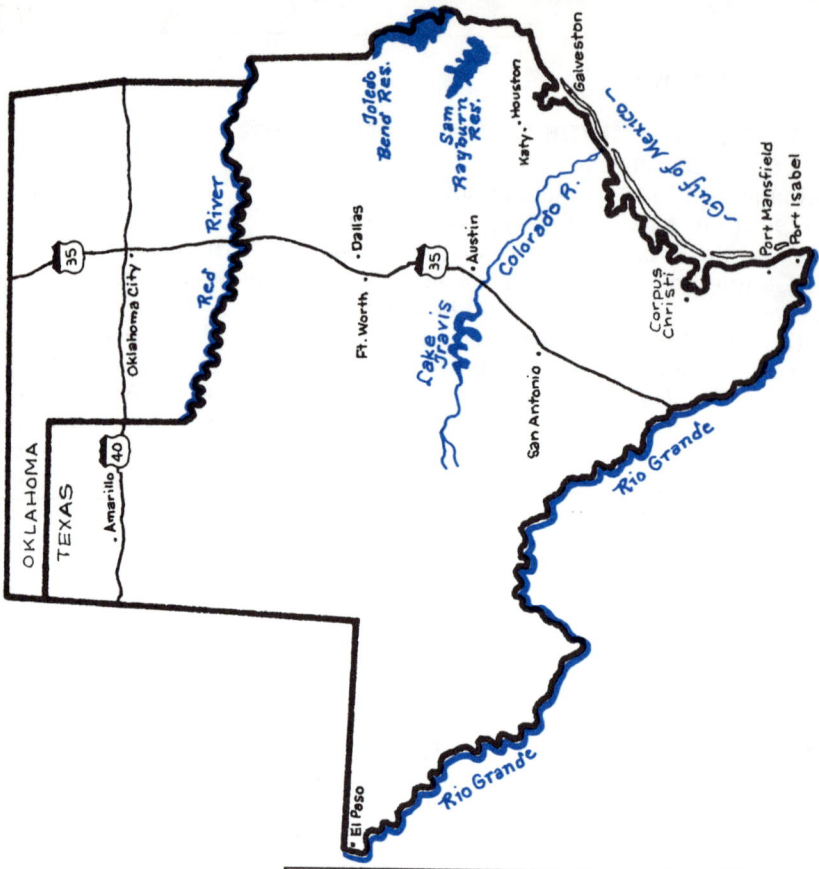

Amarillo • OKLAHOMA / TEXAS
El Paso •
Oklahoma City
Red River
Ft. Worth •
Dallas •
Austin •
Lake Travis
Colorado R.
San Antonio •
Katy • Houston
Galveston
Gulf of Mexico
Corpus Christi
Port Mansfield
Port Isabel
Toledo Bend Res.
Sam Rayburn Res.
Rio Grande

SOUTH-EASTERN TEXAS

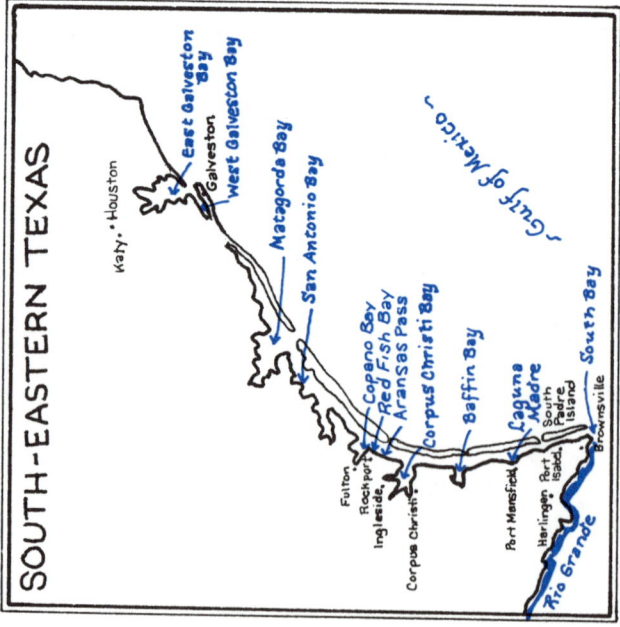

Katy • Houston
Galveston
East Galveston Bay
West Galveston Bay
Matagorda Bay
San Antonio Bay
Gulf of Mexico
Fulton
Rockport
Ingleside
Corpus Christi
Copano Bay
Red Fish Bay
Aransas Pass
Corpus Christi Bay
Baffin Bay
Laguna Madre
Port Mansfield
Harlingen
Port Isabel
South Padre Island
South Bay
Brownsville
Rio Grande

Texas

AUSTIN, TEXAS

CHRISTENSON, ALLEN (512) 444-6682, 261-7311
Address 2609 Oakhaven, Austin, TX 78704
Airport Austin **Accommodations** Austin **Operation** Guide
Fish Black bass, white bass, stripers, crappie **Season** Year-round
Water Lake Travis, Fayette County Lake, Calaveras Lake
Specialty Lake bass fishing, casting and jigging **Boats** Bass boats, pontoon
Tackle Supplied Spin, baitcast, troll **Type of Fishing** Spin, baitcast, troll
Experience 6 years **Rates** day: $150 1/2 day: $85
Guide's Notes: Lake Travis, Fayette County Lakes We fish primarily for black bass and fishing is good year round. We also fish for stripers and white bass. The best times are during winter and spring.

FULTON, TEXAS

MacQUEEN, JIM-SUNDANCE CHARTER (512) 729-4292
Address P.O. Box 936, 210 3rd St., Fulton, TX 78358
Airport Corpus Christi 30m **Accommodations** Fulton
Operation Outfitter, charter captain **Type of Fishing** Troll, spin
Fish King, blue, snapper, grouper **Season** Year-round
Water Gulf of Mexico and its bays **Tackle Supplied** Spin, baitcast, troll
Specialty Off shore salt water or deep sea fishing
Boats Raft, 32' Sports fisherman, 18' center console
Experience 5 years **Rates** day: $450 1/2 day: $315
Guide's Notes: We have fishing all year for red snapper, grouper, amberjack, warsaw, and sharks. From spring into fall the following species are available: tarpon, kings, jacks, pampano, blue runner, jewfish, dolphin, bonito, barracuda, sailfish, Atlantic marlin, and swordfish.

GALVESTON, TEXAS

BARR, EDDIE-EDDIE BARR CHARTERS (409) 763-3052
Address 7007 N. Holiday Drive, Galveston, Tx 77550
Airport Houston 50m **Accommodations** Galveston
Operation Guide, charter captain **Type of Fishing** Troll, spin, baitcast
Fish Red snapper, grouper, mackerel, ling trout **Season** Year-round
Water Gulf of Mexico, East and West Galveston Bay
Specialty Overnight shark fishing for bull, tiger lemon, hammer
Boats 25' Tiara **Tackle Supplied** Troll, spin, baitcast
Experience 15 years **Rates** day: $400 1/2 day $250

INGLESIDE, TEXAS

HEATHERINGTON, MAX-COASTAL GUIDE SERVICE (512) 758-8616
Address Box 1094, Ingleside, TX 78362
Airport Corpus Christi 18m **Accommodations** Aransas Pass 1m
Operation Guide, charter captain **Type of Fishing** Baitcast, troll
Fish Red, trout, king, bill **Season** June-Aug **Specialty** Red Fishing, Gulf Fishing
Water Red Fish Bay, Aransas Bay, Corpus Christi Bay, Gulf of Mexico
Boats 23' Outboard, 33' Bertram **Tackle Supplied** Baitcast, troll, spin
Experience 5 years **Rates** day: $150 Gulf trips day: $425/2 people
Guide's Notes: In the fall we fish the salt water flats. The fishing is casting to red fish. During the summer we troll for king mackerel, sailfish, and marlin in the Gulf of Mexico.

KATY, TEXAS

SIMMONS, LARRY-LARRY'S SPORT FISHING (713) 392-0477
Address 22903 Indian Drive, Katy, TX 77450
Airport Galveston 35m **Accommodations** Houston 70m
Operation Charter captain, outfitter **Type of Fishing** Troll, fly
Fish King, ling, dolphin, snapper, trout, sailfish **Season** Year-round
Water Galveston and Freeport offshore, Galveston Bay **Boats** Power boats
Specialty Offshore trolling & night fishing **Tackle Supplied** Spin, baitcast, troll
Experience 16 years **Rates** day: $400-600

PORT ISABEL, TEXAS

AUSTIN, CAPTAIN LOU-AUSTIN FISHING SERVICE (512) 943-6282
Address Box 1695, Port Isabel, TX 78578
Airport Brownsville 20m **Accommodations** Port Isabel
Operation Charter captain, outfitter **Type of Fishing** Spin, baitcast, troll
Fish Seatrout, redfish, flounder, all gulf species **Season** Year-round
Water Laguna Madre Bay, Gulf of Mexico
Specialty Drift fishing for trout, redfish, trolling for all offshore species
Boats 20' & 30' powerboats **Tackle Supplied** All
Experience 10 years **Rates** 1/2 day: $150-300/2 people
Guide's Notes: Port Isabel Area Fishing Calendar

January	Trout - Excellent - Some Redfish
February	Trout & Redfish - Fair to good last 2 weeks of month
March	Trout & Redfish - Excellent especially for large fish
April	Trout & Redfish - Excellent especially for large fish
May	Trout - Excellent - some Kingfish & Jackfish in Gulf
June	All fishing very good in Bay and Gulf
July	Peak month for Gulf fishing-trout & redfish good very early am
August	Peak month for Gulf fishing
September	Still good for Gulf - Some tarpon - Good for trout & redfish
October	Peak tarpon-Excellent Bay-Gulf can be good depending on weather
November	Trout & Redfish - Good to excellent
December	Trout & Redfish - Good

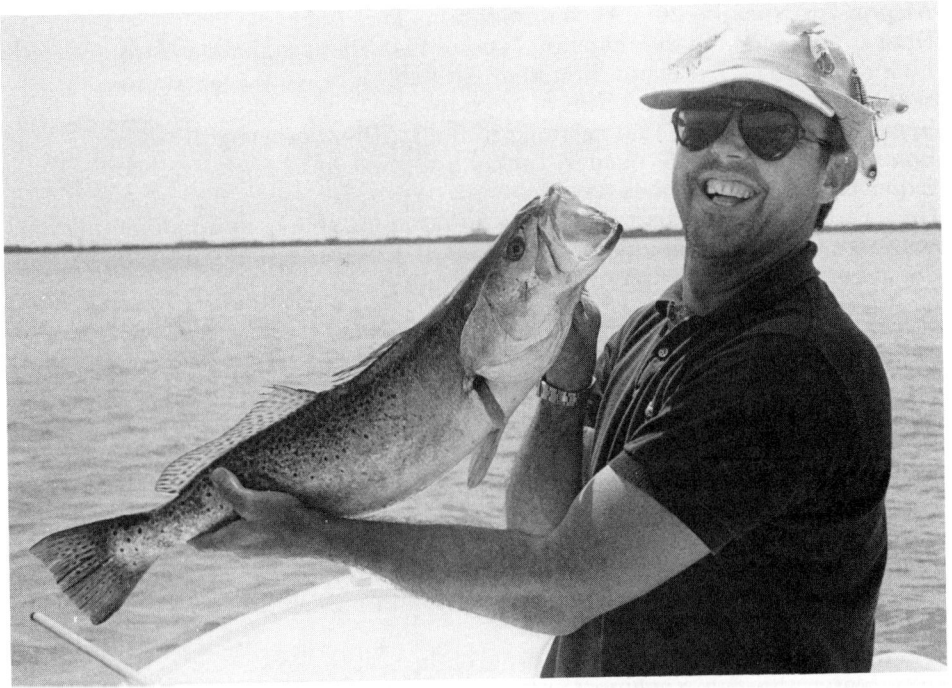

Spotted seatrout from the south Texas coast.   *Paul Bruun*

LANGFORD, CAPTAIN LARRY (512) 943-5791
Address P.O. Box 1853, Port Isabel, TX 78578
Airport Brownsville 20m **Accommodations** Port Isabel
Operation Guide, charter captain **Type of Fishing** Spin, baitcast, fly
Fish Redfish, speckled trout, flounder, snook **Season** Year-round
Water Lower Laguna Madre, Port Mansfield to Port Isabel
Specialty Some wade fishing, but mostly drift fishing lures & natural baits
Boats 19′ Ski barge for shallow water **Tackle Supplied** Spin, baitcast
Experience 5 years **Rates** 1/2 day: $150
Guide's Notes: Lower Laguna Madre Generally, I fish more for the redfish than speckled trout or flounder, mainly because they are the more aggressive fish. Also, pound for pound, they run larger here than the trout. Best times are springtime (March til June 1). The larger redfish are generally found during the fall months from October until December. In the fall it is not uncommon to see large schools of redfish from 8 to 15 pounds or more. These fish are caught both on lures (1/2 oz spoons or plactic worms) or on natural baits (usually mullet). I use the lightest tackle possible on the fish for greatest enjoyment.

THOMAS, CAPTAIN DEWITT (512) 943-3332
Address 121 Channel St., P.O. Box 1247, Port Isabel, TX 78578

Airport Brownsville 20m **Accommodations** Port Isabel
Operation Guide, charter captain **Type of Fishing** Spin, baitcast, troll
Fish Bay-specks, red drum, flounder, Gulf-shark **Season** Year-round
Water Laguna Madre Bay, Gulf of Mexico
Specialty Light tackle spin casting on the flats/light tackle gulf trolling
Boats 20′ flats boat, 25′ deep-V **Tackle Supplied** Spin, baitcast, troll
Experience 16 years **Rates** day: $450 1/2 day: $250
Guide's Notes: In the bay we mainly spincast for specks and reds on the flats
with live shrimp under a popping cork in 18 to 24 inches of water on low tide.
On about 20% of our trips, we use hardware.

PORT MANSFIELD, TEXAS

FUSTIN, CAPTAIN BOB (512) 944-2519, 821-5806
Address 732 N. Shore Dr., Port Mansfield, TX 78598
Airport Harlington 45m **Accommodations** Port Mansfield
Operation Charter captain **Type of Fishing** Spin, baitcast, troll, fly
Fish Trout, redfish, king, ling, marlin **Boats** Shallow sport scooter
Water Laguna Madre Bay, Gulf of Mexico **Tackle Supplied** Spin, baitcast, troll
Specialty Wade fishing in the bay for trout and redfish **Season** March-Nov.
Experience 5 years **Rates** day: $225
Guide's Notes: South Texas offers some of the best shallow water or flats fishing
from March through November. We wade fish for trout and redfish.

ROCKPORT, TEXAS

CLOUSE, GARY (512) 729-1520, 729-1550
Address P.O. Box 324, Rockport, TX 78382
Airport Corpus Christi 40m **Accommodations** Rockport
Operation Guide **Type of Fishing** Baitcast **Season** Year-round
Water Aransas Bay, Red Fish Bay, Corpus Bay, San Antonio Bay
Specialty Trout and redfishing in the flats **Fish** Trout, redfish, flounder
Boats Outboard, shallow draft, deep-V **Tackle Supplied** Spin, baitcast
Experience 5 years **Rates** day: $100/person (min. 3 people)

SOUTH PADRE ISLAND, TEXAS

ATKINSON, WALLY & JODY-FISHERMANS WHARF (512) 943-7818
Address P.O. Box 2097, South Padre Island, TX 78597
Airport Brownsville, 28m **Accommodations** On premises
Operation Outfitter, tackle shop, lodge **Type of Fishing** Spin, troll, fly
Fish Speckled trout, redfish, flounder, tuna **Season** Year-round
Water Laguna Madre, Gulf of Mexico **Specialty** Bay drift fishing, Gulf trolling
Boats 30′ Mako & trolling boats **Tackle Supplied** Spin, troll
Experience Varies **Rates** 1/2 day: $150

8. Midwest/Great Lakes: A fishing miracle!

Iowa, Kansas, Michigan, Minnesota, Missouri, Nebraska, Ohio, South Dakota, Wisconsin

The dominant water features of the midwest are the Great Lakes. These five lakes, largest concentration of fresh water in the world, cover a surface area roughly the size of New York, Pennsylvania, and New Jersey. A hundred years ago these lakes were superb fishing waters. The lands around them were covered with vast pine forests; the streams were gin-clear. These were the "shining waters" immortalized in Henry Wadsworth Longfellow's "Song of Hiawatha," written in 1855. Then came the sawmills, the factories, and the beginning of a long decline.

By the late 1950s, the Great Lakes fisheries were anything but great. Commercial fishing and the lamprey eel had depleted the huge stocks of indigenous lake trout. The alewife, a small form of herring that came up the St. Lawrence Seaway from the Atlantic Ocean, constituted an incredible 90% of the Great Lakes' fish population. The once great fishery was almost dead.

Nineteen sixty-six saw the stocking of Pacific salmon, along with the first successful attempts to control the lamprey. Young salmon waxed fat on millions of alewives and grew to record-breaking weights. A new era in Michigan sport fishing had begun. Later in the 1960s, the Michigan Department of Natural Resources began plants of steelhead and brown trout, and other Great Lakes states began their own plantings. The spectacular success of these efforts is now a matter of record.

Today, healthy populations of steelhead, brown trout, and three species of Pacific salmon provide fresh spawning runs every season of the year. As these fish leave the Great Lakes and enter streams, they provide anglers with the daily opportunity to catch trophy fish on light tackle.

If you hit one of these runs near its peak, you will experience world class fishing.

The state of Michigan, with almost 3400 miles of shoreline and hundreds of tributaries, offers many opportunities to fish huge spawning runs of salmon, steelhead, and brown trout. The waters most frequently fished for steelhead and salmon by the guides in this book were the Muskegon, Manistee, and Pere Marquette rivers.

The best-known brown trout stream in the state is the world-famous Au Sable, which flows from its headwaters near Grayling to an outlet into Lake Huron. Large trout can still be caught on the Au Sable, especially during the giant mayfly hatch which takes place around the end of June. Michigan also has some great black bass, walleye, and northern pike fishing, but we did not receive any response from light tackle guides who offer this type of fishing.

Although Michigan has been at the focus of the Great Lakes sport fishing revival, its neighbor to the west, Wisconsin, offers far more opportunities for guided fishing. Ninety-two Wisconsin guides responded to our questionnaire. This was the second largest response from all the states, and indicates that there is some outstanding fishing in this state.

Wisconsin, with almost 700 miles of shoreline on lakes Michigan and Superior, has great fishing for Pacific salmon, steelhead, and lake run brown trout. More than a dozen streams flowing into Lake Michigan make the Door County Peninsula one of the best places to seek these fish with light tackle. The northwest corner of the state near Ashland is another good area.

Salmon and steelhead fishing in Wisconsin is spectacular, but it represents only a fraction of the possibilities for guided fishing in this state. By far, most of the guides who responded to our questionnaire were walleye, muskie, or bass fishermen. Centers for fishing these warm water species are the Hayward and Boulder Junction areas in northern Wisconsin. Lakes and streams are literally everywhere here, so we have included maps of these areas. The most-mentioned lakes were the Minocqua Chain, the Flambeau and Chippewa Flowages, Big St. Germain Lake, Plum Lake, and North and South Twin Lakes. Good trout fishing is available on the Bois Brule, Namekagon, and Bad rivers. Popular rivers for warm water species are the Wisconsin in the central part of the state, and the Wolf, which empties into Lake Poygan on the eastern side of the state.

Minnesota, Wisconsin's neighbor to the west, offers excellent fishing for walleye, bass, and northern pike. However, a limited number of guides responded to our questionnaire, suggesting that the guiding industry in this state is much less developed than in Wisconsin. Guides concentrate on the Bemidji area and on the chain of lakes that make up Minnesota's northern border with Canada. Round, Leech, Pelican, and Deer lakes were favorites of the guides in the Bemidji area. Lake of the

Woods, Lac la Croix, and Rainy Lake were waters mentioned by the boundary water guides.

According to returns from guides in the plains states of South Dakota, Nebraska, Kansas, and Iowa, some very excellent fishing is to be had on the large impoundments of the major rivers which flow through these states. The waters of the Missouri River system most mentioned, starting in North Dakota and moving south, were lakes Sakakawea/Garrison, Oahe, and Sharpe. Other important waters in these states are Lake McConaughy in Nebraska, El Dorado Reservoir in Kansas, and Okoboji and Big Spirit Lakes in Iowa. Species available vary from lake to lake but include walleye, northern pike, striped bass, muskie, perch, and coho salmon.

The state of Missouri contains what many believe to be the largest concentration of blue ribbon bass lakes in the U.S. Lake of the Ozarks and Pomme de Terre, Truman, Stockton, and Wappapetto lakes were the ones most mentioned by the guides listed in this book. All offer excellent bass fishing; Lake Truman is currently one of the most productive bass lakes in the country. A bonus for the fisherman who is taking his wife and children on a vacation in this area, are the many fine family resorts offering swimming, tennis, and golf in addition to superb fishing.

Guide Al Denninger's 1984 record muskie.

Al Denninger

Iowa

ARNOLDS PARK, IOWA

DAVIS, JON-FISHING GUIDE SERVICE (712) 336-3355
Address Box 379, Arnolds Park, IA 51331
Airport Sioux Falls, SD 100m **Accommodations** Arnolds Park
Operation Guide **Type of Fishing** Spin, baitcast, troll
Fish Walleye, perch, panfish, northern **Season** Mar.-Nov.
Water West Okoboji Lake, Big Spirit Lake, East Okoboji Lake
Specialty Back trolling, jigging
Boats Pike boats **Tackle Supplied** Spin, baitcast, troll
Experience 2 years **Rates** day: $80 1/2 day: $50

MILFORD, IOWA

FITZGERALD, BOB (712) 338-2116
Address 1201 N Ave., Milford, IA 51351
Airport Spencer 12m **Accommodations** Okoboji Lake 2m
Operation Guide **Type of Fishing** Spin, baitcast, troll
Fish Walleye, bass, muskie, northern **Season** Year-round
Water West Okoboji, East Okoboji, Spirit and Center Lakes
Specialty Lake trolling
Boats Ranger 1600 **Tackle Supplied** Spin, baitcast, troll
Experience 15 years **Rates** 6 hours: $70/2 people

ROYAL, IOWA

McDONNELL, JIM (712) 933-5532, 332-5141 (ask for Mac)
Address Box 148, Royal, IA 51357
Airport Spencer 20m **Accommodations** Spencer 20m
Operation Guide **Type of Fishing** Spin, baitcast, troll
Fish Walleye, muskie, sm bass, panfish, pike **Season** May-Oct.
Water West Okoboji, East Okoboji, Big Spirit Lakes, Lost Island
Specialty Lake fishing, casting and trolling
Boats Canoe, outboards **Tackle Supplied** Spin, baitcast, troll
Experience 18 years **Rates** day: $85 6 hours: $75 1/2 day: $55
Guide's Notes: Peak times for walleye are June/July, muskies, July/Sept.
Author's Notes: Jim has authored a book entitled EXPLOSIVE FISHING TECHNIQUES and has written articles for FISHING FACTS magazine.

IOWA / MISSOURI

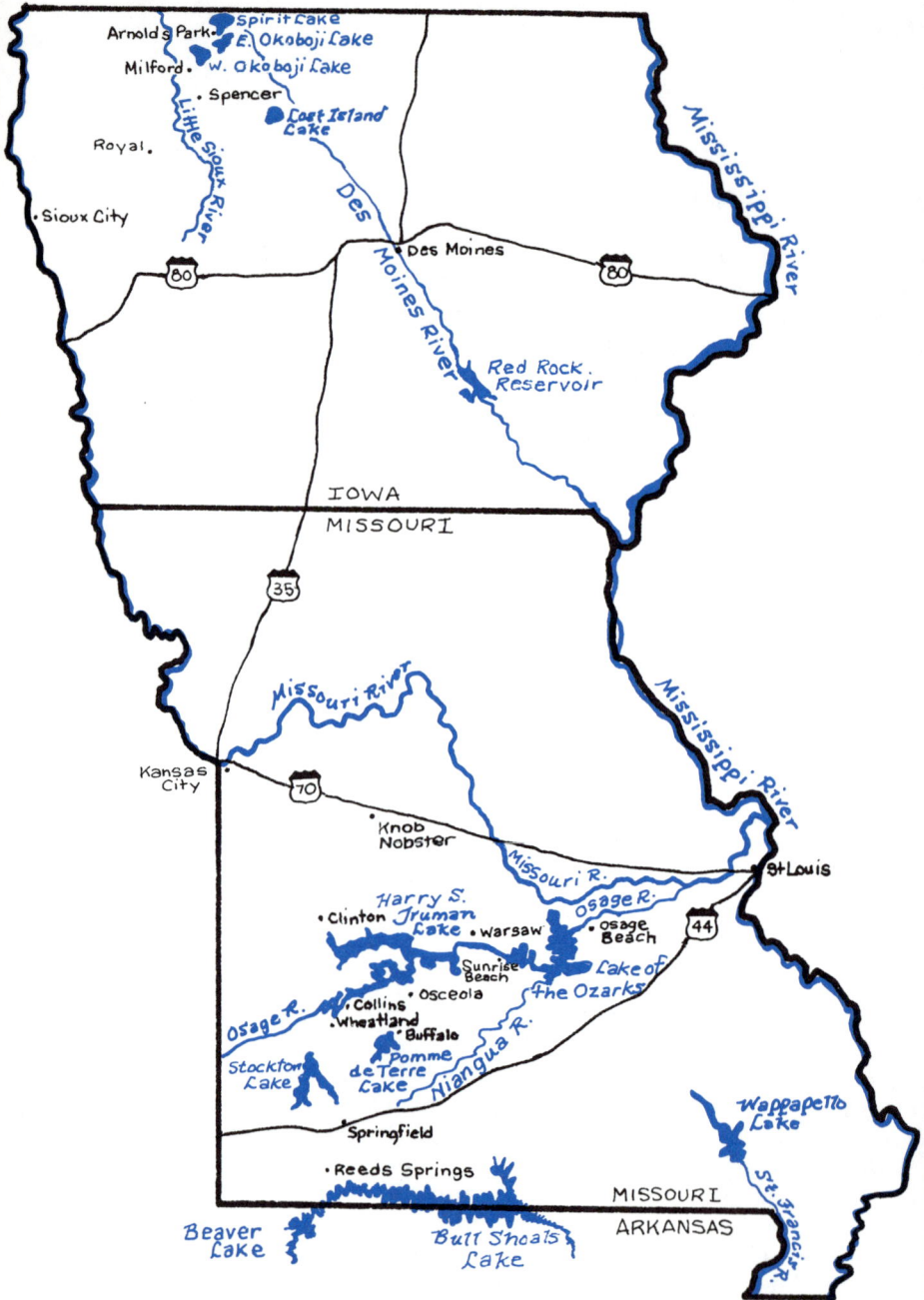

Spirit Lake
Arnold's Park
E. Okoboji Lake
Milford
W. Okoboji Lake
Spencer
Lost Island Lake
Royal
Little Sioux River
Sioux City
Des Moines River
Des Moines
80
80
Mississippi River
Red Rock Reservoir

IOWA
MISSOURI
35

Missouri River
Kansas City
70
Knob Nobster
Missouri R.
Mississippi River
St. Louis
Harry S. Truman Lake
Clinton
Warsaw
Osage R.
Osage Beach
44
Sunrise Beach
Lake of the Ozarks
Collins
Osceola
Wheatland
Osage R.
Buffalo
Niangua R.
Stockton Lake
Pomme de Terre Lake
Springfield
Wappapello Lake
Reeds Springs
St. Francis R.
MISSOURI
ARKANSAS
Beaver Lake
Bull Shoals Lake

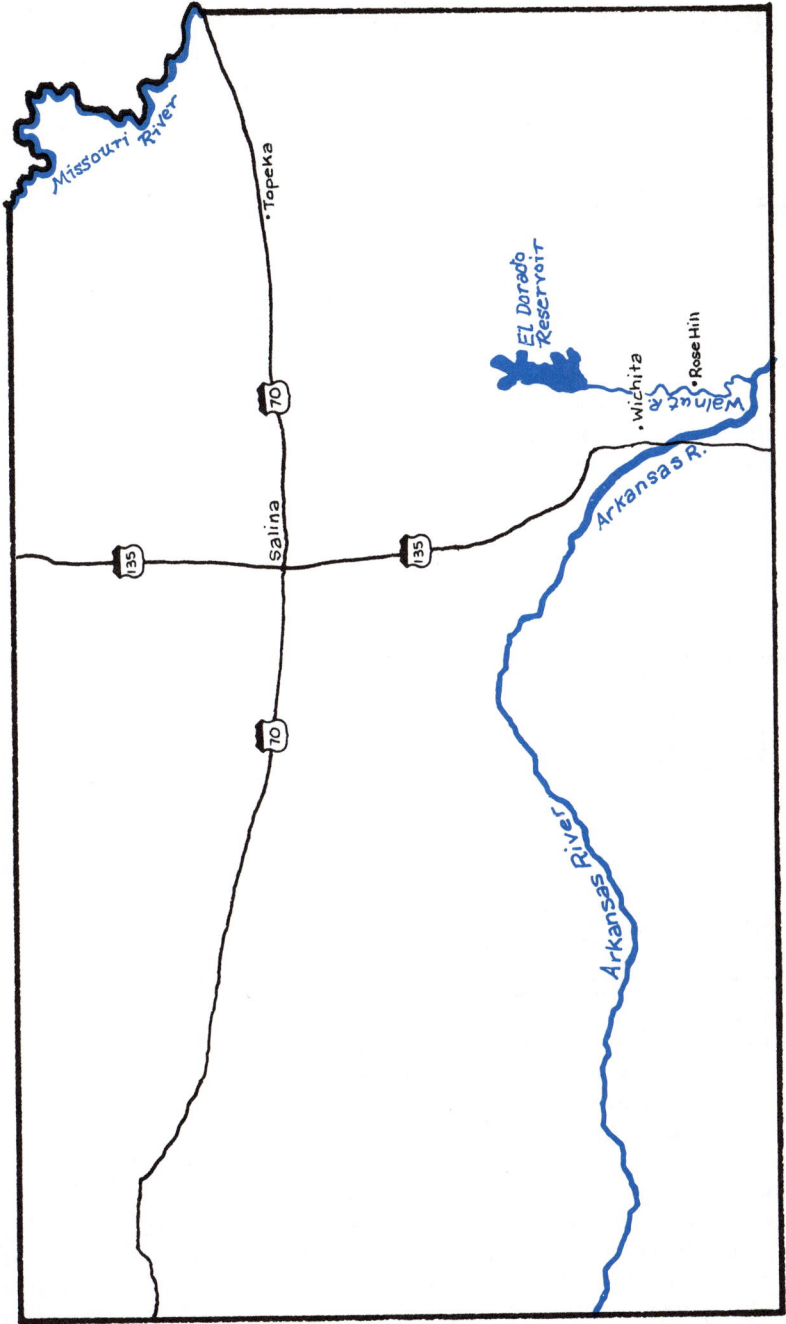

KANSAS

Kansas

ROSE HILL, KANSAS

SINKO, DON (316) 776-2059
Address 212 Reyer, Rose Hill, KS 67133
Airport Wichita 26m **Accommodations** Wichita
Operation Guide **Type of Fishing** Spin, baitcast, troll
Fish Bass, walleye, crappie **Season** April-Oct.
Water El Dorado Reservoir
Specialty Worm and jig fishing on lake
Boats Bass boat **Tackle Supplied** Spin, baitcast
Experience 4 years **Rates** day: $125 1/2 day: $75

Michigan

ADA, MICHIGAN

POBST, DICK-THORNAPPLE ORVIS SHOP (616) 676-0177
Address Box 133 Thornapple Village, Dept B, Ada, MI 49301
Airport Grand Rapids 6m **Accommodations** Grand Rapids 6m
Operation Tackle Shop, Outfitter **Type of Fishing** Fly
Fish Salmon, steelhead, trout **Season** Year-round
Water Pere Marquette, Muskegon, White, Little Manistee Rivers
Specialty Fly fishing **Boats** Canoes, drift boat **Tackle Supplied** Fly
Experience 2 years minimum experience-4 guides available
Author's Notes: We used Thornapple to set up a day of guided fishing on the Pere Marquette River. To say we had an outstanding day is an understatement. Our guide, Walt Grau, was one of the best I have ever fished with. I was left with the impression that I could rely on this operation for excellent guides, accurate information, and good service.

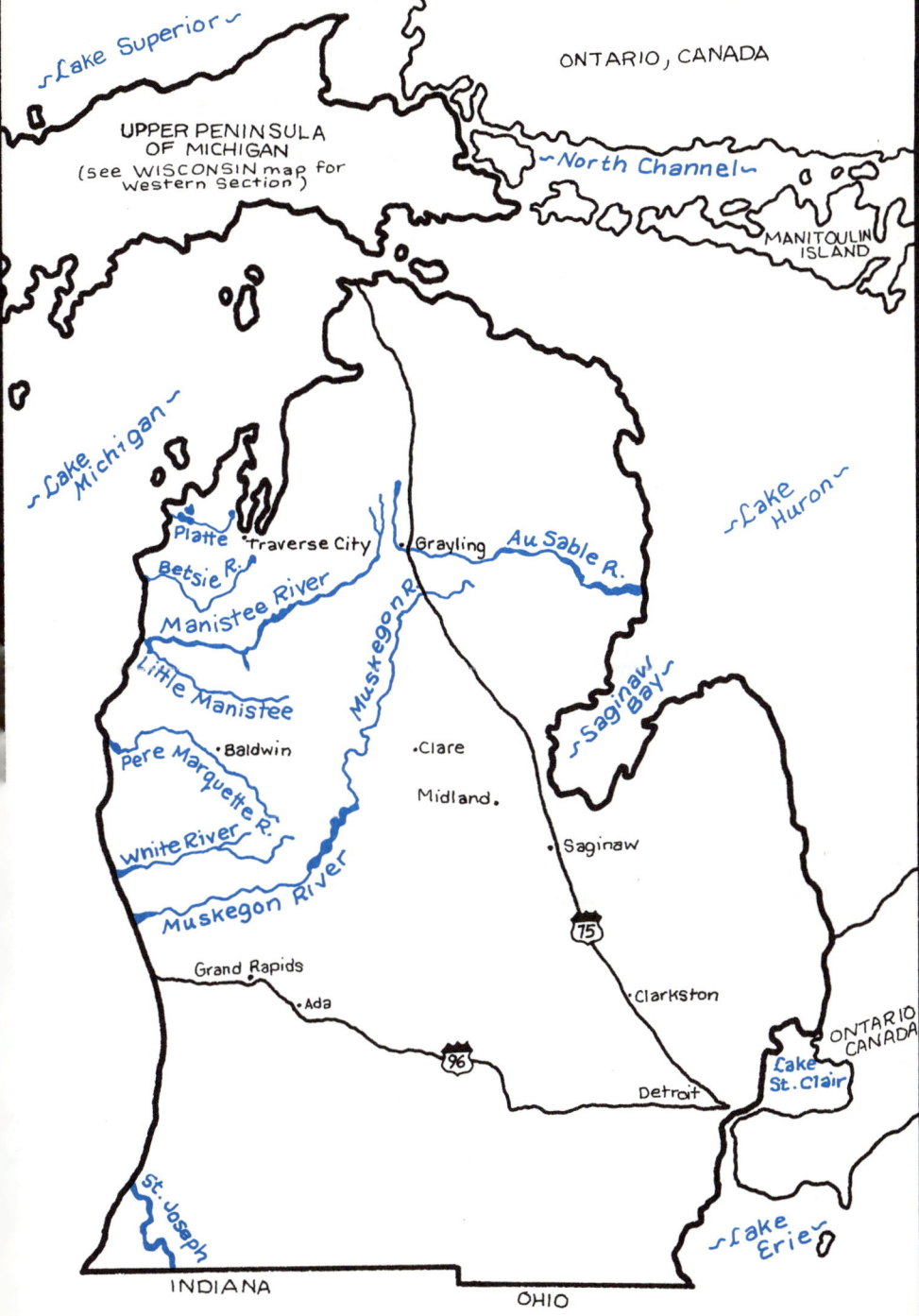

MICHIGAN

Lake Superior

ONTARIO, CANADA

UPPER PENINSULA
OF MICHIGAN
(see WISCONSIN map for
western section)

~North Channel~

MANITOULIN
ISLAND

~Lake Michigan~

~Lake Huron~

Platte
Traverse City
Grayling
Au Sable R.

Betsie R.

Manistee River

Muskegon R.

Saginaw Bay

Little Manistee

Pere Marquette R.
Baldwin
Clare

Midland

White River

Saginaw

Muskegon River

75

Grand Rapids

Clarkston

ONTARIO
CANADA

Ada

96

Lake
St. Clair

Detroit

St. Joseph

~Lake Erie~

INDIANA

OHIO

BALDWIN, MICHIGAN

NICHOLSON, ROBERT W. & CHRISTA-BALDWIN CREEK MOTEL
(616) 745-4401
Address Route 3, Box 3282, Baldwin, MI 49304
Airport Grand Rapids 72m **Accommodations** On premises
Operation Guide **Type of Fishing** Fly **Specialty** Fly fishing
Fish Steelhead, salmon, brown trout **Season** Year-round
Water Pere Marquette, Muskegon, Little Manistee Rivers
Boats Rowboat, canoes, outboard powered skiff **Tackle Supplied** Fly
Experience 10 years **Rates** day: $125
Guide's Notes: Pere Marquette River Steelhead are available to the angler from October through April. Fall fishing is best in November before the weather gets severe. Things pick up again in March, peaking the first two weeks in April. At this time the fish are spawning and easily visible to the fisherman. Summer steelhead were introduced to the Pere Marquette and other area streams in 1984. These offer the promise of fine sport through the warm months.

Chinook salmon enter the river on their spawning run in September. The action peaks around October 1st, then tapers off. These are large fish and angling is to visible groups on their redds.

Brown trout are resident the year around, with some interesting fishing for larger ones in the summer "dog days." For the beginning fly fisher May and June offer good opportunities. "Riffle Rainbows" are relatively easy to catch and provide fine sport for kids and ladies who are just getting started with the fly rod.

CLARE, MICHIGAN

SWAN, DICK (517) 386-3220
Address 3230 Oakland Drive, Clare, MI 48617
Airport Midland 40m **Accommodations** Clare
Operation Guide **Type of Fishing** Fly, spin, troll
Fish Steelhead, salmon **Season** April-Dec **Boats** Charter boat
Water Pere Marquette, Betsie, Big Manistee Rivers, Lake Michigan
Specialty Fly, spin, lake trolling **Tackle Supplied** Fly, spin, troll
Experience 10 years **Rates** day: $200 week: $1400
Author's Notes: Dick Swan is a retired school principal turned fishing guide and sports writer. He has gained national fame for developing the Noodle Rod and the techniques to fish them with, which have resulted in dozens of world line class records--we're talking about 30 pound fish on 2 pound test leaders. I have never fished with Dick, but I have watched him help clients fish for steelhead on the Betsie River. He is a very good guide. (Richard Swan, the author of this book, is no relation to Dick Swan, the guide and rod designer from Clare.)

CLARKSTON, MICHIGAN

FREELAND, MIKE-FREELAND OUTFITTERS (313) 625-4238
Address 10060 Big Lake Road, Clarkston, MI 48016
Airport Grand Rapids 100m **Accommodations** Clarkston
Operation Guide, tackle shop **Type of Fishing** Fly **Tackle Supplied** Fly
Fish Steelhead, king salmon, brown trout **Season** Year-round
Water Pere Marquette, Manistee, Little Manistee Rivers
Specialty Fly fishing for steelhead & salmon **Boats** Canoe, McKenzie
Experience 3 years **Rates** day: $175
Author's Notes: Mike was highly recommended to us by a reliable source.

GRAND RAPIDS, MICHIGAN

GRAU, WALTER (616) 495-8333, 676-0177
Address 110 Trowbridge NE, Dept. K, Grand Rapids, MI 89503
Airport Grand Rapids **Accommodations** Grand Rapids
Operation Guide **Type of Fishing** Fly, spin **Specialty** Fly fishing float trips
Fish Steelhead, king & silver salmon, brown trout **Season** Sept-April
Water Pere Marquette, Little Manistee, Betsie, Grand, White Rivers
Boats Canoes **Tackle Supplied** Spin, fly
Experience 3 years **Rates** day: $110 1/2 day: $60 week: $600
Guide's Notes: Although there is some decent summer fishing for bass and
resident stream trout, the very best fishing is for the lake run trout and salmon
species. These fish can be caught on fly tackle in the rivers from late August
thru mid-May. April is best for steelhead and October is the best for the salmon
species.

Conventional fly fishing gear can be used to catch steelhead, which are lying
behind spawning salmon, but the practical fly man will find the following rig
much more effective.

1. ROD: 10 to 10 1/2 foot noodle fly rod which balances
   with a #3 or #4 weight level fly line.
2. REEL: #72 Martin Multi-plyer fly reel
3. LINE: #3 weight level fly line or shooting monofilament line
4. LEADER: 10-16 feet with 8 pound Maxima tippet
   (go to lighter tippets in extremely clear water)
5. FLY: yarn fly, a single egg pattern, tied in the
   size and color of the natural eggs drifting in the stream.
6. WEIGHT: 1 or more split shot on a short dropper, 18-24 inches
   above the fly, use an appropriate size split shot to allow the egg fly
   to be fished naturally on the bottom as a drifting Salmon egg.

Cast the fly quartering upstream, and allow it to sink to the bottom. Then follow the drifting fly with the rod tip. The line is held off the water with the 10 foot rod to allow direct contact with the fly. When the method is fished correctly, an angler can feel a slight ticking as the split shot moves along the stream bottom. The leader is observed very carefully for a hesitation in the natural drift. The angler strikes quickly when the leader stops. Many times it will have stopped on a rock or a snag. But with luck, the angler is fast to an egg-eating steelhead.

Author's Notes: *We fished for steelhead with Walt Grau and found him to be an exceptional guide. He knew where the fish were holding and proved to be an excellent teacher of the techniques of hooking these elusive fish. The techniques he describes above may be shunned by the fly fishing purist, however, I find them quite similar to the nymphing techniques described by Charles E. Brooks in his excellent book NYMPH FISHING FOR LARGER TROUT. If you are the practical type--try it! You can always give it up after you have landed a few dozen fish!*

GRAYLING, MICHIGAN

GATES, RUSTY-GATES AU SABLE LODGE (517) 348-8462
Address Route 2 Box 2336, Stephan Bridge, Grayling, MI 49738
Airport Traverse City 50m **Accommodations** Grayling
Operation Lodge, Outfitter **Type of Fishing** Fly
Fish Brown, brook, rainbow trout **Season** April-October
Water Au Sable, Manistee Rivers, Big Creek **Specialty** Fly fishing
Boats Au Sable river boats **Tackle Supplied** Fly
Experience 20 years **Rates** day: $125

MARQUETTE, MICHIGAN

LINDQUIST, SCOTT-LUCKY LINK'S CHARTER SERVICE
(906) 228-6380, 475-5393
Address 131 W. Washington, Marquette, MI 49855
Airport Marquette **Accommodations** Marquette **Water** Lake Superior
Operation Charter captain, tackle shop **Type of Fishing** Spin, troll
Fish Lake trout, king and coho salmon, steelhead **Season** May-October
Specialty Lake trolling **Boats** 26' power cruiser **Tackle Supplied** Spin, troll
Experience 1 year **Rates** day: $225/6 people 1/2 day: $150/6 people
Guide's Notes: Lake Superior--Through the entire summer, we offer lake trout trolling with down rigger rods. During mid summer, we offer a unique opportunity to fish at Stannard Rock (a reef 40 miles north of Marquette) for native Lake Superior lake trout. Twenty pound plus lake trout can be taken by casting with light spinning tackle in shallow water. Limit catches are the rule and many fish are released. (In order to maintain this exceptional fishery we recommend that fish over ten pounds be released unless a trophy is taken for mounting.) We feel Stannard Rock offers probably the best lake trout fishery in Michigan and possibly the world. Due to the long travel time involved in making this

trip a higher rate ($400/6 people) is necessary. During August and September, coho and king salmon congregate near Marquette and we concentrate more on these species along with lake trout.
Author's Notes: Scott also owns Lindquist's Outdoor Sports, which is the Orvis outlet for the Marquette Area.

SAGINAW, MICHIGAN

GNATKOWSKI, MIKE-GNAT'S RIVER CHARTERS (517) 781-3631
Address 520 Victor Drive, Saginaw, MI 48603
Airport Tri-City 15m **Accommodations** Newaygo 7m
Operation Guide **Fish** Steelhead, salmon, trout **Season** Year-round
Water Muskegon, Pere Marquette, Au Sable and Big Manistee Rivers
Specialty Hot-shotting for steelhead and salmon, fly fishing
Boats McKenzie drift **Tackle Supplied** Fly, troll **Type of Fishing** Fly
Experience 3 years **Rates** day: $150
Guide's Notes: Muskegon River Fishing usually begins in early March for spring steelhead on the Muskegon and Pere Marquette Rivers. Hot-shotting from a Mckenzie drift boat has proven to be an exciting and productive method for anadromous species in the Great Lakes State. Steelheading continues until mid-May. May through September is prime time for fly fishing float trips for resident trout. June is best for the famous Brown Drake and Michigan "Hex" hatch. July through September is terrestrial time. September through October brings drift boating for king salmon on the mighty Muskegon. November-February is fall steelhead on the Pere Marquette and Muskegon.

SCHWIND, JOE (517) 865-6778
Address 11361 Roosevelt, Saginaw, MI 48603
Airport Tri-City 15m **Accommodations** Saginaw
Operation Guide **Type of Fishing** River float, hot-shotting, fly
Season September-June **Water** Manistee, Muskegon, Au Sable Rivers
Specialty Hot-shotting for steelhead **Fish** Steelhead, salmon
Boats McKenzie **Tackle Supplied** Fly, spin, baitcast
Experience 5 years **Rates** day: $150
Guide's Notes: Muskegon and Manistee Rivers Our steelhead run starts in early October peaking in November with bright fish trickling in all winter. Spring gives us huge runs that peak in April.

TRAVERSE CITY, MICHIGAN

WATERS, LEE G.
Address P.O. Box 306, Traverse City, MI 49684
Airport Traverse City **Accommodations** Traverse City **Operation** Guide
Fish Trout **Season** May-August **Water** Lake Michigan, local streams
Specialty Light tackle casting **Type of Fishing** Spin, baitcast, troll
Boats Canoe, outboard **Tackle Supplied** Spin, baitcast, troll
Experience 2 years **Rates** day: $135

MINNESOTA

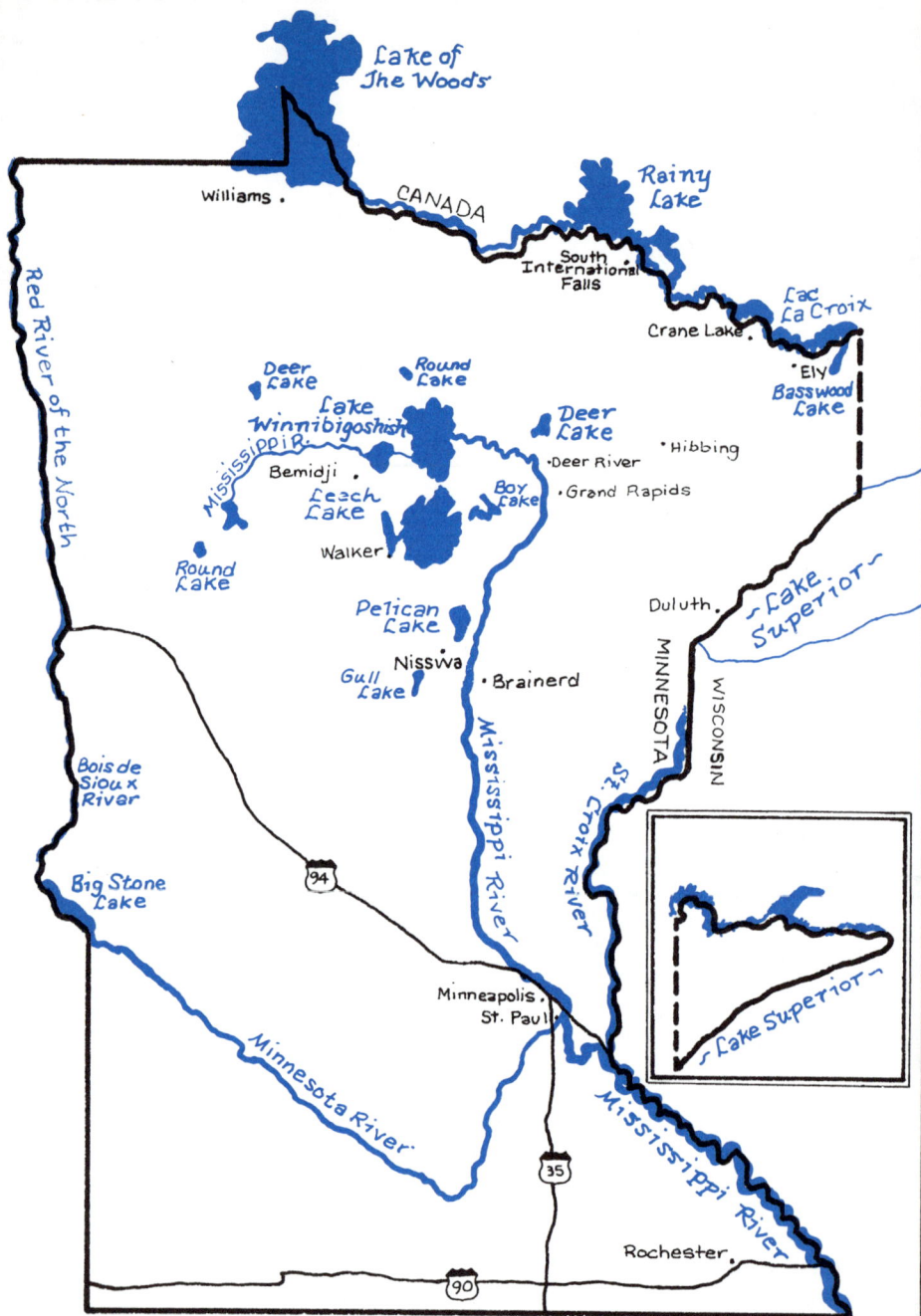

Lake of
The Woods

Williams

CANADA

Rainy
Lake

South
International
Falls

Lac
La Croix

Crane Lake

Red River of the North

Deer
Lake

Round
Lake

Lake
Winnibigoshish

Mississippi R.

Bemidji

Leech
Lake

Walker

Round
Lake

Deer
Lake

Deer River

Grand Rapids

Boy
Lake

Hibbing

Ely

Basswood
Lake

Pelican
Lake

Nisswa

Gull
Lake

Brainerd

Duluth

Lake
Superior

MINNESOTA

WISCONSIN

St. Croix River

Bois de
Sioux
River

Big Stone
Lake

94

Mississippi River

Minneapolis
St. Paul

Lake Superior

Minnesota River

35

Mississippi River

Rochester

90

Minnesota

BRAINERD, MINNESOTA

BOOS, FRED-GRAND VIEW LODGE (218) 963-2234
Address Rt. 6, Box 22, Brainerd, MN 56401
Airport Brainerd 15m **Accommodations** On premises
Operation Guide, lodge **Type of Fishing** Spin, baitcast, troll
Fish Walleye, northern pike, bass, crappie **Season** May-Oct.
Water Gull Lake, Round Lake, Pelican Lake, Boy Lake **Specialty** Lake fishing
Boats Rowboats **Tackle Supplied** Spin, baitcast, troll
Rates day: $140 1/2 day: $70

CRANE LAKE, MINNESOTA

ZUP, BILL (807) 599-2710, (218) 365-4018
Address Lac La Croix, Ontario, P.O. Crane Lake, MN 55725
Airport Hibbing 85m **Accommodations** Hibbing 85m
Operation Outfitter, lodge **Type of Fishing** All **Tackle Supplied** All
Fish Smallmouth bass, walleye, pike, lake trout **Season** May-October
Water Lac La Croix, Iron, Crouted, McAree Lakes **Specialty** Canoe trips
Aircraft Floatplanes **Boats** Rowboats, canoes, bass boats
Experience 35 years **Rates** day: $60 week: $360

DEER RIVER, MINNESOTA

NEUSTROM, TOM-DENNY'S SPORTING GOODS (218) 246-2131
Address P.O. Box 412, Deer River, MN 56636
Airport Grand Rapids 17m **Accommodations** Grand Rapids 17m
Operation Guide **Type of Fishing** All **Specialty** Walleye fishing
Fish Walleye, muskie, bass **Season** May-Nov.
Water Winnibigoshish, Deer, Jessie Lakes, Mississippi R., Big Cut Foot
Boats 16' Deep V, Lund Preditor **Tackle Supplied** Spin, baitcast, troll
Experience 14 years **Rates** day: $125 1/2 day: $65
Guide's Notes: Deer River/Grand Rapids Area Waters
   Walleye fishing is good May to November. The fishing peaks May through June and again in October through November. We mainly jig fish with leadhead jigs. Our area is recognized as one of the best in the U.S.
   Smallmouth bass We have over 12 local small bass lakes where we regularly catch and release up to 25 largemouth bass a day in the 2 - 4 pound class. Fly fishing areas are available.

Muskie fishing is late July to November 1st with August being the peak. Fishing is strictly casting with large crankbaits, jerkbaits, and bucktails.
Author's Notes: Tom was recommended to us by Larry Schoenborn, producer of "Fishing the West," a nationally syndicated television show. Tom will be featured on a future program. We understand he is an excellent guide.

ELY, MINNESOTA

BELAND, DON (218) 365-5811
Address Box 808, Ely, MN 55731
Airport Duluth 125m **Accommodations** Ely **Operation** Outfitter
Fish Smallmouth, largemouth bass, walleye, northern **Season** May-October
Water Border lakes from L. Superior to Fort Frances (west), Basswood, Rainey Lakes, Lac la Croix **Specialty** All types of fresh water fishing **Type of Fishing** All
Boats Motor boats, canoes **Aircraft** Floatplanes (as required)
Experience 35 years **Rates** day: $160 week: $1120

POSCOE, JAMES-WILDERNESS OUTFITTERS, INC. (218) 365-3211
Address 1 East Camp Street, Ely, MN 55731
Airport Duluth 110m **Accommodations** Ely
Operation Outfitter, tackle shop, lodge **Type of Fishing** All
Fish Smallmouth, largemouth bass, walleye, northern **Season** May-Oct
Water Boundary waters canoe area
Specialty Canoe and fly in fishing trips **Aircraft** Floatplane
Boats Rowboats, canoes **Tackle Supplied** All
Experience 60 years **Rates** day: $35-135

NISSWA, MINNESOTA

KOEP, MARV-NISSWA GUIDES LEAGUE (218) 963-2547
Address Box 130, Hazelwood Park, Nisswa, MN 56468
Airport Brainerd 13m **Accommodations** Nisswa
Operation Guide, tackle shop **Type of Fishing** Spin,baitcast, troll
Fish Walleye, bass, northern **Season** May-Oct **Boats** 16'-18' lund aluminum
Water Over 50 lakes of the Nisswa Area **Tackle Supplied** Spin, baitcast, troll
Specialty Back trolling for walleye, crank fishing for bass
Experience 20 years **Rates** day: $140 1/2 day: $70/2 people
Guide's Notes: Nisswa/Brainerd Area Waters
   Walleye fishing is best mid-May through June. Mid-August through October is best for bass. Northern pike fishing is best July through October. We have 12 guides booked out of our shop.

WALKER, MINNESOTA

MAAS, AL (218) 547-1600
Address Box 353, Walker, MN 56484

Airport Bemidji 40m **Accommodations** Walker **Operation** Guide
Fish Walleye, largemouth bass, muskie, northern pike **Season** May-Oct.
Water Leech Lake **Specialty** Light tackle casting for bass and muskie
Boats Bass boats, deep-V **Tackle Supplied** All **Type of Fishing** All
Experience 24 years **Rates** day: $125
Guide's Notes: Leech Lake Fish Calendar Walleye and bass are best from
mid-May to mid-June and again in the fall from September to early October.
The muskie peak is July through October and we have good northern pike year
round.

Leech Lake has plenty of largemouth bass in the 4-6 pound range. These bass
have received practically no pressure because everyone fishes for the walleye
and muskie. We take them on both lures and flies.
*Author's Notes: Al Maas appeared on Larry Shoenborn's television program
"Fishing the West" in March of 1986. The fishing on Leech Lake looked fantastic
and Al's expertise was obvious. Reliable contacts in Minnesota have confirmed
him as an excellent guide.*

WILLIAMS, MINNESOTA

PAINOVICH, NICK-ZIPPEL BAY RESORT (218) 783-6235
Address Star Route, Williams, MN 56686
Airport International Falls 75m **Accommodations** On premises
Operation Charter captain, lodge **Type of Fishing** Spin, baitcast, troll
Fish Walleye, northern, sauger, smallmouth bass **Season** May-Oct.
Water Lake of the Woods **Specialty** Lake trolling, jigging
Boats 14' Deep-V, 26' inboard **Tackle Supplied** Spin, baitcast, troll
Experience 8 years **Rates** day: $80 week: $560 1/2 day: $40
Guide's Notes: Lake of the Woods We fish May through October with mid-July
through August being our peak. Our favorite lures are Little Joe type spinners
with live bait and Shad Raps.

Missouri

BUFFALO, MISSOURI

FLETCHER, JACK L. (417) 345-2917
Address Rt 4, Box 370, Buffalo, MO 65622
Airport Springfield 30m **Accommodations** Buffalo **Operation** Guide
Type of Fishing Baitcast **Fish** Bass, crappie, walleye
Water Truman Lake, Lake of the Ozarks, Stockton, Niangua River
Boats Bass boat, johnboat **Tackle Supplied** Spin, baitcast
Experience 7 years **Rates** day: $100 1/2 day: $60
Guide's Notes: Truman Lake is famous for the hot weather months. Bass fishing catches of over 100 bass per day are not uncommon. The fishing peaks in August and September, and lots of heavy fish are caught in April and May. Heavy timber and brush make spinner baits and buzz baits the favorite on Truman. Top water lures are hot in October and November. The **Niangua River** is probably the least fished smallmouth river in Missouri and is great in May and June.

CLINTON, MISSOURI

CUSTER, STEVEN (816) 885-6346, 885-3313
Address 405 Truman Ave., Clinton, MO 64735
Airport Kansas City 100m **Accommodations** Clinton
Operation Guide **Type of Fishing** Lake bass **Boats** Bass boats
Fish Lm, white, striped bass, crappie **Season** Mar-Nov **Water** Truman Lake
Specialty Largemouth bass fishing from a bass boat **Tackle Supplied** Baitcast
Experience 1 year **Rates** day: $100 1/2 day: $65
Guide's Notes: Truman Lake is only six years old and is fast establishing itself as THE bass lake of the 1980's. It has some 55,000 acres at normal pool level and can quadruple in size when used for flood control. The flooded timber gives it unbelievable bass-catching potential. In April, 1985, the new lake record was set with a 13 lb. 9 oz. largemouth bass brought into Bucksaw Point Marina. It was only 5 ounces shy of a state record. White bass, striped bass, and crappie are also common in the lake.

DUNNING, ALBERT E. (816) 885-4813, 438-2280
Address 705 Cardinal, Clinton, MO 64735
Airport Kansas City 100m **Accommodations** Clinton **Operation** Guide
Fish Lm bass, crappie, white bass, hybrid **Season** March-Dec.
Water Lake of the Ozarks, Truman, Stockton, Pomme de Terre Lakes
Specialty Lake fishing **Type of Fishing** Spin, baitcast, troll

Boats Bass boats **Tackle Supplied** Baitcast
Experience 30 years **Rates** day: $100 week: $700

SHANKS, LARRY (816) 885-8281, 438-2841
Address Jct 7 and 13 E., Clinton, MO 64735
Airport Kansas City 100m **Accommodations** Clinton **Operation** Guide
Fish White bass, hybrid, black bass, crappie **Season** March-Nov.
Water Truman Lake, Lake of the Ozarks **Type of Fishing** Baitcast
Specialty Day trips with bass boat **Boats** Bass boats
Experience 7 years **Rates** day: $100 week: $700 1/2 day: $65

SIMMS, MIKE (816) 885-5252
Address 418 Flora, Clinton, MO 64735
Airport Kansas City 100m **Accommodations** Clinton **Operation** Guide
Fish Black bass, stripers, white bass, crappie **Season** March-Nov.
Water Truman Lake, Lake of the Ozarks **Type of Fishing** Spin, baitcast, troll
Specialty Casting and trolling **Boats** Bass boat **Tackle Supplied** All
Experience 8 years **Rates** day: $125 1/2 day: $75
Guide's Notes: For black bass fishing on **Truman Lake**, we recommend a 14
to 20 pound test line, and good medium-heavy or heavy rods with good reels.
This is almost necessary because of the brush and trees.

THOMAS, TERRY (816) 885-8296
Address 500 10th St. Terrace, Clinton, MO 64735
Airport Kansas City 100m **Accommodations** Clinton **Operation** Guide
Fish Black bass, white bass, hybrid bass **Season** June-Nov.
Water Truman Lake, Lake of the Ozarks **Type of Fishing** Lake bass
Specialty Lake fishing for black bass (flipping) **Boats** Bass boat
Experience 2 years **Rates** day: $100 1/2 day: $65

COLLINS, MISSOURI

HARRIS, RILEY (417) 275-4622, (816) 438-2939
Address Star Route, Collins, MO 64738
Airport Kansas City 91m **Accommodations** Collins **Operation** Guide
Fish Black bass, hybrids, crappie, white bass **Season** March-Dec.
Water Truman, Stockton, Pomme de Terre Lakes
Specialty Lake fishing **Type of Fishing** Spin, baitcast, troll
Boats Bass boat **Tackle Supplied** Spin, baitcast
Experience 10 years **Rates** day: $100 1/2 day: $60

KNOB NOSTER, MISSOURI

JENKINS, WALLACE (816) 563-2470, 563-5450
Address 551 North Broadway, Knob Noster, MO 65336
Airport Kansas City 110m **Accommodations** Knob Noster

Operation Guide **Type of Fishing** Spin, baitcast **Tackle Supplied** Baitcast
Fish Black bass, crappie, striped, hybrid **Season** Mar-Nov **Boats** Bass boats
Water Truman Lake, Lake of the Ozarks **Specialty** Flipping, casting
Experience 11 years **Rates** day: $100 1/2 day: $60

OSAGE BEACH, MISSOURI

VANCE, RANDY RAY-IDLE DAYS AND GALA RESORT
(314) 348-2134, 348-5274
Address P.O. Box 689, Rt 2, Box 58B-1, Osage Beach, MO 65065
Airport Resort Aire 10m **Accommodations** On premises
Operation Outfitter, lodge **Type of Fishing** Spin, baitcast **Boats** Bass boat
Fish Bass, crappie, white bass, hybrid stripers **Season** Year-round
Water Lake of the Ozarks, Osage River **Tackle Supplied** Spin, baitcast, troll
Specialty Bass and crappie fishing with artificial lures or live bait
Experience 5 years **Rates** day: $110 week: $475 1/2 day: $70
Guide's Notes: Lake of the Ozarks and Osage River Fishing Calendar Crappie
fishing is great year-round with the annual spawn taking place during April
and May. The best lures are plastic tube jigs and grubs 1/32 to 1/4 ounce weight.

Bass fishing is best from February thru June and also October and November
with the spawning during May and June. Best lures are chartreuse crankbaits
thru early April, jig and frog plastic worm for the remainder of the year until
fall, and white spinnerbait for fall.

White bass fishing is at its best February, March, June, July, September,
October and November. The fall run during September and October is outstanding. We use 1/4 ounce grubs, kastmaster spoons, roadrunners and rooster tails
for all seasons.
Author's Notes: *A reliable local contact tells us Randy has a nice resort on the
water and his guide service is excellent.*

OSCEOLA, MISSOURI

JELKS, JAY-OSCEOLA MARINA (417) 646-2670
Address Rt 2, Osceola, MO 64776
Airport Kansas City 94m **Accommodations** Osceola
Operation Outfitter, marina **Type of Fishing** Spin, baitcast, troll
Fish Bass, crappie, walleye, catfish **Season** Mar-Nov **Water** Truman Lake
Boats Bass boats **Tackle Supplied** Spin, baitcast, troll **Specialty** Lake trolling
Experience 14 years **Rates** day: $100 1/2 day: $60

REEDS SPRING, MISSOURI

KING, STACEY (417) 338-2308
Address Rt 4, Box 3290, Reeds Spring, MO 65737
Airport Springfield 50m **Accommodations** Reeds Spring **Operation** Guide

Fish Black bass **Season** Year-round **Type of Fishing** All **Boats** Bass boats **Water** White R., Beaver, Table Rock, Bull Shoals, Taneycomo Lakes **Specialty** Light tackle casting to bass **Tackle Supplied** Spin, baitcast **Experience** 16 years **Rates** day: $125 plus gas

SUNRISE BEACH, MISSOURI

PIESCHL, JACK-LODGE OF THE FOUR SEASONS (314) 374-5296
Address Box 95, Sunrise Beach, MO 65079
Airport Lake of the Ozarks 7m **Accommodations** On premises
Operation Guide, lodge **Type of Fishing** Spin, baitcast **Water** Lake of the Ozarks
Fish Lm bass, crappie, striped bass **Season** Mar-Nov **Boats** Bass boats
Specialty Flipping in top water for lm bass **Tackle Supplied** Spin, baitcast
Experience 16 years **Rates** day: $125 plus gas 1/2 day: $75 plus gas
Author's Notes: Jack is the head guide at the world class, 5 star rated, Lodge of the Four Seasons, located on Lake of the Ozarks. He has over seventy guides working for him.

The accommodations, the food, and Jack's guide services are all known to be excellent.

WARSAW, MISSOURI

BARAKS, FRED-OSAGE BLUFF MARINA (816) 438-2011, 438-2939
Address Rt #2, Box 357, Warsaw, MO 65355
Airport Springfield 80m **Accommodations** Warsaw **Operation** Guide, marina
Fish Bass, crappie, white bass hybrids, muskie **Season** Year-round
Water Truman Lake, Lake of the Ozarks, Pomme de Terre
Specialty All methods of bass and crappie fishing
Boats Bass boats, pontoon **Type of Fishing** Spin, baitcast, troll
Experience 4 years **Rates** day: $125 week: $800 1/2 day: $75
Author's Notes: Fred Baraks is President of the Truman Lake Professional Guide Association.

DOUTHIT, CHET (816) 438-5205, 438-2280
Address HCR Box 4, Rt 66, Warsaw, MO 65355
Airport Springfield 80m **Accommodations** Warsaw
Operation Guide **Type of Fishing** Baitcast
Fish Bass, crappie **Season** Apr-Nov **Specialty** Fishing for bass and crappie
Water Truman Lake, Lake of the Ozarks **Boats** Bass boats
Experience 6 years **Rates** day: $140

MITTLESTADT, CHARLIE (816) 438-2758, 438-2939
Address P.O. Box 1087, Pom-o-sa Heights, Warsaw, MO 65355
Airport Springfield 80m **Accommodations** Warsaw
Operation Guide **Type of Fishing** Spin, baitcast
Fish Black bass, crappie, white bass, hybrid bass **Season** April-Dec.

Water Truman L. **Specialty** Baitcasting for bass **Boats** Bass boats
Experience 4 years **Rates** day: $125 1/2 day: $75
Author's Notes: *Charlie is Secretary/Treasurer of the Truman Lake Professional Guides Association and helped us contact the guides from this area.*

NOVINSKA, TOM (816) 438-2903, 438-2280
Address P.O. Box 543, Warsaw, MO 65355
Airport Springfield 80m **Accommodations** Warsaw
Operation Guide **Type of Fishing** Baitcast **Tackle Supplied** Baitcast, spin
Fish Bass, crappie, hybrid, white bass **Season** Mar-Dec **Boats** Bass boats
Water Harry Truman Reservoir **Specialty** Baitcasting
Experience 7 years **Rates** day: $125 1/2 day: $70

WHEATLAND, MISSOURI

IKERD, ADRON (417) 282-6045, 477-3313
Address Rt 1, Box 91, Wheatland, MO 65779
Airport Kansas City 90m **Accommodations** Clinton 9m **Operation** Guide
Fish Bass, crappie **Type of Fishing** Spin, baitcast **Specialty** Bass fishing
Water Truman L. **Season** Apr-Nov **Boats** Bass boat **Tackle Supplied** Baitcast
Experience 5 years **Rates** day: $125

Nebraska

BRULE, NEBRASKA

ALLEN, BEN-VAN'S LAKEVIEW FISHING CAMP (308) 284-4965
Address RR #1, Box 9, Brule, NE 69127
Airport N. Platte 75m **Accommodations** On premises **Operation** Guide
Fish Walleye, trout, rainbow **Season** May-Sept **Type of Fishing** Spin, troll
Water Lake McConaughy **Specialty** Boat fishing-drifting
Boats Pontoon, 18' outboard **Tackle Supplied** Spin, baitcast, troll
Experience 15 years **Rates** day: $125 1/2 day: $70/ 2 people

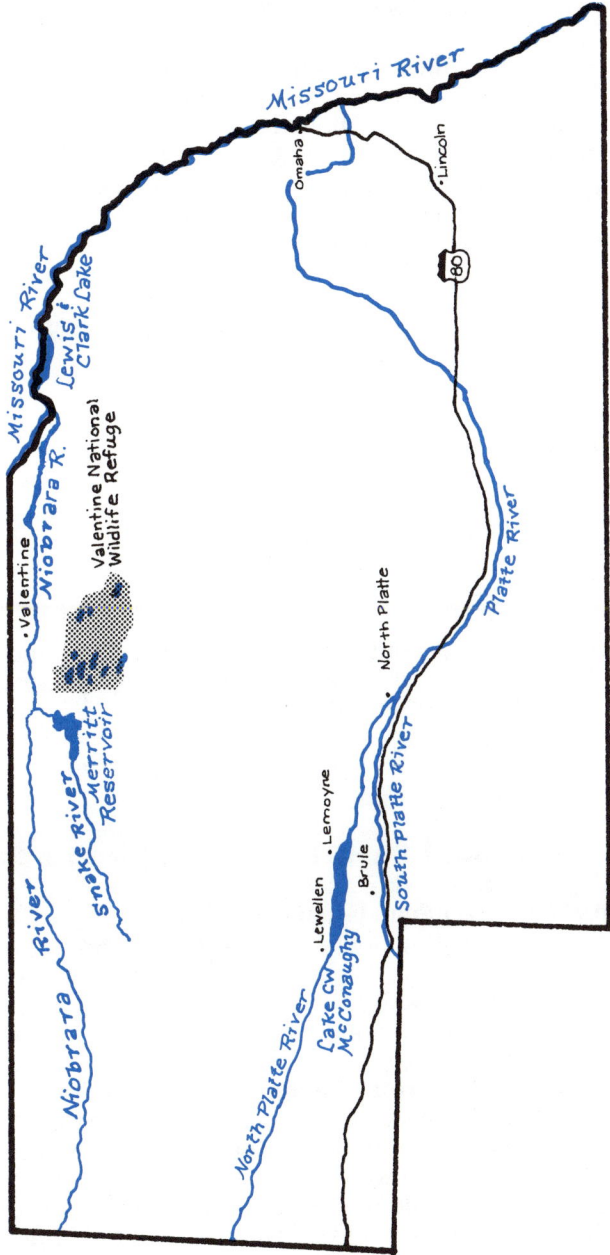

NEBRASKA

LEMOYNE, NEBRASKA

PROPST, BOB-FISHING ENTERPRISES (308) 726-2811, (605) 223-3111
Address Box 19, HCR 61, Lemoyne, NE 69146
Airport North Platte 50m **Accommodations** Lemoyne
Operation Outfitter **Fish** Walleye, rainbow, striper, bass **Season** Mar-Dec
Water L. McConaughy, Oahe Res. (SD), Garrison Res. (ND), L. Sakakawea (ND)
Specialty Trophy walleye fishing **Type of Fishing** Spin, baitcast, troll
Boats 16' Deep V, walleye rig **Tackle Supplied** Spin, baitcast, troll
Experience 32 years **Rates** day: $145
Guide's Notes: Lake McConaughy Best times for walleye are March through
April, and November, which is the best month of all. Rainbow fishing is excellent
May and June. Stripers are best October and November.
Author's Notes: Bob has written articles for FISHING FACTS Magazine, and
represents several tackle manufacturers.

LEWELLEN, NEBRASKA

WOLFORD, JERRY (308) 778-5423
Address P.O. Box 94, Lewellen, NE 69147
Airport N. Platte 80m **Accommodations** Lewellen
Operation Guide **Type of Fishing** Spin, baitcast, troll
Fish Walleye, trout, striped bass, catfish **Season** Year-round
Water Lake McConaughy **Specialty** Drift fishing for walleye and stripers
Boats 23 ft. inboard-outboard open fisher **Tackle Supplied** Spin, baitcast, troll
Experience 20 years **Rates** day: $125/up to 4 people

VALENTINE, NEBRASKA

DAVENPORT, JON-MERRITT DAM TRADING POST (402) 376-3437
Address Star Rt 1, Valentine, NE 69201
Airport N. Platte 133m **Accommodations** On premises
Operation Outfitter, tackle shop, lodge **Type of Fishing** Spin, baitcast, troll
Fish Walleye, largemouth bass, muskie, smallmouth bass **Season** May-Aug.
Water Merritt Res., Valentine Refuge Lake, Snake River **Tackle Supplied** All
Specialty Walleye and muskie fishing **Boats** Lund pro anglers
Experience 5 years **Rates** day: $160
Guide's Notes: Merrit Reservoir, Valentine Refuge Lakes Peak time for
largemouth and smallmouth bass is May and June. Walleye fishing is good May
through August with mid-May to mid-June the best time for a trophy. The best
time for a muskie trophy is mid-May to mid-June.
Author's Notes: Larry Schoenborn, producer of "Fishing the West," highly
recommended Jon Davenport as an excellent all around fishing guide.

Ohio

BURTON, OHIO

TOMASKO, BOB-BOB TOMASKO OUTDOORS (216) 834-1347

Address 14569 Hickox, P.O. Box 258, Burton, OH 44021
Airport Cleveland 60m **Accommodations** On premises
Operation Guide **Type of Fishing** Spin, baitcast, troll
Fish Walleye, muskie, pike, salmon **Season** May to ice-up
Water Pymatuning Res., Conneaut River, Mosquito Creek Lake, Lake Ontario
Specialty Boat fishing **Boats** Bass boats **Tackle Supplied** Spin, baitcast, troll
Experience 12 years **Rates** day: $125
Guide's Notes: Our inland guide service is the only professional guide service available throughout northeast Ohio and northwest Pennsylvania. We can guide you for walleyes, muskies, largemouth and smallmouth bass, northern pike, and panfish. We supply all of the bait. We can hop lakes, if that is what it takes to catch fish. When we have good days, we could start the day fishing for walleyes, then switch to the elusive muskie, and finish with some tackle busting bass. Inland guiding starts May 1st and runs thru ice-up, with late fall being the best for the trophy hunter.

EAST LIVERPOOL, OHIO

BRATT, ROY AND BETTY-OHIO RIVER FISHING GUIDE SERVICE, INC. (216) 385-8667

Address 16491 Staunton Avenue, East Liverpool, OH 43920
Airport Pittsburgh 40m **Accommodations** East Liverpool
Operation Guide **Type of Fishing** Spin, baitcast **Season** Year-round
Fish Bass, walleye, muskie, crappie **Water** Ohio River, small lakes in area
Boats Bass boats **Tackle Supplied** Spin, baitcast, troll
Experience 4 years **Rates** day: $90 1/2 day: $50
Author's Notes: Roy has gained a very good reputation in Northeast Ohio.

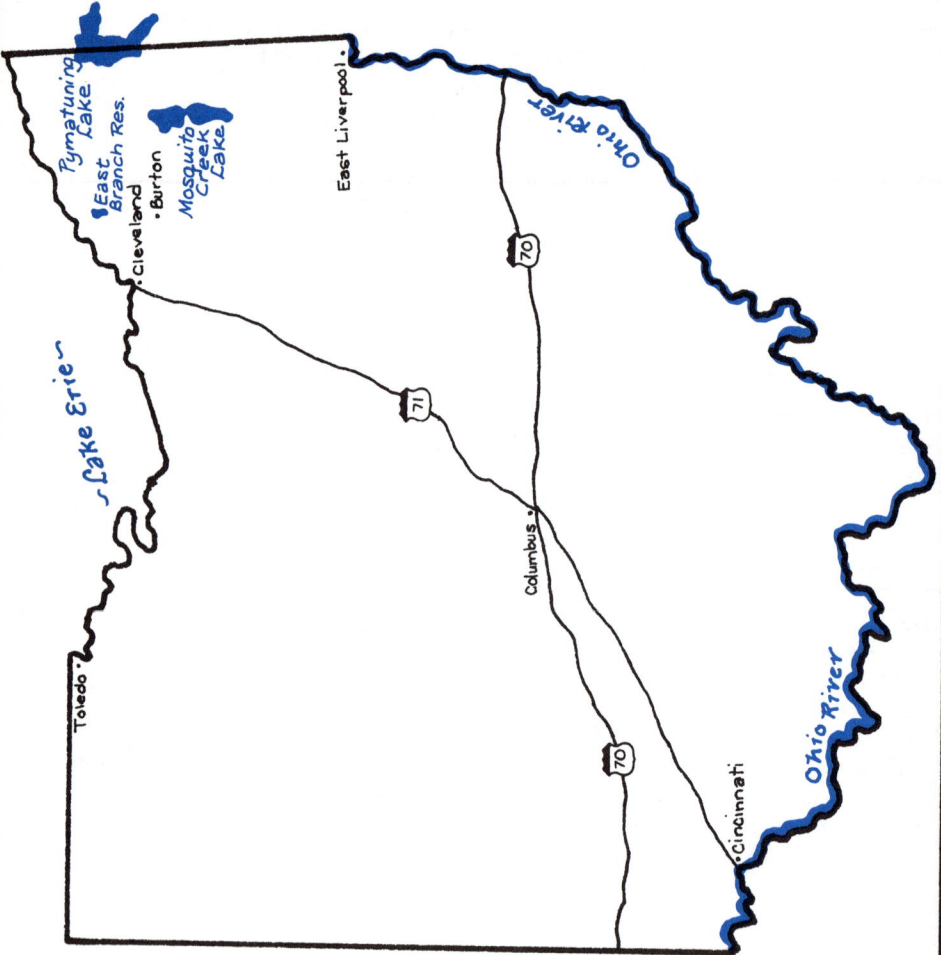

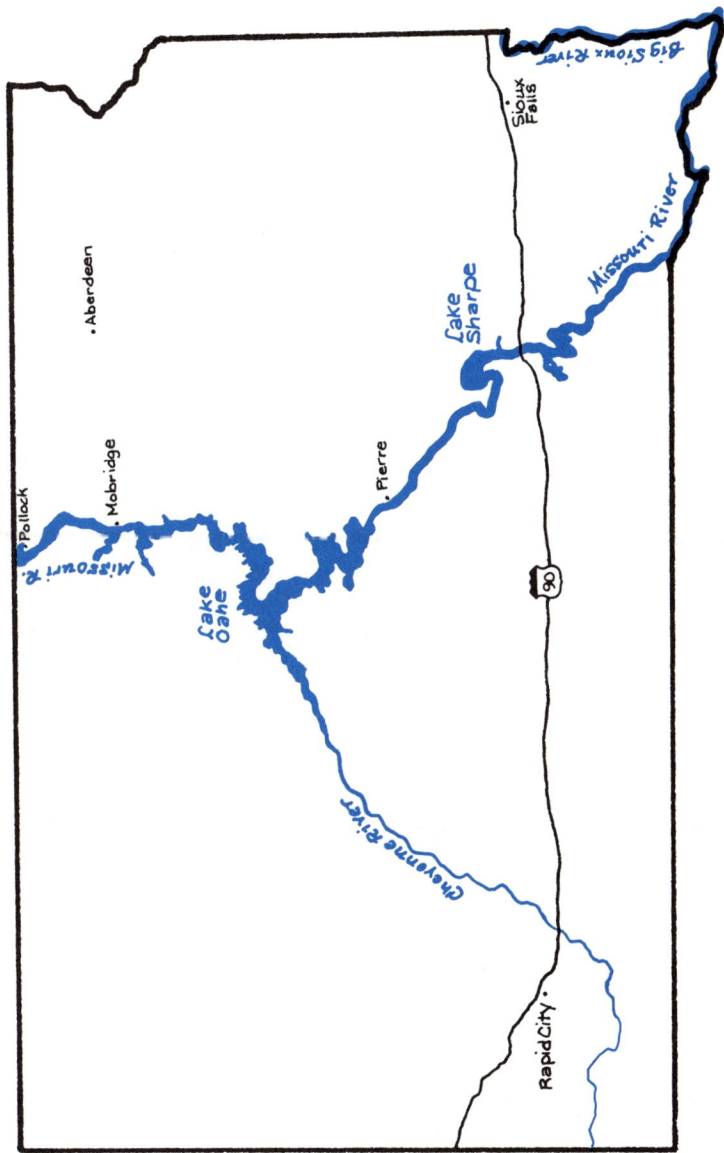

SOUTH DAKOTA

South Dakota

MOBRIDGE, SOUTH DAKOTA

DOKKEN, STEVE & MICK HAGEN (605) 845-7441
Address 111 South Main, Mobridge, SD 57601
Airport Aberdeen 100m **Accommodations** Mobridge
Operation Outfitter **Type of Fishing** Spin, baitcast, troll
Fish Walleye, northern, salmon, catfish **Season** Year-round **Water** Lake Oahe
Specialty Trolling **Boats** Outboards **Tackle Supplied** Spin, baitcast, troll
Experience 5 years **Rates** day: $115 1/2 day: $85

LIEDTKE, BRIAN (605) 845-7221
Address 808 8th Ave. W., Mobridge, SD 57601
Airport Bismarck, ND 100m **Accommodations** Mobridge **Operation** Guide
Fish Walleye, chinook, salmon **Season** June-Aug
Specialty Trolling or drifting for walleyes **Type of Fishing** Spin, baitcast, troll
Water Lake Oahe **Boats** Outboards **Tackle Supplied** Spin, baitcast
Experience 5 years **Rates** day: $140 1/2 day: $75
Guide's Notes: Lake Oahe Peak times for walleye are the last week in June and
the first two weeks in July. Early June is good if we have a warm spring. We
use spinners, crawlers and leeches trolling, jigs with minnows and crawlers or
leeches drifting.

UTTER, GREG & LORRIE-OAHE BAIT AND TACKLE (605) 845-7792
Address 622 West Grand Crossing, Mobridge, SD 57601
Airport Bismarck, ND 100m **Accommodations** Mobridge
Operation Outfitter **Type of Fishing** Spin, baitcast, troll
Fish Walleye, northern, bass, perch **Season** Year-round
Water Oahe Reservoir, Pudwill, Tatanka, McGee Dams
Specialty Lake trolling **Boats** Outboards **Tackle Supplied** All
Experience 2 years **Rates** day: $125 1/2 day: $80

PIERRE, SOUTH DAKOTA

BRAKSS, JOHN-MISSOURI RIVER PRO GUIDES ASSOC. (605) 224-6426
Address 610 N. Jackson, Pierre, SD 57501
Airport Pierre **Accommodations** Pierre
Operation Outfitter **Type of Fishing** Baitcast, troll
Fish Walleye, salmon, northern, bass **Season** Year-round
Water Lake Oahe, Lake Sharpe **Boats** Outboards **Tackle Supplied** Troll
Specialty Walleye fishing, salmon trolling
Experience 6 years **Rates** day: $145-195/2-3 people

MOORE, LEWIE-ADVENTURE GUIDE SERVICE (605) 224-0279
Address 721 Wells #7, Pierre, SD 57501
Airport Pierre **Accommodations** Pierre **Operation** Guide
Fish Walleye, salmon, white bass, northern pike **Season** Mar.-Nov.
Water Lake Oahe, Missouri River, Lake Sharpe **Type of Fishing** All
Specialty River walleye fishing and lake trolling
Boats Outboard **Tackle Supplied** Spin, troll
Experience 5 years **Rates** day: $150-200

SPENCER, DENNIS-OAHE LODGE GUIDE SERVICE (605) 224-9340
Address Box 1035, Pierre, SD 57501
Airport Pierre **Accommodations** On premises
Operation Outfitter, lodge **Type of Fishing** Baitcast,troll
Fish Salmon, walleye, northern, silver bass **Season** Year-round
Water Lake Oahe **Specialty** Lake trolling
Boats Bass boats **Tackle Supplied** Spin, baitcast, troll
Experience 5 years **Rates** day: $185 1/2 day: $100

RAY, RICK-MISSOURI RIVER PRO GUIDES ASSOC. (605) 224-5301
Address 1320 W. Capitol, Pierre, SD 57501
Airport Pierre **Accommodations** Pierre **Operation** Outfitter
Type of Fishing Baitcast, troll **Season** Year-round **Boats** Outboards
Fish Walleye, salmon, northern, bass **Water** Lake Oahe, Lake Sharpe
Specialty Walleye fishing, salmon trolling **Tackle Supplied** Troll
Experience 6 years **Rates** day: $145-195/2-3 People

POLLOCK, SOUTH DAKOTA

BAUMGARTNER, RICHARD-OAHE CAMPS BAIT AND TACKLE (605) 889-2498
Address Main Street, Pollock, SD 56748
Airport Aberdean 100m **Accommodations** Pollock
Operation Outfitter, cabins **Type of Fishing** Spin, baitcast, troll
Fish Walleye, pike, northern, salmon, bass **Season** April-Dec.
Water Oahe Reservoir (SD), Lake Oahe (ND), Lake Sakackawea (ND)
Specialty Lake trolling **Boats** Outboard **Tackle Supplied** Spin, baitcast, troll
Experience 8 years **Rates** day: $175 week: $600

WISCONSIN/
Upper Peninsula of
MICHIGAN

Wisconsin

APPLETON, WISCONSIN

MILBACH, AUBREY (414) 734-0629
Address 318 East Winnebago, Appleton, WI 54911
Airport Appleton **Accommodations** Appleton **Operation** Guide
Fish Walleye, northern, muskie, bass **Season** March-November
Water Lake Winnebago, Shawano Lake, Wolf River, area lakes
Specialty Float trips **Type of Fishing** Spin, baitcast, troll
Boats 16' & 14' outboards **Tackle Supplied** Spin, baitcast, troll
Experience 10 years **Rates** day: $80 1/2 day: $45

ARGONNE, WISCONSIN

ENGEBRETSON, JAMES-FOREST ROD & GUN SHOP (715) 649-3449
Address Box 211, Argonne, WI 54511
Airport Rhinelander 32m **Accommodations** Crandon 7m
Operation Guide, tackle shop **Type of Fishing** Spin, baitcast
Fish Muskie, walleye **Season** Year-round **Specialty** Lake casting
Water Nicolet National Forest Lakes, Whitefish, Julia, Virgin, Medicine
Boats Rowboats, antique guide boat **Tackle Supplied** Spin, baitcast
Experience 3 years **Rates** day: $150 week: $600 1/2 day: $85

ASHLAND, WISCONSIN

LA PENTER, ROGER-JOY'S PLACE (715) 682-5754
Address 2803 Front St E., Ashland, WI 54806
Airport Ashland **Accommodations** Ashland
Operation Outfitter, tackle shop **Type of Fishing** All **Tackle Supplied** All
Fish Smallmouth bass, steelhead, brown, brook **Season** Year-round
Water Lakes Superior, Namekagon, Mineral, Bad and Sioux Rivers
Specialty Fly fishing, spin fishing, light tackle **Boats** Canoes, 14'-16' deep V
Experience 20 years **Rates** day: $125 week: $500 1/2 day: $75
Guide's Notes: Our area is quite unique in the fact that we have four excellent
seasons for the angler, starting with the spring which offers a strong steelhead
run in the local streams; yarn flies and spawn sacks working best.
  May through mid-June... Smallmouth bass, coho, northern, and perch fishing
also gets started. The river and slough walleye start in early June and will last
through the summer. Some preferred baits for smallmouth fishing are "Sneaky
Petes", "Dalberg Divers", and most any chartreuse or blaze orange popper, #5

BOULDER JUNCTION, WI
AREA

Lakes and locations shown on map:

Six Lake, Moose Lake, Spider Lake, Rice Lake, Pardee Lake, Turtle-Flambeau Flowage, Cranberry Lake, Round Lake, Riley Lake, Flambeau River, Phillips

Presque Isle, Presque Isle Lake, Mercer, Manitowish Waters, Manitowish Lake, White Sand Lake, Clear Lake, Crab Lake, Twin Island Lake, Cisco Lake, Thousand Island Lake

MICHIGAN, WISCONSIN, Land o' Lakes, Lac Vieux Desert, Smoky Lake, High Lake, Fishtrap Lake

Boulder Junction, Trout Lake, Day Lake, Star Lake, Plum Lake, Lost Lake, Sayner

Big Sand Lake, North Twin Lake, South Twin Lake, Kentuck Lake, Anvil Lake, Phelps, Conover, 45, Franklin Lake, Butternut Lake

Buckatabon Lake, Pickerel Lake, Eagle Lake, Eagle River, Eagle River, St. Germain, Arbor Vitae Lake, Big Arbor Vitae Lake, Arbor Vitae, Woodruff, Minocqua, Minocqua Lake

Sandstone Lake, Pine Lake, Big Lake, Argonne, Rhinelander, Pelican Lake, Harshaw

Tomahawk Lake, Bearskin Lake, Willow Reservoir, Tomahawk R., 70, 51

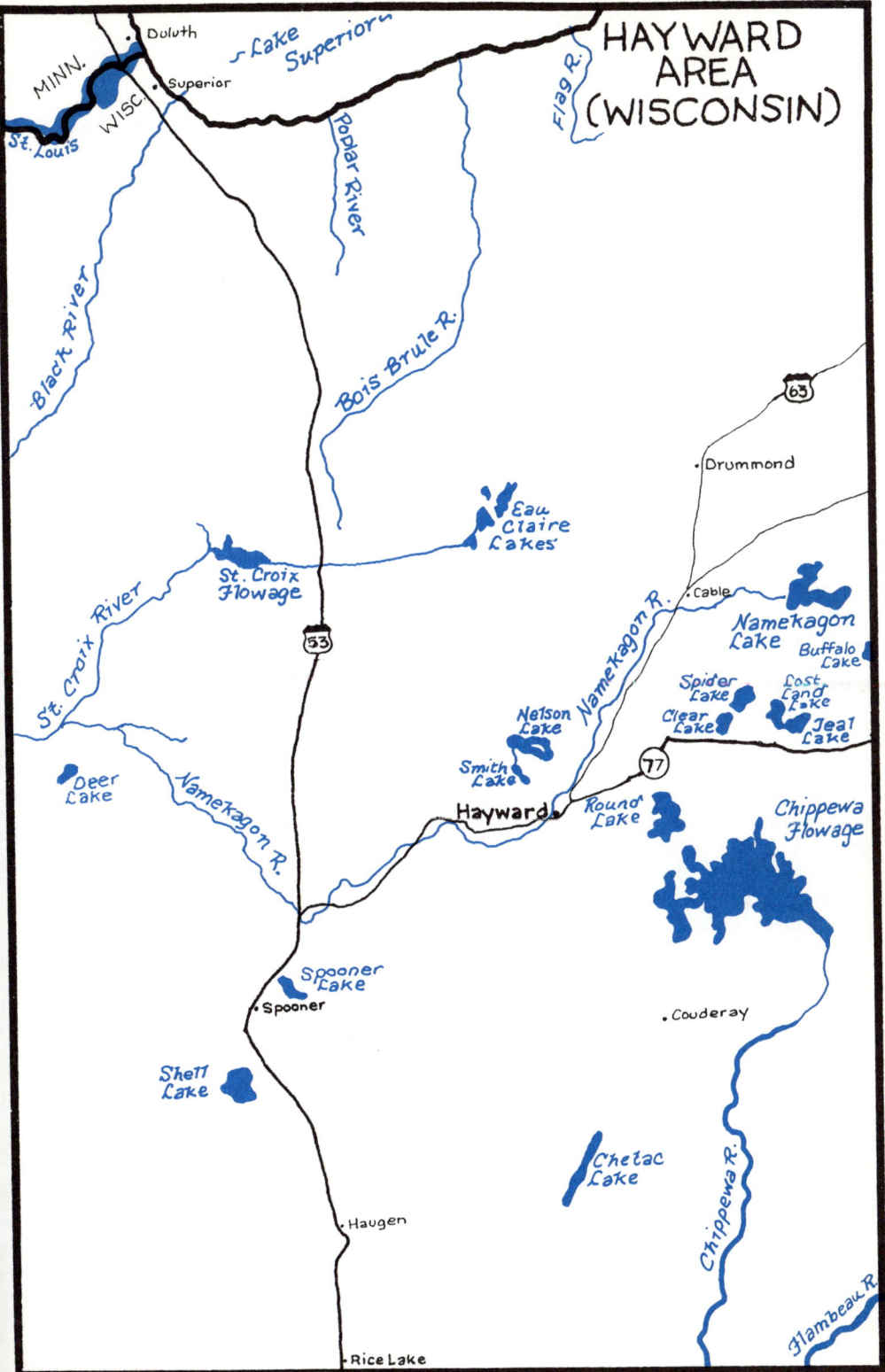

HAYWARD AREA (WISCONSIN)

MINN.

• Duluth

~Lake Superior~

St. Louis

• Superior

WISC.

Flag R.

Black River

Poplar River

Bois Brule R.

63

• Drummond

Eau Claire Lakes

St. Croix River

St. Croix Flowage

Namekagon R.

• Cable

Namekagon Lake

Buffalo Lake

Spider Lake

Lost Land Lake

Nelson Lake

Clear Lake

Teal Lake

53

Deer Lake

Namekagon R.

Smith Lake

77

Hayward •

Round Lake

Chippewa Flowage

Spooner Lake

• Couderay

• Spooner

Shell Lake

Chetac Lake

Chippewa R.

• Haugen

Flambeau R.

• Rice Lake

or #7 floating Rapalas or small rebels. The northern are taken on most any live minnow or sucker. Walleye are fished with a jig and a minnow or a crawler harness; however, later in the hot summer months a jig and leech or crawler is more productive.

As summer ends, the large brown trout move into spawn through September and October. For the fly fisherman, most any minnow imitation or small streamer will work. For the spin fisherman or caster, spawn sacks, frozen smelt, small sucker minnows, rapalas, rebels and little cleos work well.

The fall also offers another good steelhead run and some of the larger muskies will also be taken at this time. This fishing lasts into November, weather permitting.

BARABOO, WISCONSIN

HILL, SCOTT-SCOTT'S SPORT SHOP (608) 356-7338
Address 215 South Blvd., Baraboo, WI 53913
Airport Madison 40m **Accommodations** Baraboo
Operation Guide, tackle shop **Type of Fishing** Spin, baitcast, troll
Fish Walleye, bass, northern, pike **Season** March-November
Water Devils Lake, Wisconsin River, Lakes Wisconsin and Redstone
Specialty Deep water bass, river walleye, and fall pike fishing
Boats Bass boats **Tackle Supplied** Spin, baitcast, troll
Experience 2 years **Rates** day: $100 1/2 day: $50
Guide's Notes: Wisconsin River--early Spring walleye (trophy spawning time)

BOULDER JUNCTION, WISCONSIN

BEDA, JOHN-JOHN BEDA GUIDE SERVICE (715) 385-2477
Address Rte 1, Box 296, Boulder Junction, WI 54512
Airport Rhinelander 44m **Accommodations** Boulder Jct
Operation Guide, outfitter **Type of Fishing** Spin, baitcast, troll
Fish Walleye, muskie, bass, northern **Season** May-November
Water Cisco, Flambeau, Minocqua Chains, Boulder Junction waters
Specialty Walleye and muskie fishing with old fashioned shore lunch
Boats Canoes, modified bass boats **Tackle Supplied** Spin, baitcast
Experience 21 years **Rates** day: $125

BUCHER, JOE (715) 385-2646
Address P. O. Box 276, Boulder Junction, WI 54512
Airport Rhinelander 40m **Accommodations** Boulder Jct
Operation Guide **Type of Fishing** Spin, baitcast **Tackle Supplied** Spin, baitcast
Fish Muskie, walleye, large and small mouth bass **Season** May-November
Water Boulder Junction lakes and all Vilas County area **Boats** Bass boats
Specialty All forms of trophy muskie hunting, inland lake walleye
Experience 11 years **Rates** day: $120
Author's Notes: Two well known Wisconsin fishermen tell me Joe Bucher is one of the top muskie guides in the state.

CHRISTOPHERSON, GARY-BIRCHWOOD CAMPGROUND (715) 385-2882

Address Box 202, Boulder Junction, WI 54512
Airport Rhinelander 40m **Accommodations** Boulder Jct.
Operation Guide, tackle shop **Type of Fishing** Spin, baitcast, troll
Fish Walleye, muskie **Season** May-October
Water Boulder Junction waters (194 lakes) **Specialty** Lake fishing
Boats Rowboats, bass boats **Tackle Supplied** Spin, baitcast
Experience 14 years **Rates** day: $100
Author's Notes: Local contacts tell me Gary has a good reputation.

HOLLATZ, TOM-BEAR LODGE (715) 356-2507

Address Bear Lodge, Box 100, Rt 1, Boulder Junction, WI 54512
Airport Rhinelander 40m **Accommodations** Boulder Jct.
Operation Guide **Type of Fishing** Spin, baitcast
Fish Muskie, walleye, bass, northern **Boats** Rowboats, canoe
Specialty Long casting for muskies **Season** Mar-Nov
Water Mann, Trout, Allequash, Big Lakes **Tackle Supplied** Spin, baitcast
Experience 15 years **Rates** day: $95 week: $620 1/2 day: $50

SMITH, WILLIAM (715) 385-2540 823-2343

Address P.O. Box 33, Boulder Junction, WI 54512
Airport Rhinelander 40m **Accommodations** Boulder Jct.
Operation Guide **Type of Fishing** Spin, baitcast
Fish Muskie, walleye, bass, northern pike **Season** Mar-Nov
Water Big, High, Fishtrap Lakes, Cisco Chain **Specialty** Bass Fishing
Boats Bass boat **Tackle Supplied** Spin, baitcast
Experience 4 years **Rates** day: $100 week: $600 1/2 day: $65

CABLE, WISCONSIN

FORRAR, HARLEY EMERSON-NORTHWOOD LODGE (715) 794-2266

Address Rt. 2, Box 360, Cable, WI 54821
Airport Hayward 32m **Accommodations** On premises
Operation Lodge, guide **Type of Fishing** Spin, baitcast, troll **Boats** Rowboat
Fish Muskellunge, walleye, bass, northern, trout **Season** Year-round
Water Namekagon, Mineral, Spider Lakes, White River **Specialty** Lake fishing
Experience 25 years **Rates** day: $80 week: $560 1/2 day: $65

CASSVILLE, WISCONSIN

KRUGER, DALE (608) 725-5063

Address 1209 East Dewey, Cassville, WI 53806
Airport Dubuque, IA 35m **Accommodations** Cassville
Operation Guide **Type of Fishing** All **Specialty** River trolling for walleye
Fish Walleye, bass **Season** Mar-Dec **Boats** Custom built flat bottom
Water Mississippi River (Dubuque, IA to Lake City, MN)
Experience 18 years **Rates** day: $90 1/2 day: $50

CLAM LAKE, WISCONSIN

GRYZIK, WILLIAM-TALL TREES OUTPOST RESORT (715) 794-2420
Address Star Route, Clam Lake, WI 54517
Airport Duluth, MN 90m **Accommodations** On premises
Operation Lodge, guide **Type of Fishing** Spin, baitcast
Fish Muskie, walleye, crappie, bass **Season** May-October
Water Chippewa Flowage, Lost Land, Teal, Clam Lakes
Specialty Muskie fishing **Tackle Supplied** Spin, baitcast
Experience 10 years **Rates** day: $90 week:$800
Guide's Notes: Area fishing for **Northwest Wisconsin** is best May, June and
July. October and September are good muskie months.

CLEAR LAKE, WISCONSIN

ALLEN, JACK B. (715) 263-2113 263-2142
Address Box 72, Clear Lake, WI 54005
Airport Duluth, MN 50m **Accommodations** Fort Wing 2m
Operation Guide, charter captain **Type of Fishing** Fly, baitcast, troll
Fish Steelhead **Season** Sept-May **Tackle Supplied** Fly, baitcast, troll
Water Lake Superior, Flag, Bois Brule, Cranberry Rivers
Specialty Stream fishing for spring and fall steelhead **Boats** 24' inboard
Experience 20 years **Rates** day: $50/1 or 2 people

CONOVER, WISCONSIN

KRUMPLITSCH, ROBERT "MUSKY BOB" (715) 479-6292
Address 4249 Hegemann Road, Conover, WI 54519
Airport Rhinelander 32m **Accommodations** Eagle River 9m
Operation Guide **Type of Fishing** Spin, baitcast
Fish Muskie, walleye, northern pike, bass **Season** May-November
Water North and South Twin, Lac Vieux Desert, Eagle River Chain of Lakes
Specialty Casting for muskies **Boats** Bass boat **Tackle Supplied** Spin, baitcast
Experience 26 years **Rates** day: $90 5 days: $400 1/2 day: $50
Guide's Notes: Northern Wisconsin is the Muskie Capital of the world. The
peak periods for muskies in our areas are the first two weeks in July, followed
by our excellent fall fishing. Some of the lakes included are these famous waters:
North and South Twin, Lac Vieux Desert, Big Sand and Buckatabon Lakes,
which annually produce several of the top trophy muskies in the Midwest.

PLUNKETT, JIM-PLUNKETT'S GUIDE SERVICE (715) 547-6216
Address Box 394F, Star Rt., Land O' Lakes, WI 54540
Airport Wausau 90m **Accommodations** Land O' Lakes
Operation Guide **Type of Fishing** Spin, baitcast, troll
Fish Muskie, walleye, lake trout, bass **Season** Year-round
Water North Twin, Lone, Lac Vieux Desert, Palmer Lakes
Specialty Live bait techniques for walleye

The Brule River in Wisconsin.

R. Valentine Atkinson

Boats Rowboats, 16′ tuffy **Tackle Supplied** Spin, baitcast, troll
Rates day: $95 1/2 day: $65

SOBIEIC, JERRY-LAKEVIEW MOTEL (715) 545-2101
Address Box 47, Phelps, WI 54554
Airport Rhinelander 40m **Accommodations** On premises
Operation Lodge, guide **Type of Fishing** Baitcast
Fish Muskie **Season** June-August **Boats** 16′ outboard
Water North and South Twin, Lac Vieux Desert, Big Sand Lakes
Specialty Casting on inland lakes **Tackle Supplied** Baitcast
Experience 15 years **Rates** day: $90 week: $550 1/2 day: $50
Author's Notes: Local sources say Jerry is a very capable guide.

CORNELL, WISCONSIN

HEMM, JR., DONALD JOSEPH (715) 239-6184
Address Box 802, S. 8th Street, Cornell, WI 54732
Airport Eau Claire 50m **Accommodations** Cornell
Operation Guide **Type of Fishing** All
Fish Crappie, walleye, bass, muskie **Season** Year-round
Water Holcombe Flowage Area **Specialty** River fishing
Boats Rowboats, bass boats **Tackle Supplied** All
Experience 2 years **Rates** day: $65 1/2 day: $35

CRIVITZ, WISCONSIN

MLADENIK, MIKE-POPP'S RESORT (715) 854-2055, 757-3511
Address Rt. 2, Box 44, Crivitz, WI 54114
Airport Green Bay 60m **Accommodations** Crivitz
Operation Guide **Type of Fishing** Spin, baitcast
Fish Muskies, walleye, large & smallmouth bass **Season** March-Nov
Water High Falls, Caldron Falls Flowages **Tackle Supplied** Spin, baitcast
Specialty Fishing for muskies and smallmouth bass **Boats** Bass boats
Experience 6 years **Rates** day: $110 1/2 day: $60

DRUMMOND, WISCONSIN

SHUMWAY, BRUCE (715) 798-3441
Address Rt. 1, Box 82, Drummond, Wisconsin 54832
Airport Duluth, MN 80m **Accommodations** Drummond
Operation Guide **Type of Fishing** Baitcast
Fish Muskie **Season** May-Oct **Tackle Supplied** Baitcast
Water Lake Namekagon, Spider Lake, Eau Claire Chains
Specialty Muskie fishing **Boats** 15′ tri-hull guide boat
Experience 6 years **Rates** day: $100

Muskie! Virginia Peifer with guide Bruce Shumway.

Tom Kelly

Guide's Notes: I guide only for muskies on a variety of lakes in the **Hayward Area.** By fishing only muskies on a number of different lakes, I feel I can "stay" with the fish throughout the season. I like to know in advance what my client is looking for, i.e. muskie action, a first "legal" muskie, or a once in a lifetime trophy. With this information, I can better choose a suitable lake for that day's muskie hunt. All fishing is casting, not trolling.

EAGLE RIVER, WISCONSIN

DURNFORDD, HAROLD "FROGGIE" (715) 542-3038
Address 1862 County C, St. Germain, WI 54558
Airport Rhinelander 32m **Accommodations** St. Germain **Operation** Outfitter
Fish Walleye, bass, northern, muskie **Season** Year-round **Type of Fishing** All
Water Big St. Germain, Lake Tomahawk, Clear Lake, Little Arbor Vitae
Specialty Lake fishing with bass boat **Boats** Bass boat **Tackle Supplied** All
Experience 15 years **Rates** day: $100 week: $600 1/2 day: $55

GALL, ALAN W.-AL'S GUIDE SERVICE (715) 545-2127
Address 16549 Tuttle Road, Eagle River, WI 54521
Airport Rhinelander 45m **Accommodations** Eagle River
Operation Outfitter, tackle shop, lodge **Type of Fishing** Spin, baitcast, troll
Fish Muskie, walleye, lake trout, smallmouth bass **Season** Year-round
Water Twin, Kentuck, Butternut-Franklin, Anvil, Smokey Lakes
Specialty Muskie, walleye, and lake trout fishing
Boats Canoe, rowboats, 16' alumacraft **Tackle Supplied** All
Experience 6 years **Rates** day: $95 1/2 day: $65

GENZMER, GEORGE (715) 479-8093
Address 1946 N. Hwy 45, Eagle River, WI 54521
Airport Rhinelander 20m **Accommodations** Eagle River
Operation Guide **Type of Fishing** Spin **Tackle Supplied** Spin
Fish Walleye, muskie, bass, panfish **Season** Mar-Nov **Boats** Bass boats
Water Anvil, Butternut Lakes **Specialty** Lake fishing for muskie and walleye
Experience 40 years **Rates** day: $90 1/2 day: $60

HEELER, MARV-QUIET COMFORT CABINS (715) 542-3740
Address 8099 Lost Lake Drive North, St. Germain, WI 54558
Airport Rhinelander 30 **Accommodations** On premises
Operation Guide, cabins **Type of Fishing** Spin, baitcast
Fish Muskie, northern, walleye, bass **Season** March-Nov.
Water Big St. Germain, Lost, Razorback, Plum Lakes **Boats** Bass boat
Specialty Casting for all game fish **Tackle Supplied** Spin, baitcast
Experience 35 years **Rates** day: $85
Author's Notes: Marv is known locally as a very competent guide.

KRUEGER, RICK (715) 479-6251
Address 696 Meta Lake Road, Eagle River, WI 54521
Airport Rhinelander 27m **Accommodations** Eagle River

Operation Guide **Type of Fishing** Spin, baitcast **Boats** Bass boat
Fish Muskie, walleye, northern pike **Season** April-Nov.
Water Waters of Vilas County **Tackle Supplied** Spin, baitcast
Specialty Baitcasting for walleye, northern pike, and muskie
Experience 8 years **Rates** day: $125

RECHLITZ, JAMES J. (715) 479-6113, (414) 545-4642
Address 4011 Objiwa Drive, Eagle River, WI 54521
Airport Rhinelander 20m **Accommodations** Eagle River
Operation Guide **Type of Fishing** Spin **Tackle Supplied** Spin, baitcast
Fish Walleye, muskie, panfish **Season** March-November
Water Eagle River Lakes, Lakes Winnebago, Kentuck
Specialty Electric trolling, position fishing **Boats** Bass boats
Experience 2 years **Rates** day: $100 1/2 day: $50

ROSE, DICK-THE MUSKY HUNTERS (715) 479-7137
Address 3870 Chain O' Lakes Road, Eagle River, WI 54521
Airport Rhinelander 25m **Accommodations** Eagle River
Operation Guide **Type of Fishing** All **Tackle Supplied** All
Fish Muskie, walleye **Season** May-November
Water Cisco, Eagle Chains, Vilas-Oneida Counties
Specialty Casting and trolling **Boats** Bass boats, 16' tuffy rampage
Experience 31 years **Rates** day: $120 1/2 day: $100
Guide's Notes: Muskie and walleye fishing is good from May to November. At
the present time I am guide holder of 16 records including state, national and
world record line classes for muskie and walleye.
Author's Notes: *Dick Rose has an impressive record of guiding his clients to
trophy muskies and is one of the few who guide fly fishermen for muskies; a
twenty-five pounder is a wonderful experience. He is the author of THE
COMPLETE GUIDE TO MUSKY FISHING.*

SCHUMACHER, J.E.-LEISURE TYME MOTEL (715) 479-4481
Address 627 Railroad St., Hwy 45 N., Eagle River, WI 54521
Airport Rhinelander 20m **Accommodations** On premises
Operation Lodge, guide **Type of Fishing** Spin, baitcast **Season** June-Dec
Water Eagle River, Yellow Birch, Riley, Wabikon Lakes **Fish** Muskie
Boats Canoe, bass boat, rowboat **Tackle Supplied** Spin, baitcast
Experience 10 years **Rates** day: $75 week: $420 1/2 day: $40

THOMAS, DARRELL F. (715) 542-3372
Address H001, Box 102, Sayner, WI 54560
Airport Rhinelander 35m **Accommodations** Sayner **Operation** Guide
Fish Walleye, northern, muskie, bass **Season** May-Nov **Type of Fishing** Baitcast
Water Plum, Allequash, Little John, Star Lakes **Tackle Supplied** Baitcast
Specialty Walleye still fishing **Boats** Rowboats and motor
Experience 20 years **Rates** day: $90 week: $500 1/2 day: $50
Guide's Notes: I fish mostly for walleyes and northerns. Peak time is May and
June. I cook a shore lunch for my clients, fried potatoes, beans, fish, and coffee.

The charge for the lunch is about $3.00.

Author's Notes: Local contacts recommend Darrell as a skilled guide and fisherman.

EAU CLAIRE, WISCONSIN

MADSON, DARRYLL "PORKY" (715) 835-3493
Address 1911 Folsom St., Eau Claire, WI 54703
Airport Eau Claire **Accommodations** Eau Claire
Operation Guide **Type of Fishing** Spin, baitcast
Fish Bass, muskie, northern, walleye **Season** May-September
Water Deer Lake, various small lakes **Tackle Supplied** Spin, baitcast
Specialty Float trips **Boats** Rowboats, canoes, bass boats
Experience 5 years **Rates** day: $50/1 person $75/2 people
Guide's Notes: I guide on a muskie lake where the average outing will produce 8 to 10 different muskies caught, or follow ups. Yes, I said 8 to 10! June, July and August are the best months. I also take fishermen back in the woods to the many, many small glacial lakes, which are underfished and uninhabited. This type of fishing is for bass, northerns, and panfish, mostly with ultralite and artificials. July and August are the best months.

I float the **Chippewa River** below Eau Claire, Wisconsin for smallmouths, walleyes, and northerns. I have seen on these float trips, in the last 10 years, enough people to count on two hands. July and August are the best months.

FERRYVILLE, WISCONSIN

ROBERTSON, RANDY (608) 648-2105
Address Rt. #1, Box 217, Ferryville, WI 54628
Airport LaCrosse 35m **Accommodations** Lansing, IA 5m **Operation** Guide
Fish Bass, walleye, panfish **Season** Year-round **Boats** Bass boat
Water Upper Mississippi fish and wildlife refuge, Pools 8, 9, 10
Specialty Bass fishing **Tackle Supplied** Baitcast **Type of Fishing** Baitcast
Experience 8 years **Rates** day: $75
Guide's Notes: The Upper Mississippi River Fish and Wildlife Refuge maintains a healthy population of most fresh water species of fish. April, May, September and October provide excellent fishing for walleyes. We use minnow tipped jigs in the spring and crank baits in the fall. Except for June when rains raise and muddy the water levels, bass and pan fishing is excellent throughout the refuge. Structure and cover abound upon the Mississippi. Spring and summer bring vegetation that rivals Florida, to back water bays and lakes. The rolling hills with rocky limestone bluffs are a panoramic background that makes a fishing experience that will long be remembered.

FLORENCE, WISCONSIN

ERICKSON, CAL (715) 528-3280 528-3571
Address P.O. Box 56, Florence, WI 54121

Airport Iron Mountain, MI 15m **Accommodations** Florence **Operation** Guide
Fish Brown, brook trout **Season** Trout season **Type of Fishing** All
Water Pine, Popple, Brule Rivers (Michigan/Wisconsin Boarder)
Specialty River fishing for trout **Boats** Canoe **Tackle Supplied** Spin, fly
Experience 2 years **Rates** day: $50

FOND DU LAC, WISCONSIN

GUSSE, CAPTAIN RON-BLACK CAT CHARTER (414) 922-2401
Address 5612 Lake Shore Drive, Fond du Lac, WI 54955
Airport Milwaukee 60m **Accommodations** Fond du Lac
Operation Guide, charter captain **Type of Fishing** Spin, baitcast, troll
Fish Walleye, salmon, lake and brown trout **Tackle Supplied** Spin, baitcast, troll
Water Lakes Michigan, Winnabago, Big Green Lake **Season** Summer, Winter
Specialty Lake trolling and jig fishing **Boats** 22' cruiser, 18' walleye boat
Experience 20 years **Rates** day: $180 1/2 day: $90

FREMONT, WISCONSIN

REDEMANN, TUFFY (414) 446-3799
Address P.O. Box 405, 707 Theodore Street, Fremont, WI 54940
Airport Appleton 28m **Accommodations** Fremont **Operation** Guide
Fish Walleye, northern, white and black bass **Season** Year-round
Water Wolf River only **Specialty** Spring jig fishing
Boats Rowboats, bass boats, john boats, river boats
Tackle Supplied Spin, baitcast, troll **Type of Fishing** Spin, baitcast
Experience 4 years **Rates** day: $200 week: $650 1/2 day: $100
Guide's Notes: Without a doubt, April and May are the two best months for
fishing the **Wolf River** in the Fremont/Orihula area. The river is alive with fish
in these two months. Not only do the walleye make a run up river in April,
but so do catfish, northern, crappie, perch, sturgeon, and even white bass. Yep,
that's right! I've already had some great white bass fishing in the last week of
April.

GLIDDEN, WISCONSIN

HOMANN, HAL "MUSKY HAL" (715) 264-3227
Address Joy Villa Resort, Glidden, WI 54527
Airport Ironwood, MI 40m **Accommodations** On premises
Operation Guide, lodge **Type of Fishing** Baitcast, troll
Fish Walleye, northern, muskie, smallmouth bass **Season** May-Nov
Water Lake Superior, Bad River, various inland lakes
Specialty Muskie and walleye fishing **Boats** Rowboats
Experience 20 years **Rates** day: $60

HAUGEN, WISCONSIN

RASMUSSEN, JAY B. (715) 635-8540
Address P.O. Box 172, Haugen, WI 54841
Airport Eau Claire 50m **Accommodations** Haugen **Operation** Guide
Fish Muskie **Season** June-Oct **Type of Fishing** Baitcast
Water Big McKenzie, Deer, Bone, Yellow Lakes **Boats** Bass boat
Specialty Muskie fishing **Tackle Supplied** Baitcast
Experience 4 years **Rates** day: $70 week: $450

HAYWARD, WISCONSIN

CAMMACK, III, ROBERT (715) 634-3185
Address Rt. 2, Hayward, WI 54843
Airport Hayward **Accommodations** Hayward
Operation Guide **Type of Fishing** Spin, baitcast **Boats** 17' Alumicraft
Fish Walleye, crappie, muskie, bass **Season** May-Nov
Water Chippewa Flowage, Grindstone, Couderay, Round Lakes
Specialty Lake fishing **Tackle Supplied** Spin, baitcast
Experience 20 years **Rates** day: $100

DETTLOFF, JOHN-INDIAN TRAIL RESORT (715) 945-2665
Address Rte 1, Couderay, WI 54828
Airport Hayward 22m **Accommodations** On premises
Operation Guide, lodge **Type of Fishing** Baitcast **Tackle Supplied** Baitcast
Fish Muskie **Season** May-November **Water** Chippewa Flowage
Specialty Baitcasting for muskie **Boats** 16' guide boat
Experience 6 years **Rates** day: $80 1/2 day: $45
Guide's Notes: Muskie--Peak time is June 1-October 1 with late June, late August, and early September best for big fish. I use mostly surface lures and shallow running bucktails in 4 feet of water. Sunset is the prime fishing time in summer. One week after new moon and third and fourth day after full moon is best!

SISKO, STEVEN-SISKO'S PINE POINT RESORT (715) 462-3700
Address Rt. 9, Box 9338, Hayward, WI 54843
Airport Hayward **Accommodations** On premises
Operation Guide, lodge **Type of Fishing** Spin, baitcast
Fish Walleye, muskie, crappie, bass **Season** May-October
Water Chippewa Flowage, Round, Moose, Teal Lakes **Boats** Lund tri-hull
Specialty Muskie lake casting **Tackle Supplied** Spin, baitcast
Experience 13 years **Rates** day: $80 1/2 day: $50

HORICON, WISCONSIN

ZWELSDORF, ROLAND C. (414) 485-4663, 485-4632
Address 101 Main, Horicon, WI 53032

Airport Madison 50m **Accommodations** Horicon
Operation Guide, outfitter **Type of Fishing** Spin, baitcast
Fish Northern, bass, crappie **Season** April-November
Water Horicon Marsh **Boats** Rowboats, canoes
Experience 25 years **Rates** day: $80 1/2 day: $50

KEWAUNEE, WISCONSIN

PRESSNALL, LARRY-SOUTHERN COMFORT CHARTERS (414) 388-2222
Address P.O. Box 181, Kewaunee, WI 54216
Airport Green Bay 25m **Accommodations** Kewaunee
Operation Guide, charter captain **Type of Fishing** All **Season** May-Oct
Fish Chinook salmon, rainbow trout **Tackle Supplied** All
Water Lake Michigan **Specialty** Trolling**Boats** 31' slickcraft
Experience 5 years **Rates** day:$100/person
Author's Notes: *Larry Dahlberg of the* **In Fisherman** *told us about Larry Pressnall. Although Pressnall offers mostly trolling for salmon and rainbows in Lake Michigan, he has been experimenting with a new method for catching these trophy fish in the big lake with fly rods. Larry drops his clients off in float tubes in prime feeding areas. He says they average one to two fish per hour. The steelhead run to ten pounds and the salmon go over twenty. We applaud guides who develop new techniques which allow fishermen to cast to big fish with light tackle.*

Larry's success with open lake fly fishing has an interesting parallel out west at Lake Tahoe on the California/Nevada border. There, guide Rick Muller has been catching rainbows to six pounds on the surface by casting light spinning lures in water depths of over a thousand feet deep. In both lakes, this light tackle opportunity occurs in calm conditions when guides can identify current lines where small scraps of debris, insects, wood chips, pollen, etc. form wind rows on the surface. These debris slicks seem to create a natural chum line for open water rainbows and provide a hot spot for fishermen. We are looking forward to sampling this type of surface fishing this summer, and hope it offers as much potential as the reports from Pressnall and Muller indicate.

MANITOWISH WATERS, WISCONSIN

SLEIGHT, RUSS & DICK-SLEIGHT WILDWOOD RESORT (715) 543-2140
Address 166 Wildwood Road, Manitowish Waters, WI 54545
Airport Rhinelander 45m **Accommodations** On premises
Operation Resort, guide **Type of Fishing** Spin, baitcast
Fish Muskie, walleye, panfish, northern **Season** May-Nov
Water Manitowish Chain, Flambeau Flowage, Trout, Big Lakes
Specialty Lake fishing **Boats** Rowboat, canoe **Tackle Supplied** Spin, baitcast
Experience 17 years **Rates** day: $90 week: $630 1/2 day: $45

MANITOWOC, WISCONSIN

BOHACEK, THOMAS J.-FISH TRAP CHARTERS (414) 684-9534, 682-1094
Address 616 N. 6th Street, Manitowoc, WI 54220
Airport Milwaukee 87m **Accommodations** Manitowoc
Operation Guide, charter captian **Type of Fishing** Baitcast, troll
Fish Salmon, lake trout, rainbow, brown **Season** April-October
Water Lake Michigan and tributaries **Tackle Supplied** All
Specialty Lake trolling and steelhead guiding **Boats** 25' Sport craft
Experience 3 years **Rates** 1/2 day: $180
Author's Notes: Tom Bohacek has a very good reputation in the Manitowoc area.

CISLER, MICHAEL P. (414) 682-3091
Address 703 Woodlawn Drive, Manitowoc, WI 54220
Airport Green Bay 35m **Accommodations** Manitowoc
Operation Guide **Type of Fishing** Baitcast **Fish** Muskie **Season** May-Nov
Water Eagle River, Cisco Chains, North & South Twin Lakes
Specialty Casting for trophy muskie **Boats** Bass boat **Tackle Supplied** Baitcast
Experience 4 years **Rates** day: $150 week: $500 1/2 day: $100
Author's Notes: Local sources tell us Michael Cisler is a competent muskie guide.

MENASHA, WISCONSIN

NEBEL, JR., JOHN R. (715) 722-4004
Address 336 Chute, Menasha, WI 54952
Airport Appleton 3m **Accommodations** Menasha **Operation** Guide
Fish Brown, brook, bass, walleye **Season** Year-round
Water Wolf, Tomorrow, Little Wolf Rivers **Type of Fishing** Fly
Specialty Fly fishing instruction **Tackle Supplied** Fly
Experience 4 years **Rates** day: $200 1/2 day: $100
Guide's Notes: Woods and meadow streams here have good hatches, especially
the giant mayfly, hexagenia limbata (June) and most every basic hatch listed
in the books HATCHES and SELECTIVE TROUT.

MENOMONIE, WISCONSIN

BRICH, STEVEN "DOC" (715) 235-2964
Address Route 2, Box 196, Menomonie, WI 54751
Airport Eau Claire 32m **Accommodations** Menomonie
Operation Guide **Type of Fishing** Spin, baitcast, troll **Boats** Canoes, bass boat
Fish Walleye, panfish, bass, muskie **Season** June-Aug and weekends
Water Balsam-Long Lake, Chetec Chain, Amery Area Lake
Specialty Lake fishing for largemouth bass **Tackle supplied** Spin, baitcast
Experience 3 years **Rates** day: $50 week: $200 1/2 day: $30

MERCER, WISCONSIN

GRASER, PHILL-BOONIE BAITLURE, LTD. (715) 476-3570
Address 2644 County J, P.O. Box 99, Mercer, WI 54547
Airport Ironwood, MI 30m **Accommodations** Mercer
Operation Guide, tackle shop **Type of Fishing** Spin, baitcast
Fish Muskie, northern, walleye, bass **Season** May-October
Water Turtle-Flambeau Flowages, natural lakes in Iron & Vilas Counties
Specialty Backwoods waters, casting artificial lures
Boats 14' mirrocraft deep fisherman **Tackle Supplied** Spin, baitcast
Experience 8 years **Rates** day: $90 1/2 day: $50

MILLIGAN, ROBERT "DOC"-"DOC OF THE BAY" GUIDE SERVICE
(715) 476-3724
Address Box 340, Mercer, WI 54547
Airport Ironwood, MI 20m **Accommodations** Mercer **Operation** Guide
Fish Muskie, walleye, bass, trout **Season** Year-round
Water Flambeau flowage, Turtle River, Chain of Lakes, Manotwish Chain
Specialty Casting, jigging, fly casting **Type of Fishing** All
Boats Rowboat, canoe, bass boat **Tackle Supplied** Spin, baitcast
Experience 6 years **Rates** day: $75 week: $325 1/2 day: $45
Guide's Notes: I primarily guide and outfit fishermen and campers on the desolate Canadian-like waters of the **Turtle-Flambeau Flowage** in North Central Wisconsin. This 19,000 acre, island-dotted, body of water is the most wild and pristine area in Wisconsin. Large muskies and limits of 3-5 pound walleyes are not uncommon. Spring and Fall being the prime periods for the lunkers using artificial baits, and July and August being good for nice catches of bass and panfish.

MERRILLAN, WISCONSIN

PALCHIK, LEE ROY (715) 333-7093
Address RR#1, Box 182 A, Merrillan-Hatfield, WI 54754
Airport La Crosse 50m **Accommodations** Hatfield **Operation** Guide
Fish Walleye, bass, muskie, northern **Season** May-October
Water Waters of Merrillan-Hatfield Area **Type of Fishing** Spin, baitcast,troll
Specialty Lake trolling, river casting **Tackle Supplied** All **Boats** 14' outboard
Experience 3 years **Rates** day: $45

MILWAUKEE, WISCONSIN

DENNINGER, ALLEN (414) 353-5760, (715) 945-2665 (summer)
Address 10251 W. Leon Terrace, Milwaukee, WI 53224
Airport Hayward 20m **Accommodations** Hayward **Operation** Guide
Fish Muskie, walleye **Season** May-Nov **Type of Fishing** Spin, baitcast

Water Chippewa Flowage-13,000 acres **Tackle Supplied** Spin, baitcast
Specialty Casting for muskie and walleye **Boats** 15′ tri-hull
Experience 15 years **Rates** day: $90 1/2 day: $60
Guide's Notes: World famous **Chippewa Flowage:** Home of world record muskies... May--Outstanding walleye fishing using jig and minnow or leach. Also great crappie fishing. Muskie season starts the end of May through November 30. Bucktails and surface baits during most of the season are the best baits. Suckers are used in late fall. Night fishing for muskie is very productive with surface baits.
Author's Notes: Al caught the largest muskie landed in the U.S.A. in 1984, 40lbs, 2oz. at the Chippewa Flowage south of Hayward.

ENGEBRETSON, CRAIG-CRAIG'S MUSKIE CATCHERS (414) 461-2066, (715) 542-2061
Address 3725 N. 84th, Milwaukee, WI 53222
Airport Rhinelander 30m **Accommodations** Sayner **Operation** Guide
Fish Muskie (true & hybrid) **Season** June-Oct **Type of Fishing** Spin, baitcast
Water Plum, Big St. Germain, North Twin Lakes, Upper Manitowish Chain
Specialty Lake casting **Boats** Rowboat, bass boat **Tackle Supplied** Spin, baitcast
Experience 8 years **Rates** day: $100 1/2 day: $60

NEWBAUER, TOM-SPHEERI'S SPORTING GOODS (414) 466-4874, 464-2800
Address 4309 N. 91 St., Milwaukee, WI 53222
Airport Milwaukee **Accommodations** Milwaukee **Operation** Guide
Fish Bass, muskie, walleye **Season** April-Nov **Type of Fishing** Spin, baitcast
Water Pewaokee, Nagawicka, Bealah, Big Cedar Lakes **Boats** Bass boat
Specialty On-water instructional fishing **Tackle Supplied** Spin, baitcast
Experience 10 years **Rates** day: $150 1/2 day: $100

STROIK, CORNELL M. (414) 761-2115
Address 2439 W. Sycamore, Oak Creek, WI 53154
Airport Milwaukee 10m **Accommodations** Milwaukee 10m
Operation Outfitter **Type of Fishing** Spin, baitcast, troll
Fish Bass, walleye, muskie **Season** March-November
Water Wisconsin, Wolf, Mississippi, Apple Rivers
Specialty Casting for bass and muskie
Boats Rowboat, bass boat **Tackle Supplied** Spin, baitcast, troll
Experience 9 years **Rates** day: $150 week: $1000 1/2 day: $75

MINOCQUA, WISCONSIN

BOHN, GREG (715) 356-4633
Address 7850 Hwy 51 South, Minocqua, WI 54548
Airport Rhinelander 20 **Accommodations** Minocqua
Operation Outfitter **Type of Fishing** Spin, baitcast
Fish Muskie, walleye, bass, northern pike **Season** May-Oct
Water Minocqua, Flambeau Chains, Trout Lake **Boats** Bass boats

Specialty Live bait, river trips **Tackle Supplied** Spin, baitcast
Experience 20 years **Rates** day: $100 week: $625 1/2 day: $55
Guide's Notes: May is the best walleye fishing. June and July are good for river fishing. Muskie fishing is good all year and opens June 1. Fall brings beautiful colors and great fishing.

GRIES, RICHARD J. (715) 356-2503, 356-9426
Address 150 Woodland Lane, Minocqua, WI 54548
Airport Rhinelander 25m **Accommodations** Minocqua
Operation Guide **Type of Fishing** Spin, baitcast
Fish Muskie, walleye, northern pike, bass **Season** March-Nov
Water All major Vilas County waters, Lake Superior
Boats Bass boat **Tackle Supplied** Spin, baitcast
Experience 8 years **Rates** day: $110

RESCH, ROBERT (715) 356-4585
Address 970 Cedar Street, Minocqua, WI 54548
Airport Rhinelander 25m **Accommodations** Minocqua **Operation** Guide
Fish Muskie, walleye **Season** March-Nov **Type of Fishing** Fly
Water Minocqua Chain, Flambeau flowage, Trout, Big Arbor Vitae
Specialty Muskie sport fishing **Boats** 18' bone fisher **Tackle Supplied** All
Experience 6 years **Rates** day: $100
Guide's Notes: I fish winters in Florida for bonefish, tarpon, sea trout, and redfish.
Author's Notes: My contacts in Wisconsin tell me Bob is a very good guide. He specializes in fly fishing for muskie.

SARENAC, JERRY-"PRO FISHERMAN" (715) 356-9020
Address 9474 Country Club Road, Minocqua, WI 54548
Airport Rhinelander 30m **Accommodations** Minocqua
Operation Guide **Fish** Walleye, bass, muskie **Season** Year-round
Water Lakes Minocqua, Kawasasaga, Tomahawk **Type of Fishing** Spin, baitcast
Specialty Muskie fishing **Boats** bass boat **Tackle Supplied** Spin, baistcast
Experience 19 years **Rates** day: $125 1/2 day: $75 4 days or more: $100/day
Guide's Notes: Peak fishing times are May-June for walleyes and bass; end of June to the end of October is excellent for muskie and bass; and September-October for walleye.

I recommend the following lures for our area. Walleye-Jigs and lindy rigs; muskie-bucktail and jerk bait; bass-nightcrawlers, plastic worms, jig & pig, buzzard baits, deep divers.

I teach customers on specific methods when we fish depending on time of year, conditions, etc.

I fish winters in Florida on Lake Kissimee.
Author's Notes: Jerry comes highly recommended in his area.

SMITH, RUSS-SMITH BAIT MFG., CO. (715) 356-5565
Address 312 Oneida Ave., P.O. Box 462, Minocqua, WI 54548
Airport Rhinelander, 25m **Accommodations** Minocqua

Operation Guide **Type of Fishing** Spin, baitcast **Boats** 16' deep V
Fish Muskie, walleye, bass, northern pike **Season** Year-round
Water Minocqua Chain, Sayner, St. Germain, Presque Isle Lakes
Specialty Casting for muskie **Tackle Supplied** Spin, baitcast
Experience 10 years **Rates** day: $110 week: $700 1/2 day: $75
Guide's Notes: May is the best time for walleye fishing. In June, the muskie and bass get active. July and August are good muskie and northern pike fishing. September, October, and November is an excellent time to catch a "trophy" muskie. Also the walleye fishing is very good during this time.
Author's Notes: Russ is recognized as one of the best muskie hunters in the state. He owns his own lure company and manufacturers the Smity's line of muskie lures.

MONTELLO, WISCONSIN

CHRISTENSEN, DARYL (608) 296-3068
Address Box 182, Montello, WI 53949
Airport Madison 55m **Accommodations** Montello
Operation Guide **Type of Fishing** Spin, baitcast **Tackle Supplied** Spin, baitcast
Fish Northern, bass, walleye, muskie **Season** Year-round **Boats** Bass boats
Water Lakes Puckaway, Wisconsin, Buffalo Lake, Wisconsin River
Specialty Trophy northern pike and largemouth bass fishing
Experience 3 years **Rates** day: $80 week: $300 1/2 day: $40/2 people
Guide's Notes: Spring and fall are peak times for bass, pike and walleyes, although good pike and bass fishing continues throughout the summer. Walleye and pike fishing is good most of the winter. Look to fall for big pike, bass, and walleyes. March provides good fishing on Wisconsin River for walleyes.

NEENAH, WISCONSIN

GRIESBACH, STEVE (414) 725-1093
Address 419 5th Street, Neenah, WI 54956
Airport Outagamie 2m **Accommodations** Neenah
Operation Guide **Type of Fishing** Fly, spin, baitcast, troll **Season** March-Nov
Water Lake Winnebago, Butte des Morts, Wolf, Fox Rivers, Green Lake
Fish Walleye, bass, muskie, trout **Specialty** Trolling artificials and casting
Experience 10 years **Rates** varies
Guide's Notes: Lake Winnebago Area Fishing Calendar

Water	Fish	Time
Wolf and Fox Rivers	Spring walleye run	April
Lake Winnebago	Spring walleye spawn	Late April and May
Willow Creek	Trout opener	May
Little Green Lake	Muskies	May and June

ONALASKA, WISCONSIN

NELSON, NORVAL A.-ONALASKA GUIDE SERVICE (608) 783-0164
Address 1404 Lake Street, Onalaska, WI 54650

Airport La Crosse 5m **Accommodations** La Crosse 5m
Operation Guide **Type of Fishing** Spin, baitcast **Boats** Rowboats, canoes
Fish Northern, bass, muskie, crappie **Season** March-November
Water Mississippi, Black Rivers, Lakes Onalaska, Holcombe
Specialty Baitcasting **Tackle Supplied** Baitcast
Experience 5 years **Rates** day: $100 1/2 day: $50

OSHKOSH, WISCONSIN

JUEDES, GILBERT "GIB" (414) 233-3148
Address 2115 Hickory Lane, Oshkosh, WI 54901
Airport Oshkosh **Accommodations** Oshkosh **Operation** Guide
Fish Walleye, sauger, perch, black bass **Season** Year-round
Water Lake Winnebago, Lake Butte des Morts
Specialty Lake trolling **Type of Fishing** Baitcast, troll
Boats Canoes, 16' tri-hull **Tackle Supplied** Spin, baitcast, troll
Experience 4 years **Rates** 1/2 day: $60

SCHMIDT, DENNIS R.-CAPT'N WALLEYE GUIDE SERVICE (414) 233-3209
Address 1857 Minnesota St., Oshkosh, WI 54901
Airport Oshkosh **Accommodations** Oshkosh
Operation Charter captain, tackle shop **Type of Fishing** Spin, baitcast, troll
Fish Walleye, sauger, perch, white bass **Season** Year-round
Water Lakes Winnebago, Butte des Morts, Fox River
Specialty Leadhead jig fishing **Tackle Supplied** Spin, baitcast, troll
Experience 14 years **Rates** day: $150 1/2 day: $75/2 people

PHILLIPS, WISCONSIN

KELLY, DAVID A.-FLAMBEAU SPORTS (715) 339-2012
Address Luger Rt., HCR 3, Phillips, WI 54555
Airport Rhinelander 60m **Accommodations** Phillips
Operation Outfitter, tackle shop **Type of Fishing** Spin
Fish Muskie, walleye, bass, brook trout **Season** Year-round
Water Waters of Phillips' Area **Tackle Supplied** Spin, baitcast
Specialty Float fishing river trips for muskie **Boats** Rowboats, canoes
Experience 3 years **Rates** day: $75 week: $375

PLAINFIELD, WISCONSIN

BOVEE, PAUL (715) 335-6984
Address Route 1, Box 242, Plainfield, WI 54966
Airport Stevens Point 15m **Accommodations** Stevens Point **Operation** Guide
Fish Muskie **Season** March-Nov **Boats** Canoe, bass boat **Type of Fishing** Baitcast
Water Eagle River Chain, North and South Twin, Trout, Tomahawk Lakes
Specialty Lake or river float trips for muskie **Tackle Supplied** Baitcast
Experience 2 years **Rates** day: $135

PLYMOUTH, WISCONSIN

DODGE, DONALD D. (414) 893-8781
Address Rt. 2, Plymouth, WI 53073
Airport Sheboygan 3m **Accommodations** Plymouth **Operation** Guide
Fish Steelhead, brook, brown, salmon **Season** Mar-June **Type of Fishing** Fly, spin
Water Lake Michigan tributaries of Ozaukee, Sheboygan and Manitowoc counties **Specialty** Stream fishing **Boats** Canoes **Tackle Supplied** Fly, spin
Experience 2 years **Rates** day: $90 (12 hours) 1/2 day: $50
Guide's Notes: I'll be guiding mainly for steelhead (rainbow) primarily spring run, February-May, and again in the fall, September-December for our fall strain, plus fall run brook trout. Most rainbows taken will average out at over 8lbs/fish. Brookies up to 3 lbs, can be taken occasionally, 1-2 lbs are the rule.
Fishing Calendar for Wisconsin, Lake Michigan Streams - Fly Fishing and Spinning (Streamers, Flys, and Spawn Sacs)

Fish	Available
Rainbow	Mar - early May, Sept - Dec
Brookies	Mar - Apr, Sept - Nov
Chinook	Late Aug - Oct
Coho/Silvers	Oct - Dec
Browns	Sept - Dec

Fishing Calendar for Wisconsin, Lake Michigan Shoreline - Wading (Spinning)

Fish	Available
Chinook/Kings	Jul-Sept
Brown	July- Oct
Coho/Silvers	July - Sept
Rainbow	Year round chances
Brookies	Year round chances

PRAIRIE DU SAC, WISCONSIN

WAGNER, BOB-VERN LUNDES' FLY FISHING CHALET
(608) 544-4942, 437-5465 (Fly Shop)
Address Rt. 1, Box 271, Prairie du Sac, WI 53578
Airport Dane County 25m **Accommodations** Prairie du Sac
Operation Guide **Type of Fishing** Fly **Tackle Supplied** Fly
Fish Brook, brown, rainbow trout **Season** January-September
Water Catch and release streams in Southwest Wisconsin
Specialty Fly fishing small streams with light equipment for trout
Experience 2 years **Rates** day: $100 1/2 day: $60
Guide's Notes: Nymph and dry fly fishing for wild trout on 2, 3 and 4 weight rods, using standard caddis and mayfly patterns. Great spring fishing with catches of 30 or more wild fish per day is common. I specialize in catch and release.

PRESCOTT, WISCONSIN

LIVINGSTON, LEN (715) 262-5708 259-7189
Address 1357 Walnut St., Prescott, WI 54021
Airport St. Paul, MN 100m **Accommodations** Prescott
Operation Guide, tackle shop **Type of Fishing** Spin, baitcast, troll
Fish Muskie, bass, walleye, northern **Season** June-October
Water McKenzie Lakes, Spooner-Webster Area **Tackle Supplied** All
Specialty Trolling and casting for muskie and bass **Boats** Bass boat
Experience 5 years **Rates** day: $100 1/2 day: $50

PRESQUE ISLE, WISCONSIN

OLSSON, RODNEY J."ROD" (715) 686-2236
Address Rt. 1, Box 149, Presque Isle, WI 54557
Airport Ironwood, MI 40m **Accommodations** Presque Isle
Operation Guide **Type of Fishing** Spin, baitcast, troll
Fish Muskie, walleye, bass, northern **Season** March-November
Water Presque Isle, Crab, Harris, Papoose Lakes **Specialty** Lake trips
Boats Rowboats (motors available) **Tackle Supplied** Spin, baitcast, troll
Experience 20 years **Rates** day: $100

WARYE, RUSS (715) 686-2813
Address Listening Point, Presque Isle, WI 54557
Airport Rhinelander 60m **Accommodations** Presque Isle
Operation Guide **Type of Fishing** Spin, baitcast
Fish Muskie, bass **Season** May-Oct **Tackle Supplied** Spin, baitcast
Water Lakes and Streams of Vilas, Iron, and Oneida Counties
Specialty Casting for muskies **Boats** Rowboats, canoes, bass guide boats
Experience 8 years **Rates** day: $90 1/2 day: $55

PRINCETON, WISCONSIN

WELLS, RUSSELL-RUSS WELLS GUIDE SERVICE (414) 295-3258
Address 218 S. Fulton, Princeton, WI 54968
Airport Oshkosh 35m **Accommodations** Princeton
Operation Guide **Type of Fishing** Spin, baitcast, troll
Fish Walleye, northern, bass **Season** May-October
Water Big Green Lake **Tackle Supplied** Spin, baitcast, troll
Specialty General lake fishing back trolling **Boats** Bass boat
Experience 9 years **Rates** day: $110 1/2 day: $75

REEDSBURG, WISCONSIN

BETH, GENE C. (608) 524-2617, (414) 487-2828
Address R.P.D. #2, Box 194, Reedsburg, WI 53959

Airport Green Bay 35m **Accommodations** Green Bay 35m
Operation Guide **Type of Fishing** Fly, spin **Tackle Supplied** Fly
Fish Salmon, steelhead, brown **Season** Sept-Dec, Mar-Apr
Water Lake Michigan tributaries **Specialty** Fly fishing
Experience 14 years **Rates** day: $150
Guide's Notes: In Lake Michigan tributaries peak times are September until freeze up, and March through April. We use weighted streamers, sink tip fly lines, and steelhead or salmon fly patterns. Flashabou flies are exceptional.

RHINELANDER, WISCONSIN

KLABUNDE, TERRY W.-BOB'S SPORTS CENTER
(715) 282-5667, 546-2767
Address Fire No. 7900 Hwy 8 West, Rhinelander, WI 54501
Airport Rhinelander **Accommodations** Rhinelander
Operation Guide, tackle shop **Type of Fishing** All
Fish Muskie, walleye, bass, trout **Season** April-November
Water North and South Twins, Big Sand, Long Lakes, Cisco Chain
Specialty Fishing inland waters and streams
Boats Rowboats, canoes, bass boats **Tackle Supplied** All
Experience 22 years **Rates** day: $95 week: $575 1/2 day: $60
Guide's Notes: Prime fishing time is all of May to mid-June and the second week in September through October. Trout do very well on flys as well as spinners in May. Muskies do best on bucktails in May and June, then switch over to plugs for them in September and October. Beautiful fall colors appear from September 20-October 15th yearly. Don't forget your camera.

ROSS, CHARLIE (715) 362-3816
Address 4290 Oak Drive, Rhinelander, WI 54501
Airport Rhinelander **Accommodations** Rhinelander
Operation Guide **Type of Fishing** Spin, baitcast, troll **Specialty** Casting
Fish Muskie, walleye, bass, northern **Season** Year-round
Water Willow Flowage, Wisconsin River, Kentuck, Twin Lakes
Boats Rowboats, bass boats **Tackle Supplied** Spin, baitcast, troll
Experience 5 years **Rates** day: $130 week: $750 1/2 day: $90

SCHULZ, JOHN W. (715) 277-3305
Address 9178 Island Road, Harshaw, WI 54529
Airport Rhinelander, 13m **Accommodations** Harshaw
Operation Guide, outfitter **Type of Fishing** Spin, baitcast
Fish Muskie **Season** May-Nov **Water** Minocqua, Flambeau, Bearskin Chains
Specialty Muskie fishing in lakes & rivers **Boats** Customized muskie boat
Experience 4 years **Rates** day: $100 1/2 day: $55

URBAN, THOMAS J. (715) 362-3618
Address 916 Margaret St., Rhinelander, WI 54501
Airport Rhinelander **Accommodations** Rhinelander
Operation Guide **Season** Year-round **Tackle Supplied** All

Fish Muskie, walleye, northern, bass **Type of Fishing** Fly, spin, baitcast
Water Wisconsin River, Pelican Lake, Lakes Tomahawk, Minocqua
Specialty Casting for muskie and walleye **Boats** Canoe, bass boat
Experience 9 years **Rates** day: $100 week: $500 1/2 day: $60

VOBORSKY, JIM (715) 282-5709
Address 2875 South Rifle Road, Rhinelander, WI 54501
Airport Rhinelander **Accommodations** Rhinelander **Operation** Guide
Fish Muskie, walleye **Season** Year-round **Type of Fishing** Spin, baitcast
Water Oneida and Vilas County lakes **Boats** Rowboat, canoes, bass boat
Specialty Lake casting for muskie and walleye **Tackle Supplied** Spin, baitcast
Experience 17 years **Rates** day: $135

WORRALL, STEVE (715) 362-3275
Address 3790 Foster Lane, Rhinelander WI 54501
Airport Rhinelander **Accommodations** Rhinelander
Operation Guide **Type of Fishing** Spin, baitcast
Fish muskie, walleye, pike, bass **Season** March-November
Water Pelican, Enterprise Lakes, Wisconsin River, Minocqua Chain
Specialty Trophy muskie instruction **Tackle Supplied** Spin, baitcast
Experience 13 years **Rates** day: $125 week: $700

RICE LAKE, WISCONSIN

PETRY, GEORGE A. (715) 234-4921 635-2418
Address Rt. 5, Box 324, Rice Lake, WI 54868
Airport Eau Claire 60m **Accommodations** Rice Lake **Season** Year-round
Operation Outfitter **Type of Fishing** All **Specialty** Lake trolling, float trips
Fish Walleye, bass, muskie, panfish **Boats** Rowboats, canoes, bass boats
Water Long, Stone, Shell, Day Lakes, Chippewa River **Tackle Supplied** All
Experience 10 years **Rates** day: $100 1/2 day: $55

SCHOFIELD, WISCONSIN

SOPATA, JIM (715) 359-6670
Address 4403 Augustine Ave., Schofield, WI 54476
Airport Mosinee 20m **Accommodations** Schofield
Operation Guide **Type of Fishing** All **Fish** Muskie, walleye, trout
Season Mar-Nov **Boats** Rowboats, bass boats **Tackle Supplied** Spin, baitcast
Water Wisconsin River, Pelican Lake, Minocqua Chain
Experience 2 years **Rates** day: $60 1/2 day: $40

SHIOCTON, WISCONSIN

DIEMEL, HAZE S. (715) 752-3600
Address RR# 1, Box 292, Shiocton, WI 54170

Airport Clintonville 10m **Accommodations** Clintonville 10m
Operation Guide **Type of Fishing** Spin, baitcast **Water** Wolf River
Fish Northern, walleye, bass, panfish **Season** April-Oct **Specialty** Float trips
Boats Rowboats, bass boats **Tackle Supplied** Spin, baitcast
Experience 24 years **Rates** day: $85 1/2 day: $50
Guide's Notes: The **Wolf River** is a nationally know river for its spring walleye and white bass spawning runs. As there is no closed season or size limit on the Wolf, it is fished early in the year before other parts of the state are open. The Wolf also has very good fishing throughout the summer for northerns, walleye, bass, etc. The northern Wolf between Shawano and Shiocton is a much different river than it is south thru New London, Fremont, etc. The northern Wolf is more of a wilderness area, with not much boat traffic and approximately ten miles between boat landings. Much fishing is done with artificial baits such as, Rebels, Rapalas, Fat Raps, Shad Raps, spinners, jigs, etc. It has a large number of different kinds of fish. Fishing with bait you may catch 10 fish and have no two alike, including catfish.

Wilderness type campsites are available on the river (no electricity) also some boat rentals are available.

STURGEON BAY, WISCONSIN

ESPE, ROGER K.-BAYLAND SPORTS CENTER (414) 743-0056, 743-2415
Address Gitche Gumee Road, Sturgeon Bay, WI 54235
Airport Greenbay 40m **Accommodations** Sturgeon Bay
Operation Guide, tackle shop **Type of Fishing** Spin, baitcast, troll
Fish Walleye, trout, perch, bass **Season** March-Nov.
Water Sawyer Harbor, Green Bay, Lake Michigan, Sturgeon Bay
Specialty Casting, drifting, rock reefs or structure
Boats Rowboats, canoes **Tackle Supplied** Spin, baitcast
Experience 5 years **Rates** 1/2 day: $60
Guide's Notes: Door County, Wisconsin
Salona Rd.-Braunsdorf Beach-Well known for shore fishing with spoons or spawn sacs - sand and rock beach. Very good shallow water.
Sturgeon Bay ship canal-Pier fishing off both breakwalls is very good from time to time. Medium to heavy spinning tackle is adequate to catch all trout species and salmon. Spoons, spawn sacs and alewife used.
Portage Park-Good shore fishing for trout off the sand beach.
Wester's at Lilly Bay-Good shore fishing off the sand beach with spinning tackle and shallow water trolling for trout and salmon.
White Fish Bay-Good shore fishing off the sand beach with spinning tackle.
Cave Point County Park-Good shore fishing off picturesque rock cliffs.
Mouth of Heins & Hibbard's Creek-Very good fishing here in early spring (April, May, June) for brown and rainbow trout. Shallow water sand and rock beach can be fished with small boats or from shore. Both creeks are excellent trout streams in early spring.
Rowley's Bay & The Mink River-Good trolling for trout and salmon in the bay and very good northern, bass, and perch fishing up the river. The river is not a rapid running river and can be fished with any type of small boat or raft.

Gills Rock-Northport-The Ferry Docks in Gills Rock and Northport are often real good for pier fishing bass and trout.

Washington Island-Detroit Harbor is well known for jumbo perch, smallmouth bass and northerns. The harbor can be fished with any small to medium size boat. Boat launching and rental are available right at the Ferry Dock.

Sister Bay-Shallow water trout fishing early spring and summer.

Ephraim-Beautiful picturesque harbor and village with very good yacht harbor and marina facilities. Very good early spring fishing for brown and rainbow trout. Good bass fishing near the reefs and islands in mid summer. Pier fishing available.

Fish Creek-Picturesque harbor and village with very good yacht harbor and marine facilities. Very good early fishing for brown and rainbow trout. Good bass fishing near reefs and island in mid summer.

Hat Island-Judville Rd.-Good shoreline for early spring and summer trolling for brown trout.

Egg Harbor-A real hot spot for spring brown trout fishing and good for jumbo perch through summer. Very good fishing structure just South of the harbor, but access poor at Murphy County Park. Pier fishing available at the park.

The Bay of Sturgeon Bay-Flatts-Shallow 6 to 12 foot rocky and weedy area that holds every type of fish in the area-good early spring trolling for trout and later the spot for bass, perch and walleye. Very accessible with small to medium size boat.

SUPERIOR, WISCONSIN

HOEKSTRA, BUD (715) 394-6012
Address #4 Manning Ct., Superior, WI 54880
Airport Duluth, MN 9m **Accommodations** Superior **Operation** Guide
Fish Bass, walleye, northern, panfish **Season** June-August
Water All waters around Superior (60 mile radius)
Specialty Fishing for bass, walleye, northern, and panfish
Boats Rowboats, canoes **Type of Fishing** Spin, baitcast
Experience 2 years **Rates** varies
Guide's Notes: Walleyes run in **Lake Superior** and **St. Louis Bay** from about May 15 to July 15 depending on conditions. Large walleyes 6-12 pounds are caught in the **Nemadji River** at that time. After the walleye run, it's time to fish the inland lakes for bass, northerns and panfish. Large Northerns after August 15.

WEYAUWEGA, WISCONSIN

HEINZEL, JAMES (414) 867-3019
Address Rt. 1, Box 307, Weyauwega, WI 54983
Airport Appleton 40m **Accommodations** Weyauwega
Operation Guide **Type of Fishing** Spin, baitcast, troll
Fish Muskie, walleye, northern, bass **Season** March-Nov
Water Weyauwega, Julia, Minocqua Lakes, Wolf River

Specialty Muskie and Northern Lake fishing
Boats Rowboats, canoes, runabout **Tackle Supplied** Spin, baitcast
Experience 2 years **Rates** varies

WILLIAMS BAY, WISCONSIN

GATES, BRIAN L.-GENEVA LAKE BAIT & TACKLE, INC (414) 245-6150
Address Hwy 67, P.O. Box 822, Williams Bay, WI 53191
Airport Milwaukee 45m **Accommodations** WIlliams Bay
Operation Outfitter, tackle shop **Type of Fishing** Spin, baitcast, troll
Fish Bass, walleye, northern **Season** Year-round
Water Geneva, Delavan, Lauderdale Lakes, Lake Como
Specialty Drift fishing with ultra light tackle for smallmouth bass
Boats Canoe, bass boat, rowboat, deep V, pontoon **Tackle Supplied** All
Experience 22 years **Rates** day: $90 1/2 day: $60
Guides Notes: Fishing Calendar

Fish	Available	Method
Smallmouth bass	Mid May - Mid June	Drift Fishing
Walleye	July - early Aug	Night fishing
Northern	Late Sept - Oct	Casting & Trolling
Largemouth bass	Late Feb	Jigging rapalas thru ice
	Mid June	Casting, night fishing
White bass, bluegill	Spring, Summer, Fall	
Crappie, Cisco	Spring, Summer, Fall	

Author's Notes: Brian owns and operates a tackle shop on Lake Geneva. His operation was written up by Tom McNally in the CHICAGO TRIBUNE in June of 1980.

WINNECONNE, WISCONSIN

KRINGS, GREGORY (414) 582-7454
Address 200 Division St., Winneconne, WI 54986
Airport Oshkosh 16m **Accommodations** Winneconne
Operation Guide **Type of Fishing** Spin, baitcast, troll
Fish Walleye, white & black bass **Season** March-Nov **Boats** Bass boats
Water Wolf River, Winnebago, Poygan, Butte des Morts Lakes
Specialty Live bait backtrolling and casting **Tackle Supplied** Spin, baitcast
Experience 6 years **Rates** day: $110 week: $450 1/2 day: $60

ZINECKER, MIKE (414) 582-4709
Address 6445 Paulson Road, Winneconne, WI 54986
Airport Oshkosh 13m **Accommodations** Winneconne
Operation Guide **Type of Fishing** Spin, baitcast, troll
Fish Walleye, bass, bluegill, crappie **Season** April-Nov
Water Lakes Butte des Morts, Winneconne, Poygan, Wolf R.
Specialty Cane pole fishing for bluegill and crappie
Boats Bass boats **Tackle Supplied** Spin, baitcast, troll

Experience 8 years **Rates** day: $150 week: $900 1/2 day: $90
Guide's Notes: Rates include lodging.

WISCONSIN RAPIDS, WISCONSIN

ASCHENBRENNER, DICK (715) 887-3987
Address 2935 Sandy Road, Wisconsin Rapids, WI 54494
Airport Wisconsin Rapids **Accommodations** Central Wisconsin
Operation Guide **Type of Fishing** Spin, baitcast, troll **Boats** Bass boats
Water Wisconsin River system, North waters of WI, Big Eau Pleine Flowage
Fish Walleye, northern, pike, muskie, perch **Tackle Supplied** Spin, baitcast, troll
Season May-October **Specialty** Lake trolling and baitcasting for muskies
Experience 2 years **Rates** day: $100 1/2 day: $75
Guide's Notes: Wisconsin River Area has 70 miles of river with few homes or
cabins. Great walleye fishing, many northern pike and muskie, also, the bass
are just coming on strong.
    Big Eau Pleine Flowage: Excellent walleye, northern pike and some muskie,
many perch too; over 5,000 acres of water.

WOODRUFF, WISCONSIN

BUDAY, JIM (715) 356-7788, 356-3509
Address 8636 Bambi Court, Woodruff, WI 54568
Airport Rhinelander 18m **Accommodations** Minocqua 3m
Operation Guide **Type of Fishing** Spin, baitcast **Boats** 18' Lund
Fish Muskie, walleye, northern, bass **Season** May-November
Water Minocqua, Tomahawk, Gilmore, Bear Skin Lakes
Specialty Casting with artificial baits **Tackle Supplied** Spin, baitcast
Experience 13 years **Rates** day: $90 1/2 day: $55
Guide's Notes: Muskie fishing is best in June and July on **The Minocqua** and
Bearskin Lakes. **Tomahawk Lake** produces best in August and September.
Walleye fishing is best in the area in May and June. River fishing is best in the
spring and in the fall. Bucktails and jerk baits are best for muskies. Walleyes
are taken on rapala's and jig and minnows.

KUREK, GEORGE (715) 356-4920
Address AV 10515, Hwy 70 East, Arbor Vitae, WI 54568
Airport Rhinelander 30m **Accommodations** Arbor Vitae
Operation Guide **Type of Fishing** Spin, baitcast **Specialty** Casting
Fish Muskie, walleye, northern, bass **Season** Year-round
Water Arbor Vitae, Minocqua Chain, Big St. Germain, Plum Lakes
Boats Rowboats, johnboat, 16' deep-V **Tackle Supplied** Spin, baitcast
Experience 3 years **Rates** day: $85 1/2 day: $50

KUTSCHENREUTER, JIGG'S-GOLLON'S BAIT & TACKLE
(715) 356-6540, 356-4611
Address Box 741, Woodruff, WI 54568

Airport Rhinelander 26m **Accommodations** Woodruff
Operation Guide **Type of Fishing** Spin, baitcast **Tackle Supplied** Spin, baitcast
Fish Walleye, muskie, bass **Season** May-October **Specialty** General fishing
Water Flambeau Flowage, all Lakeland area lakes **Boats** Guide boat
Experience 7 years **Rates** day: $90

MOORE, DICK (715) 356-6834, 356-3509
Address 9019 Mid Lake Road, Woodruff, WI 54568
Airport Rhinelander 25m **Accommodations** Woodruff
Operation Guide **Water** Minocqua Chain **Season** May-November
Fish Muskie, walleye, bass **Type of Fishing** Baitcast
Boats V-Hull **Tackle Supplied** Spin, baitcast
Experience 10 years **Rates** day: $90 1/2 day: $55
Author's Notes: Dick Moore is recognized as one of the best muskie guides in Wisconsin.

ZINDA, THOMAS F.-TADPOLE TOMMY'S (414) 356-3509
Address 728 Elm, P.O. Box 752, Woodruff, WI 54568
Airport Rhinelander 25m **Accommodations** Woodruff
Operation Guide, tackle shop **Type of Fishing** Spin, baitcast
Fish Walleye, muskie, northern, bass **Season** March-Nov
Water Lake Tomahawk, Minocqua, Flambeau Chains
Specialty Ice fishing for fresh water species
Boats Bass boats, pike boats **Tackle Supplied** Spin, baitcast
Experience 16 years **Rates** day: $100 1/2 day: $60
Author's Notes: Tom Zinda owns and manages Tadpole Tommy's, one of the largest tackle shops in the region. They employ 19 guides and fish over 400 area lakes.

9. The Southeast: Hog bass and salt water!

Arkansas, Florida, Georgia, Kentucky, Louisiana, Tennessee, West Virginia

The South is synonymous with largemouth bass: the Florida strain of this species can grow to over twenty pounds! Throughout this entire region, largemouth are found in habitats ranging from small farm ponds to huge impoundments. Willing to take fly rod poppers and lures off the surface, they provide especially good light tackle sport. There is something special about the way largemouth bass hit a popping bug. Sometimes they hit so hard, they come out of the water; at others, they sip in a sizable lure without disturbing the surface.

The largemouth is just one of the south's exciting light tackle opportunities. There is also excellent fishing for smallmouth, stripers, huge trout, and more. The saltwater flats around the Florida Keys teem with exotic species such as tarpon, permit, mutton snapper, and bonefish.

If you have not tried light tackle saltwater fishing, you are in for a treat. The first fish I ever hooked in the salt took out line so fast, it felt like the hook was caught in a high-speed table saw. Less than three seconds later, the line snapped, and it was all over. I never did see that fish. I assume it was a big barracuda, because I had seen a couple of them earlier in the day when I was skin diving.

That's light tackle saltwater fishing! You never know what will take the fly or lure next, or how big it will be. The tarpon which migrate through the Keys in spring can weigh up to 200 pounds. On the flats, you sight fish for these monsters, and fishing takes on the feel of a big game hunt. The next time you're in Miami, take a day off, hire a guide, and fish nearby Biscayne Bay. If you hit good fishing a whole new sport will open up to you.

Good saltwater fishing can be found almost all year long in the Keys, as well as up and down both coasts, when fish are migrating through a particular area. Read what the guides say about availability of species and peak times. You will find most of the saltwater guides located in the Keys.

North from the Keys in central Florida, is some of the finest largemouth water in the United States. The canals and ponds of the Everglades are filled with largemouth bass. Since these waters are quite shallow, surface action is year-round. A little farther north lies Lake Okeechobee, Florida's largest lake, a superb largemouth bass fishery which supports a number of guides, many listed in this book.

In the tier of states just north of Florida, guides noted three man-made lakes—Lake Lanier and West Point Lake in Georgia, and Toledo Bend on the Louisiana/Texas border—for excellent largemouth, striper, and crappie fishing. Bass fishing in reservoirs like these can be very exciting, especially when the stripers are busting into schools of shad on the surface. Guides look for the tell-tale disturbance of the water's surface and for gulls circling and diving, then rush to the action with flies and lures. This is exciting sport—these landlocked striped bass can reach weights in excess of forty pounds.

Continuing north from Louisiana into Arkansas, you will encounter a tremendous variety of fishing. Located here are the highly productive lakes Ouachita, Hamilton, DeGray, and Greason, as well as the famous Bull Shoals. All of these impoundments offer excellent angling for largemouth, stripers, and crappie.

Some of the largest stream-dwelling trout in North America live in the tail waters of the White River below Bull Shoals dam, and in the Little Red River below Greer's Ferry Lake. Brown trout to thirty-three pounds and rainbows to nineteen pounds have come out of these waters. These are incredible weights for stream-dwelling trout. The light tackle angler can take these big fish with wet flies and lures.

The Buffalo River, an important White River tributary in northwestern Arkansas, has been placed under the administration of the National Park Service. Its status as a National River means that over 150 miles of its free-flowing course, from headwaters in the Ozarks to its confluence with the White, will be protected from future development. You can arrange a guided float trip to fish this scenic river for one of my favorite quarry, smallmouth bass.

Arkansas' neighbors to the northeast are the mountainous states of Kentucky and Tennessee. Here, guides fish for largemouth, crappie, and stripers on several productive impoundments, notably Watt's Bar, Barkley, and Kentucky lakes. Cave Run Lake, near Morehead in eastern Kentucky, was noted for its outstanding muskie fishing.

West Virginia guides claim that the New River is one of the country's best smallmouth streams. The scenic New River, like the Buffalo in

Arkansas, has been designated a National River. Some New River guides offer exciting white water float trips through the deep canyons in the Glen Jean area. Other important West Virginia waters listed by the guides are the Gauley, Greenbrier, Elk, and Meadow rivers. In addition to smallmouth bass, walleye, muskie, and trout are also available.

No guide listings were received from the southern states of North and South Carolina, Virginia, Maryland, Alabama, and Mississippi. These states, with hundreds of lakes and streams and hundreds of miles of coastline, must host a multitude of light tackle possibilities. Any information readers would like to offer on guided fishing in these states will be welcome for our next edition.

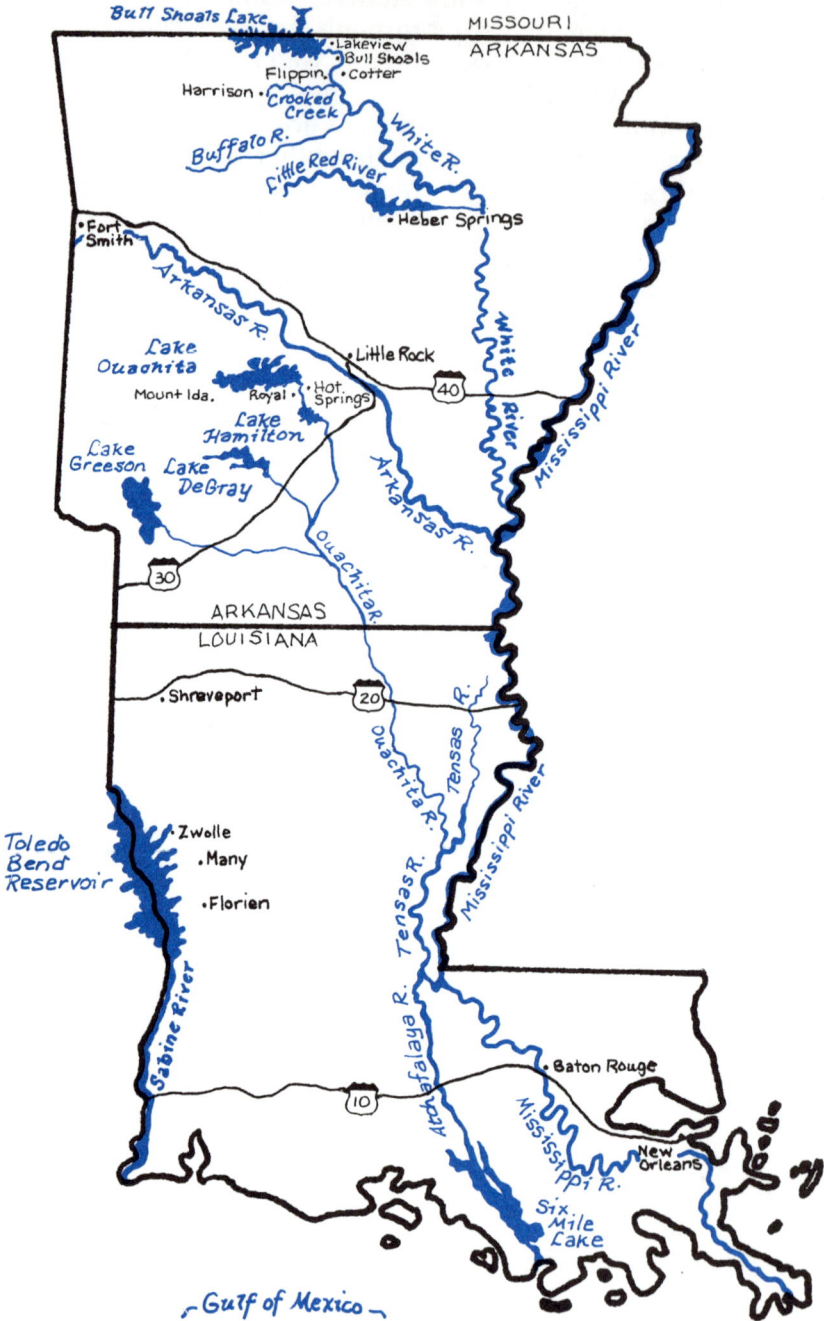

ARKANSAS / LOUISIANA

Bull Shoals Lake

MISSOURI
ARKANSAS

Lakeview
Bull Shoals
Flippin • Cotter

Harrison •
Crooked Creek

Buffalo R.
White R.
Little Red River

• Heber Springs

• Fort Smith

Arkansas R.
White River

Lake Ouachita

Mount Ida.
Royal • • Hot Springs
• Little Rock
40

Lake Hamilton

Lake Greeson
Lake DeGray

Arkansas R.

Ouachita R.
30

ARKANSAS
LOUISIANA

Ouachita R.
Tensas R.

• Shreveport
20

Toledo Bend Reservoir
• Zwolle
• Many
• Florien

Sabine River

Tensas R.
Atchafalaya R.

Mississippi River

• Baton Rouge
10

Mississippi R.
New Orleans

Six Mile Lake

~ Gulf of Mexico ~

Arkansas

BULL SHOALS, ARKANSAS

DUGA, MIKE (501) 445-4744
Address P.O. Box 228, Bull Shoals, AR 72619
Airport Harrison 50m **Accommodations** Bull Shoals **Operation** Guide
Fish Largemouth, smallmouth, spotted bass **Season** Year-round
Water Bull Shoals Lake **Specialty** Light spinning tackle for smallmouth bass
Type of Fishing Spin, baitcast **Boats** Bass boats **Rates** day: $110 plus gas
Guide's Notes: Bull Shoals Lake--Fish are available all year. Peak times are from mid-April to mid-May, late October to early December (also best top water). Summer is very good during the evenings and nights.
Author's Notes: Charlie Hoover, Sales Manager for Ranger boats, recommended Mike to us as an excellent guide.

COTTER, ARKANSAS

CAMERON, STEVE (405) 737-6174, (501) 430-5133
Address 305 E. Kerr, Midwest, OK 73110
Airport Midway 10m **Accommodations** Cotter **Operation** Outfitter
Fish Trout, bass, catfish, striper, crappie **Season** June-August
Water White River **Specialty** Fly fishing, light tackle, float fishing
Boats Johnboats **Tackle Supplied** All **Type of Fishing** All
Experience 1 year **Rates** day: $35 week: $245
Guide's Notes: The main species we have on the **White River** are rainbow and brown trout. There are also cutthroat, golden and brook trout in the river. The peak times to fish are spring, early fall, and mid-winter. We have no closed season on the river and fish can be caught from the basics like corn and red worms all the way to fly fishing using White River hoppers, mayflies, nymphs and the likes.

Brown Trout Record

Weight	Where Caught	Year
25 pounds	White River	Sept, 1963
28 lbs-3 oz	White River	Sept, 1970
31 1/2 pounds	White River	May, 1972
33 1/2 pounds	White River	March, 1977

Rainbow Trout Record

Weight	Where Caught	Year
16 lbs-2 oz	North Fork River	July, 1972
19 pounds	White River	June, 1976
19 lbs-1 oz	White River	March, 1981

Big striper from Southern reservoir.   *Del Webb Corp.*

Author's Notes: For those of us who are hung up on famous trout streams like the Madison or the Bighorn, the above records are eye openers.

FLIPPIN, ARKANSAS

DUE, TOMMY (501) 453-8260, 453-2424
Address Box 164, Flippin, AR 72634
Airport Little Rock 150m **Accommodations** Flippin **Operation** Guide
Water White River, Crooked Creek, Buffalo River **Type of Fishing** All
Specialty Spinning and baitcast float fishing **Fish** Trout, sm bass
Boats 20′ johnboats **Tackle Supplied** Spin, baitcast **Season** Year-round
Experience 24 years **Rates** day: $200

HEBER SPRINGS, ARKANSAS

GRIFFIN, LEROY-RED RIVER TROUT DOCK (501) 362-2197
Address Wilburn Rt., Box 346, Hwy 110 E and 210 E, Heber Springs, AR 72543
Airport Little Rock 60m **Accommodations** Heber Springs **Season** Year-round
Operation Tackle shop, outfitter **Type of Fishing** Spin, baitcast **Boats** Johnboats
Fish Rainbow and brown trout **Tackle Supplied** Spin, baitcast
Water Little Red River **Specialty** Trout fishing on the Little Red River
Experience 10 years **Rates** day: $85/2 people
Guide's Notes: Little Red River Trout season is open all year. The water in the Red River is drawn off the bottom of the reservoir and stays the same temperature at all times. The larger trout are caught in the winter months because of less activity on the river.
Author's Notes: Leroy has seven guides working through his shop.

LAKEVIEW, ARKANSAS

GASTON, ERIC-GASTON'S WHITE RIVER RESORT (501) 431-5202
Address #1 River Road, Lakeview, AR 72642
Airport Harrison 50m **Accommodations** On premises **Operation** Outfitter, resort
Fish Rainbow, brown, cutthroat, largemouth, white bass, crappie
Season Year-round **Water** White River, Bull Shoals **Type of Fishing** All
Specialty Twenty guides available offering all types of fishing
Boats Bass boats, 20′ johnboats with outboards **Tackle Supplied** All
Experience 9 years **Rates** day: $148
Guide's Notes: The White River is a tail water of Bull Shoals Lake. Water temperatures are constant year round and trout fishing is good all year. Peak times for trophy trout are Feb-March. Most fish are caught on lures such as count down Rapala's #9 or #7, in silver or gold, and wet flies such as big brown Wooly Worms or Sow Bugs in size #4 or #2.
Author's Notes: Both the resort and the guide service were highly recommended to us by Charlie Hoover of Ranger Boats.

MOUNT IDA, ARKANSAS

DAVIS, MARK-MOUNTAIN HARBOR RESORT (501) 867-2191, 623-8452
Address Star Rt 1, Box 305, Mount Ida, AR 71957
Airport Hot Springs 25m **Accommodations** On premises
Operation Guide **Type of Fishing** Spin, baitcast
Fish Largemouth bass, stripers, crappie, walleye **Season** Year-round
Water Lake Ouachita, Lake De Gray, Lake Hamilton, Arkansas River
Specialty Bass boat fishing **Boats** Bass boats **Tackle Supplied** Spin, baitcast
Experience 6 years **Rates** day:$125 1/2 day: $75 plus fuel/2 people
Guide's Notes: Lake Ouachita Bass are available year round and the best top
water fishing is during the spring and fall.
*Author's Notes: Mark Davis comes highly recommended by Joe Hughes of
Rebbel/Heddon lures. Joe says "Mark is one of the best guides in Arkansas and
that Mountain Harbor Resort where Mark is head guide is a world class fishing
resort."*

ROYAL, ARKANSAS

KILBY, BILL AND ROB (501) 767-3869
Address Rt. 2, Box 1205, Royal, AR 71968
Airport Little Rock 50m **Accommodations** Royal **Operation** Guide
Fish Largemouth bass, walleye, striped bass **Season** Year-round
Water Lake Ouachita, Lake Hamilton, Lake Greeson, Arkansas River
Specialty Baitcasting-spinning **Type of Fishing** Spin, baitcast
Boats Bass boats **Tackle Supplied** Spin, baitcast
Experience 15 years **Rates** day: $150
Guide's Notes: Fishing Calendar for Lake Ouachita

Fish	Season	Best Topwater
Largemouth Bass	Good all year	Mar - Jun, Sept - Dec
Striper	Good all year	May, Oct - Dec
Walleye	Peak Mar - May	

Author's Notes: Local sources say both Bill and Rob are very capable guides.

Florida

BIG PINE KEY, FLORIDA

FECHER, RAY (305) 872-2487
Address RR 1, Box 345, Big Pine Key, FL 33043
Airport Key West 20m **Accommodations** Big Pine Key
Operation Guide, charter captain **Type of Fishing** All
Fish Tarpon, bonefish, permit **Season** Year-round **Boats** 18′ flats skiff
Water Lower Florida Keys **Specialty** Fly fishing **Tackle Supplied** All
Experience 8 years **Rates** day: $225 1/2 day: $155
Guide's Notes: Lower Florida Keys--Bonefish are available year-round with the best fishing from March-November. The biggest tarpon are available from March to July with smaller fish available through November. Permit are available from February through November.
Author's Notes: Ray is known as an excellent guide.

WEJEBE, CAPTAIN JOSE-FISHING CHARTERS (305) 872-9573
Address P.O. Box 602, Big Pine Key, FL 33043
Airport Key West 30m **Accommodations** Key West 20m
Operation Guide, charter captain **Type of Fishing** All
Fish Tarpon, bonefish, permit, snook **Season** Year-round
Water Gulf of Mexico, Atlantic Ocean, Florida Bay, Everglades
Specialty Fly fishing or light tackle **Boats** Flats skiff **Tackle Supplied** All
Experience 6 years **Rates** day: $250
Author's Notes: Friends tell us that Jose is a very capable light tackle and fly fishing guide.

CLEWISTON, FLORIDA

AKRIDGE, AL (813) 983-8066
Address 612 Sabal Ave, Seminol Manor, Clewiston, FL 33440
Airport Fort Myers 60m **Accommodations** Clewiston **Operation** Guide
Fish Largemouth bass **Season** Year-round **Type of Fishing** Baitcast
Water Lake Okeechobee **Specialty** Shiner or artificial lures
Boats Bass boat **Tackle Supplied** Baitcast
Experience 6 years **Rates** day: $150 1/2 day: $100

FISCHER, BERT (813) 983-8902, 983-8930
Address Tropical Village Lot 249, Clewiston, FL 33440
Airport Fort Myers 60m **Accommodations** Clewiston
Operation Guide **Type of Fishing** Baitcast, troll **Tackle Supplied** Spin, baitcast
Fish Lm bass, crappie, bream **Season** Year-round **Boats** Bass boat

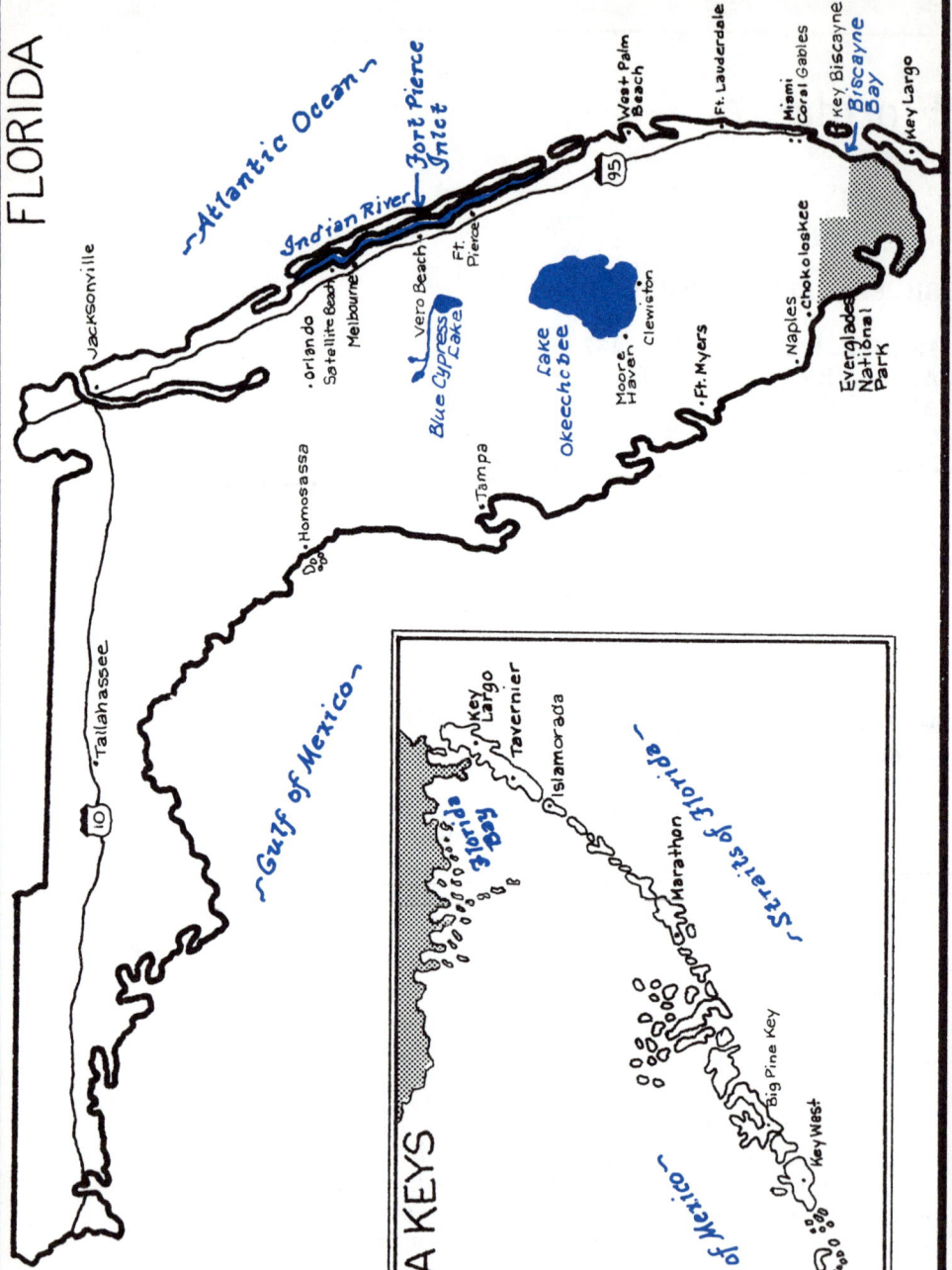

FLORIDA

Atlantic Ocean

Jacksonville

Tallahassee

10

Homosassa

Tampa

Gulf of Mexico

Orlando
Satellite Beach
Melbourne
Vero Beach
Blue Cypress Lake
Indian River
Fort Pierce Inlet
Ft. Pierce

95

West Palm Beach
Ft. Lauderdale
Miami
Coral Gables
Key Biscayne
Biscayne Bay
Key Largo

Lake Okeechobee

Moore Haven
Clewiston

Ft. Myers

Naples
Chokoloskee

Everglades National Park

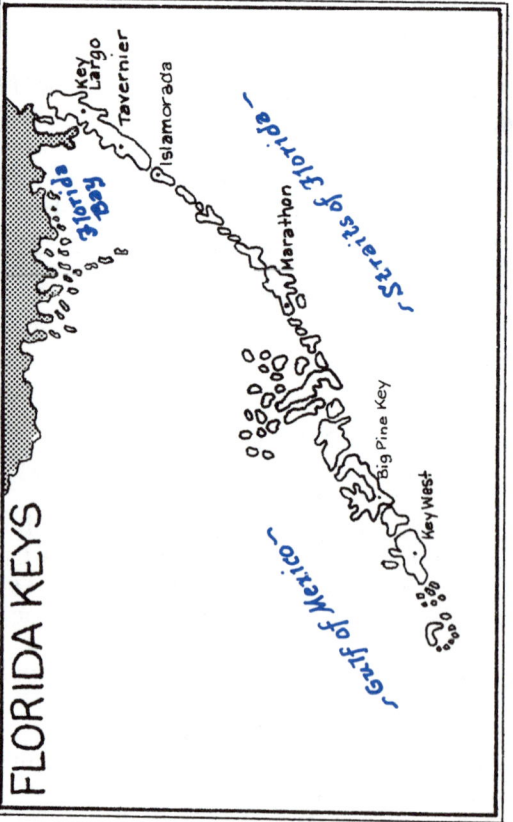

FLORIDA KEYS

Key Largo
Tavernier
Islamorada
Florida Bay
Marathon
Straits of Florida
Big Pine Key
Key West
Gulf of Mexico

Water Lake Okeechobee **Specialty** Shiner fishing for largemouth bass
Experience 13 years **Rates** day: $150 1/2 day: $100

SCHNEIDER, DANIEL (813) 983-7293, 983-7402
Address Lot 270, Tropical Mobile Village, Clewiston, FL 33440
Airport Fort Myers 60m **Accommodations** Clewiston **Operation** Guide
Fish Black bass only **Season** Oct.-May **Type of Fishing** Baitcast
Water Lake Okeechobee **Specialty** Bass boat fishing
Boats Bass boat **Tackle Supplied** Spin, baitcast
Experience 10 years **Rates** day: $150 1/2 day: $90

WAGNER, FRED (813) 983-8711
Address 444 W. Sugarland Hwy, Clewiston, FL 33440
Airport West Palm 75m **Accommodations** Clewiston
Operation Guide **Type of Fishing** Spin, baitcast
Fish Lm bass, bluegill, shell cracker, crappie **Season** Year-round
Water Lake Okeechobee **Specialty** Wild shiner and artificial for bass
Boats Bass boats **Tackle Supplied** Spin, baitcast
Experience 2 years **Rates** day: $150 1/2 day: $100

WELLS, JIM (813) 983-5741
Address 1550 Sassy Road, Clewiston, FL 33440
Airport West Palm 60m **Accommodations** Clewiston
Operation Guide **Type of Fishing** All **Season** Year-round
Fish Bass, specks, blue gill **Water** Lake Okeechobee
Boats Bass boats **Tackle Supplied** All **Specialty** Bass fishing
Experience 7 years **Rates** day: $150 1/2 day: $90

CHOKOLOSKEE, FLORIDA

OGLESBY JR., CAPTAIN CECIL (813) 695-2910
Address P.O. Box 366, Chokoloskee, FL 33925
Airport Naples 40m **Accommodations** Chokoloskee **Operation** Charter captain
Fish Snook, redfish, trout, tarpon **Season** Year-round **Type of Fishing** All
Water Ten thousand Islands of the Everglades National Park
Specialty Plug casting for snook and tarpon
Boats 16' open fisherman **Tackle Supplied** Spin, baitcast, troll
Experience 30 years **Rates** day: $180
Guide's Notes: Everglades National Park--The prime time for snook is January,
February, April, May, and June; for redfish, August-November. Trout are avail-
able year-round and tarpon are available January through March, and May
through July.

CORAL GABLES, FLORIDA

BAKER, CAPTAIN LEE W. (305) 448-1447
Address 3133 Salzedo, Coral Gables, FL 33134

Airport Miami 10m **Accommodations** Coral Gables
Operation Charter captain, guide **Type of Fishing** All
Fish Tarpon, bonefish, permit, snapper **Season** Year-round
Water Florida Keys and Key West, Biscayne Bay, Homosassa Area
Specialty Fly fishing from custom built flats skiff for big tarpon
Boats Custom flats skiffs **Tackle Supplied** All
Experience 16 years **Rates** day: $250 week: $1750 1/2 day: $150/2 people
Guide's Notes: Florida Keys--Shallow water fly fishing for big tarpon, bonefish
and permit. The best tarpon fly fishing is from March through July. Bonefish
are good all year as are permit.
*Author's Notes: Lee Baker has a national reputation as an excellent salt water
fly fishing guide.*

FORT LAUDERDALE, FLORIDA

ALLEN, JACK (305) 764-6115
Address 1324 NE 3rd Ave., Dept. H, Fort Lauderdale, FL 33304
Airport Fort Lauderdale **Accommodations** Fort Lauderdale
Operation Guide **Type of Fishing** All **Tackle Supplied** All
Fish Bass, bluegill, snook **Season** Year-round **Boats** 16' john boat
Water Everglades, Lake Okeechobee **Specialty** Bass bug fishing
Experience 16 years **Rates** day: $175 1/2 day: $115
*Author's Notes: I have known Jack Allen for eight years. He is a great person
and one of the best guides I have ever fished with.*

FORT PIERCE, FLORIDA

METZ, CAPTAIN GERALD L.-DeBROOKS FISHING CENTER (305) 465-6194
Address 3111 Kentucky Ave., Dept. I, Fort Pierce, FL 33450
Airport W. Palm Beach 60m **Accommodations** Fort Pierce
Operation Guide, charter captain **Type of Fishing** All
Fish Snook, trout, snapper, channel bass **Season** Year-round
Water Indian River, Atlantic Ocean coastal waters, Fort Pierce Inlet
Specialty Live baiting, flats fishing, wade fishing, fly fishing
Boats 17' open fishing **Tackle Supplied** All
Experience 2 years **Rates** day: $150 1/2 day: $80
**Guide's Notes: Fishing Calendar for the Indian River from Sebastian to West
Palm Beach (and coastal waters, Ft Pierce inlet)**

Fish	Available	Lure	Peak
Snook	Sept - Dec	Live bait	
Trout	Year-round	Live bait, top water plugs, fly fishing	June - Aug Nov - Mar
Channel Bass	Jan - Mar Aug - Sep		
Mangrove Snapper	June - Aug		
Tarpon	June - Aug		

Author's Notes: We fished with Jerry in April of '85 and found him to be a very capable guide.

ISLAMORADA, FLORIDA

DILLON, GARY AND ROBERT (305) 852-3096
Address P.O. Box 524, Islamorada, FL 33036
Airport Miami 75m **Accommodations** Islamorada
Operation Charter captain **Type of Fishing** Spin, troll
Fish Dolphin, sailfish, king mackerel, blackfin tuna **Season** Year-round
Water Atlantic Ocean (Straits of Florida) **Specialty** Light tackle offshore trolling
Boats 40' and 47' Sport Fisherman **Tackle Supplied** Spin, troll
Experience 11 years **Rates** day: $450 1/2 day: $325

DOVE, ROBERT L. (305) 852-8113, 664-2321
Address Box 414, Islamorada, FL 33036
Airport Marathon 35m **Accommodations** Islamorada
Operation Guide **Type of Fishing** Fly, spin
Fish Bonefish, tarpon, redfish, trout, snapper **Season** Oct-July
Water Florida Bay and Everglades, Florida Keys
Specialty Bonefish and tarpon flats fishing **Boats** Skiff **Tackle Supplied** All
Experience 20 years **Rates** day: $200 1/2 day: $150
Guide's Notes: Fishing Calendar for Islamorada

Fish	Available	Peak
Bonefish	Year-round	Spring
Tarpon		April - July
Redfish	Oct - April	
Trout	Year-round	
Snapper	Year-round	
Permit	Year-round	Spring

MORIARTY, CAPTAIN GENE-BUD & MARY'S MARINA (305) 664-8194
Address 137 Bayview Dr., Islamorada, FL 33036
Airport Marathon 20m **Accommodations** Islamorada
Operation Guide, charter captain **Type of Fishing** All **Tackle Supplied** All
Fish Bonefish, tarpon, permit, barracuda **Season** Nov-May **Boats** Skiff
Water Florida Bay, Atlantic Ocean (shallow water) **Specialty** Fly fishing
Experience 35 years **Rates** day: $200

KEY BISCAYNE, FLORIDA

CURTIS, CAPTAIN BILL (305) 361-2973
Address 320 West Heather Dr., Key Biscayne, FL 33149
Airport Miami 10m **Accommodations** Key Biscayne
Operation Guide, charter captain **Tackle Supplied** Fly, spin
Fish Bonefish, tarpon, permit, barracuda **Season** Year-round **Boats** 18' skiff

Specialty Light tackle flats fishing **Water** Biscayne Bay **Type of Fishing** Fly, spin **Experience** 27 years **Rates** day: $250 1/2 day: $190

Guide's Notes: I specialize in light-tackle sports fishing in the waters of **Biscayne Bay**--a combination of hunting and casting to the "Big Three" (bonefish, tarpon, permit). Bonefish are available year-round here. They are not as plentiful as in the Bahamas, but the average fish is larger and gives a better fight. We also have excellent tarpon fishing spring and early summer. Permit are thick here, increasing in numbers as the summer progresses-most years thru Christmas (unless we have an unusual early cold snap). We fish from the Crandon Marina, located just as you come onto Key Biscayne.

Author's Notes: A friend of mine, Curry Harbor, has fished with Bill for years and he says "Bill is the best available." We talked to other contacts that agree that Bill is an outstanding guide. No less an authority than Lefty Kreh considers Bill one of the best guides of his type in the world.

GARISTO, CAPTAIN FRANK (305) 361-5040

Address 360 Harbor Court, Key Biscayne, FL 33149
Airport Miami 10m **Accommodations** Miami **Operation** Guide, charter captain
Fish Bonefish, permit, tarpon, barracuda **Season** Year-round **Type of Fishing** All
Water Biscayne Bay, Atlantic Ocean **Specialty** Fly fishing with ultra light tackle
Boats Bonefish skiff **Tackle Supplied** All
Experience 16 years **Rates** day: $250

Guide's Notes: I offer typical flats fishing for larger than average bonefish.
Author's Notes: Frank works out of Key Biscayne, only ten miles from Miami International Airport. He is highly regarded nationally as a bonefish guide, and has won the Master Skiff Award in the Miami Metropolitan Fishing Tournament.

KEY LARGO, FLORIDA

BLEVINS, ROGER (305) 451-2349

Address P.O. Box 806, Key Largo, FL 33037
Airport Key Largo **Accommodations** Key Largo **Operation** Charter captain
Fish Grouper, snapper, grunt, dolphin **Season** Year-round
Water Atlantic Ocean, Gulf Stream, Caribbean Sea
Specialty Reef fishing with light tackle **Type of Fishing** Spin, troll
Boats 40' Head boat **Tackle Supplied** Spin, troll, baitcast
Experience 10 years **Rates** day: $300 private charter

Guide's Notes: Fishing is good year around. Big groupers come in during January and February. Dolphins run from April until September.

KEY WEST, FLORIDA

DRAKE, GILL & LINDA (305) 296-4905

Address 2 Bougainvillea, Key West, FL 33040
Airport Key West **Accommodations** Key West **Operation** Guide, charter captain
Fish Tarpon, bonefish, permit, barracuda **Season** Jan-Jun

Water Lower Keys (Gulf and Atlantic sides), Marquesas
Specialty Fly and spin casting on salt water flats **Type of Fishing** Fly, spin
Boats 16′ and 18′ shallow draft skiffs **Tackle Supplied** Fly, spin
Experience 20 years, 6 years **Rates** day: $250
Guide's Notes: Lower Flordia Keys: In January to mid-February, we fish bar-racuda and permit. From mid-February through April, we fish barracuda, per-mit, and tarpon. Mid-May through July, our fishing is primarily for migrating tarpon.
Author's Notes: Gill and Linda certainly are among the best guides in the area. Gill has written articles for several magazines including "Field and Stream," "Sports Illustrated," and "Salt Water Sportsman." Linda is one of only a few women who guide in the Keys.

ISLEY, JAN (305) 294-1864
Address 913 Georgia, Key West, FL 33040
Airport Key West **Accommodations** Key West **Operation** Guide, charter captain
Fish Bonefish, permit, tarpon **Season** Year-round **Type of Fishing** All
Water Florida Keys, Salt water flats **Tackle Supplied** All
Specialty Light tackle fishing the Florida Flats **Boats** Bonefish skiff
Experience 5 years **Rates** day: $250
Guide's Notes: Lower Florida Keys Our fishing is with light tackle in shallow water casting to visible fish, while the boat is poled across the flats. Permit are available all year with February to mid-April being prime. Tarpon are available April through July and the prime is May and June. We have bone fishing from March to October, with the peak in July and September.
Author's Notes: Our sources say Jan is an excellent guide.

MARATHON, FLORIDA

BUSCIGLIO, JR., CAPTIAN TONY (305) 743-7225
Address P.O. Box 1387, Marathon, FL 33050
Airport Marathon **Accommodations** Marathon
Operation Charter captain, tackle shop **Type of Fishing** All
Fish Bonefish, permit, tarpon, snapper **Season** Year-round
Water Lower Malecumbe Islamorada to Key West Flats
Specialty Fly fishing-all species on flats **Boats** Skiff **Tackle Supplied** All
Experience 15 years **Rates** day: $250-600
Guide's Notes: Lower Florida Keys

Fish	Available
Tarpon on Flats	All year, peak Mar - June
Tarpon on Bridge	Mar - June
Permit, Bonefish	Apr - June, Sept - Oct
Marlin	July - Dec
Sailfish, Kings, Cobia	Nov - Mar
Dolphin	June - Sept
Snapper, Grouper	All year

Author's Notes: Tony comes recommended as another top Keys guide.

JORDAN, CAPTAIN MARLENE AND JAKE (305) 743-6139
Address P.O. Box 1543, Marathon, FL 33050
Airport Marathon **Accommodations** Marathon
Operation Guide, charter captain **Type of Fishing** All
Fish Bonefish, permit, tarpon, snapper **Season** Year-round
Water Islamorada to Key West Flats **Boats** Skiffs **Tackle Supplied** All
Specialty Light tackle and fly fishing on flats for all species
Experience 7 years **Rates** day: $250-600

PEREZ, DALE (305) 289-1756
Address P.O. Box 671, Marathon, FL 33050
Airport Key West 45m **Accommodations** Marathon **Operation** Guide
Fish Bonefish, permit, tarpon **Season** Feb-Nov **Type of Fishing** All
Water Keys **Specialty** Fly fishing **Boats** 18' outboard **Tackle Supplied** All
Experience 15 years **Rates** day: $250
Guide's Notes: February is good fishing for permit, tarpon, and bonefish. Late March to early April is the best month to catch large permit (up to 50 pounds) especially on a fly and also big tarpon(to 190 pounds). April is still a great permit month but the fish are not quite as large. May to June are prime tarpon times as the tarpon are migrating. July through September are excellent tailing bonefish months. September and October are the peak bonefish times. November is still good bonefishing and you'll also find redfish in the Everglades. Best fly patterns are Cockroach and Apt #2 for tarpon.
Author's Notes: All of our contacts tell us Dale is one of the best guides in the area.

MIAMI, FLORIDA

LANDON, FLOYD (305) 667-0972
Address 7830 SW 54th Ave., Miami, FL 33143
Airport Miami **Accommodations** Miami **Operation** Guide
Fish Bonefish, tarpon, permit **Season** Year-round
Water Biscayne Bay **Specialty** Fly and spin fishing
Boats 18' skiff **Tackle Supplied** Fly, spin **Type of Fishing** Salt water flats
Experience 15 years **Rates** day: $250 1/2 day: $150
Author's Notes: Floyd has a reputation as an experienced and highly skilled guide.

MOORE HAVEN, FLORIDA

SWANSON, ARVID (813) 946-0574, 946-0544
Address P.O. Box 1055, Moore Haven, FL 33471
Airport Fort Myers 60m **Accommodations** Moore Haven
Operation Guide **Type of Fishing** All **Boats** Bass boat, airboat
Fish Bass, shellcrackers, blue bream, specks **Season** Year-round
Water L. Okeechobee **Specialty** Airboating & bass boating **Tackle Supplied** All
Experience 8 years **Rates** day: $150 1/2 day: $100
Author's Notes: Arvid is very well known to Florida bass fisherman and has an excellent reputation.

Captains Frank Catino and Rick Ruoff with bonefish near Islamorada.   *Paul Bruun*

Captain Bill Curtis and guide Paul Brunn with fly-caught bonefish.   *Paul Bruun*

SATELLITE BEACH, FLORIDA

CATINO, FRANK-CATINO'S CUSTOM ROD SHOP (303) 777-5706, 777-2793
Address 599 E. Sherwood Ave., Box 2088, Satellite Beach, FL 32937
Airport Orlando 50m **Accommodations** Satellite Beach **Season** Year-round
Operation Guide, tackle shop **Fish** Trout, tarpon, redfish, snook
Water Indian, Banana Rivers, Florida Keys off shore **Specialty** Fly fishing
Boats 16' Dolphin, 60' Hatteras **Tackle Supplied** All **Type of Fishing** All
Experience 10 years **Rates** day: $175 1/2 day: $100
Guide's Notes: Fishing Calendar for Banana and Indian Rivers

Fish	Available
Trout	April - June and Sept
Snook	Sept - Nov

Author's Notes: Frank guides the central Florida Coast out of his rod shop in Satellite Beach. He is a highly respected guide and is nationally known for developing the Catino salt water fly reel.

TAVERNIER, FLORIDA

DiMAURA, CAPTAIN PAUL W. (305) 852-9665
Address 319 Summer Sea, Tavernier, FL 33070
Airport Miami 75m **Accommodations** Tavernier
Operation Guide **Type of Fishing** All **Fish** Bonefish, tarpon, redfish, trout
Water Florida Keys, Florida Bay, Everglades National Park **Season** Year-round
Specialty Light tackle and fly fishing **Boats** 18' skiff **Tackle Supplied** All
Experience 6 years **Rates** day: $200

VERO BEACH, FLORIDA

WILLIAMS, FRANK-FRANK'S CHARTER SERVICE (305) 562-3430
Address 2826 Atlantic Blvd., Vero Beach, FL 32960
Airport Vero Beach **Accommodations** Vero Beach
Operation Guide, charter captain **Type of Fishing** All
Fish Snook, trout, redfish, snapper, bass **Season** Year-round
Water Indian River, Blue Cypress Lake **Boats** Bass boats
Specialty Casting, fly fishing, spin casting, plug casting **Tackle Supplied** All
Experience 15 years **Rates** day: $175 1/2 day: $100
Author's Notes: Dave Harbour writing in SPORTS AFIELD about Florida's east coast wrote:

"The fastest inland saltwater action is along the east coast's Indian River from Melbourne south to Ft. Pierce. When fishing the main river and its countless tributaries and bays, you never know what will blast your plug. I've found snook, tarpon, ten-pound sea trout, big channel bass, jacks, mangrove snappers, ladyfish and even flounder in this area. The best river guide I've found is Frank Williams."

Georgia

LA GRANGE, GEORGIA

MIKE, JR., TOMMY (404) 882-8186, 882-7887
Address 728 Lakewood Dr., La Grange, GA 30240
Airport Atlanta 60m **Accommodations** La Grange
Operation Outfitter **Type of Fishing** Spin, baitcast, troll
Fish Largemouth, hybrid, striped bass, crappie **Season** Year-round
Water West Point Lake **Specialty** Baitcasting and spinning with lures
Boats Bass boats **Tackle Supplied** Spin, baitcast, troll
Experience 10 years **Rates** day: $200
Guide's Notes: West Point Lake Fishing Calendar Largemouth bass and hybrid
fishing picks up in mid-February. During March, the fish move into shallower
water and from mid-April through May the fish move onto the beds. In June
through August, the lake is at its peak. September through November, the fish
are feeding heavily. Winter is the dormant period. The fishing slows December
- January but fish are still available. The best top water period is mid-April
through mid-June and September through November. The best lures are Buzz
Baits, Bang-O-Lure, Carolina rig Gotcha worms, and deep diving Crank Baits.
The size of the fish run as follows:
  Largemouth average 2 1/2 - 3 pounds, big population of 5 - 10 lb fish
  Hybrid-Stripers average 6 - 10 pounds
  Crappie average 3/4 - 1 pound
  We have several guides available and can accommodate parties of up to 20
people.
*Author's Notes: Tommy Mike has developed a new bass lure called the Gotcha
Worm. It works on a principle similar to a pair of ice tongs, it actually grabs
the fish. I have not seen this new device, but it sounds awfully deadly. Local
sources tell us Tommy is a good guide.*

SAVAGE, RON (404) 884-6232
Address Rt. 3, Box 412, La Grange, GA 30240
Airport Atlanta 50m **Accommodations** La Grange
Operation Guide **Type of Fishing** Spin, baitcast, troll
Fish Largemouth bass, hybrid bass **Season** March-Dec.
Water West Point Lake **Specialty** Baitcasting with lures
Boats Bass boats, 20ft tunnel hull **Tackle Supplied** Spin, baitcast
Experience 7 years **Rates** day: $175
Author's Notes: Ron has a reputation as a highly capable guide.

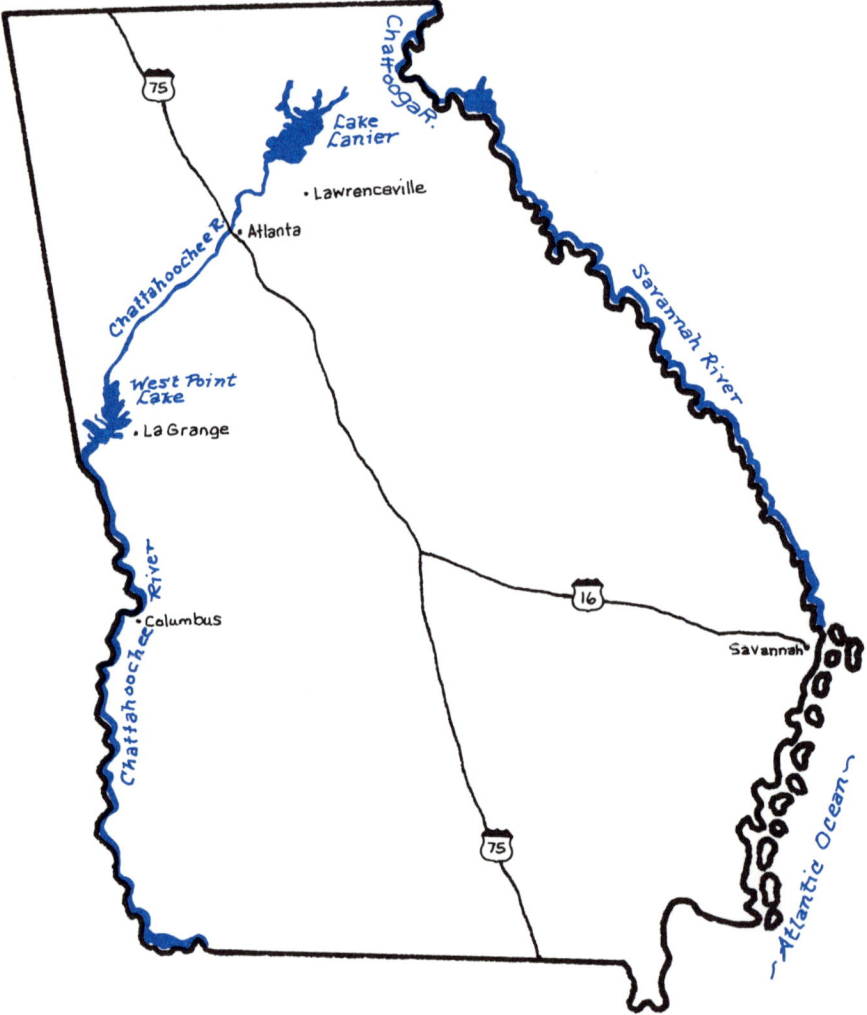

GEORGIA

75

Chattooga R.

Lake
Lanier

• Lawrenceville

Chattahoochee R.

• Atlanta

Savannah River

West Point
Lake

• La Grange

Chattahoochee River

• Columbus

16

75

Savannah•

Atlantic Ocean

LAWRENCEVILLE, GEORGIA

VANDERFORD, BILL-BILL VANDERFORD'S GUIDE SERVICE (404) 962-1241

Address 2224 Pine Point Drive, Lawrenceville, GA 30245
Airport Atlanta 60m **Accommodations** Lawrenceville
Operation Outfitter **Type of Fishing** Spin, baitcast, troll **Water** Lake Lanier
Fish Spotted, largemouth, striped bass, rainbow **Season** Year-round
Specialty Structure fishing **Boats** Bass boats **Tackle Supplied** Spin, baitcast, troll
Experience 15 years **Rates** day: $175 1/2 day: $100
Guide's Notes: I have more than 50 guides including 10 female guides.

Lanier Lake The largemouth will start coming into the shallower water in late February. They continue coming into the shallow water on into April. They stay shallow until after they spawn, and you can still catch quite a few largemouth male bass as late as June in shallow water. In fact, if the water doesn't warm up too fast, you can still catch largemouth male bass in very shallow water on into July, especially at night. After that, they pretty much drop back into the deep water where they stay until fall. In the fall they'll come again into the shallow water, not as shallow as they did in the spring, but you can catch them in 10 feet of water or less. In late fall, around the end of September or the beginning of October, they'll school with the spotted bass in deeper water and you can catch them on spoons all the way through the wintertime. They get very dormant during the winter and it is hard to locate them, but if you can locate them you can still catch them. They'll stay schooled together pretty much all the way through the wintertime.

Striped Bass More and more fishermen are discovering that striped bass have been born again in the large, freshwater impoundments like Lanier, where the largemouth was once considered king.

The stripers appeal to bass fishermen because of their staggering growth rate, which is twice that of stripers in salt water. The reason for the remarkable growth rate appears to be the simple lack of competition for food. An occasional large shad is taken by a gar, but mostly the stripers have the reservoir as an open dining table all to themselves.

Good striper fishing on Lanier really starts when the water starts to cool off in the fall, as early as the middle of October, usually lasting to March or April. The one proven way to catch stripers in Lanier is by casting large plugs. Probably the best plug is a 7-inch Redfin, made by Cotton Cordell. You do your striper fishing at night. The way to do it is to get out on a long point in maybe 25-35 feet of water and throw back toward the point. Just swim it back at a speed where it makes a "V" wake. If there are any stripers around that point, they will go after that plug. If the water is a little bit rougher, use a large Rebel plug, usually in a shad color with a black back, and pull it just under the water about the same way. These are methods that work real well for stripers all the way through the winter. Throwing these plugs, try using a 5 1/2 foot medium action graphite rod, 14 pound test line, and an Ambassador 5000. Sometimes, if a striper is active, he'll hit it 4-5 times before he gets the hook. When a striper hits, he's going to try to take 100 yards of line on his first run.

The best areas for catching big stripers in Lanier are Flat Creek and Balus Creek area; the area around Brown's Bridge; the points off the Chattahoochee channel in the Aqualand area; and around Lake Lanier Islands.

There are several reasons why stripers tend to feed at night more than in the daytime. Perhaps the most important is the fact that stripers, like many fish, are negatively phototropic. That means that they're repelled by strong light sources. Just as light penetration levels control the depth of the daylight stripers, the low intensity of light at night brings the big stripers into shallower water. Another attraction for catching nighttime stripers is artificial light. The light must come from a steady source that has been there for a period of time such as a dock or a pier light. Simply hanging a lantern or a crappie light over the side of a boat rarely attracts stripers. Normally stripers will lurk just on the border between the lighted area and the dark water. They rarely come into the light-flooded area itself. Consequently, casts around lighted piers and docks should be directed to the edges of illuminated water. For best results, you should have deep water not more than a long cast away.

Author's Notes: Bill Vanderford has a state-wide reputation as a fisherman and guide. Operating out of Stouffer's Pine Isle Resort, he employs over 40 guides.

Kentucky

CADIZ, KENTUCKY

BOWLIN, STAN (502) 924-5033
Address Rt. 2, Cadiz, KY 42211
Airport Nashville, TN 90m **Accommodations** Cadiz
Fish Black bass, sm bass, crappie, stripers **Season** Year-round
Water Lake Barkley, Kentucky Lake **Type of Fishing** Baitcast
Boats Bass boats **Tackle Supplied** Spin, baitcast **Operation** Guide
Experience 4 years**Rates** day: $100 week: $450 1/2 day: $55
Guide's Notes: Lake Barkley, Kentucky Lake
Crappie season is March to May. From late March through April they spawn and the fishing is excellent! Black Bass season is March to early December with the best fishing March, May and October. I recommend fishing with crankbaits, jig-n-pigs, worms or spinner baits. Striper fishing peaks mid-July to mid-August and the best lures are Little George and Slab Spoons. Use crankbaits for stripers off rocky points in October, November and December.

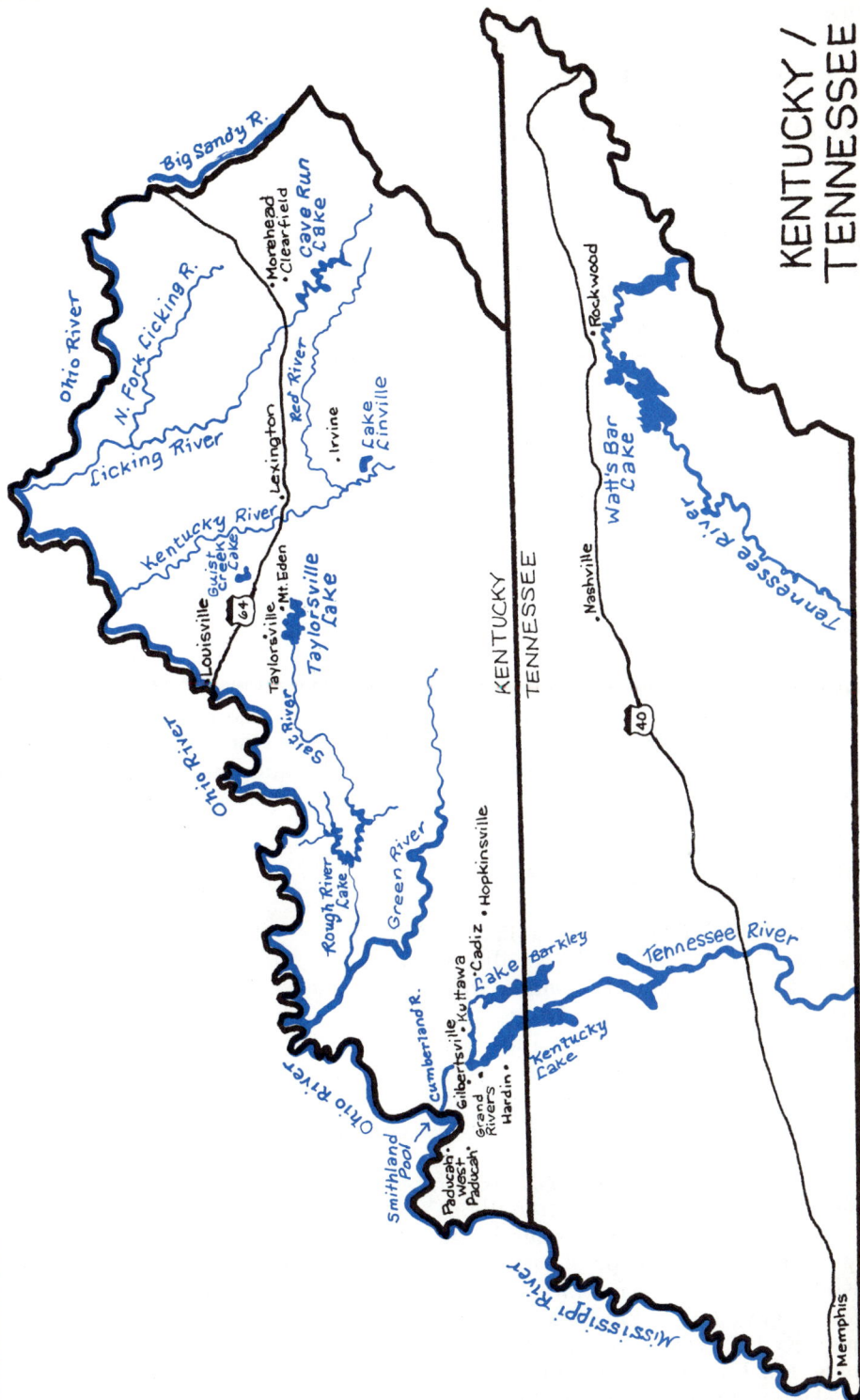

KENTUCKY / TENNESSEE

CLEARFIELD, KENTUCKY

COLLINS, MIKE (606) 784-9738
Address Box 427, Clearfield, KY 40313
Airport Lexington 65m **Accommodations** Clearfield **Operation** Guide
Fish Muskie **Season** Year-round **Type of Fishing** Spin, baitcast, troll
Water Cave Run Lake, Licking River **Specialty** Muskie fishing
Boats Bass boat, john boat **Tackle Supplied** Spin, baitcast, troll
Experience 3 years **Rates** day: $125 week: $500 1/2 day: $60
Guide's Notes: I specialize in muskie fishing only. Best times to fish are April
- May and September - December. **Cave Run Lake** offers a very good number
of 20 pound + fish. The lake record is 42 pounds. Trophy fishing is in the late fall.

JOHNSON, LARRY M.-L.J. LURES AND TACKLE (606) 784-5519
Address P.O. Box 421, Clearfield, KY 40313
Airport Lexington 65m **Accommodations** Morehead 5m **Operation** Guide
Fish Muskie, bass **Season** Year-round **Type of Fishing** Baitcast, troll
Water Cave Run Lake **Specialty** Fishing the prized muskie
Boats Bass boat **Tackle Supplied** Baitcast
Experience 5 years **Rates** day: $125 week: $400 1/2 day: $75
Guide's Notes: Cave Run Lake offers some of America's best muskie fishing.
Minor Clark fish hatchery located below the lake has stocked 8,000 muskies
per year for the last 14 years. Fisherman success is far above the national average
in Cave Run Lake with a few fish reaching near state record weight. Peak time
is spring, but October through December seems to produce the larger fish. Fall
fish are usually found in shallow coves, jerk baits and buzz baits are the top
producers.

GILBERTSVILLE, KENTUCKY

BEALS, ROBERT H. (502) 395-5533, 362-8500
Address P.O. Box 189, Gilbertsville, KY 42044
Airport Paducah 25m **Accommodations** Gilbertsville
Operation Guide **Type of Fishing** Spin, baitcast, troll
Fish Bass, crappie, sauger, striped bass **Season** Year-round
Water Kentucky, Barkley Lakes, Tennessee, Cumberland Rivers
Specialty Lake and river fishing **Boats** Bass boats **Tackle Supplied** All
Experience 13 years **Rates** day: $100 1/2 day: $50

LANE, MALCOLM-LAKELAND GUIDE SERVICE (502) 362-8124
Address Rt 2, Box 327, Gilbertsville, KY 42044
Airport Paducah 30m **Accommodations** Gilbertsville
Operation Outfitter **Type of Fishing** Spin, bait, troll
Fish Crappie, white bass, lm bass, sauger **Season** Year-round
Water Kentucky, Barkley Lakes, Smithland Pool, (on the Ohio River)
Specialty Large crappie and white bass in the jumps
Boats Bass boat **Tackle Supplied** Spin, baitcast, troll
Experience 20 years **Rates** $15/hour

GRAND RIVERS, KENTUCKY

LARKINS, BRUCE (502) 928-4554
Address Route 1, Box 181, Grand Rivers, KY 42045
Airport Paducah 15m **Accommodations** Grand Rivers
Operation Guide **Type of Fishing** Spin, baitcast, troll
Fish Bass, crappie, sauger, blue gill **Season** Year-round **Boats** Bass boats
Water Barkley, Kentucky Lakes, Smithland Pool (on the Ohio River)
Specialty Fishing for crappie, bass, & catfish **Tackle Supplied** All
Experience 4 years **Rates** $12/hour (minimum 4 hours)

HARDIN, KENTUCKY

CLARK, HAROLD (502) 354-6225
Address Rt 1, Hardin, KY 42048
Airport Paducah 45m **Accommodations** Hardin **Operation** Guide
Fish Crappie, sauger, lm bass, sm bass **Season** March-Nov
Water Kentucky Lake **Specialty** Lake trolling **Type of Fishing** Spin, baitcast, troll
Boats Bass boats **Tackle Supplied** Spin, baitcast, troll
Rates day: $80 week: $500 1/2 day: $50
Guide's Notes: Kentucky Lake is one of the best crappie and bass lakes in the United States. The peak times are April and October. Crappie are mainly caught on live bait and jigs. Bass are mainly caught on artificial worms, pig and jig, and a variety of crank, spinner and buzz baits. Western Kentucky has some of the best resorts and marinas in the United States and lots of good southern hospitality.

HOPKINSVILLE, KENTUCKY

CAYCE, DAN (502) 886-8592, 886-1231
Address 413 Henderson Dr., Hopkinsville, KY 42240
Airport Hopkinsville **Accommodations** Hopkinsville **Operation** Guide
Fish Crappie, black bass **Season** Mar-June **Type of Fishing** Spin, baitcast, troll
Water Lake Barkley, Kentucky Lake **Specialty** Crappie fishing
Boats Bass boat **Tackle Supplied** Spin, baitcast, troll
Experience 9 years **Rates** day: $80 1/2 day: $50
Guide's Notes: Barkley and Kentucky Lakes in Western Kentucky flow over 30 miles, side by side, and extend through the state of Tennessee. Crappie and bass fishing are on the upswing in February each year and usually gets better in March. Spawning of crappie takes place at 64-72 degrees, usually mid-April to mid-May. Crappie are caught on minnows and jigs in good numbers into June. Bass fishing the points, trees and gravel banks is good until spawning around the full moon near 70 degree water. Summer fishing is available on Barkley and Kentucky Lake for sauger, catfish, bluegill, some crappie, black and white bass. Fall fishing usually is good in October and November.

TVA and the Corps of Engineers maintain as stable water levels as their schedules allow. Water conditions and other fishing conditions should be checked before a trip is made.

IRVINE, KENTUCKY

COLLINS, MICHAEL D.-KENTUCKY RIVER GUIDE SERVICE (606) 723-5948
Address R.R. 2, Box 345, Irvine, KY 40336
Airport Lexington 50m **Accommodations** Irvine **Operation** Guide
Fish Black bass, muskie, crappie, trout **Season** Year-round **Type of Fishing** All
Water Kentucky, Red Rivers, Lake Linville, Cave Run Lake **Specialty** Baitcasting
Boats Bass boat, rowboats **Tackle Supplied** Spin, baitcast
Experience 8 years **Rates** day: $50 week: $300

KUTTAWA, KENTUCKY

POOL, JIM (502) 388-7554, 388-9619
Address Rt 2, Box 233, Kuttawa, KY 42055
Airport Paducah 25m **Accommodations** Suwanee 1m **Operation** Guide
Fish Crappie, bass, white bass, sauger **Season** Mar-Nov
Water Barkley, Kentucky Lakes **Specialty** Still fishing for crappie
Boats Bass boats **Tackle Supplied** Spin, baitcast **Type of Fishing** Spin, baitcast
Experience 18 years **Rates** day: $100 1/2 day: $50

MOREHEAD, KENTUCKY

WATTS, V. ALAN (606) 784-7088, 683-2033
Address Rt 4 #21, Hilltop Est., Morehead, KY 40351
Airport Lexington 60m **Accommodations** Morehead **Operation** Guide
Fish Muskie, bass, crappie **Season** Year-round **Specialty** Casting for muskie
Water Cave Run Lake, Paint Creek **Type of Fishing** Spin, baitcast, troll
Boats Bass boat **Tackle Supplied** Spin, baitcast, troll
Experience 5 years **Rates** day: $125 week: $500

MOUNT EDEN, KENTUCKY

HINES, RON-HINES' BAIT AND TACKLE (502) 839-7777
Address Rt #1, Box 106A, Mt. Eden, KY 40046
Airport Lexington 40m **Accommodations** Lawrenceburg 11m
Operation Guide, tackle shop **Type of Fishing** Spin, baitcast
Fish Bass, bluegill, crappie, catfish **Season** Mar-Nov **Tackle Supplied** All
Water Taylorsville, Rough River Lakes, Salt, Ohio Rivers
Specialty Bass fishing with artificial lures **Boats** Rowboats, bass boat
Experience 3 years **Rates** day: $75 week: $250 1/2 day: $50

PADUCAH, KENTUCKY

CHARVAT, E.-CHARVAT'S OUTBOARD MOTOR SHOP (502) 442-4172
Address 322 Elizabeth St., Paducah, KY 42001

Airport Paducah **Accommodations** Paducah **Operation** Guide, boat shop
Fish Crappie, catfish, sauger, rainbow **Season** Apr-Nov **Type of Fishing** All
Water Kentucky, Barkley Lakes, Kentucky, Barkley Dams, Tennessee River
Specialty Trolling, largemouth bass, and striped bass fishing
Boats Bass boats, house boats **Tackle Supplied** All
Experience 30 years **Rates** varies

LEIDECKER, BOBBY (502) 554-9431
Address Rt 1, Box 165, Paducah, KY 42086
Airport Paducah **Accommodations** Paducah
Operation Guide **Type of Fishing** Spin, baitcast
Fish Black bass, crappie, sauger, white bass **Season** Year-round
Water Kentucky, Barkley Lakes, Smithland Pool, Oxbow Lakes
Specialty Jig fishing for crappie **Boats** John boats **Tackle Supplied** Spin, baitcast
Experience 10 years **Rates** day: $100 1/2 day: $50
Guide's Notes: Kentucky Lake, Barkley Lake, Smithland Pool

1. Crappie Peak (April thru 1st week of May)-casting jigs over submerged brush and floating minnows.
2. Black Bass Peak (May thru 1st week of July)-casting spinner and buzzbaits over heavy cover.
3. Sauger Peak (January thru February)-bumping bottom with heavy jigs and live minnows.

TAYLORSVILLE, KENTUCKY

SNIDER, JAMES BUDDY (502) 477-2311
Address R 2, Box 265, Taylorsville, KY 40071
Airport Louisville 30m **Accommodations** Taylorsville
Operation Guide **Type of Fishing** Spin, baitcast, troll
Fish Black bass, bream, crappie, catfish **Season** Year-round
Water Taylorsville Lake, Salt River, Brashears, Guist Creeks
Specialty Lake trolling **Boats** Bass boats **Tackle Supplied** Spin, baitcast
Experience 10 years **Rates** day: $80 1/2 day: $60/2 people
Guide's Notes: Taylorsville Area Best times for bass are February through June and September through November. Bluegill are available year-round.

Louisiana

FLORIEN, LOUISIANA

DIVIS, JOHN-LANDING (318) 586-7888
Address HC-64, Box 178, Florien, LA 71429
Airport Shreveport 87m **Accommodations** Florien **Operation** Guide, marina
Fish Stripers, black bass, crappie **Season** Year-round **Boats** Bass boats
Water Toledo Bend Reservoir (south) **Tackle Supplied** Spin, baitcast, troll
Specialty Striper trolling, black bass casting **Type of Fishing** Baitcast, troll
Experience 5 years **Rates** day: $125 1/2 day: $65
Guide's Notes: Toledo Bend Reservoir The spawning period for black bass is
February and March. Night fishing is good from June through August. October
and November are the months for large black bass. Stripers and crappie are
seasonal.

MANY, LOUISIANA

FAZZIO, TOM-LAKEVIEW LODGE (318) 256-3857, 256-9261
Address Rt 1, Box 260, Many, LA 71449
Airport Shreveport 75m **Accommodations** On premises **Operation** Guide, lodge
Fish Lm bass, striped bass **Season** March-Nov. **Type of Fishing** Spin, baitcast
Water Toledo Bend Reservoir **Specialty** Worm and spinner bait fishing for bass
Boats Bass boat **Tackle Supplied** Spin, baitcast
Experience 8 years **Rates** day: $120 1/2 day: $65

ZWOLLE, LOUISIANA

WILLET, T.R. DICK-FLYING BRIDGE MARINA (318) 645-4290
Address Rt 2, Box 474E, Zwolle, LA 71486
Airport Shreveport 76m **Accommodations** Zwolle **Operation** Guide, lodge
Fish Lm bass, striped bass **Season** Year-round **Type of Fishing** Baitcast, troll
Water Toledo Bend Reservoir **Specialty** Artificial plug casting
Boats Bass boats **Tackle Supplied** Baitcast, troll
Experience 6 years **Rates** day: $120 1/2 day: $70

Tennessee

ROCKWOOD, TENNESSEE

SMITH, EVERETT S.-EAGLE LODGE RESORT (615) 354-0050
Address Route 4 Box 383, Rockwood, TN 37854
Airport Knoxville 45m **Accommodations** On premises **Operation** Guide, lodge
Fish Stripers, bass, crappie **Season** March-December **Type of Fishing** Spin
Water Watts Bar Lake, Tennessee River **Tackle Supplied** Spin, baitcast
Specialty Float fishing and live bait fishing in lake **Boats** Bass boats
Experience 6 years **Rates** day: $125 1/2 day: $70
Guide's Notes: Watts Bar Lake and the Tennessee River We have a year round
season for large and smallmouth bass, crappie, catfish and best of all stripers.
Peak times are April through October. Stripers are taken year round on live
bait. We fish the lake until mid-June and then fish the rivers where the water
is cooler. Then in October, as the water cools, we fish the lake until December.

Casting to largemouth in Tennessee.   *D. Murrian/Tenn. Wildlife Resources Agcy.*

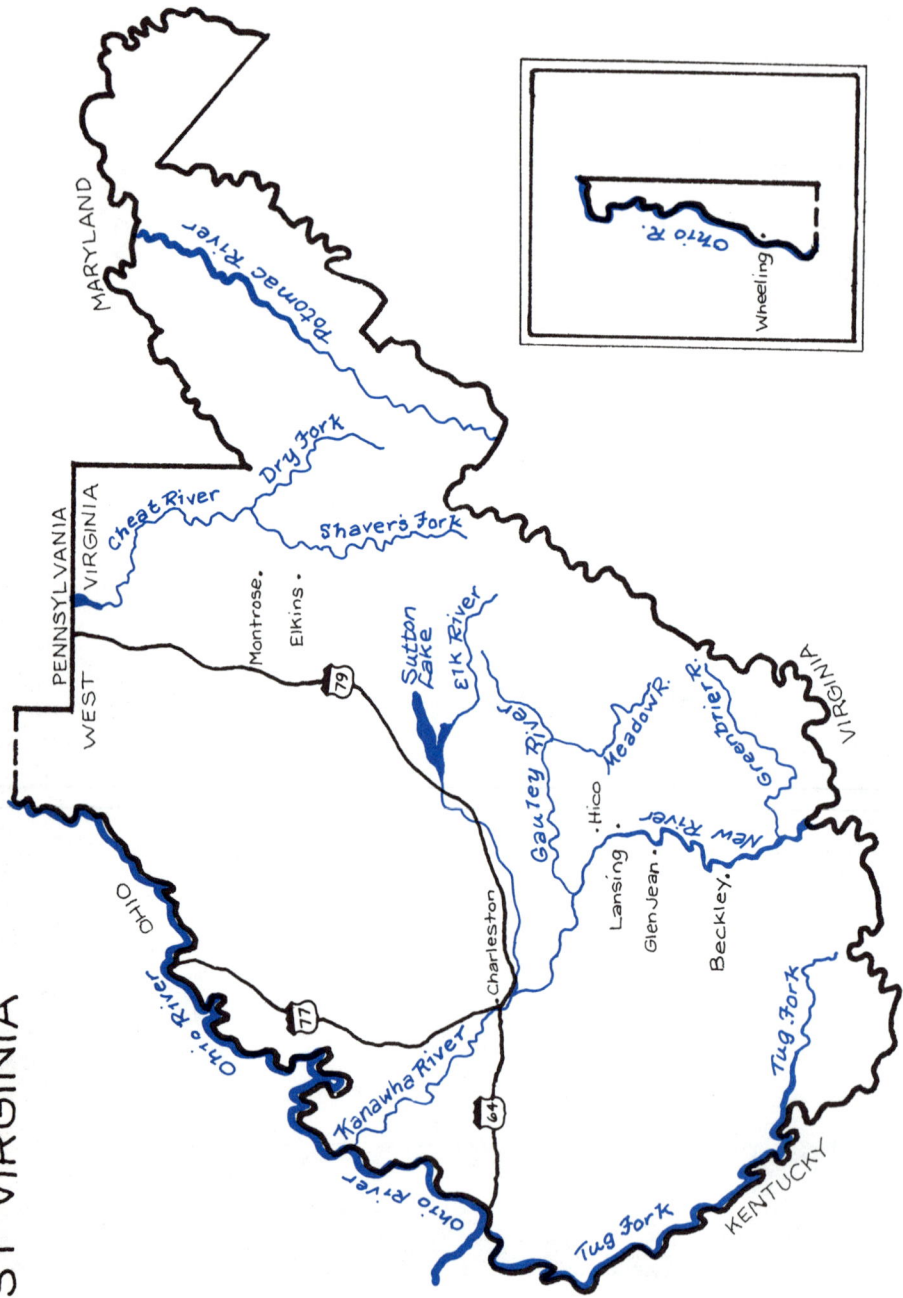

WEST VIRGINIA

MARYLAND

Potomac River

Dry Fork

Cheat River

Shavers Fork

PENNSYLVANIA

WEST VIRGINIA

VIRGINIA

Montrose

Elkins

79

Sutton Lake

Elk River

Gauley River

Meadow R.

Greenbrier R.

Hico

New River

Lansing

Glen Jean

Beckley

OHIO

Ohio River

77

Charleston

Kanawha River

64

Tug Fork

KENTUCKY

Tug Fork

Ohio River

Ohio R.

Wheeling

West Virginia

GLEN JEAN, WEST VIRGINIA

SIMMS, BILL-NEW RIVER DORIES (304)465-0747, 465-0855
Address Beury Mt. Road, Glen Jean, WV 25846
Airport Beckley 20m **Accommodations** Beckley 5m **Operation** Outfitter
Fish Sm bass, walleye, muskie **Season** Mar-Nov **Type of Fishing** All
Water New, Kanawha, Gauley Rivers, Plum Orchard L. **Tackle Supplied** All
Specialty Whitewater smallmouth bass fishing trips **Boats** McKenzies, rafts
Experience 10 years **Rates** day: $200
Guide's Notes: We fish primarily on the New River throughout the National
River boundaries. Our first choice is the Lower Gorge where access is strictly
limited by rugged terrain. Our dories and rafts make fishing possible at any
spot on any river section. Our number one choice for comfort and maneuverability, is the river dory which will hold 2 or 3 anglers. Fishing is good throughout
the summer except during periods of high water following heavy rains. Week-
days are best because there is less river use during the week. Tackle in the 6 -
10 pound range, spinning, will be most useful. For lures, rapalas, floating and
sinking 1/8 - 1/4 jigs, and #3 grubs of different colors and shapes. Waters of
the New River are host to many popular freshwater game fish. State record fish
taken from New River include the smallmouth (7.5 pounds), striped bass (21
pounds), and walleye (16.19 pounds). There are also good numbers of muskie,
spotted bass, white bass and good channel catfish in the New River.
*Author's Notes: Bill has gained national recognition for his float trips on the
New River. He was written up in SPORTS AFIELD in June, 1985, and in GONE
FISHING in January of 1986.*

HICO, WEST VIRGINIA

STANLEY, THOMAS-MOUNTAIN RIVER TOURS, INC.
(304) 658-5266, 658-5817
Address P.O. Box 88, Sunday Road, Hico, WV 25854
Airport Charleston 60m **Accommodations** Oak Hill 10m **Operation** Outfitter
Fish Sm bass, lm bass, walleye, catfish **Season** May- Oct **Type of Fishing** All
Water New, Gauley, Meadow, Greenbrier Rivers **Boats** Canoes, rafts
Specialty One day or extended overnite whitewater/float fishing trips
Experience 10 years **Rates** day: $80-160 week: $500-800 1/2 day: $40-80
Guide's Notes: New River The smallmouth bass fishing is best between mid-May
and the end of June. It picks back up in mid-September to the end of October.
New River provides the best smallmouth fishing in the state. We have never
caught less than 50 fish per day. In addition, New River provides one of the
best scenic whitewater trips in the east. Bring imitation crayfish, crankbaits,

and assorted jigs and spinners; the best natural baits are crayfish, nightcrawlers and hellgramites.

LANSING, WEST VIRGINIA

CRATOR, JEFF-CLASS VI RIVER RUNNERS, INC. (304) 574-0704
Address Ames Heights Rd, P.O. Box 76, Lansing, WV 25862
Airport Charleston 50m **Accommodations** Lansing
Operation Outfitter **Type of Fishing** Spin **Tackle Supplied** Spin
Fish Smallmouth bass **Season** June-Sept. **Water** New River, Greenbrier River
Specialty Bass fishing small rapids and pools **Boats** Rafts
Experience Varies **Rates** day: $150

MONTROSE, WEST VIRGINIA

BEAHM, BOB-PERFECTION SPORTS (304)636-6294
Address Rt. 1, Box 59, Montrose, WV 26283
Airport Elkins 4m **Accommodations** Elkins 4m **Operation** Guide, tackle shop
Fish Brown, rainbow, brook, golden trout **Season** Year-round
Water Shavers Fork, Dry Fork, Elk R., Gandy Creek **Type of Fishing** Fly, spin
Specialty Fly fishing streams **Boats** Canoes **Tackle Supplied** Fly, spin
Experience 6 years **Rates** day: $80 1/2 day: $50

TERRY, WEST VIRGINIA

ELAND, MATT-WHOLE EARTH RAFTING, INC. (304)255-6563
Address P.O. Box 4, Terry, WV 25934-004
Airport Charleston 60m **Accommodations** Beckley 7m
Operation Outfitter **Type of Fishing** Spin, baitcast
Fish Striped bass, sm bass, catfish **Season** Apr-Nov **Water** New River
Specialty Overnight custom catered fishing tours **Boats** Rafts
Experience 12 years **Rates** day: $63/person week: $500

10. The Northeast: Trout, bass, and salmon!

Connecticut, Maine, New Hampshire, New York, Pennsylvania, Vermont

The Northeast was once blessed with Atlantic salmon runs so heavy that fish literally filled the rivers. Salmon were so abundant in the early 1800s that most indentured servants coming from Europe had a clause inserted into their contracts, that they would only have to eat fish three or four times a week. Today's market price for Atlantic salmon, about twice the price of prime beef, shows how things have changed. The responses from fishing guides in this region are another indication that few of these magnificent gamefish still migrate into U.S. waters. Only one guide of forty-eight listed in this region fishes for this once-abundant king of the trout family.

Fortunately, not all northeastern gamefish have gone the way of the Atlantic salmon. Indigenous populations of bass, pike, and walleye are still healthy in the northeast, despite almost forty-three million people living there. Vast improvements have been made in pollution control and fish management. New runs of steelhead, Pacific salmon, and lake run brown trout, established on the tributaries of Lake Ontario in the past decade, rival the success of the more-publicized runs on lakes Michigan and Superior to the west. In addition, lake runs of rainbows, browns, and landlocked salmon are thriving in tributaries of Lake Champlain on the New York/Vermont border.

New York, with twenty-three listings, led the northeast in the number of guides who responded to the offer of a free listing in this book. Bass and salmon (landlocked and Pacific) were the two species most popular with the New York guides; brook and rainbow trout finished close behind. The guides concentrate on streams flowing into the southeastern corner of Lake Ontario, and on the tributaries of Lake Champlain, along the state's northeastern border. The most-mentioned Lake Ontario tributaries were the Black, Salmon, and Oswego rivers. The Boquet, the Saranac, and the Great Chezy were the favorite streams flowing into Lake Champlain.

Throughout the state, most guides offer bass fishing for both smallmouth and largemouth. These fisheries get very little attention, but offer excellent action for light tackle anglers from the spring months right through fall. The muskie, another exciting but little-publicized gamefish, is also available in New York. Lake Chautauqua on the western side of the state has produced a number of record fish; the New York Department of Environmental Conservation claims Chautauqua has more muskie for its surface area than any lake in the world.

Just one guide responded from Connecticut, New York's eastern neighbor. He described good fly fishing for brown trout on the Housatonic River, in the northwestern part of the state. Fish in the fifteen-to-seventeen-inch range are available in a special nine-mile section of the Housatonic where catch and release regulations are in effect.

New York's neighbor to the northeast, Vermont, is worth a trip just for its scenery. The countryside is dotted with nicely-kept little towns, with white churches punctuating the landscape. The trout fisherman can still find good fishing, particularly in the spring and fall when water temperatures are ideal for trout activity. The nationally famous Battenkill lies on the southern border of the state. Other streams mentioned by guides were the White, Middlebury, West, Nulhegan, New Haven, Wells, Black, and Upper Connecticut rivers. Favorite lakes included Champlain, Memphremagog, and Winona.

New Hampshire, east of Vermont, offers similar angling fare. Most guides favored Lake Winnipesaukee. Other trout waters include Umbagog and Squam lakes, and the Androscoggin and Connecticut rivers.

The state of Maine has long been famous for its brook trout and landlocked salmon fishing. Out of eight guides, seven listed these species among their favorites. Lake trout came in third of the most-sought species; smallmouth bass, mentioned by a total of three guides, finished fourth. The Penobscot and Aroostook rivers were the waters most mentioned.

South of Maine, in the state of Pennsylvania, more trout and smallmouth bass fishing can be found. A limited number of guides responded from this state, but the ones who did report good fishing on a number of small to medium-sized streams in the central part of the state. The Susquehanna River near Middletown was noted for its smallmouth bass, which can be caught on dry flies in the summer months. The Delaware River on the eastern border of the state was reported to have some good fishing for brown trout along with a good shad run.

Connecticut

LYME, CONNECTICUT

BATES, CHIP-ANGLER ADVENTURES (203) 434-9624
Address Rte 2, Lyme, CT 06371
Airport Bradley 40m **Accommodations** Lyme
Operation Booking agent for guides and charter captains
Season Year-round **Tackle Supplied** Fly **Type of Fishing** Fly
Fish Brown, bonito **Water** Housatonic River, Long Island Sound
Specialty Fly fishing/wading **Boats** 24′ formula, 29′ bayliner
Experience Varies **Rates** day: $175
Guide's Notes: The Housatonic River in Northwestern Connecticut has brown trout averaging 15-17 inches and is open year round. It has a 9 mile catch and release area and over 3 miles of fly fishing only. Excellent nymph and dry fly fishing-spring, summer and fall. Prolific insect hatches such as Hendricksons, Light Cahill, Caddis, Brown Drake, March-Browns, Blue Winged Olives, Housatonic White Fly, Tricorythodes and Black Ants are common.

Long Island Sound has Bonito up to 16 pounds, the fastest fish that swims pound for pound. Fly fishing guides fish within a few miles of the Connecticut shore specializing in fly, spin casting or trolling flies from a small boat. It is excellent light tackle sport.

Maine

ASHLAND, MAINE

LIBBY, MATT-LIBBY'S SPORTING CAMPS (207) 435-6233, 435-8274
Address Drawer V, Ashland, ME 04732
Airport Presque Isle 65m **Accommodations** Ashland
Operation Outfitter **Type of Fishing** Fly, spin, troll **Boats** Rowboats, motorboats
Fish Salmon (landlocked), brook and lake trout, bass **Season** May-Sept.
Water Millinocket Lake, Hudson Ponds, Aroostook and Allagash Rivers
Specialty Fly fishing small trophy ponds and streams **Tackle Supplied** All

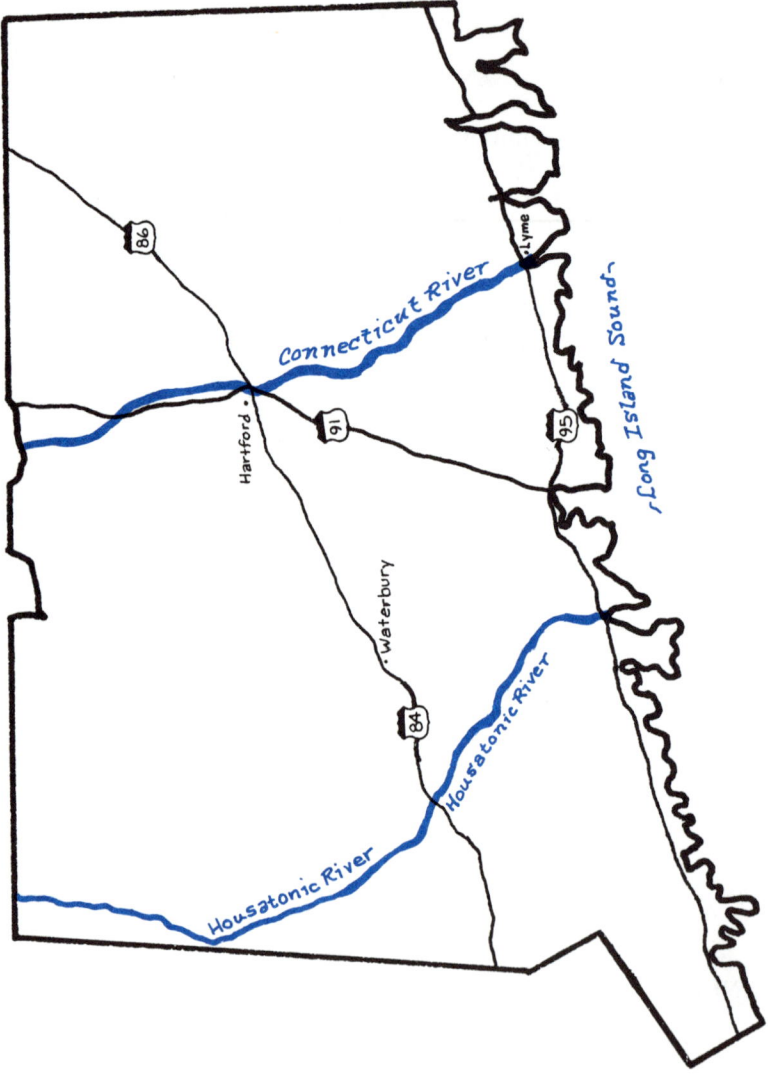

CONNECTICUT

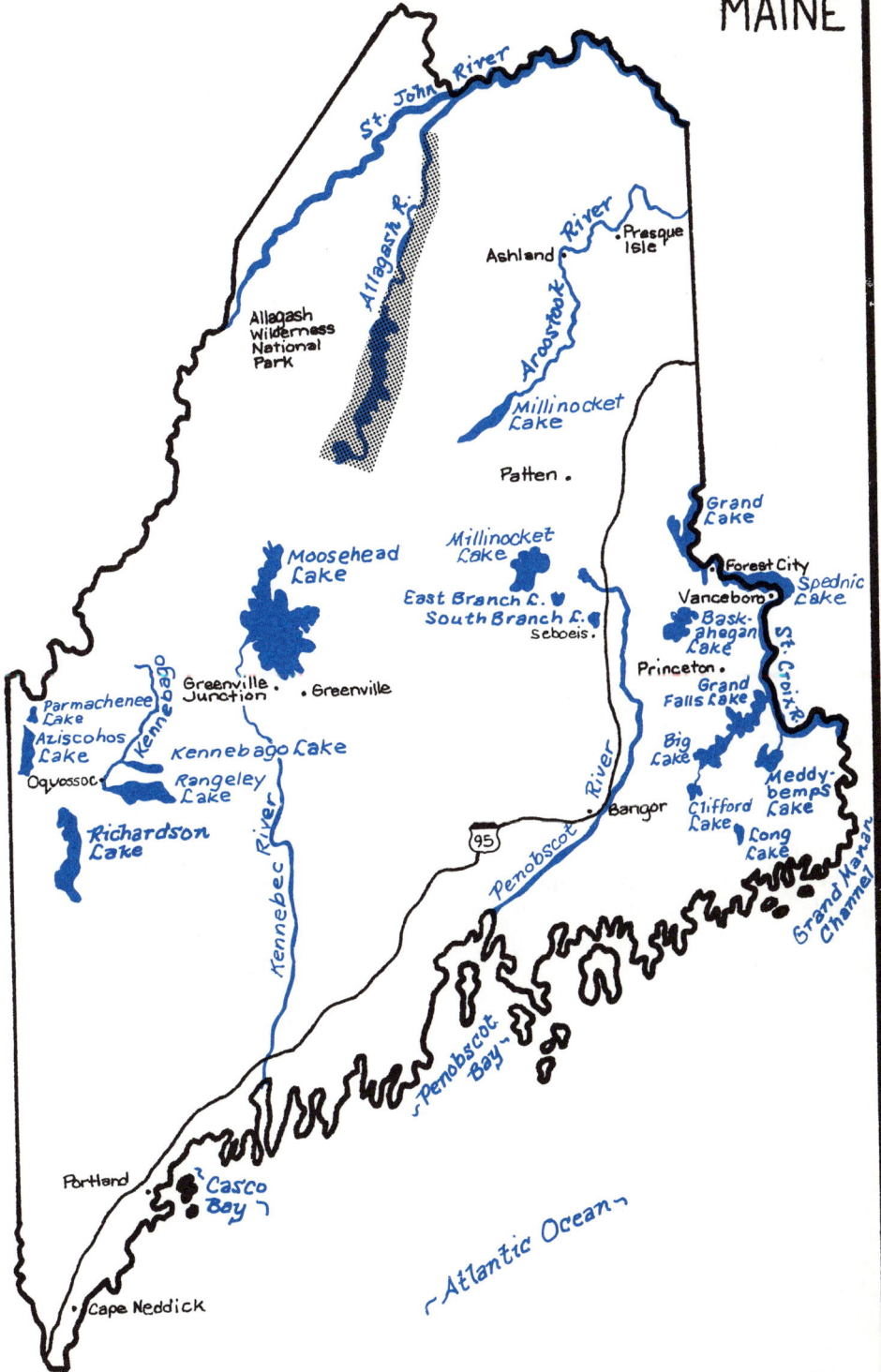

MAINE

St. John River

Allagash R.

Aroostook River

Ashland • Presque Isle

Allagash Wilderness National Park

Millinocket Lake

Patten •

Millinocket Lake

Moosehead Lake

East Branch L.
South Branch L.
Seboeis •

Grand Lake

Forest City

Spednic Lake

Vanceboro •

Bask-ahegan Lake

Princeton •

Grand Falls Lake

St. Croix R.

Kennebago

Parmachenee Lake

Aziscohos Lake

Greenville Junction

• Greenville

Kennebago Lake

Oquossoc •

Rangeley Lake

Big Lake

Clifford Lake

Meddy-bemps Lake

Long Lake

Richardson Lake

Penobscot River

Bangor •

95

Kennebec River

Grand Manan Channel

Penobscot Bay

Portland •

Casco Bay

Atlantic Ocean

• Cape Neddick

Experience 13 years **Rates** day: $175 week: $1200 1/2 day: $100
Guide's Notes: We specialize in fishing for native trout and landlocked salmon from camps in six locations encompassing 540 square miles of wilderness. Peak salmon runs are May and late September. Fly fishing for trout late May through early July. We fish 25 ponds, 7 lakes and 15 streams with experienced guides. Pack trips with horses are available to remote areas. Atlantic salmon becoming available in Aroostook River.

CAPE NEDDICK, MAINE

PETERS, CHARLES (207) 363-7709, 872-8338
Address RR 1, Box 141, Cape Neddick, ME 03902
Airport Portland 100m **Accommodations** Rangeley 30m
Operation Outfitter **Type of Fishing** Fly, troll **Boats** Rowboat, canoes
Fish Brook trout, landlocked and Atlantic salmon **Season** May-Nov.
Water Aziscohos Lake, Magalloway R., Penobscot R., Parmachenee L.
Specialty Fly fishing and lake trolling **Tackle Supplied** Fly, spin, troll
Experience 5 years **Rates** day: $100 week: $700 1/2 day: $60

FOREST CITY, MAINE

WHEATON, DALE C.-WHEATON'S FISHING LODGE
(207) 448-7723, 843-5732
Address East Grand Lake, Forest City, ME 04413
Airport Bangor 105m **Accommodations** On premises **Operation** Outfitter, lodge
Fish Sm bass, landlocked salmon, chain pickerel, perch **Season** May-Sept.
Water Spednic, E. Grand, Baskahegan Lakes, Canadian water bodies
Boats Canoes **Tackle Supplied** Fly, spin, troll **Type of Fishing** All
Experience 21 years **Rates** day: $70
Guide's Notes: We offer some of the nation's finest smallmouth bass and land-locked salmon fishing. We emphasize sport-fishing on light tackle and a catch and release philosophy.

Our guides are competent and experienced. Fishing techniques change markedly throughout the summer months, so potential guests should inquire with respect to certain periods. 1985 was the most productive landlocked salmon year in the last decade.

GREENVILLE, MAINE

LEGERE, DANNY L.-MAINE GUIDE FLY SHOP & GUIDE SERVICE
(207) 695-2266
Address Main St., P.O. Box 1202, Greenville, ME 04441
Airport Bangor 75m **Accommodations** Greenville
Operation Outfitter, tackle shop **Type of Fishing** Fly, spin, troll
Fish Landlocked salmon, brook trout **Season** May-Sept.
Water Moosehead L., Roach and West Branch of Penobscot Rivers

Boats Motorboats, canoes **Tackle Supplied** Fly, spin, troll
Experience 8 years **Rates** day: $170 week: $1190

GREENVILLE JUNCTION, MAINE

SNELL, WAYNE R.-WILSON'S ON MOOSEHEAD LAKE (207) 695-2549
Address Wilson's on Moosehead Lake, Greenville Jct, ME 04442
Airport Bangor 80m **Accommodations** On premises **Tackle Supplied** All
Operation Guide, camp **Type of Fishing** All **Boats** Canoes, outboards
Fish Salmon (landlocked), brook and lake trout **Season** Year-round
Water Moosehead Lake and East Outlet **Specialty** Lake trolling and fly fishing
Experience 1 year **Rates** day: $100 hour: $20
Guide's Notes: Fishing on **Moosehead Lake** and the **East Outlet** is world famous
for trophy landlocked salmon, brook trout over 4 pounds, and lake trout. The
fishing is excellent throughout the season from May 1 - Sept 30. The East Outlet
has been changed to fly fishing only, as of 1986, and it is an exceptional river
for landlocked salmon and brook trout.

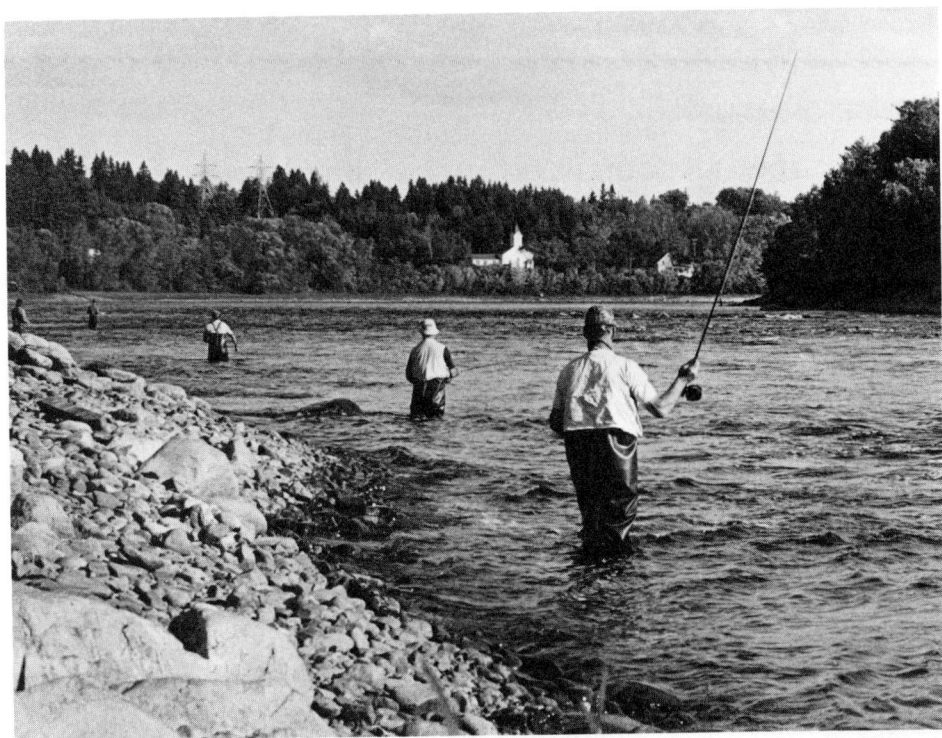

Atlantic salmon fishing in Maine.   *T. Carbone/Maine Dept. of Fisheries*

OQUOSSOC, MAINE

EASTLACK, CLAYTON 'CY'-MOUNTAIN VIEW COTTAGES (207) 864-3416
Address Rt 17, Box 284, Oquossoc, ME 04964
Airport Portland 150m **Accommodations** On premises **Operation** Guide, lodge
Fish Landlocked salmon, brook and lake trout **Season** May-Sept.
Water Rangeley and Richardson Lakes, Kennebago River
Specialty Lake trolling and fly fishing rivers **Type of Fishing** Fly, troll
Boats Canoes, outboards **Tackle Supplied** Fly, spin, troll
Experience 3 years **Rates** day: $100 1/2 day: $60

PATTEN, MAINE

YOULAND, DAVID R. (207) 764-6112, 225-3057
Address P.O. Box 499, Patten, ME 04765
Airport Presque Isle 70m **Accommodations** Ashland 47m **Type of Fishing** All
Fish Landlocked salmon, brook and lake trout **Season** May-Sept.
Water Aroostook River headwaters and watershed
Specialty Fly fishing and lake trolling **Operation** Outfitter
Boats Rowboats, canoes **Tackle Supplied** Spin, troll
Experience 14 years **Rates** day: $80

PRINCETON, MAINE

LUKACIK, EDWARD J.-LONG LAKE CAMPS (207) 796-2213
Address Long Lake Camps off West St., Princeton, ME 04668
Airport Bangor 100m **Accommodations** On premises **Operation** Outfitter, lodge
Fish Smallmouth bass **Type of Fishing** All **Specialty** Lake fishing **Boats** Canoes
Water Big, Meddybemps, Clifford Lakes, Grand Falls Flowage **Season** May-Aug.
Experience 15 years **Rates** day: $80
Guide's Notes: Big Lake, Long Lake, and surrounding waters
    The waters adjacent to the camp gives the fisherman over 400 miles of
shoreline with 65 plus islands; four lakes and three major rivers. Long Lake
Camps sits in the center. It is predominantly smallmouth bass water with a
very irregular bottom and shoreline. There is 70 feet of water at the deepest.
The entire body of water is made up of bass structure.
    The spring season is a fly casting and spin fisherman's paradise. On a good
day a fly fisherman can boat 50 bass plus -- using dry flies, hair bugs, and
poppers. Spin fishermen can have an equally enjoyable time using Jitterbugs,
Mepps, and small floating Rapalas. These tactics will change somewhat as the
summer goes on. However, fishing more than 15 feet of water is rarely needed
to fish smallmouth in these cool waters. The larger fish tend to be caught in
July and August when we sometimes use wet flies and streamers, deeper running
lures, frogs, minnows, and worms. When the mayflies hatch in July, the surface
action, again, is superb. At this time of the year the surface action is as good
as it is in early spring.

Fishing in the camp area and to the west is mostly big water with many islands, rocky points and shoals with many reefs and rock piles. Fishing east of the camp we find stumps, lily pads, and all types of bottom. The rivers near the camp have every type of fish and terrain that is in Maine. The St. Croix River valley offers the bass fisherman all types of water and structure.

SEBOEIS, MAINE

WEBSTER, BARRY-SOUTH BRANCH LAKE CAMPS (207) 732-3446, 738-2022
Address South Branch Lake Camps, Seboeis, ME 04484
Airport Bangor 45m **Accommodations** On premises **Operation** Guide, lodge
Fish Bass, trout, perch, pickerel **Season** March-Nov **Type of Fishing** All
Water South Branch, East Branch Lakes, Penobscot, Piscataquis Rivers
Specialty Fly Fishing **Boats** 14′ V-hull
Experience 5 years **Rates** week: $200/person guide service only

VANCEBORO, MAINE

MASON, KENNETH FRASER-LAKEVIEW CAMPS
(207) 788-3875, (506) 784-2918
Address Salmon Brook Road, Box 55, Vanceboro, ME 04491
Airport Bangor 100m **Accommodations** On premises **Operation** Outfitter
Fish Sm bass, salmon, brook, pickerel **Season** March-Nov. **Type of Fishing** All
Water Spednic, Paul Eery, East Grand Lakes, St. Croix River
Specialty Fly fishing **Boats** Canoes, bass boats **Tackle Supplied** All
Experience 19 years **Rates** day: $181

New Hampshire

ERROL, NEW HAMPSHIRE

BROAD, ALLEN E.-BROWN OWL CAMPS (603) 482-3274
Address Route 16, Errol, NH 03579
Airport Berlin 25m **Accommodations** On premises
Operation Guide, tackle shop, lodge **Type of Fishing** Fly, troll
Fish Salmon, brook, rainbow, brown trout **Season** May-Oct.
Water Umbagog L., Androscoggin R., remote ponds **Tackle Supplied** Fly, troll

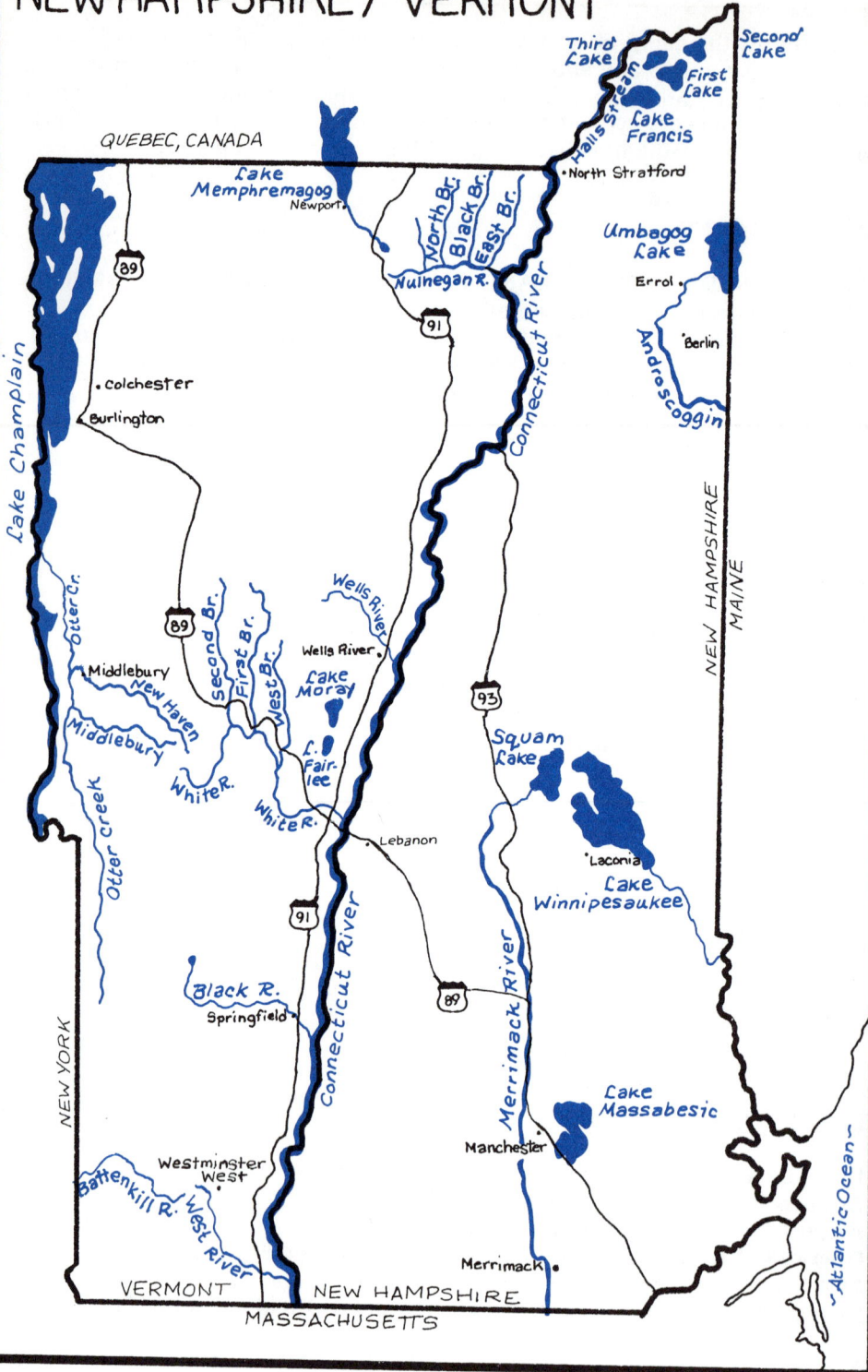

NEW HAMPSHIRE / VERMONT

QUEBEC, CANADA

Third Lake

Second Lake

First Lake

Halls Stream

Lake Francis

North Stratford

Lake Memphremagog

Newport

Umbagog Lake

North Br.

Black Br.

East Br.

Errol

Nulhegan R.

Berlin

89

Connecticut River

Androscoggin

91

Colchester

Burlington

Lake Champlain

NEW HAMPSHIRE

MAINE

Wells River

89

Second Br.

First Br.

West Br.

Wells River

Otter Cr.

Middlebury

New Haven

Lake Morey

93

White R.

Middlebury

L. Fairlee

Squam Lake

White R.

Lebanon

Laconia

Lake Winnipesaukee

Otter Creek

NEW YORK

91

Connecticut River

Merrimack River

89

Black R.

Springfield

Lake Massabesic

Westminster West

Manchester

Battenkill R.

West River

Connecticut River

Atlantic Ocean

Merrimack

VERMONT

NEW HAMPSHIRE

MASSACHUSETTS

Specialty Fly casting and fly trolling **Boats** Rowboats, canoes, outboards
Experience 7 years **Rates** day: $70 1/2 day: $45

LACONIA, NEW HAMPSHIRE

GRASSO, PETER-NORTH COUNTRY GUIDE SERVICE (603) 366-4115
Address RFD #3, Box 88, Roller Coaster Road, Laconia, NH 03246
Airport Laconia **Accommodations** Laconia
Operation Charter captain, outfitter **Type of Fishing** Spin, baitcast, troll
Fish Salmon (landlocked), lake trout **Season** April-Sept **Specialty** Lake trolling
Water Lake Winnipesaukee, Lake Francis, 1st and 2nd Connecticut Lakes
Boats 23' Deep-V, 19' center console **Tackle Supplied** Trolling
Experience 10 years **Rates** day: $150 1/2 day: $75
Guide's Notes: Lake Winnipesaukee
   From ice out (end of April) through May, landlocked salmon and trout reach their first peak. We then use downriggers and electronic fish finders to follow them through the hot summer months into the depths they require. Fishing peaks again from the 3rd week in August until the end of September as water cools and the spawning urge begins. We also offer trips to remote northern New Hampshire for trophy brown trout (end of May through September).

MANCHESTER, NEW HAMPSHIRE

BROWN, JAMES I.-THE BASS HARASSER (603) 627-9041
Address 4586 Brown Ave., Manchester, NH 03103
Airport Manchester **Accommodations** Manchester **Operation** Guide
Fish Lm bass, sm bass **Season** Apr-Oct **Type of Fishing** Spin, baitcast
Water Lake Winnipesaukee, Squam & Massabesic Lakes, Merrimack River
Specialty Baitcasting for largemouth and smallmouth bass
Boats Bass boat **Tackle Supplied** Spin, baitcast
Experience 4 years **Rates** day: $125 week: $575 1/2 day: $70
Guide's Notes: Lake Winnipesaukee and surrounding area
   The prime time for smallmouth bass is May - June. Three to four pound fish are not uncommon. Largemouth bass peak from late May through early July. Plastic worms, jigs, and topwater plugs are my favorite lures.

MERRIMACK, NEW HAMPSHIRE

FLANDERS, JIM (603) 424-4946
Address Meetinghouse Road, Merrimack, NH 03054
Airport Boston, MA 90m **Accommodations** Merrimack **Operation** Guide
Fish Lm & sm bass **Season** May-Oct **Type of Fishing** Spin, baitcast
Water Squam L., L. Winnipesaukee **Tackle Supplied** Spin, baitcast
Specialty Guide with fully rigged bass boat **Boats** Bass boats
Experience 1 year **Rates** day: $125 1/2 day: $75

Guide's Notes: Squam Lake and Lake Winnipesaukee
Bass fishing in the northeast ranks with the best in the country. Early May to mid June smallmouth fishing cannot be compared to anything you've ever seen. Light fishing pressure provides the visiting angler with a surprise beyond compare. Catch and release is encouraged.

NORTH STRATFORD, NEW HAMPSHIRE

SCHOMBURG, BILL (603) 922-5543
Address RFD Box 225, North Stratford, NH 03590
Airport Berlin 50m **Accommodations** Colebrook 12m
Operation Guide **Type of Fishing** All **Fish** Trout **Season** Year-round
Water Connecticut River, Lake Umbagog, Connecticut Lakes #1, 2, 3
Specialty River fishing for trout **Boats** Canoe **Tackle Supplied** Fly, spin
Experience 1 year **Rates** varies

New York

ASHVILLE, NEW YORK

BERRY, WARREN-FRENCHMAN GUIDE SERVICE (716) 763-8296
Address Box 231 North Maple Street, Ashville, NY 14710
Airport Erie, PA 40m **Accommodations** Lakewood 3m
Operation Guide **Type of Fishing** All **Tackle Supplied** All
Fish Muskie, walleye, bass, trout, salmon **Season** Year-round
Water Chautauqua Lake, Kinzua Reservoir, Lake Erie, Lake Ontario
Specialty Trolling for muskies on Lake Chautauqua
Boats Rowboats, canoes, bass boats, 28' sport fisherman
Experience 9 years **Rates** day: $250 1/2 day: $125
Guide's Notes: Chautauqua Lake is considered the best muskie water in the world according to our Department of Environmental Conservation. It has the most muskies per surface acre. The muskie hatchery at Prendergast Point is the largest in the country. Annually, our hourly catch rate averages just three hours per muskie. Most years we boat more than two hundred muskies.

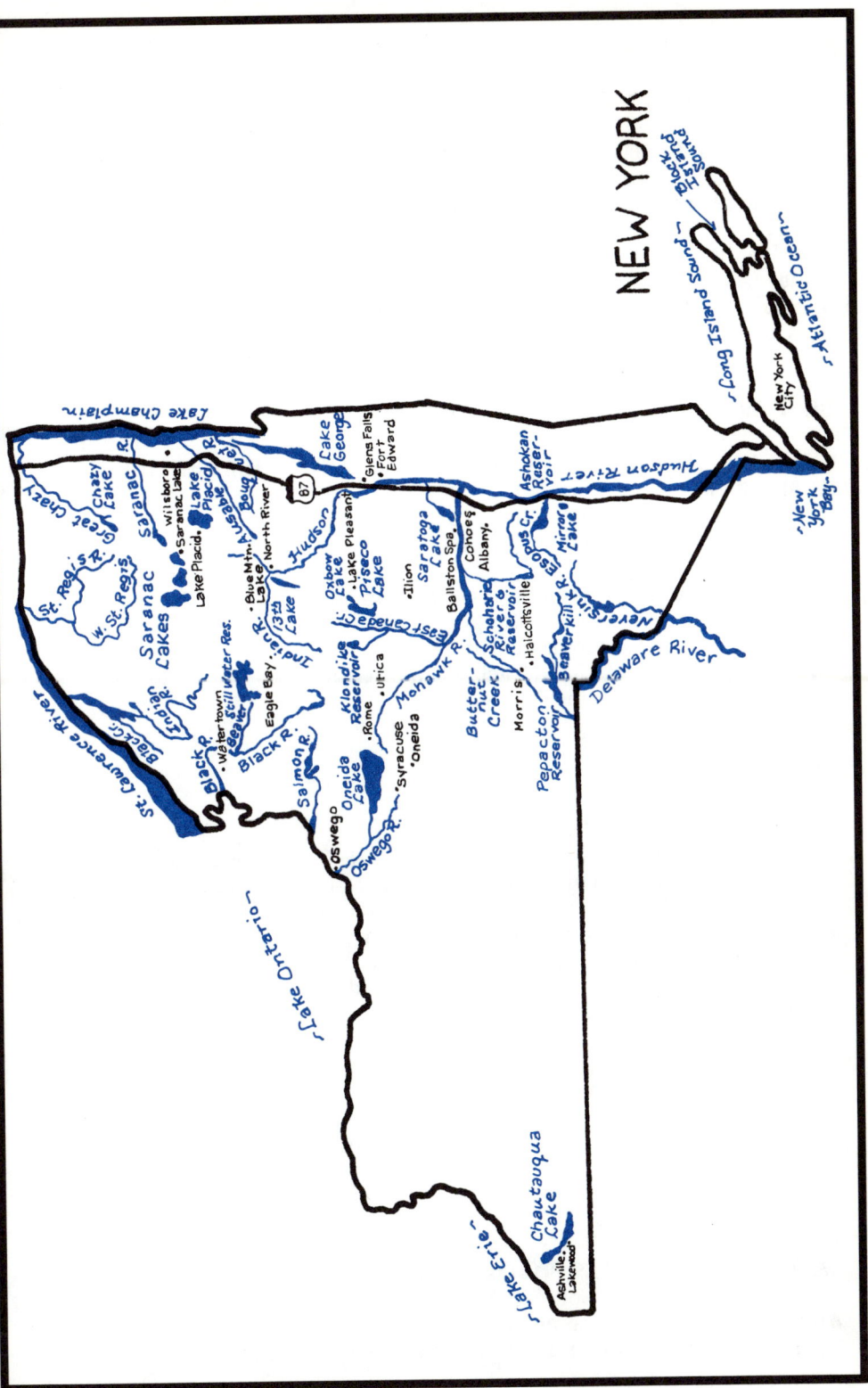

NEW YORK

BALLSTON SPA, NEW YORK

JETTE, ROGER "JIM"-MOUNTAINMAN EXPEDITIONS (518) 885-1441
Address 25 Cameron Park, Ballston Spa, NY 12020
Airport Albany 35m **Accommodations** Burnt Hills 3m
Operation Outfitter **Type of Fishing** All **Tackle Supplied** Spin, baitcast, troll
Fish Landlocked salmon, lake trout, rainbow, walleye **Season** Year-round
Water Lake George, Hudson River, Saratoga Lake, brook trout ponds
Specialty Remote brook trout fishing in ponds **Boats** Canoes, rafts
Experience 8 years **Rates** day: $80 week: $500 1/2 day: $50

BLUE MOUNTAIN LAKE, NEW YORK

CUMMINS, JOSEPH P.-BLUE MOUNTAIN LAKE GUIDE SERVICE (518) 352-7684
Address Box 111, Blue Mountain Lake, NY 12812
Airport Utica 88m **Accommodations** Blue Mountain Lake
Operation Guide **Type of Fishing** Spin, baitcast, troll
Fish Brook, lake trout, rainbow, bass **Season** May-Sept
Water Terrell, Bear, Cascade, Stephen's Ponds
Specialty Fishing for brook trout in wilderness ponds
Boats Rowboats, rafts, canoe **Tackle Supplied** Spin
Experience 10 years **Rates** day: $40

COHOES, NEW YORK

PEDONIE, JOHN JOSEPH (518) 785-1843
Address RD 1, Dunsbach Ferry Road, Box 491, Cohoes, NY 12047
Airport Albany 5m **Accommodations** Albany 5m **Operation** Guide
Fish Lake trout, salmon, walleye, pike **Season** Year-round
Water Lakes George, Champlain, Ontario, Saratoga Lake
Specialty Lake trolling **Type of Fishing** Spin, baitcast, troll
Boats Rowboats, charter boat **Tackle Supplied** Spin, baitcast, troll
Experience 6 years **Rates** day: $60/person week: $300/person
Guide's Notes: Peak Times
    Lake George - Landlocked salmon and lake trout; May, June, Aug, Sept
    Lake Ontario - All salmonoids; May through October
    Lake Champlain - Walleye, pike, bass; May thru Oct and into ice fishing
    Saratoga - Bass, pike, walleye; May thru Feb

COTTEKILL, NEW YORK

LAPP, ROGER CHARLES (914) 657-7008
Address P.O. Box 155, Cottekill NY 12419
Airport Albany 60m **Accommodations** Kingston 15m
Operation Guide, outfitter **Type of Fishing** All **Tackle Supplied** All

Fish Steelhead, brown, rainbow, salmon **Season** September-May
Water Salmon River, Lake Ontario, Esopus Creek, Ashokan Reservoir
Specialty Steelheading with fly and egg sacks
Experience 15 years **Rates** day: $130 week: $650

EAGLE BAY, NEW YORK

CARMAN, WILLIAM E. (315) 357-6076
Address Twitchell Lake, Big Moose, Eagle Bay, NY 13331
Airport Utica 70m **Accommodations** Big Moose 3m
Operation Guide **Type of Fishing** Baitcast, troll
Fish Trout **Season** May-Sept **Water** Twitchell Lake, Still Water Reservoir
Specialty Bait fishing and some trolling **Boats** Outboard motor boats
Experience 40 years **Rates** day: $25

FORT EDWARD, NEW YORK

BARBER, DAVE B. (518) 747-4811
Address Patterson Road, Fort Edward, NY 12828
Airport Glen Falls 15m **Accommodations** Fort Edward
Operation Charter captain, outfitter **Type of Fishing** Troll, spin
Fish Lake trout, salmon, brook, bass **Season** March-Nov.
Water Lake George, ponds and streams **Specialty** Lake trolling
Boats Rowboat, canoe **Tackle Supplied** Troll, spin, fly,
Experience 5 years **Rates** day: $200 week: $400 1/2 day: $150
Guide's Notes: The best salmon fishing is in the spring when the lake ice just goes out. Surface trolling with lures or streamers and sometimes drifting with minnows produces well. Summer means the use of down riggers and trolling deep for lake trout.

GLENS FALLS, NEW YORK

WINSLOW, LARRY E.-LYNX GUIDE SERVICE (518) 793-8353
Address 31 Gage Avenue, Glens Falls, NY 12801
Airport Albany 43m **Accommodations** Glens Falls
Operation Outfitter **Type of Fishing** All **Specialty** Trolling in remote ponds
Fish Lake trout, landlocked salmon, brook, rainbow **Season** Year-round
Water Lake George, Thirteenth Lake, Siamese Pond, Salmon River
Boats Rowboats, McKenzies **Tackle Supplied** Fly, spin, troll
Experience 6 years **Rates** day: $200 week: $1200

HALCOTTSVILLE, NEW YORK

HINKLEY, TIMOTHY F.-WILDERNESS GUIDE SERVICE (607) 326-7606
Address Bragg Hollow Road, Halcottsville, NY 12438

Airport Albany 60m **Accommodations** Halcottsville
Operation Outfitter **Type of Fishing** Spin **Fish** Brook trout **Season** April only
Water Headwaters of the Neversink, Esopus, Beaverkill, East Branch of the
Delaware Rivers **Specialty** Bait fishing for brook trout **Tackle Supplied** Spin
Experience 4 years **Rates** day: $100

ILION, NEW YORK

WAINWRIGHT, JOHN, JOHN BULLIS, JEFF WHITEMORE-WHITEDOG TRAIL CO. (315) 895-7850
Address 196 Second Street, Ilion, NY 13357
Airport Oneida 25m **Accommodations** Ilion **Operation** Outfitter
Fish Brook, bass, walleye, northern pike **Season** Year-round
Water Adirondack Preserve, West Canada Creek, Piseco Lake
Specialty Wilderness fishing for brook trout **Type of Fishing** All
Boats Guide boats (Adirondack type), canoes
Experience 4 years **Rates** day: $115 week: $485 1/2 day: $60
Guide's Notes: The majority of our guided fishing trips involve brook trout in
remote Adirondack Mountain streams and ponds which last from one to five
days. These adventures are generally under wilderness conditions, requiring
the backpacking of all equipment, and sleeping in tents or Adirondack lean-tos.
Fly and ultra light spinning equipment are best suited for this type of fishing.
We can supply all the necessary equipment.
  The best pond fishing is from late April to late May and throughout the
month of September. Stream fishing is good throughout the season.

LAKE PLACID, NEW YORK

FAILING, WAYNE-MIDDLE EARTH EXPEDITIONS (518) 523-9572
Address Cascade Rd, Lake Placid, NY 12946
Airport Saranac Lake 20m **Accommodations** On premises
Fish Brook, rainbow, splake, lake trout **Season** April-September
Water St. Regis Wilderness, Lake Placid, Mirror Lake **Operation** Outfitter, lodge
Specialty Trolling back ponds with a canoe **Type of Fishing** Spin, troll
Boats Rowboats, canoes, rafts (motors available) **Tackle Supplied** All
Experience 9 years **Rates** day: $100 1/2 day: $75

GALLAGHER, PATRICK (518) 523-9727
Address 58 3/4 McKinley Street, Box 306, Lake Placid, NY 12946
Airport Saranac Lake 20m **Accommodations** Lake Placid
Operation Guide **Type of Fishing** All **Boats** Rafts, canoes
Fish Brook, brown, bass, muskie **Season** March-November
Water Surrounding area ponds, rivers, streams and lakes
Specialty Hike/paddle trips for backwoods pond fishing (fly and spin)
Experience 5 years **Rates** day: $100 1/2 day: $65

HACKETT, JOSEPH P.-TAHAWUS GUIDE SERVICE (518) 523-1508

Address Box 424, Lake Placid, NY 12946
Airport Saranac Lake 20m **Accommodations** Lake Placid **Operation** Outfitter
Fish Trout, salmon, bass, pike **Season** Year-round **Type of Fishing** Fly, spin, troll
Water St. Regis Wilderness, Bouquet, Ausable Rivers, Lake Placid
Specialty Fly fishing and remote pond fishing **Tackle Supplied** Fly, spin, troll
Boats Rowboats, canoes, rafts, Adirondack guide boat
Experience 7 years **Rates** day: $125
Guide's Notes: We specialize in fly fishing, canoe fishing and remote pond angling. Also offered are horseback and floatplane trips, as well as remote pond angling from inflatable rafts. We service waters that contain rainbow, brook, brown, and lake trout; splake, kokanee and landlocked Atlantic salmon; bass, northern pike and walleyes. Some of our more productive waters include Lake Placid, Mirror Lake, the Saranacs, the St. Regis Canoe Area, the Ausable, Saranac and Boquet Rivers and numerous backwoods ponds and mountain streams.

A very successful restocking program has resulted in a Spring and Fall run of landlocked Atlantic salmon from Lake Champlain. Averaging 4-6 lbs, some run as large as 12-14 lbs. Since the first run in 1976 we have closely followed the salmon program and have enjoyed many successful days on the river. Prime dates are late April through early June, and again late September through mid-November; on the spawn run. Our salmon trips center on the **Boquet River**, with limited coverage of the **Ausable** and **Saranac Rivers**. With the introduction of a fish ladder at Willsboro Falls in 1982, an additional 40 miles of the Boquet River now offer salmon fishing opportunities.

Major Fly Hatches - Adirondack Region

Name	Observation Period
Quill Gordon	May 10 - June 2
Hendrickson	May 18 - June 5
Caddis	May 20 - June 7 *Top Hatch
Grey Fox	May 30 - June 19
March Brown	June 2 - June 18
Green Drake	June 7 - June 20
Yellow May	June 8 - July 2
Light Cahill	June 10 - July 8
Chocolate Drake	Aug 20 - Sept 18
Slate Grey Drake	Aug 26 - Oct 6

Author's Notes: Joe's references are excellent. Our contacts indicate he is one of the best freshwater guides east of the Rockies.

LAKE PLEASANT, NEW YORK

WHARTON, WILLIAM-WHARTON'S ADIRONDACK OUTFITTER (518) 548-3195

Address Oxbow Road, Lake Pleasant, NY 12108
Airport Oneida 60m **Accommodations** On premises **Operation** Outfitter

Fish Brook trout, pickerel, bass, panfish **Season** Year-round
Water Oxbow Lake, Jessup River, Spruce Lake, Indian River
Specialty Stream fishing in wilderness lakes and streams
Boats Rowboats, canoes, rafts **Type of Fishing** Spin, troll
Experience 12 years **Rates** varies
Guide's Notes: Peak season for brook trout is mid-May to mid-June.

MORRIS, NEW YORK

BIRDSALL, ROBERT P. (607) 783-2258
Address Box 48B, Birdsall Road, Morris, NY 13808
Airport Oneonta 25m **Accommodations** Oneonta 25m **Operation** Outfitter
Fish Trout, bass, pickerel, salmon **Season** March-August
Water Stillwater Res., Cooperstown Lake, Butternut Creek, Ausable River
Specialty Fly and spin fishing **Boats** Canoes **Type of Fishing** All
Experience 3 years **Rates** day: $50 week: $250 1/2 day: $40
Guide's Notes: April 15th - July 30th is best for trout. Natural baits are good
in early spring. Flies, phoebes, etc., are good in May. June and July are best for
bass. When the water level drops in the rivers, the action gets fast. Spinners,
plugs, and poppers work best.

NEW YORK CITY, NEW YORK

SAVARESE, JOHN (212) 733-4348
Address 2690 Morris Avenue, New York City, NY 10468
Airport New York City **Accommodations** New York City
Operation Guide **Type of Fishing** Spin, baitcast **Boats** Rowboats
Fish Large and smallmouth bass **Season** Year-round
Water Hudson River, Perpacton, Aschokan Reservoirs
Specialty Light tackle casting for bass **Tackle Supplied** Spin, baitcast
Experience 15 years **Rates** day: $100 week: $500 1/2 day: $50

NORTH RIVER, NEW YORK

FLANAGAN, GARY J.-EASTERN SLOPES SPECIALTY SPORTS
(518) 251-3655
Address Box 52, North River, NY 12856
Airport Albany 90m **Accommodations** On premises
Operation Guide, lodge **Type of Fishing** Fly, spin **Tackle Supplied** Spin
Fish Brook trout, landlocked salmon **Season** March-November
Water Peaked Mt., Siamese, Lower Sargeant Ponds
Specialty Remote pond fishing **Boats** Rowboats, canoes, rafts
Experience 4 years **Rates** day: $75-$125/2 people

OSWEGO, NEW YORK

DEMBECK, JOHN F.-TWO DOG OUTFITTERS (315) 343-7307, 564-6366
Address 333 West First Street, Oswego, NY 13126

Airport Syracuse 40m **Accommodations** Oswego **Type of Fishing** Fly, spin
Fish Steelhead, salmon, rainbow, brown **Season** Year-round
Water Salmon, Oswego, Delaware Rivers, Sterling Creek
Specialty Fly fishing float/wade trips **Operation** Outfitter, tackle shop
Boats McKenzies, canoes **Tackle Supplied** Fly, spin
Experience 4 years **Rates** day: $125-200

PHOENICIA, NEW YORK

GRIMM, EMIL-ESOPUS FLY FISHER (914) 688-5305
Address P.O. Box 206 Main St., Phoenicia, NY 12464
Airport Albany 45m **Accommodations** Phoenicia **Operation** Guide, tackle shop
Fish All trout, book, rainbow, brown **Season** Apr-Nov **Type of Fishing** Fly
Water All Catskill streams **Specialty** Fly fishing for trout **Tackle Supplied** Fly
Experience 10 years **Rates** day: $75-100

ROME, NEW YORK

SHEARER, JOHN S. (315) 339-3932
Address RD 5 Box 75, Rome, NY 13440
Airport Oneida 15m **Accommodations** Rome
Operation Outfitter **Type of Fishing** All **Tackle Supplied** Fly, spin
Fish Trout, bass, pickerel, bullheads, perch **Season** Year-round
Water Beaver River, Pepperbox, 5 Ponds Wilderness, Adirondacks
Specialty Wilderness backpack and canoe fishing trips **Boats** Canoes, rowboats
Experience 5 years **Rates** day: $150 week: $750

SYRACUSE, NEW YORK

DUNNING, BRUCE-LAKE ONTARIO CHARTER BROKERAGE (315) 478-7293
Address 716 James Street, Syracuse, NY 13203
Airport Syracuse **Accommodations** Syracuse
Operation Outfitter **Type of Fishing** All **Tackle Supplied** All
Fish Lake, brown, rainbow trout, coho, chinook salmon **Season** Year-round
Water Lake Ontario and its tributaries **Boats** Charter, McKenzies
Specialty Over 100 charter vessels, specialties vary
Experience 6 years **Rates** day: $278 1/2 day: $198

WATERTOWN, NEW YORK

BICKNELL, H. BICK-BICKNELL ENTERPRISES (315) 782-6684, 938-5434
Address 623 Holcomb Street, Watertown, NY 13601
Airport Watertown **Accommodations** Watertown
Operation Guide, Charter captain **Type of Fishing** Spin, troll
Fish Salmon, brown, lake trout **Season** Apr-Nov **Boats** Charter boat
Water Lake Ontario, Black, Salmon Rivers **Tackle Supplied** Spin, troll

Specialty Lake and river trolling/casting/jigging for salmon
Experience 2 years **Rates** day: $150/ 2 people $100/1 person

WILLSBORO, NEW YORK

CASAMENTO, PETER-ADIRONDACK-CHAMPLAIN GUIDE SERVICES (518) 963-7351

Address RR 297 Long Pond Lodge, Willsboro, NY 12996
Airport Burlington,VT 20m **Accommodations** On premises
Operation Guide, outfitter, lodge, tackle shop **Type of Fishing** All
Fish Lm, sm bass, pike, salmon, lake trout **Season** Year-round
Water Lake Champlain, Saranac, St. Regis River lake system, Ausable
Specialty Fly fishing, down rigger, ice fishing **Tackle Supplied** All
Boats Rowboats, bass boats, canoes, charter boats
Experience 10 years **Rates** day: $75
Guide's Notes: Lake Champlain, Saranac, Ausable, St. Regis, Bouquet Rivers

Salmon, trout and steelhead--Ice out time is usually the end of March. When the lake opens we troll short lines with spoons, streamers, and spinners. We also cast spoons and spinners from shore in certain areas. The landlocks and steelhead start making their runs up the big rivers at this time of year. We take them on a variety of lures, flies, and live bait.

The river and lakeshore fishing is great until late June. Then these fish go deep and we start the downrigger season, from July thru September. If you're a dry fly fisherman, many salmon come into the rivers throughout the summer, after rains and stay in the large pools. Many of these stay there until the spawning season in the fall. The fall run for salmon and steelhead goes from September thru November, then, once again, we shoreline fish for lakers, and salmon until ice over. Lake trout and landlocks are averaging over 5 pounds and many are taken over 10 pounds. The **Boquet River** promises to have, in the near future the largest landlocked salmon in North America with fish up to 20 lbs. Besides natural reproduction of these fish, the Department of Environmental Conservation of New York and Vermont will be stocking Lake Champlain and it's tributaries with 690 thousand trout and salmon annually.

Brown, Brook, and Rainbow Trout-- In mid-April we start fishing in the streams and rivers using worms, nymphs, and small spoons. At the beginning of May the remote ponds and lakes are ice free, and we take these trout plus landlocked salmon and lake trout. This type of fishing goes right into October. Fish can be taken on dry flies, worms, and spinners during the hottest months. We fish the famous rivers such as the Ausable, Saranac, Great Chazy, Chattaquay, and Boquet plus dozens of remote ponds and streams. No arm to arm fishing here. Try our summer float trips and hike-in fishing for trout. There is great fishing and a breath-taking view.

Walleye and Sauger-- These fish can be caught all year. The walleye and sauger spawning run starts in some rivers right after ice out (March), and later in other rivers, into June. The largest fish are caught at this time of year averaging 5 pounds, with some over 10 pounds. July, August and September, walleye are taken off certain reefs and islands in Lake Champlain, a lot at night and many are taken on downriggers. Ice fishing for walleye is big on Lake Champlain.

Northern and Muskie--Lake Champlain and the Adirondack ponds and lakes have tremendous northern pike fishing. Although they average about 5 pounds, there are a tremendous amount of them, which means, "plenty of action." There are quite a few large northerns over 10 pounds taken but are wary, after all, they didn't get big being stupid!! We offer an all day float trip to some remote ponds for northerns during the summer months and a hike-in ice fishing trip in the winter (January). Muskies go to 30 pounds and besides natural reproduction, the state stocks 50 to 80 thousand muskies annually. July, August, and September are the best times.

Largemouth and Smallmouth Bass--Many bass fishermen who come to fish with us are amazed at the amount of bass we have in the north country. It has been known as a great smallmouth fishery, but we take as many, if not more, largemouths than smallmouths. There have been a number of days in June and July when our clients have taken and released many times their limit. Spring and early summer we take the most bass and September and October the largest. Many largemouth and smallmouth bass are taken over 4 pounds, some up to 7 pounds. There are many days that a stringer of 4 pound plus bass are taken.

Pennsylvania

BERWICK, PENNSYLVANIA

BECK, BARRY AND CATHY-BECKIE'S FLY FISHING SPECIALISTS (717) 752-2011
Address 1336 Orange Street, Berwick, PA 18603
Airport Wilkes-Barre 20m **Accommodations** Bloomsburg 2m
Fish Brook, brown trout **Season** March-Nov **Operation** Guide
Water Fishing Creek-1 mile private water **Tackle Supplied** Fly
Specialty Fly fishing and fly fishing schools **Type of Fishing** Fly
Experience 4 years **Rates** day: $100
Guide's Notes: Peak dry fly fishing is in the month of June. A second peak period occurs in October when the brown trout are spawning.

CROSS FORK, PENNSYLVANIA

STONE, CHARLES A.-CROSS FORK TACKLE SHOP (717) 923-1960
Address Main Street, Cross Fork, PA 17729
Airport Williamsport 70m **Accommodations** Cross Fork

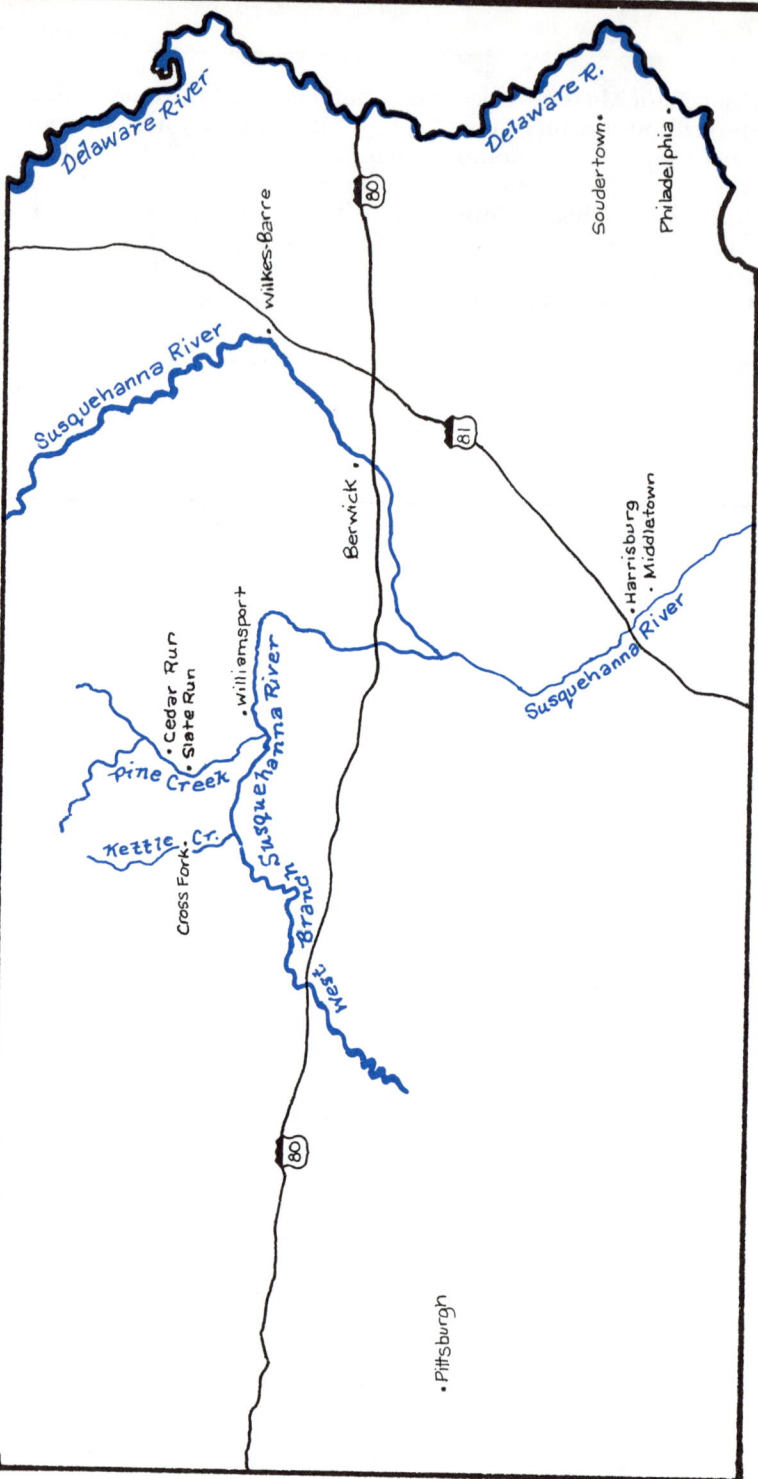

Fish Trout, bass, perch, catfish **Season** Year-round **Operation** Guide, tackle shop
Water Kettle, Cross Fork Creeks, Slate, Cedar Runs **Type of Fishing** Fly, spin
Specialty Fly fishing **Boats** Rowboat, bass boats **Tackle Supplied** All
Experience 5 years **Rates** day: $100 week: $650
Guide's Notes: We have seven "fly fishing only" trout streams and two "trophy",
lures only, smallmouth and largemouth bass streams located within twenty
miles of our shop.

MIDDLETOWN, PENNSYLVANIA

CLOUSER, BOB-CLOUSER'S FLY SHOP (717) 944-6541
Address 101 Ulrich St., Middletown, PA 17057
Airport Harrisburg 1m **Accommodations** Middletown
Operation Guide **Type of Fishing** Fly **Season** July-Oct. **Tackle Supplied** Fly
Fish Smallmouth bass **Water** Susquehanna River and its tributaries
Specialty Fly fishing for smallmouth bass **Boats** 16' john boats
Experience 20 years **Rates** day: $175
Guide's Notes: From the 1st of July to the end of September, we have dry fly
fishing for smallmouth bass every evening. We use White Miller's, Caddis
patterns and Brown Drakes. Subsurface we use nymph patterns, crayfish, and
hellgrammite patterns.
Author's Notes: Bob designed the fly pattern known as the Clouser Crayfish.

SLATE RUN, PENNSYLVANIA

FINKBINER, TOM & DEBBIE-SLATE RUN TACKLE SHOP (717) 753-8551
Address Rt 414, Slate Run, PA 17769
Airport Williamsport 50m **Accommodations** Slate Run
Operation Guide, tackle shop **Type of Fishing** Fly **Season** Year-round
Fish Brown, brook, rainbow **Water** Pine Creek, Slate Run, Cedar Run
Specialty Fly fishing for trout **Boats** Mckenzies
Experience 7 years **Rates** day: $100
Guide's Notes: Slate Run and **Cedar Run** are small mountain free stone streams
that have excellent populations of wild trout. Slate Run is a fly fishing only
stream, and Cedar Run is a trophy regulation stream. Both will produce well
for the skilled fly fisherman all season. Peak dry fly fishing is mid May to June 7th.

SOUDERTON, PENNSYLVANIA

VAN DYK, HERB-ANGLERS PRO SHOP (215) 721-4909
Address 224 Bethlehem Pike, Souderton, PA 18964
Airport Philadelphia 25m **Accommodations** Souderton
Operation Guide, tackle shop **Water** Delaware River, Martha's Vineyard
Season Apr-June, Sept-Nov **Fish** Brown, striped bass, albacore, bonito, bluefish

Specialty Fly fishing for brown trout **Tackle Supplied** Fly **Type of Fishing** Fly
Experience 4 years **Rates** day: $150
Guide's Notes: We offer guided fishing on the **Delaware River** through our
shop for brown trout and shad, and trips to **Martha's Vineyard** for striped bass,
albacore, bonito, and bluefish. Peak time for the Delaware is late April to
mid-June. For Martha's Vineyard, the peak time is September 15 to November 1.

Vermont

COLCHESTER, VERMONT
BUSHNELL, RAY-OFFSHORE CHARTERS (802) 864-1773
Address P.O. Box 26 Lake Shore Dr., Colchester, VT 05446
Airport Burlington 10m **Accommodations** Colchester
Operation Charter Captain **Type of Fishing** Troll, spin
Fish Lake trout, salmon, browns, sm bass **Season** April-Sept.
Water Lake Champlain **Specialty** Lake trolling
Boats Bass boat **Tackle Supplied** Spin, troll
Experience 5 years **Rates** day: $240 1/2 day: $175 (up to 4 people)
Guide's Notes: Best fishing is April - June.

MIDDLEBURY, VERMONT

RYDER, "RED" WILLIS (802) 388-3872
Address 93A Main St., Middlebury, VT 05753
Airport Burlington 28m **Accommodations** Middlebury
Operation Guide **Type of Fishing** All **Tackle Supplied** Fly, spin
Fish Trout, bass, northern pike **Season** May-Oct **Boats** Canoes
Water White, Battenkill, Middlebury, New Haven Rivers, Otter Creek, Lake
Winona, Bristol Pond **Specialty** Fly fishing and spinning for bass and pike
Experience 3 years **Rates** varies
Guide's Notes: Trout season runs from the 2nd Saturday in April to the last
Sunday in October. Best fly fishing is from May 10th to mid-June and from
Labor Day to season's end. We have good Hendrickson hatches around mid-May
(around 1:30 pm). Trico hatches run through the day in September and October
with the trout being very selective then.

Author's Notes: I fished with Red in late July of '84. Trout fishing was slow so we decided to try for largemouth bass on Bristol Pond. Fishing was very good, we took lots of one to one and a half pound bass on the surface. I even managed to catch my first northern pike on a fly. Red's guiding skills were excellent. He works very hard at putting you in the hot spots.

NEWPORT, VERMONT

WAGENHEIM, CHUCK-GREAT OUTDOORS TRADING CO.
(802) 334-8532, 334-2831
Address Lake Road, Newport, VT 05855
Airport Burlington 62m **Accommodations** Newport
Operation Guide, charter captain, tackle shop **Type of Fishing** Spin, troll
Fish Salmon, rainbow, bass, walleye **Water** Lake Memphremagog
Tackle Supplied Spin, troll **Season** March-Nov **Specialty** Lake trolling
Experience 7 years **Rates** day: $90/person 1/2 day: $50/person
Guide's Notes: Lake Memphremagog Spring fishing for rainbow and salmon is May to June. The peak is the last week in May and the first week in June. Fall fishing is from September to mid October. Good streamers and lures are Grey Ghost, Memphremagog Smelt, Rapalas and Sutton Spoons. We have good smallmouth bass fishing in mid summer.

Guide Red Ryder on Vermont's Bristol Pond.   *Richard Swan*

WELLS RIVER, VERMONT

DI FRANCESCO, ROCCO (802) 429-2431, 757-2830
Address RFD 1 Box 80, Wells River, VT 05081
Airport Lebanon, NH 43m **Accommodations** Wells River
Operation Guide **Type of Fishing** All **Tackle Supplied** Spin, baitcast
Fish Bass, trout, pike **Season** May-Oct **Boats** Bass boats, canoes
Water Connecticut & Wells River, Lakes Morey and Fairlee, Hall's Pond
Specialty Fly fishing for trout and bass fishing
Experience 3 years **Rates** day: $130 1/2 day: $100
Guide's Notes: Wells River Area Fish Calendar

Fish	Available	Lures
Black Bass	June, Oct	Spinner bait, rubber worm, buzz bait
Sm Bass	June - Oct	Black jig, tiny torpedo, spinner bait
Pike		Spinner bait, buzz bait
Trout	June - Sept	Any light mayfly pattern

WESTMINSTER WEST, VERMONT

DEEN, DAVID L.-STRICTLY TROUT (802) 869-3116
Address RFD 3 Box 930, Westminster West, VT 05346
Airport Springfield 20m **Accommodations** On premises
Operation Outfitter **Fish** Rainbow, brook, brown, sm bass
Water White, West, Nulhegan, Black Rivers **Season** May-Oct
Specialty Fly fishing wade and camping trips **Type of Fishing** All
Boats McKenzie, canoes, rafts, cabin cruiser
Experience 3 years **Rates** day: $100 1/2 day: $50
Guide's Notes: Strictly Trout is a booking service for out of state fishermen. There are nine guides associated with Strictly Trout, most are wade fly fishermen but some do specialize in lake fishing on Lake Champlain and providing float trips on the Upper Connecticut River. The guides cover the entire state, and about any type of fishing anyone might want while in Vermont.

Accommodations are through the country inns and bed and breakfast locations around the state, unless someone would like to camp in which case I serve as the outfitter, and can accommodate up to 4 people comfortably in either wilderness or state park camping sites. The stay in a country inn is an enjoyable part of the fishing experience.

Vermont Light Tackle Fishing Fishing around Vermont is varied depending on where you are staying. There are over a dozen major watersheds in the state. Each offers brook trout fishing at their headwaters, some are rainbow fisheries further down stream, and some are brown trout fisheries. Those watersheds which empty into the Connecticut River, Otter Creek, or Lake Champlain offer black bass fishing close to the mouths of the larger water.

The insect life is healthy, and progresses from the quills to March Brown to Hendrickson to terrestrials. Most of the major hatches are concluded by the end of June. From then on terrestrials, and midges during the day, and caddis in the evening take over the action.

Spin fishermen can have action on the larger streams and rivers throughout the season. Bait fishermen are limited to early season and immediately at the the start and after high water. Lake fishing progresses from the surface to down riggers as the waters warm. All the guides in Strictly Trout will advise clients about proper gear to meet conditions.

The guides associated with Strictly Trout are: Peter Basta, Willis "Red" Ryder, Michael Baz, Conrad Klefos, Monty Montplaisir, Captain Bill Lowell, Wayne Woodard, Dan Phillabaum, Gloria Jordan, and myself.

There are now over 30 inns or bed & breakfast locations in my book. All have been reviewed and are comfortable according to their price. There are also 4 lodges in my book as well as 6 house rental locations, rustic cabins to condos.

Without seeming immodest, Strictly Trout can get a fisherman to his kind of fishing with knowledgable local advice about conditions anywhere in Vermont and northern New Hampshire.

Author's Notes: I booked fishing guide Red Ryder through David and was very pleased. When I go back to Vermont, I will definitely call David and have him help me plan my trip.

Guide John Pizza with 28-lb. coastal chinook.

Jack Ellis

11. Western Canada:
World record steelhead !

Alberta, British Columbia, Manitoba, Northwest Territories, Saskatchewan, Yukon Territory

Western Canada is simply immense. If these provinces and territories formed a separate country, it would be the sixth largest in the world. The Northwest Territories alone account for half of this huge area. Twice the size of Alaska, they cover a mind-boggling 1,300,000 square miles, half of them north of the Arctic Circle. The climate is harsh, with short summers followed by long, cold winters. The most recent census counted fewer than 46,000 inhabitants. With a population density less than four people per 100 square miles, fishing pressure in most of the Territories is nonexistent.

Great Bear and Great Slave lakes are the Northwest Territories' best-known sport fisheries. These huge lakes, seventh and ninth largest in the world, are of particular interest to the light tackle fisherman. Huge lake trout swim near the surface of these waters during the brief summer, accessible to the angler with spinning and fly tackle. Arctic grayling, northern pike, and Arctic char also provide excellent light tackle sport.

Centers for fishing this part of the Territories are Yellowknife and Hay River, both situated on Great Slave Lake. These towns serve as jumping-off points for a number of lodges and camps in the back country. Yellowknife is the largest town in the Territories, with about 5,000 people.

In the Northwest Territories, exciting possibilities await the angler who dreams of exploring waters that may never have been fished before. Guides here speak of places most of us know little about, or have never even heard of. For example, the vast Thelon Game Sanctuary lies approximately 450 miles northeast of Yellowknife. Three major river systems— the Dubawnt, the Thelon, and the Back—flow through this remote area of the Canadian Shield. Any one of these rivers could offer a lifetime of wilderness fishing.

Another invitation to fishing adventure is Baffin Island far to the northeast. Baffin, sixth largest island in the world, is about twice the size of Great Britain, but has a population of fewer than five thousand people. If you have the time and money, you can hire an outfitter to place you on one of many remote Arctic char streams, and spend a week or more totally isolated from modern civilization.

The Northwest Territories loom large in any sportman's imagination. They are one of the last places on earth where we can experience the wilderness adventure of a lifetime. But remember, trips of this type require extensive planning, research, and experience.

Yukon Territory, 200,000 square miles of largely uninhabited wilderness, occupies the northwestern reaches of Canada between British Columbia and the Beaufort Sea. Only about 25,000 people live here, mostly in the south along the Alaskan highway and in the town of Whitehorse. Most of the Yukon is drained by the Yukon River, which originates in the lakes of northwestern British Columbia. Pacific salmon run up from the mouth of the Yukon all the way to its headwaters, a distance of more than 1700 miles.

Guides in this area also fish for Arctic char, lake trout, grayling, northern pike, and Dolly Varden. In the Destruction Bay area, they favor Kluane, Aishihik, Sekulmun, and Stevens lakes. Toobally Lakes near the town of Watson Lake, and Clair, Ken, and Lyn lakes in the Whitehorse area, were also mentioned.

British Columbia contributed more guide listings to this directory than any other province. Its spectacular fishing is best described by dividing the province into four areas: southwestern, southern interior, northern interior, and north coast. Each of these has its own identity.

On Vancouver Island, just north of Washington's Olympic Peninsula, the fishing is for silver and king salmon, steelhead, and sea run cutthroat trout. The island is laced with excellent streams, including the Stamp, Gold, Campbell, and Nimkish rivers. Runs occur all year, and fish can be taken by a variety of methods, including flies. This fishing is convenient to the angler who is planning a business trip to the city of Vancouver. It is only a short hop by scheduled seaplane to Victoria at the south end of the island, or to Campbell River in the central section. Both towns offer accommodations, car rentals, and guides who can put you on the best holes.

The Coquhala and the Vedder rivers, about two hour's drive east of Vancouver, are two more excellent steelhead streams. Both have improved considerably in recent years, thanks to good fish management and special regulations, and provide good opportunities for a Vancouver visitor to sample Canadian steelheading.

British Columbia's southern interior is famous for its Kamloops rainbows, which are found in many lakes, including Quesnel, Horsefly, Crooked, Bluff, and Sheridan, all north of Kamloops. Further north, there are more good lakes and streams in the Williams Lake, Prince George, and Hudson Hope areas. Many of these lakes host prolific insect hatches, which mean outstanding sport for the fly fisherman.

The steelhead fishing on British Columbia's coastal rivers is legendary! The famous Skeena River system, which flows into the Pacific west of Terrace, may offer the best dry fly steelhead fishing in the world. Tributaries include the storied Babine, Bulkley, and Kispiox rivers. Further south, the fabled Dean flows through Tweedsmuir Provincial Park on its course to a Pacific outlet north of Bella Coola. These are all world class waters which regularly produce bright steelhead in the twenty-five-pound class. Guides for this region are based in Terrace, Smithers, Telkwa, and Bella Coola. Check their notes for more information on these world-renowned streams.

Alberta's Bow River is gaining a reputation as one of the world's finest trout streams. It heads in the Canadian Rockies near Banff and flows east through the city of Calgary, where the best fishing is found. Rainbows and browns averaging sixteen inches are caught on daily float trips with flies and lures, but guides say that fish in the twenty to twenty-three inch range are common. Some of the largest fish are caught within the city limits of Calgary, which has a population of over 600,000 people. Take along your fly rod on your next visit!

West of Calgary, there are many fine trout streams and lakes. Guides favor Brazeau Lake and the Brazeau River, but also list the Maligne River, and Maligne and Medicine lakes near Jasper.

The prairie provinces of Saskatchewan and Manitoba both boast outstanding lake trout, walleye, and northern pike fishing. Their vast northern reaches also offer some very fine grayling fishing. Middle and Lower Foster, Shatwin, and Big Sandy lakes were mentioned by guides in northern Saskatchewan; McGavock Lake and the Laurie River system were named as favorites in Manitoba.

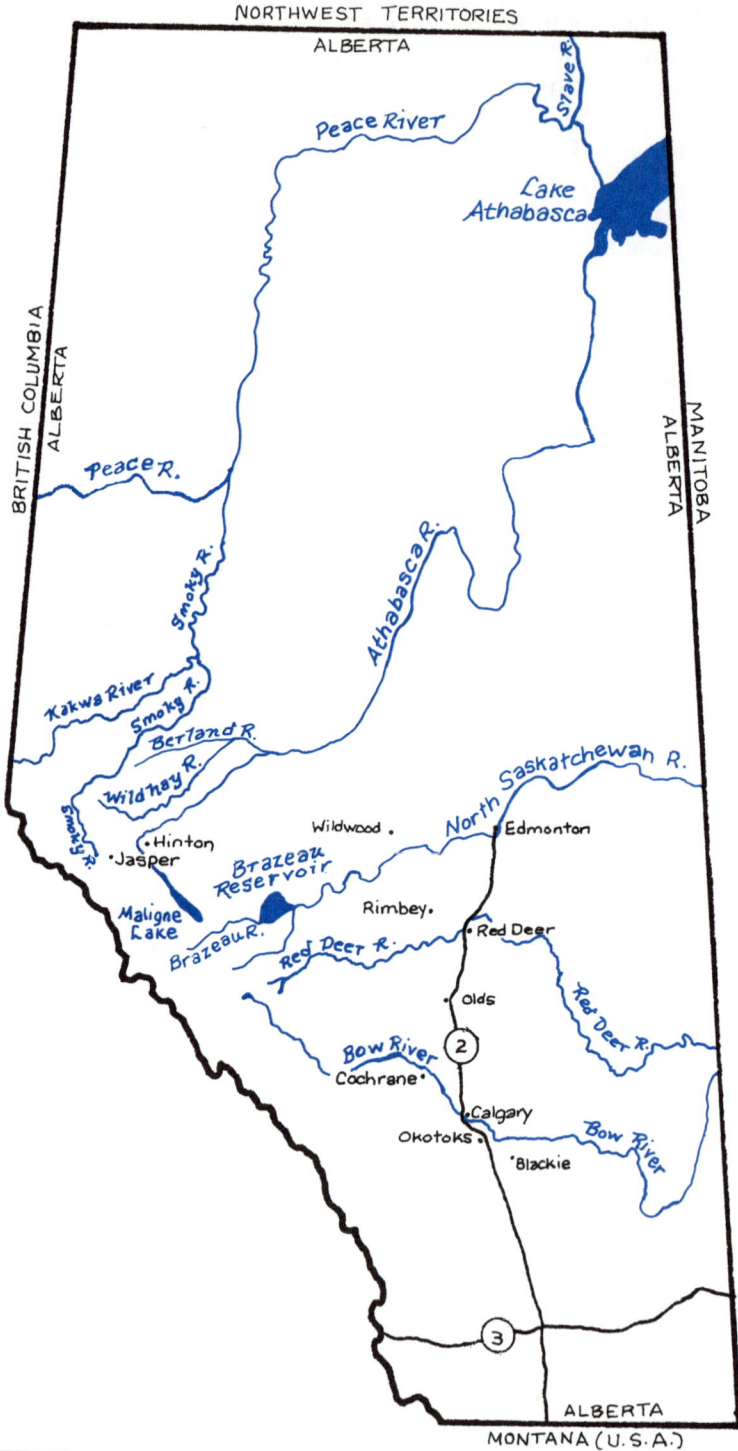

ALBERTA

NORTHWEST TERRITORIES
ALBERTA

Peace River

Stave R.

Lake Athabasca

BRITISH COLUMBIA
ALBERTA

MANITOBA
ALBERTA

Peace R.

Smoky R.

Athabasca R.

Kakwa River

Smoky R.

Berland R.

Wild'hay R.

North Saskatchewan R.

Wildwood

Edmonton

Smoky R.

Hinton
Jasper

Brazeau Reservoir

Rimbey

Red Deer

Maligne Lake

Brazeau R.

Red Deer R.

Red Deer R.

Olds

Bow River

2

Cochrane

Calgary

Okotoks

Blackie

Bow River

3

ALBERTA
MONTANA (U.S.A.)

Alberta

BLACKIE, ALBERTA

OSTERCAMP, CAM-PEKISKO OUTFITTERS (403) 684-3397
Address Box 171, Blackie, Alberta T0L 0J0
Airport Calgary 40m **Accommodations** High River 12m
Operation Outfitter **Type of Fishing** Fly, spin
Fish Rainbow, cutthroat, brown trout **Season** June-September
Water Bow river, McPhail, Carnarvon, Loomis Lakes **Boats** Rafts
Specialty Fly fishing in mountain lakes and streams
Experience 10 years **Rates** day: $100/person U.S. funds

CALGARY, ALBERTA

ANDREASEN, JOHN & BETHE-GREAT WATERS ALBERTA (403) 239-2520
Address 7903 Ranchview Drive NW, Calgary, Alberta T3G 1S7
Airport Calgary **Accommodations** Calgary
Operation Outfitter **Type of Fishing** Fly **Specialty** Fly fishing float trips
Fish Rainbow, brown trout **Season** June-October **Water** Bow River
Boats McKenzies, drift boats **Tackle Supplied** Fly
Experience 5 years **Rates** day: $190 U.S. funds
Guide's Notes: The Bow River fishing is for hard-fighting native brown and rainbow trout, averaging 15 - 19 inches with a large percentage over 20 inches. Our season runs from June 1st to mid-October and we have excellent fishing during the entire season.

The most important hatches are baetis, inermis, tricorythodes, caddis (primary hatch), and grasshoppers. The best patterns are Blue-winged Olives, Pale Morning Dun, Light Cahill, Elk-hair Caddis, Latort Hoppers, Wooly Buggers, white legged Girdle Bugs, White Maribou Muddlers, Gray Muskrat Nymph, Hare's Ear Nymph. We recommend dry fly sizes: 14 - 18, wet fly sizes: weighted sizes 4 - 6, nymph sizes: 14 - 18.

The Bow River is located in a beautiful area which offers activities and entertainment for the entire family.

GUINN, MICHAEL R.-THE WATER BOATMAN (403) 271-0799
Address 612 Queensland Dr. SE, Calgary, Alberta T2J 4G7
Airport Calgary 18m **Accommodations** Calgary
Operation Outfitter **Type of Fishing** Fly
Fish Rainbow, brown trout **Season** June-October
Water Bow River **Specialty** Fly fishing float trips
Boats Rowboats, McKenzies **Tackle Supplied** Fly

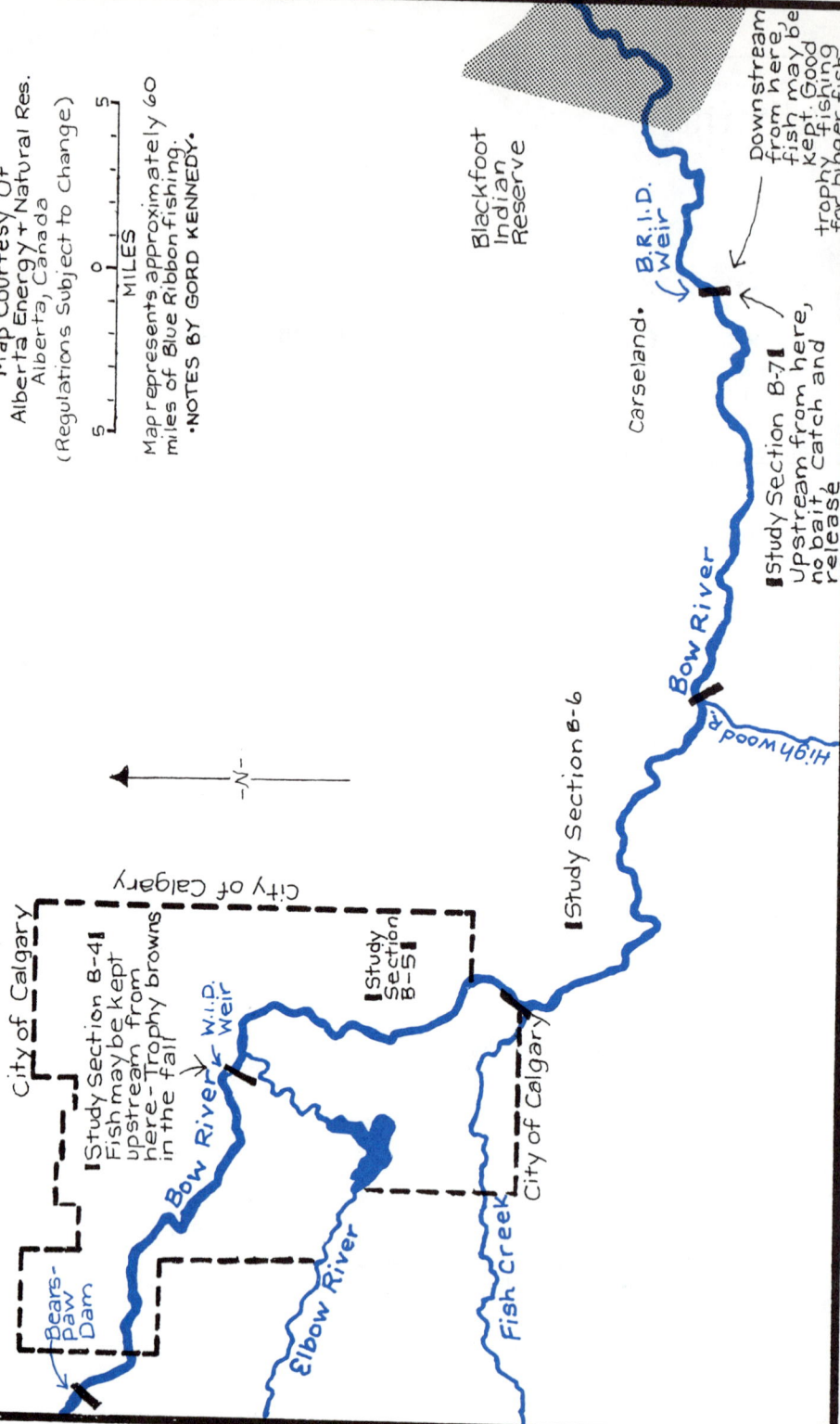

Experience 13 years **Rates** day: $200 U.S. funds
Guide's Notes: The Bow River, a world class trout stream originates from glaciers along the Continental Divide of the Canadian Rockies. A mountain river that is transformed into the fertile home of thousands of rainbow and brown trout, this stream has fast runs, deep pools and long stretches of water where weeds sway in the gentle current and rising trout unknowingly reveal their positions to the watchful angler.

The Lower Bow, a fifty mile stretch below the City of Calgary, is populated with rainbow and brown trout that average 14 to 16 inches. Fish over 20 inches are common and feed freely on the abundant hatches that come off the river and are receptive to a well presented dry fly. Large fish are easily taken on large nymphs and streamers fished near the bottom of the fast runs and deep pools. The fish of the Bow are strong, fast and high jumping fish that often gain their freedom before they can be brought to hand or net.

The Bow River offers good fishing all year but is closed each spring from April 1st to May 31st. Fishing in June is excellent except for a one to two week period when the spring runoff occurs. Fishing can be slow at this time and during years of extreme flooding, the river may be unfishable for a few days. July, August and September provide fine dry fly fishing, and September and October provide excellent fishing for trophy size brown trout using large streamer flies.

We recommend that you bring two rods, one a 5 to 8 weight outfit equipped with a floating fly line, and a 6 to 10 weight rod equipped with a high density fast sinking line. Due to the close proximity of Calgary to the mountains and the high altitude, warm clothing may be required any month of the summer season. Bring a hat, polaroid glasses, chest waders and a rain jacket. You will want a camera to record your fishing trip and the wildlife encountered along the river.

KENNEDY, GORDON-WEST WIND FISHING CHARTER, INC.
(403) 286-4359, 286-3805
Address 220 Silver Creek Way, NW, Calgary, Alberta T3B 4H5
Airport Calgary **Accommodations** Calgary
Operation Outfitter **Type of Fishing** Fly, spin
Fish Rainbow, brown trout **Season** June-October
Water Bow River **Specialty** Fly fishing float trips
Boats Drift boats, river sleds **Tackle Supplied** Fly, spin
Experience 6 years **Rates** day: $220 U.S. funds
Guide's Notes: The Bow River fishing season is June - October for rainbows and browns to 10 lbs. The average rainbow is 16 inches with fish 20 to 25 inches common. Methods are nymphing in June and dry fly late June to mid-September. (Streamers and nymphs work well all year) There are 1600 rainbows, 12 inches and up, per mile and 600 browns per mile, 12 inches and up, according to the Alberta Department of Fish and Wildlife.
Author's Notes: *Gordon will be featured fishing the Bow sometime in early January 1987 on the television program "Fishing the West."*

Calgary fisherman Curry Harbor with a nice rainbow.   *Richard Swan*

COCHRANE, ALBERTA

REISER, STAN-ALBERTA TROPHY HUNTS (403) 932-5442

Address Box 1226, Cochrane, Alberta T0L 0W0
Airport Calgary 25m **Accommodations** Cochrane
Operation Outfitter **Type of Fishing** Fly, spin, troll
Fish Rainbow, brown, cutthroat, brook **Season** July-Aug
Water Bow River, Todd Creek, Dogpound Creek
Specialty Bow River fly fishing float trips
Boats Outboards **Tackle Supplied** Spin, troll
Experience 5 years **Rates** day: $300 week: $2000
Guide's Notes: The Bow River fishery needs no introduction to most trout fishermen. The Lower Bow is basically a catch-release system, with all trout over 16 inches being released by law. This ensures the protection of the larger spawn fish and maintains a high quality fishery.

The Upper Bow is a much more sterile stream bed, but still produces good quantities of mature trout. The catch and release system on fish over 16 inches is not mandatory on this stretch. This section of river has very little land access, and therefore does not come under any great fishing pressure. On the late season trips, fishermen are treated to the Rocky Mountain Whitefish spawning run. The fish, (from 1 to 3 lbs) bite readily and are plentiful.

HINTON, ALBERTA

WILSON, DAN (403) 865-4232, 865-7988

Address 128 Sunset Trailer Court, Hinton, Alberta T0E 1B0
Airport Edmonton 190m **Accommodations** Hinton
Operation Outfitter **Type of Fishing** All **Specialty** Fly fishing float trips
Fish Rainbow, Dolly Varden, grayling, brown **Season** May-October
Water Big Beland, Wild Hay, Smokey, Bow Rivers
Boats Canoes, rafts, outboards **Tackle Supplied** Fly, spin, troll
Experience 7 years **Rates** day: $100 week: $500 1/2 day: $75
Guide's Notes: Fishing Calendar for Big Beland, Wild Hay, and Smokey Rivers

Fish	Best Time	Fishing Method	Size
Rainbow Trout (lake)	May - July	Troll, cast, fly fishing	2 to 10 lbs
Rainbow Trout (river)	July - Oct	Fly fishing, casting	1 to 5 lbs
Grayling	July - Oct	Fly fishing	1 to 3 lbs
Brook Trout (lake)	June - Aug	Trolling, fly fishing	1 to 5 lbs
Lake Trout	June - Oct	Trolling or jigs	2 to 15 lbs
Brown Trout (river)	June - Oct	Fly fishing	1 to 5 + lbs
Rocky Mtn Whitefish	May - Oct	Fly, baitcasting	1 to 5 lbs
Lake Whitefish	June - Aug	Fly fishing	1 to 10 lbs
Pike	May - Aug	Trolling, Casting	5 to 25 lbs
Cutthroat Trout	July - Aug	Casting, fly fish, baitcast	1 to 7 lbs
Dolly Varden	July - Sept	Spinners, spoons, baitcast	1 to 10 lbs
Walleye	June - July	Baitcast, jigs, spoons	2 to 12 lbs

JASPER, ALBERTA

CURRIE, LORNE-CURRIE'S TACKLE SHOP (403) 852-5650, 852-3001
Address Box 202, Jasper, Alberta T0E 1E0
Airport Edmonton 220m **Accommodations** Jasper
Operation Outfitter, tackle shop **Type of Fishing** Fly, spin, troll
Fish Rainbow, brook, steelhead, salmon **Season** April-November
Water Maligne, Medicine Lakes, Maligne River
Specialty Fly fishing and spin fishing lakes and rivers
Boats Rowboats, canoes **Tackle Supplied** Fly, spin, troll
Experience 6 years **Rates** day: $195 week: $2100 1/2 day: $170

MIDNAPORE, ALBERTA

GRINNELL, ERIC-SILVERTIP OUTFITTERS (403) 256-5018
Address Box 515, Midnapore, Alberta T0L 1J0
Airport Calgary 15m **Accommodations** Calgary 15m
Operation Outfitter **Type of Fishing** Fly **Boats** Bass boats
Fish Rainbow, brown trout **Season** June-Sept **Water** Bow River
Specialty Fly fishing float trips **Tackle Supplied** Fly
Experience 6 years **Rates** day: $225 U.S. funds
Guide's Notes: The Bow River is a large fertile river that has its source in the
icefields of the Canadian Rockies. Several dams in the vicinity of Calgary dampen
its fluctuations and it takes on the aspect of a giant spring creek. The Bow is
home to brown trout and a race of large silvery rainbows that have been likened
to steelhead. Growth rates and population densities equal or exceed those of
the famous Bighorn and Beaverhead rivers. The ultimate appeal of these fish
is that 4 pound trout rise regularly to dry flies. Fish caught average a fat 16
inches but 20-21 inch fish can be expected each day.
   Although close to the city of Calgary, there is little access to the river and
the valley is an unspoiled patchwork of grazing land, cliffs and wooded islands.
There is very little fishing pressure. Fishermen are just beginning to discover
that perhaps the finest accessible fly fishing for trout in North America occurs
on the Bow River.
   Silvertip Outfitters are the only float fishing outfit offering fishing downstream
of the Carsland Dam. This forty mile stretch has not been commercially float
fished and in fact has been fished by very few people. Much of this water is
within an Indian Reservation and we are currently negotiating access. We have
been using a motor to return upriver from this section.

OLDS, ALBERTA

ARTINDALE, G.D. (403) 335-8532
Address Box 2642, Olds, Alberta T0M 1P0
Airport Calgary 45m **Accommodations** Olds
Operation Outfitter **Type of Fishing** Fly, troll

Fish Bull trout, cutthroat, northern, walleye **Season** Year-round
Water Brazeau River, Brazeau Reservoir **Boats** Canoes
Specialty Mountain pack trips, wilderness lake fishing
Experience 6 years **Rates** day: $100/person Canadian funds

BURTON, GORD-DOUBLE DIAMOND OUTFITTERS (403) 938-7868
Address Box 313, Okotoks, Alberta T0L 1T0
Airport Calgary 30m **Accommodations** Calgary 15m
Operation Outfitter **Type of Fishing** Fly, spin
Fish Rainbow, brown, cutthroat, brook **Season** June-Aug.
Water Bow River, various mountain lakes and streams
Specialty Fly fishing float trips on the Bow River
Boats Rowboats, rafts **Tackle Supplied** Fly, spin
Experience 4 years **Rates** day: $100 and up, U.S. funds

SHORT, W.L.-BARRIER MOUNTAIN OUTFITTERS
(403) 556-6778, 556-3704
Address Box 69, Olds, Alberta T0M 1P0
Airport Calgary 120m **Accommodations** Olds
Operation Outfitter **Type of Fishing** Fly, spin **Tackle Supplied** Fly, spin
Fish Bull trout, cutthroat, brook, whitefish **Season** April-October
Water Panther, Red Deer Rivers, high mountain lakes **Specialty** Fly fishing
Experience 3 years **Rates** week: $1000

RIMBEY, ALBERTA

HATALA, JOHN H.-DOUBLE DIAMOND WILDERNESS TRAILS
(403) 843-3582, 347-1171
Address RR #3, Rimbey, Alberta T0C 2J0
Airport Edmonton 70m **Accommodations** Nordegg 35m
Operation Outfitter **Type of Fishing** All **Tackle Supplied** Spin, baitcast
Fish Cutthroat, Dolly Varden, rainbow, brown **Season** Mar-November
Water Job, Brazeau, Obstruction Lakes, Brazeau River
Specialty Spin casting, trolling and fly fishing **Boats** Rafts
Experience 15 years **Rates** day: $70 week: $550

WILDWOOD, ALBERTA

STRICKER, C.-STRICKER OUTFITTING LTD (403) 325-3961
Address Box 354, Wildwood, Alberta T0E 2M0
Airport Prince George 250m **Accommodations** Prince George 170m
Operation Outfitter **Type of Fishing** All **Boats** Canoes
Fish Dolly Varden, rainbow, grayling **Season** June-Sept.
Water Cake, Tutachi, Fredrickson, Tutcha Lakes
Specialty Fly fishing and lake trolling **Aircraft** Landplane
Experience 25 years **Rates** week: $2000 U.S. funds

BRITISH COLUMBIA

British Columbia

ANAHIM LAKE, BRITISH COLUMBIA

BLACKWELL, JOHN-MOOSE LAKE LODGE (503) 575-1152
Address General Delivery, Anahim Lake, BC VOL 1CO
Airport Anahim Lake 45m **Accommodations** On premises
Operation Outfitter, lodge **Type of Fishing** Fly, spin, troll
Fish Rainbow, kokanee **Season** May-November **Tackle Supplied** Fly, spin, troll
Water Moose Lake, Blackwater, Dean, Chelaslie Rivers
Specialty Fly fishing river trips and lake trolling **Boats** Rowboats, rafts
Experience 14 years **Rates** day: $200 week: $1100 U.S. funds
Guide's Notes: Lake fishing is good from May 25 to October 15. Stream fishing is good from July 1 to September 20 with rainbow trout to 6 pounds.

ATLIN, BRITISH COLUMBIA

ROBINSON, GARY-WILDERNESS FISHING ADVENTURES (604) 651-7503
Address Box 86, Atlin, BC VOW 1AO
Airport Whitehorse 120m **Accommodations** Atlin **Operation** Outfitter
Fish Steelhead, king, coho, trout **Season** Year-round **Type of Fishing** All
Water Nakina River, Naden Harbour **Specialty** Fly fishing
Aircraft Floatplane, helicopter **Boats** Rafts **Tackle Supplied** Fly, spin
Experience 10 years **Rates** day: $600 U.S. funds
Guide's Notes: Fishing Calendar

Fish	Available
Spring Steelhead	Apr - May
King Salmon	June - July
Coho Salmon	Mid-Aug - Oct
Winter Steelhead	Nov - Mar

Author's Notes: Our contacts tell us Gary runs a good operation.

VIG, NORMAN-NORSEMAN ADVENTURES, LTD. (604) 651-7535, 826-2559
Address P.O. Box 184, Atlin, BC VOW 1AO
Airport Whitehorse 115m **Accommodations** Atlin
Operation Outfitter, charter captain **Type of Fishing** Fly, troll
Fish Lake trout, grayling **Boats** Houseboats, 24 ft charter boat
Tackle Supplied Troll **Season** May-September
Water Atlin, Tagish Lakes **Specialty** Lake trolling and fly fishing
Experience 20 years **Rates** day: $200 week: $795

BELLA COOLA, BRITISH COLUMBIA

HILL, TONY & JUDY-NAKIA LODGE (707) 542-4242
Address C/O Fishing International, P.O. Box 2132, Santa Rosa, CA 95405
Airport Bella Coola **Accommodations** On premises **Water** Dean River
Operation Lodge, outfitter **Type of Fishing** Fly, spin **Boats** River sleds
Fish Summer run steelhead, king salmon **Season** July-September
Specialty Fly and spin fishing for trophy summer run steelhead
Experience 2 years **Rates** week: $1895/person
Guide's Notes: The Dean River There are few places on earth as spectacularly beautiful as the magnificent and incomparable Dean River. Isolated and remote, this fabled river runs its unspoiled course through the sky high, snow capped peaks and vertical stone walls of the most beautiful mountain scenery anywhere in the world -- the unsurpassed wilderness reaches of British Columbia's famed Coastal Mountains.

This river stands supreme as the home of the world's finest strain of wild, summer run steelhead, and as one of the ultimate destinations for world traveled anglers in search of the fullest measure of world class angling adventure and excitement!

Dean River stock are as bright as they come. Deepbodied fish that can go over twenty-five pounds, their translucent steel blue backs and ocean fresh flanks shimmer in the clear waters of the Dean. Anglers here are treated to explosive action on light fly tackle of all kinds - from floating lines and greased line presentations to deeply fished wets on traditional sunken line presentations.

During late June and July, strong runs of king salmon enter the stream offering serious anglers excellent sport on fly and conventional tackle. Each year, Fishing International hosts groups on this most desired of all Canadian steelhead rivers. (Fishing International)
Author's Notes: The Dean River is world famous for steelhead on the dry fly. Our contacts say this is an excellent place to experience the action.

CAMPBELL RIVER, BRITISH COLUMBIA

HARRISON, WILLIAM JOHN (604) 287-9639
Address 566 Quadra Ave., Campbell River, BC V9W 6V2
Airport Campbell River **Accommodations** Campbell River
Operation Guide **Type of Fishing** All **Specialty** Steelhead fly fishing
Fish Steelhead, chinook, coho, pink **Season** Year-round **Tackle Supplied** All
Boats Rafts, Boston Whalers **Water** Campbell, Gold, Oyster, Salmon Rivers
Experience 3 years **Rates** day: $180 Canadian funds

MAYNARD, JEREMY (604) 286-1456
Address 559 Birch St., Campbell River, BC V9W 2S9
Airport Campbell River **Accommodations** Campbell River
Operation Guide **Type of Fishing** Fly, baitcast, troll

(BRITISH COLUMBIA)
VANCOUVER ISLAND

BRITISH COLUMBIA

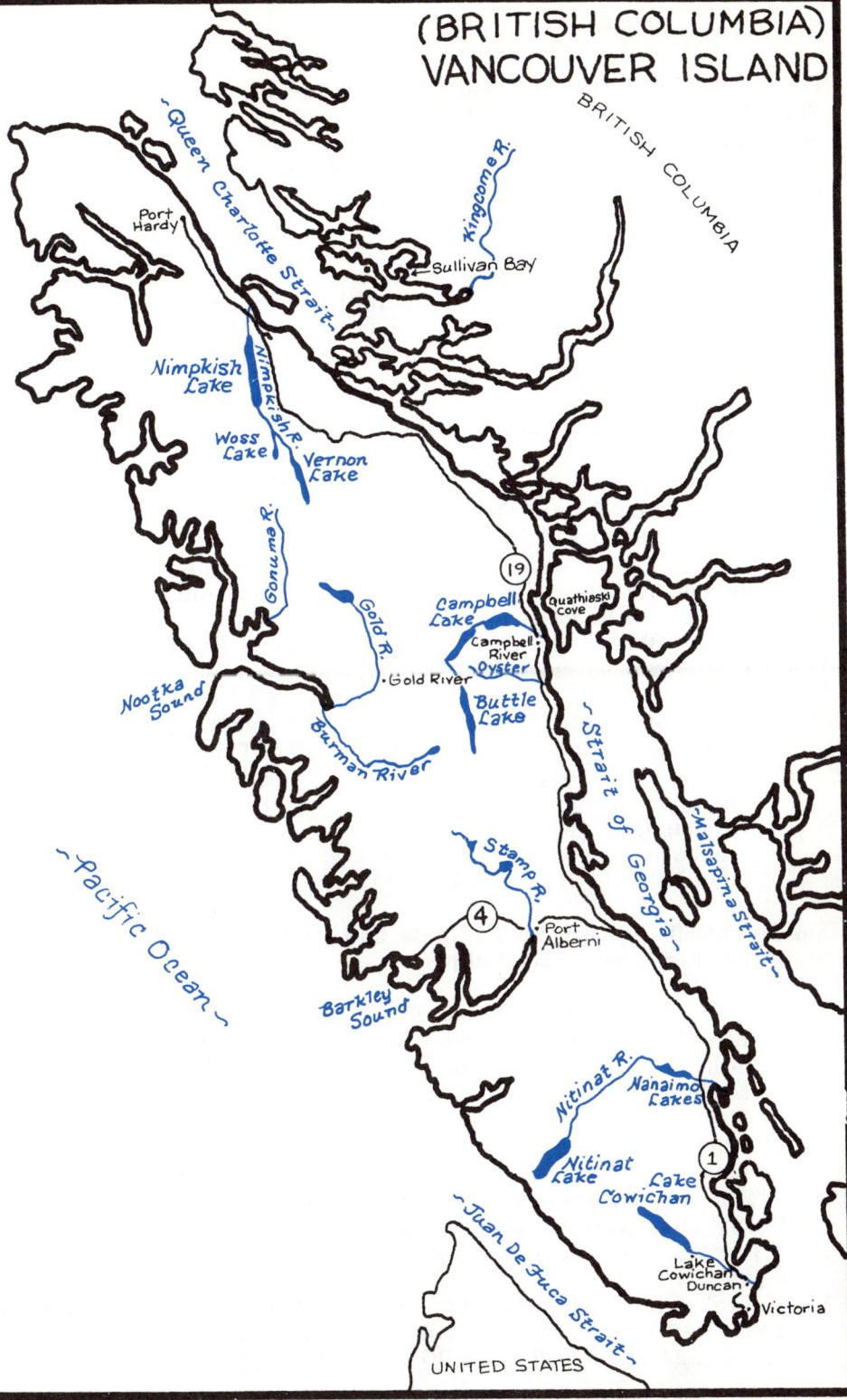

Port Hardy

~ Queen Charlotte Strait ~

Kingcome R.

Sullivan Bay

Nimpkish Lake

Nimpkish R.

Woss Lake

Vernon Lake

Gonome R.

Gold R.

Nootka Sound

Campbell Lake

19

Quathiaski Cove

Campbell River

Oyster

Gold River

Buttle Lake

Burman River

~ Strait of Georgia ~

~ Malaspina Strait ~

Stamp R.

~ Pacific Ocean ~

4

Port Alberni

Barkley Sound

Nitinat R.

Nanaimo Lakes

Nitinat Lake

Lake Cowichan

1

~ Juan De Fuca Strait ~

Lake Cowichan

Duncan

Victoria

UNITED STATES

Fish Chinook, coho, steelhead **Season** Year-round **Boats** Raft, 17′ Boston Whaler
Water Discovery Passage, Gold, Oyster, Campbell Rivers
Specialty Fly fishing for steelhead **Tackle Supplied** Fly, baitcast, troll
Experience 12 years **Rates** day: $175-300 U.S. funds
Guide's Notes: Salt water--I have a 17 foot Boston Whaler from which I fish
the strong tidal currents of Discovery Passage in front of Campbell River. The
main season is May to October. Chinooks from 10 to 50 pounds and coho from
4 to 16 pounds can be expected. Freshwater--I fish and guide on the rivers
mentioned above from November to April for winter run steelhead. The
Campbell River has a summer run of fish April to August. Steelhead weigh
from 5 to 25 pounds with 9 to 10 pounds being average. I have an 11 foot
inflatable raft for drifting the rivers.

PAULSON, JON (604) 923-4846
Address 703 Ash St., Campbell River, BC V9W 1G1
Airport Campbell River **Accommodations** Campbell River
Operation Outfitter **Type of Fishing** All
Fish Steelhead, chinook, coho **Season** Year-round
Water Campbell, Gold, Oyster, Salmon Rivers **Tackle Supplied** All
Specialty Summer run steelhead fly fishing **Boats** Rafts, outboard
Experience 3 years **Rates** day: $180-300 Canadian funds
**Guide's Notes: Winter Steelhead River Rating Guide, Campbell River Area.
(Season starts mid November and ends May 15th)**

River	Fly Rod	Float Rod	Drift Rod	Best Time	Overall Rating
Gold	4	10	8	Jan-June	10
Oyster	6	8	3	Feb-Apr	8
Salmon	6	7	8	Feb-Mar	5
Campbell	8	6	2	Dec-June	7
Nimpkish	7	5	7	Dec-Mar	4

**Summer Steelhead River Rating Guide, Campbell River Area. (Season starts
May 1st and ends November 15th)**

River	Fly Rod	Float Rod	Drift Rod	Best Time	Overall Rating
Gold	7	10	8	June-Oct	10
Marble	3	Fly only	Fly only	May-June	3
Stamp	5	8	8	July-Sep	6
Campbell	8	10	5	May-Oct	10
Kaipit	6	7	8	June-Oct	5

Note: "Float Rod" means using a float or a bobber, conventional gear.
"Drift Rod" means conventional gear, no bobber.
Ratings are on a 1 - 10 scale, with 10 being best.

VESELY, STEVE & RETTA-GYPSY FISHING CAMP Phone Main Operator:
Campbell River Radio, Sayward-Channel 28, Gypsy II N113192
Address Box 333, Campbell River, BC V9W 5B6

Airport Campbell River **Accommodations** On premises
Operation Outfitter, lodge **Type of Fishing** Fly, spin, troll
Fish King, coho, steelhead, halibut **Season** March-November
Water Wakeman Sound, Kingcome Inlet, Sutledge Inlet, Wakeman River
Boats 15 ft outboards, 22 ft inboard/outboard **Tackle Supplied** Spin, troll
Specialty Trolling, river fishing
Experience 5 years **Rates** day: $400 U.S. funds

CHILANKO FORKS, BRITISH COLUMBIA

SEVERSON, MARVIN J.-BARNEY'S LAKESIDE RESORT
Phone Puntzie Lake 1 G thru Prince George Radio Operator (BC)
Address Puntzi Lake, Chilanko Forks, BC VOL 1HO
Airport Williams Lake 100m **Accommodations** On premises
Operation Outfitter, lodge, tackle shop **Type of Fishing** Fly, spin, troll
Fish Rainbow, kokanee, Dolly Varden, steelhead **Season** May-November
Water Chilcotin, Puntzi, Tsuniah, Bluff Lakes **Tackle Supplied** Fly, spin, troll
Specialty Lake trolling, river fishing, fly & spin **Boats** Rowboats and motors
Experience 2 years **Rates** day: $100-150 Canadian funds
Guide's Notes: Spring lake fishing begins as soon as ice is off of the lakes
(approximately May 15 until freeze up in November). Angling regulations don't
allow river and stream fishing until July 1 and during spawning runs closures
do occur on the major spawning rivers.
   We are located in the Chilcotin District and home base is on Puntzi Lake.
Puntzi Lake is fished mainly by trolling using a gangtroll (Ford Fender) and
lure to catch the rainbow and 2 to 3 pound kokanee.
   Numerous lakes in the area provide excellent day trips to try for Dolly Varden,
rainbow, etc., and there is extremely good fly fishing on some of the smaller
lakes and streams.
   Road access--110 miles west of Williams Lake on Hwy 20, 65 miles are paved
with the remaining 45 miles gravel.
   Air Access--Puntzi Mountain Airstrip. Asphalt 250 ft wide and 6,000 feet
long. Elevation of 2995 feet. Approaches clear. Floatplane service from Puntzi
Lake, Barney's Lakeside Resort.

COQUITLAM, BRITISH COLUMBIA

BLAKE, ALEX N. (604) 936-9463
Address 692 Florence St., Coquitlam, BC V3J 4C8
Airport Vancouver 10m **Accommodations** Vancouver 10m
Operation Outfitter **Type of Fishing** All
Fish Steelhead, salmon, trout, bottom **Season** Year-round
Water Stamp, Vedder, Gold, Thompson Rivers **Tackle Supplied** All
Specialty Fly fishing and spin casting **Boats** Rowboats, rafts
Experience 31 years **Rates** day: $500/2 people Canadian funds
Guide's Notes: Coquhala River: We fish summer run steelhead, during the
month of August, on the Coquhala which is a wilderness stream of pure, clean

waters coming down out of rugged mountains 110 miles east of Vancouver. It is close to the road in many places and accessibility is not particularly difficult. The river consists of many good, short runs, and some good holding pools. It is easy to work a fly over most of the river, but basic casting skills must be present if success ratios are to stay on course.

These are catch and release, fly-only, waters. Barbless hooks are the law. The steelhead average five to eight pounds and are nice and bright in colour, in excellent shape for photo work. It is not uncommon to have each man hook into three fish per day. All fishing is done from the river's banks; no boats are allowed.

Proven flies are: Young's Fire Fly, the Umpqua, Red Sandy, Yellow Belle, General Practitioner (on a single hook), and Wooly Worm in black, with red tail and silver ribs.

Stamp River/Vancouver Island: The Stamp is approximately 5 hours traveling time from Vancouver and is a pristine stream where you will find very little competition from other anglers. The river flows mostly through a lightly populated area, and consists of "not too much" white water. It is about a hundred feet across in most places, and can be rafted with a small rubber raft. The Stamp has some of the best return rates for winter run steelhead and salmon in all of British Columbia.

Winter run steelhead fishing here is best from October to March. Success ratios are good, 2 fish per day is common, with the fish running up to twenty pounds. Barbless hooks are the rule, and the use of a float is the best method for covering the runs and pools. Boats and rubber rafts can be used for seeking out good holes. Heavy baitcasting outfits work best for this fishing. Artificials like spin glows, plastic single eggs, gooie bobs, and pink rubber worms work well. The weather can be wet and cold so bring warm clothing and two pair of chest waders.

Summer run steelhead fishing on the Stamp is best from July to August. The fish are bright and average five to eight pounds. It is not unusual for a skilled fisherman to hook into more than the two fish limit for the day. All fishing is done from the banks. Regulations allow bait fishing, but barbless hooks are required, and all wild steelhead must be released. We only use flies at this time of the year on the Stamp and recommend 7 and 8 weight rods. Wet-cell and fast-sink lines in weight forward tapers, with 100 yards of 20 pound backing, are best for getting to the holding fish. We use mostly wet flies such as the Umpqua, Red Sandy, Yellow Bell, and Wooly Worms in black, with red tail and silver ribs.

Chinook and coho salmon fishing on the Stamp is well known. The best time of the year is from September 15 to October 30. The chinooks run up to 50 pounds and the cohos go to 15 pounds. Bait can be used, but barbless hooks are the rule. Super heavy rods must be used to turn the big chinooks, and use of a float is the best method for working the pools. The Stamp has the highest return rates of big chinooks of any river its size, in B.C. With chinooks, coho, and steelhead all returning to the river at the same time, your success ratio is very high.

Vedder River: The Vedder is about 60 miles east of Vancouver. We fish it for winter run steelhead from December to March. I feel the Vedder will soon be rated as the number 2 river in all of B.C. because of the good work that has been done by the hatchery, situated on the river's upper reaches. It offers 10 miles of good, easy, accessible waters which average 100 ft. in width. Big steelhead up to 20 pounds have been taken. We fish from the shore and no boats are on the river. It is lightly populated along some of the shoreline, and has plenty of elbow room on most days throughout the year. Barbless hooks are required and one hatchery fish a day may be taken. The use of a float is the best method to cover the pools.

Gold River: The Gold River on Vancouver Island is a good winter-run steelhead river which fishes best from February 1st to March 31st. It is narrow and steep in places with lots of good holding pools. It has one of the highest success ratios in British Columbia for anglers that know where and how to fish it. The fish run up to 15 pounds and are super clean, as they are only a few miles from the sea. It is best fished with a float; some good lures include a Red-and White Spin Glow, in size #10; Single-Egg imitations in orange plastic, and Gooie Bobs.

Sheridan Lake: This lake is located 300 miles northeast of Vancouver, British Columbia, and offers trout fishing from May 15 through October 31. The lake is situated on a 50,000 square mile plateau at an elevation of 3,600 feet above sea level. The lake is approximately 5 miles long and 3 miles wide, with numerous large bays, channels and islands. The deepest part of the lake is 115 feet and the average depth is 15 to 40 feet deep, which makes the lake an excellent fly-fishing lake. Water is fed from underground springs and snow runoffs, which makes the water crystal clear. There is an abundance of freshwater shrimp, stone nymphs, leeches and almost every kind of bug hatch during the summer. Winds are light and the weather is warm during the summer months; the days are long for the angler (sunrise 4:30am, sunset 9:45pm). The lake is lightly populated with seasonal cabins, and many areas of the lakeshore are unpopulated.

The record rainbow is over 16 pounds in Sheridan Lake with the average being about 4 pounds. The record eastern brook is 6 pounds; the average is 2 to 3 pounds. It is not uncommon for each person to hook into 3 to 5 fish per day, but basic casting skills must be present if the success ratio is to stay on course. All fishing is done from boats.

Proven flies include: Doc Sprately, Idaho, Leech Patterns, Horsehair Nymphs, Wooly Worm and Dragon Fly. We use fly rod systems in sizes #6 to 8. Long leaders are a must (15 feet).

Author's Notes: Mr. John Kaufman, who is on the staff of Shakespeare Rod Company and has fished all over the world, told me Alex is one of the finest guides in Canada. Alex fishes throughout British Columbia and specializes in 2 to 7 day trips for 2 to 4 anglers based riverside in a 23' motor home. Mr. Kaufman says the food is very good to excellent and the fishing is superb.

DUNCAN, BRITISH COLUMBIA

ATKINSON, ALF (604) 748-9197
Address RR#3, 3939 Vaux Road, Duncan, BC V9L 2X1
Airport Victoria 40m **Accommodations** Duncan 5m **Operation** Guide
Fish Steelhead, salmon **Season** Year-round **Type of Fishing** All

Water Samsun Narrows, Cowichan, Nitnat, Kaksilah Rivers **Boats** McKenzies
Specialty Fly fishing or baitcasting **Tackle Supplied** All
Experience 15 years **Rates** day: $140 1/2 day: $75
Guide's Notes: Cowichan River
   - semi wild river
   - catch and release except for hatchery fish
   - pleasant river for day trip fishing
   - excellent steelhead fishing during winter and spring
   - subject to regulation changes inquiries should be made
     when planning a trip.

FORT SAINT JAMES, BRITISH COLUMBIA

WAIBLER, STEPHAN F.-GLEN EAGLE LODGE (604) 996-8476
Address P.O. Box 1210, Fort St. James, BC V0J 1P0
Airport Prince George 100m **Accommodations** On premises
Operation Outfitter, charter captain, lodge **Type of Fishing** Fly, spin, troll
Fish Rainbow, lake, Dolly Varden, kokanee **Season** June-October
Water Stuart and Trembleur Lake **Tackle Supplied** Fly, spin, troll
Specialty Stream fly fishing & lake trolling **Boats** Canoes, river boats, 30 ft cruiser
Experience 20 years **Rates** varies

GOLD RIVER, BRITISH COLUMBIA

MICHAUD, VAUGHN-NOOTKA SOUND SPORTS FISHING (604) 283-7194
Address Box 176, Gold River, BC V0P 1G0
Airport Campbell River 60m **Accommodations** Gold River
Operation Guide **Type of Fishing** Spin, baitcast, troll
Fish Chinook, steelhead, halibut, cutthroat **Season** Year-round
Water Nootka Sound, Gold, Burman, Gonuma Rivers
Specialty Trolling for salmon and halibut **Tackle Supplied** Spin, baitcast, troll
Boats Canoes, raft, 18 ft deep V inboard/outboard
Experience 15 years **Rates** varies

HAZELTON, BRITISH COLUMBIA

FLEMING, RON-LOVE BROTHERS & LEE LTD (604) 842-6350, 846-5648
Address RR #1, Kispiox Rd, Hazelton, BC V0J 1Y0
Airport Smithers 165m **Accommodations** Smithers 165m
Operation Outfitter **Type of Fishing** Fly, spin, troll **Boats** McKenzie
Fish Rainbow, char **Season** June-August **Tackle Supplied** Fly, spin
Water Finlay River System **Specialty** Fly fishing **Aircraft** Floatplane
Experience 15 years **Rates** week: $2500/2 people

OYSMUELLER, KARL-AURORA OUTFITTERS, LTD. (604) 842-6182
Address RR#1 Kispiox Road, Hazelton, BC V0J 1Y0

Airport Smithers 165m **Accommodations** Hazelton **Operation** Outfitter
Fish Steelhead, salmon, Dolly Varden **Season** Sept-Dec **Specialty** Fly fishing
Water Headwaters of Skeena, Kispiox Rivers **Type of Fishing** Fly, spin
Boats Outboards, raft, canoe **Tackle Supplied** Fly, spin
Experience 15 years **Rates** week: $1900

HEFFLEY CREEK, BRITISH COLUMBIA

**ROBERTSON, RICK-SUSKEENA LODGE (604) 578-7690 or
Vancouver, BC radio phone Channel 8-#N710120 "Suskeena"**
Address Box 43, Heffley Creek, BC V0E 1Z0
Airport Smithers 120m **Accommodations** On premises
Operation Outfitter, lodge **Type of Fishing** Fly, spin **Water** Sustut River
Fish Steelhead, Chinook **Season** August-October **Boats** River sleds
Specialty Fly and spin fishing for trophy steelhead and chinook
Experience 12 years **Rates** varies

HUDSON HOPE, BRITISH COLUMBIA

DAVIDSON, W.H. (604) 783-5770
Address Box 663, Hudson Hope, BC V0C 1V0
Airport Fort St. John 64m **Accommodations** Hudson Hope **Operation** Guide
Fish Dolly Varden, rainbow, grayling, char **Season** June-August **Boats** Canoes
Water All waters in Region 7 in British Columbia **Aircraft** Floatplane
Specialty Stream fishing, lake trolling **Type of Fishing** Spin, troll
Experience 3 years **Rates** day: $250 week: $500

**KYLLO, KEN-FORT GRAHAM LODGE (604) 783-5248 or
N413890 Fort Nelson Operator on Fort Wave Tower**
Address Box 238, Hudson Hope, BC V0C 1V0
Airport Fort St John 60m **Accommodations** On premises
Operation Outfitter, lodge **Type of Fishing** All
Fish Dolly Varden, rainbow, grayling, whitefish **Season** Mar-Nov
Water Williston Lake and tributary streams **Boats** River sleds
Specialty Jet boating to stream mouths for fly fishing or spin casting
Experience 32 years **Rates** day: $400 week: $2100 1/2 day: $300
Guide's Notes: We specialize in Big Dolly Varden to 18 pounds on Williston
Lake, the biggest lake in British Columbia. Our new 19 room Fort Graham Lodge
is next to one of the best fishing streams on Williston Lake.

KASLO, BRITISH COLUMBIA

FRANKLIN, GERALD IAN-LOKI GUIDES & OUTFITTERS (604) 353-2664
Address P.O. Box 755, Kaslo, BC V0G 1M0
Airport Castlegar 60m **Accommodations** Kaslo
Operation Outfitter **Type of Fishing** Fly, spin, troll

Fish Rainbow, Dolly Varden, cutthroat, kokanee **Season** January-November
Water Kootenay Lake and River, high country lakes **Specialty** Lake trolling
Boats Rowboats, 31 ft Chris Craft **Tackle Supplied** Fly, spin, troll
Experience 25 years **Rates** day: $250/person
Guide's Notes: The Gerard rainbows are a truly magnificent sport fish. Rainbows
up to 20 pounds are quite common. The record for the lake is 39 pounds,
however, Fish and Wildlife have netted fish in the Lardeau River up to 55
pounds. Also, Kootenay Lake has an excellent stock of Dolly Varden trout up
to 20 pounds and an excellent kokanee fishery.

Kootenay Lake is located in the southern central portion of British Columbia
and is approximately 100 miles long. It varies from 2 to 5 miles wide. There
is a large number of rivers and streams flowing into and out of Kootenay Lake.
The average overall depth is 400 feet (and cold!). Kootenay Lake is ice free and
can be fished year round. Peak fishing periods for fishing Kootenay Lake are
September, October, November and December, and there is another peak period
during April, May and June. Best methods for catching these large trout are
lake trolling bucktails and plugs. Also, fly fishing from an open boat in the
Kootenay River during the months of September, October, November, can be
a delight and very successful. Trout from 2 to 10 pounds are common.

Loki Guides and Outfitters also operates a heli-hiking, heli-fishing operation.
Clients are flown into high alpine lakes to a base camp and have the opportunity
to fish and explore in beautiful wilderness alpine areas. There are many alpine
lakes (38) in our area. These lakes have excellent fish stock of cutthroat and
rainbow trout to two pounds.

LAKE COWICHAN, BRITISH COLUMBIA

SAYSELL, JOE (604) 749-3062
Address Wentworth Road, Lake Cowichan, BC V0R 2G0
Airport Victoria 50m **Accommodations** Lake Cowichan
Operation Guide, charter captain **Type of Fishing** Fly, spin
Fish Steelhead, trout, salmon **Season** Year-round
Water Cowichan, Campbell, Stamp Rivers, Pacific Ocean
Specialty Fly fishing float trips, salt water mooching
Boats McKenzie, salt water runabout **Tackle Supplied** Fly
Experience 20 years **Rates** day: $200

NIMPO LAKE, BRITISH COLUMBIA

**NAUMANN, FRANK & PAULINA-CRAZY BEAR LAKE FISHING
(604) 733-5999**
Address Nimpo Lake, British Columbia, BC V0L 1R0
Airport Anahim 12m **Accommodations** On premises
Operation Outfitter, lodge **Type of Fishing** Fly, spin, troll
Fish Rainbow, steelhead, salmon **Season** June-November
Water Crazy Bear, Shetler, Paulina, Hotnarke Lakes

Specialty Fly fishing, lake spincasting **Boats** Canoes, outboards
Experience 5 years **Rates** day: $260 Canadian funds

**SCHILLER, MOE-ELIGUK LAKE LODGE (604) 742-3269 or
H42/3247 Nimpo Lake Channel J.R.**
Address General Delivery, Nimpo Lake, BC V0L 1R0
Airport Vancouver 250m **Accommodations** On premises
Operation Outfitter, lodge **Type of Fishing** Fly, troll **Specialty** Fly fishing
Fish Kamloops, rainbow **Season** May-October **Boats** Rowboats, canoes
Water Eliguk, Petrie, Squiness, Walla Lakes **Tackle Supplied** Fly, troll
Experience 5 years **Rates** day: $100 Canadian funds
Guide's Notes: Eliguk Lake
   1. Mid May through October
   2. May, June, July are peak times
   3. Hatches: sedge, mayflies, mosquitoes
   4. Fly patterns: Gil's Monsters, Nyerges Nymph, Muddlers, Doc's Spratley
   Full floating, sinking tip, and sinking line are a must. Eliguk Lake is a fly
fisherman's paradise. Wild, native rainbow trout are all on the surface, ranging
from 1 to 3 pounds. Also, there are three hike-to lakes for diversity within 2
miles of the lodge.

100 MILE HOUSE, BRITISH COLUMBIA

**MAITLAND, STUART-EUREKA PEAK OUTFITTERS-Phone N412348 on J.S.
or J.P. channel thru Williams Lake Operator**
Address Box 1332, 100 Mile House, BC V0K 2E0
Airport Williams Lake 100m **Accommodations** On premises
Operation Outfitter, lodge **Type of Fishing** Fly, spin, troll
Fish Rainbow, lake, kokanee, whitefish **Season** May-August
Water Bosk Lake, Horsefly River, Crooked, McKinley Lakes
Specialty Fly fishing for rainbow, lake trolling for char, horse pack trips
Boats Rowboats, canoes, outboards **Tackle Supplied** Fly, spin, troll
Experience 8 years **Rates** day: $170 week: $1000
Guide's Notes: Rainbow trout up to 9 pounds, but commonly 1 to 2 pounds,
are readily caught on flies and fishing is good the entire season on the lakes.
River fishing is best from July 1 to August 10. Best fly patterns: Sedge for dry
flies, Spratles, and Carys for wet patterns.

PORT ALBERNI, BRITISH COLUMBIA

THOMPSON, BRUCE (604) 724-3112, 724-2664
Address 5440 Argyle St., Port Alberni, BC V94 1T7
Airport Port Alberni **Accommodations** Port Alberni
Operation Charter **Type of Fishing** All
Fish Chinook, sockeye, coho, steelhead **Season** Year-round
Water Alberni Canal, Georgia Strait, Barkley Sound, Stamp River

Specialty Trolling, drift, lake, and fly fishing
Experience 10 years **Rates** day: $240-460 1/2 day: $140-260

PRINCE GEORGE, BRITISH COLUMBIA

CONNORS, KEITH (604) 562-7826
Address 4080 Lansdowne Road, Prince George, BC V2N 2P6
Airport Smithers 200m **Accommodations** Smithers 200m
Operation Outfitter **Type of Fishing** All **Water** Finlay, Stikine Rivers
Fish Rainbow, grayling, lake, Dolly Varden **Season** July-September
Specialty Fly and spin, fishing **Aircraft** Floatplanes
Boats River sleds, canoes, McKenzies **Tackle Supplied** Spin, troll
Experience 10 years **Rates** week: $2800 U.S. funds
Guide's Notes: Fly-in freshwater fishing. Excellent fly fishing August and September for rainbow trout and grayling (2-4 pounds). Dolly Varden and lake trout fishing is superior from early July to September (5-35 pounds). A large number of remote lakes to choose from, also stream and river fishing.

UNRALL, ROY-TROPHY FISHING EXPEDITIONS (604) 563-1152
Address RR#4, Site 12, Comp. #1, Prince George, BC V2N 2J2
Airport Prince George **Accommodations** Prince George
Operation Outfitter **Type of Fishing** All **Season** Year-round
Fish King, silver, steelhead **Water** Skeena, Kalum, Copper Rivers
Specialty Jet boat fishing for king salmon and steelhead, float and fly fishing
Boats Inboard **Tackle Supplied** Spin, baitcast
Experience 4 years **Rates** day: $300 week: $2000 1/2 day: $160
Guide's Notes: Fishing Calendar

Fish	Available	Peak
Chinook (kings)	May - Aug	July 28
Coho (silvers)	Aug 10 - Oct 15	Sept 15
Steelhead	Year-round	Late Aug

Larger steelhead tend to be caught in late August but winter and spring fishing is excellent. Fly fishing is also very good.

QUATHIASKI COVE, BRITISH COLUMBIA

NELSON, BILL (604) 285-3129, 285-3329
Address Box 186, Quathiaski Cove, BC V0P 1N0
Airport Campbell River 8m **Accommodations** Quathiaski
Fish Chinook, coho, steelhead **Season** March-October
Water Coastal waters of B.C., Campbell River **Operation** Guide
Specialty Fly fishing in ocean and rivers **Type of Fishing** Fly, troll
Boats McKenzies, Boston Whalers **Tackle Supplied** Spin, fly, troll
Experience 12 years **Rates** day: $210 1/2 day: $108 U.S. funds
Guide's Notes: I fly fish only for salmon during the summer season. We can teach casting and also offer fly trolling techniques for those unable to cast. This is all salt water fishing.

Author's Notes: In the recently published book *FLY FISHING FOR PACIFIC SALMON*, the author thanks Bill for his help and calls him a "guide extraordinaire".

RADIUM, BRITISH COLUMBIA

TEGART, H. CODY-PALLISER RIVER GUIDES & OUTFITTERS (604) 347-9274
Address Box 238, Radium, BC V0A 1M0
Airport Cranbrook 90m **Accommodations** Radium
Operation Outfitter **Type of Fishing** Fly, spin
Fish Cutthroat **Season** August **Boats** Rafts
Water Palliser River, Queen Mary Lake **Aircraft** Helicopter
Experience 10 years **Rates** day: $200

SMITHERS, BRITISH COLUMBIA

BUNN, CHARLIE-CHARLIE'S FISH 'N' FUR (604) 847-3355, 847-9681
Address Box 113, Smithers, BC V0J 2N0
Airport Smithers **Accommodations** Smithers **Operation** Guide
Fish Steelhead **Season** September-October **Type of Fishing** Fly, spin
Water Bulkley, Morice River **Boats** River sled, raft **Tackle Supplied** Spin
Specialty Wet and dry fly fishing, casting with lures
Experience 9 years **Rates** day: $250 week: $1500 U.S. funds
Guide's Notes: The peak season on the **Buckley** and **Morice** rivers for steelhead is from mid-September to the end of October. Early in this period we have exciting dry fly fishing. After mid- October, we use wet flies. I also accommodate spin fishermen as well as fly fishermen. We encourage catch and release.

MILTENBERGER, GARY-STEELHEAD VALHALLA LODGE (604) 847-5367
Address RR #1 Trout Creek, Smithers, BC V0J 2N0
Airport Smithers **Accommodations** On premises **Operation** Outfitter, lodge
Fish Steelhead, salmon, trout **Season** April-October **Type of Fishing** All
Water Sustut, Skeena, Bulkley, Kalum Rivers **Boats** River sleds, rafts
Specialty Fly fishing for steelhead **Aircraft** Floatplanes
Experience 10 years **Rates** week: $3000/person U.S. funds
Guide's Notes: Of all of the famous steelhead rivers in northern British Columbia, probably the best known and least fished is the Sustut River.
   The Sustut River is a fairly large river by western standards, runs around 1,500 to 3,000 cfs during the fishing season, and is normally low and clear during the autumn months. Ranging from 25 to 100 yards wide, the pools and runs that you will fish vary from 50 yards to over a quarter-mile in length, and nearly all of them have more than ample backcasting room for fly fishing. The best fly water is three to eight feet deep although some pools of the upper river are up to 15 feet deep. The lower 12 miles of the Sustut consists of a series of long, wide pools and runs that comprise some of the most classical steelhead water that you will ever see. The upper eight miles is canyon type water, with deep, narrow pools interspersed with short but productive runs. Much of the

upper water is still virgin, having never been fished before 1984 when we started our camp, and many of the upper pools and runs are still unnamed, awaiting the day when one of our customers beaches a steelhead thereby entitling him to christen the pool. In good light conditions when the water is low you will be able to see the fish in some pools. Unlike many western steelhead streams the wading is fairly easy on the Sustut, however, felt soles on your boots are a must as the rocks are quite slippery. We navigate the river in safe, comfortable 24 ft wood/fiberglass riverboats powered by 50 hp jet outboard motors which gives us access to over 50 different pools and runs in 20 miles of river. Normally, six to ten pools will be fished each day by two fishermen and their guide.

The Fishing Calendar: What is probably the largest run of chinook (king) salmon in the entire Skeena drainage enter the Sustut in early August and continue running through the end of that month. Steelhead usually begin to appear around the third week of August and continue to run until late November or early December when the river freeezes. We open our camp the second week of August through mid-November. Prime time fly fishing for steelhead is from September 1 until October 21, and fly fishing parties will be given booking preference during that time period. Parties wishing to fish for chinooks in August or for steelhead after October 21 should come equipped to fish with lures as well as flies.

There is no certain week or time during the period of September 1 to October 21 that we can predict with any degree of certainty that the fishing will be best; if that were the case we would price those time periods accordingly. There seems to be a fairly consistent number of fish in the river after the third week of August, with the best fishing being determined more by water levels and the weather than the calendar. For those willing to fish in cooler weather, some of the best fishing of the steelhead season can occur in late October and early November.

The Fish: Having travelled nearly 300 miles from the ocean, the chinooks are fairly coloured by the time they reach the Sustut. These fish run from 10 to 50 pounds, and average in the 20 to 25 pound range. They will take a fly but only grudgingly. Although coloured, these fish are very strong, and heavy tackle is required for them. The Sustut steelhead average 15 pounds in size, with many running to 20 pounds, a significant number weighing in the low 20's and a few in the mid to high 20's and low 30's. Some of the steelhead are bright and some are coloured, and they will come to a fly quite well. The females generally run from 8 to 20 pounds, while the males normally range from 14 to over 30 pounds. We also have a fair number of Dolly Varden char ranging from a pound up to 10 pounds that average around 2 pounds, and a few rainbows that run from a pound to three pounds. All of these are wild fish.

Tackle: Lines, tippets, and leaders should be at least 12 lb. test. Rods should be 8-1/2 to 10-1/2 feet in length and should be able to handle nine to 11 weight shooting heads or 20 lb. test line. Reels should be good quality and be able to handle a minimum of 200 yards of line. All standard steelhead lures and flies work well on the Sustut. A small selection of lures and flies will be available at the lodge, but you should try to bring a week's supply with you.

NORTHLAND ANGLING GUIDE SERVICE (604) 847-9234
Address RR #2, Babine Lake Rd, Site 53, Smithers, BC V0J 2N0
Airport Smithers **Accommodations** On premises
Operation Outfitter, lodge **Type of Fishing** Fly, spin
Fish Steelhead, salmon, trout **Season** May-November
Water Babine, Bulkley, Skeena, Morice Rivers
Specialty Fly fishing **Boats** River sleds **Tackle Supplied** Spin, fly
Experience 4 years **Rates** day: $300 week: $2100

O'NEILL, MIKE-KIT-EX-CHEN GUIDING SERVICES (604) 847-4166
Address Box 2214, Smithers, BC V0J 2N0
Airport Smithers **Accommodations** Smithers **Operation** Outfitter
Fish Chinook, steelhead, coho, trout **Season** April-November
Water Skeena, Nass, Bulkley, Kalum Rivers **Type of Fishing** Baitcast, troll
Specialty Lure fishing for record class salmon and steelhead
Boats River sled, canoe **Tackle Supplied** Baitcast, spin
Experience 2 years **Rates** day: $290 week: $1900 1/2 day: $200 Canadian funds

STERZER, RANDOLPH M.-BABINE RIVER RAINBOW LODGE (604) 943-1213 or Radio Van N710005 Channel 1 or 8
Address Box 3399, Smithers, BC V0J 2N0
Airport Smithers **Accommodations** On premises **Operation** Outfitter, lodge
Fish Trout, steelhead **Season** March-November **Type of Fishing** Fly, spin
Water Babine River and Lake, Kwinageese, Nass Rivers **Specialty** Fly fishing
Boats River sleds, bass boats **Tackle Supplied** Troll, fly **Aircraft** Floatplane
Rates day: $100 week: $499
Guide's Notes: Babine Lake is 136 miles long and is open to all types of fishing. The river system is for fly fishing. Our upper Nass River Steelhead Camp is steelhead only.

WICKWIRE, BOB-SILVER HILTON STEELHEAD LODGE (707) 542-4242
Address C/O Fishing International, P.O. Box 2132, Santa Rosa, CA 95405
Airport Smithers **Accommodations** On premises
Operation Outfitter, lodge **Fish** Steelhead **Season** August-October
Specialty Fly fishing and light tackle spin fishing for steelhead
Boats River sleds **Aircraft** Helicopter **Water** Babine River
Experience 25 years **Rates** week: $2050/person U.S. funds
Guide's Notes: Bob Wickwire's new Silver Hilton Steelhead Lodge has recently opened up a new and previously unfished section of the fabled Babine River. Boasting superb accommodations and the finest equipment available, including three 22 foot jet sleds, the new lodge offers the serious steelheader the opportunity of a lifetime: wild, fresh run trophy Babine River steelhead in excess of twenty five pounds.

These are the sea run trout that have made angling history on one of the most challenging and magnificent streams in the world. Long prized as one of the truly great strains of British Columbia steelhead, these wild Skeena fish glow with all the colors of their truly remarkable rainbow heritage. Females are sleek and bright, glowing in the river's light and will go to twenty pounds. The immense bucks are powerful steelhead that exhibit the deep slash of rainbow along their heavily muscled flanks and a rich peppering of dark rainbow along a light olive back. These are steelhead of awesome proportions and it is always the males that break the records.

The section of the river we fish is untouched by the outside world. Access is by helicopter only. Each week ten anglers have exclusive privileges to over fifteen miles of private quality fly fishing water as well as many productive runs for the lure fisherman.

SULLIVAN BAY, BRITISH COLUMBIA

MURRAY, CRAIG-NIMMO BAY RESORT (604) 956-4000
Address C/O Sullivan Bay P.O., Sullivan Bay, BC V0N 3H0
Airport Sullivan Bay **Accommodations** On premises
Operation Outfitter, lodge **Type of Fishing** All
Fish Steelhead, chinook, coho, cutthroat **Season** December-October
Water Mainland inlets of coast **Tackle Supplied** Fly, spin, troll
Specialty Heli-fishing **Aircraft** Helicopters **Boats** Outboards
Experience 5 years **Rates** day: $300-700
Guide's Notes: Fishing Calendar

Fish	Available	Method
Winter Steelhead	Dec - May	Spin, drift
Summer Steelhead	July 15 - Oct	Spin, fly
Chinook Salmon	May - July	Spin, troll
Coho Salmon	July 15 - Sept 30	Spin, fly, troll
Cutthroat trout	Mar 1 - June 30	Spin, fly
Dolly Varden	May - Sept	Spin, fly
Pink Salmon	July - Sept 15	Spin, fly

Author's Notes: Nimmo Bay Resort was featured on ESPN's fishing show, "The Fishing Hole." I have not been there personally, but I was very impressed with the operation from the television coverage.

TELKWA, BRITISH COLUMBIA

SCHADRECH, COLLIN-RIVERS WEST TOURS (604)846-5336
Address P.O. Box 250, Telkwa, BC V0J 2X0
Airport Smithers 8m **Accommodations** On premises
Operation Outfitter, lodge **Type of Fishing** Fly
Fish Steelhead, rainbow **Season** Aug-Nov/May-June
Water Bulkley, Morice Rivers, Kispiox Area
Specialty Steelhead fishing with dry fly **Boats** McKenzies
Experience 6 years **Rates** week: $1200-1600/person U.S. funds
Guide's Notes: For more than 15 years we have fished the fabulous Skeena River system. The fabled rivers of this region are the Bulkley, Babine, Kispiox and the Morice. All four offer excellent fishing, but the Bulkley is the crowning jewel, for on the Bulkley the "dry fly" reigns supreme.

Bulkley River

All the record steelhead come from the Skeena river system. A quirk of nature has these fish stay much longer than normal (up to two years) in fresh water. This in turn has the returning adults much larger in size than any other steelhead system in the world.

The Bulkley River has the largest run of summer steelhead and the most stable water flow in the Skeena drainage and in British Columbia. Also it has the most favourable water temperature from the beginning to the end of the season of all major steelhead rivers, and could well be the reason why the Bulkley River steelhead have the unique characteristic to actively take dry flies.

In keeping with its many pluses, the Bulkley has a very moderate flow gradient that makes for easy wading. It is easily one of the great rivers of the world by virtue of the incredible array of fishable holding water at nearly all river levels. The steelhead in this system range in size from 20 to 40 inches, the average is 30 inches or 11-1/2 pounds. Each year our guests hook fish of over 30 pounds on dries.

The Bulkley and Dry Flies

The traditional method of steelhead fishing dictated that only occasionally could you take steelhead on the surface or with a dry fly. However, the Bulkley River steelhead willingly take dry flies with reckless abandon.

It was only by accident that we stumbled on this unique characteristic of the Bulkley steelhead. We use the word stumbled almost literally for we find most of the fish in less than three feet of water and often less than 30 feet from the shore.

The traditional method of steelheading with standard shooting heads restricted fishing to only the deepest pools and runs. Experimenting, we used sink tip lines and standard wet flies and found that most fish took the fly when still on the surface. Naturally we thought if these fish took so readily on the surface why not use a dry line. The results with the dry line and wet flies were even more productive, why not use dry flies?

In 1978, the great fly experiment began, and by the end of that season the prototype of the "Bulkley Mouse" was born. The following two seasons we fished the Bulkley River almost exclusively with the "Mouse", with unprecedented results. By 1980 we found we could bring steelhead to the surface from any depth of water throughout our entire fall season.

During these experimental years non-believers of the dry fly method fished with sink tips and standard shooting heads with insignificant catches as compared with those using dry flies.

Since 1980 the "Bulkley Mouse" has been fished on all of British Columbia's major summer steelhead rivers with only sporadic success except on the Bulkley River. There is no other river that can offer you the dry fly steelhead fishing experience the Bulkley can.

It is a unique and exciting experience to take a steelhead on a dry fly. In our three month season last fall our guests hooked over 1,431 steelhead on dry flies. Rivers West Tours would like to share this classic steelhead opportunity with you.

The angler will generally average 14 fish a week hooked on the dry fly, approximately 1 fish a day on the beach. However, the highly skilled fly fisherman can do much better than this depending on conditions. Fish range from 3 to 30 pounds

Author's Notes: Huge steelhead on the dry fly is one of the most exciting types of fishing there is. This is Collin's specialty, and he is located in the premier area of the world for it.

TERRACE, BRITISH COLUMBIA

DOLL, STAN (604) 635-4686
Address 5131 McConnell Ave., Terrace, BC V8G 4W9
Airport Terrace **Accommodations** Terrace
Operation Guide **Type of Fishing** All **Boats** River sleds, raft
Fish Steelhead, chinook, coho, cutthroat **Season** Year-round
Water Skeena, Kalum, Copper, Kitimat Rivers
Specialty Fishing with a jet sled **Tackle Supplied** Spin, baitcast
Experience 6 years **Rates** day: $200 week: $1400 1/2 day: $150

JUDZENTIS, GORDON-WATER WITCH EXCURSIONS
(604) 638-8476, 635-5583
Address 3643 Cottonwood Crescent, Terrace, BC V8G 5C8
Airport Terrace **Accommodations** On premises
Operation Outfitter, lodge **Type of Fishing** Fly, baitcast
Fish Chinook, slamon, steelhead, coho **Season** April-December
Water Skeena, Kwinimass, Ecstall Rivers, Work Channel
Specialty River fishing **Aircraft** Floatplane
Boats River sleds **Tackle Supplied** Spin, baitcast, troll
Experience 5 years **Rates** day: $400 week: $1050

OWEN, BRYAN-BIGFISH COUNTRY GUIDES (604) 638-0462
Address P.O. Box 684, Terrace, BC V8G 4B8
Airport Terrace **Accommodations** Terrace
Fish Steelhead, chinook, coho, trout **Season** Year-round
Water Skeena, Copper, Kitimat, Kalum Rivers **Operation** Outfitter
Specialty Drift Boat-Jet boat river fishing **Type of Fishing** All
Boats River sleds, McKenzies, raft **Tackle Supplied** Baitcast, fly
Experience 5 years **Rates** day: $400 week: $2800 U.S. funds
Guide's Notes: Fishing Calendar

Fish	Available
Steelhead	Year-round
Salmon (river)	May - Oct
Salmon (ocean)	Year-round

The Skeena River's run of summer run steelhead is from August to September. This is the largest summer run of steelhead in the world.
Author's Notes: We are told by a reliable source that Bryan owns one of the best operations in the area.

SCHMIDERER, MARTIN-EXCLUSIVE FLY FISHING LTD. (604) 635-9597
Address Box 1093, Terrace, BC V8G 4V1
Airport Terrace **Accommodations** On premises
Operation Outfitter, lodge **Type of Fishing** Fly
Fish Steelhead, king and silver salmon, Dolly Varden **Season** March-August
Water Skeena system and 11 coastal streams **Tackle Supplied** Fly
Specialty Fly fishing for steelhead with dry flys, catch and release only
Aircraft Floatplane, helicopter **Boats** River sleds, rafts
Experience 10 years **Rates** week: $1800 U.S. funds
Author's Notes: Martin has an excellent reputation, and his operation is recognized as one of the best for the serious fly fisherman.

WILLIAMS LAKE, BRITISH COLUMBIA

SCHREIBER, KAY-JENS-LINGFIELD CREEK RANCH
Address Box 4264, Williams Lake, BC V2G 2V3
Airport Williams Lake **Accommodations** On premises
Operation Guide, ranch, tackle shop **Type of Fishing** Spin, troll
Fish Trout, Dolly Varden, steelhead, salmon **Season** May-October
Water Chilko Lake and River, Tsuniah Lake, Atnarko River
Boats Rowboats, canoes, 18ft lund, sailboat **Tackle Supplied** Spin, troll
Experience 10 years **Rates** day: $100 week: $600 1/2 day: $60

DYE, JAMES "JIM"-DYMON CHARTERS (604) 392-7210, 392-7600
Address 1136 Latin Avenue, Williams Lake, BC V2G 2J9
Airport Williams Lake **Accommodations** On premises
Operation Guide, charter captain, lodge **Type of Fishing** All
Fish Rainbow, lake, char, Dolly Varden **Season** April-November
Water Quesnel Lake **Specialty** Lake trolling **Tackle Supplied** All
Experience 17 years **Rates** day: $350 1/2 day: $175

Manitoba

BISSETT, MANITOBA

GRAPENTINE, BYRON O.L-BISSET OUTFITTERS (204) 277-5262
Address Lot 5, Antonio Road, Bissett, Manitoba R0E 0J0
Airport Winnipeg 150m **Accommodations** Bissett

MANITOBA

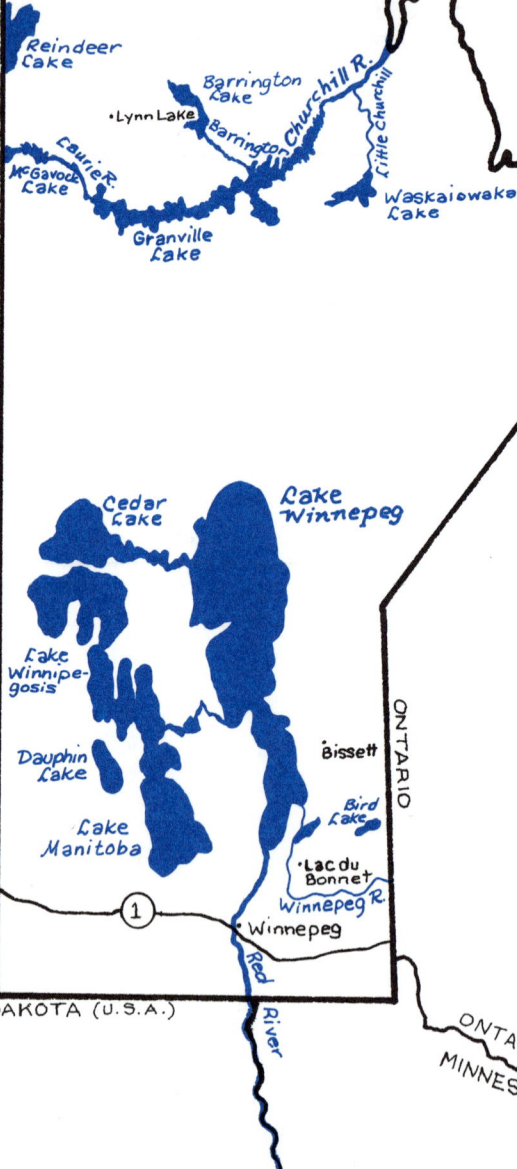

NORTHWEST TERRITORY

MANITOBA

~ Hudson Bay ~

Reindeer Lake

Barrington Lake

Churchill R.

•Lynn Lake

Barrington

Little Churchill

Laurie R.

McGavock Lake

Waskaiowaka Lake

Granville Lake

SASKATCHEWAN

Cedar Lake

Lake Winnepeg

Lake Winnipe-gosis

ONTARIO

Dauphin Lake

•Bissett

Bird Lake

Lake Manitoba

•Lac du Bonnet

Winnepeg R.

①

•Winnepeg

NORTH DAKOTA (U.S.A.)

Red River

ONTARIO

MINNESOTA (U.S.A.)

Operation Outfitter **Type of Fishing** Spin, baitcast, troll
Fish Walleye, northern pike, trout, catfish **Season** Year-round
Water Various lakes of the Bissett area **Boats** Rowboats, canoes
Specialty Lake fishing within 100 miles of Bissett **Aircraft** Floatplane
Experience 10 years **Rates** Please phone or write
Guide's Notes: We specialize in small untouched lakes where no lodges are set up. We use a small 185 Cessna aircraft for flying in and out of the small lakes. The hooks most used are jigs and spinner combinations. The fish caught are walleye, northern, trout and catfish.

LAC DU BONNET, MANITOBA

GUENTHER, BLAINE-NOPIMING LODGE (204) 884-9275
Address Box 723, Lac du Bonnet, Manitoba R0E 1A0
Airport Winnipeg 115m **Accommodations** On premises
Operation Guide, lodge **Type of Fishing** Spin, baitcast, troll **Season** Year-round
Water Bird, Oasis, Tulabi, Elbow Lakes **Fish** Walleye, northern, sm bass
Specialty Lake fishing-Bird for walleye, Oasis for northern
Boats Rowboats with motors, canoes, bass boat
Experience 3 years **Rates** day: $75 week $325 1/2 day: $45

LYNN LAKE, MANITOBA

MERZ, JACK-LAURIE RIVER LODGE 1-800-426-2533 or
THOMPSON, MANITOBA MOBILE YJ5-3606
Address McGavock Lake, P.O. Box 550, Lynn Lake, Manitoba R0B 0W0
Airport Lynn Lake 30m **Accommodations** On premises **Operation** Guide, lodge
Fish Walleye, northern pike, whitefish, lake trout, grayling **Season** June-Sept
Water McGavock Lake, Laurie River System **Type of Fishing** All
Specialty Lake fishing through river chains **Aircraft** Floatplane
Boats Rowboats, 18' lunds with motors **Tackle Supplied** Spin, baitcast, troll
Experience 15 years **Rates** week: $1595/person US funds
Guide's Notes: We have excellent fishing for trophy walleye, northern pike, lake trout, and Arctic grayling. Much of the fishing is done out of the front door of our 4 star rated lodge on McGavock Lake, which is located 30 miles southwest of Lynn Lake, Manitoba. We also offer fly-outs to other nearby lakes and streams which offer daily fishing in total solitude. We are particularly happy to say our trophy northern pike fishing has been preserved by emphasizing a catch and release policy over the past several years. All types of fishing are available, including spin casting, fly fishing, and trolling. Fly fishermen can catch trophy northern pike on streamers and will find outstanding Arctic grayling fishing on dry flies.
Author's Notes: *Homer Circle, Fishing Editor of SPORTS AFIELD tells me: "Laurie River Lodge is an excellent buy for each dollar spent per man hour of fishing and fish caught. The fishing is for walleye, lake trout, and northern pike."*

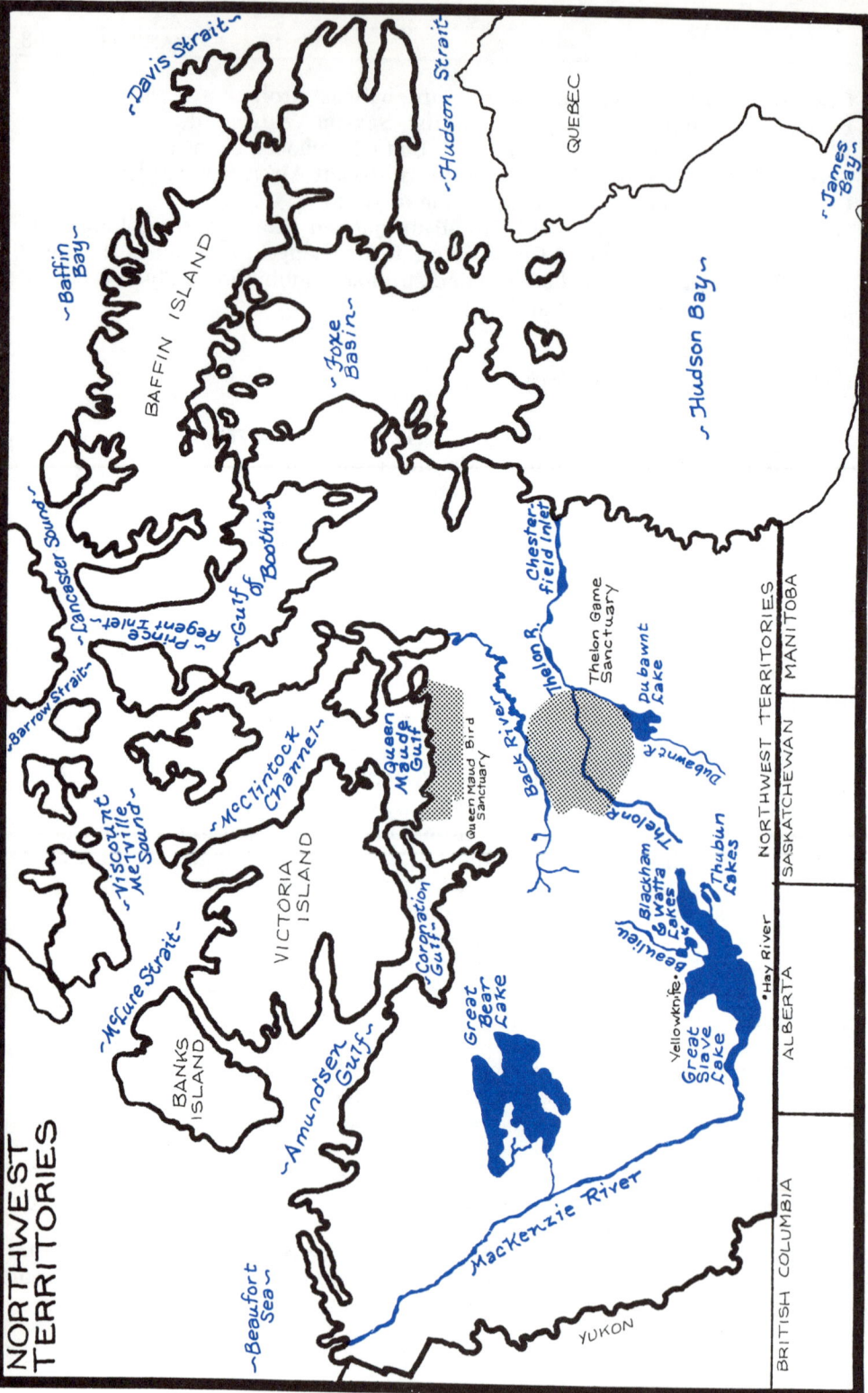

NORTHWEST TERRITORIES

BANKS ISLAND

VICTORIA ISLAND

BAFFIN ISLAND

QUEBEC

Davis Strait

Baffin Bay

Hudson Strait

James Bay

Hudson Bay

Foxe Basin

Lancaster Sound

Prince Regent Inlet

Gulf of Boothia

Barrow Strait

Viscount Melville Sound

McClintock Channel

Chesterfield Inlet

Back River

Thelon R.

Thelon Game Sanctuary

Dubawnt Lake

Dubawnt R.

Thelon R.

Queen Maude Gulf

Queen Maud Bird Sanctuary

McClure Strait

Amundsen Gulf

Coronation Gulf

Great Bear Lake

Beaufort Sea

MacKenzie River

YUKON

BRITISH COLUMBIA

ALBERTA

SASKATCHEWAN

MANITOBA

NORTHWEST TERRITORIES

Hay River

Yellowknife

Great Slave Lake

Blackham & Watta Lakes

Beaulieu

Thubun Lakes

Northwest Territories

BAFFIN ISLAND, NORTHWEST TERRITORIES

FABER, JOHN-CLEARWATER FISHING CAMP (519) 759-0880
Address Faber Travel Ltd., Lynden Park Mall, 84 Lynden Rd,
Brantford, Ontario N3R 6B8
Airport Pangnirtling 90m **Accommodations** On premises
Operation Outfitter **Type of Fishing** Fly, spin, troll
Fish Arctic char **Season** July-Aug **Boats** Outboards
Water Clearwater Fjord, Baffin Island **Specialty** Still fishing and trolling
Experience 2 years **Rates** week: $3000/person Canadian funds

GREAT BEAR LAKE, NORTHWEST TERRITORIES

BAUER, R.A.-GREAT BEAR LODGE (605) 336-2008
Address 707 East 41st St., Suite 124, Sioux Falls, SD 57105
Airport Yellowknife 300m **Accommodations** On premises
Operation Lodge **Type of Fishing** All **Season** July-Aug
Fish Lake trout, Arctic grayling, northern pike, Arctic char
Water Great Bear Lake **Aircraft** Floatplanes
Rates week: $1895/person
Guide's Notes: Great Bear Lake Our lodge is located on Great Bear Lake in the
Northwest Territories of Canada. Our season runs July and August. Types of
fish are lake trout, Arctic grayling, northern pike and Arctic char. The lake
trout run up to 40 pounds. We have superb grayling fishing for fish that run 2
to 4 pounds.

DOLINSKY, ERNIE & MAVIS-BRANSONS LODGE (403) 962-6363
Address P.O. Box 2600, Spruce Grove, Alberta T0E 2C0
Airport Spruce Grove **Accommodations** On premises
Operation Outfitter, lodge, tackle shop **Type of Fishing** All
Fish Lake trout, Arctic char, Arctic grayling, pike **Season** July-Aug
Water Great Bear Lake, NWT and Arctic drainage rivers and ocean
Specialty All forms of fishing-predominantly spinning (trolling & casting) & fly
Boats Outboard **Tackle Supplied** All
Experience 12 years **Rates** week: $2000/person
Guide's Notes: Great Bear Lake We are a fly-in fishing lodge near the Arctic
Circle, Northwest Territories, offering trophy lake trout, char and grayling fish-
ing. Our season is July and August only. The trips include food, accommoda-
tions, and a 10 hour/day guide service with two fishers per boat.

HAY RIVER, NORTHWEST TERRITORIES

WEBB, JACK & BONNIE-THUBUN LAKE LODGE (403) 874-6416, 874-2950
Address Box 480, Hay River, NWT X0E 0R0
Airport Edmonton, Alberta **Accommodations** On premises
Operation Outfitter, lodge **Season** June-Sept **Tackle Supplied** Fly, baitcast, troll
Fish Lake trout, northern pike, pickerel, whitefish **Type of Fishing** All
Water North, South, and Middle Thubun Lakes, La Perriere Lake
Specialty Lake trolling, spin casting, or fly fishing **Boats** 14 ft & 16 ft Lunds
Experience 2 years **Rates** day: $95/person week: $1820/person-Canadian funds

YELLOWKNIFE, NORTHWEST TERRITORIES

BRICKER, JERRY-FRONTIER FISHING LODGE (403) 433-4914, 370-3501
Address P.O. Box 4550, Edmonton, Alberta T6E 5G4
Airport Yellowknife 115m **Accommodations** On premises
Operation Outfitter, lodge **Type of Fishing** Fly, spin, troll
Fish Lake, grayling, northern, white **Season** June-Sept **Boats** Outboards
Water Great Slave, Stark Lakes, Stark, Snowdrift Rivers **Tackle Supplied** All
Experience 25 years **Rates** week: $1740/person U.S. funds
Guide's Notes: Lake Trout The surface-fighting "Lakers" of the Territories are similar by scientific definition to the lake trout of southern Canada, but that is where the similarity ends. Their behavior on the end of a line must be experienced to be believed. Veteran anglers compare their behavior and fighting qualities with that of the brook trout. This applies particularly to the lake trout in the 10-pound and under class. Lake trout are found all through the lake and run up to our 59 pound record. It is common to catch 30 to 40 pounders.

Arctic Grayling are found in the Stark River, a few hundred yards from the lodge, and average between 1 and 2 pounds although they have been caught up to 5 pounds. They will take wet or dry flies and some types of metal lures.

Northern Pike The angling interest in big "northerns" in the Precambrian Lakes of the provinces has been somewhat overshadowed by the abundance and fighting qualities of the lake trout. However, there are plenty of targets for the avowed pike fisherman in the lake which run between five and fifteen pounds, and fish in the 25-30 pound class have been caught. Try them with a streamer.

Whitefish For those wanting a change, a fly or jig will do the trick. The world record (12 lbs, 9 oz.) was caught in front of our lodge during 1972.

Fishing Tackle Flexible trolling rod, 6 or 7 feet long. Your favorite casting rod and 6 to 35 pound test line. Heavy duty snaps and swivels. Spoons such as all size Dardevles, Half Waves, William's Wobblers. Spinning outfit, with small Dardevles, small spoons or spinners, such as Mepps. The trout hit savagely and show a preference for red-on-white, silver, copper, gold or yellow. For the ultimate, a spinning or casting reel with 6 to 8 pound test line is ideal all round sporting gear. Bring a fly rod with a wide assortment of dry flies, and light leaders for grayling. Recommended flies include the Par Bell, Black Gnat, Silver Doctor, Grey and Brown Hackles and light and dark Cahills on a number 10 or 12 hook. When the fish are feeding on larvae, nymphs are particularly effective.

Many of our guests are also fishing northern and lakers on fly rods for the ultimate in sport.

Author's Notes: Below is a quote describing the fishing here by Ken Schultz, Associate Fishing Editor, FIELD AND STREAM:

"I was surprised and impressed to find such fabulous grayling fishing in the Stark River, so close to the lodge, and a delight on ultralight spinning tackle or fly rods. The lake trout of Great Slave, of course, were large, plentiful, and hard-fighting. Top this off with beautiful surroundings, superb shore lunches, and warm, hospitable accommodations and you have a first-class experience."

QUICK, YVONNE-ARCTIC FISHING LODGES & OUTFITTERS
(403) 873-4036, 873-3626
Address Box 806, Yellowknife, NWT X1A 2N6
Airport Yellowknife **Accommodations** Yellowknife
Operation Outfitter, lodge **Type of Fishing** Fly, spin, troll
Fish Lake trout, Arctic grayling, northern pike, whitefish **Season** May-Sept.
Water Great Slave Lake, Watta Lake, Buckham Lake, Beaulieu River
Specialty Lake trolling, fly fishing, river and stream fishing
Boats Rowboats, canoes, raft **Tackle Supplied** Fly, spin, troll
Experience 10 years **Rates** day: $185/person week: $1275/person U.S. funds
Guide's Notes: Our main lodge on **Watta Lake** is located in the rugged unspoiled beauty of Canada's Northwest Territories. Isolated and accessible only by air, it gives one the feeling of being in another world. Watta Lodge has exclusive rights to all of the lake, to ensure privacy and the best of undisturbed fishing.

Buckham Lake - just 5 miles east of the main lodge, offers great lake trout fishing for the adventurous fisherman. Boats, motors, guides, and if you decide to stay over, a small tent camp fully equipped is at your disposal.

Beaulieu River provides shallows where the mighty, great northern pike lie waiting for you to cast your line in their direction, and have the time of your life. On the south of the lake where the Beaulieu heads for Great Slave Lake, are rapids where Arctic grayling are plentiful and have been caught up to 4 pounds in size.

FAESS, THOMAS H.-EAST WIND ARCTIC TOURS & OUTFITTERS
(403) 874-2170
Address P.O. Box 2728, Yellowknife, NWT X1A 2R1
Airport Yellowknife **Accommodations** On premises
Operation Outfitter, lodge **Type of Fishing** All **Season** June-Sept
Fish Lake trout, Arctic grayling, northern pike, Arctic char
Water Thelon, Dubawnt, Back Systems **Boats** Canoes, rafts, outboards
Specialty Lake trolling for trout, fly fishing for grayling **Tackle Supplied** All
Experience 21 years **Rates** week: $2200 Canadian funds
Guide's Notes: Yellowknife Area of Northwest Territories, Canada Exclusive Arctic trophy fishing (small group, high service) in the most remote regions of the Arctic Northwest Territories barren grounds. Based from our main lodge on Lynx Lake, the headwaters of the Thelon River, we sponser trophy fishing expeditions for lake trout, Arctic grayling, northern pike, and Arctic char via quality watercraft (boats, rafts, canoes), fly outs via float aircraft, and overland

hiking on the tundra. All fishing adventures can be combined with wildlife photo safaris in the lodge area, and into the Thelon Game Sanctuary and Queen Maud Gulf Migratory Bird Sanctuary, the two most remote Arctic wildlife refuges in the world. 3 months of open (ice-free) water systems provide excellent shallow water lake trout opportunities throughout the short open season. Fly fishing is excellent all season for Arctic grayling. Fly out trips can be arranged during the run of Arctic char into the sea.

ROBERTSON, GREG-BLUEFISH SERVICES (403) 873-4818 MOBILE JJ3-6808
Address Box 1266, Yellowknife, NWT X1A 2N9
Airport Yellowknife **Accommodations** Yellowknife **Operation** Outfitter
Fish Arctic grayling, lake trout, pike **Season** June-Sept **Type of Fishing** All
Water Great Slave Lake **Specialty** Shore fishing for grayling
Boats Rafts, 19' & 16' outboards **Tackle Supplied** Spin, baitcast
Experience 10 years **Rates** day: $140 week: $800 1/2 day: $80
Guide's Notes: Great Slave Lake For grayling, Mepps and Panther Martin spinners are very effective. June 15 through October 1 is good fishing. The peak is July 15 through August 15. Light spinning gear or fly rods work well.
     Lake trout fishing is good July 1 through August 30. The peak is July 15 through August 15. We use medium weight spinning gear. Large Dardevle lures are effective. It is common to catch 10 pound fish; trophies run to 30 pounds.

Saskatchewan

LA RONGE, SASKATCHEWAN

BRUNANSKI, TRENT-FOSTER LAKE LODGE (306) 233-5489, 425-3176
Address Box 977, La Ronge, Saskatchewan, Canada S0J 1L0
Airport La Ronge 100m **Accommodations** On premises
Operation Outfitter, lodge **Type of Fishing** Fly, spin, troll
Fish Northern pike, lake trout, Arctic grayling **Season** June-Sept.
Water Middle Foster, Lower Foster, Shatwin, Big Sandy Lakes
Specialty Fly fishing, spin, trolling **Boats** 14 ft outboards **Aircraft** Floatplane
Experience 5 years **Rates** varies

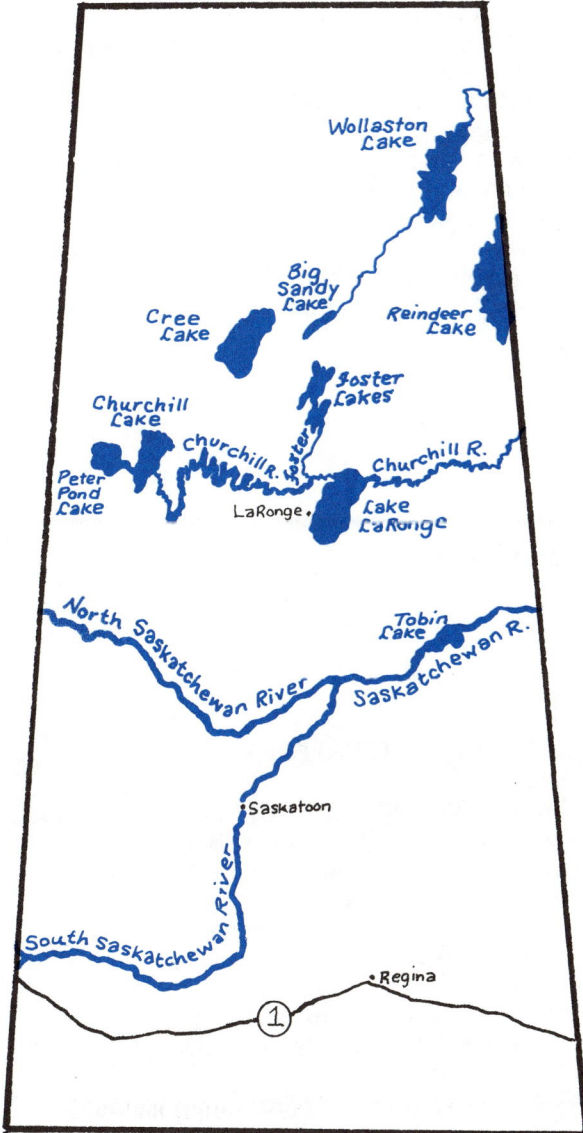

SASKATCHEWAN

Wollaston Lake

Big Sandy Lake

Cree Lake

Reindeer Lake

Foster Lakes

Churchill Lake

Churchill R.

Foster

Churchill R.

Peter Pond Lake

LaRonge

Lake LaRonge

North Saskatchewan River

Tobin Lake

Saskatchewan R.

Saskatoon

South Saskatchewan River

Regina

1

SASKATOON, SASKATCHEWAN

WOLOSHYN, MIKE & LENA-SCOTT LAKE CAMP, LTD (306) 384-8834
Address Box 909, Saskatoon, Saskatchewan, Canada S7K 3M4
Airport Stony Rapids 50m **Accommodations** Stony Rapids 50m
Operation Outfitter **Fish** Lake trout, northern pike **Season** June-Sept.
Water Scott, Premier, Wignes Lakes, area streams **Type of Fishing** All
Specialty Lake trolling and casting **Boats** Outboards **Tackle Supplied** Troll
Experience 12 years **Rates** week: $2800 US funds
Guide's Notes: Scott Lake
　Lake trout--Shallow trolling and some casting in the early part of the season. Trolling as fish go deeper and water continues to warm up. Very deep in August, excellent time for trophy size fish. Spawn in late August to early September, fastest action at spawning time, casting, spinning or trolling. Spoons are best for trolling. Spoons or spinners are good for casting.
　Northern Pike--Found in weedy, shallow bays and sometimes along rocky shorelines. Good action all season wherever found.

Yukon Territory

DESTRUCTION BAY, YUKON TERRITORY

McBRIDE, HOWARD & YVONNE-KLUANE LAKE TOURS (403) 841-4411
Address Destruction Bay, Yukon Territory Y0B 1H0
Airport Whitehorse 167m **Accommodations** Destruction Bay
Operation Outfitter **Type of Fishing** Fly, spin, troll
Fish Lake trout, grayling, northern pike **Season** June-Sept.
Water Kluane, Aishihik, Sekulmun, Stevens Lakes
Specialty Lake trolling, fly fishing, spin casting
Boats Raft, 18 ft aluminum **Tackle Supplied** Fly, spin, troll
Experience 27 years **Rates** day: $140 1/2 day: $85

RODTKA, WAYNE-KLUANE LAKE TOURS (403) 841-4411
Address General Delivery, Destruction Bay, Yukon Territory Y0B IH0
Airport Whitehorse 167m **Accommodations** Destruction Bay
Operation Outfitter **Type of Fishing** Fly, spin, troll
Fish Lake trout, grayling, northern pike, rainbow **Season** June-Sept.
Water Kluane, Aishihik, Sekulmun, Stevens Lakes

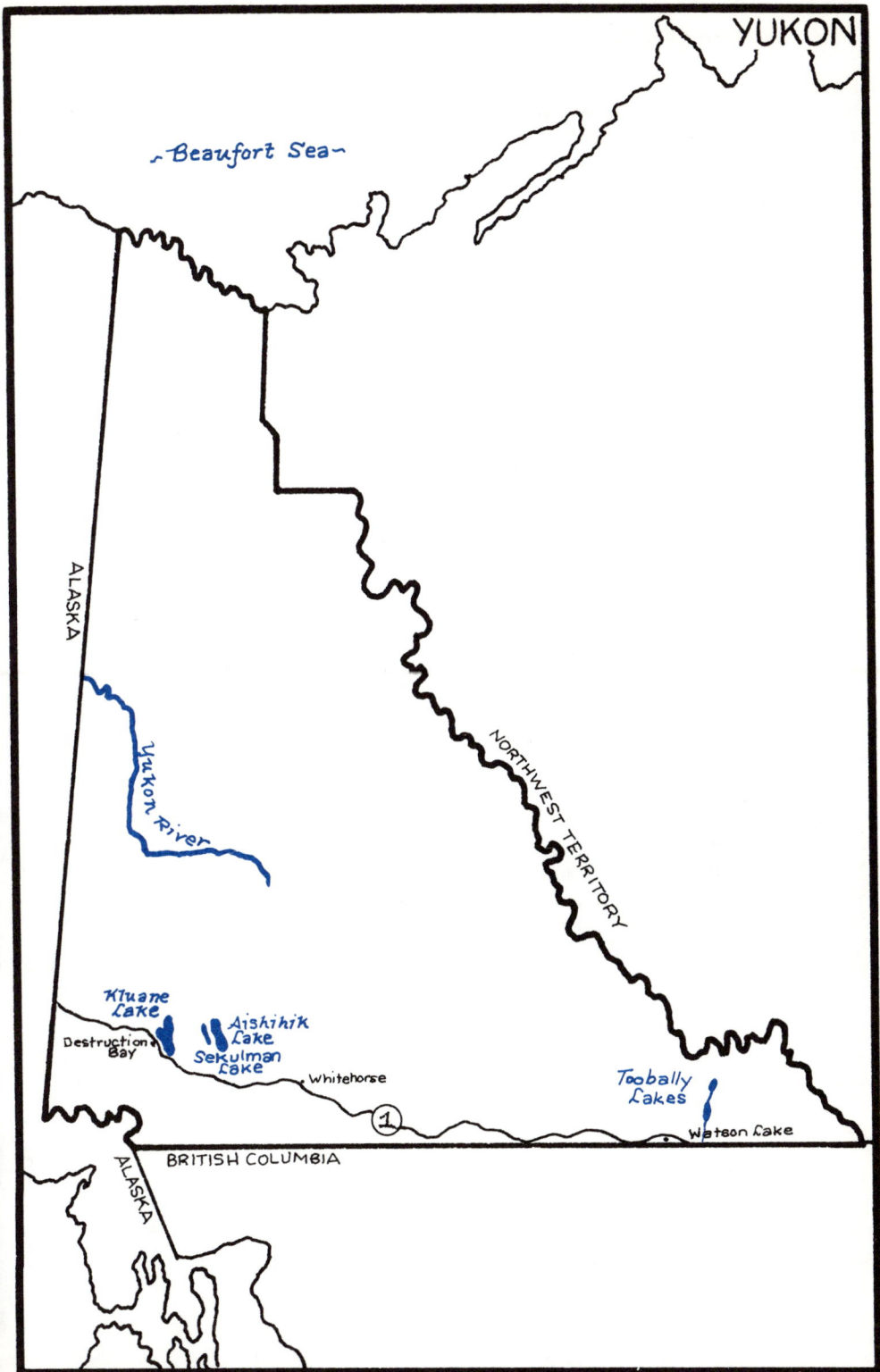

YUKON

~Beaufort Sea~

ALASKA

Yukon River

NORTHWEST TERRITORY

Kluane Lake

Destruction Bay

Aishihik Lake

Sekulman Lake

Whitehorse

Toobally Lakes

Watson Lake

(1)

BRITISH COLUMBIA

ALASKA

Specialty Lake trolling, spin casting, fly fishing
Boats Raft, 18ft aluminum **Tackle Supplied** Fly, spin, troll
Experience 2 years **Rates** day: $140 1/2 day: $85 Canadian funds
Guide's Notes: Fishing packages offer our fishermen some of the Yukon's finest sport and trophy fishing either by trolling or fly fishing. We fish for lake trout, northern pike weighing up to 40 pounds and Arctic grayling from 1 to 4 pounds, with side trips for rainbow trout. We also catch Dolly Varden, kokanee and salmon (in season) in the south and southwestern Yukon, including Kluane National Park.

WATSON LAKE, YUKON TERRITORY

SCHNIG, LARRY & MAGGIE-TOOBALLY LAKES FISHING CAMPS (604) 774-2876, (403) 536-2231
Address 5624 Alpine Road, Fort Nelson, BC VOC 1R0
Airport Watson Lake 7m **Accommodations** Watson Lake 7m
Operation Outfitter, lodge **Type of Fishing** Fly, spin, troll
Fish Lake trout, northern pike, Arctic grayling, Dolly Varden **Season** Jan-Mar
Specialty Fly fishing for grayling and whitefish, trophy lake trout trolling
Boats Rowboats, river sleds, canoes, 16 ft aluminum
Tackle Supplied Fly, spin, troll **Water** Toobally Lakes
Experience 18 years **Rates** day: $350 week: $1050 US funds

WHITEHORSE, YUKON TERRITORY

PEACOCK, JOHN E.-PEACOCK'S YUKON CAMPS (403) 667-2846
Address 77 Alsek Rd S., Whitehorse, Yukon Territory Y1A 3K5
Airport Whitehorse **Accommodations** Whitehorse **Operation** Outfitter
Fish Lake trout, northern pike, Arctic grayling **Season** June-September
Water Claire, Ken, 10 mile, Lyn Lakes **Aircraft** Floatplane
Specialty Lake trolling for trout, casting for northern & grayling
Boats 14 ft Aluminum **Tackle Supplied** Spin, troll **Type of Fishing** All
Experience 10 years **Rates** week: $600 Canadian funds

12. Eastern Canada: Atlantic salmon & brookies!

New Brunswick, Newfoundland/Labrador, Nova Scotia, Ontario, Prince Edward Island, Quebec

From Ontario's western border to the town of St. Johns, Newfoundland, eastern Canada spans almost 2000 miles. Most of the land, with the exception of the Maritime Provinces, sits on the Canadian Shield, a plateau scraped clean by recurrent glaciers. When the glaciers retreated, they left this barren, rocky land littered with hundreds of thousands of lakes; five of these, known as the Great Lakes, constitute one sixth of the fresh water in the world. These myriad lakes, along with their connecting streams, are eastern Canada's claim to fishing fame.

Ontario, westernmost of these six provinces, is Canada's "Great Lakes State," with an incredible 4,700 miles of freshwater coastline along its international border. A generation ago these waters, devastated by pollution, over-fishing, and the lamprey eel, were nearly devoid of sport fish. Today, pollution control and other measures have greatly improved this situation. Increased numbers of salmon and steelhead now run up several Ontario rivers, providing extensive light tackle opportunities.

Although thousands of smaller lakes dot the Ontario landscape, the largest number of guides in this directory are based in the Boundary Waters region; they guide fishing on Lake of the Woods, Lac Seul, Marmion Lake, and Lake Superior. Species found here are lake trout, walleye, northern pike, and smallmouth bass; there is also some excellent muskie fishing near the U.S. border.

Northern Ontario, stretching over 600 miles from Lake Superior to Hudson Bay, is a huge, roadless wilderness. Most transportation is by floatplane, so fishing can be fair to excellent, depending on how many visitors an individual lake or stream has received. The Attawapiskat and Albany rivers, which drain into James Bay, were cited by guides for their excellent speckled (brook) trout fishing. Other good streams in northern Ontario include the Winisk, Severn, and Black Duck rivers. Lakes in this area provide lots of northerns and pickerel.

Quebec, eastern Canada's largest province, hosts a variety of fishing possibilities. Its 600,000 square miles contain over a million lakes and countless miles of streams. The population is concentrated in a narrow band along the southern border, so most of Quebec's vast northern expanse is still wilderness.

The brook trout is to Quebec what the largemouth bass is to Florida. Found in thousands of clear, cool streams and lakes throughout the province, it signifies high-quality sport to the light tackle angler. This beautiful fish, actually a member of the char family, grows to record size in the headwaters of Quebec's interior streams. Many guides fish for brook trout in the Lake Mistassini region near Chibougamau. The lake itself contains big trout; guides report that they can be caught on dry flies during the month of June. The Toceque and Cheno rivers, tributaries on the north end of the lake, receive excellent spawning runs from mid-August to mid-September. The Broadback River, which rises in this region, is one of the best brook trout streams in the world. Brookies from four to seven pounds are taken every week; some even larger are caught each year.

The Arctic char in Quebec's far northern streams provide excellent light tackle sport, particularly during the late summer and early fall when large numbers of bright fish arrive from the sea daily. Native Inuit operate a fish camp on the Tunulik River, which empties into Ungava Bay near Fort Chimo. Fresh run char on this stream average five to twenty pounds, and fishing is outstanding during the months of July and August. Fishing on the Tunulik is restricted to flies and lures.

The Atlantic salmon, largely vanished from the northeastern U.S., is still Quebec's most revered game fish. It spawns on rivers of the Gaspé Peninsula, such as the storied Grand Cascapedia, York, Bonaventure, and Matapédia. However, no responses were received from guide operations on these streams, the primary reason being that most of the fishing rights are privately held. The only Quebec salmon guides who responded are on the George River, which flows into Ungava Bay not far from the Tunulik, and on the St. Paul near Blanc Sablon. St. Paul salmon average six to eight pounds, but can run up to twenty.

North of Blanc Sablon lies the mainland portion of Newfoundland called Labrador. This is a wild, sparsely populated land covered with evergreen forests, except in the far northern peninsula, where tundra prevails. It is one of the best fishing areas in eastern Canada; here, as in Quebec, fishing is for trophy brook trout, salmon, and Arctic char. Some of the best Atlantic salmon rivers in the world are located here.

The three most famous are the Hunt, the Adlatok, and the Eagle, which all rise in the western mountains and flow through dense evergreen forests to the Atlantic. According to Labrador guides, the salmon which run these rivers are larger and contain fewer grilse than those in most other Canadian streams.

The Umiakovik River, three hundred miles north of Goose Bay, flows into the Labrador Sea through the craggy peaks and rocky fiords of the North Coast. It boasts one of the finest Arctic char runs on the Atlantic. I have never caught an Arctic char, but the owners of a fish camp on the Umiakovik say that a fresh run char fights as hard as a bright salmon. Apart from its fighting qualities, the Arctic char is symbolic of the far north. Its beauty, its delicate flesh, and the unspoiled surroundings it has chosen for a home make it a worthy prize for the venturesome angler.

Labrador's trackless interior is famous for some of the finest brook trout fishing in all the world. The Minipi River and Eagle River watersheds are two of the best places to seek large brookies. Fish from the Eagle average a respectable two to three pounds—fish from the Minipi average an amazing four pounds! Both of these rivers also hold numerous fish in the seven to eight pound range.

Fish camps on all of these Labrador rivers are reached by charter plane from Goose Bay. Accommodations and guide services vary greatly all across eastern Canada, so you should carefully review all information you obtain, and talk to someone who has been to the camp you are considering.

The island of Newfoundland, off the southeast coast of Labrador, offers more salmon and brook trout opportunities. This is a more populous area, so the fishing may not be quite as good, although streams are much more accessible. It is possible for a business traveler to take a day or two off from a visit to Gander and try his luck.

Prince Edward Island, smallest of the Canadian provinces, lies in the Gulf of St. Lawrence between New Brunswick and Nova Scotia. It is less than 175 miles long and only about thirty miles wide, but three of its rivers—the West, the Morell, and the Dunk—offer sea run brook trout and an occasional salmon. The brookies run up to six pounds and can be caught wading with flies and lures.

Nova Scotia is one of Canada's most picturesque provinces. Grassy green hills and forested mountains slope down to the blue Atlantic; the colorful old port towns and harbors date to the 1700s. Nova Scotia, about 375 miles long and 100 miles wide, lies southeast from the coast of New Brunswick, to which it is connected by a narrow strip of land less than twenty miles wide. The major airports are at Halifax and Sydney. The fishing on Nova Scotia is for Atlantic salmon and seatrout (sea-run brook trout). Guides here name the Margaree and the Medway as their favorite rivers; fishing is best in late spring and early fall for both salmon and seatrout. Also, guided fishing for stripers and smallmouth bass begins in May, and good fishing continues through the summer months.

New Brunswick, largest of the Maritime Provinces, offers some of the best Atlantic salmon fishing in Canada. Of the six guide operations which responded to our questionnaire, four are located on the world-famous Miramichi River. The Miramichi and other New Brunswick salmon rivers were put under strict catch and release regulations in 1984. This change, along with the prohibition of commercial netting in the river mouths, has already increased the number of returning salmon. 1985 was the best year since 1970; at the time of this writing, this trend seems to be continuing.

Two other very good Atlantic salmon rivers are represented by fish camps listed in this book. The Restigouche, in northern New Brunswick, and the Tobique, a tributary to the St. John, have also experienced increases in salmon runs in recent years due to new conservation measures. The airport most convenient to the Miramichi and Tobique rivers is at Fredericton; the best air connection for the Restigouche is Charlo. From these towns, rental cars and good paved roads can bring anglers to the fishing.

New Brunswick

BLACKVILLE, NEW BRUNSWICK

WADE, HERB-WADE'S FISHING LODGE (506) 472-6454
Address 143 Main St., Fredricton, New Brunswick
Airport Fredericton 70m **Accommodations** On premises **Tackle Supplied** Fly
Operation Lodge **Type of Fishing** Fly **Water** Main Southwest Miramichi River
Fish Atlantic salmon **Season** Apr 15-May 15, June 15-Sept 30
Experience 40 years **Specialty** Fly fishing only **Boats** Canoes, outboards
Rates day: $245/person Canadian funds, includes guide, food, lodging
Guide's Notes: Main Southwest Miramichi River From July 1 to September
30, there are always fish in the river. Standard salmon fly patterns are effective.
Author's Notes: Experienced fishermen from this area tell me Herb runs an
outstanding lodge.

DOAKTOWN, NEW BRUNSWICK

GASTON, FLOYD-MIRAMICHI SALMON CLUB (506) 365-2289
Address Doaktown, New Brunswick, E0C 1G0
Airport Fredericton 60m **Accommodations** On premises
Operation Lodge, outfitter **Type of Fishing** Fly
Fish Atlantic salmon, trout **Season** April 15 - Sept 30
Water Miramichi River **Specialty** Fly fishing only **Boats** Canoes
Experience 20 years **Rates** day $165/person Canadian funds, includes meals,
lodge, guide. 3 day minimum
Guide's Notes: Miramichi River We have two seasons for salmon. The first is
from April 15 to May 15 for spring salmon which are fish that have spawned
and are on their way back to the ocean. The regular season is from July through
September. Anglers can keep grilse up to about five pounds. All adult salmon
must be released.
Author's Notes: Reliable contacts tell us this is an excellent operation.

MILLS, ALEX-OLD RIVER LODGE (506) 365-7568
Address RR #2, Doaktown, New Brunswick, E0C 1G0
Airport Fredericton 70m **Accommodations** On premises
Operation Outfitter, lodge **Type of Fishing** Fly
Fish Atlantic salmon, sea run brook trout **Season** April 15-May 15, June-Oct 1
Water Main Southwest Miramichi River and tributaries
Specialty Fly fishing only **Boats** 20 ft Canoes **Experience** 10 years
Rates day: $206/person Canadian funds, includes food, guide, lodging

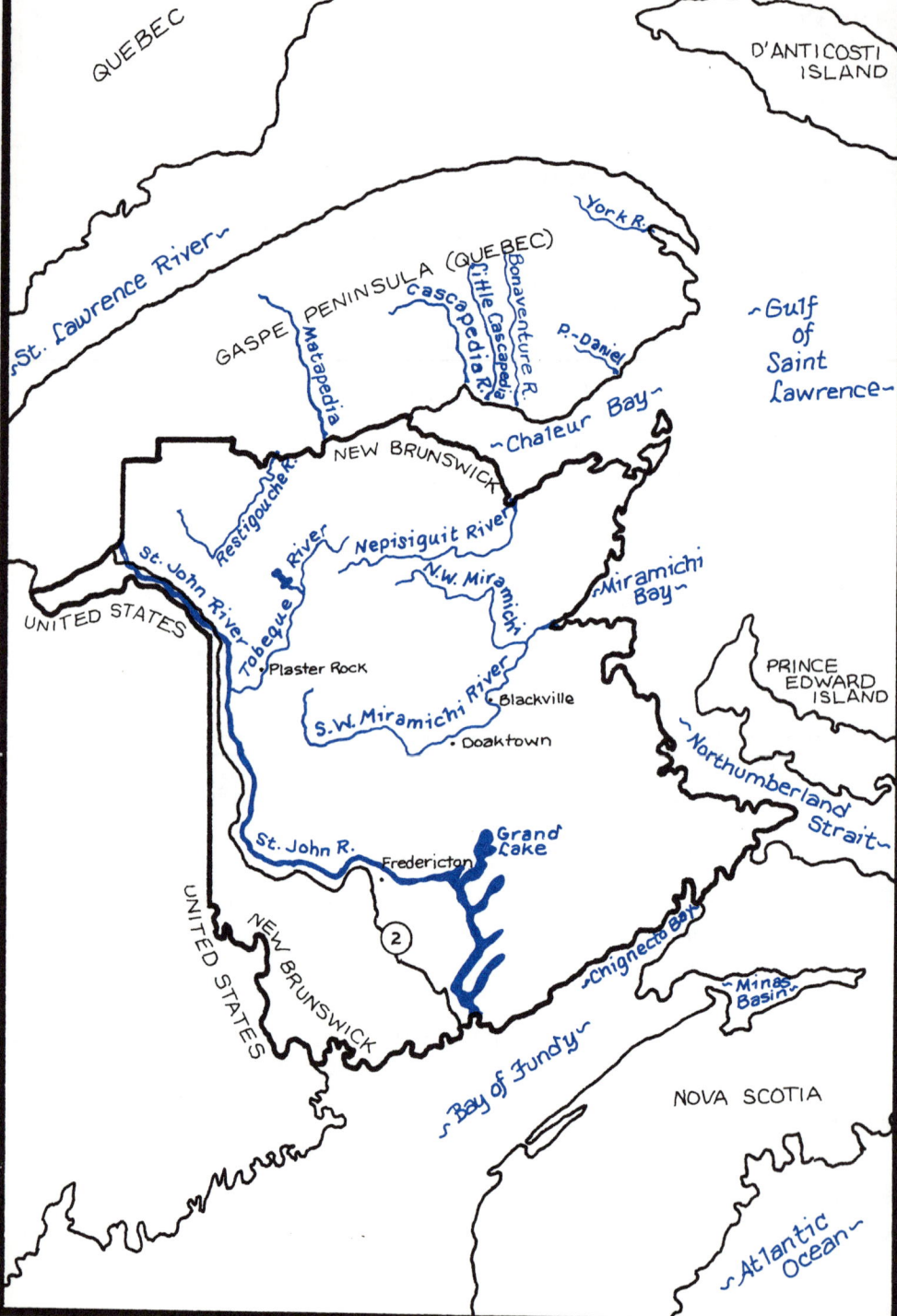

NEW BRUNSWICK

QUEBEC

D'ANTICOSTI ISLAND

St. Lawrence River

York R.

GASPE PENINSULA (QUEBEC)

Matapedia

Cascapedia R.

Little Cascapedia

Bonaventure R.

P.-Daniel

Gulf of Saint Lawrence

NEW BRUNSWICK

Chaleur Bay

Restigouche R.

Nepisiguit River

Tobeque River

N.W. Miramichi

Miramichi Bay

St. John River

UNITED STATES

Plaster Rock

S.W. Miramichi River

Blackville

Doaktown

PRINCE EDWARD ISLAND

Northumberland Strait

St. John R.

Fredericton

Grand Lake

2

UNITED STATES

NEW BRUNSWICK

Chignecto Bay

Minas Basin

Bay of Fundy

NOVA SCOTIA

Atlantic Ocean

Guide's Notes: The Miramichi River has tremendous variety and includes everything from wilderness runs to "big" river fishing. In the past four years the commercial netting has been stopped and a catch and release policy has been instated for salmon over 25 inches. 1985 was the best year since 1970. We feel the fishing will continue to improve.

Author's Notes: This is another excellent salmon lodge. The owner, Alex Mills, is President of the New Brunswick Guides and Outfitters Association. He tells me the most popular fly patterns on the Miramichi are hair wings.

McNAMEE, NEW BRUNSWICK

WILSON, KEITH-WILSON'S SPORTING CAMPS LTD. (506) 365-7962
Address McNamee, New Brunswick, E0C 1P0
Airport Fredericton 80m **Accommodations** On premises
Operation Lodge, outfitter **Type of Fishing** Fly
Fish Atlantic salmon, sea run brook trout **Season** April 15 - Oct 15
Water Main Southwest Miramichi River, Cains River
Experience 5 years **Specialty** Fly fishing only **Boats** Canoes, outboards
Rates day: $180 Canadian funds, includes food, lodging, guide
Author's Notes: Wilson's Sporting Camps have been owned and operated by the same family for over sixty years. It has an excellent reputation as one of the best camps in the area.

PLASTER ROCK, NEW BRUNSWICK

KING, ALLISON & HELEN-LITTLE BALD PEAK LODGE (506) 356-2354
Address RR #1, Plaster Rock, New Brunswick E0J 1W0
Airport Fredericton 170m **Accommodations** On premises
Operation Lodge **Type of Fishing** Fly **Boats** 22 ft canoes
Fish Atlantic salmon **Season** July 1 - Sept 15 **Tackle Supplied** Fly
Experience 10 years **Water** Tobique River **Specialty** Fly fishing only
Rates day: $165/person U.S. funds, includes food, lodging, guide service
Guide's Notes: The Tobique River is a tributary to the Saint John River. The season opens July 1 and there are generally good numbers of salmon in the river by July 15. We always know exactly how many fish have entered the river because all the Tobique salmon are netted and trucked around barrier dams on the lower part of the system. A very accurate count is made during this transfer. We fish about fifty miles of the river which is all public. Our lodge is limited to nine guests so it is never crowded on the river. Because of the new conservation measures, we are seeing substantial increases in our salmon runs and we are optimistic this trend will continue.

Author's Notes: Allison and Helen run a very fine operation. It has been highly recommended by a number of contacts.

TIDEHEAD, NEW BRUNSWICK

**PINKHAM, VIRGINIA-PINKHAM'S FISHING LODGE
(207) 435-6954, (506) 753-3644**
Address P.O. Box M, Ashland, ME 04732, or Group 3 Box 6,
Tidehead, New Brunswick E0K 1K0
Airport Charlo 20m **Accommodations** On premises **Season** June-Sept
Operation Guide, lodge **Type of Fishing** Fly **Fish** Atlantic salmon
Water Restigouche River **Boats** 26 ft canoes with motors
Specialty Fishing for salmon **Tackle Supplied** Fly
Experience 20 years **Rates** day: $350 3 days: $1050
Guide's Notes: Restigouche River The largest salmon run is in June. During
early July, the arriving fish are a mix between adult salmon and grilse. In late
July and August most of our fishing is for grilse. We have four and a half miles
of private water.
Author's Notes: *This operation is rated excellent by our contacts.*

Newfoundland/Labrador

GANDER, NEWFOUNDLAND

BENNETT, BILL-GANDER AVIATION LIMITED (709) 256-3421
Address P.O. Box 250, Gander, Newfoundland A1V 1W6
Airport Gander **Accommodations** Gander
Operation Outfitter **Type of Fishing** Fly **Tackle Supplied** Fly, spin
Fish Atlantic salmon, speckled trout, Arctic char **Season** June-Sept.
Water Michael's, Sandhill Rivers, Newfoundland, Sitdown Pond
Specialty Fly fishing **Aircraft** Floatplanes **Boats** Canoes
Experience 25 years **Rates** week: $1800 Canadian funds
Guide's Notes: Prime time for Atlantic Salmon is July 15 to August 20. Prime
times for Arctic char and speckled trout are June 25 through August 10.

GOOSE BAY, LABRADOR

HOUSE, CLYDE-HUNT RIVER CAMPS LTD. (709) 896-8049
Address P.O.Box 307, Stn A, Goose Bay, Labrador A0P 1S0
Airport Goose Bay **Accommodations** Goose Bay
Operation Outfitter, lodge **Type.of Fishing** Fly, spin, troll

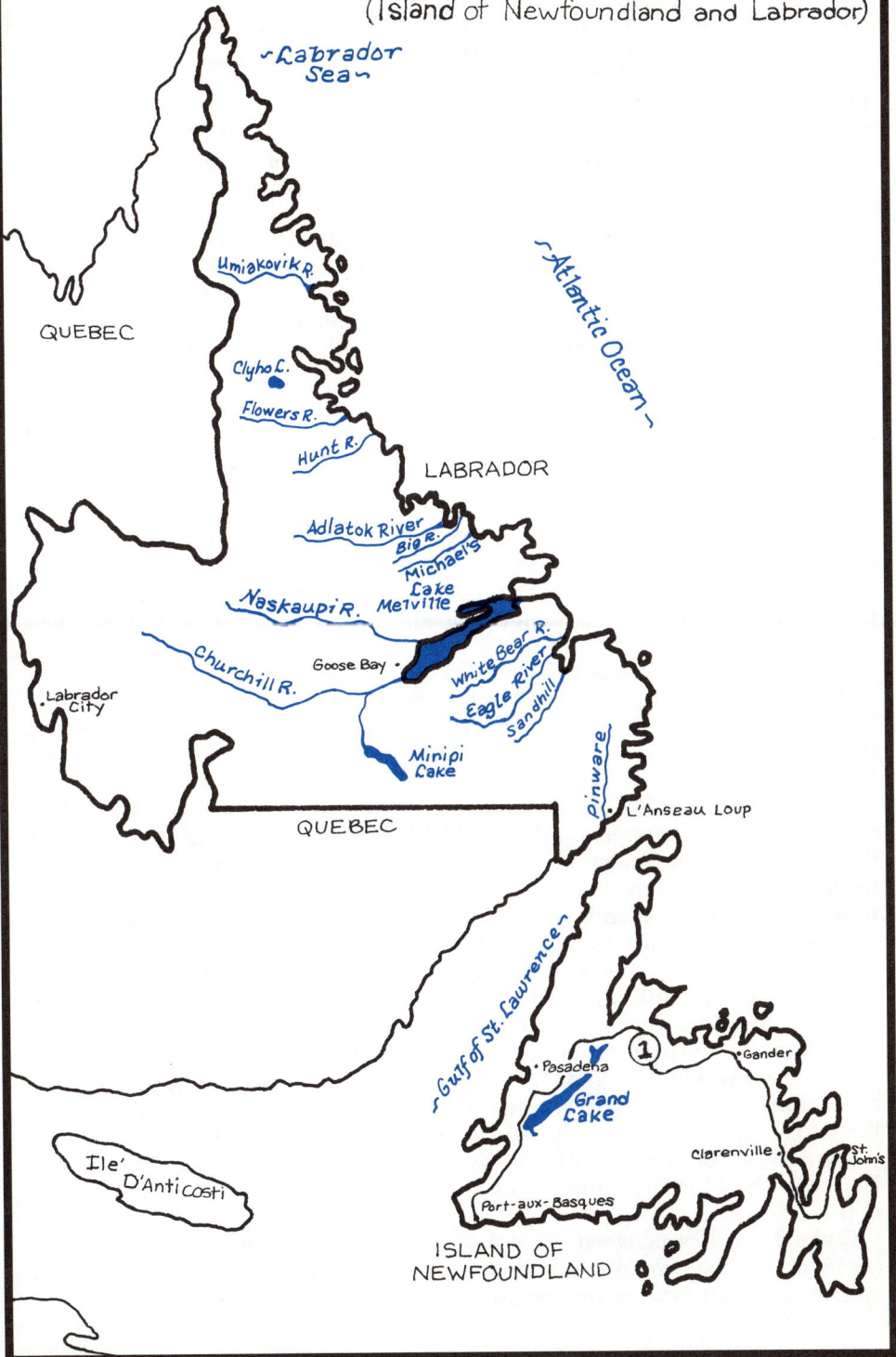

NEWFOUNDLAND
(Island of Newfoundland and Labrador)

Labrador Sea

Atlantic Ocean

QUEBEC

Umiakovik R.

Clyho L.

Flowers R.

Hunt R.

LABRADOR

Adlatok River
Big R.

Michael's Lake
Lake Melville

Naskaupi R.

Churchill R.

Goose Bay

White Bear R.

Eagle River

Sandhill

Labrador City

Minipi Lake

QUEBEC

Pinware

L'Anseau Loup

Gulf of St. Lawrence

Pasadena

1

Gander

Grand Lake

Clarenville

St. John's

Ile' D'Anticosti

Port-aux-Basques

ISLAND OF NEWFOUNDLAND

Fish Salmon, trout, char, pike **Season** March-November
Water Eagle, Hunt Rivers, Clyho, Nipisish Lake
Specialty Fly fishing **Aircraft** Floatplanes, helicopters
Boats River boats **Tackle Supplied** Fly, spin
Experience 20 years **Rates** week: $1600-2100/person U.S. funds
Guide's Notes: Hunt River Camps LTD. operates one Salmon Lodge on the
Hunt River, one Speckled Trout Lodge on the Eagle River and one Char Lodge
at Clyho Lake.

The **Hunt River** One of the most northerly salmon rivers of Labrador, the
Hunt flows near the 56th parallel, entering the ocean near Hopedale, 150 miles
north of Goose Bay. Compared to other salmon streams, it is a medium size
river already known for its large fish. Salmon commonly run around 10 or 12
pounds and may exceed 20 pounds on occasion. Large salmon dominate the
catch and very few grilse are taken.

Rock-filled with frequent gravel bars, the Hunt is the type of stream which
can produce consistently good fishing throughout its length. Most water can
be fished by wading although boats are available for travel and fishing wherever
required. Most of the fishing takes place on a series of pools that mark the
upper part of the river, only a five-minute boat ride from camp. Here you can
wade, fish from a boat or stand on a convenient rock. A well-marked portage
trail along the river bank will take you to the "Big Falls". From there, the central
section of the river, consisting of a five mile series of pools and rapids, is
covered by boat. Along with salmon, you will run into some real good wilderness
fishing for speckled trout and Arctic char.

The best wet flies for the Hunt are Black Dose, Black Doctor, Silver Tip (black
and green), Green Highlander, Blue Charm and Silver Grey. Dry flies: Wulffs
(white and grey), Royal Coachman, Brown Fairy and Irresistible. Size of flies
depends on water conditions and may vary from #4 through 10, with #6 and
8 generally used.

Park Lake is just 64 miles southeast of Goose Bay, in the shadow of the
towering Mealy Mountains, at the Head Waters of the mighty Eagle River, where
the clear mountain waters from melting snow and ice flow into countless
tributaries and streams, that make up the main watershed for the Eagle. Here
in abundance, the lakes and rivers are teeming with spectacular speckled trout.

Park Lake is the most popular and has the best speckled trout fishing in all
of Newfoundland and Labrador. The speckles here are running up to 6 pounds
and over. Northern pike up to 15 pounds are common, and 15-20 pound salmon
frequent the pools from August through September.

The size of dry fly used is in the range of #10 through 16 and of the high
floating variety which includes all the Wulff patterns, very notably the Irresistible and many of the classic dry trout flies. In wet flies, streamers and nymphs,
the size range is most generally #6 through 12, but the variety of patterns used
with success is endless. Over the years, the most consistently successful pattern
has been the Muddler Minnow or similarly tied patterns with the head of
clipped deer hair.

Clyho Lake lies between 55 and 56 degrees North, approximately in the
centre of the vast Labrador wilderness, where there are still thousands of lakes
and streams that have never been fished because of their inaccessibility.

The lake is approximately 5 miles long and is fed by three rock-studded streams that are winding down between the mountains from numerous unseen lakes, which are fed by glacier-like melting ice and snow left over from a long cold winter. The main char fishing stream is located on the south shore of the lake, approximately four miles from the outlet. Directly across the lake is a second stream where there is also excellent char fishing. At the outlet, the river winds its way through dozens of pools as it flows to the ocean just 3 miles away.

SHANNON, G.W. "JERRY"-KLUB KAVISILIK (613) 623-2659
Address P.O. Box 104 RR1, Arnprior, Ontario K7S 3G7
Airport Goose Bay 170m **Accommodations** On premises
Operation Outfitter, lodge **Type of Fishing** Fly, spin
Fish Salmon, char, brook, ouananiche **Season** June-Sept
Water Flowers R., lakes and rivers of Labrador area **Boats** Rowboats, canoes
Specialty Fly fishing **Aircraft** Floatplane **Tackle Supplied** Spin, fly
Experience 18 years **Rates** day: $300/person week: $2260/person Canadian funds

HAPPY VALLEY, LABRADOR

COOPER, JACK E.-MINIPI CAMPS (709) 896-2891, 896-3024
Address P.O. Box 340, Stn B, Happy Valley, Labrador A0P 1E0
Airport Goose Bay 55m **Accommodations** Goose Bay 55m **Season** June-Oct
Operation Outfitter, lodge, tackle shop **Type of Fishing** Fly, troll
Fish Brook trout, Arctic char, northern pike **Tackle Supplied** Fly
Water Anne Marie, Minonipu, Minipi Lakes **Aircraft** Helicopter
Specialty Fly fishing, canoe trips, survival expeditions **Boats** Canoes, outboards
Experience 17 years **Rates** week: $2000 - 4000/2 people 1 guide, week: $1600 - 2600/person 1 guide U.S. funds
Guide's Notes: The large **Minipi River** (approximately 30 miles in length) flowing from the western end of Minipi Lake itself, offers terrific action for brook trout in the 1/2 to 5 pound class. One hundred brookies or more per person per day is not uncommon.

Northern Pike--Attaining proportions as large as 30 pounds, this is a ferocious game fish made for great sport, especially when taken on dry fly. Eighteen pounders have been landed in the Anne Marie watershed, and the Minipi itself yields monsters from the "Alligator Swamp" in the 25-30 pound plus class.

Arctic Char, while in the system, are taken sporadically, and tend to remain mysterious and elusive.
Author's Notes: *Local sources tell us that Jack Cooper runs some of the best fishing camps in Eastern Canada.*

MICHELIN, REGINALD F.-LABRADOR WILDERNESS EXPEDITIONS (709) 896-8605
Address 6 Paddor Road, Happy Valley-Goose Bay, Labrador A0P 1E0
Airport Goose Bay 3m **Accommodations** Goose Bay
Operation Outfitter, lodge **Type of Fishing** Fly, spin

Fish Salmon, char, trout, pike **Season** Year-round **Boats** Canoes, aluminum boats
Water Double Mer Lake, Lake Melville, Smallwood Reservoir, Grand Lake
Specialty Fly fishing float trips and lake trolling **Tackle Supplied** Fly, spin, troll
Experience 13 years **Rates** day: $300

HAPPY VALLEY, NEWFOUNDLAND

PAOR, PETER & ALMA-GOOSE BAY OUTFITTERS, LTD
(709) 896-2423, 753-0550
Address Box 171, Happy Valley, Labrador, Newfoundland A0P 1E0
Airport Goose Bay 800m **Accommodations** Happy Valley 1m
Operation Outfitter **Type of Fishing** Fly **Water** Eagle River
Fish Salmon, trout **Season** June-Sept **Boats** Motor boats
Specialty Fly fishing **Aircraft** Helicopters
Experience 17 years **Rates** week: $2300/person (Salmon camps), $1500/person
(Trout camps) Canadian funds
Guide's Notes: We have 5 lodges and camps.

Lower Eagle River Salmon Lodge is located directly at picturesque Eagle Falls, the loveliest spot on the river. The number of Atlantic salmon comprising the Eagle River's average salmon run is of course unknown, but using figures supplied by Canada's Department of Fisheries, we may conclude that the run is tremendous. The Eagle River is one of a half dozen or so of the very great salmon rivers of the world. Pratfall Rock Pool, a joy to wade, and year in and year out the best pool on the river, is five minutes from camp.

Historically, the first run of Atlantic salmon appears on the Eagle River a few days either side of July first, though vanguards appear earlier. The fishing holds up well until September 15th, the last day of the fishing season in Labrador.

The fishing for the fine sea-run brook trout which inhabit the lower reaches of the Eagle River is excellent all season long. These fellows average two to three pounds, and provide a splendid opportunity for a mixed bag of two superb gamefish.

The White Bear River is three miles north of and parallel to the Eagle River. It is a fine salmon river in its own right, and many of our anglers leave the Eagle for a day of exploring and fishing on the White Bear. This is a much smaller river than the Eagle, and it is very rarely fished.

Adlatok River Atlantic Salmon Camp Located some 125 miles north of Goose Bay, the Adlatok is one of the two or three rivers which represent the northernmost range of the Atlantic salmon in Labrador. The waters of this river are gin-clear, owing to the rocky terrain which surrounds it and forms the riverbed. On bright days, when the sun is high in the sky, one can stand on the river's high banks and peering down into its crystal depths, gradually identify magnificent Atlantic salmon patiently finning in the current.

Because some of the Adlatok's holding areas are only a few hundred yards above the sea, the salmon caught by anglers fishing from our camp are exceedingly strong, bright fish, many still bearing sea-lice. And for those of you who enjoy fishing with dry flies, these fresh fish will take a floater as readily as any salmon we've seen, particularly those which stop to rest in the smooth-flowing Top Pool.

The Adlatok is a medium-sized salmon river with a good reputation for large fish (they'll average well over ten pounds) and a relatively small percentage of grilse. The salmon run usually begins in mid July and lasts well past the last day of the fishing season which in Labrador is September 15. The Adlatok is an excellent late season river.

Little Minipi Brook Trout Camp Since its discovery in 1966, the fabulous Minipi watershed has been the subject of many articles in the leading outdoor periodicals, and with good reason. Located sixty-five miles southwest of Goose Bay, and accessible only by float-equipped aircraft, the beautiful, wild lakes and rivers of the area are one of a kind in the world, for they harbor a strain of brook trout which, for average size and beauty, is unequalled anywhere. The average brook trout caught by anglers fishing from our lodge is approximately twenty-two inches long and weighs four pounds. Most of our anglers catch at least one trout near six pounds or more, and every year, trout of over 7-1/2 pounds are taken. The largest brook trout taken from our waters weighed 9-1/2 pounds and over the years our waters have produced many trout in this weight range and we know there still are many more. For those of you interested in catching some very large eastern brook trout on flies, we invite you to try our Little Minipi Lodge. We think it's the best there is.

Little Minipi's outlet is a charming medium-sized brook trout stream. Physically, Minipi's outlet resembles some of the fine freestone streams of the northeastern United States. There are smooth, deep slicks, friendly little riffles, and big, swirling pools, all of which have productive moments in the course of a season's angling.

Fly fishing only is a strictly enforced camp rule, and while you may catch as many trout as you wish, you may kill only one trout during your stay at Minipi.

Eagle River Trout Fishing Lodge Our beautifully located lodge lies at the fast-flowing thoroughfare between two small lakes. The fishing is excellent in the rocky, wadable areas directly in front of camp, and of course lake fishing from a boat is available as well.

Our river system forms a considerable portion of the headwaters of the Eagle River. While all of the waters in this watershed are freestone, limestone-like slicks are numerous, and they are a joy to the dry-fly fisherman. Within a short distance of camp, one can fish in virtually any type of water he prefers, from the smoothly-flowing slicks to chuckling riffles and swirling pools in the best tradition of the freestone stream. And best of all, Eagle River waters are filled with big, brawling specimens of salvelinus fontinalis, the beautiful Eastern Brook Trout. The fish at Eagle River average between two and three and a half pounds, with some fish reaching six pounds. The largest fish taken at Eagle River in 1974 weighed 7-1/2 pounds, but fish of this size are not common.

Umiakovik Arctic Char Camp Our newest camp provides top-notch angling for Arctic char at Umiakovik Lake, three hundred miles north of Goose Bay. The rugged beauty of the area surrounding our camps is breathtaking, with craggy, lichen-covered cliffs forming a lovely backdrop to the diamond-clear lake. And of course, the angling in this fjord-like setting is superb. Umiakovik's char are fresh, silvery sea-run fish, and they average right around five pounds in weight. There are a good number of fish over ten and up to fifteen pounds.

We explored northern Labrador quite thoroughly before deciding upon our present location, and we think it is without equal for consistent action and size and quantity of the quarry. The Arctic char, like its smaller cousin, the brook trout, is a very beautiful gamefish, with deep blue or greenish blue back and upper sides, and silver lower sides. Many individuals have a powder-blue tint on the lower sides with small pink spots along the median line. As char approach ripeness during the spawning season, the body coloration changes from silvery through orange to bright red and deep vermillion. On any trip to Umiakovik, you will test your mettle against both red and silver char, and of course this fine gamefish makes a rare and beautiful mount for your trophy room at either stage of developement.

Arctic char are very strong fish, and in fact no less an authority than A. J. McClane has written that in the fresh, sea-run form, they are, pound to pound, every bit as powerful as a grilse (Atlantic salmon). Char are lightning fast swimmers as well, and in a typical battle will leap as many as a half dozen times, taking you well into your backing before turning the first time. And because char are not netted to the extent salmon are, they are present at Umiakovik in great numbers. Both stream fishing and lake fishing are available within a short walk from camp, and there is a guide for each pair of anglers.

Fly fishing for Arctic char is a relatively new sport, and fly designs and equipment are not as standardized as they are in salmon and trout fishing. Apparently, however, brightly dressed flies fished deeply and slowly are attractive to char. The brightly dressed brook trout patterns have done well at Umiakovik, as have imitations of some of the forage fish found there, the sculpin and the smelt among them. Some of the steelhead patterns used on the west coast should be effective as well. Bring a selection of flies that range in size from four through ten. For spin fishing we have found the red and white Dardevle works best. Bring all sizes.

Author's Notes: *Peter has a reputation for running a high quality camp.*

L'ANSE AU LOUP, NEWFOUNDLAND

NORMORE, DENNIS-LUCKY STRIKE LODGE (709) 927-5520, 927-5657
Address P.O. Box 27, L'Anse Au Loup, Labrador, Newfoundland A0K 3L0
Airport Deer Lake 200m **Accommodations** L'anse Au Loup
Operation Guide, lodge **Type of Fishing** Fly **Tackle Supplied** Fly
Fish Atlantic salmon, sea-run trout **Season** June-Aug **Boats** Rowboats
Water Pinware and Forteau Rivers **Specialty** Fly fishing
Experience 15 years **Rates** day: $150 week: $750 U.S. funds

MOUNT PEARL, NEWFOUNDLAND

BURTON, VINCE-LABRADOR SPORTSFISH, LTD (709) 364-1001, 364-6160
Address 11 Markland St., St. John's, Newfoundland A1E 4A8
Airport Goose Bay 500m **Accommodations** On premises

Operation Outfitter, lodge **Type of Fishing** Fly **Season** June-Sept.
Fish Atlantic salmon, Arctic char, speckled trout
Water Eagle River, Flowers River **Boats** River boats **Tackle Supplied** Fly
Specialty Fly fishing **Aircraft** Floatplanes, helicopters
Experience 25 years **Rates** week: $3000-4000 Canadian funds
Guide's Notes: The Flowers River is located 166 miles north of Goose Bay and
runs out into Flowers (James Lane) Bay. It's a very large stream and consists
of sandy bottoms throughout the river. It's a beautiful piece of water and runs
some 50 miles inland from the bay.

Our lodge is located some 15 miles up river. Most of the salmon fishing is
done up and down stream by river boats and by wading the pools. Char fishing
is done right at the lodge and throughout the river.

The river has a high percentage of salmon, up to 18 pounds - many taken
from 7 - 12 pounds. The average size is between 4 and 5 pounds.

Fishing is from July 25 to September 15, fly fishing only for salmon and lure
fishing is permitted for char from the sand bar in the steady and the char pools
in the river. The char are from 2 to 5 pounds.

The Eagle River is one of the longest and most productive streams of central
Labrador. It ranks among the top half dozen great Atlantic salmon rivers of the
world. Gathering itself in its alpine headwaters, this 100 mile plus waterway
drains an extensive watershed as it flows eastward near the 53rd parallel - A
beautiful stream with primeval charm beyond description.

We are located on a fabulous stretch of water located some 15 miles from
the mouth of the river. We fish, when the water is high, with boats but normally
you can wade most pools, even where the water is high. The largest fish caught
last year was 18 pounds. Several were caught between 10-15 pounds. The
average size is between 4-6 pounds.

Fishing customarily begins in mid-July at this lodge and continues into September. There are peak periods, subject to local conditions, as on any other
salmon stream but with such a short season and the legendary heavy run of
salmon, you may expect consistent fishing at any time. It is, of course, fly
fishing only on the Eagle River.

PASADENA, NEWFOUNDLAND

SKINNER, R.W.-BIG RIVER FISHING CAMP (709) 686-2242
Address P.O. Box 250, Pasadena, Newfoundland, A0L 1K0
Airport Deer Lake 11m **Accommodations** On premises
Operation Outfitter, lodge **Specialty** Fly fishing **Water** Big River
Fish Atlantic salmon, sea run speckled, land locked salmon
Experience 26 years **Rates** varies
Guide's Notes: Big River One hundred twenty miles northeast of Goose Bay
Airport, Goose Bay, Labrador and completely inaccessible except by float equip-
ped aircraft is a river known as Big River.

This river drains a very extensive lake system. At White Bear Lake it gathers
up all its tributaries, becomes a large body of water and heads east to the
Atlantic Ocean some forty miles away.

Through a series of very rough rapids it runs through deep gorges extending over some five or six miles. Midway in its journey to the sea, the river hurries off the high country into a wide, heavily forested valley where it breaks into a chain of long deep pools and moderate rapids. The last such rapid occurs about five miles from the sea. Here the river is broken into a number of channels by islands built up over the years by its own effort. It is here on the North Bank overlooking a smooth flowing and spent river we have constructed our lodge.

The Atlantic salmon usually enters this river the second week in July and the last run of fish, the male grilse usually put in an appearance about August 25. The latest date that I have accomodated guests is September 4. On that date five fish were taken the largest being 8 pounds.

The appearance of sea run trout is usually about one week later than the Atlantic salmon and can be taken at will from about July 20 on.

The largest salmon taken to date was 22 pounds and the largest sea run trout is 7-1/2 pounds. The proportion of salmon to grilse is about fifty to fifty.

Rattling Brook which flows into the estuary of Big River is a tremendous piece of trout fishing water but the closeness of the falls to the sea limits the fishing area to one pool with accommodations for two or three rods. Sea run trout and Atlantic salmon accumulate here in enormous numbers.

SHOAL HARBOUR, NEWFOUNDLAND

PLOUGHMAN, GENE-THORBURN AVIATION LIMITED
(709) 466-7823, 466-7046
Address P.O. Box 213, Shoal Harbour, Newfoundland A0C 2L0
Airport Gander 90m **Accommodations** Clarenville 2m
Operation Outfitter **Type of Fishing** All **Boats** Canoes, power boats
Fish Speckled trout, landlocked salmon **Season** May-Sept.
Water Jubilee Lake, Island Pond West, Meelpaeg, Meta Pond
Specialty Trolling and fly fishing **Aircraft** Floatplane
Rates day: $250 week: $1200
Guide's Notes: Fishing is good from May 1st until September 15th. However, bait normally produces better catches during the early spring and summer with fly fishing being popular from July 1st until the season closes on September 15th.

Nova Scotia

ANNAPOLIS, NOVA SCOTIA

GAUTHIER, MARIE & ROBERT-CLEARWATER OUTFITTERS (902) 638-3509
Address RR 2, Annapolis, Nova Scotia B0S 1A0
Airport Yarmouth 100m **Accommodations** On premises
Operation Outfitter, lodge **Type of Fishing** All
Fish Bass, trout **Season** April-November **Boats** Canoes, bass boat
Water Annapolis River, area lakes and streams **Tackle Supplied** All
Specialty Bass and trout fishing (fly, float, troll)
Experience 12 years **Rates** week: $1200 U.S. funds
Guide's Notes: Annapolis River For trout, the peak time is May. For bass and striped bass, the peak starts in April and runs to November. There are spring and fall runs of large bass. Timing varies according to tides, feeding available, etc.

COUNTRY HARBOUR, NOVA SCOTIA

MASON, REID S. (902) 328-2366
Address RR 1 Country Harbour, Guysborough County, Nova Scotia B0H 1J0
Airport Halifax 200m **Accommodations** Sherbrooke 20m
Operation Guide **Type of Fishing** Fly, spin, troll **Boats** River boat
Fish Salmon, trout **Season** May-September **Tackle Supplied** Fly, spin
Water St. Mary's, Country Harbour, Salmon Rivers
Specialty Salmon and trout fly fishing (wading or boat)
Experience 3 years **Rates** day: $125 week: $750 1/2 day: $60
Guide's Notes: St. Mary's River
  May - June is the peak time for large salmon depending on the water level. The smaller salmon (3-5 pounds) peak about the first two weeks in July. The method for fishing the large salmon is from boats or wading, depending on conditions. Grilse or smaller salmon are usually taken by wading. Current regulations require us to release all large salmon. The combined effects of all the conservation measures over the past two years are bringing the salmon back very well.

GLACE BAY, NOVA SCOTIA

OSMOND, EUGENE (902) 849-2805
Address 38 McIntyre Lane, Glace Bay, Nova Scotia B1A 4R9
Airport Sydney 10m **Accommodations** Sydney 10m
Operation Guide **Type of Fishing** All **Boats** Rowboat, river sled

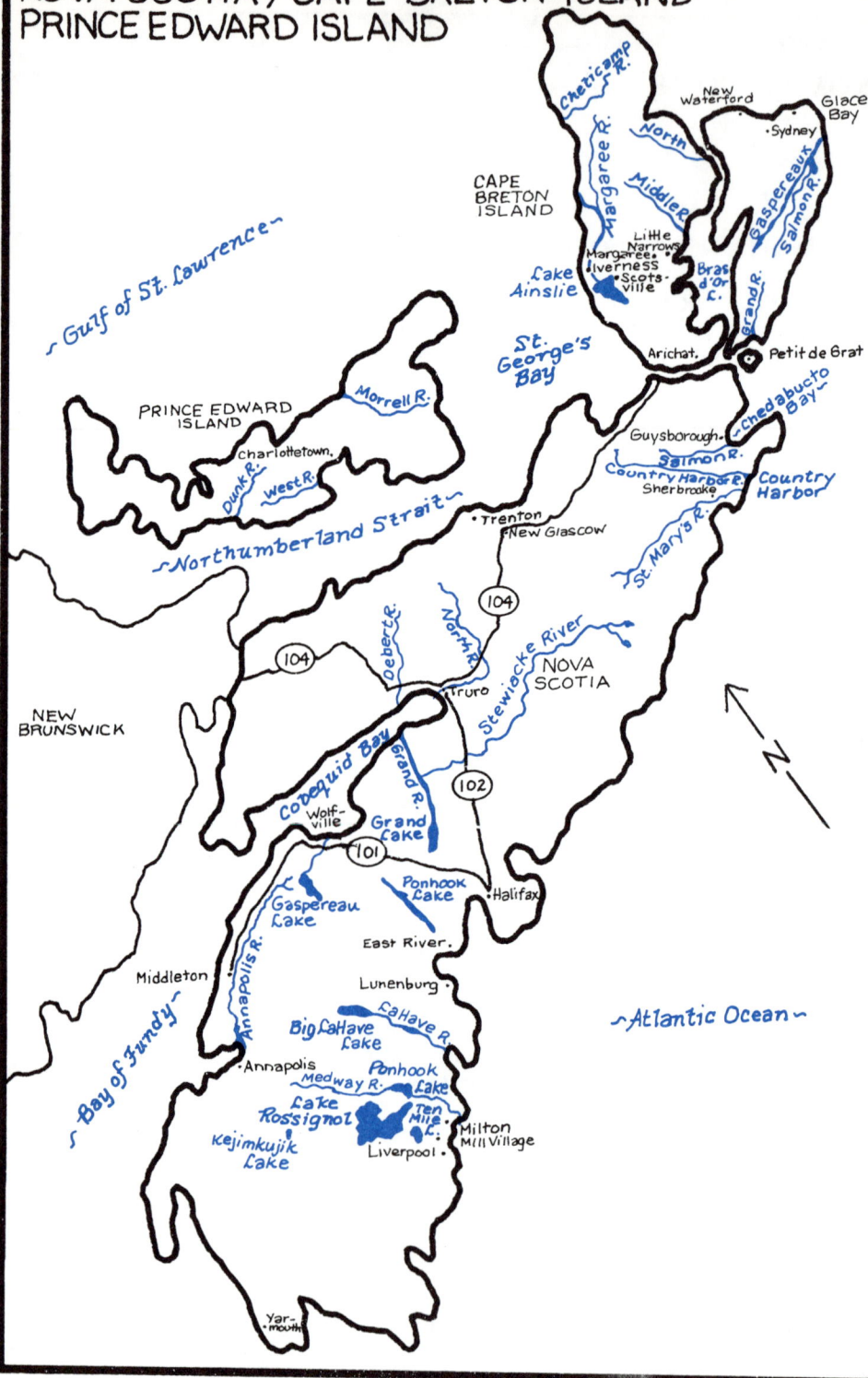

NOVA SCOTIA / CAPE BRETON ISLAND
PRINCE EDWARD ISLAND

CAPE BRETON ISLAND

New Waterford
Glace Bay
Sydney

Cheticamp R.
Margaree R.
North R.
Middle R.

Little Narrows
Margaree
Inverness
Scotsville

Gaspereaux R.
Salmon R.

Lake Ainslie

Bras d'Or L.
Grand R.

Arichat
Petit de Grat

St. George's Bay

Gulf of St. Lawrence

PRINCE EDWARD ISLAND

Morrell R.
Charlottetown
Dunk R.
West R.

Guysborough
Chedabucto Bay
Salmon R.
Country Harbor R.
Sherbrooke
Country Harbor

Trenton
New Glasgow

Northumberland Strait

NOVA SCOTIA

St. Mary's R.

104
Debert R.
North R.
104
Truro
Stewiacke River

NEW BRUNSWICK

Cobequid Bay
Grand R.
Wolfville
Grand Lake
102

101
Gaspereau Lake
Ponhook Lake
Halifax

Annapolis R.
East River

Middleton

Bay of Fundy

Lunenburg

Big LaHave Lake
LaHave R.

Annapolis
Medway R.
Ponhook Lake

Lake Rossignol
Ten Mile L.
Milton
Mill Village
Kejimkujik Lake
Liverpool

Atlantic Ocean

Yarmouth

N

Fish Trout, smelt, mackerel, cod **Season** Year-round **Tackle Supplied** All
Water Bras d'Or Lakes, Red Islands, Soldiers Cove, Framboise L.
Specialty Trout fishing, fly or spin on lakes and streams
Experience 3 years **Rates** day: $180
Guide's Notes: Bras d'Or Lakes Rainbow trout fishing is very good on Bras d'Or Lakes for the months of July, August, and September. The type of bait found to be effective is crawdad which is found in sandy grassy areas along the beach. The means of fishing is to have lines free from lures, spinners, etc., and have one small hook baited with a live crawdad. Catches can vary from 1 to 6 pounds.

HALIFAX, NOVA SCOTIA

CORBETT, GARY NEIL (902) 429-2994, 354-4341
Address Box 1001, Halifax, Nova Scotia B3J 2X1
Airport Halifax **Accommodations** Halifax
Operation Charter captain, outfitter **Fish** Salmon, trout, bass, cod
Water Kejimkujik and Rossignol Lakes **Season** March-August
Specialty Fly fishing, deep sea, lake trolling **Type of Fishing** All
Boats Rowboats, canoes, bass boat, outboards **Tackle Supplied** All
Experience 10 years **Rates** day: $300 1/2 day: $100
Guide's Notes: Trout is best from late April through May 25. Atlantic salmon is best in June. We deep lake fish for landlocked salmon (Grand Lake) and striped bass all summer. Deep sea fishing is best in June. We offer an expensive exclusive service for 2 people maximum on a daily basis. We let you know exactly when to come. We know when the fishing is good.

INVERNESS, NOVA SCOTIA

HERBERT, MAGGIE (902) 258-3320, 258-2096
Address RR#2, North Lake Ainslie, Inverness, Nova Scotia B0E 1N0
Airport Sydney 90m **Accommodations** Scotsville 2m
Operation Guide **Type of Fishing** Fly, spin, troll **Boats** Canoes
Fish Brook, rainbow, salmon **Season** March-Oct **Tackle Supplied** Fly, spin
Water SW Margaree, Middle Rivers, Lake Ainslie
Specialty Small brook fly fishing for wild brook trout
Experience 3 years **Rates** day: $50-60 1/2 day: $30-35
Guide's Notes: SW Margaree River and Lake Ainslie We have wild brook trout up to 15 inches, larger sometimes in Lake Ainslie. Best fishing is May - September. Hexagenia hatch in mid to late July. Sea run brook trout are available from early June to July. Searching patterns include Caddis and Wulff's. Beautiful rural area for family vacations including historic sites, ocean beaches, Salmon River, Cabot Trail nearby - all public water. Bald eagles summer here at Lake Ainslie.

LITTLE NARROWS, NOVA SCOTIA

McCARTY, EDWARD (902) 756-2442
Address Campbell Road, Little Narrows, Nova Scotia B0E 1T0
Airport Sydney 75m **Accommodations** Margaree 1m **Operation** Guide
Fish Atlantic salmon **Season** June-October **Type of Fishing** Fly
Water Margaree River **Specialty** Fly fishing-wading **Tackle Supplied** Fly
Experience 6 years **Rates** day: $70 week: $490 1/2 day: $40
Guide's Notes: Margaree River The fly fishing season for Atlantic salmon on
the Margaree River is June 1 - October 15. July is the peak time for the summer
run and September 15 - October 15 the peak for the fall run.

MAHONE BAY, NOVA SCOTIA

ERNST, WELTON B. (902) 624-8580
Address RR#3 Mahone Bay, Lunenburg County, Nova Scotia B0J 2E0
Airport Halifax 70m **Accommodations** Mahone Bay 12m
Operation Outfitter **Type of Fishing** All
Fish Salmon, trout, bass, whitefish **Season** March-May
Water Lahave River, Lakes Sixty, Mushmusk, Churchs
Specialty Lake trolling **Boats** Rowboats, canoes, rafts
Experience 4 years **Rates** day: $75/family $50/person week: $500 1/2 day: $40

MARGAREE FORKS, NOVA SCOTIA

HALDEMAN, RONALD W.-ATLANTIC SALMON FLY SHOP
(902) 248-2920 June-October, (215) 495-5035 November-May
Address Margaree Forks, Nova Scotia B0E 2A0
Airport Sydney 60m **Accommodations** Margaree Forks
Operation Outfitter, tackle shop **Type of Fishing** Fly
Fish Atlantic salmon **Season** June- October **Water** Margaree River
Specialty Fly fishing for Atlantic salmon **Tackle Supplied** Fly
Experience 7 years **Rates** day: $110 week: $700 1/2 day: $60

MARGAREE VALLEY, NOVA SCOTIA

ROSS, GREG-ATLANTIC SALMON FLY SHOP (902) 248-2728, 248-2920
Address RR #1, Margaree Valley, Nova Scotia B0E 2C0
Airport Sydney 70m **Accommodations** Margaree Valley
Operation Guide **Type of Fishing** Fly **Tackle Supplied** Fly
Fish Atlantic salmon, brook trout **Season** June-October
Water Margaree River **Specialty** Fly fishing
Experience 5 years **Rates** day: $100 week: $700 1/2 day: $50 Canadian funds

MILL VILLAGE, NOVA SCOTIA

CROFT, JOHN F. (902) 677-2406, 354-3453
Address RR #1, Mill Village, Queens County, Nova Scotia B0J 2H0
Airport Halifax 100m **Accommodations** Liverpool 8m
Operation Guide **Type of Fishing** All **Specialty** Fly fishing
Fish Speckled trout, salmon **Season** April-July
Water Medway River and surrounding area
Boats Rowboats, river punts **Tackle Supplied** All
Experience 10 years **Rates** day: $125 week: $600 1/2 day: $100

CONRAD, SCOTT 677-2679
Address RR #1, Mill Village, Queens County, Nova Scotia B0J 2H0
Airport Halifax 90m **Accommodations** Liverpool 8m
Operation Guide **Type of Fishing** All **Boats** Rowboats, canoe
Fish Salmon, trout, kiacks, eels **Season** April-Sept **Specialty** Fly fishing
Water Medway River and surrounding areas **Tackle Supplied** All
Experience 3 years **Rates** day: $150 week: $750 1/2 day: $75

MILTON, NOVA SCOTIA

BREEN, DONALD J.-BEAVER ISLAND LODGE (902) 354-4354
Address 10 Mile Lake, P.O. Box 402, Milton, Queens County, NS B0T 1P0
Airport Halifax 90m **Accommodations** On premises
Operation Outfitter, tackle shop, lodge **Type of Fishing** All
Fish Atlantic salmon, brook, brown **Season** Year-round **Tackle Supplied** All
Water Lakes Rossignol, Ponhook, 10 Mile Molega, Medway River
Specialty Fly, lake and spin fishing **Boats** Canoes, outboards
Experience 28 years **Rates** day: $250 week: $1600
Guide's Notes: Fishing Calendar for Lake Rossignol and Medway River

Fish	Peak Times
Brook Trout	April 15 - June 15 and Sept 15 - Oct 30
Brown Trout	May 15 - July 1 and Sept 15 - Oct 30
Atlantic Salmon	May 25 - July 15 and Sept 15 - Oct 31
Striped Bass	May 15 - Oct 30
Smallmouth Bass	June 15 - Oct 1

NEW WATERFORD, NOVA SCOTIA

DEMETER, GEORGE (902) 862-8978
Address 3168 Sunset Dr., New Waterford, Nova Scotia B1H 1K9
Airport Sydney 14m **Accommodations** New Waterford
Operation Guide **Type of Fishing** All **Fish** Trout, salmon
Season April-October **Water** All lakes of Cape Breton Island
Specialty Off shore salmon fishing
Experience 5 years **Rates** day: $50

PETIT DE GRAT, NOVA SCOTIA

SAMSON, VENARD J. (902) 226-2519
Address Box 43, Petit de Grat, Cape Breton, Nova Scotia B0E 2L0
Airport Sydney 80M **Accommodations** Arichat 5m
Operation Guide, charter captain **Type of Fishing** Spin, baitcast, troll
Fish Trout **Boats** Rowboats, 38 ft Cape Island boat
Water Grand Lake and River, Tillard, Shaw's, and Benoit's Lakes
Specialty Lake trolling **Season** June-November
Experience 8 years **Rates** day: $100 week: $500 1/2 day: $75

SHERBROOKE, NOVA SCOTIA

BEAVER, AUBREY-EASTERN VALLEY OUTFITTERS (902) 522-2283
Address P.O. Box 40, Sherbrooke, Nova Scotia B0J 3C0
Airport Halifax 10m **Accommodations** On premises
Operation Outfitter, lodge **Type of Fishing** All **Fish** Salmon, brook
Water St. Mary's River **Specialty** Fly fishing for Atlantic salmon
Boats Rowboats, river sleds **Tackle Supplied** All
Experience 15 years **Rates** week: $850 U.S. funds
Guide's Notes: St. Mary's River is known for its very large salmon and clearly-defined pools. A superb dry fly stream, the St. Mary's season generally lasts from late May until August. It was these waters that inspired the highly successful MacIntosh dry fly.

Fish	Available	Hatch	Available
Atlantic Salmon	June	May Fly	Mid May
Grisle	Last week in June	Green Drake	Sept
	July & Sept	Caddis	June
Trout	May - June & Sept		

SYDNEY, NOVA SCOTIA

ELWORTHY, LES W.L. (902) 539-8638
Address 1901 George St., Sydney, Nova Scotia B1P 1P5
Airport Sydney **Accommodations** Sydney
Operation Guide **Type of Fishing** All **Specialty** Fly fishing
Fish Salmon, speckled, rainbow, brown **Season** June-October
Water Margaree, Cheticamp, North, Grand Rivers
Experience 10 years **Rates** day: $80 week: $500

TRENTON, NOVA SCOTIA

RANKIN, BILL (902) 752-7710
Address 30 Forge St., Box 308, Trenton, Nova Scotia B0K 1X0
Airport Halifax 100m **Accommodations** New Glasgow 1m

Operation Guide **Type of Fishing** All **Boats** McKenzies
Fish Speckled, rainbow, sea run, brown **Season** July-August
Water Bras d'Or Lakes, Cape Breton River & Streams, Guysborough Lakes,
Margaree River **Specialty** Fly and bait fishing **Tackle Supplied** All
Experience 6 years **Rates** day: $150 week: $700 1/2 day: $100

TRURO, NOVA SCOTIA

SIMMS, DOUGLAS IAN-ATLANTIC ANGLER (902) 893-2991
Address RR #3, Old Courthouse Branch, Truro, Nova Scotia B2N 5B2
Airport Halifax 35m **Accommodations** Truro
Operation Outfitter **Type of Fishing** Fly **Specialty** Fly fishing in streams
Fish Atlantic salmon **Season** October **Tackle Supplied** Fly
Water Stewiacke, Folly, Salmon, Debert Rivers **Boats** Canoes
Experience 15 years **Rates** day: $200 week: $2000
Guide's Notes: Stewiacke River Atlantic Salmon fishing is best in this area the
month of October. Fly fishing only!

System 6 to 8 is recommended for equipment. Current legislation dictates
the releasing of mature salmon so only grilse can be retained. Limit 2 per day,
10 total. Fish run 3-1/2 to 5 pounds.

WOLFVILLE, NOVA SCOTIA

SENEY, RON (902) 542-9595, 542-7711
Address 5 Locust St., Wolfville, Nova Scotia B0P 1X0
Airport Halifax 75m **Accommodations** Wolfville
Operation Outfitter **Type of Fishing** All **Boats** Rowboat
Fish Speckled, striped bass, sea trout, sm bass **Season** Year-round
Water Gaspereau Lake and River, Lake Pleasant Watershed, Sixty Lake
Specialty River fishing (fly or spin) **Tackle Supplied** Fly, spin
Experience 4 years **Rates** day: $75 week: $300 1/2 day: $50
Guide's Notes: Fishing Calendar Gaspereau Lake and River Area

Fish	Season	Lures/Flies
Speckled trout	May - mid July	Victory 190 Spinners
Smallmouth Bass	July - August	#1 Silver Mepps, Dardevles, poppers
Sea trout	May and August	Flies, Victory 290 Spinners
Striped Bass	July - August	

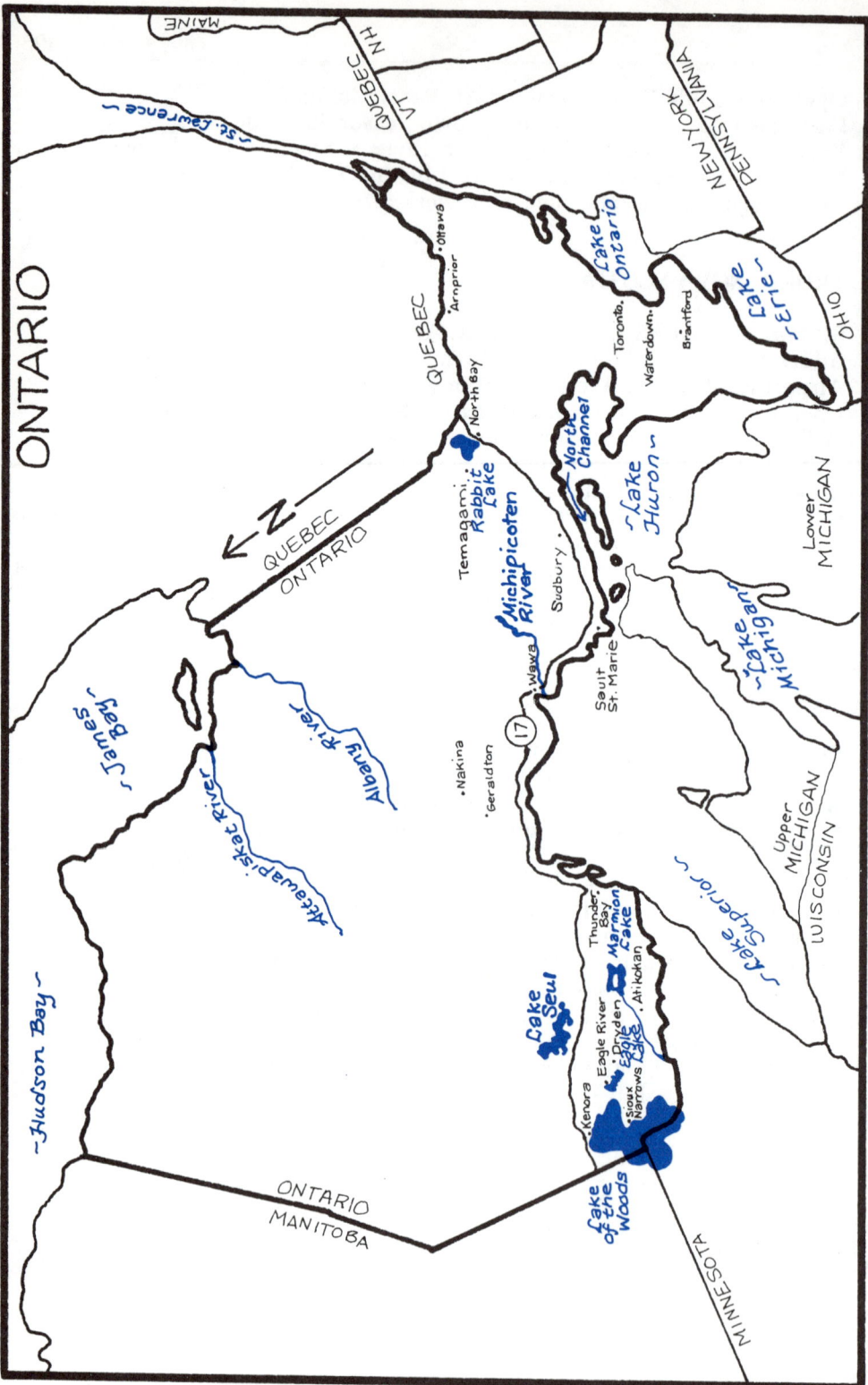

Ontario

ATIKOKAN, ONTARIO

BENINGER, PAT-CANADIAN WILDERNESS OUTPOSTS (807) 929-3561
Address Box 100, Atikokan, Ontario P0T 1C0
Airport Thunder Bay 100m **Accommodations** On premises
Operation Outfitter, lodge, tackle shop **Type of Fishing** Spin, baitcast, troll
Fish Walleye, lake, smallmouth bass, northern **Season** May-October
Water Marmion, Venorain, Entwine, Highrock Lakes
Specialty Lake trolling and spin casting for walleye and trout
Boats Canoes, outboards **Tackle Supplied** Spin, baitcast, troll
Experience 19 years **Rates** day: $60/person week: $400/person

EAGLE RIVER, ONTARIO

LANDON, FRANK (807) 938-6894
Address Eagle Lake Reserve #27, Eagle River, Ontario P0V 1S0
Airport Eagle River **Accommodations** Eagle River
Operation Guide **Type of Fishing** Baitcast, troll **Water** Eagle Lake, Lac Seul
Fish Muskie, walleye, northern **Season** May-October
Specialty Baitcasting **Boats** 16 ft Lunds **Tackle Supplied** Baitcast, troll
Experience 30 years **Rates** day: $60 U.S. funds
Guide's Notes: Eagle Lake Muskie fishing peaks in the months of June and July
through September. Surface baits and jerk baits are popular at this time.

MEAWASIGE, RAYMOND
Address General Delivery, Eagle River, Ontario P0V 1S0
Airport Dryden 28m **Accommodations** Eagle River **Boats** 16 ft Lund
Operation Guide **Type of Fishing** Baitcast, troll **Water** Outpost Lake
Fish Walleye, northern, muskie, sm bass **Season** May-October
Specialty Lake trolling for walleye and northern, casting for muskie
Experience 31 years **Rates** day: $100 week: $700

GERALDTON, ONTARIO

BAXTER, LAWRENCE-BAXTER BROTHERS WILDERNESS CAMPS
(807) 935-2707
Address RR#1, Murillo, Ontario P0T 2G0
Airport Geraldton 60m **Accommodations** On premises **Season** May-September
Operation Outfitter, outpost camps **Type of Fishing** Fly, spin, troll
Fish Speckled, pickerel, northern **Specialty** Fly, spincast, troll, and jig fishing

Water Albany, Attawapiskat Rivers **Boats** Rowboats (motors available), canoes
Rates day: $65 Canadian funds

MANITOULIN ISLAND, ONTARIO

PHILLIPS, BOB-THE ISLAND LODGE (416) 532-3144, (705) 285-4343
Address 259 Rusholme Road, Toronto, Ontario M6H 2Y9
Airport Sudbury 70m **Accommodations** On premises
Operation Guide, lodge **Type of Fishing** Spin, baitcast, troll
Fish Sm bass, northern, lm bass, muskie **Season** June-September
Water North Channel, Lake Huron **Specialty** Lake trolling
Boats Outboards **Tackle Supplied** Spin, baitcast
Experience 20 years **Rates** day: $250 week: $1400

NAKINA, ONTARIO

GOLDER, G.R. "BUD"-ESNAGAMI WILDERNESS LODGE & AIR SERVICE (807) 329-5209
Address Esnagami Lodge, Nakina, Ontario P0T 2H0
Airport Geraldton 35m **Accommodations** On premises
Operation Outfitter, lodge **Type of Fishing** Fly, spin,troll
Fish Brook, walleye, northern **Season** May-October
Water Canadian National Rail Line North to James & Hudson Bays
Specialty River fishing, fly-in areas only **Aircraft** Floatplanes
Boats Rowboats, canoes, river sleds, rafts
Experience 25 years **Rates** week: $600/person

SIOUX NARROWS, ONTARIO

HOLLAND, DON-SIOUX NARROWS HOTEL (807) 226-5224
Address Box 60, Sioux Narrows, Ontario P0X 1N0
Airport Kenora 50m **Accommodations** On premises
Operation Outfitter, lodge **Type of Fishing** Spin, baitcast, troll
Fish Walleye, northern, muskie, lake trout, bass **Season** May-November
Water Lake of the Woods **Tackle Supplied** Spin, baitcast, troll
Specialty Daily enclosed cruiser trips **Boats** Cruisers
Experience 15 years **Rates** day: $200 1/2 day: $125
Guide's Notes: Fishing Calendar for Lake of the Woods

Fish	Available
Muskie	Aug - Oct
Walleye	May 15 - Oct
Northern	May 15 - Oct
Bass	June - July
Lake Trout	May - Sept

TEMAGAMI, ONTARIO

MAURER, DIETER-MORTORBITCHUAN LODGE (705) 569-3573
Address Box 147, Temagami, Ontario P0H 2H0
Airport North Bay 60m **Accommodations** On premises
Operation Outfitter, lodge **Type of Fishing** Spin, baitcast, troll
Fish Lake trout, northern, walleye, sm bass **Season** March-August
Water Rabbit Lake, Mortorbitchuan River **Boats** Canoes, outboards, inboards
Experience 14 years **Rates** day: $50
Guide's Notes: Rabbit Lake peak time for walleye is the third Saturday of May
through mid-June.

THUNDER BAY, ONTARIO

OJIBWAY COUNTRY WILDERNESS CAMPS (416) 689-7925
Address P.O. Box 1230, Waterdown, Ontario 1OR 2H0
Airport Thunder Bay **Accommodations** Thunder Bay
Operation Outfitter, lodge **Type of Fishing** Baitcast, troll
Fish Walleye, northern, trout, whitefish **Season** May-October
Water Machewaian, Windsor, Kenozhe, Peninsular, Beteau Lakes
Specialty Lake fishing and float trips **Boats** Canoes, outboards
Aircraft Floatplanes **Rates** week: $500 U.S. funds

WAWA, ONTARIO

LAPHAM, DALE-REDWOOD MOTEL (705) 856-2705
Address Box 202, Wawa, Ontario P0S 1K0
Airport Wawa **Accommodations** On premises
Operation Outfitter, charter captain, motel **Type of Fishing** Fly, spin, troll
Fish Lake, rainbow, salmon, brook **Season** April-November
Water Lake Superior, Michipicoten River **Specialty** Lake trolling and float trips
Boats Canoes, bass boats, raft, charter boat **Tackle Supplied** Spin, troll
Experience 20 years **Rates** day: $200 week: $900 1/2 day: $100 Canadian funds

Prince Edward Island

CHARLOTTETOWN, PRINCE EDWARD ISLAND

FITZGERALD, MIKE-ISLAND RODS AND FLIES LTD. (902) 675-3278
Address P.O. Box 2163, Charlottetown, Prince Edward Island C1A 8B9
Airport Charlottetown **Accommodations** Charlottetown
Operation Outfitter, tackle shop **Type of Fishing** All **Tackle Supplied** Spin, fly
Fish Sea run brook, rainbow, Atlantic salmon **Season** March-Nov.
Water West, Morell, Dunk Rivers **Specialty** Fly fishing **Boats** Canoes
Experience 4 years **Rates** day: $65 1/2 day: $45
Guide's Notes: West, Morell and Dunk Rivers Our main fishery consists of sea run brook trout. These fish can exceed 6 pounds. The season runs from April 15 through September 30. Peak times are mid-May to mid-July and mid-August to the end of September. We have several runs, usually, related to the above times. Both lures and flies are used but mainly flies from June on. Small boats and canoes are used, however, wading is the major form of fishing.

Quebec

BLANC SABLON, QUEBEC

ST. PAUL SALMON CLUB (203) 434-9624
Address C/O Angler Adventures, Rte 2, Lyme, CT 06371
Airport Blanc Sablon **Accommodations** Blanc Sablon **Operation** Guide
Fish Atlantic salmon **Season** July-Sept **Type of Fishing** Fly
Water St. Paul River **Specialty** Fly fishing for Atlantic salmon
Experience 15 years **Rates** week: $2250 Canadian funds
Guide's Notes: St. Paul River--Generally the St. Paul gets two Atlantic salmon runs, one in mid-July and one in mid-August. The average salmon are 6-8 pounds, while trophy fish run about 20 pounds.

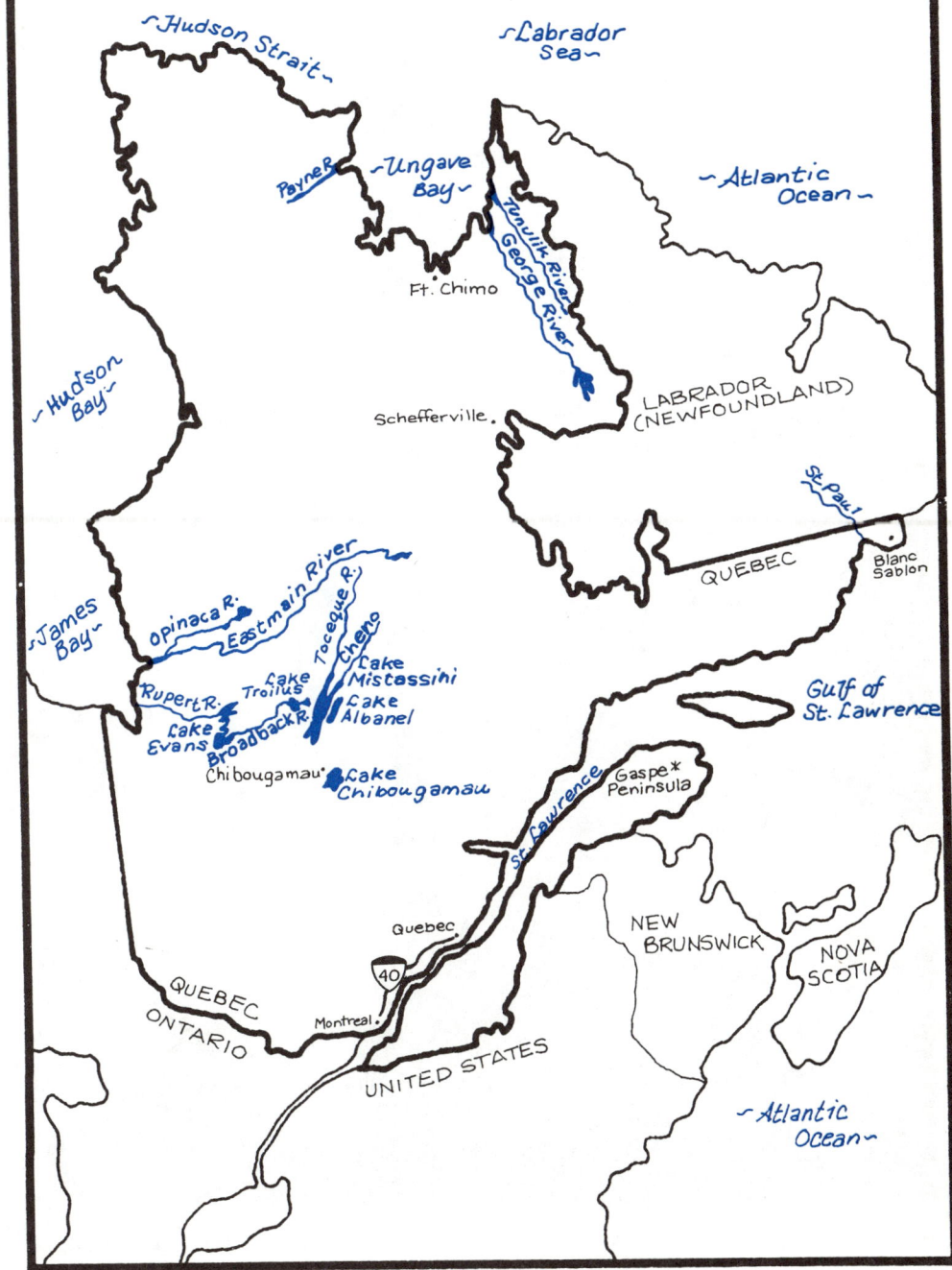

QUEBEC
*See New Brunswick for Gaspe Peninsula detail.

~Hudson Strait~

~Labrador Sea~

Payne R.

~Ungave Bay~

~Atlantic Ocean~

Tunulik River

George River

Ft. Chimo

~Hudson Bay~

Schefferville

LABRADOR (NEWFOUNDLAND)

St. Paul

QUEBEC

Blanc Sablon

~James Bay~

Opinaca R.

Eastmain River

Toceque R.

Cheno

Lake Mistassini

Rupert R.

Lake Troilus

Lake Albanel

Lake Evans

Broadback R.

Gulf of St. Lawrence

Chibougamau

Lake Chibougamau

St. Lawrence

Gaspe* Peninsula

Quebec

40

QUEBEC

ONTARIO

Montreal

NEW BRUNSWICK

NOVA SCOTIA

UNITED STATES

~Atlantic Ocean~

Atlantic salmon from a Quebec river.

A. Boucher/Quebec M.L.C.P.

FORT CHIMO, QUEBEC

SNOWBALL, ROBERT-TUNULIK RIVER FISHING CAMP (514) 844-8641
Address C/O Steve Ashton, Destinature, 1410 Stanley St.,
Room 520, Montreal, Quebec H3A 1P8
Airport Fort Chimo **Accommodations** On premises **Operation** Lodge
Fish Arctic char **Season** July-August **Type of Fishing** All
Water Tunulik River **Specialty** Light tackle and fly fishing
Boats 24 ft freighters, canoes **Tackle Supplied** Lures and flies only
Rates week: $2100 U.S. funds
Guide's Notes: Tunulik River Fishing Camp This camp is run by Inuit (Eskimo) Natives. Accommodations are finished plywood cabins with hot showers. Toilets are outdoor chemical type. Fishing is for trophy Arctic char from 5-20 pounds. Fishing is excellent the entire season.

LAKE MISTASSINI, QUEBEC

LOUIS JOLLIET CAMP (800) 245-1950, (412) 935-1577
Address C/O Kathy Carlson, Frontiers, P.O. Box 161, Wexford, PA 15090
Airport Chibougamau 100m **Accommodations** On premises
Operation Outfitter, lodge **Type of Fishing** All **Boats** 20 ft outboards
Fish Brook, walleye, lake trout, pike **Season** June-Sept.
Water Lake Mistassini **Specialty** Lake fishing, casting, trolling
Experience 25 years **Rates** week: $1894 Canadian funds
Guide's Notes: Lake Mistassini--Brook trout peaks are in June and again in late August through early September. Dry fly fishing for these big brookies (up to 5 pounds) is possible in June. The late summer and early fall fishing is mainly with lures and streamers. Pike are available all season and can be taken on surface lures and streamers to 15 pounds.

KINNIK, MATTHEW-CHENO RIVER OUTPOST CAMP (514) 844-8641
Address C/O Steve Ashton, Destinature, 1410 Stanley St.,
Room 520, Montreal, Quebec H3A 1P8
Airport Chibougamau 100m **Accommodations** On premises
Operation Outfitter, camp **Type of Fishing** Fly, spin **Season** Aug 20-Sept. 7
Fish Speckled trout, brook trout **Water** Cheno, Toceque Rivers
Specialty Light tackle trophy brook trout fishing **Boats** Canoes
Experience 2 years **Rates** week: $1075 U.S. funds

MORIN HEIGHTS, QUEBEC

WHITE, BOB-SQUARE-TAIL LODGE (514) 226-3119, 226-2049
Address P.O. Box 442, Morin Heights, Quebec J0R 1H0
Airport Chibougamau 76m **Accommodations** On premises
Operation Outfitter, lodge **Type of Fishing** Fly, spin, troll **Aircraft** Floatplane
Fish Brook, walleye, northern, lake **Season** June-Sept

Water Broadback, Rupert, Martin Rivers, Troilus Lake
Specialty Fly fishing, fly-out outpost fishing **Boats** Rowboats, canoes
Experience 30 years **Rates** week: $1200/person U.S. funds
Guide's Notes: The Broadback River System--The Broadback River has its beginnings in the high-lands of central Quebec, about 375 miles due north of Montreal. Spawned by a series of glacial formed lakes, the river flows westward for 200 miles before it loses its identity in the marsh lands of lower James Bay. It is only the headwaters though, or upper 50-75 miles, that the brookie angler need concern himself with, because it is here in the cool clear waters of the mountains that the Square-Tails are able to obtain their record breaking size. Here also are to be found lake trout, northern pike, walleye and whitefish. It is mainly the brookie though, that makes this area the mecca for trophy trout angling. A fisherman can normally expect to catch a trophy of 4-7 pounds and even larger fish are taken annually.

 Rupert River--The Rupert River is a tremendous body of water that has to be seen to be appreciated. It is more a series of lakes, connected by rapids, than a continuous river. There are stretches of river to suit the preferences of the most discriminating fisherman - from wide shallow stretches, to the smaller feeder streams favoured by many fly fishermen; and between, are endless miles of wilderness lakes where trophy pike grow in excess of 25 pounds. We would like to impress on you that we have so much water to fish, that it is possible to explore waters that have never been fished before.

 Lake Troilus--This lake is at the lodge doorstep, with numerous islands, bays, and small feeder streams to fish and explore. While our lake is quite large, there is never a wind problem - few large open stretches of water makes this lake very safe for boating.

 Fishing Tackle--For spin fishing we recommend 8 pound test line and bring at least one line change and one extra rod and reel per party. Also bring plenty of small and medium sized spoons and spinners, with some large spoons for pike fishing. For fly fishing, an assortment of wet and dry flies of various sizes and patterns and some large streamers. A 6-8 pound test leader is recommended, and a sinking line is an asset for fishing swifter stretches of the river.
Author's Notes: Respected contacts tell us this is a very good operation.

SHEFFERVILLE, QUEBEC

WEDGE HILLS LODGE (514) 844-8641
Address C/O Steve Ashton, Destinature, 1410 Stanley Street,
Room 520, Montreal, Quebec H3A 1P8
Airport Shefferville 170m **Accommodations** On premises **Operation** Lodge
Fish Brook, lake trout, Atlantic salmon **Type of Fishing** All **Water** George River
Specialty Light tackle and fly fishing **Boats** Rafts, freighter, canoes
Experience 5 years **Rates** week: $1900-2200 U.S. funds

13. Bahamas, Belize, Mexico: Salt water!

Saltwater fishing is not a sport for the faint of heart. In ocean waters, fish weighing several hundred pounds, once hooked, may take hours of hard work to land. Long sizzling runs and spectacular jumps can press the angler to his physical limits. On occasion, a furious fish will join the startled fisherman in his boat, creating pandemonium and a very dangerous situation. The use of light tackle equipment makes this game much more difficult and exciting. The thrill of seeing a big tarpon or permit take your lure or fly in shallow water cannot be described; it must be experienced.

Some of the best light tackle saltwater fishing in the world is found in the shallow waters off the Bahama Islands, Belize, and Mexico. Most of these exotic fishing grounds are only a few hours away from major U.S. cities by scheduled airlines. Bonefish, tarpon, snook, snapper, permit, and barracuda are just some of the explosive game fish which swim in these waters.

The Bahamas, off the east coast of southern Florida, stretch southward for over two hundred miles. The climate is warm, with temperatures in the low eighties all year. Ocean breezes fan the sun-drenched beaches, making air conditioning unnecessary. On the islands, the tensions of the world soon vanish, replaced by the sound of waves on the beach and the music of steel drum bands. But out on the saltwater flats, another form of tension builds as your guide quietly poles you toward huge schools of bonefish tailing in the noonday sun. Andros, Long, and Grand Bahama Islands, described in the following pages, are typical of the spectacular fishing to be found in the Bahamas. In addition to bonefish, you will find tarpon, permit, and barracuda in large numbers.

Belize, a former British colony, lies between Mexico and Guatemala. Turneffe Island, 25 miles off its coast, is world-famous for its huge bonefish schools. These fish, which average two to four pounds, may represent the largest concentration of bonefish in the the world. Tarpon and snapper are also available. A modern fish camp located here offers guides who specialize in light tackle methods.

Jutting out into the Gulf of Mexico north of Belize, Mexico's Yucatan Peninsula offers a mixed bag of light tackle saltwater game fish: bonefish, tarpon, barracuda, ladyfish, cobia, snook, snapper, and jack crevalle. Fishing is excellent at the resorts of Boca Paila and Pez Maya; the beaches and swimming are superb. Good connections into this area are available through the international airports of Cancun and Cozumel.

The Baja Peninsula extends from the California border almost 800 miles south to the town of Cabo San Lucas. The Baja is an arid, sun-baked strip of land, roughly 100 miles wide, which separates the Pacific Ocean from the fertile waters of the Sea of Cortez (Gulf of California). A wide variety of marine species migrate along its shores, and many inhabit the area all year.

The village of Loretto, about three quarters of the way down the peninsula's east coast, fishes well for yellowtail in March and April, and is a hot spot for dorado in June and July. Several fine hotels and excellent light tackle guides are available here.

Cabo San Lucas on the southern tip of the Baja is a fabulous year-round playground best known for its trolling fishery for big marlin. Outstanding light tackle opportunities are just developing, thanks to improved fishing methods and the use of fast small boats which can quickly reach surface-feeding fish. Two world fly fishing records for marlin were set here in 1985, but there is also great fishing for roosterfish, yellowfin tuna, and dorado. The Humboldt ocean current maintains a constant water temperature, providing year-round action. There are many good hotels in the area, and excellent airline connections are available into the the resort town of La Paz.

Across the Sea of Cortez, eighty miles from the town of Los Mochis, lies Lake Baccarac. This recently-filled impoundment is perhaps the hottest largemouth bass lake in North America. An average day fishing it will yield many four pound bass, and a few up to eight pounds. Special regulations have been placed on the lake to help maintain the large numbers of trophy-sized fish. Baccarac's one drawback is that it is not easy to get to. Scheduled airline service to Los Mochis is available, but only from Mexico City. An alternative for a group of fishermen is to charter a direct flight from a southern city such as Phoenix or El Paso.

A travel agency which specializes in light tackle fishing is an absolute must when planning a trip to Mexico or any foreign country. It is the only way to be reasonably sure you will experience the kind of fishing you are looking for at your destination.

Bahamas

ANDROS ISLAND, BAHAMAS

LEADON, RUPERT-POINT OF VIEW GUIDE SERVICE (707) 542-4242
Address C/O Fishing International, P.O. Box 2132, Santa Rosa, CA 95405
Airport Androstown 25m **Accommodations** On premises
Operation Guide, lodge **Type of Fishing** All **Boats** Skiffs
Fish Bonefish, tarpon, barracuda, snapper **Season** Year-round
Water Salt water flats of Andros Island **Tackle Supplied** All
Specialty Light tackle casting and fly fishing on salt water flats
Rates week: $1300/person U.S. funds
Guide's Notes: Fishing Andros Island The vast flats surrounding the eastern side of Andros Island offer the light tackle enthusiast a variety of fishing that can only be described as extraordinary. The famed North and Middle Bights, the legendary west side, the fabulous oceanside flats of Umbrella Cay and Curly Creek Sound, and the expansive backcountry waters of Fresh Creek provide classic wading and poling flats in a near wilderness, virgin water environment.

There are many in the angling fraternity that rate these waters as the finest bonefishing in the world. Bonefish are found here in incredible numbers - with tremendous schools of smaller fish in the 2 to 5 pound class and lots of larger fish which run 6 to 9 pounds that travel in smaller groups ranging from several fish to a dozen or so.

Double-figure fish of world-record class size usually work the flats as singles, doubles and triples. Stalking tailing bonefish in this weight class is an experience never to be forgotten. In addition to the bonefishing, anglers can try their luck with tarpon, barracuda, a variety of snappers, grouper, jacks and shark.

The Areas You'll be Fishing Fresh Creek, a tremendous inlet with miles of secluded lagoons, islands and bays, offers the most consistent fishing on the island. Because of the large numbers of fish here combined with the well-protected flats, this area can be highly productive during windy or cloudy conditions.

Although the bonefish are not as large as those found on the oceanside flats or west side of Andros Island, the sheer number of bonefish one encounters more than makes up for their smaller size range. Bonefish will average 2 to 5 pounds with a good sprinkling of 6 to 8 pounders. Yes, an angler can expect good action on Fresh Creek!

The oceanside flats, well protected by a large barrier reef running the entire length of the island, can provide some of the most exciting fishing to be found anywhere. On the low tide, feeding bonefish (and at times, permit) will nose their way up on the banks, tailing on small crustaceans and baitfish.

ISLANDS of the BAHAMAS

LONG ISLAND

Clarence Town

South Point

Stella Maris

Simms

Cape Santa Maria

Mannas

South Bight

North Bight

Middle Bight

Kemp Bay

Moxey Town

Andros Town

Oceanside Flats

Coakley Town

Nicholls Town

New Town

San Andros

West Side

Deep Water Cay

High Rock

GRAND BAHAMA ISLAND

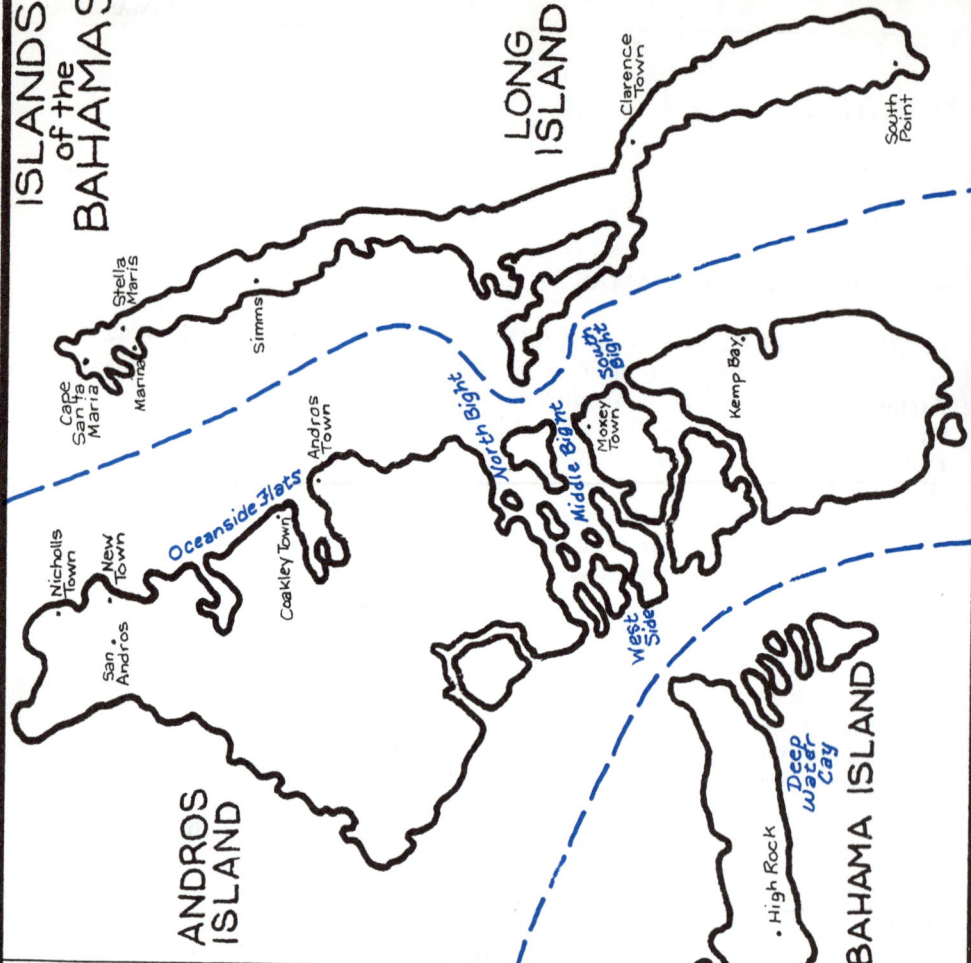

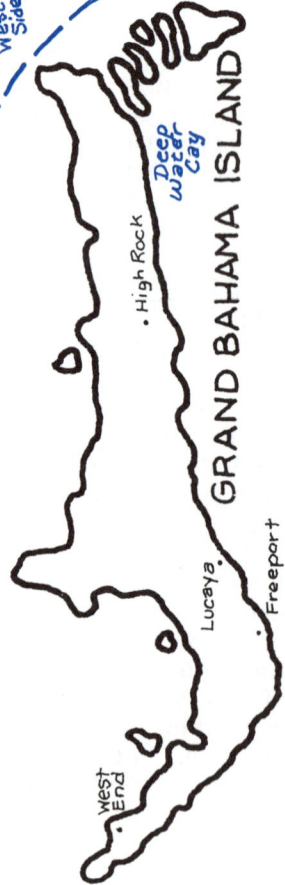

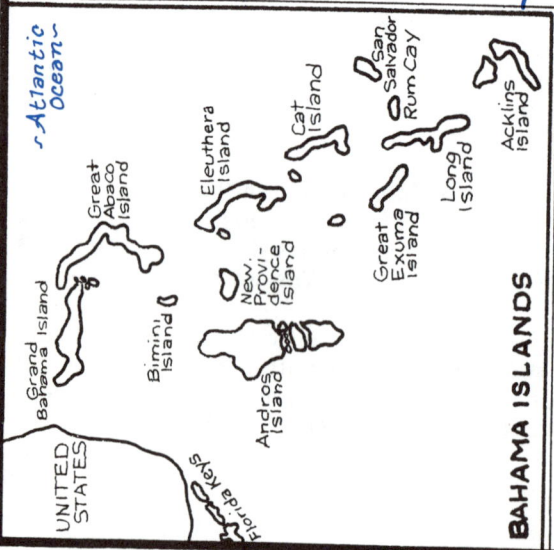

ANDROS ISLAND

Atlantic Ocean

Grand Bahama Island

Great Abaco Island

Eleuthera Island

Cat Island

San Salvador

Rum Cay

Acklins Island

New Providence Island

Great Exuma Island

Long Island

Bimini Island

Andros Island

UNITED STATES

Florida Keys

BAHAMA ISLANDS

West End

Lucaya

Freeport

These are the flats that have already yielded several world-record bonefish to anglers such as Dr. Rod Neubert who took two record bones in one day. Anything can happen out here... big permit will often surprise you, giant barracuda cruise the edges of the reefs, mutton snapper ride the tails of rays... This kaleidoscope of marine life must be seen to be believed.

The North and Middle Bights of Andros Island consist of an immense interior archipelago dotted with hundreds of cays in all shapes and sizes. The variety of flats are incredible. There is Big Wood Cay with seven miles of bright white hard sand flats to wade. On the falling tide, there's the famous Dressing Room, a "fish funnel," where bonefish will swim by your boat in battalions.

Traveling through the maze of islands will put you in the Middle Bight where you can wade or fish from your skiff. This area is well-known by many as "big fish water," where parts have nicknames such as "Home of the Giants," "Bonefish Boulevard," and "Animal House."

Twenty more minutes of running will put the adventurous angler on the legendary west side where you'll encounter hundreds of bonefish that have never seen a fly. This is bonefishing...as good as it ever gets!

Author's Notes: *This is an excellent choice for a week of bonefishing.*

Poling the flats for bonefish in the Bahamas.   *Paul Bruun*

GRAND BAHAMA ISLAND, BAHAMAS

DEEP WATER CAY (800) 245-1950, (412) 935-1577
Address C/O Frontiers, P.O. Box 161, Wexford, PA 15090
Accommodations On premises **Operation** Guide, charter captain, lodge
Fish Bonefish, permit, barracuda, snapper **Season** Year-round
Water Salt water flats and reefs of Grand Bahama Island **Type of Fishing** All
Specialty Light tackle casting and fly fishing on the salt water flats
Experience 15 years **Rates** week: $1410/person U.S. funds
Author's Notes: Chris Child of Frontiers tells me this is one of his favorite bonefishing resorts.

LONG ISLAND, BAHAMAS

TAYLOR, LENNOX (809) 336-2106
Address C/O Stella Maris Inn, P.O. Box 30-105, Long Island, Bahamas
Airport Stella Maris 3m **Accommodations** Stella Maris 3m
Operation Guide, charter captain **Type of Fishing** Fly, baitcast
Fish Bone, and all reef fish **Season** Year-round **Specialty** Bone fishing
Water Long Island North West, Adderley's, Glenton's, Cape Santa Maria's Bay
Boats Outboards **Tackle Supplied** Fly, baitcast
Experience 20 years **Rates** day: $75 1/2 day: $65 U.S. funds
Guide's Notes: Inshore fishing for bonefish is a spinning and fly rodder's paradise! Average bones caught per day...15 to 20, from 3 to 12 pounds. Average school of bonefish sighted per day...five to six, with 200 to 300 per school. They can be caught from an anchored boat, from the beach, or while wading in water one foot in depth. We have 3 excellent bonefish bays within 1/2 to five miles from our dock.

Belize

BELIZE CITY, BELIZE

BENNETT, DAVE-TURNEFFE ISLAND LODGE (412) 935-1577
Address C/O Frontiers, P.O. Box 161, Wexford, PA 15090
Airport Belize City 30m **Accommodations** On premises

MEXICO/BELIZE

UNITED STATES

Gulf of Mexico

Yucatán Peninsula

Boca Paila, Pez Maya

Cancun

Cozumel Island

Turneffe Islands

Belize City

BELIZE

GUATEMALA

HONDURAS

• Mexico City

• Guadalajara

• Mazatlán

Lake Baccarac

• Los Mochis

La Paz

Hotel Las Arenas

Cabo San Lucas

Loreto

Gulf of California

~ Pacific Ocean ~

UNITED STATES

Operation Guide, lodge, charter captain **Type of Fishing** All
Fish Bonefish, permit, tarpon, snapper **Season** October-July
Water Salt water flats around Turneffe Island **Boats** Bonefish skiffs
Specialty Light tackle casting and fly fishing on the salt water flats
Experience 15 years **Rates** week: $1250/person
Guide's Notes: Fishing Calendar of Turneffe Island

Fish	Available
Bonefish	Oct-July
Tarpon	Apr-June

*Author's Notes: This is a world famous bonefishing spot, and our contacts tell
us it is an excellent operation.*

Mexico

BAJA CALIFORNIA, MEXICO

HOTEL PUNTA COLORADO (818) 703-1002
Address Box 2573, Canoga Park, CA 91306
Accommodations On premises **Operation** Charter captain, operation, lodge
Type of Fishing Fly fishing, deep sea **Boats** 28 to 32 ft cruisers, 22 ft skiffs
Fish Sail, dorado, wahoo, roosterfish **Season** October-July
Water Sea of Cortez, East Cape **Tackle Supplied** Troll, casting
Specialty Big game fishing **Rates** day: $70

CANCUN, QUINTANA ROO, MEXICO

SUAREZ, ROMAN LOPEZ Y-MUNDO MARINO PHONE# 30554
Address Apartado Postal 569, Cancun, Q. Roo, Mexico 77500
Airport Cancun 15k **Accommodations** Cancun **Operation** Guide, marina
Fish Bonefish, tarpon, snook, permit **Season** Year-round
Water Shallow water, marsh, deep water lagoon, fresh water springs
Specialty Light tackle casting **Type of Fishing** All
Boats 16 ft ski barge, 14 ft Boston Whaler **Tackle Supplied** Spin, baitcast
Experience 8 years **Rates** day: $200 1/2 day: $100 U.S. funds
Guide's Notes: Cancun, Mexico Area Peak season for snook is from December
to April although we have all species all year-round.

Author's Notes: A few years back I spent a week's vacation at a hotel in Cancun. I had my fishing gear but was unable to locate a light tackle guide. When I got back home, the following appeared in SPORTS AFIELD's travel section: "On a recent trip [to Cancun], I caught and released nine bonefish and seven tarpon in one morning, using a fly rod. The tarpon were all less than 50 pounds, but I'm told there are considerably bigger ones in remote tidal inlets that were too far away for our limited time. This area's best guide is a personable young man named Roman Lopez."

LAKE BACCARAC, MEXICO

CHAPMAN, JR., BILL-CHAPMAN'S EXECUTIVE RESORTS
(800) 245-1950, (412) 935-1577
Address C/O Frontiers, P.O. Box 161, Wexford, PA 15090
Airport Los Mochis 100m **Accommodations** On premises
Operation Lodge, outfitter **Type of Fishing** All **Water** Lake Baccarac
Fish Largemouth bass **Season** Year-round except September
Specialty Light tackle casting to bass **Boats** V-hulled outboards
Experience 3 years **Rates** 2-1/2 days and 3 nights: $825/person U.S. funds
Guide's Notes: Lake Baccarac is unique! It is situated about 1,000 feet above Los Mochis (at sea level) in a picturesque valley with green forested mountain peaks surrounding this 30,000 acre lake. It was first fished in 1983. Not only can you anticipate great numbers of bass, but you have the expectancy of catching trophy fish in the 4-10 pound class daily with surface plugs, plastic worms or spinner or crank baits on light to medium weight spinning or casting tackle, and with popping bugs on the fly rod. The record bass taken was 12-1/2 pounds in January, 1985.

There is no commercial fishing for bass on the lake nor will there ever be, unlike Lake Guerrero and Lake Dominguez, where the big fish potential is almost nil but where you can still catch 100 cookie-cutter one pound fish each day. This is a new concept in lake management in Mexico, and it should insure that quality bass fishing for big fish remains constant for years to come. We also offer superb dove hunting. (Scott Fitzgerald/Frontiers.)
Author's Notes: I have not visited Lake Baccarac but our contacts indicate this is probably the hottest largemouth bass fishing in North America.

LAS ARENAS, MEXICO

WALLER, LANI-HOTEL LAS ARENAS (707) 542-4242
Address C/O Fishing International, P.O. Box 2132, Santa Rosa, CA 95405
Airport La Paz 35m **Accommodations** On premises
Operation Guide, lodge **Type of Fishing** All
Fish Dorado, bonita, roosterfish, yellowtail **Season** Year-round
Water Sea of Cortez (Gulf of California) **Boats** 22 ft glass-pongas
Specialty Light tackle casting to salt water game fish
Experience 4 years **Rates** day: $80/2 people

Guide's Notes: Peak time for light tackle is May through August. What is unique about this area is it offers fabulous surface casting to dorado, bonito, roosterfish and yellowtail. The guide chums these fish up to the surface where they can be caught with a variety of lures including fly rod poppers. (Lani Waller/Fishing International)

Author's Notes: Hotel Las Arenas can offer explosive surface fishing for exciting salt water species that are normally only caught deep casting or trolling. If you are interested in this type of fishing you should contact Lani Waller (West Coast Fishing Editor for FLY FISHERMAN) at Fishing International. Lani has personally checked out and organized the local guides to provide this type of fishing experience.

YUCATAN PENINSULA, MEXICO

GONZALEZ, JAVIER-BOCA PAILA FISHING LODGE
(800) 245-1950, (412) 935-1577
Address C/O Frontiers, P.O. Box 161, Wexford, PA 15090
Airport Cozumel 50m **Accommodations** On premises
Operation Lodge, guide **Type of Fishing** All **Boats** Bonefish skiffs
Fish Bonefish, permit, tarpon, snapper **Season** October-July
Water Local salt water flats, Ascension Bay **Tackle Supplied** Fly, spin
Specialty Fly, spin, and baitcasting for bonefish and permit
Aircraft Landplane **Experience** 17 years **Rates** week: $1275/person
Guide's Notes: Boca Paila What Boca Paila has more than anything else is vast numbers of bonefish, and the often absolute ideal conditions to encounter them. Average size is 2-1/2 to 3 pounds, but there are a number of 5 pounders and better. At 4 pounds and up, the bonefish is capable of the reel-screaming antics for which they are known. A 5 pound bonefish will make two or three runs with every bit as much authority as a 20 pound Atlantic salmon. The permit is probably a better fish on light tackle than the Atlantic salmon, or at least comparable to a big salmon.

There are a few other fish on the flats. Tarpon, baby size up to 40 pounds, snook, jack crevalle, various snapper, a few small sharks and barracuda are constantly cruising the flats. When they're in a taking mood, they will take flies and are a lot of fun. You can cast successfully in the surf right in front of the cottages and take bonefish, permit and other species. This is blind casting and a lot of fun. The boca at certain tide times can be productive for tarpon, snook, barracuda, permit and jacks.

Seasonal Implications Prime time on the flats is definitely from March through the first of August. The end of November until the end of February is popular because of the winter getaway syndrome, but during these months, people face a greater weather risk for ideal fishing conditions on the flats, perhaps a 30 percent chance of excessive wind or overcast. Although our January group had bad weather, the two weeks prior were great, and it looked like fine stable weather was settling in when we left.

Summer temperatures might be a little warmer but shouldn't be oppressive. At camp they compensate by fishing earlier, taking a longer midday break, and fishing later in the evening due to longer days. We found that temperatures ranged from the low 60's on cloudy, windy, days up to the mid-80's when it was quiet, sunny and still. Sleeping temperatures were great each night. (Chris Child/Frontiers)

Author's Notes: I visited Boca Paila a few years ago and was very impressed. The water is beautiful and the facilities excellent. The lodge is still under the management of the Gonzalez family and Chris Child of Frontiers tells me the fishing is as good if not better than ever. If you are looking for a nice quiet place in the sun to take your family, which has a great beach, an excellent swimming area, and some of the best light tackle fishing in the world, you will love Boca Paila.

PEZ MAYA RESORT, MEXICO (707) 542-4242

Address C/O Fishing International, P.O. Box 2132, Santa Rosa, CA 95405
Operation Lodge, outfitter **Type of Fishing** All **Water** Salt water flats
Fish Bonefish, tarpon, barracuda, snapper **Season** Year-round
Specialty Light tackle casting on the flats **Boats** Bonefish skiffs
Experience 12 years **Rates** week: $1400/person
Guide's Notes: Fish are available year round. Best weather is from mid March through September and the month of December.
Author's Notes: This is a well established light tackle fishing resort situated on a beautiful secluded beach of the Yucatan Peninsula. They have a very good reputation.

Index

Boldface *numbers indicate notes by the author or a guide.*

ELAND, MATT 302
Elephant Butte Reservoir 196
ELIGUK LAKE LODGE 353
EHARDT, LARRY 120
EKSTROM, DAN 143
El Capitan Lake 76, 154
El Dorado Reservoir 213 , 218
EL RIO GUIDE SERVICE 205

426

About the Author

Richard Swan was born in 1943, in Traverse City, Michigan, where he began fishing with his dad as a young boy. After attending the University of Michigan he moved to the West Coast to work in the ski industry; currently, he resides in Reno, Nevada, with his wife and two children. His interest in angling greatly intensified after a guided float trip on the Madison river in 1973 introduced him to the sport of fly fishing. Since then, Richard has fished with guides throughout North America. Much of his spare time is spent behind the oars of his own white-water raft, plying the Truckee River in search of trout. In 1982 he patented and began marketing Glacier Glove®, a neoprene glove designed specifically for cold weather angling. Today he travels the West marketing ski equipment, and fishes whenever possible. *Light Tackle Fishing Guides of North America* is his first book.

Production notes.

This book was written on the author's Apple® Macintosh™ computer. Typesetting codes were placed directly into the text through the Stylo-Type 1™ software program designed by Gary Duarte of Type/Setting Net/Work, Reno, Nevada. It was typeset in Melior directly on a high-resolution typesetting machine. Two hundred casebound copies were signed and numbered by the author.